ESSENTIALS OF MARKETING RESEARCH

ESSENTIALS OF MARKETING RESEARCH

WILLIAM G. ZIKMUND
Oklahoma State University

THOMSON

SOUTH-WESTERN

Australia · Canada · Mexico · Singapore · Spain · United Kingdom · United States

THOMSON

SOUTH-WESTERN

Essentials of Marketing Research, 2e
William G. Zikmund

Editor-in-Chief:
Jack Calhoun

Team Leader:
Melissa Acuña

Acquisitions Editor:
Steve Hazelwood

Developmental Editor:
Mary H. Draper
Draper Development

Marketing Manager:
Nicole Moore

Production Editor:
Amy McGuire

Manufacturing Coordinator:
Diane Lohman

Production House:
Lifland et al., Bookmakers

Compositor:
Parkwood Composition

Printer:
Quebecor World
Versailles, KY

Internal Designer:
Ann Small Design

Cover Designer:
Michael H. Stratton

Cover Photographer/Illustrator:
Humberto Calzada

Photography Manager:
Deanna Ettinger

Photo Researcher:
Susan Van Etten

Library of Congress Cataloging-in-
Publication Data

Zikmund, William G.
    Essentials of marketing research /
William G. Zikmund.—2nd ed.
        p. cm
    Includes index.
    ISBN 0-324-18257-0
    1. Marketing research. I. Title

HF5415.2.Z537 2002
658.8'3—dc21   2002069599

TO SYBIL

BRIEF CONTENTS

PART 2 DESIGNING RESEARCH STUDIES

Contents

PART 5 ANALYSIS AND REPORTING

PART 6 COMPREHENSIVE CASES WITH COMPUTERIZED DATABASES

*E*ssentials of Marketing Research, Second Edition presents a lively picture of marketing research in sixteen chapters. Although it is shorter than my other textbook, *Exploring Marketing Research*, Eighth Edition, it shares that book's same objective: to give students a basic understanding of the scope of marketing research, using an applied approach with interesting practical applications. *Essentials of Marketing Research* is also contemporary, reflecting the emergence of our digital age.

Since the first edition of *Essentials of Marketing Research* was published, the use of the Internet for marketing research has come of age. I am certain that technological developments and social diffusion of the Internet will dramatically shape the future of marketing research. As the Internet becomes increasingly representative of the U.S. population, innovative marketing research techniques that can uniquely be administered online will become standard. In the 21st century, marketing research on the Internet has moved out of the introductory stage of its product life cycle into the growth stage. Many aspects of Internet marketing are discussed in this book.

I believe a student's first exposure to the subject of marketing research should create an appreciation of the full range of marketing research activities in businesses and other organizations. This book was written under the assumption that few students will truly appreciate the marketing research process if their first exposure to the material requires them to study an exhaustive technical handbook filled with advanced statistical techniques and abstract research designs.

During my student years, my professors presented marketing research as a dynamic, creative, and enjoyable pursuit. This approach turned out to be more accurate than the dry, analytical image of marketing research presented in most marketing research textbooks. My own experience in the marketing research industry and in teaching marketing research for many years at the university level has convinced me that students enrolled in their first course in marketing research require a topically relevant and exciting text. I have put forth my best effort to communicate the energy and creativity of marketing research without compromising integrity or accuracy.

In writing a shorter book, I have not simply pared down the coverage to the essentials of marketing research but have organized many topics in a unique way. For example, the material on data analysis is organized to show the big picture of data analysis rather than to focus on advanced techniques that undergraduate students have difficulty understanding.

ORGANIZATION OF THE BOOK

The organization of *Essentials of Marketing Research* follows the logic of the marketing research process. The book begins by discussing the scope of marketing research. It provides an overview of problem definition and the entire marketing research process. A discussion of global information systems and the Internet follows. The many new information technologies and new methodologies for collecting data are covered at this point. Next, the need for exploratory research and secondary data collection is explained. Research designs for primary data collection, surveys, observation research, and experiments are discussed next. A practical explanation of measurement and questionnaire design follows. Sampling designs and sample size are examined. Finally, basic data analysis is explained and a conceptual overview of advanced data analysis is presented.

SUPERIOR PEDAGOGY

More than other marketing research textbooks, *Essentials of Marketing Research,* Second Edition addresses students' need to comprehend all aspects of the marketing research process. To achieve these objectives, the book includes the following features:

- **Learning objectives** at the beginning of each chapter preview the important topics in that chapter. Students can also use the objectives to determine whether they understand the major points of the chapter.

- **Opening vignettes** describe marketing research challenges in actual businesses that most students will recognize.

- **What Went Right?** and **What Went Wrong?** features describe successes and failures of marketing research strategies. For example, the What Went Right? feature in Chapter 7 describes how Avon moved its research online to collect valuable market information from its sales reps, a successful strategy that saved time and money.

- **Exploring Research Ethics** use interesting, compelling examples to reveal how biased or unethical behavior can thwart the marketing research process. **Exploring Marketing Research Issues** illustrate key points from the chapter and delve deeper into related marketing research topics.

- **An accessible, interesting writing style** continues to be a hallmark of the book. With a careful balance between theory and practice and a sprinkling of interesting examples, the writing style helps clarify rather than mystify. In addition, the text offers comprehensive rather than superficial treatment of topics.

- **A review of statistical theory** in Chapter 13 provides students with an overview of the basic aspects of statistics theory. Because this managerially oriented book is a marketing research text and not a statistics monograph, students are given the tools they need to review and comprehend statistical theory. Even students with rusty statistical skills will benefit from a quick review of the basic statistical concepts in Chapter 13.

- **Key terms** within the chapters and in the margins help students recognize and retain important marketing research and statistical terminology. Learning the vocabulary of marketing research is essential to understanding the topic. *Essentials of Marketing Research* facilitates this learning in three ways. First, key concepts are in boldface type and are completely defined when they first appear in the text. Second, all key terms and concepts are listed at the end of each chapter, and many terms are highlighted in a marginal glossary. Third, a Glossary that lists all key terms and definitions appears at the end of the book for handy reference. A Glossary of Frequently Used Symbols is also included.

- **Questions for Review and Critical Thinking** promote student involvement in the classroom by prompting them to think about topics beyond the text's coverage. Review materials enhance students' understanding of key concepts.
- **Ethics questions,** identified by a special icon, are included in each chapter. New technology has raised interest in privacy issues, and these ethics questions pose compelling questions for students to explore.
- **Exploring the Internet** activities provide considerable value for students of marketing research. A serious effort has been made to provide current URLs for numerous worthwhile Internet links. These are not just a bunch of shallow links to trivial places, but links to educational sites a professor will want his or her students to visit to learn more about a concept. Internet activities range from consulting the Census Bureau's Population Clock to being participants in Internet surveys.
- **Extensive cases and video cases** illustrate marketing research concepts and build knowledge and research skills. These cases present interesting, real-life research situations that require students to make thoughtful decisions. They offer the opportunity for active participation in a decision-making process, one of the most effective forms of learning. The video cases portray actual research activities for brands and companies, such as Fisher-Price, I-Zone by Polaroid, Ben and Jerry's, and Burke, Inc.

COMPREHENSIVE INSTRUCTOR RESOURCES

Materials that supplement the content of the text are available to help instructors perform their vital teaching function. The extensive learning package provided with *Essentials of Marketing Research* includes a Test Bank, a computerized Test Bank (which uses ExamView Testing Software), a comprehensive Instructor's Manual, PowerPoint presentation slides, databases for several cases, a videocassette containing case materials, and online marketing resources available at http://zikmund.swcollege.com.

- **Instructor's Resource CD-ROM** (ISBN: 0-324-182597) contains all of the instructor resources on one easy-to-use CD-ROM, including the Test Bank, computerized testing software, Instructor's Manual, PowerPoint presentation slides, and data sets for several cases.
- **The Test Bank,** prepared by Tom Quirk of Webster University, has been carefully written to provide a variety of questions covering every major concept in the book. Each question has been scrutinized to eliminate ambiguity, and questions have been selected to provide varying levels of difficulty. Each question is accompanied by the page number from the book where the answer may be located.
- **ExamView** is an easy-to-use automated testing program that allows instructors to create exams by using provided questions, modifying questions, or adding new questions.
- **Instructor's Manual and Transparency Masters** assist with lecture presentation by offering detailed and comprehensive lecture outlines, solutions to all assignments, and transparency masters. Each case and video case solution includes the objective of the case, a brief summary of the case, and recommended questions and solutions.

- **PowerPoint presentation slides** summarize and illustrate key concepts in each chapter. These slides are both available on the Instructor's Resource CD-ROM and downloadable from the Web site at http://zikmund.swcollege.com.
- **Excel and SPSS data sets** are available for several cases. Students may download the data sets from http://zikmund.swcollege.com. Data sets are also included on the Instructor's Resource CD-ROM.
- **A Comprehensive Video Library** (ISBN: 0-324-181507) introduces students to marketing research challenges in a variety of interesting businesses. Video cases guide students through problem analysis, problem solving, and application of chapter concepts. Suggested solutions and teaching notes for the video cases are included in the Instructor's Manual.
- **Web Resources** at http://zikmund.swcollege.com provide the latest information about what's new and what's cool in marketing research. The site features links to other research-related sites, tips about using the supplemental video library, and much more.

RESOURCES FOR STUDENTS

In addition to its coverage of the latest information technology, *Essentials of Marketing Research,* Second Edition includes the following new student resources:

- **A partnership with WebSurveyor,** a specialist in Web-based marketing research, has made it possible to greatly enhance student learning by providing sample surveys, response scales, question libraries, and survey results developed specifically for this text. WebSurveyor activities appear both in the text and on the companion Web site. The WebSurveyor desktop software is available to students who purchase new books that contain a WebSurveyor postcard with a serial number. Students with serial numbers should go to http://zikmund.swcollege.com, click on the textbook, click the WebSurveyor button, and follow the steps for registering. Students who need to purchase a serial number should go to http://zikmund. swcollege.com, click on the textbook, click the WebSurveyor button, and follow the steps for purchasing access to the software.
- **The dedicated Web site** http://zikmund.swcollege.com has been developed especially for the new edition. The site includes chapter quizzes that allow students to test and retest their knowledge of chapter concepts, downloadable PowerPoint slides, the very best online marketing research resources available, data sets for all the cases, crossword puzzles, and much more.
- **InfoTrac College Edition** is packaged free with each new text. This fully searchable online database gives professors and students 24-hour access to full-text articles from a variety of well-known periodicals and scholarly journals.
- **SPSS–Student Version** brings affordable, professional statistical analysis and modeling tools to a student's own computer. Based on the professional version of one of the world's leading desktop statistical software packages, SPSS 10.0 for Windows–Student Version (ISBN: 0-324-108699) includes an easy-to-use interface and comprehensive online help that lets students learn statistics, not software.

ACKNOWLEDGMENTS

Many colleagues contributed ideas for this text in particular and made suggestions that greatly enhanced all of my marketing research books. For their insightful feedback, I thank the following people:

Gerald Albaum, *University of Oregon*
William Bearden, *University of South Carolina*
Joseph A. Bellizzi, *Arizona State University–West*
James A. Brunner, *University of Toledo*
F. Anthony Bushman, *San Francisco State University*
Thomas Buzas, *Eastern Michigan University*
Roy F. Cabaniss, *Huston-Tillotson College*
Michael d'Amico, *University of Akron*
Ron Eggers, *Barton College*
H. Harry Friedman, *City University of New York–Brooklyn*
Ron Goldsmith, *Florida State University*
Larry Goldstein, *Iona College*
David Gourley, *Arizona State University*
Jim Grimm, *Illinois State University*
Al Gross, *Robert Morris College*
Don Heinz, *University of Wisconsin*
Craig Hollingshead, *Texas A&M University–Kingsville*
Victor Howe, *University of Kentucky*
Roy Howell, *Texas Tech University*
Rhea Ingram, *University of Kentucky*
P. K. Kannan, *University of Maryland*
Susan Kleine, *Arizona State University*
David B. Klenosky, *Purdue University*
C. S. Kohli, *California State University–Fullerton*
Jerome L. Langer, *Assumption College*
James H. Leigh, *Texas A&M University*
Larry Lowe, *Bryant College*
Karl Mann, *Tennessee Technological University*
Charles R. Martin, *Wichita State University*
Marlys Mason, *Oklahoma State University*
Tom K. Massey, *University of Missouri–Kansas City*
Sanjay Mishra, *University of Kansas*
G. M. Naidu, *University of Wisconsin–Whitewater*
Charles Prohaska, *Central Connecticut State University*
Alan Sawyer, *University of Florida*
Robert Schaffer, *California State University–Pomona*
Leon G. Schiffman, *City University of New York–Baruch*
K. Sivakumar, *University of Illinois at Chicago*
Mark Speece, *Central Washington University*
Harlan Spotts, *University of Wisconsin–Parkside*
Wilbur W. Stanton, *Old Dominion University*
Bruce L. Stern, *Portland State University*

James L. Taylor, *University of Alabama*
Gail Tom, *California State University–Sacramento*
Deborah Utter, *Boston College*
David Wheeler, *Suffolk University*
Richard Wilcox, *Carthage College*
Margaret Wright, *University of Colorado*
Clifford E. Young, *University of Colorado–Denver*
William Lee Ziegler, *Bethune Cookman College*

Essentials of Marketing Research, Second Edition was completed because of the hard work of a team of people at South-Western Publishing. Behind the scenes, Bob Lynch, Dave Shaut, Jack Calhoun, Melissa Acuña, and Mike Roche made the acquisition of the Dryden Press and the transition to South-Western seamless. Steve Hazelwood and Mary Draper offered support during all stages of the book. I owe a particular debt to the highly organized Mary Draper, who coordinated many developmental activities, insisted that others meet their deadlines, and was always responsive to my requests. The attentive copyediting and permissions work by Quica Ostrander, Sally Lifland, and others at Lifland et al., Bookmakers is greatly appreciated. Photo research by Susan Van Etten made the book more attractive. Barbara Fuller Jacobsen's management and Amy McGuire's execution of the production tasks related to composition and printing were key factors in the quality improvements in this edition. I appreciate working with such fine professionals.

For debts extending over a longer period and less directly, I wish to thank Leo Aspinwall, Philip Cateora, Charles Hinsderman, Jerome Scott, and William Stanton.

William G. Zikmund
June 2002

A native of the Chicago area, William G. Zikmund now lives in Tulsa, Oklahoma. He is a professor of marketing at Oklahoma State University. He received a Bachelor of Science degree in marketing from the University of Colorado, a Master of Science degree in marketing from Southern Illinois University, and a Ph.D. in business administration with a concentration in marketing from the University of Colorado.

Before beginning his academic career, Professor Zikmund worked in marketing research for Conway/Millikin Company (a marketing research supplier) and Remington Arms Company (an extensive user of marketing research). Professor Zikmund also has served as a marketing research consultant to several business and nonprofit organizations. His applied marketing research experiences range from interviewing respondents and coding questionnaires to designing, supervising, and analyzing entire research programs.

During his academic career, Professor Zikmund has published dozens of articles and papers in a diverse group of scholarly journals ranging from the *Journal of Marketing* to *Accounting Review* to the *Journal of Applied Psychology.* In addition to *Essentials of Marketing Research,* Professor Zikmund has written *Exploring Marketing Research, Business Research Methods, Marketing, Effective Marketing,* and a work of fiction, *A Corporate Bestiary.*

Professor Zikmund is a member of professional organizations including the American Marketing Association, the Academy of Marketing Science, the Association for Consumer Research, the Society for Marketing Advancement, the Marketing Educators' Association, and the Association of Collegiate Marketing Educators. He has served on the editorial review boards of the *Journal of Marketing Education, Marketing Education Review,* the *Journal of the Academy of Marketing Science,* and the *Journal of Business Research.*

ESSENTIALS OF MARKETING RESEARCH

W hen Kraft introduced Easy Mac, executives were certain they had a hit on their hands.[1] After all, the product was an extension of the ever-popular Kraft Macaroni and Cheese brand that held a place in American culture just a couple of notches below mom and apple pie. As a single-serving microwave version of the classic brand, Easy Mac leveraged the consumer's desire for speed and convenience of preparation. The hope: That the easier-to-make product would find additional uses, like snacks and quick meals. But Easy Mac's launch didn't live up to expectations. Although the product had a respectable first year, executives at Kraft were disappointed. They had expected Easy Mac to capture a 5 percent share of the market, but actual market share was only half that figure. Brand managers were puzzled. They were convinced that Easy Mac was a good product, since it performed well in the microwave and tasted like the original. What was holding it back?

According to a survey of more than 2,000 people, consumers were aware of Easy Mac, but perceptions of the product were lower than expected. Interviews with consumers who were aware of Easy Mac but hadn't purchased it revealed skepticism about its taste and quality. This surprised brand managers, who had assumed that the strength of the Kraft Macaroni and Cheese name would assure consumers that the product tasted good. Another dilemma: The product took several steps to prepare—you didn't just pop a premade entrée into the microwave—and consumers were confused about this. Yet, when Kraft execs looked at the marketing research findings from consumers, they found a wide gap among those who had tasted Easy Mac. Fifty-five percent of users said that the product tasted good, compared with 20 percent who said it did not. What's more, once non-users tasted the product and were told how to prepare it, their opinions fell in line with those of users. Kraft execs

What you will learn in this chapter

- To understand the importance of marketing research as a management decision-making tool.

- To recognize that the essence of marketing research is to fulfill the marketing manager's need for knowledge of the market.

- To define *marketing research.*

- To explain the difference between basic and applied marketing research.

- To understand that marketing research is a means for implementing the marketing concept.

- To discuss the various categories of marketing research activities.

- To describe the managerial value of marketing research and its role in the development and implementation of marketing strategy.

- To understand when marketing research is needed and when it should not be conducted.

were convinced that the problem was with the communication, not the product.

Kraft decided to reformulate the ad campaign. In a series of focus group interviews, mothers revealed that they like the product because older kids could make it for themselves. Easy Mac allowed kids to become more self-reliant and lightened mom's workload. Kraft and its ad agency, FCB Worldwide, decided to shift away from the more generic consumer benefit of convenience to a more focused one: "Older kids can make it themselves." FCB created the "Siblings" campaign—slice-of-life vignettes that give mothers a sense of eavesdropping on their kids. In one, a school-age boy enjoys a steaming bowl of Easy Mac. His little sister asks if mom made it for him. When the brother explains that he made it himself, the sister further questions him, asking if "Mom knows" he performed this culinary feat on his own. "It was her idea," he says. Advertising research revealed that the "Siblings" ad scored higher than previous commercials. Consumer research showed moms liked the way the sister and brother gently teased each other. "It's totally believable. It reminds me of my household," said a Chicago mother. However, the advertising research also revealed that the taste message still wasn't strong enough. So the final commercial shows the brother and sister talking about how good Easy Mac tastes.

After the "Siblings" campaign, research showed Kraft Easy Mac had increases in both brand and ad awareness. The product saw a 30 percent increase in sales, making it the most successful macaroni and cheese line extension ever. Although many factors determined Easy Mac's success, marketing research exerted a major influence. At Kraft and thousands of other organizations, marketing research is an important managerial tool.

This chapter defines marketing research and discusses its role in marketing decision making. ■

THE NATURE OF MARKETING RESEARCH

Marketing research covers a wide range of phenomena. In essence, it fulfills the marketing manager's need for knowledge of the market. The manager of a food company may ask, "Will a package change improve my brand image?" The sales manager of a sporting goods firm may ask, "How can I monitor my sales and retail trade activities?" A marketing manager in the industrial tools market may ask, "To whom am I losing sales? From whom am I taking sales?" Marketing questions such as these require information about how customers, distributors, and competitors will respond to marketing decisions. Marketing research is one of the principal tools for answering such questions because it links the consumer, the customer, and the public to the marketer through information—information used to identify and define marketing opportunities and problems; to generate, refine, and evaluate marketing actions; to monitor marketing performance; and to improve the understanding of marketing as a process.[2]

The task of marketing research is to help specify and supply accurate information to reduce the uncertainty in decision making. Although marketing research provides information about consumers and the marketplace for developing and implementing marketing plans and strategies, it is not the only source of information. Every day marketing managers translate their experiences with marketing phenomena into marketing strategies. Information from a manager's experiences frequently is used in an intuitive manner because of the time pressures of business decisions or because the problem does not warrant more formal methods. However, the primary task of marketing management is effective decision making. Relying on seat-of-the-pants decision making—decision making without systematic inquiry—is like betting on a long shot at the racetrack because the horse's name is appealing. Occasionally there are successes, but in the long run intuition without research can lead to disappointing results. Marketing research helps decision makers shift from intuitive information gathering to systematic and objective investigating.

Marketing Research Defined

marketing research
The systematic and objective process of generating information to aid in making marketing decisions.

Marketing research is defined as the systematic and objective process of generating information to aid in making marketing decisions. This process includes specifying what information is required, designing the method for collecting information, managing and implementing the collection of data, analyzing the results, and communicating the findings and their implications.[3]

This definition suggests first that research information is not intuitive or haphazardly gathered. Literally, *research* (re-search) means "to search again." The term connotes patient study and scientific investigation wherein the researcher takes another, more careful look at the data to discover all that is known about the subject.

Second, if the information generated or the data collected is to be accurate, the marketing researcher must be objective. The need for objectivity was cleverly stated by the 19th-century American humorist Artemus Ward: "It ain't the things we don't know that gets us in trouble. It's the things we know that ain't so." The researcher should be detached and impersonal rather than biased, attempting to support his or her preconceived ideas. If the research process is contaminated by bias, its value is considerably reduced.

As an example, a developer owned a large area of land and wished to build a high-prestige shopping center. He wanted a research report to demonstrate to prospective retailers that there was a large market potential for such a center. He conducted his survey exclusively in an elite neighborhood. Not surprisingly, the findings showed that a large percentage of the respondents wanted a high-prestige shopping center. Results of this kind are misleading and should be disregarded. The importance of striving for objectivity cannot be overemphasized; without objectivity, research is valueless.

This definition of marketing research also points out that the objective of research is to facilitate the managerial decision-making process for all aspects of the firm's marketing mix: pricing, promotion, distribution, and product decisions. The definition is not restricted to any one aspect of the marketing mix. By providing the necessary information on which to base decisions, marketing research can reduce the uncertainty of a decision and thereby decrease the risk of making the wrong decision. However, research should be an aid to managerial judgment and not a substitute for it.

Finally, this definition of marketing research is limited by one's definition of marketing. Certainly research in the marketing area of a for-profit corporation is marketing research. A broader definition of marketing research, however, includes nonprofit organizations such as the American Heart Association, the San Diego Zoo, and the Boston Pops Orchestra. Each of these organizations exists to satisfy social needs, and each requires marketing skills to produce and distribute the products and services people want. Hence, marketing research may be conducted by organizations that are not business organizations.

Basic Research and Applied Research

basic (pure) research
Research conducted to expand the boundaries of knowledge itself or to verify the acceptability of a given theory.

applied research
Research undertaken to answer questions about specific problems or to make decisions about particular courses of action.

One purpose of conducting marketing research is to develop and evaluate concepts and theories. **Basic** or **pure research** attempts to expand the limits of knowledge. It is not aimed at solving a particular pragmatic problem. It has been said that there is nothing as practical as a good theory. Although this is true in the long run, basic marketing research findings generally cannot be immediately implemented by a marketing executive. Basic research is conducted to verify the acceptability of a given theory or to learn more about a certain concept. **Applied research** is conducted when a decision must be made about a specific real-life problem. Our focus is on applied research: studies undertaken to answer questions about specific problems or to make decisions about particular courses of action or policies.

This discussion emphasizes applied research because most students will be oriented toward the day-to-day practice of marketing management. It is aimed at students and researchers who will be exposed to short-term, problem-solving research conducted for businesses or nonprofit organizations. However, the procedures and techniques used by applied and basic researchers do not differ substantially; both employ the scientific method to answer the question at hand. Broadly defined, the **scientific method** refers to the techniques and procedures used to recognize and understand marketing phenomena. In the scientific method, empirical evidence (facts derived from observation or experimentation) is analyzed and interpreted to confirm or disprove prior conceptions. In basic research, testing these prior conceptions or hypotheses and then making inferences and conclusions about the phenomena lead to the establishment of general laws about the phenomena. Use of the scientific method in applied research ensures objectivity in gathering facts and testing creative ideas for alternative marketing strategies. The essence of research, whether basic or applied, lies in the scientific method. Much of this book deals with scientific methodology. Thus, the techniques of basic and applied research differ largely in degree rather than substance.

scientific method
Systematic techniques or procedures used to analyze empirical evidence in an unbiased attempt to confirm or disprove prior conceptions.

THE MARKETING CONCEPT

marketing concept
The marketing philosophy that stresses a consumer orientation, emphasizes long-range profitability, and suggests the integration and coordination of marketing and other organizational functions.

Although this book focuses on marketing research, marketing managers should understand how marketing research fits into the broader scope of marketing. Research is one of the primary tools that enables firms to implement the philosophical idea of the marketing concept. The **marketing concept** is the most central idea in marketing thinking. It has evolved over time as production- and engineering-oriented firms have responded to changes in the economic environment to become marketing-oriented firms. The marketing concept is a threefold concept concerned with

1. Consumer orientation
2. Long-run profitability rather than sales volume
3. Cross-functional perspective

Consumer Orientation

According to the marketing concept, marketers must view the consumer as the pivotal point around which the business revolves. Simply put, the firm creates products, whether goods, services, or both, with consumers' needs in mind. Many marketing theorists and operating marketing managers believe that the satisfaction of consumers' wants is the justification for a firm's existence.

The Partnership for a Drug Free America is a nonprofit organization that conducts applied research. Its research indicated that the Partnership should target younger children. As a result, it created a public service announcement called "Big Ol' Bug" to appeal to children ages 6 to 8. The rock music lyrics include the line "I'd rather eat a big ol' bug than ever take a stupid drug."

Yoplait Go-Gurt, yogurt packaged in a three-sided tube designed to fit kids' lunchboxes, had more than $100 million in sales its first year on the market. The development of Go-Gurt clearly illustrates a consumer orientation. The company's consumer research about regular yogurt showed that moms and kids in their "tweens" wanted convenience and portability. Some brands, like Colombo Spoon in a Snap, offered the convenience of having a utensil as part of the packaging/delivery system. However, from what Yoplait marketers learned about consumers, they thought kids would eat more yogurt if they could "lose the spoon" and eat yogurt anywhere, anytime. Moms and kids participating in a taste test were invited to sample different brand-on-the-go packaging shapes—long tubes, thin tubes, fat tubes, and other shapes—without being told how to handle the packaging. One of the company's researchers said, "It was funny to see the moms fidget around, then daintily pour the product onto a spoon, then into their mouths. The kids instantly jumped on it. They knew what to do."[4] Squeezing Go-Gurt from the tube was a big plus. The kids loved the fact that the packaging gave them permission to play with their food, something parents always tell them not to do. Go-Gurt is a fun, convenient product that allows consumers the freedom to eat whenever and wherever they want. Yoplait realized that knowledge of consumers' needs, coupled with product research and development, leads to successful marketing strategies and that industry leadership—indeed, corporate survival—depends on satisfying consumers.

Long-Run Profitability

Consumer orientation does not mean slavery to consumers' every fleeting whim. Implicit in the marketing concept is the assumption of the continuity of the firm within a competitive environment. The firm must make a profit to survive in the long run. Most consumers would prefer to have a Porsche priced under $15,000. However, the production costs of this car exceed that figure, and the firm surely would fail if it attempted to satisfy this desire.

The second aspect of the marketing concept argues against profitless volume, or sales volume for the sake of volume alone. Marketing cost analysis has taught numerous firms that 20 percent of their customers have been responsible for 80 percent of their profits and that salespeople have spent too much time on unprofitable accounts. The marketing concept suggests that these firms should reevaluate selling to small, unprofitable accounts.

A Cross-Functional Perspective

Marketing personnel do not work in a vacuum, isolated from other company activities. The actions of people in areas such as production, credit, and research and development may affect an organization's marketing efforts. Similarly, the work of marketers will affect activities in other departments. Problems are almost certain to arise from a lack of an integrated, companywide effort. Marketers need to take a cross-functional perspective.

Problems occur when the marketing department views focusing on consumer needs as its sole responsibility. Indeed, other functional areas' goals may conflict with customer satisfaction or long-term profitability. For instance, the engineering department may want long lead times for product design, with simplicity and economy as major design goals. Marketing, however, may prefer short lead times and more complex designs with custom components and optional features for multiple models. The finance department may want fixed budgets, strict spending justifications, and prices that cover costs, whereas the marketing department may seek flexible budgets, liberal spending rationales, and below-cost prices to develop markets quickly.

Similar differences in outlook may be found in other functional areas of the organization, and these may be sources of serious conflicts. When a firm lacks organizational procedures for communicating marketing information and coordinating marketing efforts, the effectiveness of its marketing programs will suffer.

Keeping Customers and Building Relationships

So far, we have talked about getting customers, but keeping customers is equally important. Marketers want customers for life. Effective marketers work to build long-term relationships with their customers. The term *relationship marketing* communicates the idea that a major goal of marketing is to build long-term relationships with the parties that contribute to the company's success.

Once an exchange is made, effective marketing stresses managing the relationships that will bring about additional exchanges. Effective marketers view making a sale not as the end of a process but as the start of the organization's relationship with a customer. Satisfied customers will return to a company that has treated them well if they need to purchase the same product in the future. If they need a related item, satisfied customers know the first place to look.

Marketing Research: A Means for Implementing the Marketing Concept

Satisfying the consumer is a major goal of marketing. One purpose of marketing research is to obtain information that identifies consumers' problems and needs, bridging the information gap between marketing executives and consumers. Researching consumer needs in this way enables firms to fulfill the marketing concept.

Rubbermaid's new-product development process epitomizes this function.[5] Every new Rubbermaid product starts with research that asks one simple question: What's wrong with existing products? No consumer problem is considered too small, no concern too finicky. One marketing research study uncovered an inner secret of the bathroom: Women found it distasteful that family members' toothbrushes touched one another in the toothbrush holder. After finding what was wrong, Rubbermaid's new-product team went back to the lab and created a toothbrush holder that angled each brush outward to prevent the offending contact.

H. J. Heinz knew that kids under 12 are the biggest ketchup consumers. So it conducted research among kids and moms to see if it could increase customer satisfaction and enhance its relationship with its customers. Researchers observed kids and how they used Heinz's traditional ketchup bottles. They concluded that the bulky bottle made it difficult for kids to control the pour—they squirted ketchup in blobs and often made messy spills. To make kids a lot happier, Heinz introduced EZ Squirt, vitamin C–fortified ketchup in an hourglass-shaped package designed especially for kids. The new plastic bottle is easy for kids to hold with two hands. Its narrow nozzle allows kids to apply (and draw) a ketchup stream on their food. Best of all, however, EZ Squirt ketchup is green. The green color was also the result of research with kids, who said they would like to see ketchup in some color other than red. Blue and other colors were investigated, but researchers concluded that green was the best place to start because it had more "kitchen logic."[6]

Consider another example from Rubbermaid of how marketing research found a natural answer to consumers' needs. The company now markets a shower caddy that has a dispenser that can hold a shampoo bottle upside down. Why? Research showed that many consumers wanted to make sure they could use the last drop of their shampoo, but they hated to stand in the shower waiting for those last drops.

In research about children's lunchboxes, parents indicated they often worried about where to put milk money, allergy medicines, keys, and other small items their kids needed to take to school. When Rubbermaid came out with its backpack lunchbox, which was designed to slip easily into a backpack, it built in a change holder.

Measuring consumer satisfaction is another means of determining how well a company is fulfilling the marketing concept. Customer satisfaction research can ascertain whether an organization's total quality management program is meeting customer expectations and management objectives. General Electric's major-appliance division sends the questionnaire shown in Exhibit 1.1 to customers after repair calls to determine how well the company is accomplishing its objective of consumer satisfaction. The questionnaire asks whether the appointment was scheduled promptly, whether the repair person showed up on time and was polite, and if the customer was satisfied with the service. Customer satisfaction surveys such as this tend to be standardized and ongoing so that performance can be compared against previously established standards. These measures lead to the evaluation of managers according to consumers' perceptions of quality, in addition to the evaluation of actual operational quality.

Marketing research can also help prevent commercialization of products that are not consumer oriented. Sometimes ideas that look like technological breakthroughs in the laboratory fall flat when presented to consumers. For example, a powdered pain reliever was supposed to be a soothing remedy because it was to

| EXHIBIT 1.1 | MARKETING RESEARCH MAY MEASURE CONSUMER SATISFACTION[7] |

 QUALITY OF SERVICE SURVEY

Please rate the service you recently received from GE Factory Service (product and date shown on the reverse side). Consider all service calls required for this particular problem. Indicate your answers by checking the appropriate box for each question.

1. When you called for service were you able to get through on the first call without getting a busy signal? .... YES ☐ NO ☐

2. When you called, were you placed on hold? .... YES ☐ NO ☐

3. Did the person you talked with on the phone give you the feeling that he/she really cared about your problem? .... YES ☐ NO ☐

4. What day was your appointment scheduled for? .... SAME DAY ☐ NEXT DAY ☐ 3RD DAY ☐ 4TH DAY ☐ LATER ☐

5. Was this the day you most preferred? .... YES ☐ NO ☐

6. If not, what day would you have most preferred? .... SAME DAY ☐ NEXT DAY ☐ 3RD DAY ☐ 4TH DAY ☐ LATER ☐

7. When was the technician scheduled to arrive? .... AM 8-12 ☐ PM 12-5 ☐ EVENING AFTER 5 ☐ ALL DAY 8-5 ☐

8. Was this time of day you most preferred? .... YES ☐ NO ☐

9. Did the technician come on the scheduled day? .... YES ☐ NO ☐

10. Did the technician arrive during the scheduled time period? .... YES ☐ NO ☐

11. Did the technician give you the feeling he/she really cared about your problem? ... YES ☐ NO ☐

12. Did the technician seem to be knowledgeable and competent about your product? ... YES ☐ NO ☐

13. Did the technician explain what was done to fix your problem? .... YES ☐ NO ☐

14. Were the charges on the invoice explained to you? .... YES ☐ NO ☐

15. Considering the service you received, how would you rate the charges for:

	NO CHARGE INVOLVED	VERY REASONABLE	REASONABLE	UNREASONABLE	VERY UNREASONABLE
LABOR (incl. home call)	☐	☐	☐	☐	☐
PARTS	☐	☐	☐	☐	☐
TOTAL CHARGE	☐	☐	☐	☐	☐

16. How many trips were required to complete the repair? ... 1 ☐ 2 ☐ 3 ☐ 4 ☐ MORE THAN 4 ☐

17. Overall, how would you rate our technician? ... EXCELLENT ☐ GOOD ☐ FAIR ☐ POOR ☐

18. If a part was needed to complete the repair, was the part: ... AVAILABLE ON SERVICE TRUCK ☐ MAILED TO YOU ☐ BROUGHT BACK LATER BY A TECHNICIAN ☐ NO PART NEEDED ☐

19. If a part was ordered, how many days did it take for you to get the part? ... NO PART ORDERED ☐ SAME DAY ☐ 1-4 DAYS ☐ 5-9 DAYS ☐ MORE THAN 9 DAYS ☐

20. **Considering all these questions, how satisfied are you with the overall service you received?** ... VERY SATISFIED ☐ SATISFIED ☐ NEITHER SATISFIED/DISSATISFIED ☐ DISSATISFIED ☐ VERY DISSATISFIED ☐

21. **If you needed to replace the product you had repaired, how likely would you be to buy the General Electric or Hotpoint brand?** ... DEFINITELY WOULD BUY GE/HOTPOINT ☐ PROBABLY WOULD BUY GE/HOTPOINT ☐ MIGHT OR MIGHT NOT BUY GE/HOTPOINT ☐ PROBABLY WOULD NOT BUY GE/HOTPOINT ☐ DEFINITELY WOULD NOT BUY GE/HOTPOINT ☐

22. Please add any comments you have about the service you received.

_____

_____

_____

_____

be mixed with milk. It did not soothe customers, however. Research showed that the public thought this great step forward was a step backward in convenience of usage. Someone forgot to consider the consumer benefit.

By improving efficiency, research also facilitates profitability. For instance, during the introduction of a new product, accurate forecasting of the product's potential sales volume is an essential basis for estimating its profitability. A firm considering the introduction of a low-calorie candy bar might rely on a test-market experiment to determine the optimal price for this new concept. Extensive testing should be done to ensure that the marketing program is fine-tuned to maximize the firm's profitability while satisfying the consumer.

Analysis of data may also be a form of marketing research that can increase efficiency. Marketing representatives from Exxon Chemical Company used laptop computers to present a complex set of calculations to sales prospects to show them the advantage of Exxon products over competitors'. Such analysis of research data improves the salesperson's batting average and the firm's efficiency.

Because of the importance of company efforts, a marketing researcher must be knowledgeable not just about marketing research but about the entire spectrum of marketing activities.

THE MANAGERIAL VALUE OF MARKETING RESEARCH FOR STRATEGIC DECISION MAKING

The primary managerial value of marketing research comes from its ability to reduce uncertainty. Research generates information that facilitates decision making about marketing strategies and tactics.

Developing and implementing a marketing strategy involves four stages:

TO THE POINT

The secret of success is to know something nobody else knows.

ARISTOTLE ONASSIS

1. Identifying and evaluating opportunities
2. Analyzing market segments and selecting target markets
3. Planning and implementing a marketing mix that will satisfy customers' needs and meet the objectives of the organization
4. Analyzing marketing performance.[8]

Identifying and Evaluating Opportunities

Before developing a marketing strategy, an organization must determine where it wants to go and how to get there. Marketing research can help answer these questions by investigating potential opportunities to identify attractive areas for company action.

Marketing research may provide diagnostic information about what is occurring in the environment. A simple description of some social or economic activity, such as trends in consumer purchasing behavior, may help managers recognize problems and identify opportunities to enrich marketing efforts.

One reason for Mattel Toys' success in the rapidly changing toy market is the company's commitment to consumer research. Much of its success may be traced to the way it goes about identifying opportunities for its new products. For example, marketing research showed that instead of military, spy, or sports heroes, young boys preferred fantasy figures. Boys spend much time fantasizing about good versus evil. Research showed that timeless fantasy figures, both ancient and futuristic, were visually exciting, and because they were timeless, boys could do more with them. Several lines of action figures, including Rock 'Em Sock 'Em Robots and Max Steel toys, benefited from this research. Video games by Gameboy and Xbox also reflect an awareness of this research finding.

The purpose of a research study on running shoes was to investigate the occasions or situations associated with product use—that is, when individuals wore their running shoes. The researchers found that most owners of running shoes wore the shoes while walking, not running. Also, most of this walking was part of a normal daily activity like shopping or commuting to work. Many of the people who wore running shoes for routine activities considered the shoes an alternative to other casual shoes. This research ultimately led to the development of the walking shoe designed for comfortable, everyday walking.

Market opportunities may be evaluated using many performance criteria. In many cases marketing research supplies the information to determine which opportunities are best for the organization. For example, the performance criterion of market demand typically is estimated using marketing research techniques.

Estimates of market potential or predictions about future environmental conditions allow managers to evaluate opportunities. Accurate sales forecasts are among the most useful pieces of planning information a marketing manager can have. Complete accuracy in forecasting the future is not possible, because change is constantly occurring in the marketing environment. Nevertheless, objective forecasts of demand or changing environments may be the foundations on which marketing strategies are built.

Analyzing and Selecting Target Markets

The second stage of marketing strategy development is to analyze market segments and select target markets. The American Marketing Association found that more than 90 percent of the organizations it surveyed engaged in research to determine market characteristics and trends.[9] Marketing research is a major source of information for determining which characteristics of market segments distinguish them from the overall market.

Market segmentation studies at Harley-Davidson provide a good example of this essential activity. Marketing research depicts the Harley-Davidson motorcycle purchaser as a 46-year-old male (80 percent) with some college (44 percent). He is likely to be married (72 percent) and to have no children (55 percent). The average Harley owner lives in a household with an annual income of $78,000.[10]

Planning and Implementing a Marketing Mix

Using the information obtained in the two previous stages, marketing managers plan and execute a marketing mix strategy. However, marketing research may be needed to support specific decisions about any aspect of the marketing mix. Often the research is conducted to evaluate alternative courses of action. For example, advertising research investigated whether a particular actress, one of Hollywood's most beautiful women, would make a good spokesperson for a specific brand of hair coloring. She was filmed in some test commercials to endorse the brand, but the commercials were never aired, because although viewers recognized her as an outstanding personality in the test commercials, they did not perceive her as a user of home hair-coloring kits or as an authority on such products.

Managers face many diverse decisions about marketing mixes. The following examples highlight selected types of research that might be conducted for each element of the marketing mix.

Product Research Product research takes many forms and includes studies designed to evaluate and develop new products, measure perceptions of the quality of goods and services, and learn how to adapt existing product lines. Concept testing exposes potential customers to new product ideas to judge the concept's acceptance and feasibility. Product testing reveals a product prototype's strengths and weaknesses or determines whether a finished product performs better than competing brands or according to expectations. Brand name evaluation studies investigate whether a name is appropriate for a product. Package testing assesses size, color, shape, ease of use, and other attributes of a package. Total quality management studies involve routinely asking customers to rate a product against its competitors.

Product research encompasses all applications of marketing research that seek to develop product attributes that will add value for consumers. When Chee-tos became the first major brand of snack food to be made and marketed in China, product taste tests revealed that traditional cheese-flavored corn puffs Chee-tos did not appeal to Chinese consumers. So the company conducted consumer research with 600 different flavors to learn which flavors would be most appealing. Among the flavors Chinese consumers tested and disliked were ranch dressing, nacho, Italian pizza, Hawaiian barbecue, peanut satay, North Sea crab, chili prawn, coconut milk curry, smoked octopus, caramel, and cuttlefish. Research did show that consumers liked some flavors. So, when Chee-tos were introduced in China, they came in two flavors: savory American cream and zesty Japanese steak.

Pricing Research　Most organizations conduct pricing research. A competitive pricing study is a typical marketing research project of this type. However, research designed to discover the ideal price for a product or to determine if consumers will pay a price high enough to cover cost is not uncommon. Pricing research may also investigate when to offer discounts or coupons, explore whether certain critical product attributes determine how consumers perceive value, or determine if a product category, such as soft drinks, has price gaps among national brands, regional brands, and private labels.[11]

Research may answer many questions about price. Is there a need for seasonal or quantity discounts? Are coupons more effective than price reductions? Is a brand price elastic or price inelastic? How much of a price difference will best differentiate items in the product line?.

Distribution Research　Golden Books traditionally distributed its small hardcover children's books with golden spines through upscale book retailers. When it researched where its customers would prefer to purchase Golden Books, the company learned that mass merchandisers, grocery stores, and drug stores would be just as popular as the upscale stores as distribution channels. Williams-Sonoma, Sears, and KB Toys are among the many major retailers that have researched home shopping services via the Internet. New interactive media and home delivery as a means of distribution have the potential to revolutionize channel-of-distribution systems, and millions of dollars are being spent to research this alternative. Although most distribution research does not have the dramatic impact of the research on Internet shopping systems, research focused on developing and improving the efficiency of channels of distribution is important to many organizations.

A typical study in the distribution area may be conducted to select retail sites or warehouse locations. A survey of retailers or wholesalers may be conducted because the actions of one channel member can greatly affect the performances of other channel members. Distribution research often is needed to gain knowledge about retailers' and wholesalers' operations and to learn their reactions to a manufacturer's marketing policies.

The 3M Corporation surveys its industrial distributors anonymously to determine how they feel about doing business with each of their suppliers, including 3M. The purpose of the research is to investigate distributors' attitudes

British Airways' marketing research revealed that many business travelers find air travel a frustrating experience—full of hassles from the office to the airport to a hotel or a meeting and back again. Air travelers want to know they're being cared for. With these findings in mind, executives at British Airways made a decision to alter its service. The airline relaunched its Club Europe business-class services to smooth business travelers' paths, providing them more time and space, and above all, eliminating the hassles. The new Club Europe service, whose cost exceeded 70 million British pounds, includes new seats, more business lounges, limousines at taxi rates, and speedier service through customs at Heathrow's Terminal One.[12]

about relationships with sales representatives, ordering procedures, on-time delivery, training of distributor personnel, product quality, and many other activities that help build long-term relationships.

Promotion Research   Research that investigates the effectiveness of premiums, coupons, sampling deals, and other sales promotions is classified as promotion research. Promotion research includes buyer motivation studies to generate ideas for copy development, media research, and studies of advertising effectiveness. However, the most time, money, and effort are spent on advertising research.

The marketing research findings of Zale's, a large jewelry retailer, helped in the creation of advertising with large, one-word headlines that simply asked, "Confused?" "Nervous?" or "Lost?" The advertisements overtly acknowledged the considerable emotional and financial risks consumers face in jewelry purchases. Research had shown that typical consumers felt unable to determine the relative quality of various jewelry items, believed jewelry purchases were expensive, and needed reassurance about their purchases, especially because they often purchased jewelry for someone else.

Media research helps an advertiser decide whether television, newspapers, magazines, the Internet, or other media alternatives are best suited to convey the advertiser's message. Choices among media alternatives may be based on research that shows how many people in the target audience each advertising vehicle can reach.

The Integrated Marketing Mix   The individual elements of the marketing mix do not work independently. Hence, many research studies investigate various combinations of marketing ingredients to gather information to suggest the best possible marketing program.

Analyzing Marketing Performance

After a marketing strategy has been implemented, marketing research may serve to inform managers whether planned activities were properly executed and are

SUPER BOWL 2002: A HIGHLY EFFECTIVE ADVERTISING MEDIUM

The 2002 Super Bowl game was one of the most exciting games in Super Bowl history, and the television audience for the game was estimated at more than 130 million viewers.[13]

But did the match between New England and St. Louis give advertisers what they were looking for: an audience who watched the ads and remembered them? Yes. Advertisements on the Super Bowl left a far more enduring impression with viewers than did advertisements on Monday Night Football or a football playoff game.

Research conducted by Ipsos-ASI with male TV viewers the day after the Super Bowl and after two previous football games shows that the Super Bowl delivered what it promised . . . and in a big way.

Ipsos-ASI, which has tested more than 40,000 commercials since it was founded in 1962, found that the Super Bowl far exceeded the ability of other football games to deliver the hard-to-reach male audience. With Super Bowl ads costing close to $2 million for 30 seconds, and some specifically created for this game, Isos-ASI wanted to see whether the Super Bowl delivers a bigger and more attentive audience than any other game of the year. And the answer unequivocally is, yes it does. For example, the advertising researchers found that 45 percent of the audience reported that they had watched all of the 56 paid ads in any given quarter during the Super Bowl, compared with only 9 percent who watched the ads during Monday Night Football and NFC Championship games.

In Internet interviews with adult males conducted the day after each of the three games, Ipsos-ASI found:

- 88 percent could remember the name of at least one of the advertisers in the Super Bowl, while only 29 percent could remember an advertiser from Monday Night Football and only 33 percent could recall ads from the NFC Championship.
- The average viewer could remember 3.2 advertisers from the Super Bowl, compared to less than 1 advertiser from Monday Night Football and the NFC Championship.
- 32 percent claimed to have watched all the ads during the halftime show. Only 9 percent watched all the ads during halftime on Monday Night Football, and 13 percent watched halftime ads during the NFC Championship game.
- Pepsi and Budweiser fared the best during the Super Bowl. Two-thirds of the audience could remember those companies' advertising.

performance-monitoring research
Research that regularly, sometimes routinely, provides feedback for evaluation and control of marketing activity.

accomplishing what they were expected to achieve. In other words, marketing research may be conducted to obtain feedback for evaluation and control of marketing programs.

Performance-monitoring research refers to research that regularly, sometimes routinely, provides feedback for evaluation and control of marketing activity. For example, most firms continuously monitor wholesale and retail activity to ensure early detection of sales declines and other anomalies. In the grocery and drug industries, sales research may use Universal Product Codes on packages read by electronic scanners and computerized checkout counters to provide valuable information about each brand's retail sales volume and market share. Market–share analysis and sales analysis are the most common forms of performance-monitoring research. Almost every organization compares its

Tan Auténtica y Original Como Nuestra Gente

current sales with previous sales and with competitors' sales. However, marketing performance analysis is not limited to the investigation of sales figures.

Performance-monitoring research is especially important for the continuous improvement of product and service quality necessary for a successful total quality management program.[15] Implementing a total quality management program requires considerable measurement. It involves routinely asking customers to rate a product or service against its competitors, measuring employee attitudes, and monitoring company performance against benchmark standards. Because these activities use marketing research extensively, marketing research with external customers and with employees in the organization (internal customers) contributes much to a total quality management program.

United Airlines' Omnibus in-flight surveys provide a good example of performance-monitoring research for quality management. United routinely selects sample flights and administers questionnaires concerning in-flight service, food, and so forth. The Omnibus survey is conducted quarterly to determine who is flying and for what reason. It enables United to track demographic changes and monitor customer ratings of its services on a continuing basis and to gather vast amounts of information at low cost. The information regarding customer reaction to services can be compared over time. For example, suppose United decided to change its menu for in-flight meals. The results of the Omnibus survey might indicate that shortly after a menu change, customers' ratings of food and meals declined. Information gathered continuously is extremely valuable because it allows management to quickly spot similar trends in passengers' ratings of airport lobbies, gate-line waits, or cabin cleanliness. Thus, management can act rapidly to improve deficiencies.

When analysis of marketing performance indicates that things are not going as planned, marketing research may be required to explain why something went wrong. Detailed information about specific mistakes or failures is frequently sought. If a general problem area is identified, breaking down industry sales volume and a firm's sales volume into different geographical areas may yield explanations for specific problems. Exploring problems in greater depth may indicate which managerial judgments were erroneous.

WHEN IS MARKETING RESEARCH NEEDED?

A marketing manager confronted with two or more alternative courses of action faces the initial decision of whether to conduct marketing research. The determination of the need for marketing research centers on (1) time constraints, (2) the availability of data, (3) the nature of the decision to be made, and (4) the value of the research information in relation to costs. Exhibit 1.2 outlines the criteria for determining when to conduct marketing research.

Time Constraints

Systematic research takes time. In many instances, management believes that a decision must be made immediately, allowing no time for research. Decisions sometimes are made without adequate information or thorough understanding of market situations. Although making decisions without researching a situation is not ideal, the urgency of a situation sometimes precludes the use of research.

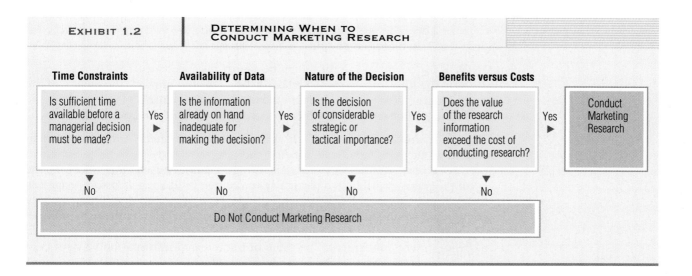

| EXHIBIT 1.2 | DETERMINING WHEN TO CONDUCT MARKETING RESEARCH |

Time Constraints   **Availability of Data**   **Nature of the Decision**   **Benefits versus Costs**

Is sufficient time available before a managerial decision must be made? → Yes → Is the information already on hand inadequate for making the decision? → Yes → Is the decision of considerable strategic or tactical importance? → Yes → Does the value of the research information exceed the cost of conducting research? → Yes → Conduct Marketing Research

No ↓   No ↓   No ↓   No ↓

Do Not Conduct Marketing Research

Availability of Data

Often managers already possess enough information to make sound decisions without conducting marketing research. When they lack adequate information, however, research must be considered. Managers must ask themselves if the research will provide the information needed to answer the basic questions about a decision. Furthermore, if a potential source of data exists, managers will want to know how much it will cost to obtain the data.

If the data cannot be obtained, research cannot be conducted. For example, many African nations have never conducted a population census. Organizations engaged in international business often find that data about business activity or population characteristics that are readily available in the United States are non-existent or sparse in a developing country. Imagine the problems facing marketing researchers who wish to investigate market potential in places like Uzbekistan, Yugoslavian Macedonia, and Rwanda.

Nature of the Decision

The value of marketing research will depend on the nature of the managerial decision to be made. A routine tactical decision that does not require a substantial investment may not seem to warrant a substantial expenditure for marketing research. For example, a computer company must update its operator's instruction manual when it makes minor product modifications. The research cost of determining the proper wording to use in the updated manual is likely to be too high for such a minor decision. The nature of the decision is not totally independent of the next issue to be considered: the benefits from conducting the research versus the costs of the research. In general, however, the more strategically or tactically important the decision, the more likely it is that research will be conducted.

Benefits versus Costs

There are both costs and benefits to conducting marketing research. Earlier we discussed some of the managerial benefits of marketing research. Of course, conducting research to obtain these benefits requires an expenditure of money. In any decision-making situation, managers must identify alternative courses of action, then weigh the value of each alternative against its costs. Marketing research can be thought of as an investment alternative. When deciding whether to make a decision without research or to postpone the decision in order to conduct research, managers should ask three questions:

1. Will the payoff or rate of return be worth the investment?
2. Will the information gained by marketing research improve the quality of the marketing decision enough to warrant the expenditure?
3. Is the proposed research expenditure the best use of the available funds?

For example, *TV-Cable Week* was not test marketed before its launch. Although the magazine had articles and stories about TV personalities and events, its main feature was program listings, channel by channel, showing the exact programs available to a particular subscriber. Producing a custom magazine for each individual cable TV system in the country required developing a costly computer system. Since that development necessitated a substantial expenditure, one that could not be scaled down for research, conducting research was judged to be an unwise investment. The value of the research information was not positive, because its cost exceeded its benefits. Unfortunately, pricing and distribution problems became so compelling after the magazine was launched that the product was a marketing failure. Nevertheless, managers, lacking the luxury of hindsight, made a reasonable decision not to conduct research. They analyzed the cost of the information (that is, the cost of test marketing) relative to the potential benefits of the information.

MARKETING RESEARCH IN THE 21ST CENTURY

Marketing research, like all business activity, has been strongly influenced by two major trends in business: increased globalization and the rapid growth of the Internet and other information technologies. These trends will continue, and likely accelerate, as the 21st century progresses. We consider their significance for marketing research here.

Global Marketing Research

Marketing research has become increasingly global and will become more so in the 21st century. Some companies have extensive international marketing research operations. Upjohn conducts marketing research in 160 different countries. A. C. Nielsen International, known for its television ratings, is the world's largest marketing research company. Two-thirds of its business comes from outside the United States.[16]

Companies that conduct business in foreign countries must understand the nature of those particular markets and judge whether they require customized marketing strategies. For example, although the 15 nations of the European Union share a single formal market, marketing research shows that Europeans do not share identical tastes for many consumer products. Marketing researchers have found no such thing as a typical European consumer; language, religion, climate, and centuries of tradition divide the nations of the European Union. Scantel Research, a British firm that advises companies on color preferences, found inexplicable differences in the ways Europeans take their medicine. The French prefer to pop purple pills, but the English and Dutch favor white ones. Consumers in all three countries dislike bright red capsules, which are big sellers in the United States. This example illustrates that companies that do business in Europe must judge whether they need to adapt to local customs and buying habits.[17]

Although the nature of marketing research can differ around the globe, the need for marketing research is universal. Throughout this book, we will discuss the practical problems involved in conducting marketing research in Europe, Asia, Latin America, the Middle East, and elsewhere.

Growth of the Internet

The Internet is transforming society. Time is collapsing. Distance is no longer an obstacle. Crossing oceans requires only a mouse click. People are connected 24 hours a day, 7 days a week. "Instantaneous" has a new meaning.[18]

The Internet is a worldwide network of computers that allows users access to information and documents from distant sources. Many people believe that the Internet is the most important communications medium since television. It has certainly changed the way millions of people think about getting and distributing information. And, of course, obtaining and communicating information is the essence of marketing research. Consider that a researcher seeking facts and figures about a marketing issue may find more extensive information on the

The world economy has become global, and corporations market products in many countries. People think of their home culture as the normal way of life, but consumers in other cultures often have different values, beliefs, and behaviors. Marketing research helps marketers understand cultural differences. Colgate-Palmolive is a progressive company that conducts marketing research around the world. Colgate-Palmolive used marketing research when it introduced a new and improved toothpaste in Colombia.

Internet more quickly than by visiting a library. Another researcher who is questioning people from around the globe may do so almost instantaneously with an Internet survey and get responses 24 hours a day, 7 days a week. Visitors to an organization's Web site may find that online questions are personalized, because the site incorporates information technology that remembers the particular "click-stream" of the Web pages they visited. These few examples illustrate how the Internet and other information technologies are dramatically changing the face of marketing research.

In the 21st century, marketing research on the Internet is moving out of the introductory stage of its product life cycle into the growth stage. The rest of this book reflects this change. Throughout the book, we will discuss the latest information technologies and their application to marketing research. Marketing research via the Internet has come of age.

SUMMARY

Marketing research is a tool companies use to discover consumers' wants and needs so that they can satisfy those wants and needs with their product offerings. Marketing research is the marketing manager's source of information about market conditions. It covers topics ranging from long-range planning to near-term tactical decisions.

Marketing research is the systematic and objective process of generating information—gathering, recording, and analyzing data—to aid marketing decision making. The research must be systematic, not haphazard. It must be objective to avoid the distorting effects of personal bias. Basic or pure research aims to expand knowledge of a concept or to verify the acceptability of a theory. Applied research seeks to address specific problems or aid in decisions about particular courses of action.

Marketing research is a means of implementing the marketing concept, the most central idea in marketing. The marketing concept says that a firm must be oriented toward both consumer satisfaction and long-run profitability (rather than short-run sales volume). Further, all aspects of the firm need to be integrated to achieve these goals.

Marketing research can help implement the marketing concept by identifying consumers' problems and needs, improving efficiency, and evaluating the effectiveness of marketing strategies and tactics.

The development and implementation of a marketing strategy involves four stages: (1) identifying and evaluating opportunities, (2) analyzing market segments and selecting target markets, (3) planning and implementing a marketing mix that will satisfy customers' needs and meet the objectives of the organization, and (4) analyzing marketing performance. Marketing research helps in each stage by providing information for strategic decision making.

Managers also use marketing research to determine what went wrong with past marketing efforts, describe current events in the marketplace, and forecast future conditions.

A marketing manager determines whether marketing research should be conducted based on (1) time constraints, (2) availability of data, (3) the nature of the decision to be made, and (4) the benefits versus the costs of the research information.

Key Terms and Concepts

marketing research
basic (pure) research

applied research
scientific method

marketing concept
performance-monitoring research

Questions for Review and Critical Thinking

1. Is it possible to make sound marketing decisions without conducting marketing research? What advantages does research offer to the decision maker over seat-of-the-pants decision making?
2. An advertising agency's slogan is "People listen to us because we listen to them." Has this firm integrated the marketing research function with the marketing concept?
3. Name some products that logically might have been developed with the help of marketing research.
4. In your own words, define *marketing research* and describe its task.
5. Which of the following organizations are likely to use marketing research? Why? How?
   a. Manufacturer of breakfast cereals
   b. Manufacturer of nuts, bolts, and other fasteners
   c. The Federal Trade Commission
   d. A hospital
   e. A computer software publisher
6. An automobile manufacturer is conducting research in an attempt to predict the type of car consumers will desire in the year 2020. Is this effort basic or applied research? Explain.
7. The owner of 22 restaurants was asked how he does marketing research. He answered that he does it by driving around in a pickup truck after midnight: "I stay up late. If it's midnight and I don't have anything else to do, I drive around town and look at the lines in front of places. I'll look at the trash and see if a guy's doing business. If he's got a real clean bunch of trash cans and an empty dumpster, he's not doing any business. I find out a lot by talking to my vendors. I ask the bread guy how many boxes of buns the drive-in down the street is buying. Very few restaurateurs do that. But that's the way I research my market." Is this marketing research?
8. Comment on the following statements:
   a. Marketing managers are paid to take chances with decisions. Marketing researchers are paid to reduce the risk of making those decisions.
   b. A marketing strategy can be no better than the information on which it is formulated.
   c. The purpose of research is to solve marketing problems.
9. In what specific ways can marketing research influence the development and implementation of marketing strategy?
10. What is the relationship between marketing research and customer satisfaction?

Exploring the Internet: What Is Ahead?

Exploring the Internet is a feature that will give you an opportunity to use the Internet to gain additional insights about marketing research. The Internet is discussed in depth in Chapter 2, and Internet exercises are included in each of the remaining chapters.

The home page for this textbook is at

http://Zikmund.swcollege.com

You may also go directly to the marketing research online supplemental materials at

http://www.swcollege.com/marketing/
mr_online/mr_online_main.html

The author's home page is at

http://www2.bus.okstate.edu/mktg/
zikmund/index.htm

"Where will you stick it?"[19] If you hear those words from a young teen brandishing a brightly colored camera, relax. You aren't being attacked or insulted. To the contrary, your friend probably just wants to take your picture. "Where will you stick it?" is Polaroid's slogan for its new I-Zone pocket camera, the firm's first consumer-product introduction in more than 20 years. The product is also aimed at a new target market for a Polaroid product: teens. Polaroid, famous for its instantly developing film, has come up with a new filmstrip with a sticky back that turns tiny photos into instant stickers. Kids can snap a photo, pull out the strip, wait a few seconds for the picture to develop, then peel it off the strip and stick it anywhere—on a notebook, on a jacket or hat, on a key chain, on a purse, or on a bicycle. Within months of its launch, the I-Zone became the number-1–selling camera in the United States.

How did the I-Zone zoom to the top of the charts so quickly? Polaroid made a commitment to integrated marketing communications in researching the market, getting the product to the right consumers, and promoting it. First, they did the research and discovered that teens now have more spending power than any other generation of teens before them. "Polaroid decided to enter the kids' market because the kids' market right now is the biggest it's ever been in history," says Mary Courville, an I-Zone marketing executive. Second, they divided the market further, into preteens—tweens—and older teenagers. Girls seem to be most interested in taking pictures, so the Polaroid team focused there. Third, they thought "outside the box" about different uses for a camera. For instance, the younger girls actually view the camera as a fashion accessory—so a sleek design in fashionable bright colors was important. By thinking creatively, the team came up with whole new ways to use a camera. "It's not about taking pictures to put in a photo album," explains Courville. This is "a cool camera that allows kids to be creative and have fun. It's about play and doing what you want to do." The I-Zone's sticky film lets young photographers become artists. They can take their camera anywhere and stick their pictures anywhere.

Courville stresses that Polaroid couldn't have come up with either the product or the promotion that followed without integrated communications among the marketing, public relations, advertising, and promotion staff. "We're a very tight group," she says. "We're always together." They conducted focus groups and field tests together. They met with the advertising agency together. "We are just always talking to each other," she says. "Always, always, always." Not only does this increase the efficiency with which the product is launched, it keeps the message to the consumer consistent. The consumer sees the same message through television commercials, magazine or Internet ads, and various promotions.

What exactly is the message? For Polaroid in general, says Courville, it's about instant gratification. "Only Polaroid can give you that photograph instantly. Only Polaroid can enliven your time, your party, right then. Polaroid is the only one that allows you to capture the moment instantly." I-Zone takes it a step further by giving kids instant pictures that they can use to transform and personalize something else—a backpack, a belt buckle, a baseball cap.

In addition to advertising in traditional media as well as the Internet, Polaroid decided to hook up with the popular teen group the Backstreet Boys, becoming a sponsor of their "Into the Millennium" tour. "Sponsorship allowed us wonderful promotional opportunities," comments Courville. Since the group's biggest fans are girls age 14 to 17, the match was perfect. The Backstreet Boys actually used the I-Zone cameras during their concerts, and girls were invited on stage to have their pictures taken with band members, with I-Zone cameras, of course. Polaroid distributed cameras to fans at concerts so they could take pictures of each other and the band. Results were so positive that Polaroid decided to sponsor another pop singer, Britney Spears, the following year. "This sponsorship is the perfect combination of music, fun, and friendship—all key aspects of our target consumers' lifestyle. Polaroid is committed to giving teens and tweens exactly what they want." Even the stars themselves seem hooked on I-Zone. "I'm psyched to be working with Polaroid," says Spears. "The I-Zone is the coolest way for me and my fans to have fun taking pictures. We can stick them everywhere." That's just what Polaroid has in mind.

Questions

1. What is the marketing concept? Does it appear that Polaroid has adopted it?
2. What aspects of the I-Zone marketing mix might have been influenced by or based on marketing research?
3. What role should marketing research play in a consumer products organization such as Polaroid?

VIDEO CASE 1.2   WBRU

WBRU, an independent radio station based in Providence, Rhode Island, plays a variety of formats and appeals to a diverse group of listeners. Student volunteers play jazz in the very early morning, modern rock during the day, and retro music at noon. Fridays at midnight, listeners experience the best in techno, big beat, drum 'n' bass, and remixes. Weekdays at 3, WBRU hands over the reins to its listeners—they pick the music. Every Wednesday night at 10, the station's "Breaking-and-Entering" segment broadcasts 4 hours of new music. Contests and sweepstakes with many free prizes are included in the programming.

WBRU is not a large corporate station with a large budget; it sees itself as a cool, fun station. Much time is spent seeking creative ways to please both listeners and advertisers.

Questions
1. Does a small independent station like WBRU need marketing research information, or is creative marketing enough?
2. What type of marketing research might WBRU find useful?

VIDEO CASE 1.3   BEN & JERRY'S

Ben & Jerry's Homemade, Inc., the Vermont-based manufacturer of ice cream, frozen yogurt, and sorbet, was founded in 1978 in a renovated gas station in Burlington, Vermont, by childhood friends Ben Cohen and Jerry Greenfield, with a $12,000 investment ($4,000 of which was borrowed).[20] They soon became popular for their innovative flavors, made from fresh Vermont milk and cream. The company currently distributes ice cream, low-fat ice cream, frozen yogurt, sorbet, and novelty products nationwide, as well as in selected foreign countries, in supermarkets, grocery stores, convenience stores, franchised Ben & Jerry's scoop shops, restaurants, and other venues.

Ben & Jerry's product strategy is to differentiate its super premium brand from other ice cream brands. The brand image reflects high quality, uniqueness, and a bit of amusement. Its all-natural flavors have unique names. For example, "Chubby Hubby" has chunks of chocolate-covered peanut-butter-filled pretzels in a rich vanilla malt ice cream with deep ripples of fudge and peanut butter. Other names in the company's line of ice creams include Cherry Garcia, Bovinity Divinity, Dilbert Totally Nuts, New York Super Fudge Chunk, Chunky Monkey, and From Russia with Buzz.

The new product development process and flavor-naming process are a top priority at Ben & Jerry's. For example, Phish Food ice cream was developed as a unique product with a fun name associated with the band Phish. Ben Cohen had been a neighbor of members of Phish since the band's early years as favorites on the local music scene. When Ben & Jerry's suggested mixing up a Phish ice cream to celebrate their shared Vermont roots, the band agreed. So Ben & Jerry's concocted a chocolate ice cream with chewy marshmallow nougat, a thick caramel swirl, and a school of fudge fish in every pint. Most marshmallow variegates disappear into nothingness. The company took great pains to make sure that the marshmallow was the way it was meant to be. With Phish Food you can see, taste, and feel the white streaks of marshmallow. The Phish Food package is a departure from Ben & Jerry's traditional graphics. The pint container is designed with images from Phish's concert light show, featuring Phish band members Trey Anastasio, Mike Gordon, Jon Fishman, and Page McConnell on the pint lid, along with Ben and Jerry.

Question
What role does marketing research play in new product development and brand name development for a company like Ben & Jerry's?

GLOBAL INFORMATION SYSTEMS AND THE INTERNET

The last things likely to come to mind when you walk into Starbucks are complex data warehouses and business intelligence software. How about insurance, then? Probably not.[1]

But Zurich U.S., a leader in business and casualty insurance, is paid to think about risk management, not caffeine rushes. And Zurich U.S. has come up with a way to use the highest-tech database technology to help Starbucks and other big-liability customers manage and minimize insurance claims.

Zurich's product, an Internet-based service called Risk-Intelligence, lets its clients view insurance data in any number of ways. For a company like Starbucks, which doles out coffee all day to hundreds of thousands of possibly clumsy consumers, RiskIntelligence means a better chance to control claims.

The RiskIntelligence data management software allows users to view data from many different angles. Some use the metaphor of a Rubik's Cube, because the data can be twisted and turned in order to discern patterns. Correlations and relationships among data that are not otherwise obvious can be revealed.

Starbucks uses many different floor designs in its 3,500 North American retail locations. So, Starbucks' executives might, for example, look at its claims data to see whether there were more falls from spills in stores with a specific foot-traffic pattern. The executives might further drill down to find out that accidents were more frequent at certain times of the day. Good analytical tools could also reveal that these things happen mostly in a certain region of the country during a certain time of the year. This all could result in decisions that would help minimize those risks—and help the company handle its claims more effectively in general. RiskIntelligence gives clients like Starbucks much more up-to-date information than did the old way, which consisted of mailing out disks with static reports to customers once a month.

What you will learn in this chapter

- To distinguish among data, information, and knowledge.
- To identify the four characteristics of information.
- To understand the importance of global information systems.
- To understand decision support systems.
- To explain the nature of online information services.
- To recognize the major categories of databases.
- To explain the functions of electronic data interchanges.
- To explain the significance of the Internet.
- To understand the basics of navigating the World Wide Web.

23

Starbucks' use of RiskIntelligence, a computerized decision support system, illustrates how the management of information has changed in recent years. This chapter discusses the nature of decision support systems within the context of knowledge management and global information systems. It goes on to discuss the dramatic implications of the Internet on marketing research. ■

DATA VERSUS INFORMATION

data
Facts or recorded measures of certain phenomena.

information
Any body of facts in a format suitable for decision making or in a context that defines the relationship between two pieces of data.

Marketing managers must distinguish between data and information. **Data** are simply facts or recorded measures of certain phenomena; **information** is a body of facts in a format suitable to support decision making or define the relationship between two pieces of data. To see the difference between data and information, consider that Toys Я Us records thousands of unsummarized facts. A store clerk feeds data into the computer system each time he or she enters a transaction into a cash register. The data are simultaneously entered into a computerized inventory system. These data lack any meaning, however, until managers instruct the information system to translate the data into product sales totals by store, by county, or by state, or into forecasts for future time periods.

THE CHARACTERISTICS OF VALUABLE INFORMATION

Not all information is valuable to decision makers. Marketing information is useful if it helps a marketing manager make a decision. Information can be evaluated using four characteristics: relevance, quality, timeliness, and completeness.

Relevance

Information is relevant if it suits the needs of the marketer. The decision maker gets exactly what he or she wants from relevant information. Information is relevant if it clarifies the questions the decision maker faces.

Quality

Information quality depends on the degree to which the information represents the true situation. High-quality information is accurate, valid, and reliable. High-quality data present a good picture of reality.

For example, the author regularly receives two catalogs from Bloomingdale's, one addressed to Mr. Zikmund and one to Mr. Vikmund. Bloomie's mailing list has problems with its information quality.

Information quality is a critical issue in marketing research, and it will be discussed throughout this textbook.

Timeliness

Marketing is a dynamic field in which out-of-date information can lead to poor decisions. Marketing information must be timely, that is, provided at the right time.

Computerized information systems can record events and dispense relevant information soon after a transaction takes place. A great deal of marketing information becomes available almost at the moment a transaction occurs. Computer technology has redefined standards for timely information.

Completeness

Information completeness means having the right quantity of information. Marketing managers must have sufficient information about all aspects of their decisions. For example, a researcher investigating Eastern European markets may

As the 21st century begins, countries' borders are becoming more open to facilitate international marketing. The 15-nation European Union is becoming a single market, and companies that are marketing in Europe have a high demand for electronic data interchange systems and multilingual software for global information systems.

plan to analyze four former Soviet-bloc countries. Population statistics and information on inflation rates may be available for all four countries. However, information about disposable personal income may be available for only three of the countries. If facts about disposable personal income or another economic characteristic cannot be obtained, the information is incomplete. Often incomplete information leads decision makers to conduct marketing research.

GLOBAL INFORMATION SYSTEMS

The well-being of a multinational corporation—indeed, the health of any business organization that plans to prosper in the 21st century—will depend on information about the world economy and global competition. Contemporary marketers require timely and accurate information from countless sources to maintain competitive advantages.

Increased global competition and technological advances in interactive media have given rise to global information systems. A **global information system** is an organized collection of computer hardware, software, data, and personnel designed to capture, store, update, manipulate, analyze, and immediately display information about worldwide business activities. A global information system is a tool for providing past, present, and projected information on internal operations and external activity. It organizes and integrates data from production, operations, marketing, finance, accounting, and other business functions. Using satellite communications, high-speed microcomputers, electronic data interchanges, fiber optics, CD-ROM data storage, fax machines, and other technological advances in interactive media, global information systems are changing the nature of business.

Consider a simple example. At any moment, United Parcel Service (UPS) can track the status of any shipment around the world. UPS drivers use handheld electronic clipboards called delivery information acquisition devices (DIADs) to record appropriate data about each pickup or delivery. The data are then entered

global information system
An organized collection of computer hardware, software, data, and personnel designed to capture, store, update, manipulate, analyze, and immediately display information about worldwide business activity.

into the company's main computer for record keeping and analysis. A satellite telecommunications system allows UPS to track any shipment for a customer.

With so much diverse information available in a global information system, organizations have found it necessary to determine what data, information, and knowledge are most useful to particular business units.

DECISION SUPPORT SYSTEMS

decision support system
A computer-based system that helps decision makers confront problems through direct interaction with databases and analytical software programs.

customer relationship management (CRM)
A decision support system that brings together numerous pieces of information about customers and their relationship with the company.

An organization may have several, even many, decision support systems that are components of its larger global information system. A marketing **decision support system** is a computer-based system that helps decision makers confront problems through direct interaction with databases and analytical software programs. The purpose of a decision support system is to store data and transform them into organized information that is easily accessible to marketing managers.

Most major corporations have a decision support system to facilitate **customer relationship management (CRM)**. A CRM system might bring together numerous pieces of information about customers, sales, marketing effectiveness, company responsiveness, and market trends.[3] The goal of the CRM system is to describe customer relationships in sufficient detail that managers, salespeople, customer service representatives, and perhaps the customers themselves can access information directly, match customer needs with satisfying product offerings, remind customers of service requirements, know what other products a customer has purchased, and so forth.[4] Once a CRM system is established, an executive might query the system to investigate how much repeat business a product is getting or to learn whether special efforts are needed to retain certain types of customers. An efficient CRM system should give a service representative in a call center the ability to retrieve a complete record of a customer's interactions with the company seconds after the customer provides identification information.

Decision support systems serve specific business units within a company, operating within the context of the global information system. No single decision support system is independent of the more comprehensive global information system.

Exhibit 2.1 illustrates a decision support system. Raw, unsummarized data are inputs to the decision support system. Data collected in marketing research projects are a major source of this input, but the data may be purchased or collected by accountants, sales managers, production managers, or company employees other than marketing researchers. Effective marketers spend a great deal of time and effort collecting information for input into the decision support system. Useful information is the output of a decision support system. A decision support system requires both databases and software.

Databases and Data Warehousing

database
A collection of raw data arranged logically and organized in a form that can be stored and processed by a computer.

A **database** is a collection of raw data arranged logically and organized in a form that can be stored and processed by a computer. A customer mailing list is one type of database. Population characteristics may be recorded by state, county, and city in another database. Databases often reside in computer storage devices such as hard-disk drives, but other types of databases may be maintained by vendors of information services.

Because most companies compile and store many different databases, they often develop data warehousing systems. *Data warehousing* is the term managers of information technology use to refer to the process that allows important data

EXHIBIT 2.1 | DECISION SUPPORT SYSTEM

Decision Support System

Input ▶ Database ◀▶ Software ▶ Output

collected from day-to-day computer systems (often called operational systems) to be stored and organized into separate systems designed for simplified access.[5] More formally, data warehousing refers to the multitiered, computerized storage of current and historical data. Data warehouse management requires that the detailed data from operational systems be extracted and transformed so that layers of summarized data "tables" can be stored (warehoused) to make the various databases consistent. Organizations that use data warehousing may integrate databases from both inside and outside the company.[6]

The development of data warehouses requires database management software to provide easy access to the data.

software
Various types of programs that tell computers, printers, and other hardware what to do.

business intelligence software
Computer programs that permit managers to restructure and analyze data in extensive data warehouses to discover significant patterns and relationships.

Software

The **software** portion of a decision support system consists of various types of programs that tell computers, printers, and other hardware what to do. Advances in database management, spreadsheet, and statistical software have revolutionized access to and analysis of business data. A decision support system's **business intelligence software** allows managers to combine and restructure databases, diagnose

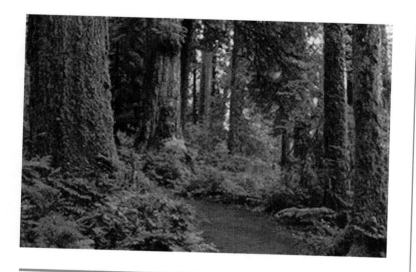

Facing a public increasingly critical of logging in national forests, the U.S. Forest Service uses an information system and a technique called "seen-area analysis" to plan national forests. The information system helps foresters tuck clear-cuts behind ridges, shield them from view with "beauty strips"—veneers of trees maintained to hide bare patches—and identify areas where they can use one of several "partial cut" techniques to subtly thin the forest without ruining the view.

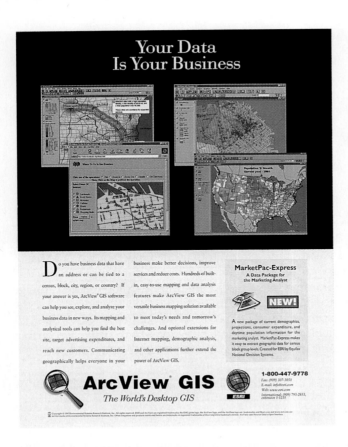
ESRI's ArcView databases and computer software for creating colorful maps allow researchers to exhibit marketing data by geographical area such as zip code, census tract, or sales territory. ArcView integrates visualization and data management tools, making customization of maps an easy point-and-click task.

relationships, discover patterns, estimate variables, and otherwise analyze various databases. For instance, suppose a bank has a listing of all its customers in its data warehouse. Analysts can create a new database of high-volume customers using certain analytical procedures. They can also analyze the demographic structure of this group and make projections about the group's future savings behavior based on economic forecasts and other forecasted trends. The bank could then use its CRM software to build a personalized mailing list based on any customer characteristic or behavioral pattern.

Most of today's business intelligence software is so user-friendly that it is easy for nonexperts to maintain direct control over the computer's tasks and outcomes. A manager can sit at a computer terminal and instantaneously retrieve personalized data files and request special, creative analyses to refine, modify, or generate information in a tailor-made format suited specifically for evaluating particular consequences or alternatives. User-friendly graphical software enables managers to convert endless columns of numbers to colored charts, graphs, and maps almost instantaneously. For example, members of PepsiCo's business planning group can generate on demand hundreds of charts and graphs that compare sales and earnings for each division with past performance and corporate projections.

Input Management

To this point, we have focused on the organization and accessibility of computerized information. Now let's look at the input function in detail.

Input includes all the numerical, text, voice, and image data that enter the decision support system. Systematic accumulation of pertinent, timely, and accurate data is essential to the success of a decision support system. Clearly, the input function must be managed.

Decision support system managers, systems analysts, and programmers are responsible for the decision support system as a whole, but many functions within an organization provide input data. Marketing researchers, accountants, corporate librarians, sales personnel, production managers, and many others within the organization help to collect data and provide input for the decision support system. Input data can also come from external sources.

Exhibit 2.2 shows four major sources of input for marketing data: internal records, proprietary marketing research, marketing intelligence, and outside vendors/external distributors of data. Each source can provide valuable input.

Internal records, such as accounting reports of sales and inventory figures, provide considerable data that may become useful information for marketing managers. An effective data collection system establishes orderly procedures to ensure that data about costs, shipments, inventory, sales, and other aspects of regular operations are routinely collected and entered into the computer.

Marketing research has already been defined as a broad set of procedures and methods. To clarify the decision support system concept, let's consider a narrower view of marketing research. **Proprietary marketing research** emphasizes the company's gathering of new data. Few proprietary marketing research procedures and methods are conducted regularly or continuously. Instead, research projects conducted to study specific company problems generate data; this is proprietary marketing research. Most of this book deals with this kind of marketing research. Providing managers with nonroutine data that otherwise would not be available is a major function of proprietary marketing research.

The term *marketing intelligence* has been defined in a variety of ways. A restrictive and specialized definition works best: A marketing intelligence system consists of a network of sources and regular procedures by which marketing executives obtain information about nonrecurrent developments in the external marketing environment.

proprietary marketing research
The gathering of new data to investigate specific problems.

EXHIBIT 2.2	FOUR MAJOR SOURCES OF MARKETING INPUT FOR DECISION SUPPORT SYSTEMS
Source	**Examples**
Internal records	Customer profiles, orders, goods-in-process inventory, product-line sales histories
Proprietary marketing research	Survey findings, test market results
Marketing intelligence	E-mail logs of comments and complaints, discovery of price changes by competitors, news of industry technology
Outside vendors and external distributors	Industry sales trends, competitors' market shares, demographic trends

INSIGHT FROM MICROSOFT

Bill Gates offers some insight into internal input into decision support systems.[7]

One of the first ways Microsoft began using information tools internally was by phasing out printed computer reports. In many companies, when you go into a top executive's office you see books of bound computer printouts with monthly financial numbers, dutifully filed away on a shelf. At Microsoft, those numbers are made available only on a computer screen. When someone wants more detail, he or she can examine it by time period, locale, or almost any other way. When we first put the financial reporting system on-line, people started looking at the numbers in new ways. For example, they began analyzing why our market share in one geographic area was different from our share somewhere else. As we all started working with the information, we discovered errors. Our data-processing group apologized. "We're very sorry about these mistakes," they said, "but we've been compiling and distributing these numbers once a month for five years and these same problems were there all along and no one mentioned them." People hadn't really been using the print information enough to discover the mistakes.

For example, Procter & Gamble discovered a need to change its slogan for Puritan Oil, "Make it his oil for life," through marketing intelligence. Ongoing investigations of consumer complaints received on the company's toll-free telephone number indicated that the slogan was considered sexist. Consumers didn't like the new theme, even though it was only slightly changed from the earlier "Make it your oil for life." Toll-free numbers and consumer correspondence are two of many sources of intelligence about external environments.

Sales people work in firms' external environments and thus routinely provide essential marketing intelligence. Sales representatives' call reports frequently alert managers to changes in competitors' prices and new-product offerings.

Outside vendors and external distributors market information as their products. Many organizations specialize in the collection and publication of high-quality information. One outside vendor, the A. C. Nielsen Company, provides television program ratings, audience counts, and information about the demographic composition of television viewer groups. Other vendors specialize in the distribution of information. Public libraries have always purchased information, traditionally in the form of books, and they have served as distributors of this information.

Media representatives often provide useful data about their audiences' characteristics and purchasing behavior. *Advertising Age,* the *Wall Street Journal, Sales and Marketing Management,* and other trade and business-oriented publications are important sources of information. These publications keep managers up-to-date regarding the economy, competitors' activities, and other aspects of the marketing environment.

Companies called *data specialists* record and store certain marketing information. Computer technology has changed the way many of these organizations supply data, favoring the development of computerized databases.

Computerized Data Archives

Historically, collections of organized and readily retrievable data were available in printed form at libraries. The *Statistical Abstract of the United States,* which is filled with tables of statistical facts, is a typical example. Printed copies of this book can be found in most public and corporate libraries. In recent years, the *Statistical Abstract* has also become available on CD-ROM and on the Internet. The entire 2000 census is also available in print as well as on CD-ROM. Many census databases can be accessed on the Internet. As the 21st century progresses, even more data will be stored in digitized form in computerized data archives.

Numerous computerized search and retrieval systems and electronic databases are available as subscription services or in libraries. A researcher can query the library computer to learn whether the library owns a particular book and whether that book is on the shelf or checked out. Today, business people can use personal computers to access online information search and retrieval services, such as Dow-Jones News Retrieval and Bloomberg Financial Markets, without leaving their offices. In fact, some information services can be accessed from remote locations via digital wireless devices.

Computerized database searches offer the most efficient and exhaustive way to find published information. Most online information services use *electronic indexing systems* that function much like the *periodic indexes* found in book form in libraries. For example, an electronic indexing system may allow a researcher to search for information by subject. A subject index is an information resource that contains lists of references to other database resources, categorized by subject, usually in a hierarchy. Most online information services also have software that allows a researcher to do keyword searches for information in their databases.

Modern library patrons can command a computer to search indexes and retrieve databases from a range of vendors. Major wholesalers or online vendors of *bibliographic databases* include PROQUEST, INFOTRAC, DIALOG (Dialog Information Services, Inc.), LEXIS-NEXIS, and Dow Jones News Retrieval Services. These services index information and provide access to computer-readable databases to business people and scholars.

DIALOG, for example, maintains more than 600 databases. A typical database may have a million or more records, each consisting of a one- or two-paragraph abstract that summarizes the major points of a published article along with bibliographic information. One of the DIALOG databases, ABI/INFORM, abstracts significant articles in more than 1,000 current business and management journals. Many computerized archives provide more than abstracts of published articles and journals. The *New York Times* database and the Dow Jones Text-Search Services are full-text databases that allow the retrieval of an entire article or document. ABI/INFORM offers full-text versions of the articles on CD-ROM.

Exhibit 2.3 illustrates the services provided by two popular vendors of information services that electronically index numerous databases. For a more extensive listing, see the *Gale Directory of Databases.*[8]

Several types of databases from outside vendors and external distributors are so fundamental to decision support systems that they deserve further explanation.

Statistical Databases   Statistical databases contain numerical data for market analysis and forecasting. Often demographic, sales, and other relevant marketing variables are recorded by geographical area. Geographic information systems use these *geographical databases* and powerful software to prepare computer maps of relevant variables. Companies such as Claritas, Urban Decision

EXHIBIT 2.3 | TWO VENDORS OF INFORMATION SERVICES AND ELECTRONIC INDEXING

Vendors	Selected Databases	Type of Data
DIALOG	ABI/INFORM	Summaries and citations from over 1,000 academic management, marketing, and general business journals with full text of more than 500 of these publications
	ASI (American Statistics Index)	Abstracts and indexes of federal government statistical publications
	PROMT (The Predicast Overview of Markets and Technologies)	Summaries and full text from 1,000 U.S. and international business and trade journals, industry newsletters, newspapers, and market research studies; information about industries and companies, including the products and technologies they develop and the markets in which they compete
	Investext	Full text of over 2 million company, industry, and geographic research reports written by analysts at more than 600 leading investment banks, brokerage houses, and consulting firms worldwide
Dow Jones News Retrieval	Business Newsstand	Articles from the *New York Times, Los Angeles Times, Washington Post,* and other leading newspapers and magazines
	Historical Market Data Center	Historical data on securities, dividends, and exchange rates
	Web Center	Information obtained from searches of corporate, industry, government, and news Web sites

Systems, and CACI all offer geographic/demographic databases that are widely used in industry.

Known as *scanner data,* or single-source data, the wealth of product and brand sales information collected by optical scanners in supermarkets and other retail outlets is another example of statistical data. (The term *single-source* data refers to the ability of these systems to gather several types of interrelated data, such as purchase, sales promotion, and advertising frequency data, from a single source in a format that will facilitate integration, comparison, and analysis.) As the number of scanner-equipped stores continues to increase, scanner systems are replacing human record keeping for in-store auditing. Substituting mechanized record keeping for human record keeping results in greater accuracy and rapid feedback about store activity.

One weakness of single-source scanner data is that the largest stores, such as supermarkets, mass merchandisers, and warehouse retailers, are the most likely to have scanner systems, causing the sampling base of stores to be less than perfectly representative. However, things are changing. A. C. Nielsen and the National Housewares Manufacturers Association formed a partnership to provide data generated by the Universal Product Codes scanned at housewares retailers' checkouts. The Universal Product Code (UPC) contains information on the category of goods, the manufacturer, and product identification based on size, flavor, color, and so on. Nevertheless, if a large percentage of a product category's sales occur in small stores or in vending machines (for example, candy), which tend not to have scanners, the marketer should be aware that the scanner data may not be representative.

Financial Databases   Competitors' and customers' financial data, such as income statements and balance sheets, may interest managers. These are easy to access in financial databases. CompuStat publishes an extensive financial database on thousands of companies, broken down by industry and other criteria. To illustrate the depth of this pool of information, consider CompuStat's Global Advantage, which offers extensive data on 6,650 companies in more than 30 countries in Europe, the Pacific Rim, and North America.

Video Databases   Video databases and streaming media are having a major impact on the marketing of many goods and services. For example, movie studios provide clips of upcoming films and advertising agencies put television commercials on the Internet. (See www.adcritic.com.) McDonald's maintains a digital archive of television commercials and other video footage to share with its franchisers around the world. The video database enables franchisers and their advertising agencies to create local advertising without filming the same types of scenes already archived. Just imagine the value of digital video databases to advertising agencies' decision support systems.

Networks and Electronic Data Interchange

Individual personal computers can be connected through networks to other computers. Networking involves linking two or more computers to share data and software.

electronic data interchange (EDI)
The linking of one company's computer system with another company's system to allow the sharing of data and software.

Electronic data interchange (EDI) systems integrate one company's computer system directly with another company's system. Much of the input to a company's decision support system may come through networks from other companies' computers. Companies such as Computer Technology Corporation and Microelectronics market data services that allow corporations to exchange business information with suppliers or customers. For example, every evening Wal-Mart transmits millions of characters of data about the day's sales to its apparel suppliers. Wrangler, a supplier of blue jeans, for instance, shares the data and a model that interprets the data. It also shares software applications that act to replenish stocks in Wal-Mart stores. This decision support system lets Wrangler's managers know when to send specific quantities of specific sizes and colors of jeans to specific stores from specific warehouses. The result is a learning loop that lowers inventory costs and leads to fewer stockouts.

WHAT IS THE INTERNET?

Internet
A worldwide network of computers that allows users access to information and documents from distant sources.

The **Internet** is a worldwide network of computers that allows users access to information and documents from distant sources. Because it is a combination of a worldwide communication system and the world's largest public library, containing a seemingly endless range of information, many people believe the Internet is the most important communications medium since television.

The Internet has changed the way millions of people get and distribute information. It is estimated that more than 269 million users in Europe, the Pacific Rim, and North America can access the Internet from a home computer.[9] For many years the number of users doubled annually, making the Internet the fastest-growing communication medium in history.

Computer communication and resource discovery are two central functions of the Internet. Electronic mail or messaging is the most widespread communication function. For example, users send messages on the Internet by **e-mail** (electronic mail) to ask questions of experts or, in other ways, communicate with individuals who share similar interests. Just as a letter delivered by a postal worker requires an address, so does e-mail. An e-mail address consists of two parts, separated by the @ symbol. The name of the user's mailbox is on the left-hand side. The name of the system on which the mailbox resides is on the right-hand side. System, or domain, names have two or more fields, separated by dots, and can follow many different naming schemes, such as by country (.uk, .jp) or by type of activity (.com, .org).

e-mail
Electronic mail used to communicate over the Internet.

The domain is typically a company name, institutional name, or organizational name associated with the **host** computer. For example, *Forbes* magazine's Internet edition is located at forbes.com. The "com" indicates this domain is a commercial site. Educational sites end in "edu," government sites end in "gov," and other types of organizations end in "org."

host
Any computer that has access to other computers on the Internet. One or more people may log on to a host computer through their personal computers.

The Internet allows instantaneous and effortless access to a great deal of information. Noncommercial and commercial organizations make a wealth of data and other resources available on the Internet. For example, the U.S. Library of Congress provides full text of all versions of House and Senate legislation and full text of the *Congressional Record*. The Internal Revenue Service makes it possible to download an income tax form. Thomson Learning (http://thomsonlearning.com) and its South-Western college division (http://www.swcollege.com) have online directories that allow college professors to access information about the company and its textbooks.

The Internet began in 1969 as an experimental hookup among computers at Stanford University, the University of California at Santa Barbara, the University of California at Los Angeles, and the University of Utah, in conjunction with the Department of Defense.[10] The Defense Department was involved because it wanted to develop a communications network that could survive nuclear war. The Internet gradually grew into a nationwide network of connected computers, and now it is a worldwide network often referred to as the "information superhighway." The Internet has no central computer; instead, each message sent bears an address code that lets the sender forward a message to a desired destination from any computer linked to the Net. Many benefits of the Internet arise because the Internet is a collection of thousands of small networks, both domestic and foreign, rather than a single computer operation. These many small networks of host and **server** computers contain millions of databases that are accessible to Internet users, mostly without fees.

server
A computer that provides services on the Internet.

In the following pages we discuss the World Wide Web and how to use the Internet for research. However, keep in mind that the Internet is constantly changing. The description of the Internet, especially home page addresses, may be out of date by the time this book is published. Be aware that the Internet of today will not be the Internet of tomorrow.

Navigating the Internet

Anyone with a computer and a modem can access the Internet by subscribing to a gateway company known as an Internet service provider (ISP), such as America Online, AT&T WorldNet, Earthlink, or WorldCom. In addition, many college and university campus networks also offer Internet access either in common user laboratories or through off-campus dial-up services.

The **World Wide Web (WWW)** refers to that portion of the Internet made up of servers that support a retrieval system that organizes information into documents called Web pages. World Wide Web documents, which may include graphic images, video clips, and sound clips, are formatted in special programming languages, such as HTML (HyperText Markup Language) and XML (Extensible Markup Language), that allow information to be displayed, linked, and shared on the Internet.

Over the past few years, many universities, government agencies, academic associations, newspapers, TV networks, libraries, and corporations have decided to provide information on the Internet. Parties that furnish information on the World Wide Web are called **content providers.** Content providers maintain Web sites. A **Web site** consists of one or more Web pages with related information about a particular topic; for example, a university Web site might include pages about the university's mission, courses, and faculty. The introductory page or opening screen is called the **home page** because it provides basic information about the

World Wide Web (WWW)
A portion of the Internet that is a system of computer servers that organize information into documents called Web pages.

content provider
A party that furnishes information on the World Wide Web.

Web site
One or more Web pages with related information about a particular topic.

home page
The introductory page or opening screen of a Web site.

purpose of the document along with a menu of selections or links that lead to other screens with more specific information. Thus, each page can have connections, or **hyperlinks,** to other pages, which may be on any computer connected to the Internet. People using the World Wide Web may be viewing information that is stored on their host computer or on a machine halfway around the world. The World Wide Web allows users to point and click on where they want to go and to call up video, sound bytes, and graphics from different participating computer networks around the world.

To access the World Wide Web, the typical home user needs a Web **browser,** which is a software program with a graphical user interface that enables the user to display Web pages as well as navigate the Internet.[11] Popular Web browsers, such as Netscape Navigator and Microsoft Explorer, make it easy to move from Web site to Web site on the World Wide Web (often called navigating the Net, navigation, or surfing). With these Web browsers even a novice on the Internet can search for information by simply pointing and clicking on graphics that resemble the familiar Windows or Macintosh interface. The links to other documents are usually highlighted in another color, underlined, or identified by a unique icon. Often the user may be linked to a series of expanded menus or navigation buttons containing descriptions of the contents of various Web pages around the Internet. The user moves the cursor to highlighted words or colorful icons and then clicks the mouse button to immediately go to the file, regardless of what server it may be stored on. At this point the user can either read or download the material. By clicking on "U.S. Government Information" in one electronic document, for example, a Netscape user might connect to a computer in Washington, D.C. with more information. A few more clicks, and the user could be perusing files from the U.S. Census Bureau or the Small Business Administration.

Most Web browsers also allow the user to enter a **Uniform Resource Locator (URL)** into the program. The URL is really just a Web site address that Web browsers recognize. A Web site is any computer host acting as a location that can be accessed with the browser software. Many Web sites allow any user or visitor access without previous approval. However, many commercial sites require that the user have a valid account and password before access is granted.

A researcher who wants to find a particular site or document on the Internet or is just looking for a resource list on a particular subject can use one of the many Internet search engines. A **search engine** is a computerized directory that allows anyone to search the World Wide Web for information in a particular way. Some search titles or headers of documents, others search words in the documents themselves, and still others search other indexes or directories. Yahoo (http://www.yahoo.com) and Excite (http://www.excite.com) offer such a broad array of resources and services that they are also called *portals*. A person using Yahoo will find lists of broad categories on topics such as art, business, entertainment, and government. Clicking on one of these topics leads to other subdirectories or home pages. An alternative way to use a search engine is to type keywords and phrases associated with the search and wait for a list of Web sites to be displayed.

Some of the most comprehensive and accurate search engines are

Yahoo	http://www.yahoo.com
Google	http://www.google.com
Hotbot	http://www.hotbot.com
Go network	http://www.go.com
Excite	http://www.excite.com

hyperlinks
Connections from one Web page to other Web pages, which may be on any computer connected to the Internet.

browser
A software program with a graphical user interface that enables the user to display Web pages as well as navigate the Internet.

Uniform Resource Locator (URL)
A Web site address that Web browsers recognize.

search engine
A computerized directory that allows anyone to search the World Wide Web for information in a particular way.

Lycos	http://www.lycos.com
Alta Vista	http://www.altavista.com
WebCrawler	http://www.webcrawler.com

Some specialized search engines provide unique services tailor-made for a particular industry or for a specific task. For example, http://gallery.yahoo.com provides a means for finding images available on the Internet.

Interactive Media and Environmental Scanning

Because people who use the Internet interact with their computers, it is an **interactive medium.** A user clicks a command, and the computer responds in sophisticated ways, so the user and equipment can have a continuing conversation. Two or more individuals who communicate one-to-one via e-mail using an Internet service provider are also using interactive media. So are individuals who communicate with many senders and receivers via bulletin boards. Because of its vastness, the Internet is an especially useful source for scanning many types of changes in the environment. **Environmental scanning** entails all information gathering that is designed to detect indications of environmental changes in their initial stages of development.

Ford Motor Company maintains an Internet-based relationship marketing program that, among other things, helps the auto maker scan its environment using the Internet. Its dealer Web site creates a centralized communication service linking dealers via an Internet connection. Its buyer Web site allows prospective buyers to visit a virtual showroom and to get price quotes and financial information. Its owner Web site allows an owner who registers and supplies pertinent vehicle information to get free e-mail and other ownership perks—perhaps a free Hertz upgrade or an autographed photo of a Ford-sponsored NASCAR driver. In return, Ford collects data at all levels, which allows managers to scan for trends and apply what they learn at a local level.

Information Technology

The terms *pull technology* and *push technology* describe how data are sent over the Internet. When a Web page isn't delivered until a browser requests it, it is said to be pulled. The opposite of pull is push. Push technology sends data to a user's computer without a request being made.

Smart information delivery (known by a variety of technical names, including *push phase technology*) allows a Web site, such as the Yahoo portal, to become a one-on-one medium for each individual user. Today's information technology uses "smart agents" or "intelligent agents" to deliver customized content to the viewer's desktop. **Smart agent software** is capable of learning an Internet user's preferences and automatically searching out information at selected Web sites and then distributing the information to a user's computer for later viewing. MyYahoo and MyExcite are portal services that personalize Web pages. Users can get stock quotes relevant to their portfolios, news about favorite sports teams, local weather, and other personalized information. Users can customize the sections of the service they want delivered. With push technology, pertinent content is delivered to the viewer's desktop without the user having to do the searching.

Push technology may employ surveys of customer preferences, or it may use cookies. **Cookies,** or "magic cookies," are small computer files that a content provider can save onto the computer of someone who visits its Web site. The cookie allows the content provider's computer to track other Web sites visited by the user and store these Web sites in a file that uses the cookie in place of the person's name (which in most cases the content provider never knows). If a person looks up a weather report by keying a zip code into a personalized Web page, the computer can note that. This is a clue that tells where the person lives (or maybe where he or she may be planning to visit). The computer might note whether a user looks up stock quotes. Then the next time the person visits the Web site the computer might serve up an ad for a restaurant in Seattle, Washington, or an online brokerage firm, depending on what the computer has managed to learn. Information technology is having a major impact on the nature of marketing research. We will explore this topic in several places throughout this book.

Intranets

intranet
A company's private data network that uses Internet standards and technology.

An **intranet** is a company's private data network that uses Internet standards and technology.[12] The information on an intranet—data, graphics, even video and voice—is available only inside the organization. Thus, a key difference between the Internet and an intranet is that security software programs, or "firewalls," are installed to limit access to only those employees authorized to enter the system.[13]

A company uses Internet features, such as electronic mail, Web pages, and browsers, to set up an intranet, which is a communications and data resource for that company. Company information is accessible using the same point-and-click technology used on the Internet. Managers and employees use links to get complete, up-to-date information. An intranet lets authorized personnel, some of whom previously were isolated on departmental local area networks, look at product drawings, employee newsletters, sales forecasts, and other sources of company information. Whether the information comes from a spreadsheet or a word-processing document is not an issue for the user of an intranet. Managers and employees do not have to worry about the format of the information. In short, setting up an intranet involves adding Web-like functionality to an organization's existing global information system.

SUMMARY

Increased global competition and technological advances in interactive media have spurred development of global information systems. A global information system is an organized collection of computer hardware, software, data, and personnel designed to capture, store, update, manipulate, analyze, and immediately display information about worldwide business activity.

Marketing managers distinguish between data and information. Data are simply facts or recorded measures of certain phenomena; information refers to a body of facts in a format that facilitates decision making or that defines relationships between two pieces of data.

Information can be evaluated based on four characteristics: relevance, quality, timeliness, and completeness. Relevant information provides the information a marketer needs. High-quality information is accurate, valid, and reliable; it presents a good picture of reality. Timely information is obtained at the right time. Computerized information systems can record events and present information soon after a transaction takes place, thus improving timeliness. Complete information is the right quantity of information. Marketing managers must have sufficient information to relate all aspects of their decisions together.

A computer-based marketing decision support system helps decision makers confront problems through direct interaction with databases and analytical software. A decision support system stores data and transforms them into organized information that is easily accessible to marketing managers.

A database is a collection of raw data arranged logically and organized in a form that can be stored and processed by a computer. Marketing data come from four major sources: internal records, proprietary marketing research, marketing intelligence, and outside vendors and external distributors. Each source can provide valuable input.

Numerous database search and retrieval systems are available by subscription or in libraries. Computer-assisted database searching has made the collection of external data faster and easier. Marketers refer to many different types of databases.

Although personal computers work independently, they can connect to other computers in networks to share data and software. Electronic data interchange (EDI) allows one company's computer system to join directly to another company's system.

The Internet is a worldwide network of computers that allows users access to information and documents from distant sources. It is a combination of a worldwide communication system and the world's largest public library. The World Wide Web (WWW), a system of thousands of interconnected pages, or documents, can be easily accessed with Web browsers and search engines.

Key Terms and Concepts

data	electronic data interchange (EDI)	browser
information	Internet	Uniform Resource Locator (URL)
global information system	e-mail	search engine
decision support system	host	interactive medium
customer relationship management (CRM)	server	environmental scanning
	World Wide Web (WWW)	smart agent software
database	content provider	cookies
software	Web site	intranet
business intelligence software	home page	
proprietary marketing research	hyperlinks	

Questions for Review and Critical Thinking

1. What is the difference between data and information? Provide examples.
2. What are the characteristics of useful information?
3. What type of databases might be found in the following organizations?
   a. Holiday Inn
   b. A Las Vegas gambling casino
   c. Anheuser-Busch
4. If a manufacturer sells directly to retailers, what type of marketing intelligence information would you expect to find in the company's decision support system?

5. What type of questions could a brand manager of a packaged goods firm expect to answer with the company's decision support system?
6. What makes a decision support system successful?
7. What are the four major sources of input for a decision support system?
8. Give three examples of computerized databases that are available at your college or university library.
9. In your own words, describe the Internet. What is its purpose?
10. How can an intranet help manage knowledge?

Exploring the Internet

1. Go to your school's computer center to learn how to obtain an e-mail address and how to establish an account that allows you to access the Internet. Get instructions on how to access the Internet using your local computer system.
2. The Spider's Apprentice is a Web site that provides many useful tips about using search engines. Go to http://www.monash.com/spidap.html, then click on The Spider's Apprentice to learn the ins and outs of search engines.
3. Use a Web browser to visit Yahoo at http://www.yahoo.com. You will see a list of the major search categories. Click on Business and Economics. What additional search categories become available to you?
4. CEO Express (http://www.ceoexpress.com), Brint.com (http://www.brint.com/), the American Marketing Association's Marketing Power (http://www.marketingpower.com), and WorldOpinion (http://www.worldopinion.com) provide information about research topics and links to other Web pages. These pages will be extremely useful in your study of many marketing research topics. Visit these sites often during your study of marketing research.
5. For a useful business and personal tool go to http://www.mapblast.com. Describe the site.
6. To learn more about data warehousing, go to http://www.knowledgecenters.org/ or to http://www.datawarehousing.org.
7. Use the Internet to see if you can find information to answer the following questions:
    a. What is the weather in Denver today?
    b. What are four restaurants in the French Quarter in New Orleans?
    c. What is the population of Brazil?

From his office window overlooking the main floor of the Harvard Cooperative Society, CEO Jerry Murphy can glance down and see customers shopping.[14] They make their way through the narrow aisles of the crowded department store, picking up a sweatshirt here, trying on a baseball cap there, checking out the endless array of merchandise that bears the Harvard University insignia.

Watching Murphy, you can well imagine the Coop's founders, who started the store in 1882, peering through the tiny windowpanes to keep an eye on the shop floor. Was the Harvard Square store attracting steady traffic? Were the college students buying enough books and supplies for the Coop to make a profit? Back then, it was tough to answer those questions precisely. The owners had to watch and wait, relying only on their gut feelings to know how things were going from minute to minute.

Now, more than a hundred years later, Murphy can tell you, down to the last stockkeeping unit, how he's doing at any given moment. His window on the busi-

ness is the PC that sits on his desk. All day long it delivers up-to-the-minute, easy-to-read electronic reports on what's selling and what's not, which items are running low in inventory and which have fallen short of forecast. In a matter of seconds, the computer can report gross margins for any product or supplier, and Murphy can decide whether the margins are fat enough to justify keeping the supplier or product on board. "We were in the 1800s, and we had to move ahead," he says of the $55 million business.

Questions
1. What is a decision support system? What advantages does a decision support system have for a business like the Harvard Cooperative Society?
2. How would the decision support system of a small business like the Harvard Cooperative Society differ from that of a major corporation?
3. Briefly outline the components of the Harvard Cooperative Society's decision support system.

THE MARKETING RESEARCH PROCESS: AN OVERVIEW

What you will learn in this chapter

- To classify marketing research as either exploratory research, descriptive research, or causal research.
- To list the stages in the marketing research process.
- To identify and briefly discuss the various decision alternatives available to the researcher during each stage of the research process.
- To explain the difference between a research project and a research program.

Suppose you are assigned to take charge of the marketing research effort when R. J. Reynolds Tobacco Company is developing an almost smokeless cigarette. You are told that the smokeless cigarette does not burn tobacco and greatly reduces the production of harmful substances linked to health concerns. R. J. Reynolds' executives believe it will be the world's cleanest cigarette. The new cigarette is lit like a normal cigarette; then a carbon heat source at its tip generates warm air that passes through tobacco extract, flavorings, and glycerine to form smoke that tastes like cigarette smoke. The cigarette includes carbon monoxide and nicotine at levels similar to low-tar brands now on the market. However, because the tobacco does not burn, most of the combustion products linked to cancer and other health risks are eliminated or greatly reduced. The new cigarette produces almost no sidestream smoke, and after the first few puffs there is no ash and no odor. Further, the exhaled smoke dissipates quickly. The cigarette does not burn down. It remains lit for as long as a king-size cigarette does and extinguishes itself.

Will a smokeless cigarette appeal to smokers? Will nonsmokers be more tolerant of a smokeless cigarette? In what situations will a smokeless cigarette be preferred to a regular cigarette? The research process can help answer questions such as these, but what form should the research take? Should a laboratory taste test be conducted? Should a survey of nonsmokers be part of the research strategy?

This chapter discusses how managers make decisions about research strategies and tactics. It provides an overview of the types of research designs and briefly discusses the stages in the research process. ■

INFORMATION REDUCES UNCERTAINTY

Marketing research provides information to reduce uncertainty. It helps focus decision making. Sometimes marketing researchers know exactly what their marketing problems are and design careful studies to test specific hypotheses. For example, a soft-drink company introducing a new vanilla cola might want to know whether a gold or a silver label would make the packaging more effective. This problem is fully defined, and an experiment may be designed to answer the marketing question with little preliminary investigation.

In more ambiguous circumstances, management may be totally unaware that a marketing problem exists. For example, suppose McDonald's managers notice that Mo's Burgers, a competitor in the Japanese market, introduced Mo's Roast Katsu Burger, a roast pork cutlet drenched in traditional Japanese katsu sauce and topped with shredded cabbage. The managers may understand little about Japanese consumers' feelings about this menu item. In this case, some exploratory research will yield insights into the nature of this problem.

To understand the variety of research activity, it is beneficial to categorize the types of marketing research.

TYPES OF MARKETING RESEARCH

Marketing research can be classified on the basis of either technique or function. Experiments, surveys, and observational studies are just a few common research techniques. Classifying research by its purpose or function shows how the nature of the marketing problem influences the choice of methods. The nature of the problem will determine whether the research is (1) exploratory, (2) descriptive, or (3) causal.

Exploratory Research

exploratory research
Initial research conducted to clarify and define a problem.

Exploratory research is conducted to clarify ambiguous problems. Management may have discovered a general problem but may need research to gain a better understanding of the dimensions of the problem and to aid analysis. Exploratory research is not intended to provide conclusive evidence from which to determine a particular course of action. Usually exploratory research is conducted with the expectation that subsequent research will be required to provide such conclusive evidence. Rushing into detailed surveys before less expensive and more readily available sources of information have been exhausted can lead to serious mistakes.

For example, suppose a Chinese fast-food restaurant chain is considering expanding its hours and product line with a breakfast menu. Exploratory research with a small number of current customers might find a strong negative reaction to eating a spicy vegetable breakfast at a Chinese fast-food outlet. Thus, exploratory research might help crystallize a problem and identify information needed for future research.

Descriptive Research

descriptive research
Research designed to describe characteristics of a population or a phenomenon.

The major purpose of **descriptive research**, as the name implies, is to describe characteristics of a population or a phenomenon. Marketing managers frequently need to determine who purchases a product, accurately portray the size of the market, identify competitors' actions, and so on. Descriptive research seeks to determine the answers to *who, what, when, where,* and *how* questions.

Love knows no limits.

With 353 horses, the power is Herculean. The handling, telepathic. And the brakes, breathtaking.   Add a roof that disappears as swiftly as its taillights, and you have pure, unremitting love.

Descriptive research shows that the Internet is changing new car shopping and purchasing patterns. In 2000, while only 4 percent made the actual purchase online, 40 percent of new car purchasers gathered information about their cars online. And, 85 percent of BMW buyers go to the Internet before making a purchase.[1]

Descriptive research often helps segment and target markets. For example, marketing researchers conducted descriptive surveys to identify the characteristics of consumers who purchase organic food products. Such consumers tend to live in larger cities with populations over 500,000. More than half live on the coasts, with the majority residing on the West Coast. The most frequent buyers of organic foods are affluent men and women ages 45–54 (36 percent) and 18–34 (35 percent).[2] Interestingly, consumers who buy organic foods are not very brand oriented—81 percent of them cannot name a single organic brand.

Descriptive research often is used to reveal the nature of shopping or other consumer behavior. *Bride* magazine's descriptive research revealed that the average bride tried on 12 wedding gowns; one in five considered more than 21 dresses before choosing the right one; and 20 percent cried when they found it.[3]

Accuracy is of paramount importance in descriptive research. While they cannot completely eliminate errors, good researchers strive for descriptive precision. Suppose a study seeks to describe the market potential for portable MP3 music players. If the study does not precisely measure sales volume, it will mislead the managers who are making production scheduling, budgeting, and other decisions based on it.

Unlike exploratory research, descriptive studies are based on some previous understanding of the nature of the research problem. Although the researcher may have a general understanding of the situation, the conclusive evidence that answers questions of fact necessary to determine a course of action has yet to be collected. Many circumstances require descriptive research to identify the reasons consumers give to explain the nature of things. In other words, a diagnostic analysis is performed when consumers are asked questions such as "Why do you feel that way?" Although they may describe why consumers feel a certain way, the findings of a descriptive study such as this, sometimes called *diagnostics,* do not provide causal evidence. Frequently descriptive research attempts to determine the extent of differences in needs, attitudes, and opinions among subgroups.

Causal Research

causal research
Research conducted to identify cause-and-effect relationships among variables.

The main goal of **causal research** is to identify cause-and-effect relationships among variables. Exploratory and descriptive research normally precede cause-and-effect relationship studies. In causal studies, researchers typically have an expectation about the relationship to be explained, such as a prediction about the influence of price, packaging, advertising, and the like on sales. Thus, researchers must be quite knowledgeable about the subject. Ideally, the manager wants to establish that one event (say, a new package) is the means for producing another event (an increase in sales). Causal research attempts to establish that when we do one thing, another thing will follow. The word *cause* is common in everyday conversation, but from a scientific research perspective, a true causal relationship is impossible to prove. Nevertheless, researchers seek certain types of evidence to help them understand and predict relationships.

A typical causal study has management change one variable (for example, advertising) and then observe the effect of the change on another variable (such as sales). Some evidence for causality comes from the fact that the cause precedes the effect. In other words, having an *appropriate causal order of events,* or temporal sequence, is one criterion for causality that must be met to be able to establish a causal relationship. If a consumer behavior theorist wishes to show that an attitude change causes a behavior change, one criterion that must be established is that the attitude change precedes the behavior change.

concomitant variation
The way in which two phenomena or events vary together.

In the example above, some evidence of concomitant variation exists, because advertising and sales appear to be associated. **Concomitant variation** occurs when two phenomena or events vary together. When the criterion of concomitant variation is not met—that is, when no association exists among the variables—reason suggests that no causal relationship exists. If two events vary together, one event may be the cause; however, concomitant variation by itself is not sufficient evidence for causality because the two events may have a common cause; that is, both may be influenced by a third variable. For instance, a large number of ice cream cones were sold one morning at Atlantic City's beach. That afternoon, a large number of drownings occurred. Most of us would not conclude that eating ice cream causes drowning; more likely, on that day the beach was crowded and the number of people probably influenced both ice cream sales and drownings. The effect could have been produced in other ways. Thus, causation requires more than concomitant variation and a proper time sequence between the occurrence of two events. There may be several plausible alternative explanations for the observed relationship.[4]

Consider a presidential candidate who reduces advertising expenditures near the end of the primary campaign race and wins many more delegates in the remaining primaries. To infer causality—that reducing advertising increased the number of delegates—may be inappropriate, because the presumed cause of the increase in delegates may not have been the real cause. It is more likely that near the end of the race, marginal candidates withdrew. The real cause probably was unrelated to advertising.

In these examples, the third variable that is the source of the spurious association is a very salient factor readily identifiable as the true influence of change. However, within the complex environment in which managers operate, identifying alternative or complex causal facts can be difficult. A researcher can never be completely certain that the causal explanation is adequate.

EXHIBIT 3.1 | TYPES OF MARKETING RESEARCH

| | | Uncertainty | |
| Absolute Ambiguity | | | Complete Certainty |

Degree of Problem Definition	Exploratory Research (Ambiguous Problem)	Descriptive Research (Partially Defined Problem)	Causal Research (Problem Clearly Defined)
Possible situation	"Our sales are declining and we don't know why."	"What kind of people are buying our product? Who is buying our competitor's product?"	"Will buyers purchase more of our product in a new package?"
	"Would people be interested in our new product idea?"	"What features do buyers prefer in our product?"	"Which of two advertising campaigns is more effective?"

Note: The degree of uncertainty of the research problem determines the research methodology.

Uncertainty Influences the Type of Research

The uncertainty of the research problem is related to the type of research project. As Exhibit 3.1 illustrates, exploratory research is conducted during the early stages of decision making, when the decision situation is ambiguous and management is very uncertain about the nature of the problem. When management is aware of the problem but lacks some knowledge, descriptive research is usually conducted. Causal research requires sharply defined problems.

STAGES IN THE RESEARCH PROCESS

As previously noted, marketing research can take many forms, but systematic inquiry is a common thread. Systematic inquiry requires careful planning and an orderly investigation. Marketing research, like other forms of scientific inquiry, involves a sequence of highly interrelated activities. The stages of the research process overlap continuously, and it is somewhat of an oversimplification to state that every research project follows a neat, ordered sequence of activities. Nevertheless, marketing research often follows a generalized pattern. Exhibit 3.2 shows the stages: (1) problem discovery and definition, (2) planning a research design, (3) sampling, (4) gathering the data, (5) processing and analyzing the data, and (6) formulating the conclusions and preparing the report.

In practice, the stages overlap chronologically and are functionally interrelated; sometimes the later stages are completed before the earlier ones. Sometimes the earlier stages of research influence the design of the later stages.

Alternatives in the Research Process

The researcher must choose among a number of alternatives during each stage of the research process.[5] On a map, some paths are better charted than others; some are difficult to travel, and some

EXHIBIT 3.2 | FLOWCHART OF THE MARKETING RESEARCH PROCESS

Note: Diamond-shaped boxes indicate stages in the research process in which a choice of one or more techniques must be made. The dotted line indicates an alternative path that skips exploratory research.

are more interesting and beautiful than others. Rewarding experiences may be gained during the journey. It is important to remember that there is no single right or best path for all journeys. The road one takes depends on where one wants to go and the resources (money, time, labor, and so on) available for the trip. The map analogy is useful for the marketing researcher because each stage of the research process offers several paths to follow. In some instances, time constraints may dictate that the quickest path will lead to appropriate research. In other circumstances when money and human resources are plentiful, the appropriate path may be quite different. Exploration of the various paths of marketing research decisions is the primary purpose.

The following sections briefly describe the six stages of the research process. (Each stage is discussed in greater depth in later chapters.) Exhibit 3.2 shows the decisions researchers must make in each stage. Our discussion of the research process begins with problem discovery and definition, because most research projects are initiated to remedy managers' uncertainty about some aspect of the firm's marketing program.

As Exhibit 3.2 shows, the research process begins with problem discovery. Identifying the problem is the first step toward its solution. In general usage, the word *problem* suggests that something has gone wrong. Actually, the research task may be to clarify a problem, define an opportunity, or monitor and evaluate current operations. The concept of problem discovery and definition must encompass a broader context that includes analysis of opportunities. Note that the initial stage is problem *discovery* rather than *definition*. The researcher may not have a clear-cut statement of the problem at the outset of the research process; often, only symptoms of the problem are apparent at that point. Sales may be declining, but management may not know the exact nature of the problem. Thus, the problem statement often is made only in general terms; what is to be investigated is not yet specifically identified.

Albert Einstein noted that "the formulation of a problem is often more essential than its solution."[6] This is good advice for marketing managers. Too often they concentrate on finding the right answer rather than asking the right question. Many managers do not realize that defining a problem may be more difficult than solving it. In marketing research, data that are collected before the nature of the marketing problem is carefully thought out probably will not help solve the problem.

It should be emphasized that the word *problem* refers to the managerial problem (which may be a lack of knowledge about consumers or advertising effectiveness) and the information needed to help solve it. Defining the problem must precede determination of the purpose of the research. Frequently the marketing researcher will not be involved until line management has discovered that some information about a particular aspect of the marketing mix is needed. Even at this point, the exact nature of the problem may be poorly defined. Once a problem area has been discovered, the marketing researcher can begin the process of precisely defining it.

Defining the Problem

In marketing research, the adage "a problem well defined is a problem half solved" is worth remembering. This adage emphasizes that an orderly definition of the research problem lends a sense of direction to the investigation. Careful attention to the **problem definition stage** allows the researcher to set the proper research objectives. If the purpose of the research is clear, the chances of collecting necessary and relevant information and not collecting surplus information will be much greater.

Ascertain the Decision Makers' Objectives   As a staff person, the research investigator must attempt to satisfy the decision makers' objectives: those of the brand manager, sales manager, and others who requested the project. Management and organizational theorists suggest that the decision maker should express goals to the researcher in measurable terms. Unfortunately, this rarely occurs. Instead, the decision maker is likely to state his or her objectives in a

problem definition stage
The stage in which management seeks to identify a clear-cut statement of the problem or opportunity.

A SEA HORSE'S TALE

Once upon a time, a Sea Horse gathered up his seven pieces of eight and cantered out to find his fortune.[7] Before he had traveled very far he met an Eel, who said,

"Psst. Hey, bud. Where ya goin'?"

"I'm going out to find my fortune," replied the Sea Horse, proudly.

"You're in luck," said the Eel. "For four pieces of eight you can have this speedy flipper, and then you'll be able to get there a lot faster."

"Gee, that's swell," said the Sea Horse, and paid the money and put on the flipper, and slithered off at twice the speed. Soon he came upon a Sponge, who said,

"Psst. Hey, bud. Where ya goin'?"

"I'm going out to find my fortune," replied the Sea Horse.

"You're in luck," said the Sponge. "For a small fee I will let you have this jet-propelled scooter so that you will be able to travel a lot faster."

So the Sea Horse bought the scooter with his remaining money and went zooming through the sea five times as fast. Soon he came upon a Shark, who said,

"Psst. Hey, bud. Where ya goin'?"

"I'm going out to find my fortune," replied the Sea Horse.

"You're in luck. If you'll take this shortcut," said the Shark, pointing to his open mouth, "you'll save yourself a lot of time."

"Gee, thanks," said the Sea Horse, and zoomed off into the interior of the Shark, there to be devoured.

The moral of this fable is that if you're not sure where you're going, you're liable to end up someplace else—and not even know it.

---

vague, generalized form, leaving it up to the researcher to determine what those objectives really are. In so doing, the researcher may well be performing his or her most useful service to the decision maker.[8]

Isolate and Identify the Problem, Not the Symptoms

Anticipating the many influences and dimensions of a problem is impossible for any researcher or executive. For instance, a firm may have a problem with its advertising effectiveness. The possible causes of this problem may be low brand awareness, the wrong brand image, the wrong media, or perhaps too small a budget. Management's job is to isolate and identify the most likely causes. Certain occurrences that appear to be the problem may be only symptoms of a deeper problem.

iceberg principle
The principle that the dangerous part of many marketing problems is neither visible to nor understood by marketing managers.

The Iceberg Principle The **iceberg principle** helps explain why so many marketing research projects begin without clear objectives or adequate problem definitions (see Exhibit 3.3). A sailor on the open sea notices only the 10 percent of an iceberg that extends above the surface of the water; 90 percent of the iceberg is submerged. The dangerous part of many marketing problems, like the submerged portion of the iceberg, is neither visible to nor understood by marketing managers. If the submerged portions of the problem are omitted from the problem definition (and subsequently from the research design), the decisions

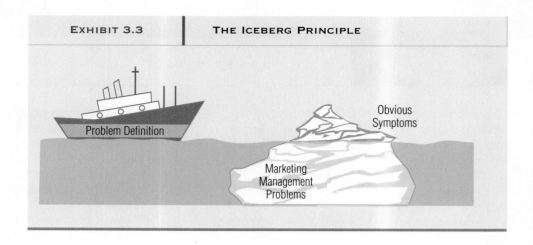

EXHIBIT 3.3 | THE ICEBERG PRINCIPLE

based on the research may be less than optimal. Omission of important information or faulty assumptions about the situation can be extremely costly. Exhibit 3.4 illustrates how symptoms may mask the nature of the true problem.

Identification of Key Variables

A crucial aspect of problem definition is identification of key variables. The term *variable* is important in research. A **variable** is anything that varies or changes in value. Because a variable represents a quality that can exhibit differences in value, usually in magnitude or strength, it may be said that a variable generally is anything that may assume different numerical or categorical values. For example, attitudes toward airlines may be a variable ranging from positive to negative. Each attribute of airlines' services, such as safety, seat comfort, and baggage handling, is a variable.

In statistical analysis, a variable is identified by a symbol, such as X. Categories or numerical values may then be associated with this symbol. Gender may be categorized as male or female; thus, gender is a **categorical** or **classificatory variable**, since it has a limited number of distinct values. On the other hand, sales volume may encompass an infinite range of numbers; it is a **continuous variable**, one that can have an infinite number of values.

In causal research, the terms *dependent variable* and *independent variable* are frequently used. A **dependent variable** is a criterion or a variable that is to be predicted or explained. An **independent variable** is a variable that is expected to influence the dependent variable. For example, average sales compensation may be a dependent variable that is influenced or predicted by an independent variable such as number of years of experience. These terms are discussed in greater detail in the chapters on experimentation and data analysis.

Research Questions and Hypotheses

The objective of the problem definition stage is to prepare a written statement that clarifies any ambiguity about what the research is intended to accomplish. Formulating a series of research questions and hypotheses adds clarity to the statement of the marketing problem. For example, a personal computer company made the following statement about an advertising problem: In the broadest sense, the marketing problem is to determine the best ways [the company] can communicate with potential purchasers of laptop computers.

variable
Anything that may assume different numerical or categorical values.

categorical (classificatory) variable
A variable that has a limited number of distinct values.

continuous variable
A variable that has an infinite number of possible values.

dependent variable
A criterion or variable to be predicted or explained.

independent variable
A variable that is expected to influence a dependent variable.

EXHIBIT 3.4 | SYMPTOMS CAN BE CONFUSING

Organization	Symptoms	Problem Definition Based on Symptom	True Problem
20-year-old neighborhood swimming association in a mid-size city	Membership has been declining for years. New water park with wave pool and water slides moved into town a few years ago.	Neighborhood residents prefer the expensive water park and have negative image of swimming pool.	Demographic changes: Children in this 20-year-old neighborhood have grown up. Older residents no longer swim.
Manufacturer of palm-size computers with Internet access	Distributors complain prices are too high.	Investigate business users to learn how much prices need to be reduced.	Sales management: Distributors do not have adequate product knowledge to communicate product's value.
Microbrewery	Consumers prefer the taste of competitor's brand.	What type of reformulated taste is needed?	Package: Old-fashioned package influences taste perception.

- How familiar are consumers with the various brands of computers?
- What attitudes do consumers have toward these brands?
- How important are the various factors for evaluating the purchase of a laptop computer?
- How effective are the communications efforts of the various competitive marketers in terms of message recognition?

Research questions clarify what is perplexing managers and indicate what issues have to be resolved. A research question is the researcher's translation of the marketing problem into a specific inquiry.

A research question can be too vague and general if stated in terms such as "Is advertising copy X better than advertising copy Y?" Advertising effectiveness can be variously measured by sales, recall of sales message, brand awareness, intention to buy, and so on. Asking a more specific research question (e.g., "Which advertisement has a higher day-after recall score?") helps the researcher design a study that will produce pertinent information.

The goal of defining the problem is to state the research questions clearly and to develop well-formulated hypotheses. A **hypothesis** is an unproven proposition or possible solution to a problem. Hypothetical statements assert probable answers to research questions. A hypothesis is a statement about the nature of the world; in its simplest form, it is a guess. A sales manager may hypothesize that salespeople who show the highest job satisfaction will be the most productive. An advertising manager may hypothesize that if consumers' attitudes toward a product are changed in a positive direction, consumption of the product will increase. Problem statements and hypotheses are similar. Both state relationships, but problem statements are interrogative while hypotheses are declarative. Sometimes the two types of statements are almost identical in substance. An important difference, however, is that hypotheses usually are more specific than problem statements; typically they are closer to the actual research operations and empirical testing.

hypothesis
An unproven proposition or supposition that tentatively explains certain facts or phenomena; a probable answer to a research question.

Hugh Dubberly, creative director of Netscape, advocates the following step-by-step process to help clearly define the problem to be solved:[9]

"How do we define the problem? Begin by assembling all the relevant players in a room. Ask each player to describe the unmet need, or in other words, to suggest the cause of the problem. Write down each suggestion. Nothing you will do on the project will be more important. With each suggestion, ask in turn for its cause. And then the cause of the cause. And then the cause of the cause of the

cause. Keep at it like a 2-year-old. By the time everyone in the room wants to strangle you, you will very likely have found the root cause of the problem.

"After you've developed the problem statement, you need to be sure to gain consensus on it from all the relevant parties. Failure to get 'buy-in' from all the right people at this stage creates the potential for trouble later in the process. Someone who hasn't agreed on the definition up front is likely to want to change it later."

---

research objective
The researcher's version of the marketing problem; it explains the purpose of the research in measurable terms and defines standards for what the research should accomplish.

The **research objective** is the researcher's version of the marketing problem. After the research questions or hypotheses have been stated, the research project's objectives are derived from the problem definition. They explain the purpose of the research in measurable terms and define standards for what the research should accomplish. In addition to explaining the reasons for conducting the project, research objectives help ensure that the scope of the research project will be manageable.

In some instances, the marketing problem and the project's research objectives are identical. However, the objectives must specify the information needed to make a decision. Identifying the needed information may require that managers or researchers be extremely specific, perhaps even listing the exact wording of the question in a survey or explaining exactly what behavior might be observed or recorded in an experiment. Statements about the required precision of the information or the source of information may be required to clearly communicate exactly what information is needed. Many product buying decisions, for example, are made by both husband and wife. If so, the husband–wife decision–making unit is the unit of analysis. The objective of obtaining X information about research questions from this unit should be specifically stated.

The research objectives should be limited to a manageable number. Fewer study objectives make it easier to ensure that each will be addressed fully.

Managers Often Neglect the Problem Definition Stage

Although problem definition probably is the most important stage of the research process, it frequently is a neglected area of marketing research. Too many researchers forget that the best place to begin a research project is at the end. Knowing what is to be accomplished determines the research process. An error or omission in problem definition is likely to be a costly mistake that cannot be corrected in later stages of the process.

Exploratory Research Techniques

Exploratory research usually is conducted during the initial stage of the research process. The preliminary activities undertaken to refine the problem into researchable form need not be formal or precise. The purpose of the exploratory research process is to progressively narrow the scope of the research topic and transform ambiguous problems into well-defined ones that incorporate specific research objectives. By investigating any existing studies on the subject, talking with knowledgeable individuals, and informally investigating the situation, the researcher can progressively sharpen the concepts. After such exploration, the researcher should know exactly which data to collect during the formal phases of the project and how to conduct the project. Exhibit 3.2 indicates that managers and researchers must decide whether to use one or more exploratory research techniques. As Exhibit 3.2 indicates, this stage is optional.

The marketing researcher can employ techniques from four basic categories to obtain insights and gain a clearer idea of the problem: secondary data analysis, pilot studies, case studies, and experience surveys. These are discussed in detail in Chapter 5. This section briefly discusses secondary data and focus group interviews, the most popular types of pilot studies.

Secondary Data   *Secondary data,* or *historical data,* are data previously collected and assembled for some project other than the one at hand. (*Primary data* are gathered and assembled specifically for the project at hand.) Secondary data often can be found inside the company, at a public or university library, or on the Internet. In addition, some firms specialize in providing information, such as economic forecasts, that is useful to many organizations. The researcher who gathers data from the *Census of Population* or the *Survey of Current Business* is using secondary sources.

A literature review—a survey of published articles and books that discuss theories and past empirical studies about a topic—is an almost universal first step in academic research projects. A literature survey also is common in many applied research studies. Students who have written term papers should be familiar with using computer search systems, indexes to published literature, and other library sources to compile bibliographies of past research.

Consider a bank that wishes to determine the best sites for additional automated teller machines. A logical first step would be to investigate the factors that bankers in other parts of the country consider important. By reading articles in banking journals, management might quickly discover that the best locations are inside supermarkets located in residential areas where people are young, highly educated, and earning higher-than-average incomes. These data might lead the bank to investigate census information to determine where in the city such people live. Reviewing and building on the work already compiled by others is an economical starting point for most research.

pilot study
A collective term for any small-scale exploratory research technique that uses sampling but does not apply rigorous standards.

Pilot Studies   The term **pilot study** covers a number of diverse research techniques. Pilot studies collect data from the ultimate consumers or the actual subjects of the research project to serve as a guide for a larger study. When the term *pilot study* is used in the context of exploratory research, it refers to a study whose data collection methods are informal and whose findings may lack precision.[10] For instance, a downtown association concerned with revitalization of the central business district conducted a very flexible survey using open-ended questions. The interviewers were given considerable latitude to identify changes needed in the shopping area. The results of this survey suggested possible topics for formal investigation.

The focus group interview is a more elaborate kind of exploratory pilot study that has become increasingly popular in recent years. The focus group session brings together six to ten people in a loosely structured format; the technique is based on the assumption that individuals are more willing to share their ideas when they are able to hear the ideas of others. Information obtained in these studies is qualitative and may serve to guide a subsequent quantitative study.

For example, the Philadelphia Museum used focus groups to investigate how well its exhibits and shows were catering to the public. A local resident who had never visited the museum mentioned that he was not aware of any important artwork at the museum. Another participant in the same focus group assumed that the museum would be filled with "pictures I would not understand. . . . I've seen art where it looked like kids splashed paint." These findings (confirmed by other research) influenced the museum to reinstate an image of van Gogh's *Sunflowers* on the cover of its brochures.[11]

We have looked at two basic methods of exploratory research, but such research does not have to follow a standard design. Because the purpose of exploratory research is to gain insights and discover new ideas, researchers may use considerable creativity and flexibility. Data generally are collected using several exploratory techniques. Exhausting these sources usually is worth the effort because the expense is relatively low. Further, insights into how and how not to conduct research may be gained from activities during the problem definition stage. If the conclusions made during this stage suggest marketing opportunities, the researcher is in a position to begin planning a formal, quantitative research project.

Statement of Research Objectives   A researcher must initially decide precisely what to research. After identifying and clarifying the problem, with or without exploratory research, the researcher should make a formal statement of the problem and the research objectives. This statement delineates the type of information to be collected and provides a framework for the scope of the study.

A typical research objective might seek to answer a question such as "To what extent did the new pricing program achieve its objectives?" In this sense, the statement of the problem is a research question.

The best expression of a research objective is a well-formed, testable research hypothesis. A *hypothesis* is a statement that can be refuted or supported by empirical data. For example, an exploratory study might lead to the hypothesis that a market share decline recognized by management is occurring predominantly among households in which the head of the household is 45 to 65 years old with an income of $45,000 per year or less. Another hypothesis might be that concentrating advertising efforts in monthly waves (rather than conducting continuous advertising) will cause an increase in sales and profits. Once the hypothesis has been developed, the researcher is ready to select a research design.

Planning the Research Design

research design stage
The stage in which the researcher determines a framework for the research plan of action by selecting a basic research method.

research design
A master plan that specifies the methods and procedures for collecting and analyzing needed information.

After the researcher has formulated the research problem, he or she must develop the research design as part of the **research design stage.** A **research design** is a master plan that specifies the methods and procedures for collecting and analyzing the needed information; it is a framework for the research plan of action. The objectives of the study determined during the early stages of the research are included in the design to ensure that the information collected is appropriate for solving the problem. The researcher also must determine the sources of information, the design technique (e.g., survey or experiment), the sampling methodology, and the schedule and cost of the research.

Selection of the Basic Research Method Here again, the researcher must make a decision. Exhibit 3.2 shows the four basic design techniques for descriptive and causal research: surveys, experiments, secondary data, and observation. The objectives of the study, the available data sources, the urgency of the decision, and the cost of obtaining the data will determine which method to choose. We will consider the managerial aspects of selecting the research design later.

Surveys The most common method of generating primary data is through surveys. Most people have seen the results of political surveys by Gallup or Harris Interactive, and some have been respondents (members of a sample who supply answers) to marketing research questionnaires. A *survey* is a research technique that gathers information from a sample of people using a questionnaire. The task of writing a list of questions and designing the format of the printed or electronic questionnaire is an essential aspect of the development of a survey research design. Research investigators may choose to contact respondents by telephone, by mail, in person, on the Internet, or through another communication medium. An advertiser spending $2,000,000 for 30 seconds of commercial time during the Super Bowl may telephone people to quickly gather information concerning their responses to the advertising. A forklift truck manufacturer trying to determine a cause for low sales in the wholesale grocery industry might choose an Internet questionnaire because the appropriate executives are hard to reach by telephone. A manufacturer of a birth control device for men might determine the need for a versatile survey method wherein an interviewer can ask a variety of personal questions in a flexible format. Personal interviews are expensive, but they are valuable because investigators can use visual aids and supplement the interviews with observations. Each of these survey methods has advantages and disadvantages. The researcher's task is to find the most appropriate way to collect the needed information.

Dentyne Ice's survey research objective was to understand what goes on in the hearts and minds of young men and women in the 15–24 age range when they're at that crucial moment before the first kiss.[12] The research showed that without question, there is the nervous anticipation of one's first kiss with a new love interest. Marketing research helped develop a series of ads to put 15–24-year-old characters in humorous situations that illustrate variations of using gum to freshen breath before a first kiss. One commercial for Dentyne Ice features a young man closing in for a kiss with an attractive someone. At that moment, he imagines himself surrounded by every guy she's ever kissed before—all of them issuing taunts and generally undermining his resolve. Happily, there's a quick confidence-booster available, in the form of Dentyne Ice.

Experiments Marketing *experiments* hold the greatest potential for establishing cause-and-effect relationships. Experimentation allows investigation of changes in one variable, such as sales, while manipulating one or two other variables, perhaps price or advertising, under controlled conditions. Ideally, experimental control provides a basis for isolating causal factors by eliminating outside, or exogenous, influences. Thus, an experiment controls conditions so that one or more variables can be manipulated to test a hypothesis.

Test marketing is a frequently used form of marketing experimentation. Chelsea, Anheuser-Busch's "not-so-soft soft drink," illustrates the usefulness of marketing experiments. Anheuser-Busch first introduced Chelsea as a drink with a slight alcoholic content—about 0.4 percent—that was a socially acceptable alternative to beer for adults who did not want to get intoxicated. During an experiment to test market the "not-so-soft soft drink" and the "not-so-sweet" concept, a Virginia nurses' association and some religious groups strongly criticized the company and the new product. These critics suggested that Anheuser-Busch had introduced a product that might encourage children to become beer drinkers. They contended that Chelsea was packaged like beer and looked, foamed, and poured like it. The criticism led the brewery to suspend production, advertising, and promotion of the drink. Later it reintroduced the product as a soft drink with only "a trace of alcohol" as a "natural alternative" to soft drinks, with not-so-sweet and stylish attributes. Similar problems occurred in the second experiment. This experiment pointed out to Anheuser-Busch that an extraneous variable, alcohol level, caused an inadvertent miscommunication: Consumers confused the original Chelsea with beer.

Secondary Data for Descriptive and Quantitative Analysis Like exploratory research studies, descriptive and causal studies use previously collected data. Although the terms *secondary* and *historical* are interchangeable, we will use the term *secondary data*. An example of a secondary data study is the use

Direct marketers often conduct experiments to determine how to increase response to pamphlets, catalogs, or Internet offerings. Experiments have shown that the wording of headline copy and prices can greatly influence the success of direct marketing.

of a mathematical model to predict sales on the basis of past sales or a correlation with related variables. Manufacturers of color printers for personal computers may find that sales are highly correlated with discretionary personal income. To predict future market potential, projections of disposable personal income may be acquired from the government or a university. This information can be manipulated mathematically to forecast sales. Formal secondary data studies have benefits and limitations similar to those of exploratory studies that use secondary data, but generally the quantitative analysis of secondary data is more sophisticated.

Observation   The objective of many research projects is merely to record what can be observed—for example, the number of automobiles that pass by a proposed site for a gas station. This can be mechanically recorded or observed by humans. Research personnel known as *mystery shoppers* may act as customers to observe actions of sales personnel or do comparative shopping to learn prices at competing outlets.

The main advantage of the observation technique is that it records behavior without relying on reports from respondents. Observational data are often collected unobtrusively and passively without a respondent's direct participation. For instance, A. C. Nielsen Company uses a "people meter" attached to television sets to record the programs each household member is watching. This eliminates the possible bias of respondents stating that they watched the president's State of the Union address rather than a situation comedy on another station.

Observation is more complex than mere "nose counting," and the task is more difficult than the inexperienced researcher would imagine. Several things of interest, such as attitudes, opinions, motivations, and other intangible states of mind, simply cannot be observed.

The "Best" Research Design   It is argued that there is no single research design and there are no hard-and-fast rules for good marketing research. This does not mean, however, that the researcher faces chaos and confusion. It means that the researcher can choose among many alternative methods to solve a problem. An eminent behavioral researcher has stated this concept quite eloquently:

> There is never a single, standard, correct method of carrying out a piece of research. Do not wait to start your research until you find out the proper approach, because there are many ways to tackle a problem—some good, some bad, but probably several good ways. There is no single perfect design. A research method for a given problem is not like the solution to a problem in algebra. It is more like a recipe for beef Stroganoff; there is no one best recipe.[13]

Consider the researcher who must forecast sales for the upcoming year. Some commonly used forecasting methods are surveying executive opinion, collecting sales force composite opinions, surveying user expectations, projecting trends, and analyzing market factors.

The ability to select the most appropriate research design develops with experience. Inexperienced researchers often jump to the conclusion that the survey method is the best design because they are most familiar with this method. When Chicago's Museum of Science and Industry wanted to determine the relative popularity of its exhibits, it could have conducted a survey. Instead, a creative researcher familiar with other research designs suggested a far less expensive alternative: an unobtrusive observation technique. The researcher suggested that the museum merely keep track of the frequency with which the floor tiles in front of the various exhibits had to be replaced, indicating where the heaviest traffic occurred. When this was done, the museum found that the chick-hatching exhibit was the most popular. This method provided the same results as a survey but at a much lower cost.

After determining the proper design, the researcher moves on to the next stage: planning the sample.

Sampling

sampling stage
The stage in which the researcher determines who is to be sampled, how large a sample is needed, and how sampling units will be selected.

Although the sampling plan is outlined in the research design, the **sampling stage** is a distinct phase of the research process. For convenience, however, we will treat the sample planning and the actual sample generation processes together in this section.

If you take your first bite of steak and conclude that it needs salt, you have just conducted a sample. *Sampling* involves any procedure that uses a small number of items or a portion of the population to make a conclusion regarding the whole population. In other words, a sample is a subset from a larger population. If certain statistical procedures are followed, a researcher need not select every item in a population because the results of a good sample should have the same characteristics as the population as a whole. Of course, when errors are made, samples do not give reliable estimates of the population. A famous example of error due to sampling is the 1936 *Literary Digest* fiasco. The magazine conducted a survey and predicted that Republican Alf Landon would win over Democrat Franklin D. Roosevelt by a landslide in that year's presidential election. This prediction was wrong—and the error was due to sample selection. The postmortems showed that *Literary Digest* had sampled its readers and telephone subscribers. In 1936 these people were not a representative cross-section of voters, because in those days, people who could afford magazine subscriptions and phone service were generally well-to-do—and a disproportionate number of them were Republicans.

This famous example suggests that the first sampling question to ask is "Who is to be sampled?" The answer to this primary question requires the identification of a *target population*. Defining this population and determining the sampling units may not be easy. If, for example, a savings and loan association surveys people who already have accounts for answers to image questions, the selected sampling units will not represent potential customers. Specifying the target population is a crucial aspect of the sampling plan.

The next sampling issue concerns sample size. How big should the sample be? Although management may wish to examine every potential buyer of a product or service, doing so may be unnecessary as well as unrealistic. Typically, larger samples are more precise than smaller ones, but proper probability sampling can allow a small proportion of the total population to give a reliable measure of the whole. A later discussion will explain how large a sample must be to be truly representative of the universe, or population.

The final sampling decision concerns choosing how to select the sampling units. Students who have taken a statistics course generally understand simple random sampling, in which every unit in the population has an equal and known chance of being selected. However, this is only one type of sampling. For example, a cluster sampling procedure may reduce costs and make data-gathering procedures more efficient. If members of the population are found in close geographical clusters, a sampling procedure that selects area clusters rather than individual units in the population will reduce costs. Rather than selecting 1,000 individuals throughout the United States, it may be more economical to first select 25 counties and then sample within those counties. This will substantially reduce travel, hiring, and training costs. In determining the appropriate sampling plan, the researcher will have to select the most appropriate sampling procedure for meeting the established study objectives.

There are two basic sampling techniques: probability sampling and nonprobability sampling. In a *probability sample,* every member of the population has a known, nonzero probability of selection. If sample units are selected on the basis of personal judgment (for example, a test market city is selected because it appears to be typical), the sample method is a *nonprobability sample.* In reality, the sampling decision is not a simple choice between two methods. Simple random samples, stratified samples, quota samples, cluster samples, and judgmental samples are among the many methods for drawing a sample. A full discussion of these techniques must be postponed to a later chapter.

Data Gathering

data-gathering stage
The stage in which the researcher collects the data.

Once the research design (including the sampling plan) has been formalized, the process of gathering or collecting information, the **data-gathering stage,** may begin. Data may be gathered by humans or recorded by machines. Scanner data illustrate electronic data collection by machine.

Obviously, the numerous research techniques involve many methods of data gathering. The survey method requires some form of direct participation by the respondent. The respondent may participate by filling out a questionnaire or interacting with an interviewer. If an unobtrusive method of data gathering is used, the subjects do not actively participate. For instance, a simple count of motorists driving past a proposed franchising location is one kind of data-gathering method. However the data are collected, it is important to minimize errors in the process. For example, the data gathering should be consistent in all geographical areas. If an interviewer phrases questions incorrectly or records a respondent's statements inaccurately (not verbatim), major data collection errors will result.

Often there are two phases to the process of gathering data: pretesting and the main study. A *pretesting phase* using a small subsample may determine whether the data-gathering plan for the *main study* is an appropriate procedure. Thus, a small-scale pretest study provides an advance opportunity for an investigator to check the data collection form to minimize errors due to improper design, such as poorly worded or organized questions. There is also a chance to discover confusing interviewing instructions, learn if the questionnaire is too long or too short, and uncover other such field errors. Tabulation of data from the pretests provides the researcher with a format of the knowledge that may be gained from the actual study. If the tabulation of the data and statistical results does not answer the researcher's questions, the investigator may need to redesign the study.

Data Processing and Analysis

After the fieldwork has been completed, the data must be converted into a format that will answer the marketing manager's questions. This is part of the **data-processing and analysis stage.** Data processing generally begins with editing and coding the data. *Editing* involves checking the data collection forms for omissions, legibility, and consistency in classification. The editing process corrects problems such as interviewer errors (an answer recorded on the wrong portion of a questionnaire, for example) before the data are transferred to the computer.

Before data can be tabulated, meaningful categories and character symbols must be established for groups of responses. The rules for interpreting, categorizing, recording, and transferring the data to the data storage media are called *codes.* This coding process facilitates computer or hand tabulation. If computer analysis is to be used, the data are entered into the computer and verified. Computer-assisted (online) interviewing is an example of the impact of technological change on the research process. Telephone interviewers, seated at computer terminals, read survey questions displayed on the monitor. The interviewers ask the questions and then type in the respondents' answers. Thus, answers are collected and processed into the computer at the same time, eliminating intermediate steps that could introduce errors.

Analysis   *Analysis* is the application of logic to understand the data that have been gathered. In its simplest form, analysis may involve determining consistent patterns and summarizing the relevant details revealed in the investigation. The appropriate analytical technique for data analysis will be determined by management's information requirements, the characteristics of the research design, and the nature of the data gathered. Statistical analysis may range from portraying a simple frequency distribution to very complex multivariate analysis, such as multiple regression. Later chapters will discuss the most popular techniques for statistical analysis.

Conclusions and Report Preparation

As mentioned earlier, most marketing research is applied research aimed at facilitating a marketing decision. An important but often overlooked aspect of the marketing researcher's job is to look at the analysis of the information collected and ask "What does this mean to management?" The final stage in the research

**conclusions and
report preparation stage**
The stage in which the researcher
interprets information and draws
conclusions to be communicated to
decision makers.

process, the **conclusions and report preparation stage,** consists of interpreting the information and making conclusions for managerial decisions.

The research report should effectively communicate the research findings. All too many reports are complicated statements of technical aspects and sophisticated research methods. Frequently, management is not interested in detailed reporting of the research design and statistical findings but wishes only a summary of the findings. If the findings of the research remain unread on the marketing manager's desk, the study will have been useless. The importance of effective communication cannot be overemphasized. Research is only as good as its applications.

Marketing researchers must communicate their findings to a managerial audience. The written report serves another purpose as well: It is a historical document that will be a record that may be referred to later, if the research is to be repeated or if further research is to be based on what has come before.

THE RESEARCH PROPOSAL

research proposal
A written statement of the research
design that includes a statement of
the purpose of the study and a
detailed, systematic outline of procedures associated with a particular
research methodology.

Now that we have outlined the research process, a brief discussion of research proposals is in order. The **research proposal** is a written statement of the research design. It always includes a statement explaining the purpose of the study (research objectives) or a definition of the problem. It systematically outlines the particular research methodology and details the procedures that will be followed during each stage of the research process. Normally the research proposal includes a schedule of costs and deadlines. Exhibit 3.5 illustrates a short research proposal for the Internal Revenue Service that explored public attitudes toward a variety of tax-related issues.

THE RESEARCH PROGRAM STRATEGY

Our discussion of the marketing research process began with the assumption that the researcher wishes to gather information to achieve a specific marketing objective. We have emphasized the researcher's need to select specific techniques to solve one-dimensional problems, such as identifying market segments, selecting the best packaging design, or test marketing a new product.

However, if you think about a firm's marketing mix activity over a given period of time (such as a year), you will realize that marketing research is not a one-shot activity—it is a continuous process. An exploratory research study may be followed by a survey, or a researcher may conduct a specific research project for each aspect of the marketing mix. If a new product is being developed, the different types of research might include market potential studies to identify the size and characteristics of the market, product usage testing to record consumers' reactions to prototype products, brand name and packaging research to determine the product's symbolic connotations, and test marketing the new product. Because research is a continuous process, management should view marketing research at a strategic planning level. The **program strategy** refers to the firm's overall plan to use marketing research. It is a planning activity that places a series of marketing research projects in the context of the company's marketing plan.

program strategy
The overall plan to conduct a series
of marketing research projects; a
planning activity that places each
marketing project in the context of
the company's marketing plan.

The marketing research program strategy can be likened to a term insurance policy. Conducting marketing research minimizes risk and increases certainty. Each research project can be seen as a series of term insurance policies that make the marketing manager's job a bit safer.

EXHIBIT 3.5 | AN ABBREVIATED VERSION OF A RESEARCH PROPOSAL FOR THE IRS[14]

Purpose of the Research

The general purpose of the study is to determine the taxpaying public's perceptions of the role of the IRS in administering the tax laws. In defining the limits of this study, the IRS identified the study areas to be addressed. A careful review of those areas led to the identification of the following specific research objectives:

1. To identify the extent to which taxpayers cheat on their returns, their reasons for doing so, and approaches that can be taken to deter this kind of behavior
2. To determine taxpayers' experience and level of satisfaction with various IRS services
3. To determine what services taxpayers need
4. To develop an accurate profile of taxpayers' behavior relative to the preparation of their income tax returns
5. To assess taxpayers' knowledge and opinions about various tax laws and procedures

Research Design

The survey research method will be the basic research design. Each respondent will be interviewed in his or her home. The personal interviews are generally expected to last between 35 and 45 minutes, although the length will vary depending on the previous tax-related experiences of the respondent. For example, if a respondent has never been audited, questions on audit experience will not be addressed. Or, if a respondent has never contacted the IRS for assistance, certain questions concerning reactions to IRS services will be skipped.

Following are some questions that will be asked.

Did you or your spouse prepare your federal tax return for (year)?

☐ Self
☐ Spouse
☐ Someone else

Did the federal income tax package you received in the mail contain all the forms necessary for you to fill out your return?

☐ Yes
☐ No
☐ Didn't receive one in the mail
☐ Don't know

If you were calling the IRS for assistance and someone were not able to help you immediately, would you rather get a busy signal or be asked to wait on hold?

☐ Busy signal
☐ Wait on hold
☐ Neither
☐ Don't know

During the interview the taxpayer will be asked to complete a self-administered questionnaire containing sensitive questions such as the following:

Have you ever claimed a dependent on your tax return that you weren't really entitled to?

☐ Yes
☐ No

Sample Design

A survey of approximately 5,000 individuals located in 50 counties throughout the country will provide the database for this study. The sample will be selected on a probability basis from all households in the continental United States.

Eligible respondents will be adults over the age of 18. Within each household an effort will be made to interview the individual who is most familiar with completing the federal tax forms. When there is more than one taxpayer in the household, a random process will be used to select the taxpayer to be interviewed.

Data Gathering

The fieldworkers of a consulting organization will conduct the interviews.

Data Processing and Analysis

Standard editing and coding procedures will be utilized. Simple tabulation and cross-tabulations will be utilized to analyze the data.

Report Preparation

A written report will be prepared, and an oral presentation of the findings will be made by the research analyst at the convenience of the IRS.

Budget and Time Schedule

[Any complete research proposal should include a schedule of how long it will take to conduct each stage of the research and a statement of itemized costs.]

SUMMARY

Marketing research provides information to reduce uncertainty. The clarity with which the research problem is defined determines whether exploratory, descriptive, or causal research is appropriate. Exploratory research is appropriate when management knows only the general nature of a problem; it is used not to provide conclusive evidence but to clarify problems. Descriptive research is conducted when management has some understanding of the nature of the problem; such research is used to provide a more specific description of the characteristics of a population. Causal research identifies cause-and-effect relationships when the research problem has been narrowly defined.

Research proceeds in a series of six interrelated phases. The first is problem definition, which may include exploratory research using secondary data, experience surveys, or pilot studies. Once the problem is defined, the researcher selects a research design. The major designs are surveys, experiments, observation, and secondary data analysis. Creative research design can minimize the cost of obtaining reliable results. After the design has been selected, a sampling plan is chosen, using a probability sample, a nonprobability sample, or a combination of the two. The design is put into action in the data-gathering phase. This phase may involve a small pretest before the main study is undertaken. In the analysis stage the data are edited and coded, then processed, usually by computer. The results are interpreted in light of the decisions management must make. Finally, the analysis is presented to decision makers in a written or oral report. This last step is crucial, because even an excellent project will not lead to proper action if the results are poorly communicated.

The research proposal is a written statement of the research design.

Quite often research projects are conducted together as parts of a research program. Such programs can involve successive projects that monitor an established product or a group of projects undertaken for a proposed new product to determine the optimal form of various parts of the marketing mix.

Key Terms and Concepts

exploratory research	hypothesis	data-gathering stage
descriptive research	research objective	data-processing and analysis stage
causal research	pilot study	conclusions and report preparation
concomitant variation	research design stage	stage
problem definition stage	research design	research proposal
iceberg principle	sampling stage	program strategy

Questions for Review and Critical Thinking

1. For each of the following situations, decide whether the research should be exploratory, descriptive, or causal.
   a. Establishing the functional relationship between advertising and sales

   b. Investigating consumer reactions to the idea of a new laundry detergent that prevents shrinkage in hot water

   c. Identifying target market demographics for a shopping center

d. Estimating sales potential for concrete vibrators in a northwestern sales territory

2. Describe a research situation that allows one to infer causality.

3. In the following nine-dot square, connect all nine dots using no more than four straight lines and without lifting the pencil from the paper. What does the solution of this problem suggest about the solutions of problem definition situations?

$$\begin{matrix} \bullet & \bullet & \bullet \\ \bullet & \bullet & \bullet \\ \bullet & \bullet & \bullet \end{matrix}$$

4. Why is the problem definition stage of the research process probably the most important stage?

5. What is the iceberg principle?

6. Do the stages in the research process follow the scientific method? Explain.

7. Which research design seems appropriate for the following situations?
   a. The manufacturer and marketer of flight simulators and other pilot-training equipment wish to forecast sales volume for the next 5 years.
   b. A local chapter of the American Lung Association wishes to identify the demographic characteristics of individuals who donate more than $500 per year.
   c. A major petroleum company is concerned about the increasing costs of marketing regular leaded gasoline and is considering dropping this product.
   d. A food company researcher wishes to know what types of food are carried in brown-bag lunches to learn if the company can capitalize on this phenomenon.

8. What purpose does the research proposal serve?

9. What role should managers play in the development of the research proposal?

10. Comment on the following statements:
    a. "The best marketing researchers are prepared to rethink and rewrite their proposals."
    b. "The client's signature is an essential element of the research proposal."

11. Should the marketing research program strategy be viewed as a strategic planning activity? Why or why not?

Exploring the Internet

1. Use a Web browser to go to the Gallup Organization's home page at: http://www.gallup.com. The Gallup home page changes regularly. However, it should provide an opportunity to read the results of a political poll. After reading the results of one of Gallup's polls, click on How Polls Are Conducted. List the various stages of the research process and how they were followed in Gallup's project.

2. Use a Web browser to access Lycos (http://www.lycos.com). What keyword topics can be investigated? How might the information you find help you design a research project?

3. Go to the Advertising Research Foundation's home page at http://www.arfsite.org. What research information can you access?

Fisher-Price's action-figure collection Rescue Heroes, as well as the CBS TV show with the same name, is popular with boys age 3 and up. The Rescue Heroes characters' mission is to help and rescue with courage, perseverance, resourcefulness, and nonviolent problem solving. The product line consists of action figures (such as Jake Justice Police Officer, Wendy Waters Firefighter, and Rocky Canyon Mountain Ranger), vehicles (for example, Rescue Heroes Quick Response Helicopter), and command centers. Additional details about the characters may be found online at www.fisher-price. com/us/rescueheroes/.

Fisher-Price uses marketing research extensively in its new product development process. Rescue Heroes went from an identified need to a commercial product line with the help of a multistage research program. Through exploratory research, the company learned that there was a gap in toys available for preschool and early elementary school boys. Little boys liked the idea of action figures that their older brothers and friends played with, but those toys were difficult for them to understand and handle. The findings led Fisher-Price to coin the term KAGO—"Kids Are Getting Older"—meaning younger children want more grown-up toys.

Research with moms indicated their toy preferences. The moms liked the idea of imaginative play with action figures, but they clearly did not want their young children playing with toys that had violent overtones. As a result of these research findings and creative thinking, Fisher-Price came up with the idea of age-appropriate action figures. After much marketing research, the com-

pany learned that young boys had trouble with the figures toppling over. The product concept was refined so that the new action figures would have wide feet for stability.

During the marketing research process, Fisher-Price's researchers conduct focus group interviews to test new toy concepts. They interview both kids and moms in search of ideas for toys that have play value—the tangible features and intangible allure that entice a child to interact with and have fun with a toy. Fisher-Price tried versions of the action figure line in its play laboratory, a large nursery overflowing with toys and equipped with a wall of one-way mirrors and microphones dangling from the ceiling so that researchers can observe children using the toys.

Fisher-Price conducted extensive in-home testing around the country. After the boys played with the toys at home, researchers interviewed the parents about price and asked if they would buy the toys.

Questions

1. Using the flowchart in Exhibit 3.2, outline the steps in the research process that you would recommend that Fisher-Price take in evaluating an idea for a new toy.

2. What type of outcome might Fisher-Price expect from its exploratory research efforts?

3. Describe the program strategy for Rescue Heroes. How did the early research projects influence subsequent research objectives?

The SꙊool was a singles bar in Chicago's Rush Street area. This area, located on Chicago's Near North Side by the Gold Coast, is approximately seven blocks long and three blocks wide and is popular for evening entertainment.

The SꙊool once was one of the most popular spots on Rush Street. There had always been wall-to-wall people on Friday afternoons, but lately the crowds had begun to go elsewhere.

A marketing research consultant who patronized The SꙊool because it was two blocks from her home knew the manager, Judy Burton, well. After some discussions with Burton, the consultant sent a letter proposing that The SꙊool conduct some marketing research. (See Case Exhibit 3.2-1.)

Questions

1. Has the research problem been adequately defined?
2. Evaluate the research proposal.

CASE EXHIBIT 3.2-1	**THE SꙊOOL'S MARKETING RESEARCH PROPOSAL**

Dear Judy:

Here is a brief outline of what I believe The SꙊool must consider if it is to regain its popularity on Rush Street. As you know, The SꙊool's management has changed the decor and exterior of The SꙊool, hired exceptional bands, and used various other promotions to improve business. In spite of this, a decline in The SꙊool's popularity has been evidenced. As these efforts have not brought back the crowd The SꙊool once had, I suggest The SꙊool undertake a marketing research investigation of consumer behavior and consumer opinions among Rush Street patrons.

I recommend this project because The SꙊool once had what it takes to be a popular bar on Rush Street and should still have the potential to regain this status. Most likely, the lack of patronage at The SꙊool is caused by one or both of the following factors:

1. A change in the people or type of people who patronize Rush Street bars
2. A change in the opinions of The SꙊool held by people who patronize Rush Street bars

The problem for The SꙊool's management is to determine the specifics of the change either in the people or in the opinions of the regular patrons of Rush Street and The SꙊool.

Determining what type of information is desired by The SꙊool's management depends on some underlying facts about the popularity of the bars on Rush Street. An assumption must be made concerning this question: Does the crowd (weekend and Wednesday patrons) go where the regulars go, or do the regulars go where the crowd goes? If you believe that the regulars follow the crowd, a general investigation should be conducted to test why the masses go to the popular bars. If the assumption is made that a bar is popular because there are always people (regulars) there, the best method to increase business is to get a regular following who will attract the crowd.

Of course, the optimal position is to appeal to both the regulars and the crowd. Thus, there are numerous areas for investigation:

- Who visits Rush Street bars? What are the group characteristics?
- What motivates these people to go to the various bars and thus makes them popular? For example, to what extent does the number of stag girls in the bars bring about more patrons? (Note: Remember that The SꙊool, Rush-up, Filling Station, and Barnaby's had female servers at the start of their popularity. Could this have been a factor in their appeal?) How important is bartender rapport with the patrons?
- What do drinkers like and dislike about The SꙊool?
- What is the awareness among beer drinkers of Pete's Wicked Ale quality? Do they like it? How does having several microbrewery beers on tap affect a bar's popularity?
- What image does The SꙊool project? Is it favorable or unfavorable? Has it lost the image it once had because it is trying to be the Store Annex, Barnaby's, Rush-up, and The SꙊool combined? Is the decor

consistent? How can a favorable image be restored in the minds of Rush Street drinkers? You might think The Skool can appeal to all Rush Street people, but you can't be all things to all people. A specialization of image and customers may bring back the crowd for The Skool.

- How important is it to be first with a new promotion? For example, did Barnaby's idea of starting a wine and chicken feast make it the place to go to, at least in the short run? If a food promotion would go over, what should The Skool try?

There are many ways in which The Skool would benefit if it conducted a marketing research survey. Of course, the above suggestions for investigation are not all-inclusive, as I have not had a chance to talk with you to determine which areas are the most important. If you would like to have me submit a formal research proposal to determine how The Skool can improve its business, I will be happy to talk with you any evening.

Sincerely yours,

Lisé Johnson

THE HUMAN SIDE OF MARKETING RESEARCH: Organizational and Ethical Issues

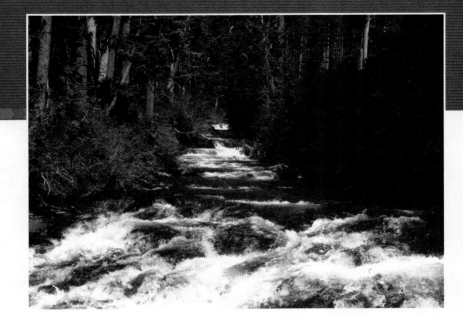

What you will learn in this chapter

- To recognize the degree of marketing research sophistication in various organizations.

- To discuss the organizational structure of marketing research in various organizations.

- To identify the various individual job titles within the marketing research industry.

- To understand the role that research suppliers and research contractors play in the marketing research industry.

- To explain why ethical questions are philosophical questions.

- To describe the three parties involved in most research situations and discuss how the interaction among them may identify a series of ethical questions.

- To discuss the rights and obligations of the respondent, the researcher, and the client sponsor.

- To discuss selected issues such as deception, privacy, and advocacy research from the perspective of each of the three parties.

A research manager and a sales manager had to cross a swiftly flowing river.[1] The sales manager immediately flung off his clothes, dove in, and, with many furious strokes and the help of a strong downstream current, finally managed to cross the river. With much loud huffing and puffing, he emerged, pounded his chest, and proudly told everyone of his exploit. The research manager, in the meantime, carefully calculated the speed of the current; observed the location of shoal water and sandy bottom, the height of the banks, and other factors; determined the best starting point; and quietly waded across. Upon arriving on the other side, he didn't say anything to anyone.

While this story undoubtedly stereotypes sales managers and marketing researchers, it should be remembered that most jokes originate as some form of complaint. The story makes some salient points about the difference between line and staff marketing managers.

Most of this text deals with research methodology and the research process. However, several organizational, managerial, and ethical issues are important concerns. In this chapter, we investigate the human side of marketing research. First, we explore the role of research in the organization and the part researchers play. Then we discuss the roles of research suppliers and contractors. Finally, we look at a variety of ethical issues that confront managers and marketing researchers. ■

EXHIBIT 4.1 | **RESEARCH DEPARTMENT MISSION STATEMENT**

The research mission is to:

Support the company's strategy by providing the highest quality marketing intelligence upon which strategic and tactical decisions are based.

The Department will accomplish its mission by:

■ Providing ad hoc marketing information which is relevant to the issues, appropriate (in terms of accuracy, timeliness, and risk), and commensurate with the true needs of the marketing decision maker.

■ Integrating market/marketing information in a total intelligence to facilitate the identification, development, and execution of significant, long-term strategic planning.

■ Exercising leadership in accumulating relevant marketing experience and utilizing it to develop a knowledge base about marketing and the marketing process.

■ Exercising leadership in the development of research methods which will significantly improve marketing decision making.

■ Maintaining a high degree of consistency of methodology to facilitate decision making across our many businesses.

■ Maintaining assurance of objectivity in the collection, analysis, interpretation, and use of marketing information.

THE MISSION OF THE RESEARCH DEPARTMENT

A mission statement identifies the marketing research department's purpose within the organization. It explains what the department hopes to accomplish.

Exhibit 4.1 presents the mission statement of the marketing research department of a large packaged-goods corporation. It shows the importance of a complete program of research that meets the needs of decision makers. It also suggests that the mission of the research department is a key factor in the success of a research function within an organization.

An executive at another large corporation has stressed that the research mission should be integrated with other units in the organization:

> The most successful research departments are those whose mission is directly linked to the decision makers' needs. In most cases this means the research department must be a valued, integrated, and active part of the company's marketing process.
>
> Conversely, those research departments that have not been successful seem to be independent of the decision makers' needs. Such departments tend to be isolated and operate within a vacuum. Their output may be technically precise, but it is rarely put to use because research is independent of the decision makers.[2]

TO THE POINT

To manage a business is to manage its future; and to manage the future is to manage information.

MARION HARPER

DEGREE OF MARKETING RESEARCH SOPHISTICATION

As business people have come to recognize that marketing research is a useful decision-making tool, its use has become more widespread. An organization's willingness to use research generally parallels its acceptance of the marketing concept. Just as some firms remain in the production-oriented stage, some ignore or are ignorant of marketing research. In some companies, the use of marketing research has evolved from a stage in which managers make decisions intuitively to a stage of **research sophistication,** in which managers have considerable experience in the proper use of research techniques. Marketing management's attitudes toward research methodology can range along a continuum from ignorance of research and intuition-centered decision making to sophisticated, research-centered decision making (see Exhibit 4.2). For purposes of discussion, we can identify three levels of marketing research sophistication.

Stage of Intuitive Decision Making

Marketing managers in this stage may be ignorant about marketing research; or they may believe that research methodology should be confined to the ivory tower of academia or, at best, to technical research conducted elsewhere in the organization. These managers depend heavily on intuition and experience and obtain their information informally.

Stage of Sophistication

In this stage, marketing research has become a proactive force to identify decision makers' information needs. Marketing managers in this advanced stage recognize the potential of research to improve the decision-making process. They recognize that a fortune teller is probably a better bargain than poor research. They also recognize that while good research does not completely eliminate uncertainty, it can be an economically warranted means of at least reducing that uncertainty.[3]

Stage of Development

Most companies are neither completely ignorant nor completely informed about what marketing research can and cannot do. They have passed beyond intuitive decision making. They are in the process of developing research sophistication. Companies may use marketing research for the first few times on blind faith. Marketing managers in this stage naively believe that the result of the application of research methodology is the decision itself rather than the information on which to base a good decision. They fail to see that good research can only reduce uncertainty; it cannot eliminate it. Managers who are just developing a knowledge of research seem most impressed with complex research they are not capable of evaluating. Some statistical analysis in a research report impresses these managers. Show them the same analysis in the form of computer graphics and they are awestruck.

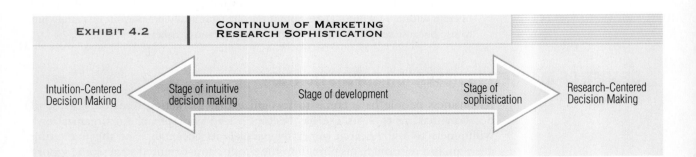

EXHIBIT 4.2   CONTINUUM OF MARKETING RESEARCH SOPHISTICATION

Intuition-Centered Decision Making — Stage of intuitive decision making — Stage of development — Stage of sophistication — Research-Centered Decision Making

Over time managers gain experience and become increasingly familiar with marketing research. They begin to use research more often and to recognize occasions when it should be applied.

Sometimes marketing managers become disillusioned as they develop more research sophistication, perhaps even to the point of feeling betrayed by marketing research. These managers become very cynical because decisions they have made based on research have proven to be costly mistakes. Such vulnerability arises from a failure to distinguish good from bad research or from an assumption that good research effectively makes a management decision.

This is a learning stage. Companies employ marketing research, but they do not exploit its full potential. Gradually, they increase their research sophistication.

ORGANIZATIONAL STRUCTURE OF MARKETING RESEARCH

TO THE POINT

The longer the title, the less important the job.

GEORGE McGOVERN

A survey of companies that belonged to the American Marketing Association found that 76 percent reported having formal marketing research departments. Formal research departments are most common among consumer goods firms, manufacturers, and retailers. Larger companies are more likely to have marketing research departments.[4]

The place of marketing research in an organization and the structure of the research department vary substantially, depending on the firm's acceptance of the marketing concept and its stage of marketing research sophistication. Given that research and the decision makers are linked together, the best organizational structure allows the research department to report as high up in the senior management ranks as possible—at least to the senior marketing vice president and preferably higher. The research department should also be able to have as broad a perspective across the company as possible. This arrangement facilitates the flow of information, which the research department manages, interprets, and communicates. Improper placement of the marketing research department can isolate it. Researchers may lack a voice in executive committees when they have no continuous relationship with marketing management. Sometimes the research department is positioned at an inappropriately low level.

Marketing Research as a Staff Function

Research departments that perform a staff function must wait for management to request assistance. Often the research department uses the term **client** to refer to line management for whom it performs services.

client
Term often used by a research department to refer to line management for whom it performs services.

The research department responds to clients' requests and is responsible for design and execution of all research. It should function as an internal consulting organization that develops action-oriented, data-based recommendations.

In a small firm, the vice president of marketing may be in charge of marketing research. This officer generally will have the sales manager collect and analyze sales histories, trade association statistics, and other internal data. If a survey needs to be conducted, an advertising agency or a firm that specializes in marketing research will be contracted to do the job. At the other extreme, a large company such as Procter & Gamble may staff its research departments with more than 100 people.

director of marketing research
The head of a research department, who provides leadership and integrates staff-level activities by planning, executing, and controlling the marketing research function; sometimes called *director of marketing information systems*.

In a medium-size firm, the research department might include a director of marketing research and individuals with titles such as *research analyst, research assistant,* and *manager of decision support systems*. The **director of marketing research**, chief information officer, or director of marketing information systems provides leadership and integrates staff-level activities. The director of marketing research plans, executes, and controls the marketing research function. This person typically serves on executive committees that identify competitive opportunities and formulate marketing strategies for the organization. The director's responsibility is to provide the research point of view on these strategic issues. In many cases, the director serves as an internal consultant to the organization about consumer behavior and strategic business issues.[5]

A **research analyst** is responsible for client contact, project design, preparation of proposals, selection of research suppliers, and supervision of data collection, analysis, and reporting activities.[6] Normally the research analyst is responsible for projects for all or several of a medium-size firm's products. He or she works with product or division management and makes recommendations based on analysis of collected data. A junior analyst, or **research assistant** (or associate), provides technical assistance with questionnaire design, analysis of data, and so on. The **manager of decision support systems,** or the manager of customer relationship management, supervises the collection and analysis of sales, inventory, and other periodic data. Sales forecasts for product lines usually are developed using analytical and quantitative techniques. Sales information is provided to satisfy the planning, analysis, and control needs of decision makers. The manager of decision support systems may be assisted by a **forecast analyst,** who provides technical assistance such as running computer programs and manipulating data to forecast sales.

The marketing research function in a medium-size firm may be performed by personnel within a planning department. These individuals may plan or design research studies and then contract with outside firms that supply research services such as interviewing or data processing.

As marketing research departments grow, they tend to specialize by product or strategic business unit. Marriott Corporation has a director of marketing research for lodging (e.g., Marriott Hotels and Resorts, Courtyard by Marriott, and Fairfield Inn) and a director of marketing research for contract services and restaurants (e.g., Roy Rogers, Big Boy, and Senior Living Services). Each business unit's research director reports to the vice president of corporate marketing services. Many large organizations have **managers of customer quality research,** who specialize in conducting surveys to measure consumers' satisfaction with product quality.

Exhibit 4.3 illustrates the organization of the marketing research department of a major firm. Within this organization the centralized marketing research department conducts research for all of the division's product groups. This department is typical of a large research department that conducts much of its own research, including fieldwork. The director of marketing research reports to the vice president of marketing.

The department in Exhibit 4.3 does not use outside marketing research contractors. This is rare; nevertheless, using a full-service department as an example facilitates discussion of the interface between the marketing research department and other departments.

Cross-Functional Teams

As more companies rise to the challenge of the global information age and the need to act quickly, old forms of organizational structures are fading fast. Today, everyone in a progressive organization, from accountants to engineers, engages in a unified effort to consider all issues related to the development, production, or marketing of new products.

research analyst
The person responsible for client contact, project design, preparation of proposals, selection of research suppliers, and supervision of data collection, analysis, and reporting activities.

research assistant
The person who provides technical assistance with questionnaire design, analysis of data, and so on.

manager of decision support systems
The person who supervises the collection and analysis of sales data and other recurring data.

forecast analyst
The person who provides technical assistance such as computer analysis to forecast sales.

manager of customer quality research
The person who specializes in conducting surveys to measure consumers' satisfaction and perceptions of product quality.

(by product groupings)

aConducts research to improve total quality management in production.
bConducts research that cuts across product lines or involves competitive marketing practices or characteristics of customer groups.
cConducts research that cuts across product lines to measure the effectiveness of promotional activities.
dConducts research aimed at gaining a basic understanding of various elements of the marketing process.

cross-functional teams
Teams composed of individuals from various organizational departments, such as engineering, production, finance, and marketing, who share a common purpose.

Cross-functional teams are composed of individuals from various organizational departments, such as engineering, production, finance, and marketing, who share a common purpose. Current management thinking suggests that cross-functional teams help organizations focus on a core business process, such as customer service or new-product development. Working in teams reduces the tendency for employees to focus single-mindedly on an isolated functional activity. The use of cross-functional teams to help employees improve product quality and increase customer value is a major trend in business today.

At trend-setting organizations, many marketing research directors are members of cross-functional teams. New-product development, for example, may be done by a cross-functional team of engineers, finance executives, production personnel, marketing managers, and marketing researchers who take an integrated approach to solve problems or exploit opportunities. In the old days, marketing research may not have been involved in developing new products until long after many key decisions about product specifications and manufacturing had been made. Today, marketing researchers' input is part of an integrated team effort. Researchers act as both business consultants and providers of technical services. Researchers working in teams are more likely to understand the broad purpose of their research and less likely to focus exclusively on research methodology.

At General Motors the goal of the marketing research department is to provide cost-effective market understanding that will allow General Motors to beat competitors to opportunities for existing and new products. The marketing research department's primary mission is to provide relevant, accurate, usable, and timely market information. The director of research says, "Our added value is found when we participate as an active and equal member of the decision-making team. This active role must be accomplished by being perceived as coming to the team without a personal point of view, as that perception could negatively affect the credibility of our primary mission."[7]

The effective cross-functional team is a good illustration of the marketing concept in action. It reflects an effort to satisfy customers by using all of the organization's resources. Cross-functional teams are having a dramatic impact on views of the role of marketing research within the organization.

RESEARCH SUPPLIERS AND CONTRACTORS

research supplier
A commercial marketing research service that conducts marketing research activity for clients.

The marketing research manager (in smaller firms, the marketing manager) must also interact with **research suppliers,** or commercial marketing research services. Although a great deal of marketing research activity is conducted in private companies' marketing research departments, much of it is also carried out by firms that may be variously classified as marketing research consulting companies (for example, Market Facts, Inc.), advertising agencies (such as J. Walter Thompson), suppliers of syndicated research services (such as Roper Starch Worldwide), interviewing agencies, universities, and government agencies. The growth of global business and the trend toward being a "right-sized" organization focusing on core competencies has led to a greater emphasis on working with research suppliers as partners.

syndicated service
A marketing research supplier that provides standardized information for many clients.

No matter how large a firm's marketing research department is, some projects are too expensive to perform in-house. A **syndicated service** is a marketing research supplier that provides standardized information for many clients. For example, J. D. Power and Associates sells research on customers' ratings of automobile quality and their reasons for satisfaction. Most automobile manufacturers and their advertising agencies subscribe to this syndicated service because it provides important industrywide information gathered from a national sample of thousands of car buyers. By specializing in this type of customer satisfaction research, J. D. Power gains certain economies of scale.

Syndicated services can provide expensive information economically to numerous clients because the information is specific not to one client but to many. Such suppliers offer standardized information to measure media audiences, collect wholesale and retail distribution data, and conduct other forms of data gathering.

standardized research service
A research organization that has developed a unique methodology for investigating a specialty area, such as advertising effectiveness.

A number of organizations supply **standardized research services** at the request of individual clients. Typically the research organization has developed a unique methodology for investigating a specialty area, such as advertising effectiveness or brand name evaluation. These research suppliers will conduct studies for individual clients using the same methods they use for other clients. ACNielsen BASES is an organization that collects information throughout the new-product development process, from initial concept screening through test marketing. The BASES system can evaluate initiatives relative to other products in a competitive environment. For example, a client can compare its Day-After Recall scores with average scores for a product category.

Even when a firm could perform a research task in-house, research suppliers may be able to conduct the project at a lower cost, faster, and from a completely objective perspective. A company that wishes to quickly evaluate a new advertising strategy may find that an ad agency's research department is able to provide technical expertise on copy development research that is not available within the company itself.

Limited-service research suppliers specialize in particular research activities, such as field interviewing or data processing. Full-service research suppliers contract for entire ad hoc marketing research projects. The client usually controls these marketing research agencies or management consulting firms, but the research supplier handles most of the operating details of these **custom research** projects, tailoring them to the client's unique needs. A custom research supplier may employ individuals with titles that imply relationships with clients such as *account executive* or *account group manager,* as well as functional specialists with titles such as *statistician, librarian, director of field services, director of data processing,* and *interviewer.*

custom research
A marketing research study designed for an individual client and tailored to the client's unique needs.

A. C. Nielsen, IMS Health, Information Resources, VNU, NFO World Group, The Kantar Group, and Westat are among the top U.S. research suppliers. Most of these firms provide a variety of services ranging from design activities to fieldwork. Their services are not covered in detail here because they are discussed throughout the book.

In many cases the marketing research manager's job is primarily administrative: hiring interviewing services, data-processing services, and so on. When it is necessary to hire outside research suppliers or contractors, the marketing researcher must be able to evaluate such specialized services. An analogy is the make-or-buy decision in the factory: The researcher can hire a research service to conduct the project or conduct the project with in-house personnel.

ETHICAL ISSUES IN MARKETING RESEARCH

As in all human interactions, ethical issues arise in marketing research. This book considers various ethical issues concerning fair business dealings, proper research techniques, and appropriate use of research results. The remainder of this chapter addresses society's and managers' concerns about the ethical implications of marketing research.

Ethical Questions Are Philosophical Questions

Ethical questions are philosophical questions. There is no general agreement among philosophers about the answers to such questions. However, the rights and obligations of individuals generally are dictated by the norms of society. **Societal norms** are codes of behavior adopted by a group; they suggest what a member of a group ought to do under given circumstances. This section reflects

societal norms
Codes of behavior adopted by a group that suggest what a member of that group ought to do under given circumstances.

Market Facts is a leading U.S.-based full-service global marketing research consulting and information company. As a research supplier, Market Facts conducts custom research tailored to clients' needs.

the author's perceptions of the norms of our society (and undoubtedly his own values to some extent).[8]

General Rights and Obligations of Concerned Parties

Most research situations involve three parties: the researcher, the sponsoring client (user), and the respondent (or subject). The interaction of each party with one or both of the other two identifies a series of ethical questions. Consciously or unconsciously, each party expects certain rights and feels certain obligations toward the other parties. Every society imposes a set of normatively prescribed expectations of behavior (including rights and obligations) associated with a social role, such as researcher, and another, reciprocal role, such as respondent. Certain ethical behaviors may be expected only in specific situations, while other expectations may be more generalized. Conflicting perspectives about behavioral expectations may create ethical problems. For instance, several ethical issues concern the researcher's expected rights versus those of the respondent/subject. A number of questions arise because researchers believe they have the right to seek information, but subjects believe they have a right to privacy. A respondent who says, "I don't care to answer your question about my income" believes he or she has the right to refuse to participate. Yet some researchers will persist in trying to get that information. In general, a fieldworker is expected not to overstep the boundary society places on consumer privacy.

For each of the subject's rights, the researcher has a corresponding obligation. For example, the individual's right to privacy dictates that the researcher has an obligation to protect the respondent's anonymity. When that respondent discloses information about personal matters, it is assumed that such information will be guarded from all people other than the researcher.

Rights and Obligations of the Respondent

The ethical issues vary somewhat depending on whether the participant has given willing and informed consent. The rights of a participant in an unobtrusive observation study differ from a survey respondent's rights because he or she has not willingly consented to be a subject of the research.

The Obligation to Be Truthful   When a subject provides willing consent to participate, he or she is generally expected to provide truthful answers. Honest cooperation is the main obligation of the respondent or subject.

Privacy   *Privacy* refers to the issue of whether a respondent chooses to answer a researcher's questions; a person may choose to protect her privacy by not answering. *Confidentiality* refers to the obligation on the part of the researcher not to reveal the identity of an individual research subject. A person who waives her right to privacy by agreeing to answer a researcher's questions nonetheless has a right to expect that her answers and her identity will remain confidential.

Americans relish their privacy. A major polling organization has indicated that almost 80 percent of Americans believe the collecting and giving out of personal information without their knowledge is a serious violation of their privacy.[9] Hence, the right to privacy is an important issue in marketing research. This issue involves the subject's freedom to choose whether to comply with the investigator's request. Traditionally, researchers have assumed that an individual makes an *informed choice*. However, critics have argued that elderly, low-income, poorly educated, and other disadvantaged individuals may be unaware of their right to choose. They have further argued that an interviewer may begin with some vague explanation of the research's purpose, initially ask questions that are relatively innocuous, and then move to questions of a highly personal nature. It has been suggested that subjects be informed of their right to be left alone or to break off the interview at any time. Researchers should not follow the tendency to "hold on" to busy respondents. However, this view definitely is not universally accepted in the research community.

Another aspect of the privacy issue is illustrated by this question: "Is a telephone call that interrupts someone's favorite television program an invasion of privacy?" The answer to this issue, and to most privacy questions, lies in the dilemma of where the individual's rights end and society's need for better scientific information on consumer preferences takes over. Generally, interviewing firms have set certain standards of common courtesy, for example, not to interview late in the evening and at other inconvenient times. However, several critics may never be appeased. The computerized interview (sometimes called a "junk phone call") has stimulated increased debate over this aspect of the privacy issue. As a practical matter, respondents may feel more relaxed about privacy issues if they know who is conducting the survey. Thus, it is generally recommended that

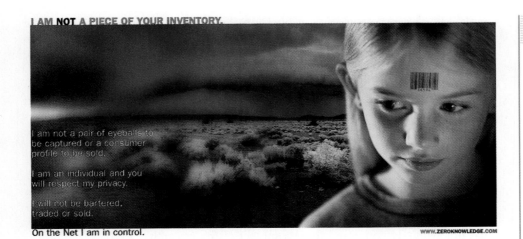

I AM NOT A PIECE OF YOUR INVENTORY.

I am not a pair of eyeballs to be captured or a consumer profile to be sold.

I am an individual and you will respect my privacy.

I will not be bartered, traded or sold.

On the Net I am in control.

WWW.ZEROKNOWLEDGE.COM

Privacy on the Internet is a growing concern for many consumers. Zero-Knowledge Systems offers software to protect the privacy of Internet users.

field interviewers indicate they are legitimate researchers by passing out business cards, wearing name tags, or in other ways identifying the names of their companies.

In an observation study, the major ethical issues concern whether the observed behavior is public or private. Generally it is believed that unobtrusive observation of public behavior in places such as stores, airports, and museums is not a serious invasion of privacy. However, recording private behavior with hidden cameras and the like represents a violation of this right. For example, a survey showed that approximately 95 percent of research directors and line marketing executives disapproved of the practice of observing women through a one-way mirror as they try on bras.[10]

Deception In a number of situations, the researcher creates a false impression by disguising the purpose of the research. At least at the outset of the research, the researcher is not open and honest. Bluntly stated, to avoid biased reactions, the researcher lies to subjects. Deception or concealment may be used if a researcher would otherwise be unable to observe or straightforwardly ask about the phenomenon of interest and hold all other factors constant. Generally, such deception is justified under two conditions: (1) The researcher ensures that no physical danger or psychological harm will result from the deception, and (2) the researcher takes personal responsibility for informing the respondent of the concealment or deception after the research project ends.

The issue of deception is interrelated with the subject's right to be informed and with the means-to-an-end philosophical issue. The primary question is "Does a minor deception substantially increase the value of the research?" Suppose a survey research project involves contacting busy executives. Pretending to be calling long distance might improve the response rate, but is this a justifiable means to this end?

A distinction has been made between deception and discreet silence. The ethical question concerning the apparent content of a questionnaire versus the true purpose of the research has been cleverly stated as follows:

> Must we really explain, when we ask the respondent to agree or disagree with the statement, "prison is too good for sex criminals; they should be publicly

whipped or worse," it is really the authoritarianism of his personality we are investigating, and not the public opinion on crime and punishment?[11]

The Right to Be Informed   It has been argued that subjects have a right to be informed of all aspects of the research. This includes information about its purpose and sponsorship. The argument for the researcher's obligation to protect this right is based on the academic tradition of informing and enlightening the public.

A pragmatic argument for providing respondents with information about the nature of the study concerns the long-run ability of researchers to gain cooperation from respondents. If the public understands why survey or Internet information has been collected and that the researchers may be trusted with private information, it may be easier in the long run to conduct research. Several research suppliers have suggested that public relations work is needed to convince consumers of the integrity of the research industry.

Rights and Obligations of the Researcher

General business ethics should be a standard for marketing research firms and marketing research departments. Our concern is not with issues such as bribery or the welfare and safety of employees but with ethical issues that are specifically germane to marketing research practices.

More has been written about the ethics of researchers than about those of the other two parties because this group's purpose is clearly identifiable. Researchers have obligations to both subjects and clients as well as corresponding rights. A number of professional associations have developed standards and operating procedures for ethical practices by researchers. These **codes of ethics** show that there are several opinions about the nature of ethical practices. Several major issues invite further exploration.

code of ethics
A set of guidelines that states the standards and operating procedures for ethical practices by researchers.

The Purpose of Research Is Research   It is considered unacceptable to misrepresent a sales tactic as marketing research. The Federal Trade Commission has indicated that it is illegal to use any plan, scheme, or ruse that misrepresents the true status of the person making the call as a door-opener to gain admission to a prospect's home, office, or other establishment. This sales ploy is considered unethical as well as illegal. No research firm should engage in any practice other than scientific investigation.

Objectivity   This book stresses the need for objective scientific investigation to ensure accuracy. Researchers should maintain high standards to ensure that their data are accurate. Further, they must not intentionally try to prove a particular point for political purposes.

Misrepresentation of Research   Research companies (and clients) should not misrepresent the statistical accuracy of their data, nor should they overstate the significance of the results by altering the findings. Basically, the researcher has the obligation to both client and subjects to analyze the data honestly and to report the actual data collection methods correctly. For example, the failure to report a variation from a technically correct probability sampling procedure is ethically questionable. Likewise, any major error that has occurred during the course of the study should not be kept secret from management or the sponsor. Hiding errors or variations from proper procedures tends to distort or shade the results. A more blatant breach of the researcher's responsibilities would be the outright distortion of data.

HERTZ WAS NOT AMUSED

A few years ago, a magazine called *Corporate Travel* published the results of a consumer survey of the travel industry.[12] In the category of rental cars, the magazine declared Avis the winner of what was to be its first annual Alfred Award, named for Alfred Kahn, former chairman of the Civil Aviation Board. Avis, not surprisingly, quickly launched an advertising campaign touting its standing in the poll.

Joseph Russo, vice president for government and public affairs at Avis's archrival, Hertz, was not amused. He called the magazine's editor and asked if he could see a press release and any other material that might explain the survey's results and methodology. "We've won virtually every other poll that's ever been done," said Russo. (Indeed, surveys like these are popularity contests that tend to favor bigger competitors over smaller ones; and they are almost impossible to duplicate or verify.) "So we wanted to see if we were missing the boat."

But Russo said he could not get much information about the survey. "I said, 'How many people voted in this? Was it bigger than a bread basket'"

It turned out that the survey responses had disappeared under mysterious circumstances. The magazine's marketing manager, who had overseen the poll, had left the magazine. "A search of their files has also failed to turn up any statistical tabulation or record of the responses for any category," wrote the president of *Corporate Travel's* parent to Hertz. Meanwhile, said Russo, "We had corporate accounts saying, 'I see you guys came in after Avis.'"

Eventually Hertz filed suit against the publisher of the magazine and Avis, charging false advertising. "We said if we allow this to go on, anyone will be able to do anything on the basis of a survey," Russo said. The parties settled, with Avis agreeing to stop calling itself the car rental company of choice among business travelers.

Protecting the Right to Confidentiality of Both Subjects and Clients   A number of clients may desire a list of favorable sales prospects generated from a research survey in the business-to-business market. It is the researcher's responsibility to ensure that the privacy and anonymity of the respondents are preserved. If the respondent's name and address are known, this information should not be forwarded to the sponsoring organization under any circumstances.

Information a research supplier obtains about a client's general business affairs should not be disseminated to other clients or third parties. The client or user of marketing research has a number of rights and obligations. The primary right is to expect objective and accurate data from the research supplier. The client should also be able to expect respect for any instructions of confidentiality.

Dissemination of Faulty Conclusions   The American Marketing Association's marketing research code of ethics states that "a user of research shall not knowingly disseminate conclusions from a given research project or service that are inconsistent with or not warranted by the data." A dramatic example of a violation of this principle occurred in an advertisement of a cigarette smoker study. The advertisement compared two brands and stated that "of those expressing a preference, over 65 percent preferred" the advertised brand to a competing brand. The misleading portion of this reported result was that most respondents did *not* express a preference; they indicated that both brands tasted about the same. Thus, only a very small percentage of those studied actually revealed a preference, and the results were somewhat misleading. Such shading of results violates the obligation to report accurate findings.

Competing Research Proposals   Consider a client who has solicited several bids for a marketing research project. The client asks the research supplier that wins the bid to appropriate ideas from the proposal of a competing research supplier and include them in the research study. This practice generally is regarded as unethical.

Rights and Obligations of the Client Sponsor (User)

Ethical Behavior between Buyer and Seller   The general business ethics expected between a purchasing agent and a sales representative should hold in the marketing research situation. For example, if the purchasing agent has already decided to purchase a product (or research proposal) from a friend, it would be unethical for that person to solicit competitive bids that have no chance of being accepted just to fulfill a corporate purchasing policy stating that a bid must be put out to some number of competitors.

An Open Relationship with Research Suppliers   The client sponsor has the obligation to encourage the research supplier to objectively seek out the truth. To encourage this objectivity, a full and open statement of the problem, an explication of constraints in time and money, and any other insights that may help the supplier anticipate costs and problems should be provided. In other words, the research sponsor should encourage efforts to reduce bias and to listen to the voice of the public.

An Open Relationship with Interested Parties   Conclusions should be based on the data. A user of research should not knowingly disseminate conclusions from a research project or service that are inconsistent with or not warranted by the data. Violation of this principle is perhaps the greatest transgression a client can commit. Justifying a political position that is not supported by the data poses serious ethical questions. Indicating that the data show something in order to make a sale is also ethically questionable.

advocacy research
Research undertaken to support a specific claim in a legal action.

Advocacy research, research undertaken to support a specific claim in a legal action, puts a client in a unique situation. Advocacy research, such as a survey conducted to show that a brand name is not a generic name, differs from research that traditionally has been intended for internal use only. The conventional factors, such as sample size, people to be interviewed, and questions to be asked, are weighed against cost when making an internal decision. A court's opinion of the value of advocacy research may be based exclusively on sampling design or some methodological issue. Thus, the slightest variation from technically correct sampling procedures may be magnified by an attorney until a standard marketing research project no longer appears adequate in the judge's eye. How open should the client be in the courtroom?

The ethics of advocacy research present a number of serious questions. Consider the following quote:

> Almost never do you see a researcher who appears as an independent witness, quite unbiased. You almost always see a witness appearing either for the FTC or for the industry. You can almost predict what is going to be concluded by the

witness for the FTC. And you can almost predict what will be concluded by the witness for industry. That says that research in this setting is not after full truth and it is not dispassionate in nature. And for those of us who consider ourselves to be researchers, that is a serious quandary.[13]

Advocacy researchers do not necessarily bias results intentionally. However, attorneys rarely submit advocacy research evidence that does not support their clients' positions.

The question of advocacy research is one of objectivity: Can the researcher seek out the truth when the sponsoring client wishes to support its position at a trial? The ethical question stems from a conflict between legal ethics and research ethics. Although the courts have set judicial standards for marketing research methodology, perhaps only the client and the individual researcher can resolve this question.[14]

Privacy   Suppose a database company is offering a mailing list compiled by screening millions of households to obtain brand usage information. The information would be extremely valuable to your firm, but you suspect a fake survey was used to obtain the data. Would it be ethical to purchase the mailing list? Deceiving respondents about the purpose of a survey and subsequently selling their names as part of a user mailing list is certainly unethical. The client as well as the research supplier has the obligation to maintain respondents' privacy. Sales managers who know a marketing survey of their business-to-business customers has been keyed to increase the response rate must resist the temptation to seek those accounts that are the hottest prospects.

Commitment to Research   Some potential clients have been known to request research proposals from research suppliers when there is a low probability that the research will be conducted. For example, a research consultant's opinion may be solicited even though management is not really planning research and funds have not been allocated for the project. Obtaining an outsider's opinion of a company problem via a research proposal provides an inexpensive consultation. If the information supports a given manager's position in an ongoing debate within the company, it could be used politically rather than as a basis for research. Most research practitioners believe that because the research supplier must spend considerable effort planning a custom-designed study, the client has the obligation to solicit proposals only for seriously considered projects.

Pseudo-Pilot Studies   Clients should be open about the marketing problem to be investigated. However, there is a special case of this problem. Sometimes a client suggests that a more comprehensive study is in the planning stages, and the proposal on which the research supplier is bidding is a pilot study. The client may say something like "I don't want to promise anything, but you should know that this is the first in a very ambitious series of studies we are planning to undertake, and if you sharpen your pencil in estimating cost . . . ."[15] The research consultant is told that if he or she does a good job during the pilot study stages, there will be an additional major contract down the line. Too often such pilot studies lead to nothing more; the comprehensive study never materializes, and the consultant must absorb a loss.

A Final Note on Ethics

Certainly there are unethical researchers in the world, and a number of shady dealings do occur. But marketing researchers are no different from other business people—or from people in general, for that matter. One may occasionally encounter a researcher who produces a report on fabricated findings. Likewise, interviewers occasionally cheat by filling out the questionnaires themselves. Under some circumstances even honest researchers take shortcuts, some of which may be ethically questionable. However, researchers, like most business people, generally are ethical people. The answer to the question "What is ethical?" is not easy; only one's conscience can prevent any questionable practice.

SUMMARY

Different firms have different degrees of marketing research sophistication. Firms in the first stage of sophistication ignore research and rely on intuition. Firms in the second stage are naively impressed with marketing research and expect it to remove all risk from marketing decisions. During this development stage managers may become disillusioned with research because they have made costly mistakes based on poor research findings. A firm in the last stage has a realistic appreciation for marketing research and uses it as a tool to reduce risk rather than to foretell the future.

A marketing research function may be organized in any number of ways depending on a firm's size, business, and stage of research sophistication. Marketing research managers must remember they are managers, not just researchers.

There are various individual job titles in the marketing research industry. Some of the most common include director of marketing research, research analyst, research assistant, manager of decision support systems, forecast analyst, and manager of customer quality research.

Research suppliers and contractors can augment the research staff of a small firm, or they can provide services impossible for even large firms to handle internally.

There is no general agreement about the answers to the ethical questions that surround marketing research. However, societal norms suggest codes of conduct that are appropriate in given circumstances. There are three concerned parties in marketing research situations: the researcher, the sponsoring client (user), and the respondent (subject). Each party has certain rights and obligations. The respondent's rights include the right to privacy and the right to be informed about all aspects of the research; the subject's main obligation is to give honest answers to research questions. The researcher is expected to adhere to the purpose of the research, maintain objectivity, avoid misrepresenting research findings, protect subjects' and clients' rights to confidentiality, and avoid shading research conclusions. The client is obligated to observe general business ethics when dealing with research suppliers, avoid misusing research findings to support its aims, respect research respondents' privacy, and be open about its intentions to conduct research and about the marketing problem at hand. A serious challenge to objectivity occurs when advocacy research—research conducted to support a specific legal claim—is undertaken.

Key Terms and Concepts

research sophistication
client
director of marketing research
research analyst
research assistant
manager of decision support
   systems

forecast analyst
manager of customer quality
   research
cross-functional teams
research supplier
syndicated service
standardized research service

custom research
societal norms
code of ethics
advocacy research

Questions for Review and Critical Thinking

1. What are the stages of marketing research sophistication? Name some companies that you think are in each of these stages.
2. What might the organizational structure of the research department be like for the following organizations?
   a. A large advertising agency
   b. A founder-owned company that operates a 20-unit restaurant chain
   c. Your college or university
   d. An industrial marketer with four product divisions
   e. A large consumer products company
3. What problems do marketing research directors face in their roles as managers?
4. To whom should marketing research be accountable?
5. Identify a research supplier in your area, and determine what syndicated services and other services are available to clients.
6. Go to your library to learn the job titles and responsibilities for the various types of marketing research jobs. (Hint: One of the best sources is Thomas Kinnear and Ann Root, eds., *1994 Survey of Marketing Research* [Chicago: American Marketing Association, 1995].)
7. What do you think would be the best way to find work in marketing research?
8. Name some marketing research practices that may be ethically questionable.
9. What actions might the marketing research industry take to convince the public that marketing research is a legitimate activity and that firms that misrepresent their intentions and distort findings to achieve their aims are not "true" marketing research companies?
10. Page through your local newspaper to find an article based on survey research results. Does the article outline the study's methodology? Could this research have been considered advocacy research?

11. Comment on the ethics of the following situations:
   a. A food warehouse club advertises "savings up to 30 percent" after a survey showed a range of savings from 2 to 30 percent below average prices for selected items.
   b. A radio station broadcasts the following message during a syndicated rating service's rating period: "Please fill out your diary."
   c. A sewing machine retailer advertises a market test and indicates that the regular price will be cut to one-half for 3 days only.
   d. A researcher tells a potential respondent that an interview will last 10 minutes rather than the 30 minutes he or she actually anticipates.
   e. A respondent tells an interviewer that she wishes to cooperate with the survey, but her time is valuable and therefore she expects to be paid for the interview.

12. Comment on the following interview:

Interviewer:	Good afternoon, sir. My name is Mrs. Johnson, and I am with Counseling Services. We are conducting a survey concerning Memorial Park. Do you own a funeral plot? Please answer yes or no.
Respondent:	(pauses)
Interviewer:	You do not own a funeral plot, do you?
Respondent:	No.
Interviewer:	Would you mind if I sent you a letter concerning Memorial Park? Please answer yes or no.
Respondent:	No.
Interviewer:	Would you please give me your address?

Exploring the Internet

1. ESOMAR is the World Association of Opinion and Marketing Research Professionals. The organization was founded in 1948 as the European Society for Opinion and Marketing Research. Its online ESOMAR Directory of Research Organizations, listing over 1,500 research organizations in 100 countries, can be found at http://www.esomar.nl/directory.htm.

2. Go to http://www.elavidge.com/Our%20Mission.htm to find the mission statement of Elrick and Lavidge, a leading marketing research company.

3. Use a Web browser to go to the NPD, Inc. home page at http://www.npd.com. Select About NPD and Careers. What would a career in marketing research be like at NPD?

4. Many Internet sites list job opportunities and information that is useful for job applicants. Use your Web browser to search for marketing management and marketing research jobs at the following addresses:

   http://www.jobs.hotjobs.com

   http://www.careerpath.com

   http://www.monster.com

5. One purpose of the United Kingdom's Market Research Society is to set and enforce the ethical standards to be observed by research practitioners. Go to its Web site at http://www.marketresearch.org. Click on its code of conduct and evaluate it in light of the AMA's code.

6. The American Asociation for Public Opinion Research (AAPOR) and the World Association for Public Opinion Research (WAPOR) are professional societies of individuals engaged in public opinion research, market research, and social research. Links to commercial organizations, government agencies, academic institutions, and non-profit organizations conducting marketing research can be found in its bluebook at http://www.aapor.org/bluebook/. Another source, WorldOpinion (http://www.worldopinion.com), profiles and provides links to top research firms in the United States, as well as major international organizations.

7. Epicurious is a gourmet food–oriented Web site. Its privacy policy can be found at http://www.epicurious.com by clicking on Read Our Privacy Policy. Evaluate the policy.

The question, in the midst of a telephone poll, was as shocking as it was designed to be: Would you still favor Rudy Silbaugh, a Republican candidate for the Wisconsin state assembly, if you knew he voted to give guns back to juveniles who had used them in crimes?[16]

Mr. Silbaugh and other Wisconsin Republicans filed a lawsuit because of that damaging assertion, which the Republican Party said was made recently by a telemarketing firm calling on behalf of Democratic candidates. But they recognize the campaign tactic, having used it themselves.

It's known as "push polling," and it has increasingly become implemented at the last minute of political campaigns when the airwaves have grown saturated with political messages.

For years, campaign pollsters have conducted surveys of a few hundred voters to test the potency of negative information for later use in broad attacks, such as television advertising. What's different about push polling, though not easy to trace, is the use of phone calls as the means of disseminating attacks to thousands of voters at a time. But unlike the case with TV ads or direct-mail brochures, federal law doesn't require congressional campaigns to identify who's paying for the calls.

"If people want to lie, cheat, and steal, they should be held accountable," said Representative Tom Petri, Republican of Wisconsin, who complains that during a campaign anonymous callers told constituents that he was a tool of Japanese auto dealers and responsible for the savings and loan mess.

In Colorado, the campaign of Democratic Governor Roy Romer, who was reelected, complained to the state attorney general that opponent Bruce Benson's campaign used push polling in violation of a Colorado statute forbidding anonymous campaigning.

The advocacy in question, according to a script obtained by the governor's aides, asked voters if they'd be more or less likely to support Mr. Romer if they knew that "there have been nearly 1,300 murders in Colorado since Romer was first elected and not one murderer has been put to death." Follow-up questions informed voters that the state parole board "has granted early release to an average of four convicted felons per day every day since Romer took office," that Mr. Romer spent "one out of every four days outside of Colorado" during his four-year term, and that he "is being sued for mismanaging the state's foster-care system."

The attorney general declined to prosecute, but Romer campaign manager Alan Salazar complained the lack of accountability of push polling, as well as the enhanced credibility of an attack delivered personally to voters, makes the practice worrisome.

Questions
1. Why do political organizations conduct push polls? Is push polling a legitimate form of marketing research?
2. Is push polling ethical?

EXPLORATORY RESEARCH AND QUALITATIVE ANALYSIS

The woman chose a story that she remembered from her child-hood.[1] One Christmas she waited in giddy excitement to find out what was in the biggest package under the tree. It had the best wrapping paper. She could hardly imagine what it might be. But after she unwrapped the gift, it turned out to be something so ordinary that she hardly remembers what it was, only the disappointment that it didn't live up to the promise of its package.

The short story, written by a woman who had just finished looking at an early version of the PT Cruiser, was the impetus that prompted designers to take another look at the interior. They redesigned it from standard, fixed seating to the more adaptable, unexpected interior that appears in the production car.

The team studying the design of the PT Cruiser read through hundreds of similar stories, looking for clues they could translate into action. . . . But rather than relying on focus groups, as they might have in the past, the team used a different type of qualitative research. Consumers met for 3 hours to look at the vehicle, discuss it, and then write stories. The environment is more relaxed than a focus group, and the goal is not to get people to recommend changes but to get them to tap into less tangible feelings via their creative writing. "Sometimes people just don't know how to say what they really think about a vehicle." Creative writing often draws it out.

Exploratory research serves as a source for developing ideas that are then subjected to further research investigation. At Chrysler, exploratory research helped reduce some of the risks of introducing a new, unconventional vehicle in the ever-changing automobile industry. This chapter discusses the various exploratory research techniques used in marketing research. ■

What you will learn in this chapter

■ To understand the differences between qualitative research and quantitative research.

■ To explain the purposes of exploratory research.

■ To identify the four general categories of exploratory research.

■ To explain the advantages and disadvantages of experience surveys, case study methods, focus group interviews, projective techniques, depth interviews, and other exploratory research techniques.

■ To identify when exploratory techniques are appropriate and to understand their limitations.

■ To understand how technology is changing the nature of exploratory research.

EXPLORATORY RESEARCH: WHAT IT IS AND WHAT IT IS NOT

exploratory research
Initial research conducted to clarify and define the nature of a problem.

When a researcher has a limited amount of experience with or knowledge about a research issue, **exploratory research** is a useful preliminary step. It helps ensure that a more rigorous, conclusive future study will not begin with an inadequate understanding of the nature of the marketing problem.

Conclusive research answers questions of fact necessary to determine a course of action. Exploratory research, on the other hand, never has this purpose. Most, but certainly not all, exploratory research designs provide *qualitative* data. Usually, exploratory research yields greater understanding of a concept or crystallizes a problem rather than providing precise measurement, or *quantification*. A researcher may search for numbers to indicate economic trends, but exploratory research does not involve rigorous mathematical analysis. Any source of information may be informally investigated to clarify which qualities or characteristics are associated with a product, situation, or issue.

Alternatively, the purpose of quantitative research is to determine the quantity or extent of some phenomenon in the form of numbers. Most exploratory research is not quantitative. This chapter discusses exploratory research under the assumption that its purpose is qualitative.

Exploratory research may be a single investigation or a series of informal studies to provide background information. Researchers must be creative in the choice of information sources to be investigated. They must be flexible enough to investigate all inexpensive sources that may possibly provide information to help managers understand a problem. This flexibility does not mean that researchers need not be careful and systematic when designing exploratory research studies. Most of the techniques discussed in this chapter have limitations. Researchers should be keenly aware of the proper and improper uses of the various techniques.

WHY CONDUCT EXPLORATORY RESEARCH?

The purpose of exploratory research is intertwined with the need for a clear and precise statement of the recognized problem. Researchers conduct exploratory research for three interrelated purposes: (1) to diagnose a situation, (2) to screen alternatives, and (3) to discover new ideas.

Diagnosing a Situation

We already have seen that situation analysis is necessary to clarify a problem's nature. Exploratory research helps diagnose the dimensions of problems so that subsequent research projects will be on target; it helps set priorities for research. In some cases, exploratory research helps orient management by gathering information on an unfamiliar topic. A research project may not yet be planned, but information about an issue will be needed before a marketing strategy can be developed.

For example, when an advertising agency got an account for a new coffee containing chicory, the firm began the research process with exploratory research to diagnose the situation. The researchers learned that almost nobody had heard of chicory. It wasn't being used, and nobody seemed to know how to use it. This led to the hypothesis that the advertising could portray the chicory ingredient any way the client wanted.

Screening Alternatives

When several opportunities, such as new-product ideas, arise at once, but budgets don't allow trying all possible options, exploratory research may be used to determine the best alternatives. Many good products are not on the market because a company chose to market something better. Exploratory research may indicate that some new-product ideas are unworkable. An exploratory look at market data (size, number, and so on) may depict a product alternative as not feasible because the market is too small. This aspect of exploratory research is not a substitute for conclusive research; however, such studies can yield certain evaluative information.

Concept testing is a frequent reason for conducting exploratory research. **Concept testing** is a general term for many different research procedures, all of which have the same purpose: to test some sort of stimulus as a proxy for a new, revised, or repositioned product or service. Concept testing portrays the functions, uses, and possible applications for the proposed good or service. Typically, consumers are presented with a written statement or filmed representation of an idea and asked if they think it is new and different, if they would use it, whether they like it, and so on. Concept testing is a means of evaluating ideas by providing a feel for their merits prior to the commitment of any research and development, manufacturing, or other company resources.

Keebler's Sweet Spots, a combination of shortbread cookie and chocolate drop, was more than a cookie—it was almost a candy.[2] When Keebler researched the positioning concept for Sweet Spots, it considered two alternative concepts: (1) an upscale product for the self-indulgent cookie eater and (2) a lunchbox filler for children.

Researchers look for trouble signals in consumer evaluations of concepts to reduce the number of concepts under consideration or improve them to avoid future problems. For example, marketers scrapped a concept for a men's shampoo that claimed to offer a special benefit to hair damaged by overexposure to the sun, heat from a hair dryer, or heavy perspiration after exploratory research showed that consumers thought the product was a good idea for someone with an outdoor lifestyle but not for themselves.[3] Early research indicated that although the product was seen as unique, the likelihood of persuading men that it matched their self-images was low.

Discovering New Ideas

Marketers often conduct exploratory research to generate ideas for new products, advertising copy, and so on. For example, automobile marketers have consumers design their dream cars using computerized design systems similar to those used by automotive designers. This exploratory research might generate ideas that would never have occurred to the firms' own designers.[4]

Uncovering consumer needs is a great potential source of product ideas. One goal of exploratory research is to first determine what problems consumers have with a product category. When research has to determine what kinds of products people will buy, there is a difference between asking people about what they want or need and asking them about their problems. When you ask a customer what he or she wants in a dog food, the reply likely will be "Something that is good for the dog." If you ask what the problems with dog food are, you may learn that "the dog food smells bad when it is put into the refrigerator."[5] Once research has identified problems, the marketing job is to find solutions.

concept testing
Any exploratory research procedure that tests some sort of stimulus as a proxy for an idea about a new, revised, or repositioned product, service, or strategy.

TO THE POINT

The cure for boredom is curiosity. There is no cure for curiosity.

DOROTHY PARKER

CATEGORIES OF EXPLORATORY RESEARCH

There are many techniques for investigating undefined research problems. Several of the most popular qualitative techniques are discussed in the next section. However, the purpose, rather than the technique, determines whether a study is exploratory, descriptive, or causal. For example, telephone surveys (discussed in Chapter 7) are sometimes used for exploratory purposes, although they are used mainly for descriptive research. The versatile qualitative techniques discussed in this chapter tend to be used primarily, but not exclusively, for exploratory purposes.

A manager may choose from four general categories of exploratory research methods: (1) experience surveys, (2) secondary data analysis, (3) case studies, and (4) pilot studies. Each category provides various alternative ways to gather information.

EXPERIENCE SURVEYS

If management decides that an idea is worthwhile, a decision maker may spend some time personally analyzing the situation. In attempting to gain insight into the problems at hand, researchers may discuss the concepts with top executives and knowledgeable individuals, both inside and outside the company, who have had personal experience in the field. These conversations constitute an informal **experience survey.**

experience survey
An exploratory research technique in which individuals who are knowledgeable about a particular research problem are questioned.

People who are knowledgeable about the area to be investigated often are willing to share their experiences with others (competitors excluded, of course). For example, a firm that is ready to launch a new product may discuss the general nature of the product with some of its key retailers and wholesalers. Members of the company's sales force also may be valuable sources of information. The purpose of such discussions is to exhaust the information available from relatively inexpensive sources before gathering expensive primary data. While the interviews with knowledgeable individuals may reveal nothing conclusive, they may help define the problem more formally.

Exploratory research during situation analysis may be quite informal. Input from knowledgeable people both inside and outside the company may come merely from informal conversations. To simply get ideas about the problem, the marketing manager, rather than the research department, may conduct an experience survey. An experience survey may consist of a small number of interviews with some carefully selected people. Some formal questions may be asked, but the respondents generally will be allowed to discuss the questions with few constraints. Knowledgeable people who are articulate on a particular subject should be selected; the researcher is not trying to establish a representative probability sample. The purpose is to help formulate the problem and clarify concepts rather than to develop conclusive evidence.

SECONDARY DATA ANALYSIS

Another economical and quick source of background information is trade literature. Searching through such material is exploratory research with secondary data. Basic theoretical research rarely is conducted without extensive reviews of the literature or reviews of similar research reports.

Using secondary data may be equally important in applied research. Suppose the brand manager of a company that manufactures dental hygiene products is

A chain saw manufacturer received from its Japanese distributor a recommendation to modify its product with a drilling attachment on the sprocket (replacing the chain and guide bar) so that the chain saw could be used as a mushroom-planting device. The distributor indicated that many such units had been sold in Japan. However, an experience survey with only one individual, the president of the Mushroom Growers Association, indicated that the product was not feasible in the United States. Most Americans favor a white, cultured mushroom grown in enclosed areas or caves rather than the variety of mushrooms grown on wood in Japan. The mushroom expert indicated that Americans believe too many superstitious tales about poisonous mushrooms and would not change their eating habits to include the Japanese variety.

contacted by an inventor of a tongue cleaner. The inventor states that her stainless steel device cleans the tongue deposits that cause bad breath. Shortly thereafter, the brand manager finds information in the library that explains the practice of tongue cleaning: It began centuries ago and is a common practice among certain Asian people. If the problem had concerned an existing product, the manager's situational analysis might have begun with an analysis of sales records by region and by customer or some other source of internal data.

Investigating data that have been compiled for some purpose other than the project at hand, such as accounting records or trade association data, is one of the most frequent form of exploratory research. Because this is also a technique for conclusive research (both descriptive and causal research), a separate chapter (Chapter 6) is devoted to the investigation of secondary sources.

CASE STUDIES

case study method
An exploratory research technique that intensively investigates one or a few situations similar to the problem situation.

The purpose of the **case study method** is to obtain information from one or a few situations that are similar to the researcher's problem situation. For example, a bank in Montana may intensively investigate the marketing activities of an innovative bank in California. A shirt manufacturer interested in surveying retailers may first look at a few retail stores to identify the nature of any problems or topics that a larger study should investigate.

The primary advantage of the case study is that an entire organization or entity can be investigated in depth with meticulous attention to detail. This highly focused attention enables the researcher to carefully study the order of events as they occur or to concentrate on identifying the relationships among

TGI FRIDAY'S

Because TGI Friday's thought the Navy was an extremely efficient food handler, perhaps more efficient than for-profit companies, the restaurant wanted to understand the sources of that efficiency.[6] Friday's executives concluded that successful imitation of the Navy's food-handling operations might help the firm gain some expertise and lead to increased proficiency in performing its service. This matter was of particular interest to Friday's because the firm's strategy called for building smaller restaurants with almost the same number of seats as were included in the older designs (5,700 square feet with 210 seats, compared to 9,200 square feet with 240 seats). These smaller designs place a premium on handling food efficiently.

To study the Navy's food-based work processes, Friday's CEO spent a day aboard the nuclear submarine *USS West Virginia*. His visit occurred when a crew of 155 was engaged in a 70-day voyage. Because the submarine had a crew on duty 24 hours per day, the Navy served four meals daily in an extremely confined space. A quick calculation shows that 4 daily meals, for 70 days, for 155 people, is more than 43,000 meals.

The Navy was pleased to let Friday's use its operations as a case study. According to one Navy official, "These aren't things we want to keep secret. All of our food service research and development is funded by American tax dollars."

functions, individuals, or entities. A fast–food restaurant chain may test a new menu item or a new store design in a single location to learn about potential operating problems that could hinder service quality before launching the change throughout the chain.

Conducting a case study often requires the cooperation of the party whose history is being studied. A successful franchisee may be willing to allow the franchisor access to records and reports. Intensive interviews or detailed discussions with the franchisee and his or her employees may provide insights into a situation. The researcher has no standard procedures to follow; she or he must be flexible and attempt to glean information and insights wherever possible. This freedom to search for whatever data an investigator deems important makes the success of any case study highly dependent on the alertness, creativity, intelligence, and motivation of the individual performing the case analysis.

As with all exploratory research, the results from case studies should be seen as tentative. Generalizing from a few cases can be dangerous, because most situations are atypical in some sense. The bank in Montana may not be in a market comparable to the one in California. Even if situations are not directly comparable, however, a number of insights can be gained and hypotheses suggested for future research. Obtaining information about competitors may be very difficult because they generally like to keep the secrets of their success to themselves. Thus, researchers may have limited access to information other firms consider confidential.

TO THE POINT

I never predict. I just look out the window and see what is visible— but not yet seen.

PETER DRUCKER

PILOT STUDIES

The term *pilot study* covers a number of diverse research techniques. Within the context of exploratory research, the term indicates that some aspect of the research (e.g., fieldwork) will be on a small scale. Thus, a **pilot study** is a research project that involves sampling but relaxes the rigorous standards used to obtain precise quantitative estimates from large representative samples.

In one kind of pilot study, researchers or managers try to experience what consumers experience to gain inexpensive and valuable insights. Without indicating their real positions with the company, researchers or managers may wait on customers, ride in repair trucks, and answer telephones. For example, the chairperson of Avis occasionally gets in line with airport customers waiting for cars or works behind the counter to get customer reactions. This form of pilot study may yield true comprehension of the situation to be investigated.

A pilot study generates primary data, but usually for qualitative analysis. This characteristic distinguishes pilot studies from research that gathers background information using secondary data. Some researchers refer to pilot studies that generate qualitative information as *qualitative research*. The primary data usually come from consumers or other subjects of ultimate concern rather than from knowledgeable experts or case situations. This distinguishes pilot studies from experience surveys and case studies. Major categories of pilot studies include focus group interviews, projective techniques, and depth interviews.

Focus Group Interviews

The focus group interview has become so popular that many advertising and research agencies consider it the only qualitative research tool. As noted in Chapter 3, a **focus group interview** is an unstructured, free-flowing interview with a small group of people. It is not a rigidly constructed question–and–answer session but a flexible format that encourages discussion of a brand, advertisement, or new-product concept. The group meets at a central location at a designated time; typically, it consists of a moderator or interviewer and six to ten participants, although larger groups are sometimes used. The participants may range from consumers talking about hair coloring, petroleum engineers talking about problems in the "oil patch," or children talking about toys. The moderator introduces the topic and encourages group members to discuss the subject among themselves. Ideally, the discussion topics emerge at the group's initiative. Focus groups allow people to discuss their true feelings, anxieties, and frustrations, as well as the depth of their convictions, in their own words. The primary advantages of focus group interviews are that they are relatively fast, easy to execute, and inexpensive. In an emergency situation, three or four group sessions can be conducted, analyzed, and reported in less than a week at a cost substantially lower than that of other attitude-measurement techniques. Remember, however, that a small group of people will not be a representative sample no matter how carefully they are recruited. Focus group interviews cannot take the place of quantitative studies.

The flexibility of focus group interviews offers some advantages, especially when compared with the rigid format of a survey. Numerous topics can be discussed and many insights can be gained, particularly with regard to variations in consumer behavior in different situations. Responses that would be unlikely to emerge in a survey often come out in group interviews: "*If* it is one of the three brands I sometimes use and *if* it is on sale, I buy it; otherwise, I buy my regular brand" or "*If* the day is hot and I have to serve the whole neighborhood, I make Kool-Aid; otherwise, I give them Dr Pepper or Coke." If a researcher is investigating a target group to determine who consumes a particular beverage or why a consumer purchases a certain brand, situational factors must be taken into account. If the researcher does not realize the impact of the occasion on which

Synergy among focus group participants can trigger a chain of responses that help diagnose situations. During a focus group interview of people who had never visited the J. Paul Getty Museum, a middle-aged man said, "I've been told there's heavy, very classical type of art, somewhat stuffy and standoffish. It's the kind of place you wouldn't want to take your kids and let them run around." An older woman agreed: "I get the impression it's a little stuffy and has old art." A younger man put in his two cents' worth: "I was driving up past Malibu and I saw the sign. I'd never heard of it before. I thought it was a place where they were going to show you how to refine oil or something." [7]

the particular beverage is consumed, the results of the research may be general rather than portraying the consumer's actual thought process. A focus group elicits situationally specific responses: on a hot day the whole neighborhood gets Kool-Aid; but if there are just a few kids, they get Dr Pepper or Coke.

A baby products company's research provides an interesting example of the type of information focus group interviews can reveal. The company wanted to understand what is of critical importance to mothers of young babies. After a series of initial focus groups, researchers discovered, not surprisingly, that a baby's health is what is most important to a young mother. The company, which planned to target Hispanic Americans, next wanted answers to several questions: What is a healthy baby? Is a healthy baby the same for an Anglo mom as for an Hispanic one? What does a healthy baby look like, and what does an unhealthy baby look like, to Hispanic mothers? [8]

The researchers designed a study that compiled video images and still photos of babies at different stages of development, at different levels of activity (sleeping, sitting, walking, running, crawling), in different moods, and with different physiques (heavier babies and slimmer babies). In focus groups, both Anglo (non-Hispanic) and Hispanic mothers viewed videos and stacks of baby pictures. In their reactions to the images, the mothers unconsciously projected their feelings about what was healthy and what was not healthy. The study revealed very interesting information: A healthy baby for an Anglo mother is not the same as a healthy baby for an Hispanic mom. An Hispanic mom looks for a baby who is chubby, has rosy cheeks, and looks into his mother's eyes and not the camera. What a non-Hispanic mother might consider a fit, carefree baby might be considered skinny and not well-cared-for by Hispanic moms. There were other bits of interesting information. Healthy Hispanic babies always wear shoes—or at the very least, clean socks. Non-Hispanic mothers thought that a barefoot baby was healthy, carefree, and happy.

Focus groups often are used for concept screening and concept refinement. The concept may be continually modified, refined, and retested until management believes it is acceptable.

The advantages of focus group interviews stem from group *synergy* and the emphasis on the group rather than on the individual.[9] The combined effort of the group will produce a wider range of information, insights, and ideas than will the cumulation of separately secured responses from a number of individuals. A bandwagon effect often operates in a group interview situation. A comment by one individual often triggers a chain of responses, a brainstorming of ideas, from the other participants.

Because no individual is required to answer any given question in a group interview, a participant's responses can be more spontaneous and less conventional. Ideas often drop out of the blue. This often affords the moderator the opportunity to develop an idea to its full potential.

In a well-structured group, the individual usually finds some comfort in the fact that his or her feelings are similar to those of others in the group and that each participant can expose an idea without being obliged to defend it or follow through and elaborate on it. With the security the group provides, participants are more likely to be candid, because the focus is on the group rather than on the individual.

Finally, a group interview session can be observed by several people; this provides a check on the consistency of the interpretations. Further, the session can be tape recorded or even videotaped. Later, detailed examination of the recorded session can offer additional insight and help clear up disagreements about what happened.

Group Composition   The ideal size of the focus group is six to ten relatively similar people. If the group is too small, one or two members may intimidate the others. Groups that are too large may not allow for adequate participation by each group member. Homogeneous groups seem to work best. Because group members share similar lifestyles, experiences, and communication skills, the session does not go off track with numerous arguments and different viewpoints stemming from diverse backgrounds.

When the Centers for Disease Control and Prevention tested public-service announcements about AIDS through focus groups, it discovered that single-race groups and multicultural groups reacted differently.[10] By conducting separate focus groups, the organization was able to gain important insights about which creative strategies were most appropriate for targeted versus broad audiences.

For example, a typical homogeneous group might be made up of married, full-time homemakers with children at home; such a group would not include unmarried, working women. Having first-time mothers in a group with women who have three or four children reduces the new mothers' participation. Even if they differ in their opinions, new mothers defer to the more experienced mothers for advice; thus, first-time mothers and experienced mothers would be in separate groups.

Researchers who wish to collect information from different types of people should conduct several focus groups; for example, one focus group might consist only of men and another only of women. Thus, a diverse sample may be obtained even though each group is homogeneous. Most focus group experts believe that four focus group sessions (often in different cities) can satisfy the needs of exploratory research.

Environmental Conditions   The group session may take place at the research agency, the advertising agency, a hotel, or one of the subjects' homes. Research suppliers that specialize in conducting focus groups operate from commercial facilities that have videotape cameras in observation rooms behind one-way mirrors and microphone systems connected to tape recorders and speakers to allow observation by others outside the room. Some researchers suggest that a "coffee klatch" or "bull session" atmosphere can be established in the commercial research facility to ensure that the mood of the sessions will be as relaxed and natural as possible. More open and intimate reports of personal experiences and sentiments might be obtained under these conditions.

moderator
The person who leads a focus group discussion.

The Moderator   The **moderator's** job is to develop a rapport with the group and promote interaction among its members. The moderator should be someone who is really interested in people, who listens carefully to what others have to say, and who can readily establish rapport and gain people's confidence and make them feel relaxed and eager to talk. Careful listening is especially important, because the group interview's purpose is to stimulate spontaneous responses. The moderator should ensure that everyone gets a chance to speak. The moderator also should focus the discussion on the areas of concern. When a topic is no longer generating fresh ideas, the effective moderator changes the flow of discussion. The moderator does not give the group total control of the discussion, but normally has prepared questions on topics that concern managers. However, the timing of these questions in the discussion and the manner in which they are raised are left to the moderator's discretion. The term *focus group* thus stems from the moderator's task: He or she starts out by asking for a general discussion, but usually focuses in on specific topics during the session.

Planning the Focus Group Outline   Effective focus group moderators prepare discussion guides to help ensure that a group covers all topics of interest. The **discussion guide** begins with a written statement of the prefatory remarks to inform the group about the nature of the focus group. It then outlines topics or questions to be addressed in the group session.

discussion guide
A document prepared by a focus group moderator that contains remarks about the nature of the group and outlines the topics or questions to be addressed.

Focus Groups as Diagnostic Tools   Researchers use focus groups predominantly as a means of conducting exploratory research. Focus groups can be helpful in later stages of a research project, but the findings from surveys or other quantitative techniques raise more questions than they answer. Managers who are puzzled about the meaning of survey research results may use focus groups to better understand what consumer surveys indicate. In such a situation, the focus group supplies diagnostic help after quantitative research has been conducted.

Videoconferencing and Streaming Media   The videoconferencing industry has grown dramatically in recent years. And as the ability to communicate via telecommunications and videoconferencing links has improved in quality, the number of companies using these systems to conduct focus groups has increased. With traditional focus groups, managers often watch the moderator lead the group from behind one-way mirrors. If the focus group is being conducted out of town, management personnel usually have to spend more time in airplanes, hotels, and taxis than they do watching the group session. With videoconferenced focus groups, managers can stay home.

TYPICAL CONSUMERS OR PROFESSIONAL RESPONDENTS?

Clients that lack physical facilities for conducting focus groups regularly hire research suppliers that specialize in focus group research. What is a research supplier's responsibility when recruiting individuals to participate in a focus group? Should respondents be recruited because they will make the session go well or because they are typical consumers?

A disturbing example of a lack of objectivity in research occurred when managers of a client organization observed a focus group interview being conducted by a research supplier that had previously worked for the client on other projects. They noticed that some of the respondents looked familiar. A review of the video recordings of the session found that, to make the session go smoothly, the focus group moderators had solicited subjects who in the past had been found to be very articulate and cooperative. It is questionable whether such "professional respondents" can avoid playing the role of expert.

Focus Vision Network of New York is a business research company that provides videoconferencing equipment and services for clients. The Focus Vision system is modular, which allows it to be wheeled around to capture close-ups of each group member. The system operates via a remote keypad that allows observers in a far-off location to pan the focus group room or zoom in on a particular participant. The system allows executives and managers at remote locations to send messages to the moderator. For example, while new product names were being tested in one focus group, an observing manager had an idea and contacted the moderator, who tested the new name on the spot.[11]

streaming media
Multimedia content, such as audio or video, that can be accessed on the Internet without being downloaded first.

Streaming media consist of multimedia content such as audio or video that is made available in real time over the Internet or a corporate intranet, with no download wait and no file to take up space on a viewer's hard disk.[12] This new technology for digital media delivery allows researchers to "broadcast" focus groups that can be viewed online. The offsite manager uses RealOne Player or Microsoft Media Player to view a focus group on a computer rather than at a remote location. Except for a decrease in quality of the video when there are bandwidth problems, the effect is similar to videoconferencing.

online focus group
A focus group whose members carry on their discussion through an Internet chat room.

Interactive Media and Online Focus Groups The use of the Internet for qualitative exploratory research is growing rapidly. The term **online focus group** refers to a qualitative research effort in which a group of individuals provide unstructured comments by entering their remarks into a computer connected to the Internet. The group participants keyboard their remarks either during a chat room format or when they are alone at their computers. Because respondents enter their comments into the computer, transcripts of verbatim responses are available immediately after the group session. Online groups can be quick and cost-efficient. However, because there is less interaction between participants, group synergy and snowballing of ideas may be diminished.

A research company may set up a private chat room on its company Web site for focus group interviews. Participants in these chat rooms feel that their anonymity is very secure. Often they will make statements or ask questions they would never pose under other circumstances.[13] This can be a major advantage for a company investigating sensitive or embarrassing issues.

Many focus groups using the chat room format involve a sample of participants who are online at the same time, typically for about 60 to 90 minutes. Because participants do not have to be together in the same room, the number of participants in these online focus groups can be much larger than in traditional focus groups. Twenty-five participants or more is not uncommon for the simultaneous chat room format. Participants can be at widely separated locations, even in different time zones, because the Internet does not have geographical restrictions. Of course, a major disadvantage is that only individuals with Internet access can be selected for an online group. (The nature of Internet samples will be discussed in depth in Chapters 7 and 12.)

The job of an online moderator resembles that of an in-person moderator. However, the online moderator should possess fast and accurate keyboard skills or be willing to hire an assistant who does. Ideally, the discussion guide is downloaded directly onto the site so the moderator can, with one click, enter a question into the dialogue stream.[14]

A problem with online focus groups is that the moderator cannot see body language and facial expressions (bewilderment, excitement, interest, etc.) to interpret how people are reacting. Also, the moderator's ability to probe and ask additional questions on the spot is reduced in online focus groups, especially those in which group members are not participating simultaneously.[15] Research that requires focus group members to actually touch something (such as a new easy-opening packaging design) or taste something cannot be performed online.

The complexity of the subject will determine the exact nature and length of an online focus group. For many online projects the group discussion can continue for 24 or 48 hours or even longer. Cross Pen Computing Group tested the appeal of an advertising campaign for a new product called CrossPad with an online brainstorming group that ran for 5 days.[16]

As the session's time expands, so may the number of participants. Some sessions involve quite a large number of participants, perhaps as many as 200. Whether these online chat sessions are true focus groups or not is a matter of some minor debate. However, these online research projects do have their purpose. For example, Nickelodeon uses an online format to learn about a variety of subjects from a group of viewers. These kids use personal computers and the Internet to talk with each other and with network researchers about pets, parents, peeves, and pleasures. Kids post notes on the computer bulletin board whenever they want to. Three times a week they log on for scheduled electronic conferences, during which Nickelodeon researchers lead discussions to answer questions such as "Is this a good scoring methodology for a game show?" or "Do kids understand if we show a sequence of program titles and air times?" On one occasion, the kids told researchers they were confused by the various locations shown in a segment of *The Tomorrow People,* a futuristic series with events occurring around the world. Realizing that the sight of a double-decker bus wasn't enough to allow a modern kid to identify London, the producers wrote the name of the city on the screen.[17]

Although we have not yet discussed Internet surveys, it is important to make a distinction between online focus groups, which provide qualitative information, and Internet surveys, which provide quantitative findings. Chapter 7 discusses technological challenges and how to administer Internet surveys. (Much of that discussion is also relevant for researchers wishing to conduct online focus groups.)

Shortcomings   The shortcomings of focus groups are similar to those of most qualitative research techniques, as discussed later in this chapter. However, here we must point out two specific shortcomings of bringing people together for focus groups. First, focus groups require sensitive and effective moderators; without a good moderator, self-appointed participants may dominate a session, giving somewhat misleading results. If participants react negatively toward the dominant member, a "halo effect" on attitudes toward the concept or topic of discussion may occur. This situation should be carefully avoided. Second, some unique sampling problems arise with focus groups. Researchers often select focus group participants because they have similar backgrounds and experiences or because screening indicates that the participants are more articulate or gregarious than the typical consumer. Such participants may not be representative of the entire target market.

Projective Techniques

There is an old story about asking a man why he purchased a Mercedes. When asked directly why he purchased a Mercedes, he responds that the car holds its value and does not depreciate much, that it gets better gas mileage than you'd expect, or that it has a comfortable ride. If you ask the same person why a neighbor purchased a Mercedes, he may well answer, "Oh, that status seeker!" This story illustrates that individuals may be more likely to give true answers (consciously or unconsciously) to disguised questions. Projective techniques seek to discover an individual's true attitudes, motivations, defensive reactions, and characteristic ways of responding.

The assumption underlying these methods lies in Oscar Wilde's observation: "A man is least himself when he talks in his own person; when he is given a mask he will tell the truth." In other words, advocates of projective techniques assume that when directly questioned, respondents do not express their true feelings because they are embarrassed about answers that reflect negatively on their self-concepts; they wish to please the interviewer with the "right" answer, or they cannot reveal unconscious feelings of which they are unaware. However, if respondents are presented with unstructured, ambiguous stimuli, such as cartoons or inkblots, and are allowed considerable freedom to respond, they will express their true feelings.

projective technique
An indirect means of questioning that enables a respondent to project beliefs and feelings onto a third party or an inanimate object or into a task situation.

A **projective technique** is an indirect means of questioning that enables respondents to project beliefs and feelings onto a third party, onto an inanimate object, or into a task situation. Respondents are not required to provide answers in any structured format. They are encouraged to describe a situation in their own words with little prompting by the interviewer. Individuals are expected to interpret the situation within the context of their own experiences, attitudes, and personalities and to express opinions and emotions that may be hidden from others and possibly from themselves. The most common projective techniques in marketing research are word association tests, sentence completion methods, third-person techniques, and thematic apperception tests.

word association test
A projective technique in which the subject is presented with a list of words, one at a time, and asked to respond with the first word that comes to mind.

Word Association Tests   During a **word association test**, the subject is presented with a list of words, one at a time, and asked to respond with the first word that comes to his or her mind. Both verbal and nonverbal responses (such as hesitation in responding) are recorded. For example, a researcher who reads a list of job tasks to sales employees expects that the word association technique will reveal each individual's true feelings about the job tasks. A sales representative's first thought presumably is a spontaneous answer because the subject does not have enough time to think about and avoid making admissions that reflect poorly on himself or herself.

Word association frequently is used to test potential brand names. For example, a liquor manufacturer attempting to market a clear-colored light whiskey tested the brand names Frost, Verve, Ultra, and Master's Choice. Frost was seen as upbeat, modern, clean, and psychologically right; Verve was too modern; Ultra was too common; and Master's Choice was not upbeat enough.[18]

Interpreting word association tests is difficult, and the marketing researcher should make sure to avoid subjective interpretations. When there is considerable agreement in the free-association process, the researcher assumes the test has revealed the consumer's inner feelings about the subject. Word association tests are also analyzed by the amount of elapsed time. For example, if the researcher is investigating alternative advertising appeals for a method of birth control, a hesitation in responding may indicate that the topic arouses some sort of emotion (and the person may be seeking an "acceptable" response). The analysis of projective technique results takes into account not only what respondents say but also what they do not say.

Word association tests also can be used to pretest words or ideas for questionnaires. This enables the researcher to know beforehand whether and to what degree the meaning of a word is understood in the context of a survey.

Sentence Completion Method

The **sentence completion method** is also based on the principle of free association. Respondents are required to complete a number of partial sentences with the first word or phrase that comes to mind. For example:

People who drink beer are _____.

Imported beer is most liked by _____.

A person who drinks a microbrewery's red ale is _____
_____.

Answers to sentence completion questions tend to be more extensive than responses to word association tests. The intent of sentence completion questions is more apparent, however.

Third-Person Technique and Role Playing

The Iowa Poll once asked, "Will you wind up in heaven or hell?" Nearly all Iowans believed they would be saved, but one-third described a neighbor as a "sure bet" for hell.[19]

Almost literally, providing a mask is the basic idea behind the **third-person technique.** Respondents are asked why a third person (for example, a neighbor) does what he or she does or what she or he thinks about a product. For example, male home owners might be told:

> We are talking to a number of home owners like you about this new type of lawn mower. Some men like it the way it is; others believe that it should be improved. Please think of some of your friends or neighbors, and tell us what they might find fault with on this new type of lawn mower.

Respondents can transfer their attitudes to neighbors, friends, or coworkers. They are free to agree or disagree with an unknown third party.

Role playing is a dynamic reenactment of the third-person technique in a given situation. The **role-playing technique** requires the subject to act out someone

A child placed in a role-playing situation may be better able to express her true feelings. A child may be told to pretend she is a parent talking to a friend about toys, food, or clothing. Thus, the child does not feel pressure to express her own opinions and feelings directly.

else's behavior in a particular setting. For example, a child in a role-playing situation might use a pretend telephone to describe the new cookie she has just seen advertised. She projects herself into a mother role. Many researchers who specialize in research with children believe the projective play technique can be used to determine a child's true feelings about a product, package, or commercial. Young children frequently have their own meaning for many words. A seemingly positive word such as *good,* for example, can be a child's unflattering description of the teacher's pet in his class. In a role-playing game, the child can show exactly what he thinks "good" means.

Role-playing is particularly useful in investigating situations in which interpersonal relationships are the subject of the research—for example, salesperson–customer, husband–wife, or wholesaler–retailer relationships.

thematic apperception test (TAT)
A projective technique that presents a series of pictures to research subjects and asks them to provide a description of or a story about the pictures.

Thematic Apperception Test (TAT)

A **thematic apperception test (TAT)** presents subjects with a series of pictures in which consumers and products are the center of attention. The investigator asks the subject to tell what is happening in the pictures and what the people might do next. Hence, themes (*thematic*) are elicited on the basis of the perceptual-interpretive (*apperception*) use of the pictures. The researcher then analyzes the contents of the stories the subjects relate.

The picture or cartoon stimulus must be sufficiently interesting to encourage discussion but ambiguous enough not to disclose the nature of the research project. Clues should not be given to the character's positive or negative predisposition. A pretest of a TAT investigating why men might purchase chain saws used a picture of a man looking at a very large tree. The research subjects were home owners and weekend woodcutters. When confronted with the picture of the imposing tree, they almost unanimously said they would get professional help from a tree surgeon. Thus, early in the pretesting process, the researchers found out that the picture was not sufficiently ambiguous for the subjects to identify with the man in the picture. If subjects are to project their own views into the situation, the environmental setting should be a well-defined, familiar problem, but the solution should be ambiguous.

CIGARETTE SMOKING: ARE SMOKERS BEING HONEST WITH THEMSELVES?

Cigarette smoking in public spaces is an emotionally charged and hotly debated issue. Direct, undisguised questioning may not be the best alternative because cigarette smoking seems to trigger ego defense mechanisms. Marketing researchers directly questioned 179 smokers who believed cigarettes to be a health hazard about why they continued to smoke. The majority answered, "Pleasure is more important than health"; "Moderation is OK"; "I like to smoke." Such responses suggest that smokers are not dissatisfied with their habit. However, in another portion of the study, the researchers used the sentence completion method.

Respondents were asked to respond with the first thing that came to mind after hearing the sentence "People who never smoke are _____." The answers were "better off," "happier," "smarter," "wiser," "more informed." To "Teenagers who smoke are _____," smokers responded with "foolish," "crazy," "uninformed," "stupid," "showing off," "immature," "wrong." The sentence completion test indicated that smokers are anxious, uncomfortable, dissonant, and dissatisfied with their habit. The sentence completion test elicited responses the subjects would not have given otherwise.

Frequently, the TAT consists of a series of pictures with some continuity so that stories may be constructed in a variety of settings. The first picture might portray two women discussing a product in a supermarket; in the second picture, a person might be preparing the product in the kitchen; the final picture might show the product being served at the dinner table.

picture frustration
A version of the TAT that uses a cartoon drawing for which the respondent suggests a possible dialogue between the characters.

Cartoon Tests   The **picture frustration** version of the TAT uses a cartoon drawing for which the respondent suggests a possible dialogue between the characters. Exhibit 5.1 is a purposely ambiguous illustration of an everyday occurrence. The two office workers are shown in a situation and the respondent is asked what the woman might be talking about. This setting could be used for discussions about products, packaging, merchandise displays, store personnel, and so on.

Several other projective techniques apply the logic of the TAT. *Construction techniques* request that consumers draw a picture, construct a collage, or write a short story to express their perceptions or feelings. For example, children hold in their heads many pictures that they are unable to describe in words. Asking a child to "Draw what comes to your mind when you think about going shopping" enables the child to use his or her visual vocabulary to express feelings.[20]

Depth Interviews

depth interview
A relatively unstructured, extensive interview in which the interviewer asks many questions and probes for in-depth answers.

Motivational researchers who want to discover reasons for consumer behavior may use relatively unstructured, extensive interviews during the primary stages of the research process. A **depth interview** is similar to a client interview conducted by a clinical psychologist or psychiatrist. The researcher asks many questions and probes for additional elaboration after the subject answers. In contrast to projective techniques, the subject matter of a depth interview is generally undisguised.

EXHIBIT 5.1 | PICTURE FRUSTRATION VERSION OF TAT

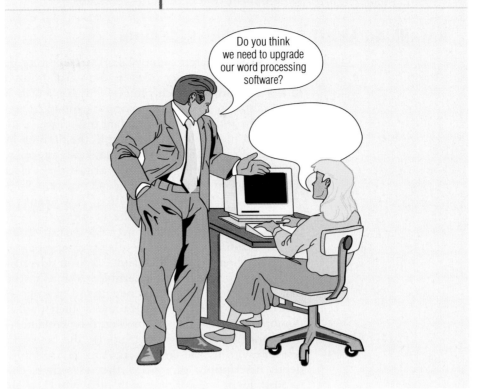

The interviewer's role is extremely important in the depth interview. He or she must be a highly skilled individual who can encourage the respondent to talk freely without influencing the direction of the conversation. Probing questions such as "Can you give me an example of that?" and "Why do you say that?" stimulate the respondent to elaborate on the topic. The interviewer constantly strives to get the respondent to reveal and elaborate on his or her emotions and or motivations.

International marketing researchers find that in certain cultures, depth interviews work far better than focus groups. They provide a quick means to assess buyer behavior in foreign lands.

The depth interview may last more than an hour and requires an extremely skilled interviewer; hence, it is expensive. In addition, the area for discussion is largely at the discretion of the interviewer, so the success of the research depends on the interviewer's skill—and, as is so often the case, skilled people are hard to find. A third major problem stems from the need to record both surface reactions and subconscious motivations of the respondent. Analysis and interpretation of such data are highly subjective, and it is difficult to settle on a true interpretation.

An example of conflicting claims is illustrated by a study of prunes done by two organizations. One study used projective techniques to show that people considered prunes to be shriveled, tasteless, and unattractive; symbolic of old age and parental authority (thus disliked); and associated with hospitals, peculiar people, and the Army. The other study stated that the principal reason people did not like prunes was the fruit's laxative property.

Finally, alternative techniques, such as focus groups, can provide much the same information depth interviews do.

A WARNING ABOUT EXPLORATORY RESEARCH

Exploratory research cannot take the place of conclusive, quantitative research. Nevertheless, a number of firms use what should be exploratory studies as the final, conclusive research project. This has led to incorrect decisions. The most important thing to remember about exploratory research techniques is that they have limitations. Most of them are qualitative, and interpretation of the findings typically is judgmental. For example, the findings from projective techniques can be vague. Projective techniques and depth interviews were frequently used in the 1950s by practitioners who categorized themselves as motivational researchers. They produced some interesting and occasionally bizarre hypotheses about what was inside the buyer's mind, such as "A woman is very serious when she bakes a cake because unconsciously she is going through the symbolic act of giving birth" and "A man buys a convertible as a substitute mistress."[21]

Unfortunately, bizarre hypotheses cannot be relegated to history. Not so long ago, researchers at the McCann-Erickson advertising agency interviewed low-income women about their attitudes toward insecticides. The women indicated that they strongly believed a new brand of roach killer sold in little plastic trays was far more effective and less messy than traditional bug sprays. Rather than purchase the new brand, however, they remained stubbornly loyal to their old bug sprays. Baffled by this finding, the researchers did extensive qualitative research with female consumers. After reviewing the women's drawings and in-depth descriptions of roaches the researchers conclude that women subconsciously identified roaches with men who had abandoned them. Spraying the roaches and watching them squirm and die was enjoyable—so by using the spray, the women both gained control over the roaches and vented their hostility toward men.[22] Evidently, conclusions based on qualitative research may be subject to considerable interpreter bias.

Findings from focus group interviews likewise may be ambiguous. How should a facial expression or a nod of the head to be interpreted? Have subjects fully grasped the idea or concept behind a nonexistent product? Have respondents overstated their interest because they tend to like all new products? Because of such problems in interpretation, exploratory findings should be considered preliminary.

Another problem with exploratory studies deals with the ability to make projections from the findings. Most exploratory techniques use small samples, which may not be representative because they have been selected on a probability basis. Case studies, for example, may have been selected because they represent extremely good or extremely bad examples of a situation rather than the average situation.

Before making a scientific decision, the researcher should conduct a quantitative study with an adequate sample to ensure that measurement will be precise. This is not to say that exploratory research lacks value; it simply means that such research cannot deliver what it does not promise. The major benefit of exploratory research is that it generates insights and clarifies marketing problems for hypothesis testing in future research. One cannot determine the most important attributes of a product until one has identified those attributes. Thus, exploratory research is extremely useful, but it should be used with caution.

However, occasions do arise when the research process should stop at the exploratory stage. If a cheese producer conducts a focus group interview to get a feel for consumers' reactions to a crispy snack food made from whey (the product left over from cheesemaking) and exploratory findings show an extremely negative reaction by almost all participants, the cheese manufacturer might decide not to continue the project.

One researcher suggests that the greatest danger in using exploratory research to evaluate alternative advertising copy, new-product concepts, and so on is not that a poor idea will be marketed, because successive steps of research will prevent that. The real danger is that a good idea with promise may be rejected because of findings at the exploratory stage. On the other hand, when everything looks positive in the exploratory stage, the temptation is to market the product without further research. Instead, after conducting exploratory research, marketing management should determine whether the benefits of the additional information would be worth the cost of further research. In most cases where a major commitment of resources is at stake, conducting the quantitative study is well worth the effort. Many times good marketing research only documents the obvious. However, the purpose of business is to make a profit, and decision makers want to be confident that they have made the correct choice.

SUMMARY

Qualitative research is subjective in nature. Much of the measurement depends on evaluation by the researcher rather than rigorous mathematical analysis. Quantitative research determines the quantity or extent of an outcome in numbers. It provides an exact approach to measurement.

This chapter focused on qualitative exploratory research. Exploratory research may be conducted to diagnose a situation, screen alternatives, or discover new ideas. It may take the form of gathering background information by investigating secondary data, conducting experience surveys, scrutinizing case studies, or utilizing pilot studies. The purpose of the research, rather than the technique, determines whether a study is exploratory, descriptive, or causal. Thus, the techniques discussed in this chapter are primarily but not exclusively used for exploratory studies.

The case study method involves intensive investigation of one particular situation that is similar to the problem under investigation.

Focus group interviews are unstructured, free-flowing group sessions that allow individuals to initiate and elaborate on the topics of discussion. Interaction among respondents is synergistic and spontaneous, characteristics that have been found to be highly advantageous.

As the ability to communicate via the Internet, telecommunications, and videoconferencing links improves, a number of companies are using the new media to conduct focus group research and other forms of exploratory research.

Projective techniques are an indirect means of questioning respondents. Some examples are word association tests, sentence completion tests, the third-person technique and role playing, and thematic apperception tests.

Depth interviews are unstructured, extensive interviews that encourage a respondent to talk freely and in depth about an undisguised topic.

Although exploratory research has many advantages, it also has several shortcomings and should not take the place of conclusive, quantitative research. Knowing where and how to use exploratory research is important. Many firms make the mistake of using an exploratory study as a final, conclusive research project. This can lead to decisions based on incorrect assumptions. Exploratory research techniques have limitations: The interpretation of the findings is based on judgment, samples are not representative, the techniques rarely provide precise quantitative measurement, and the ability to generalize the qualitative results is limited.

Key Terms and Concepts

exploratory research	moderator	sentence completion method
concept testing	discussion guide	third-person technique
experience survey	streaming media	role-playing technique
case study method	online focus group	thematic apperception test (TAT)
pilot study	projective technique	picture frustration
focus group interview	word association test	depth interview

Questions for Review and Critical Thinking

1. Comment on the following remark by a marketing consultant: "Qualitative exploration is a tool of marketing research and a stimulant to thinking. In and by itself, however, it does not constitute market research."
2. What type of exploratory research would you suggest in the following situations?
   a. A product manager suggests development of a nontobacco cigarette blended from wheat, cocoa, and citrus.
   b. A research project has the purpose of evaluating potential brand names for a new insecticide.
   c. A manager must determine the best site for a convenience store in an urban area.
   d. An advertiser wishes to identify the symbolism associated with cigar smoking.
3. Evaluate the following concept statement for a new frozen food product:

   INTRODUCING CHICKEN MARINADE MEALS FROM CREATE-A-MEAL!
   Now you can quickly and easily make delicious, marinated chicken and serve the perfect side dish too, with new Chicken Marinade Meals from Create-A-Meal! It comes with both a highly flavored marinade for your chicken and a pasta/vegetable medley to complete the meal—a delicious traditional dinner has never been easier. Simply add your chicken to the special two-minute marinade and broil. Cook the combination of flavored pasta or potatoes and crisp, colorful Green Giant vegetables, and serve with the chicken for a delicious home-cooked meal.

   Varieties:
   - Roasted Garlic Herb with Pasta Primavera
   - Teriyaki with Oriental Pasta/Vegetable Medley
   - Mesquite Chicken with Roasted Potatoes and Vegetables
   - Lemon Pepper Chicken with White Cheddar Rotini and Broccoli
   - Honey Mustard Chicken with Garden Herb Pasta and Vegetables
   - Red Wine Chicken with Roasted Potatoes and Vegetables

   Found in your grocer's freezer case
   Suggested Retail Price, $4.09
   Servings: 4
   Size: 21 oz. bag

4. What benefits can be gained from case studies? What dangers, if any, do they present? In what situations are they most useful?
5. What is the function of a focus group? What are its advantages and disadvantages?
6. If a researcher wanted to conduct a focus group with teenagers, what special considerations might be necessary?
7. A focus group moderator plans to administer a questionnaire before starting the group discussion about several new product concepts. Is this a good idea? Explain.
8. Discuss the advantages and disadvantages of the following focus group techniques:
   a. A videoconferencing system that allows marketers to conduct focus groups in two different locations with participants who interact with each other

b. A system that uses telephone conference calls for group sessions

9. A packaged goods manufacturer receives many thousands of customer letters a year. Some are complaints, some are compliments. They cover a broad range of topics. Are these letters a possible source for exploratory research? Why or why not?

10. How might exploratory research be used to screen various ideas for advertising copy in television commercials?

 11. Most projective techniques attempt to assess a respondent's true feelings by asking indirect questions rather than using direct questions that could give the respondent a good idea about the researcher's true motives. Does the use of this technique constitute deception?

Exploring the Internet

1. How might the following organizations use an Internet chat room for exploratory research?
   a. A zoo
   b. A computer software manufacturer
   c. A video game manufacturer
2. Connect with a special-interest Internet bulletin board such as one for college students. Conduct an online focus group exploring what criteria students use to choose destinations for spring break.
3. The Looking Glass has a state-of-the-art focus group facility. Go to http://www.tlgonline.com to see a video presentation of the layout of the facility.

4. A filmmaker spent a year documenting his son's high school marching band. The film *The Band* provides a crash course in the life and times of the modern teenager. Transcripts of separate parent and teenage groups can be found at http://www.pbs.org/pov/theband/focus/.
5. To learn about streaming media, go to http://www.realnetworks.com and click on Internet Media.

On July 13, 1997, Mr. Campagna, the marketing manager for Hamilton Power Tools, was anxiously awaiting his meeting with the marketing research firm. He felt the findings from the marketing research would change Hamilton from a sales-oriented company to a firm that would adopt the consumer-oriented philosophy of the marketing concept.

For more than 45 years Hamilton Power Tools had been marketing industrial products by catering to the construction and industrial tool markets. Its construction product lines included power trowels, concrete vibrators, generators, and powder-actuated tools. Its industrial products were primarily pneumatic tools: drills, screwdrivers, and so on. One of its products, the gasoline-powered chain saw, was somewhat different from traditional construction and industrial tools. The chain saw line had been added in 1949 when John Hamilton, Sr. had the opportunity to acquire a small chain saw manufacturer. Hamilton believed that construction workers would have a need for gasoline-powered chain saws. He acquired the business to diversify the company into other markets.

During the 1990s the chain saw market was rapidly changing, and Hamilton Power Tool executives began to realize they needed some expert marketing advice. Mr. Campagna felt that a major change in the company's direction was on the horizon. Campagna had been in the chain saw business for 15 years. Reports from trade publications, statistics from the Chain Saw Manufacturers' Association, and personal experience had led him to believe that the current chain saw industry was composed of roughly the following markets: professionals (lumberjacks), farmers, institutions, and casual users (home or estate owners with many trees on their lots). The casual user segment was considered to be the future growth market. Campagna wished to ensure that Hamilton would not make any mistakes in marketing its product to this segment of weekend woodcutters who once or twice a year used a chain saw to cut firewood or prune trees in the backyard.

In March 1997, when chain saw sales began to slow down because of the seasonal nature of the business, Campagna and Ray Johnson, the chain saw sales manager, had a meeting with John Hamilton, Sr. Although Hamilton believed they had been doing well enough in chain saw sales over the past decade, Campagna and Johnson were able to persuade the aging executive that some consumer research was necessary. After talking with several marketing research firms, Hamilton Power Tools hired Consumer Metrics of Chicago to perform two research projects. The first was a thematic apperception test (TAT).

The TAT research was completed in the first week of July. Campagna arranged for a meeting with the marketing research firm the following week. As Dale Conway and Frank Baggins made their presentation of the results of the survey of chain saw users, Campagna thought back to the day Consumer Metrics had originally suggested the idea of a TAT to John Hamilton. Conway had sold him on the idea with his argument that motivational research was widely used in consumer studies to uncover people's buying motives. Conway had mentioned that Consumer Metrics had recently hired a young, bright MBA. This MBA—Baggins, as it turned out—had specialized in consumer psychology and marketing research at a major state university. Conway had thought that Baggins was one of the best-qualified people to work on this type of project. Since Hamilton Power Tools had had no experience in consumer research, Campagna had been eager to proceed with the in-depth TAT.

Conway told Campagna, Hamilton, and Johnson that in the TAT respondents are shown a series of pictures and are asked to express their feelings about the people in the pictures. He told Campagna that although the present study was exploratory, it could be used to gain insights into the reasons people make certain purchases. He also suggested that the test would be a means of gaining the flavor of the language people use in talking about chain saws, and it could be a source of new ideas for copywriting.

Campagna remembered that at one time he had thought this project wouldn't be very worthwhile; however, he also realized he did not know that much about the consumer market. During the initial meeting with the research firm, it had been proposed that an exploratory research project be conducted within the states of Illinois and Wisconsin to obtain some indication of the attitudes of potential casual users toward chain saws. The researcher had suggested a TAT. Campagna had not known much about this type of research and needed time to think. After a week's deliberation, he called Conway and told the researchers to go ahead with the project. Case Exhibit 5.1.1 shows the TAT used by the researchers.

At the meeting, Conway and Baggins carefully presented the research results. They pointed out that in the TAT study several screening questions were asked at the beginning of the interview. The findings of this study were based on those respondents who either planned to purchase a chain saw in the next 12 months, already owned a chain saw, or had used a chain saw in the past. The presentation closely followed the written report submitted to Campagna. The findings were as follows:

The first picture (Exhibit A in Case Exhibit 5.1.1) shown to the respondent was of a man standing looking at a tree. The interviewer asked the respondent the following question:

Exhibit A	Exhibit B	Exhibit C	Exhibit D

I have a problem which you may find interesting. Here's a picture of a man who is thinking about the purchase of a chain saw. Suppose that such a man is your neighbor. What do you suppose he is thinking about?

After the respondent's initial answer, the following probing question was asked:

Now, if he came to you for advice and you really wanted to help him, what would you tell him to do? Why do you think this would be the best thing for him to do?

Initial responses seemed to center around what the man would do with the tree. Many respondents expressed an interest in the tree and were concerned with preservation. It seemed that pride in having a tree that added beauty to one's property was important to some respondents. Some of the typical responses were as follows:

He's thinking about cutting the tree down.

Why cut a whole tree when you can save part of it?

He could trim out part of those trees and save some of them.

We lose trees due to disease and storm damage.

Trees beautify property and make it more valuable.

I don't like to destroy trees.

Considering the alternatives to buying and using a chain saw was the next step many of the respondents took. Basically, the ultimate consumer sees the alternatives to the purchase of a chain saw as

1. Using a hand saw
2. Hiring a tree surgeon
3. Renting or borrowing a chain saw

These alternatives were in the respondents' minds partly because they were concerned about the cost of doing the job. They seemed to be worried about the investment in a chain saw, about whether it paid to buy one for a small, one-time job. (Another reason for the alternatives came out in responses to a later picture.) Some quotations illustrate this line of thinking:

He's thinking how to go about it. He will use his hand saw.

He doesn't have to invest in a chain saw for only one tree.

He's thinking about how to get the tree down—the cost of doing it himself versus having someone else do it.

Have him cut it down himself, it's not too big a tree. He'll save the cost.

He's thinking whether it pays for a couple of trees.

If it would be worth it. How much longer with an axe.

He's thinking whether he should do it himself or get someone else do it for him. Get someone who knows what he is doing.

He's thinking he'll rent a chain saw for a small area and would buy one for a large area.

The best way to get a job done. Chain saw is faster, but a hand saw is cheaper. Depends on how much work he has to do.

An interesting comment made by two respondents was "He's thinking about Dutch elm disease." The area had recently been hit by that disease. The respondents were projecting their situations into the TAT pictures.

Other statements were made concerning the ease and speed of using a chain saw. Some questions regarding the characteristic performance of a chain saw were raised in response to this question; however, Exhibit B covered this area more adequately. This picture showed two men standing in a chain saw store looking at a chain saw. The question asked was as follows:

Here is a picture of the same man in a chain saw store. Suppose he's a friend of yours—your next-door neighbor, perhaps. Tell me what you think he will talk about with the store clerk.

The issue most frequently raised was how the chain saw worked. An equal number of respondents wanted to know first how much it cost. Weight (lightness) was the next most frequently raised issue. Horsepower was of concern for many of the respondents. Other subjects they thought the man would talk about with the clerk were maintenance and availability of repair, performance (what size tree the chain saw would cut), durability and expected life, safety (what safety features the chain saw had), and ease of starting the chain saw. In relation to price, respondents had the following types of comments:

Well, price is the most important, of course.

He's wondering how he will pay for it.

One respondent said, "He's not considering price; price means nothing compared to safety." One individual was concerned whether the chain would come off the "blade" (respondents referred to the guide bar as a "blade" rather than a "guide bar").

Various other issues were raised by respondents, including

Ease of handling

Length of blade

Which was the best brand?

Whether it had direct drive

Whether it had a gas protector

Self-lubrication

The warranty (guarantee)

Ease of controls

Specifications

Availability of credit

Possibility of mixing oil and gas

Exhibit C showed a man cutting a felled tree with the chain saw. Respondents were asked:

The man in the picture is the same man as in the last picture. He purchased the chain saw he was looking at. Knowing that he purchased the chain saw, what can

you tell me about him? Can you tell me anything about the character and personality of this man?

A follow-up question was

What do you suppose this man is thinking about while he's using his chain saw?

A common response was that the man was satisfied. Typical responses were "He's pleased," "He's happy he bought the chain saw," "Lots of time saved," and "He's happy with the chain saw; he made the right decision." Many favorable overtones to using a chain saw were given—for example,

Sure beats bucking with an axe.

He's thinking about speed of getting through, time saved.

How much easier it is to cut a tree down with a chain saw than a hand saw.

He seems to be saying, "Why didn't I buy a chain saw sooner?"

Respondents in general seemed to think the man was using the chain saw for the first time.

Very prominent in many respondents' answers was the fear of using a chain saw—it seemed to be a major reason why people would not purchase one. Some typical comments were

He's a little frightened. He doesn't know how to go about it, but he's willing to learn.

If he gets caught in that blade . . .

He's watching what he's doing—he could lose a limb.

He might be somewhat apprehensive about the use of it.

He looks scared of it.

He better think safety.

In general, the test, as it is designed to do, made the respondents project their own personalities and backgrounds onto the character of the man in the pictures. Respondents described the man in a variety of ways. He was described as a blue-collar worker, an office worker laboring after hours and on weekends, a somewhat wealthy man able to afford a chain saw, and a homeowner. A number of responses indicated that he was a do-it-yourselfer, a man who liked to "do his own thing." "Farmer" was another more than scattered response. Associations with an outdoorsman, a man who liked to keep in shape, were also indicated. One quotation seems to sum it all up:

This seems to be his first job. He seems to be happy about it. He seems to think the chain saw will lighten his workload. He looks like he has not owned many power tools. He looks excited. He seems like he will be able to do a lot of cleanup work that he would not have

been able to do without the chain saw. The chain saw is sure an improvement over the hand saw. It's faster, easier to use.

The fourth picture (Exhibit D) showed a man and woman seated before a fireplace. The question read,

Here's a picture of the same man as in the previous pictures, sitting and talking with a woman. What do you suppose they're talking about?

An analysis of the fourth picture in the projection test showed that respondents felt the man and woman in the picture were happy, content, cozy, and enjoying the fireplace. The man was "enjoying the fruits of his labor." It came out very strongly that a man who uses a chain saw is proud of himself after he cuts the wood; he thinks his cutting of wood with a chain saw is a job well done. Some typical comments:

He's very happy to cut his own wood for his fireplace—real proud of himself.

He's telling her how much he saved by cutting it himself.

They're talking about the logs, how pleased he is with himself.

He's thinking about the beauty of the fire, fire logs he himself sawed from their property.

The people projecting onto the picture seemed to think that because the job was well done, purchasing a chain saw was worthwhile:

The man in the picture is saying, "The chain saw pays for itself. There's a $300 job, and you will be able to use the chain saw afterwards."

Work's done, and there's enough for winter, and he has trees for winters to come.

What a good buy that chain saw was. Cut wood costs, save money.

The woman in the picture was also very happy; she was satisfied and probably thinking about the future. But most of all she was very proud of her husband. This came out very strongly. For example,

The woman is looking to the enjoyment of the fireside and of the money saved because they cut their own wood. She might have questioned the investment before this, before sitting in front of the fireplace.

She is proud of her husband.

She is pleased the tree is down.

The woman is probably proud of the fireplace and starting the fire. He's probably thinking about the wood he sawed.

The man and woman are congratulating each other on finally getting around to buying a chain saw and cutting firewood.

She is complimenting him on his ability and on how handy it is to have a man around the house.

She is also thinking that possibly it was easier for her husband to use a chain saw.

The woman didn't care about the chain saw, but she was satisfied. The husband's concern over his wife's approval of this investment was also brought out by this picture—evidently men were worried that their wives would not see the value of a chain saw purchase. Also, there were implications that the man should be tired after using the chain saw—"and he had to work hard in the afternoon to get the logs for the fireplace."

After the presentation, Campagna was reasonably impressed. He asked Hamilton what his opinion was. Hamilton said, "This is all very interesting, but I don't see how it can lead to greater profits in our chain saw division."

Questions

1. How should Conway and Baggins respond to Hamilton's final comment?
2. Is Hamilton investigating the casual-user market segment correctly?
3. What conclusions would you draw from the thematic apperception test? Do you feel this is a valid and reliable test?
4. What specific recommendations would you make to Campagna concerning the casual-user chain saw market?

VIDEO CASE 5.2 **TRADING CARDS FOCUS GROUP**

A manufacturer of baseball cards, football cards, and other sport and novelty cards had never conducted business research with its customers. The president of the company decided that they needed to learn more about their customers. He instructed his business research department to conduct a focus group with some boys in the fourth grade.

Questions

1. Outline what you would like to learn in the focus group.
2. What problems might arise when conducting a focus group with children?

SECONDARY DATA RESEARCH IN A DIGITAL AGE

What you will learn in this chapter

- To discuss the advantages and disadvantages of secondary data.
- To give typical examples of secondary data analysis conducted by marketing managers.
- To understand the nature of model building with secondary data.
- To discuss and give examples of the various internal and proprietary sources of secondary data.
- To describe the concept of data mining.
- To describe the channels of distribution for external sources of secondary data.
- To identify and give examples of various external sources of secondary data.

alifornia's 30-year-old ethnic makeover hit a national benchmark at the millennium: the first big state with no racial majority.[1] Census 2000 figures show that California's non-Hispanic white population shrank to 46.7 percent of the state's 33,871,648 residents, while Hispanic and Asian minorities grew at rapid rates. Blacks' share of the population changed little in the 1990s. Since 1970, the state's Hispanic population has more than quadrupled to 10.9 million from 2.4 million. Its share climbed from 12.1 percent of the population to 32.4 percent. Nearly one-third of all Hispanics in the United States live in California.

California also had the highest proportion of people in any large state who said they were of more than one race, 4.7 percent. That's nearly double the national average of 2.4 percent. The multiracial share in the next closest big states were 3.1 percent in New York, 2.5 percent in Texas, 2.4 percent in Florida, and 1.9 percent in Illinois.

The Census Bureau's data show a nation that is less white, more ethnic, more urban and suburban, and Sun Belt–oriented. Those trends are driven home dramatically in California, home of nearly one in eight Americans. They were evident in the 1980s, but they gained greater momentum in the 1990s.

Demographers say the state provides an early glimpse of the United States in the distant future, a time late in the century when some states will still have non-Hispanic white majorities, but most won't. Nationally, non-Hispanic whites will become known as the largest minority.

The Golden State's growing ethnicity and multiracial character make it a melting pot unlike any other place else in the United States, but most of the rest of the country is not moving in the same direction as quickly. Only two much smaller states, Hawaii and New

Mexico, have no racial majorities. The Census Bureau projects that by 2010 the United States still will be more than two-thirds non-Hispanic white.

These facts about the population of California and that of the United States illustrate the richness and value of secondary data. They also illustrate that analysis and interpretation are important activities. This chapter discusses how to conduct research with secondary data in a digital age and examines many of the diverse sources for secondary data. ■

SECONDARY DATA RESEARCH

secondary data
Data that have been previously collected for some purpose other than the one at hand.

Secondary data are data gathered and recorded by someone else prior to and for purposes other than the current project. Secondary data usually are historical and already assembled. They require no access to respondents or subjects.

Advantages

The primary advantage of secondary data comes from their availability. Obtaining them is almost always faster and less expensive than acquiring primary data. This is particularly true when electronic retrieval is used to access data that are stored digitally. In many situations, collection of secondary data is instantaneous.

Consider the money and time saved by researchers who obtained updated population estimates for a town during the interim between the 2000 and 2010 censuses. Instead of doing the fieldwork themselves, they could acquire estimates from a firm dealing in demographic information or from sources such as Claritas or PCensus. Many of the activities normally associated with primary data collection (for example, sampling and data processing) are eliminated by using secondary data.

In some instances, data cannot be obtained using primary data collection procedures. For example, a manufacturer of farm implements could not duplicate the information in the *Census of Agriculture* because much of the information there (for example, amount of taxes paid) might not be accessible to a private firm.

Disadvantages

An inherent disadvantage of secondary data is that they were not designed specifically to meet the researchers' needs. Thus, researchers must ask how pertinent the data are to a particular project. To evaluate secondary data, researchers should ask questions such as these:

▩ Is the subject matter consistent with our problem definition?
▩ Do the data apply to the population of interest?
▩ Do the data apply to the time period of interest?
▩ Do the data appear in the correct units of measurement?
▩ Do the data cover the subject of interest in adequate detail?

Consider the following typical situations:

▩ A researcher interested in forklift trucks finds that the secondary data on the subject are included in a broader, less pertinent category encompassing all industrial trucks and tractors. Further, the data were collected 5 years earlier.
▩ An investigator who wishes to study individuals earning more than $125,000 per year finds the top category in a secondary study reported at $100,000 or more per year.

- A brewery that wishes to compare its per-barrel advertising expenditures with those of competitors finds the units of measurement differ, because some report point-of-purchase expenditures with advertising, while others do not.
- Data from a previous warranty card study show where consumers prefer to purchase the product, but provide no reasons.

Each of these situations shows that even when secondary information is available, it can be inadequate. The most common reasons secondary data do not adequately satisfy research needs are (1) outdated information, (2) variation in definition of terms, (3) different units of measurement, and (4) lack of information to verify the data's accuracy. Exhibit 6.1 illustrates a series of questions that should be asked to evaluate secondary data before they are used.

Information quickly becomes outdated in our rapidly changing environment. Because the purpose of most studies is to predict the future, secondary data must be timely to be useful.

Every primary researcher has the right to define the terms or concepts under investigation to satisfy the purpose of his or her primary investigation. This is little solace, however, to the investigator of the African American market who finds secondary data reported as "_____ percent nonwhite." Variances in terms or variable classifications should be scrutinized to determine if differences are important. The populations of interest must be described in comparable terms. Researchers frequently encounter secondary data that report on a population of interest that is similar but not directly comparable to the population the researcher is investigating. For example, Arbitron (http://www.arbitron.com) reports its television audience estimates by geographical areas known as ADI (Areas of Dominant Influence). An ADI is a geographic area consisting of all counties in which the home market commercial television stations receive a preponderance of total viewing hours. This unique population of interest is used exclusively to report television audiences. The geographical areas used in the census of population, such as Metropolitan Statistical Areas, are not comparable to ADIs.

A researcher might be interested in learning the demographic profile of Texas two-step dancers. The first step in the research process might be fact finding using secondary data.

EXHIBIT 6.1 | EVALUATING SECONDARY DATA[2]

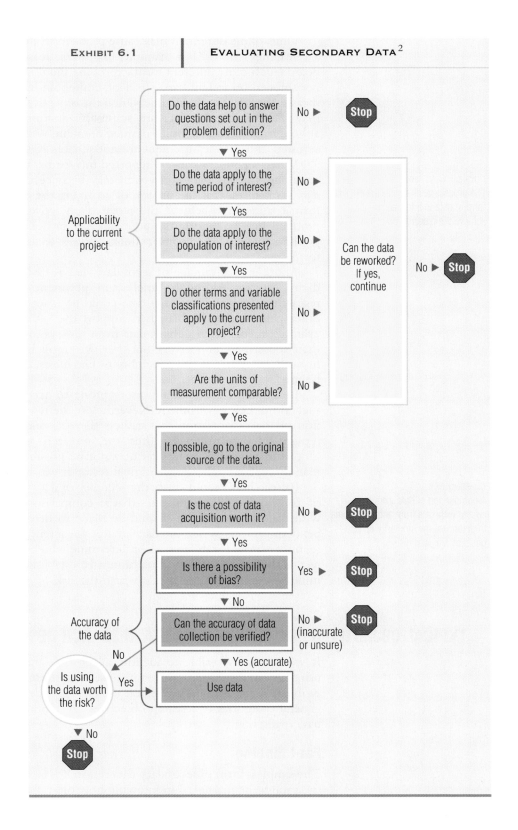

Units of measurement may cause problems if they do not conform exactly to a researcher's needs. For example, expressing lumber shipments in millions of board feet is quite different from expressing them in billions of ton-miles of lumber shipped on freight cars. Head-of-household income is not the same unit of measure as total family income. Often the objective of the original primary study may dictate that the data are summarized, rounded, or reported such that, although the original units of measurement were comparable, aggregated or adjusted units of measurement are not suitable in the secondary study.

When secondary data are reported in a format that does not exactly meet the researcher's needs, data conversion may be necessary. **Data conversion** (also called *data transformation*) is the process of changing the original form of the data to a format suitable to achieve the research objective. For example, sales for food products may be reported in pounds, cases, or dollars. An estimate of dollars per pound may be used to convert dollar volume data to pounds or another suitable format.

Another disadvantage of secondary data is that the user has no control over their accuracy. Although timely and pertinent secondary data may fit the researcher's requirements, the data could be inaccurate. Research conducted by other persons may be biased to support the vested interest of the source. For example, media often publish data from surveys to identify the characteristics of their subscribers or viewers, but they will most likely exclude derogatory data from their reports. If the possibility of bias exists, the secondary data should not be used.

Investigators are naturally more prone to accept data from reliable sources such as the U.S. government. Nevertheless, the researcher must assess the reputation of the organization that gathers the data and critically assess the research design to determine whether the research was correctly implemented. Unfortunately, such evaluation may not be possible if the manager lacks information explaining how the original research was conducted.

Researchers should verify the accuracy of data whenever possible. **Cross-checks** of data from multiple sources—that is, comparison of the data from one source with data from another—should be made to determine the similarity of independent projects. When the data are not consistent, researchers should attempt to identify reasons for differences or determine which data are most likely to be correct. If the accuracy of the data cannot be established, the researcher must determine whether using the data is worth the risk.

data conversion
The process of changing the original form of data to a format suitable to achieve the research objective; also

cross-check
A comparison of data from one source with data from another source to determine the similarity of independent projects.

TYPICAL OBJECTIVES FOR SECONDARY DATA RESEARCH DESIGNS

It would be impossible to identify all possible purposes of marketing research using secondary data. However, it is useful to illustrate some common marketing problems that secondary research designs can address. Exhibit 6.2 shows three general categories of research objectives: fact finding, model building, and database marketing.

Fact Finding

The simplest form of secondary data research is fact finding. A marketer of frozen food might be interested in knowing how often frozen pizza is consumed in the United States. Secondary data available from National Eating Trends, a service of

EXHIBIT 6.2

EXHIBIT 6.2	COMMON RESEARCH OBJECTIVES FOR SECONDARY DATA STUDIES

Broad Objective	Specific Research Example
Fact-finding	Identifying consumption patterns Tracking trends
Model building	Estimating market potential Forecasting sales Selecting trade areas and sites
Database marketing	Enhancing customer databases Developing prospect lists

The NPD Group, Inc. (http://www.npd.com), show that U.S. households serve frozen pizza an average of 11 times per year, most often for dinner (59 percent), followed by lunch (32 percent). Nielsen Marketing Research data indicate that the deluxe combination is the best-selling type of frozen pizza in the country, at 34 percent. Next is pepperoni, at 25 percent; then cheese, at 21 percent; followed by sausage, beef/hamburger, and Canadian bacon. According to the Nielsen data, frozen pizza preferences tend to be regional. More than half the frozen pizzas sold in the New York area are plain cheese. In Dallas, frozen pepperoni pizza outsells frozen sausage pizza three to one, whereas in Chicago, sausage is twice as popular as pepperoni. Canadian bacon has its largest share in Minneapolis.[3] These simple facts would interest a researcher who was investigating the frozen-foods market. Fact finding can serve more complex purposes as well.

Identification of Consumer Behavior for a Product Category

A typical objective for a secondary research study might be to uncover all available information about consumption patterns for a particular product category or to identify demographic trends that affect an industry. For example, this chapter began with a description of demographic characteristics of the California market. This example illustrates the wealth of factual information about trends and behavior patterns one can obtain by carefully collecting and analyzing secondary data.

market tracking
The observation and analysis of trends in industry volume and brand share over time.

Trend Analysis   Marketers watch for trends in the marketplace and the environment. **Market tracking** is the observation and analysis of trends in industry volume and brand share over time. Scanner research services and other organizations provide facts about sales volume to support this work.

Almost every large consumer goods company routinely investigates brand and product category sales volume using secondary data. This type of analysis typically involves comparisons with competitors' sales or with the company's own sales in comparable time periods. It also involves industry comparisons among different geographic areas. Exhibit 6.3 shows the trend in cola market share relative to the total carbonated soft drink industry.

environmental scanning
Information gathering and fact finding designed to detect indications of environmental changes in their initial stages of development.

Environmental Scanning   In many instances, the purpose of fact finding is simply to study the environment to identify trends. **Environmental scanning**

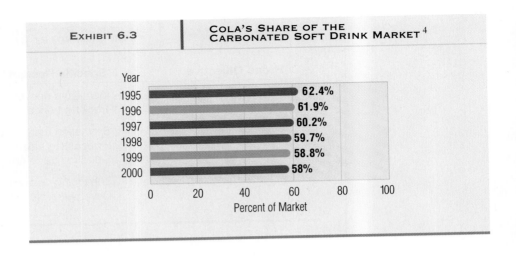

EXHIBIT 6.3 | COLA'S SHARE OF THE CARBONATED SOFT DRINK MARKET [4]

entails information gathering and fact finding designed to detect indications of environmental changes in their initial stages of development. As mentioned in Chapter 2, the Internet can be used for environmental scanning; however, there are other less recurrent means, such as periodic review of contemporary publications and reports. For example, environmental scanning for information about members of the Millennium Generation (also called Generation Y) showed them to be enthusiastic about activities that their parents or grandparents enjoyed during their leisure time, especially if the older Generation-X cohort sneered at it. In particular, it showed that today's teens find bowling and swing dancing appealing. As a result of scanning the environment, Brunswick began promoting Cosmic Bowling—bowling in a darkened alley lit only by glow-in-the-dark lanes, pins, balls, and flashing laser lights.[5]

A number of online information services, such as Dow Jones News Retrieval (http://www.dowjones.com), routinely collect news stories about industries, product lines, and other topics of interest that have been specified by the researcher. As we mentioned in Chapter 2, push technology is an Internet information technology that automatically delivers content to the researcher's or manager's desktop.[6] Push technology uses "electronic smart agents" to find information without the researcher having to do the searching. A "smart agent" is a custom software program that can filter, sort, prioritize, and store information for later viewing.[7] This frees the researcher from doing the searching. The true value of push technology is that the researcher who is scanning the environment can specify the kinds of news and information desired, have it quickly delivered to his or her computer, and view it at leisure.

Model Building

model building
The use of secondary data to help specify relationships between two or more variables; can include the development of descriptive or predictive equations.

Another general objective for secondary research, model building, is more complicated than simple fact finding. **Model building** involves specifying relationships between two or more variables, perhaps extending to the development of descriptive or predictive equations. Models need not include complicated mathematics, though. In fact, decision makers often prefer simple models that everyone can readily understand over complex models that are difficult to comprehend. For example, market share is company sales divided by industry sales. Although some may not think of this simple calculation as a model, it represents a mathematical model of a basic relationship.

The director of MIT's Media Lab, Nicholas Negroponte, thinks of a smart agent "as a computerized English butler. An agent builds a model of you, which can be likened to the process of human-to-human acquaintanceship. The longer you know somebody, the better you can guess what they mean (versus say), what they want (versus ask for) and what they do (versus say they do). So, too, with agents.

One type of agent looks at millions of bits zooming past and tries to pick out the ones that are of interest to you. Like catching fly balls.

Another type of agent works in the network. They go searching and sifting through stacks of libraries, reading daily newspapers, and joining electronic chat groups, to find answers to specific questions or topics that may interest you."[8]

We will illustrate model building by discussing three common objectives that can be satisfied with secondary research: estimating market potential, forecasting sales, and selecting sites.

Estimating Market Potential for Geographic Areas

Marketers often estimate market potential using secondary data. In many cases exact figures are published by a trade association or another source. However, when the desired information is unavailable, the researcher may estimate market potential by transforming secondary data from two or more sources. For example, managers may find secondary data about market potential for a country or other large geographic area, but this information may not be broken down into smaller geographical areas, such as by metropolitan area, or in terms unique to the company, such as sales territory. In this type of situation, researchers often need to make projections for the geographic area of interest.

An extended example will help explain how secondary data can be used to calculate market potential. A marketer of crackers is contemplating building a processing plant in Europe. Managers wish to estimate market potential for the United Kingdom, Germany, Spain, Italy, and France. Secondary research uncovered data for per capita cracker consumption and population projections for the year 2005. The data for the five European countries appear in Exhibit 6.4. (The

	(1) Population Projection for 2005 (thousands)	(2) Annual per Capita Cracker Consumption (U.S. $)	(3) Market Potential Estimate (thousands of dollars)
EXHIBIT 6.4		**MARKET POTENTIAL FOR CRACKERS IN EUROPE**	
Country			
United Kingdom	58,408	9.48	553,708
Germany	82,399	1.91	157,382
Italy	56,264	4.33	243,623
France	59,612	3.56	212,219
Spain	39,225	.62	24,320

data on per capita cracker consumption were obtained from A. C. Nielsen Company.[9] The population estimates are based on information from the *CIA Factbook* database.)

To calculate market potential for Italy in the year 2005, multiply that country's population in the year 2005 by its per capita cracker consumption:

$$56,264 \times 4.33 = 243,623$$

In Italy the market potential for crackers is $243,623 thousand, or $243,623,000. As Exhibit 6.4 reveals, although Germany's population is much higher, it has a much lower market potential.

Of course, the calculated market potential for each country in Exhibit 6.4 is a simple estimate. The marketer might recognize that dollar sales volume will be influenced by each country's inflation rate and other variables. Past inflation rates, also found in secondary data sources, could be added to the calculation to improve the estimate.

Forecasting Sales Marketing managers need information about the future. They need to know what company sales will be next year and in future time periods. Sales forecasting is the process of predicting sales totals over a specific time period.

Accurate sales forecasts, especially for products in mature, stable markets, frequently come from secondary data research that identifies trends and extrapolates past performance into the future. Marketing researchers often use internal company sales records to project sales. A rudimentary model would multiply past sales volume by an expected growth rate. A researcher might investigate a secondary source and find that industry sales are expected to grow by 10 percent; multiplying company sales volume by 10 percent would give a basic sales forecast.

Exhibit 6.5 illustrates trend projection using a moving average projection of growth rates. Average ticket prices for a major league baseball game are secondary data from Team Marketing Report (http://www.teammarketing.com). The moving average is the sum of growth rates for the past 3 years divided by 3 (number of years). The resulting number is a forecast of the percentage increase in ticket price for the coming year.

Year	Average Ticket Price ($)	Percentage Rate of Growth (Decline) from Previous Year	3-Year Moving Average Rate of Growth (Decline)
1994	10.45	—	—
1995	10.65	+1.9	—
1996	11.20	+5.1	—
1997	12.36	+10.4	+5.8
1998	13.59	+10.0	+8.5
1999	14.91	+9.7	+10.0
2000	16.67	+11.9	+10.5
2001	18.99	+13.9	+11.8

EXHIBIT 6.5 — SALES FORECAST USING SECONDARY DATA AND THE MOVING AVERAGE METHOD

Forecast of average ticket price for 2002: $18.99 + ($18.99 × .118) = $21.23

Using the 3-year average growth rate of 11.8 percent for the 1999, 2000, and 2001 sales periods, we can forecast the average ticket price for 2002 as follows:

$$\$18.99 + (\$18.99 \times .118) = \$21.23$$

Moving average forecasting is best suited to a static competitive environment. More dynamic situations make other sales forecasting techniques more appropriate.

Statistical trend analysis using secondary data can be much more advanced than in this simple example. Many statistical techniques build forecasting models using secondary data. This chapter emphasizes secondary data research rather than statistical analysis. Chapter 15, Differences Between Groups and Relationships and Variables, explains more sophisticated statistical model building techniques for forecasting sales.

Analysis of Trade Areas and Sites   Marketing managers examine trade areas and use **site analysis techniques** to select the best locations for retail or wholesale operations. Secondary data research helps managers make these site selection decisions. Some organizations, especially franchisers, have developed special computer software based on analytical models to select sites for retail outlets. The researcher must obtain the appropriate secondary data for analysis with the computer software.

The **index of retail saturation** offers one way to investigate retail sites and describe the relationship between retail demand and supply.[10] It is easy to calculate once the appropriate secondary data are obtained:

$$\text{Index of retail saturation} = \frac{\text{Local market potential (demand)}}{\text{Square feet of retailing space}}$$

For example, Exhibit 6.6 shows the relevant secondary data for shoe store sales in a 5-mile radius surrounding a Florida shopping center. These types of data can be purchased from vendors of market information such as Urban Decision Systems. First, local market potential (demand) is estimated by multiplying population times annual per capita shoe sales. The index of retail saturation is

site analysis techniques
Techniques that use secondary data to select the best locations for retail or wholesale operations.

index of retail saturation
A calculation that describes the relationship between retail demand and supply.

Exhibit 6.6	Secondary Data for the Calculation of an Index of Retail Saturation
1. Population	261,785
2. Annual per capita shoe sales	$54.43
3. Local market potential (line 1 × line 2)	$14,249,000
4. Square feet of retail space used to sell shoes	94,000 sq. ft.
5. Index of retail saturation (line 3/line 4)	152

$$\text{Index of retail saturation} = \frac{\$14,249,000}{94,000}$$

$$= 152$$

This index figure can be compared with those of other areas to determine which sites have the greatest market potential with the least amount of retail competition. An index value above 200 is considered to indicate exceptional opportunities.

Data Mining

Large corporations' decision support systems often contain millions or even hundreds of millions of records of data. These complex data volumes are too large to be understood by managers. Consider, for example, a credit card company collecting data on customer purchases. Each customer might make an average of ten transactions in a month, or 120 per year. With 3 million customers and 5 years of data, it's easy to see how record counts quickly grow beyond the comfort zone for most humans.[11]

Two points about data volume are important to keep in mind. First, relevant marketing data are often in independent and unrelated files. Second, the number of distinct pieces of information each data record contains is often large. When the number of distinct pieces of information contained in each data record and data volume grow too large, end users don't have the capacity to make sense of it all. Data mining helps clarify the underlying meaning of the data.

The term **data mining** refers to the use of powerful computers to dig through volumes of data to discover patterns about an organization's customers and products. It is a broad term that applies to many different forms of analysis. For example, **neural networks** are a form of artificial intelligence in which a computer is programmed to mimic the way that human brains process information. One computer expert put it this way:

> A neural network learns pretty much the way a human being does. Suppose you say "big" and show a child an elephant, and then you say "small" and show her a poodle. You repeat this process with a house and a giraffe as examples of "big" and then a grain of sand and an ant as examples of "small." Pretty soon she will figure it out and tell you that a truck is "big" and a needle is "small." Neural networks can similarly generalize by looking at examples.[12]

Wal-Mart uses data mining. Wal-Mart's information system houses more than 7 terabytes of data on point of sale, inventory, products in transit, market statistics, customer demographics, finance, product returns, and supplier performance. The data are mined to develop "personality traits" for each of Wal-Mart's 3,000-plus outlets, which Wal-Mart managers use to determine product mix and pre-

data mining
The use of powerful computers to dig through volumes of data to discover patterns about an organization's customers and products. It is a broad term that applies to many different forms of analysis.

neural network
A form of artificial intelligence in which a computer is programmed to mimic the way that human brains process information.

MARRIOTT VACATION CLUB INTERNATIONAL

Marriott Vacation Club International, the nation's largest seller of vacation time-share condos, has slashed the amount of junk mail it has to send out to get a response.[13] How? With a computer, a database, and some help from Acxiom Corporation, which specializes in data processing of secondary data for marketers.

What Marriott is doing is called data mining. This is the science of combing through digitized customer files to detect patterns. Marriott starts with names, mostly of hotel guests. Digging into a trove of motor vehicle records, property records, warranty cards, and lists of people who have bought by mail, Acxiom enriches the prospect list. It adds

such facts as the customers' ages, estimated incomes, what cars they drive, and if they golf. Then Marriott uses complex computer programs (neural networks) to figure out who is most likely to respond to a mailed flyer.

Using these clues, Marriott is able to cast its net a little more narrowly and catch more fish. Data mining has increased the response rate to Marriott's direct-mail, time-share pitches to certain hotel guests from 0.75 percent to 1 percent. That seems like a slim gain, but it makes a big difference to a company that sent out 3 million glossy solicitations at a cost of up to $1.50 each in a single year.

---

sentation for each store. Wal–Mart's data–mining software looks at individual items for individual stores to decide the seasonal sales profile of each item. The data–mining system keeps a year's worth of data on the sales of 100,000 products and predicts which items will be needed in each store.[14]

Market basket analysis is a form of data mining that analyzes anonymous point-of-sale transaction databases to identify coinciding purchases or relationships among products purchased and other retail shopping information.[15] Consider this example about patterns in customer purchases: Osco Drugs mined its databases provided by checkout scanners and found that when men go to its drugstores to buy diapers in the evening between 6:00 P.M. and 8:00 P.M., they sometimes walk out with a six-pack of beer as well. Knowing this behavioral pattern, it's possible for a supermarket chain to lay out its stores so that these items are closer together.[16]

The example of a credit card company with large volumes of data illustrates a data–mining application known as *customer discovery*. The credit card company will probably track information about each customer: age, gender, number of children, job status, income level, past credit history, and so on. Very often the data about these factors will be mined to find the patterns that make a particular individual a good or bad credit risk.[17]

When a company knows the identity of the customer who makes repeated purchases from the same organization, an analysis can be made of sequences of purchases. *Sequence discovery,* the use of data mining to detect sequence patterns, is a popular application among direct marketers, such as catalog retailers. A catalog merchant has information for each customer, revealing the sets of products that the customer buys in every purchase order. A sequence discovery function can then be used to discover the set of purchases that frequently precedes the purchase of, say, a microwave oven. As another example, sequence discovery used

This advertisement's copy says "To our data mining system, they're twins. Because both order milk with their hamburgers." The discovery of such similarities is the goal of market basket analysis.

on a set of insurance claims could lead to the identification of frequently occurring medical procedures performed on patients, which in turn could be used to detect cases of medical fraud.

Data mining requires sophisticated computer resources, and it is expensive. That's why companies like DataMind, IBM, Oracle, Information Builders, and Acxiom Corporation offer data-mining services. Customers send the databases they want analyzed and let the data-mining company do the "number crunching."

Database Marketing and Customer Relationship Management

As we have already mentioned, a CRM (customer relationship management) system is a decision support system that manages the interactions between an organization and its customers. A CRM maintains customer databases containing customers' names, addresses, phone numbers, past purchases, responses to past promotional offers, and other relevant data such as demographic and financial data. **Database marketing** is the practice of using CRM databases to develop one-to-one relationships and precisely targeted promotional efforts with individual customers.

> **database marketing**
> The use of customer databases to promote one-to-one relationships with customers and create precisely targeted promotions.

For example, a fruit catalog company CRM contains a database of previous customers, including what purchases they made during the Christmas holidays. Each year the company sends last year's gift list to customers to help them send the same gifts to their friends and relatives.

Because database marketing requires vast amounts of CRM data compiled from numerous sources, secondary data are often acquired for the exclusive purpose of developing or enhancing databases. The transaction record, which often lists the item purchased, its value, customer name, address, and zip code, is the building block for many databases. This may be supplemented with data customers provide directly, such as data on a warranty card, and by secondary data purchased from third parties. For example, credit services may sell databases about applications for loans, credit card payment history, and other financial data. Several companies, such as Donnelley Marketing (with its BusinessContentFile and ConsumerContentFile services) and Claritas (with PRIZM), collect primary data and then sell demographic data that can be related to small geographic areas, such as those with a certain zip code. (Remember that when the vendor collects the data, they are primary data, but when the database marketer incorporates the data into his or her database, they are secondary data.)

Now that some of the purposes of secondary data analysis have been addressed, it is appropriate to discuss sources of secondary data.

SOURCES OF SECONDARY DATA

Chapter 2 classified secondary data as either internal to the organization or external. Modern information technology makes this distinction seem somewhat simplistic. Some accounting documents are indisputably internal records of the organization. Researchers in another organization cannot have access to them. Clearly, a book published by the federal government and located at a public library is external to the company. However, in today's world of electronic data interchange, the data that appear in a book published by the federal government may also be purchased from an online information vendor for instantaneous access and subsequently stored in a company's decision support system.

internal and proprietary data
Secondary data that originate inside the organization.

Internal data should be defined as data that originated in the organization, or data created, recorded, or generated by the organization. **Internal and proprietary data** is perhaps a more descriptive term.

Internal and Proprietary Data Sources

Most organizations routinely gather, record, and store internal data to help them solve future problems. An organization's accounting system can usually provide a wealth of information. Routine documents such as sales invoices allow external financial reporting, which in turn can be a source of data for further analysis. If the data are properly coded into a modular database in the accounting system, the researcher may be able to conduct more detailed analysis using the decision support system. Sales information can be broken down by account or by product and region; information related to orders received, back orders, and unfilled orders can be identified; sales can be forecast on the basis of past data.

Researchers frequently aggregate or disaggregate internal data. Other useful sources of internal data include salespeople's call reports, customer complaints, service records, warranty card returns, and other records. For example, a computer service firm used internal secondary data to analyze sales over the previous 3 years, categorizing business by industry, product, purchase level, and so on. The company discovered that 60 percent of its customers represented only 2 percent of its business and that nearly all of these customers came through telephone directory advertising. This simple investigation of internal records showed that, in effect, the firm was paying to attract customers it did not want.

External Data: The Distribution System

external data
Data created, recorded, or generated by an entity other than the researcher's organization.

External data are generated or recorded by an entity other than the researcher's organization. The government, newspapers and journals, trade associations, and other organizations create or produce information. Traditionally, this information has been in published form, perhaps available from a public library, trade association, or government agency. Today, however, computerized data archives and electronic data interchange make external data as accessible as internal data. Exhibit 6.7 illustrates some traditional and some modern ways of distributing information.

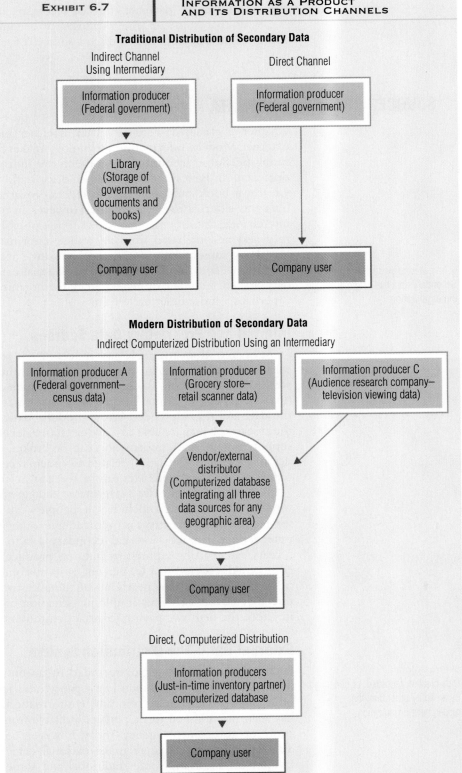

EXHIBIT 6.7 | **INFORMATION AS A PRODUCT AND ITS DISTRIBUTION CHANNELS**

Traditional Distribution of Secondary Data

Indirect Channel Using Intermediary

Direct Channel

Information producer (Federal government)

Library (Storage of government documents and books)

Information producer (Federal government)

Company user

Company user

Modern Distribution of Secondary Data

Indirect Computerized Distribution Using an Intermediary

Information producer A (Federal government—census data)

Information producer B (Grocery store—retail scanner data)

Information producer C (Audience research company—television viewing data)

Vendor/external distributor (Computerized database integrating all three data sources for any geographic area)

Company user

Direct, Computerized Distribution

Information producers (Just-in-time inventory partner) computerized database

Company user

Information as a Product and Its Distribution Channels

Because secondary data have value, they can be bought and sold like other products. And just as bottles of perfume or plumbers' wrenches may be distributed in many ways, secondary data also flow through various channels of distribution. Many users, such as the Fortune 500 corporations, purchase documents and computerized census data directly from the government. However, many small companies get census data from a library or another intermediary or vendor of secondary information.

Libraries   Traditionally, libraries' vast storehouses of information have served as a bridge between users and producers of secondary data. The library staff deals directly with the creators of information, such as the federal government, and intermediate distributors of information, such as abstracting and indexing services. The user need only locate the appropriate secondary data on the library shelves. Libraries provide collections of books, journals, newspapers, and so on for reading and reference. They also stock many bibliographies, abstracts, guides, directories, and indexes, as well as offering access to basic databases.

The word *library* typically connotes a public or university facility. However, many major corporations and government agencies also have libraries. A corporate librarian's advice on sources of industry information or the United Nations librarian's help in finding statistics about international markets can be invaluable.

The Internet   The Internet is, of course, a new source of distribution of much secondary data. Its creation has added an international dimension to the acquisition of secondary data. For example, http://www.libraryspot.com provides links to online libraries, including law libraries, medical libraries, and music libraries. Its reference desk features links to calendars, dictionaries, encyclopedias, maps, and other sources typically found at a traditional library's reference desk.

Chapter 2 discussed how to access and use the Internet. Exhibit 6.8 lists some of the more popular Internet addresses where secondary data may be found.

Vendors   The information age offers many channels besides libraries through which to access data. Many external producers make secondary data available directly from the organizations that produce the data or through intermediaries, which are often called *vendors*. Vendors such as the Dow Jones News Retrieval Service now allow managers to access thousands of external databases via desktop computers and telecommunications systems. Hoover's (http://www.hoovers.com) specializes in providing information about thousands of companies' financial situations and operations.

Producers   Classifying external secondary data by the nature of the producer of information yields five basic sources: publishers of books and periodicals, government sources, media sources, trade association sources, and commercial sources. The following section discusses each type of secondary data source.

Books and Periodicals   Books and periodicals found in a library are considered by some researchers to be the quintessential secondary data source. A researcher who finds books on a topic of interest obviously is off to a good start.

Professional journals, such as the *Journal of Marketing, Journal of Marketing Research, Journal of the Academy of Marketing Science, Marketing Research: A Magazine*

EXHIBIT 6.8

SELECTED INTERNET SITES FOR SECONDARY DATA

Name	Description	URL
Yahoo!	Portal that serves as a gateway to all kinds of sites on the Web.	http://www.yahoo.com
CEOexpress	The 80/20 rule applied to the Internet. A series of links designed by a busy executive for busy executives.	http://www.ceoexpress.com
The New York Public Library Home Page	Library resources and links available online.	http://www.nypl.org
Census Bureau	Demographic information from the U.S. Census Bureau.	http://www.census.gov
Statistical Abstract of the United States	Highlights from the primary reference book for government statistics.	http://www.census.gov/stat_abstract
STAT-USA/Internet	A comprehensive source of U.S. government information that focuses on economic, financial, and trade data.	http://www.stat-usa.gov/
Advertising Age magazine	Provides content on marketing media, advertising, and public relations.	http://www.adage.com
Inc. Online	*Inc.* magazine's resources for growing a small business.	http://www.inc.com
Wall Street Journal Interactive	Provides a continually updated view of business news around the world.	http://www.wsj.com
CNN Money	Provides business news, information on managing a business and managing money, and other business data.	http://money.cnn.com
NAICS—North American Industry Classification System	Describes the new classification system that replaced the SIC system.	http://www.census.gov/epcd/www/naics.html
MapQuest	Allows users to enter an address and zip code and see a map.	http://www.mapquest.com
Business Europe	Provides links to obtain information about European countries.	http://www.businesseurope.com
Brint.com: The BizTech Network	Business and technology portal and global network for e-business, information, technology, and knowledge management.	http://www.brint.com

of Management and Application, and *The Public Opinion Quarterly,* as well as commercial business periodicals such as the *Wall Street Journal, Fortune,* and *Business Week,* contain much useful material. *Sales and Marketing Management's Survey of Buying Power* is a particularly useful source of information about markets. To locate data in periodicals, indexing services such as the *ABI/INFORM* and *Business Periodicals Index* and the *Wall Street Journal Index* are very useful. Guides to data sources also are helpful. For example, *American Statistical Index* and Business Information Sources are very valuable sources.

Government Sources   Government agencies produce data prolifically. Most of the data published by the federal government can be counted on for accuracy and quality of investigation. Most students are familiar with the U.S. Census of Population, which provides a wealth of data.

The Census of Population is only one of many resources that the government provides. Banks and savings and loan companies rely heavily on the *Federal Reserve Bulletin* and the *Economic Report of the President* for data relating to research on financial and economic conditions. Builders and contractors use the information in the *Current Housing Report and Annual Housing Survey* for their research. The *Statistical Abstract of the United States* is an extremely valuable source of information about the social, political, and economic organizations of the United States. It abstracts data available in hundreds of other government publications and serves as a convenient reference to more specific statistical data.

The federal government is a leader in making secondary data available on the Internet. Visit FedWorld (http://www.fedworld.gov) for a central access point and links to many of these important documents. STAT-USA/Internet is another authoritative and comprehensive source of U.S. government information that focuses on economic, financial, and trade data. It contains the following types of information:

- More than 18,000 market research reports on individual countries and markets compiled by foreign experts at U.S. embassies
- Economic data series, current and historical, such as gross domestic product, balance of payment, and merchandise trade
- Standard reference works, such as the *Economic Report of the President,* the *Budget of the United States Federal Government,* and the *World Fact Book*
- Worldwide listings of businesses interested in buying U.S. products

The STAT-USA/Internet Web address is http://www.stat-usa.gov/. However, only subscribers who pay a fee have access to this service.

State, county, and local government agencies can also be useful sources of information. Many state governments publish state economic models and forecasts, and many cities have metropolitan planning agencies that provide data about the population, economy, transportation system, and so on. These are similar to federal government data but are more current and are structured to suit local needs.

Many cities and states publish information on the Internet. Many search engines have directory entries that allow easy navigation to a particular state's Web site. A researcher using Yahoo, for example, needs only to click Regional Information to find numerous paths to information about states.

Media Sources   Information on a broad range of subjects is available from broadcast and print media. *CNN Financial News* and *Business Week* are valuable sources for information on the economy and many industries. *Money* magazine commissioned a research study about all aspects of Americans' financial affairs, and the report of this survey is available free to potential advertisers. Data about the readers of magazines and the audiences for broadcast media typically are profiled in media kits and advertisements.

Information about special-interest topics may also be available. *American Woodworker* magazine reports there are nearly 19.6 million woodworkers in the United States: 17.2 million of these are amateurs, whereas 2.4 million are professionals. *American Woodworker* also provides demographic information on woodworkers: 84 percent are male, 78 percent are married, the average age is 45, and the average household income is $48,000.[18]

Data such as these are plentiful because the media like to show that their vehicles are viewed or heard by advertisers' target markets. These types of data should be evaluated carefully, however, because often they cover only limited aspects of a topic. Nevertheless, they can be quite valuable for research, and they are generally free of charge.

Trade Association Sources   Trade associations, such as the Food Marketing Institute or the American Petroleum Institute, serve the information needs of a particular industry. The trade association collects data on a number of topics of specific interest to firms, especially data on market size and market trends. Association members have a source of information that is particularly germane to their industry questions. For example, the Newspaper Advertising Bureau (NAB) has catalogued and listed in its database the specialized sections that are currently popular in newspapers. The NAB has surveyed all daily, Sunday, and weekend newspapers in the United States and Canada on their editorial content and makes this information, along with data on rates, circulation, and mechanical requirements, available to advertisers.

Commercial Sources   Numerous firms specialize in selling and/or publishing information. For example, the Polk Company publishes information on the automotive field, such as average car values and new-car purchase rates by zip code. Many of these organizations offer information in published formats and as CD-ROM or Internet databases. The following discussion of several of these firms provides a sampling of the diverse data that are available.

Market Share Data   A number of syndicated services supply either wholesale or retail sales volume data based on product movement. Information Resources, Inc. collects market share data using Universal Product Codes (UPC) and optical scanning at retail store checkouts. Its INFOSCAN is a syndicated store-tracking service that collects scanner data weekly from more than 32,000 supermarket, drug, and mass merchandiser outlets across the United States. It also tracks sales in France, Germany, Greece, Italy, the Netherlands, Spain, and the United Kingdom.

Although it is best known for its television rating operations, A. C. Nielsen also has a scanner-based marketing and sales information service called ScanTrack. This service gathers sales and marketing data from a sample of more than 4,800 stores representing more than 800 retailers in 50 major U.S. markets. As part of Nielsen's Retail Measurement Service, auditors visit the stores at regular intervals to track promotions to customers, retail inventories, displays, brand distribution, out-of-stock conditions, and other retail marketing activity. Scanner data allow researchers to monitor sales data before, during, and after changes in

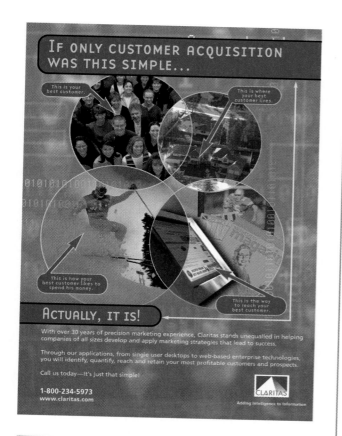

Many firms specialize in computerized census and demographic data.

advertising frequency, price changes, distribution of free samples, and similar marketing tactics.

Wal–Mart recently introduced its own in-store scanner system called RetailLink. It offers its key suppliers online access to relevant data free of charge.[19]

Many primary data investigations use scanner data to measure the results of experimental manipulations such as altering advertising copy. For example, scanning systems combined with consumer panels are used to create electronic test markets. Systems based on UPC bar codes and similar technology have been implemented in factories, warehouses, and transportation companies to research inventory levels, shipments, and the like.

Demographic and Census Updates   A number of firms, such as CACI Marketing Systems and Urban Information Systems, offer computerized U.S. census files and updates of these data broken down by small geographic areas, such as zip codes. Many of these research suppliers provide in-depth information on minority customers and other market segments.

Consumer Attitude and Public Opinion Research   Many research firms offer specialized syndicated services that report findings from attitude research and opinion polls. For example, Yankelovich provides custom research, tailored for specific projects, and several syndicated services. Yankelovich's public opinion research studies, such as the voter and public attitude surveys that appear in *Time* and other news magazines, are a source of secondary data. One of the firm's services is the *Yankelovich MONITOR*, a syndicated annual census of changing social values and an analysis of how they can affect consumer marketing. The *MONITOR* charts the growth and spread of new social values, characterizes the types of customers who support the new values and those who continue to support traditional values, and outlines the ways in which people's values affect purchasing behavior.

Harris Interactive is another public opinion research firm that provides syndicated and custom research for business. One of its services is its ABC News/Harris survey. This survey, released three times per week, monitors the pulse of the American public on topics such as inflation, unemployment, energy, attitudes toward the president, elections, and so on.

Consumption and Purchase Behavior Data   NPD's *National Eating Trends* (NET) is the most detailed database available on consumption patterns and trends for more than 4,000 food and beverage products. This is a syndicated source of data about the types of meals people eat and when and how they eat them. The data, called *diary panel data*, are based on records of meals and diaries kept by a group of households that have agreed to record their consumption behavior over an extended period of time.

National Family Opinion (NFO), Marketing Research Corporation of America (MRCA), and many other syndicated sources sell diary panel data about consumption and purchase behavior. Since the advent of scanner data, diary panels are more commonly used to record purchases of apparel, hardware, home furnishings, jewelry, and other durable goods, rather than purchases of nondurable consumer packaged goods.

Advertising Research   Advertisers can purchase readership and audience data from a number of firms. W. R. Simmons and Associates measures magazine audiences; Arbitron measures radio audiences; A. C. Nielsen Media Measurement estimates television audience ratings. By specializing in collecting and selling audience information on a continuing basis, these commercial sources provide a valuable service to their subscribers.

Assistance in measuring advertising effectiveness is another syndicated service. For example, Roper Starch Worldwide measures the impact of advertising in magazines. Readership information can be obtained for competitors' ads or the client's own ads. Respondents are classified as noted readers, associated readers, or read-most readers.

Burke Marketing Research provides a service that measures the extent to which respondents recall television commercials aired the night before. It provides product category norms, average DAR (day-after recall) scores, and DAR scores for other products.

An individual advertiser would be unable to monitor every minute of every television program before deciding on the appropriate ones in which to place advertising. However, numerous clients, agencies, television networks, and advertisers can purchase the Nielsen television ratings service.

SINGLE-SOURCE DATA: INTEGRATED INFORMATION

A. C. Nielsen Company offers data both from its television meters and from scanner operations. The integration of these two types of data helps marketers investigate the impact of television advertising on retail sales. In other ways as well, users of data find that merging two or more diverse types of data into a single database offers many advantages.

EXHIBIT 6.9 | EXAMPLES OF SINGLE-SOURCE DATABASES

CACI Marketing Systems http://www.caci.com	Provides industry-specific marketing services, such as customer profiling and segmentation, custom target analysis, demographic data reports and maps, and site evaluation and selection. CACI offers demographics and data on businesses, lifestyles, consumer spending, purchase potential, shopping centers, traffic volumes, and other statistics.
PRIZM by Claritas Corporation http://www.claritas.com	PRIZM, which stands for Potential Rating Index for Zip Markets, is based on the "birds-of-a-feather" assumption that people live near others who are like them. PRIZM combines census data, consumer surveys about shopping and lifestyle, and purchase data to identify market segments. Colorful names such as Young Suburbia and Shot Guns and Pickups describe 40 segments that can be identified by zip code. Claritas also has a lifestyle census in the United Kingdom (http://www.claritas.co.uk).
MRI Cable Report—Mediamark Research Inc. http://www.mediamark.com	Integrates information on cable television viewing with demographic and product usage information.

PRIZM by Claritas Corporation, CACI, ClusterPlus by SMI, Mediamark Research Inc., and many other syndicated databases report product purchase behavior, media usage, demographic characteristics, lifestyle variables, and business activity by geographic area such as zip code. Although such data are often called *geodemographic*, they cover such a broad range of phenomena that no one name is a good description. These data use small geographic areas as the unit of analysis.

single-source data
Diverse types of data offered by a single company. The data are usually integrated on the basis of a common variable such as geographic area or store.

The marketing research industry uses the term **single-source data** for diverse types of data offered by a single company. Exhibit 6.9 identifies several major marketers of single-source data.

SOURCES FOR GLOBAL RESEARCH

As business has become more global, so has the secondary data industry. The Japan Management Association Research Institute, Japan's largest provider of secondary research data to government and industry, maintains an office in San Diego. The Institute's goal is to help U.S. firms access its enormous store of data about Japan to develop and plan their business there. The office in San Diego provides translators and acts as an intermediary between Japanese researchers and U.S. clients.

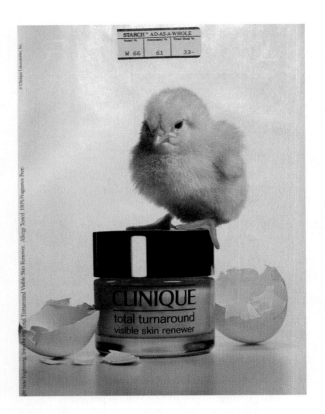

STARCH™ AD-AS-A-WHOLE

Noted %	Associated %	Read Most %
W 66	61	33~

CLINIQUE
total turnaround
visible skin renewer

Starch Readership Service measures the impact of advertising. People who recognize the ad are classified as noted readers, associated readers, or read-most readers.

Secondary data compiled outside the United States have the same limitations as domestic secondary data. However, international researchers should watch for certain pitfalls that frequently are associated with foreign data and cross–cultural research. First, data may simply be unavailable in certain countries. Second, the accuracy of some data may be called into question. This is especially likely with official statistics that may be adjusted for the political purposes of foreign governments. Finally, although economic terminology may be standardized, various countries use different definitions and accounting and recording practices for many economic concepts. For example, different countries may measure disposable personal income in radically different ways. International researchers should take extra care to investigate the comparability of data among countries.

The U.S. government and other organizations compile databases that may aid international marketers. For example, *The European Union in the US* (http://www.eurunion.org/) reports on historical and current activity in the European Union. It is a comprehensive reference guide that provides information about laws and regulations, a detailed profile of each European Union member state, investment opportunities, sources of grants and other funding, and other information about business resources.

The U.S. government offers a wealth of data about foreign countries. *The CIA Factbook* and the *National Trade Data Bank* are especially useful. Both can be accessed using the Internet. The National Trade Data Bank (NTDB), the U.S. government's most comprehensive source of world trade data, illustrates what is available.

EXHIBIT 6.10 | EXAMPLES OF INFORMATION CONTAINED IN THE NTDB

Agricultural commodity production and trade
Basic export information
Calendars of trade fairs and exhibitions
Capital markets and export financing
Country reports on economic and social policies and trade practices
Energy production, supply, and inventories
Exchange rates
Export licensing information
Guides to doing business in foreign countries
International trade terms directory
How-to guides
International trade regulations/agreements
International trade agreements
Labor, employment, and productivity

Maritime and shipping information
Market research reports
Overseas contacts
Overseas and domestic industry information
Price indexes
Small business information
State exports
State trade contacts
Trade opportunities
U.S. export regulations
U.S. import and export statistics by country and commodity
U.S. international transactions
World Fact Book
World minerals production

The National Trade Data Bank was established by the Omnibus Trade and Competitiveness Act of 1988.[20] Its purpose was to provide "reasonable public access, including electronic access" to an export promotion data system that was centralized, inexpensive, and easy to use.

The U.S. Department of Commerce has the responsibility for operating and maintaining the NTDB and works with federal agencies that collect and distribute trade information to keep the NTDB up-to-date. The NTDB has been published monthly on CD-ROM since 1990. Over 1,000 public and university libraries offer access to the NTDB through the Federal Depository Library system.

The National Trade Data Bank consists of 133 separate trade- and business-related programs (databases). By using it, small- and medium-sized companies get immediate access to information that until now only Fortune 500 companies could afford.

The NTDB includes lists of export opportunities by industry, country, and product; foreign companies or importers looking for specific products; how-to market guides; demographic, political, and socioeconomic conditions in hundreds of countries; and much more. The NTDB offers one-stop shopping for trade information from more than 20 federal sources. You do not need to know which federal agency produces the information: All you need to do is consult NTDB.

Some of the specific information that can be obtained from the NTDB are listed in Exhibit 6.10.

SUMMARY

Secondary data are data that have been gathered and recorded previously by someone else for purposes other than those of the current researcher. Secondary data usually are historical and do not require access to respondents or subjects. Primary data are data gathered for the specific purpose of the current researcher.

The chief advantage of secondary data is that they are almost always less expensive to obtain than primary data. Generally, they can be obtained rapidly and may provide information not otherwise available to the researcher. The disadvantage of secondary data is that they were not intended specifically to meet the researcher's needs. The researcher must examine secondary data for accuracy, bias, and soundness. One way to do this is to cross-check various available sources.

Secondary research designs address many common marketing problems. There are three general categories of secondary research objectives: fact-finding, model building, and database marketing. A typical fact finding study might seek to uncover all available information about consumption patterns for a particular product category or to identify business trends that affect an industry. Model building is more complicated; it involves specifying relationships between two or more variables. Model building need not involve a complicated mathematical process, but it can help marketers to estimate market potential, forecast sales, select sites, and accomplish many other objectives. The practice of *database marketing*, which involves maintaining customer databases with customers' names, addresses, phone numbers, past purchases, responses to past promotional offers, and other relevant data such as demographic and financial data, is increasingly being supported by marketing research efforts.

Managers often get data from internal proprietary sources such as accounting records. Data mining is the use of powerful computers to dig through volumes of data to discover patterns about an organization's customers and products.

External data are generated or recorded by an entity other than the researcher's organization. The government, newspaper and journal publishers, trade associations, and other organizations create or produce information. Traditionally this information has been distributed in published form, either directly from producer to researcher or indirectly through intermediaries such as public libraries. Modern computerized data archives, electronic data interchange, and the Internet have changed the distribution of external data, making them almost as accessible as internal data.

The marketing of multiple types of related data by single-source suppliers has radically changed the nature of secondary data research.

As business has become more global, so has the secondary data industry. International researchers should watch for certain pitfalls that can be associated with foreign data and cross-cultural research.

Key Terms and Concepts

secondary data	model building	database marketing
data conversion	site analysis techniques	internal and proprietary data
cross-check	index of retail saturation	external data
market tracking	data mining	single-source data
environmental scanning	neural network	

Questions for Review and Critical Thinking

1. Secondary data have been called the first line of attack for marketing researchers. Discuss this description.
2. Suppose you wish to learn about the size of the soft-drink market, particularly root beer sales,

growth patterns, and market shares. Indicate probable sources for these secondary data.
3. Over the past 5 years, a manager has noted a steady growth in sales and profits for her division's product line. Does she need to use any sec-

ondary data to further evaluate her division's condition?

4. Identify some typical research objectives for secondary data studies.

5. How might a retailer such as Victoria's Secret use data mining?

6. What would be the best source for the following data?
   a. Population, average income, and employment rates for Oregon
   b. Maps of U.S. counties and cities
   c. Trends in automobile ownership
   d. Divorce trends in the United States
   e. Median weekly earnings of full-time, salaried workers for the previous 5 years
   f. Annual sales of the top ten fast-food companies
   g. Top ten Web sites ranked by number of unique visitors
   h. Attendance at professional sports events

7. Suppose you are a marketing research consultant and a client comes to your office and says, "I must have the latest information on the supply of and demand for Maine potatoes within the next 24 hours." What would you do?

8. Find the following data in the *Survey of Current Business* for May 2001:
   a. U.S. gross domestic product for the first quarter of 2001
   b. Exports of goods and services for December 2000
   c. Imports of goods and services for December 2000

9. Use the most recent *Sales and Marketing Management Survey of Buying Power* to find the total population, median age, and total retail sales for (a) your hometown (or county) and (b) the town (or county) in which your school is located.

10. Use secondary data to learn the size of the U.S. golf market and to profile who golfs.

11. A newspaper reporter reads a study that surveyed children and then reports that a high percentage of children recognize Joe Camel, cigarette spokescharacter, but fails to report that the study also found that a much higher percentage of children indicated very negative attitudes toward smoking. Is this a proper use of secondary data?

Exploring the Internet

1. The home page for BRINT Research Initiative (Business Research, Management Research & Information Technology Research) is at http://www.brint.com/. It contains links to hundreds of information-based Web sites. Visit this site and identify several interesting sources you can go to from there.

2. PopClocks estimate the U.S. and world populations. Go to the Census Bureau home page (http://www.census.gov), navigate to the population section, and find today's estimate of the U.S. and world populations.

3. Visit the Small Business Administration's home page at http://www.sbaonline.sba.gov. What type of information can be accessed?

4. Use the Internet to learn what you can about Indonesia.
   a. Use a Web browser to go to http://www.asiadragons. com/ and click on Indonesia.
   b. Visit the *CIA World Factbook* (http://www.cia.gov/cia/publications/factbook/).
   c. Go to Infoseek or Google and use "Indonesia" as a search word.
   What kinds of information are available from these sources?

5. FIND/SVP is a company that provides information about many different industries. Go to the FIND/SVP home page at http://www.findsvp.com. Select an industry. What industry information is available?

6. Go to Statistics Norway at http://www.ssb.no/. What data, if any, can you obtain in English? What languages can be used to search this Web site? What databases might be of interest to the business researcher?

7. Go to Statistics Canada at http://www.statcan.ca. What languages can be used to search this Web site? What databases might be of interest to the business researcher?

8. *Martindale's Health Science Guide's Reference Desk* is hosted by the University of California, Irvine Libraries, http://www.lib.uci.edu/. Going to http://www-sci.lib.uci.edu/HSG/Ref.html will take you to The Reference Desk, where there are hyperlinks to a vast amount of information.

9. Go to the University of Michigan library's Statistical Resources on the Web at http://www.lib.umich.edu/libhome/Documents.center/ and click on Statistics. You will find links to secondary data for Agriculture, Business and Industry, Demographics, Economics, Education, Energy, Environment, Finance, Foreign Government Data Sources, and many other subjects. Visit the site and report what you find.

"Decorating one's home is an extremely personal and information-intensive decision," says Andrew L. Brooks, president and CEO of Furniture.com.[21] Decorating in general, and furniture shopping in particular, can be a frustrating, time-consuming, and intimidating experience for many people. Few people relish dragging spouses or kids from furniture store to furniture store to sit on sofas and order swatches. And many consumers are just plain afraid to make a decision—what if the color or style is "wrong"? What if the dining room table is too big for the room? Furniture.com is determined to change all that.

Unlike other Internet businesses. Furniture.com is not an online start-up company. The idea to sell furniture on the Web actually began with the owner of a brick-and-mortar furniture store called Empire Furniture Showroom in downtown Worcester, Massachusetts. Steven Rothschild and his partner, Misha Katz, launched the first version of the online company from the Worcester store in the late 1990s. Rothschild is now company chairman and Katz is vice president of new technology. Throughout the changes the company has undergone, however, it has maintained a clear mission, as articulated by Brooks: "To take a shopping experience in the traditional world, which is not particularly easy, to re-create it, and to make it fun, easy, and accessible to everybody."

Rothschild and Katz recognized an opportunity. "The traditional brick-and-mortar environment hasn't been very good to furniture consumers," explains Brooks. "The average consumer needs to go to five or six retail establishments. That potentially ruins five or six weekend days with kids in tow, trying to find the perfect place. That is often a frustrating exercise." With more and more consumers flocking to the Internet to do their shopping, Furniture.com took advantage of a strategic window to attract customers early and keep them coming back for more. The company offers over 50,000 items from 140 manufacturers through its site, and it provides free delivery and setup. Most brick-and-mortar stores offer only 4,000 to 10,000 items, and many charge for delivery beyond a few miles.

Connecting all these pieces of furniture with the right customers requires strategic and tactical planning. Perhaps the company's most important strategy is considering the impact of every decision its managers make on the consumer. "Examples of that include multiple ways to search," explains Brooks. "You can search on our site by room, by piece, and by very specific criteria. . . . What sets us apart is the extent to which we have identified real consumer needs. We then found technology that can provide solutions as opposed to technology for

technology's sake." To that end, customers can build their own virtual showroom at the Web site, filled with their favorite pieces of furniture to see what the finished product will look like. The Room Planner, Style Guide, Furniture Finder, and Personal Shopper features of Furniture.com's site are all implementations of the overall strategy.

Furniture.com's strengths include the following:

- Its huge selection—as already mentioned, the company offers over 50,000 items, much more than competitors
- Its service—customer service is open around the clock, by phone, live Internet chat, or e-mail, and sales reps contact customers after delivery to make certain the right items arrived on time
- Its freedom from having to hold inventory—most items are shipped directly from manufacturers.

Its one major weakness is the fact that currently the company does not offer cash refunds; instead, customers receive an exchange or store credit. Since furniture is a major purchase for most consumers, having $500 or $1,000 tied up in store credit could be a problem. However, Furniture.com does have a "no questions asked" return policy, and the company pays return shipping fees.

Looking toward future growth, Furniture.com has entered into several strategic alliances with other organizations. The company now has online advertising agreements with MSN Internet service, Yahoo!, and Lycos as part of a move to strengthen its position in the e-commerce marketplace. Indeed, Furniture.com's position is already at the head of its class. In review after review, the company receives high marks for selection and service. *Entertainment Weekly* calls the site "best of breed." *Access* rates the company with four stars, and *PC Magazine* reports, "The smartest furniture shoppers are heading to Furniture.com." That's a satisfying image for Furniture.com's founders: smart shoppers buying products from a smart company.

Questions

1. What type of research objectives might Furniture.com be able to satisfy by using secondary data?
2. Suggest some external data sources and the channel of distribution Furniture.com might use to obtain data from these sources.
3. Doing business on the Internet is uncharted waters for most companies. How useful is marketing research when most people have little or no experience with a new type of shopping?

CASE 6.2   BLACK AND TAN ADVERTISING, INC.

Black and Tan, Inc. is a medium–sized advertising agency known for its creative marketing planning. A client, Joseph S. Yarbrough Brewing Company, has been extremely pleased with its long-standing relationship with the agency.

One Friday during a business lunch with the client, at which the agency's principals conscientiously consumed the client's product, Black, the agency's president, suggested to Yarbrough that the brewery was not advertising to a major market segment. Black explained that the Asian American market was the fastest-growing minority market in the country and was projected to become a major market segment by 2010. He indicated that there were at least 10 million Asian Americans in the United States.

The client seemed more interested in maintaining quality control on his product than in what Black was saying. The agency president wisely allowed the conversation to drift for a while.

Later, Black again brought up the subject of the Asian American market. Yarbrough said, "Right now, I've got other priorities. And to be quite honest with you, I think that most Asian Americans are mainstream. They watch network TV. They read the same stuff as the average working person. But I'll tell you something: If you can come up with some hard data to show me that this market really deserves serious consideration, I'll give it a try."

Questions

1. What secondary sources might Black and Tan use to determine the exact size of the Asian American market?
2. What characteristics are peculiar to the Asian American market? List and discuss some of these characteristics.
3. Prepare a research presentation for Yarbrough.

VIDEO CASE 6.3   THE CENSUS BUREAU: CENSUS 2000

Fact-finding is one of America's oldest activities.[22] In the early 17th century, a census was taken in Virginia, and people were counted in nearly all of the British colonies that became the United States. Following independence, there was an almost immediate need for a census of the entire nation. The first census was taken in 1790. The census counted 3.9 million inhabitants. Down through the years, the nation's needs and interests evolved and have become more complex. Today there is a need for statistics to help people understand what is happening and to form a basis for planning.

The Census Bureau is part of the U.S. Department of Commerce. Its mission is to be the preeminent collector and provider of timely, relevant, and quality data about the people and economy of the United States.

The censuses of population and housing are taken every 10 years in the year ending in 0. The census of

population reports on population characteristics by geographical areas and provides detailed statistics on age, sex, race, Hispanic origin, marital status, and household relationship characteristics for states, counties, and places of 1,000 or more inhabitants. The economic censuses, covering manufacturing, retail, wholesale, and services industries, are taken every 5 years in the years ending with 2 and 7.

Questions

1. Why do we need a census of population? What good does it do the average person?
2. What is the population undercount? Is it equal among all demographic groups?
3. What types of marketing efforts might help the Census Bureau increase citizen participation in the census?

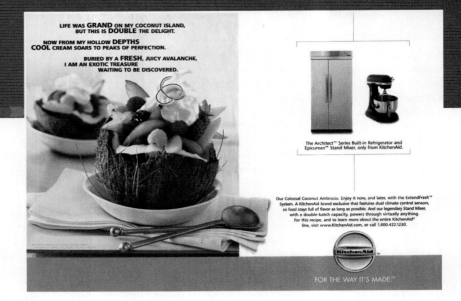

The Architect™ Series Built-in Refrigerator and Epicurean™ Stand Mixer, only from KitchenAid.

CHAPTER 7

SURVEY RESEARCH

What you will learn in this chapter

- To understand the advantages of using surveys.
- To discuss the type of information that may be gathered in a survey.
- To recognize that few surveys are error-free.
- To distinguish between random sampling error and systematic error.
- To classify the various types of systematic error and give examples of each type.
- To discuss how response error may be an unconscious misrepresentation or a deliberate falsification.
- To classify surveys according to method of communication.
- To distinguish between cross-sectional surveys and longitudinal surveys.

Although KitchenAid is best known for its Stand Mixer, the company markets a full line of small and large kitchen appliances, including dishwashers and refrigerators.[1] A couple of years ago, the countertop appliance division was doing fine, but sales for the company's larger appliances were declining. The KitchenAid team had to figure out a way to transfer brand equity from its small-appliance division to its large appliances—and they had to do it without increasing their marketing budget.

Researchers started with an analysis of data from 8 years of warranty card surveys for all of KitchenAid's products and with an analysis of the database from the 40,000 households who participate in NFO Worldwide's consumer panel surveys. The KitchenAid researchers learned that across all products, their brand signified "high quality" to customers, but that only their countertop line of appliances had the reputation for innovation. In a subsequent exploratory research study, researchers discovered consumers weren't interested in the appliance for the appliance's sake. They were interested in what the appliance could do for them—help them to prepare delicious foods and be able to entertain friends and family while serving their culinary creations. To confirm and quantify these preliminary findings, KitchenAid conducted a segmentation study. Based on the survey results, management decided to focus on "the culinary-involved," a segment of consumers who were heavy users of kitchen appliances and who believed in having the best products for their homes. These household chefs were passionate about cooking, and most important to KitchenAid, the segment cut across all demographic groups: It wasn't confined to upper-income households.

Past research had shown that consumers actively use magazines to plan their major appliance purchases, often tearing pages out of home and lifestyle magazines to file away for ideas and inspiration, so KitchenAid planned a print-only campaign. One magazine ad featured a picture of lemon soufflé pancakes dominating more than three-quarters of one page. The pancakes are drizzled in a creamy lemon sauce and topped with raspberries. On the page facing the picture, beneath the smaller images of the large and small appliances that helped to prepare the dish, the text invited the reader to visit the company's Web site for the recipe. These ads ran in 59 publications, ranging from *Architectural Digest* to *People.*

What was the payoff of this research and advertising effort? After the first 6 months of 2000, when the campaign started, sales for both countertop and major appliances were showing double-digit growth. In the first 2 months of the campaign, contacts to KitchenAid's 800 number and its Web site were more than three times what they were over the previous year, and hit rates to the site were up nearly 60 percent. Most satisfying: The marketing team produced these results using 64 percent of its budget from the previous year—and without use of a television advertising presence. ■

THE NATURE OF SURVEYS

respondent
The person who answers an interviewer's questions or provides answers to written questions.

survey
A method of collecting primary data in which information is gathered by communicating with a representative sample of people.

Surveys require asking a representative sample of people, called **respondents,** for information using either verbal or written questions. Questionnaires or interviews collect data face to face, over the telephone, by mail, or through other means of communication. Thus, a **survey** is a method of primary data collection based on communication with a representative sample of individuals.

Surveys provide a quick, inexpensive, efficient, and accurate means of assessing information about a population. Surveys are quite flexible, and, when properly conducted, extremely valuable to the manager.

As we discussed in Chapter 1, marketing research has proliferated since the general adoption of the marketing concept. The growth of survey research is related to the simple idea that the best way to find out what consumers think, is to *ask* them.

Properly conducted surveys can be quite accurate. However, many surveys conducted today are a waste of time and money because they are poorly designed or improperly implemented. As one writer describes,

> Samples are biased; questions are poorly phrased; interviewers are not properly instructed and supervised; and results are misinterpreted. Such surveys are worse than none at all because the sponsor may be misled into a costly area. Even well-planned and neatly executed surveys may be useless if, as often happens, the results come too late to be of value or are converted into a bulky report which no one has time to read.[2]

The disadvantages of specific forms of survey data collection (personal interview, telephone, mail, Internet, and other self-administered formats) are discussed later in the chapter. However, errors are common to all forms of surveys, so it is appropriate to describe them generally.

ERRORS IN SURVEY RESEARCH

A manager who is evaluating the quality of a survey must estimate its accuracy. Exhibit 7.1 outlines the various forms of survey error. The two major sources of survey error are random sampling error and systematic error.

EXHIBIT 7.1 | CATEGORIES OF SURVEY ERRORS

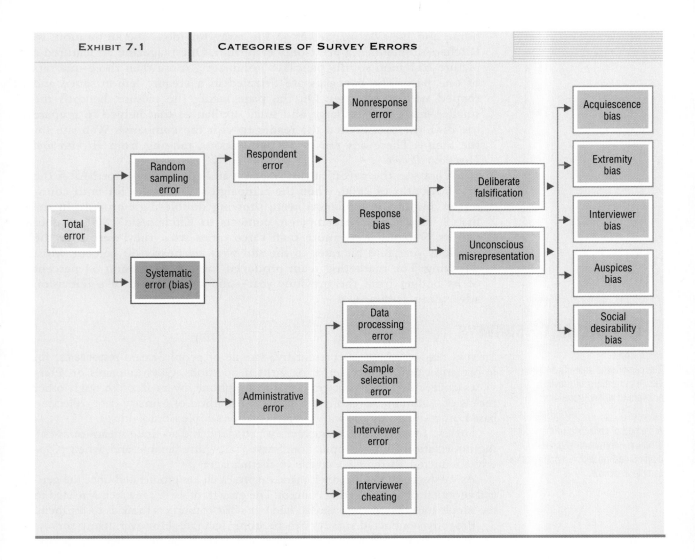

Random Sampling Error

random sampling error
A statistical fluctuation that occurs because of chance variation in the elements selected for a sample.

Most surveys try to portray a representative cross-section of a particular target population. Even with appropriate probability samples, however, statistical errors will occur because of chance variation. Without increasing sample size, these statistical problems are unavoidable. However, **random sampling errors** can be estimated; Chapter 13 will discuss these in greater detail.

Systematic Error

systematic error
Error resulting from some imperfect aspect of the research design or from a mistake in the execution of the research.

Systematic error results from some imperfect aspect of the research design or from a mistake in the execution of the research. Because all sources of error other than those introduced by the random sampling procedure are included, these errors or biases are also called *nonsampling errors*. A **sample bias** exists when the results of a sample show a persistent tendency to deviate in one direction from the true value of the population parameter.

sample bias
A persistent tendency for the results of a sample to deviate in one direction from the true value of the population parameter.

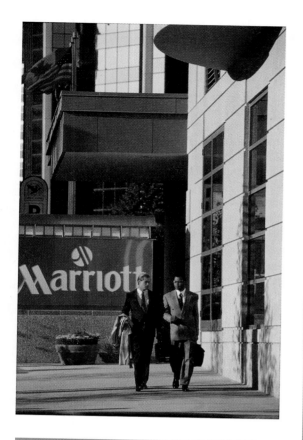

Marketing managers at Marriott Corporation know that people want a hotel room to feel residential, because they see a hotel room as a home away from home. Customers prefer a clearly marked place to sit down, straight furniture legs, light walls, big bathrooms, spacious desk areas, and a long telephone cord.

How did Marriott Corporation, the largest operator of hotels in the country, learn about its customers' preferences? Simple! Marketing researchers have built an assortment of fake hotel rooms modeled on the competition and conducted surveys to test consumers' reactions. Customers walk through and rate the rooms.

The many sources of error that in some way systematically influence answers can be divided into two general categories: respondent error and administrative error. These are discussed in the following sections.

RESPONDENT ERROR

respondent error
A category of sample bias resulting from some respondent action or inaction such as nonresponse or response bias.

Surveys ask people for answers. If people cooperate and give truthful answers, the survey will likely accomplish its goal. If these conditions are not met, nonresponse error or response bias, the two major categories of **respondent error,** may cause a sample bias.

Nonresponse Error

nonresponse error
The statistical differences between a survey that includes only those who responded and a perfect survey that would also include those who failed to respond.

Few surveys have 100 percent response rates. A researcher who obtains an 11 percent response to a five-page questionnaire concerning various brands of spark plugs may face a serious problem. To be able to use the results, the researcher must be sure that those who did respond to the questionnaire were representative of those who did not.

The statistical differences between a survey that includes only those who responded and a perfect survey that would also include those who failed to respond are referred to as a **nonresponse error.** This problem is especially acute in mail and Internet surveys, but it also threatens telephone and face-to-face interviews.

OBSTACLES TO CONSUMER RESEARCH

Many managers view consumer research as a necessary precursor to product introduction.[3] Unfortunately, innovative products that lack much in common with existing products often prove this attitude wrong. Hairstyling mousse is now a massive hit, yet its initial U.S. market tests flopped. People said it was "goopy and gunky," and they did not like its feel when it "mooshed" through their hair. Similarly, when the telephone answering machine was consumer tested, it faced an almost universally negative reaction, since most individuals felt that using a mechanical device to answer a phone was rude and disrespectful. Today, of course, many people regard their answering machines as indispensable and would dread scheduling daily activities without them. In the same vein, the computer mouse flunked its initial testing. Surveys indicated that potential customers found it awkward and unnecessary.

Surveys about new food products face terrible problems. For one, a person's desire for food is powerfully influenced by the ambience of the meal, dining companions, and what foods were eaten recently, all of which confound the results of survey research. Even more erratic results come from studies of children's food, such as a new cereal or snack. The responses of kids are strongly swayed by how well they like the people doing the test and the playthings available. Worse, kids quickly change their minds. In a taste test of several foods, a child can judge one food the best but an hour later proclaim the same food "icky."

Marketing researchers must be aware of the potential problems when deciding exactly which research design will best solve their research problems.

---

nonrespondent
A person who is not contacted or who refuses to cooperate in the research.

no contact
A person who is not at home on the first or second contact, or who is otherwise inaccessible.

refusal
A person who is unwilling to participate in a research project.

self-selection bias
A bias that occurs because people who feel strongly about a subject are more likely to respond than people who feel indifferent about it.

People who are not contacted or who refuse to cooperate are called **nonrespondents**. A nonresponse occurs if someone is not at home at the time of both the initial call and a subsequent callback. The number of **no contacts** in survey research has been increasing because of the proliferation of answering machines and growing use of caller ID to screen telephone calls.[4] A parent who must juggle the telephone and a half-diapered child and who refuses to participate in the survey because he or she is too busy is also a nonrespondent. **Refusals** occur when people are unwilling to participate in the research. No contacts and refusals can seriously bias survey data.

Self-selection bias is a problem that frequently plagues self-administered questionnaires. In a restaurant, for example, a customer on whom a server spilled soup, a person who was treated to a surprise dinner, or others who feel strongly about the service are more likely to complete a self-administered questionnaire left at the table than individuals who are indifferent about the restaurant. Self-selection biases distort surveys because they overrepresent extreme positions while underrepresenting responses from those who are indifferent.

After receiving a refusal from a potential respondent, an interviewer can do nothing other than be polite. The respondent who is not at home when called or visited should be scheduled to be interviewed at a different time of day or on a different day of the week.

With a mail survey, the researcher never really knows whether a nonrespondent has refused to participate or is simply indifferent. Researchers know that those who are most involved in an issue are more likely to respond to a mail survey. Later we will discuss several techniques for encouraging respondents to reply to mail surveys.

Response Bias

response bias
A bias that occurs when respondents either consciously or unconsciously tend to answer questions with a certain slant that misrepresents the truth.

A **response bias** occurs when respondents tend to answer questions with a certain slant. People may consciously or unconsciously misrepresent the truth. If a distortion of measurement occurs because respondents' answers are falsified or misrepresented, either intentionally or inadvertently because they have forgotten the exact details, the resulting answers have a response bias.

Response bias can arise from the question format, the question content, or some other stimulus. For example, bias can be introduced by the situation in which the survey is administered. The results of two in-flight surveys concerning aircraft preference illustrate this point. Passengers flying on B-747s preferred B-747s to L-1011s (74 percent versus 19 percent), while passengers flying on L-1011s preferred L-1011s to B-747s (56 percent versus 38 percent). The difference in preferences appears to have been largely a function of the aircraft the respondents were flying on when the survey was conducted, although sample differences may have been a factor. A likely influence was the respondent's satisfaction with the plane on which he or she was flying when surveyed. In other words, in the absence of any strong preference, the respondent may simply have identified the aircraft traveled on and indicated that as his or her preference.[5]

Occasionally people deliberately give false answers. Deliberate falsification may occur when people misrepresent answers to appear intelligent, to conceal personal information, to avoid embarrassment, and so on.

Types of Response Bias

There are five specific categories of response bias: acquiescence bias, extremity bias, interviewer bias, auspices bias, and social desirability bias. These categories overlap and are not mutually exclusive. A single biased answer may be distorted for many complex reasons; some misrepresentations may be deliberate and some unconscious.

Nonresponse error can be high when conducting international marketing research. People in many cultures do not share Americans' views about providing information. In Mexico citizens are reluctant to provide information over the phone to strangers. In many Middle Eastern countries many women would refuse to be interviewed by a male interviewer.

Acquiescence Bias Some respondents are very agreeable; these yea-sayers accept all statements they are asked about. This tendency to agree with all or most questions is particularly prominent in new-product research. Questions about a new product idea generally elicit some **acquiescence bias** because respondents give positive connotations to most new ideas. For example, Spaulding, Rawlings, and Mizuno found that consumers responded favorably when asked about pump baseball gloves (which have a mechanism similar to those on pump basketball shoes). However, when these expensive gloves hit the market, they sat on the shelves. When conducting new-product research, researchers should recognize the high likelihood of acquiescence bias.

Extremity Bias Some individuals tend to use extremes when responding to questions; others always avoid extreme positions and tend to respond more neutrally. Response styles vary from person to person, and extreme responses may cause an **extremity bias** in the data.

Interviewer Bias Response bias may arise from interplay between interviewer and respondent. If the interviewer's presence influences respondents to give untrue or modified answers, the survey will be marred by **interviewer bias.** Many homemakers and retired people welcome an interviewer's visit as a break in routine activities. Respondents may give answers they believe will please the interviewer rather than the truthful responses. Respondents may wish to appear intelligent and wealthy—of course they read *Scientific American* rather than *Spin*.

The interviewer's age, sex, style of dress, tone of voice, facial expressions, or other nonverbal characteristics may have some influence on a respondent's answers. If an interviewer smiles and makes a positive statement after a respondent's answer, the respondent will be more likely to give similar responses. In a research study on sexual harassment against saleswomen, male interviewers may generate less candid responses than female interviewers would.

Many interviewers, contrary to instructions, shorten or rephrase questions to suit their needs. This potential influence on responses can be avoided to some extent if interviewers receive training and supervision that emphasize the necessity of appearing neutral.

Auspices Bias Suppose the National Rifle Association is conducting a study on gun control. The answers to the survey may be deliberately or subconsciously misrepresented because respondents are influenced by the organization conduct-

acquiescence bias
A category of response bias that results because some individuals tend to agree with all questions or to concur with a particular position.

extremity bias
A category of response bias that results because some individuals tend to use extremes when responding to questions.

interviewer bias
A response bias that occurs because the presence of the interviewer influences answers.

In Asia, cultural values about survey research differ from those in the United States. Asians have less patience with the abstract and rational question wording commonly used in the United States. Researchers must be alert for culture-bound sources of response bias in international marketing research. For example, the Japanese do not wish to contradict others, leading to a bias toward acquiescence and yea-saying.

National Restaurant Association research shows that when it comes to diet there is considerable response bias. In response to survey questions, Americans say they intend to be virtuous in their eating (fresh fruit and bran muffins), but what they actually eat (many hamburgers) doesn't reflect what they say.

ing the study. If a national committee on gun control conducted the same study, respondents' answers might vary from those given in an NRA survey because of **auspices bias.**

auspices bias
Response bias that results because respondents are influenced by the organization conducting the study.

social desirability bias
Bias in responses caused by respondents' desire, either conscious or unconscious, to gain prestige or appear in a different social role.

Social Desirability Bias   A **social desirability bias** may occur either consciously or unconsciously because the respondent wishes to create a favorable impression or save face in the presence of an interviewer. Answering that one's income is only $30,000 a year might be difficult for someone whose self-concept is that of an upper-middle-class person "about to make it big." Incomes may be inflated, education overstated, or perceived respectable answers given to gain prestige. In contrast, answers to questions that seek factual information or responses about matters of public knowledge (zip code, number of children, and so on) usually are quite accurate. An interviewer's presence may increase a respondent's tendency to give an inaccurate answer to sensitive questions such as "Did you vote in the last election?" "Do you have termites or roaches in your home?" or "Do you have dandruff?"

ADMINISTRATIVE ERROR

administrative error
An error caused by the improper administration or execution of the research task.

The results of improper administration or execution of a research task are **administrative errors.** They are caused by carelessness, confusion, neglect, omission, or some other blunder. Four types of administrative error are data-processing error, sample selection error, interviewer error, and interviewer cheating.

CUSTOMER SURVEYS: DON'T TELL, JUST ASK

You've just dropped your car off at the dealership for service and a manager politely informs you that you will be asked to answer a quality survey by phone after the work is completed.[6] Or, you've just walked out of the supermarket and a store employee unexpectedly grills you about the convenience and speed of service you just received. In which of the two situations are you likely to be more critical? Hands down: You find more faults at the dealership.

No, not because some drivers are skeptical about service pricing at their dealerships. Consumer research shows that when people are told in advance that they will be asked to respond to a survey, they look for problems more actively. Companies want to satisfy their customers, so they are frequently conducting surveys about quality and satisfaction. People who expect to evaluate are decidedly more negative. In fact, merely asking people to state their expectations before they receive service makes them more negative—even though their predispositions may have been quite positive. For example, people who are asked if they think they will like a movie before seeing it will be more negative than people who are not asked beforehand.

Data-Processing Error

data-processing error
A category of administrative error that occurs because of incorrect data entry, incorrect computer programming, or other procedural errors during the data-processing stage.

Data processed by computer, like data processed by any arithmetic or procedural process, are subject to error because they must be edited, coded, and entered into the computer by people. The accuracy of data processed by computer depends on correct data entry and programming. **Data-processing errors** can be minimized by establishing careful procedures for verifying each step in the data-processing stage.

Sample Selection Error

sample selection error
An administrative error caused by improper sample design or sampling procedure execution.

Sample selection error is systematic error that results in an unrepresentative sample because of an error in either the sample design or the execution of the sampling procedure. Executing a sampling plan free of procedural error is difficult. A firm that selects its sample from the phone book will encounter some systematic error, because unlisted numbers are not included. Stopping female respondents during daytime hours in shopping centers excludes working people who shop by mail, by telephone, or on the Internet. In other cases, the wrong person may be interviewed. Consider a political pollster who randomly selects telephone numbers for a sample rather than basing the sample on a list of registered voters. Unregistered 17-year-olds may be willing to give their opinions, but they are the wrong people to ask because they cannot vote.

Interviewer Error

interviewer error
Mistakes made by interviewers who fail to record survey responses correctly.

Interviewers' abilities vary considerably. **Interviewer error** is introduced when interviewers record answers, but check the wrong responses or are unable to write fast enough to record answers verbatim. Or, selective perception may cause interviewers to misrecord data that do not support their own attitudes and opinions.

Interviewer Cheating

interviewer cheating
The practice by interviewers of filling in fake answers or falsifying questionnaires.

Interviewer cheating occurs when an interviewer falsifies entire questionnaires or fills in answers to questions that have been intentionally skipped. Some interviewers cheat to finish an interview as quickly as possible or to avoid questions about sensitive topics.

If interviewers are suspected of faking questionnaires, they should be told that a small percentage of respondents will be called back to confirm whether the initial interview was actually conducted. This should discourage interviewers from cheating.

Now that we have examined the sources of error in surveys, you may have lost some of your optimism about survey research. Don't be discouraged! The discussion emphasized the bad news because it is important for marketing managers to realize that surveys are not a panacea. There are, however, ways to handle and reduce survey errors. Much of the remainder of this book discusses various techniques for reducing bias in marketing research. The good news lies ahead!

CLASSIFYING SURVEY RESEARCH BY METHOD OF COMMUNICATION

Now that we have discussed the various advantages and disadvantages of surveys in general, we will classify surveys according to the method of communication used.

Survey data are obtained when individuals respond to questions asked by interviewers (interviews) or to questions they have read (questionnaires). Interviewers may communicate with respondents face to face or over the telephone. In a sample survey using a self-administered questionnaire, distribution by mail is the most common way to obtain a representative sample, but other means of distribution, such as via the Internet, are growing in popularity. Each technique for conducting surveys has its merits and shortcomings.

USING INTERVIEWS TO COMMUNICATE WITH RESPONDENTS

Interviews can be categorized based on the medium the researcher uses in communicating with individuals and recording data. For example, interviews may be conducted door-to-door, in shopping malls, or on the telephone. Traditionally, interview results have been recorded using paper and pencil, but computers are increasingly supporting survey research.

We begin our discussion of interviewing by examining the general characteristics of face-to-face personal interviews. Then we look at the unique characteristics of door-to-door personal interviews and personal interviews conducted in shopping malls. In the next section, we investigate telephone interviewing.

PERSONAL INTERVIEWS

personal interview
An interview that gathers information through face-to-face contact with individuals.

A **personal interview** is a form of direct communication in which an interviewer asks respondents questions face to face. This versatile and flexible method is a two-way conversation between interviewer and a respondent.

Advantages of Personal Interviews

Marketing researchers find that personal interviews offer many unique advantages. One of the most important is the opportunity for feedback.

The Opportunity for Feedback Personal interviews provide an opportunity to give feedback to the respondent. For example, in a personal interview a consumer who is reluctant to provide sensitive information may be reassured that his or her answers will be strictly confidential. Personal interviews offer the lowest chance of misinterpretation of questions because the interviewer can clarify any difficulties respondents have with the instructions or questions. Circumstances may dictate that at the conclusion of the interview, the respondent be given additional information concerning the purpose of the study. This is easily accomplished with the personal interview.

Probing Complex Answers An important characteristic of personal interviews is the opportunity to follow up by probing. If a respondent's answer is too brief or unclear, the researcher may probe for a more comprehensive or clearer explanation. In **probing,** the interviewer asks for clarification or expansion of answers using standardized questions such as "Can you tell me more about what you had in mind?"

Although interviewers are expected to ask questions exactly as they appear on the questionnaire, probing allows them some flexibility. Depending on the research purpose, personal interviews vary in the degree to which questions are structured and in the amount of probing required. The personal interview is especially useful for obtaining unstructured information. Skilled interviewers can handle complex questions that cannot easily be asked in telephone or mail surveys.

Length of Interview If the research objective requires an extremely lengthy questionnaire, personal interviews may be the only alternative. Generally, telephone interviews last less than 10 minutes, whereas a personal interview can be much longer, even up to 3 hours.

Completeness of Questionnaires The social interaction between a well-trained interviewer and a respondent in a personal interview increases the likelihood that the respondent will answer all the items on the questionnaire. The respondent who grows bored with a telephone interview may terminate the interview at his or her discretion simply by hanging up. Self-administration of a mail questionnaire, on the other hand, requires more effort by the respondent. Rather than write lengthy responses, however, the respondent may fail to complete some of the questions. **Item nonresponse**—failure to provide an answer to a question—is less likely to occur when an experienced interviewer asks questions directly.

Props and Visual Aids Interviewing respondents face to face allows the investigator to show them new product samples, sketches of proposed advertising, movie clips, or other visual aids. In a survey to determine whether a super-lightweight chain saw should be manufactured, visual props were necessary because the concept of weight is difficult to imagine. Two small chain saws currently on the market and a third, wooden prototype disguised and weighted to look and feel like the proposed model were put in the back of a station wagon. Respondents were asked to go to the car, pick up each chain saw, and compare them. This research could not have been done in a telephone interview or mail survey.

High Participation The presence of an interviewer generally increases the percentage of people willing to complete the interview. Respondents typically are required to do no reading or writing; all they have to do is talk.

---

probing
The verbal prompts made by an interviewer when the respondent must be motivated to communicate his or her answer more fully; used to get respondents to enlarge on, clarify, or explain answers.

item nonresponse
Failure by a respondent to answer a question on a questionnaire.

Entryware data collection software from Techneos Systems (http://www.techneos.com) can be used on Palm handheld computers to automate personal interviews. Using easy-to-carry handheld computers increases the time efficiency of interviewers and eliminates the need for later data entry.

People enjoy sharing information and insights with friendly and sympathetic interviewers.

Disadvantages of Personal Interviews

Personal interviews also have some disadvantages. Respondents are not anonymous and therefore may be reluctant to provide confidential information to another person. Suppose a survey asked top executives, "Do you see any major internal instabilities or threats (people, money, material, etc.) to the achievement of your marketing objectives?" Many managers may be reluctant to answer this sensitive question honestly in a personal interview in which their identities are known.

Interviewer Influence   Some evidence suggests that demographic characteristics of the interviewer influence respondents' answers. For example, one research study revealed that male interviewers produced larger amounts of interviewer variance than female interviewers in a survey in which 85 percent of the respondents were female. Older interviewers who interviewed older respondents produced more variance than other age combinations, while younger interviewers who interviewed younger respondents produced the least variance.[7]

Differential interviewer techniques may be a source of bias. The rephrasing of a question, the interviewer's tone of voice, or the interviewer's appearance may influence the respondent's answer. Consider the interviewer who has conducted 100 personal interviews. During the next one, he or she may lose concentration and either selectively perceive or anticipate the respondent's answer. The interpretation of the response may differ somewhat from what the respondent intended. Typically the public thinks of the person who does marketing research as a dedicated scientist. Unfortunately, some interviewers do not fit that ideal. Considerable interviewer variability exists. Cheating is possible; interviewers may cut corners to save time and energy, faking parts of their reports by dummying up part or all of the questionnaire. Control over interviewers is important to ensure that difficult, embarrassing, or time-consuming questions are handled in the proper manner.

Lack of Anonymity of Respondent   Because a respondent in a personal interview is not anonymous and may be reluctant to provide confidential information to another person, researchers often spend considerable time and effort to phrase sensitive questions to avoid social desirability bias. For example, the interviewer may show the respondent a card that lists possible answers and ask the respondent to read a category number rather than verbalize a sensitive answer.

Cost   Personal interviews are expensive, generally more so than mail, Internet, or telephone surveys. The geographic proximity of respondents, the length and complexity of the questionnaire, and the number of people who are nonrespondents because they could not be contacted (not-at-homes) will all influence the cost of the personal interview.

Door-to-Door Interviews and Shopping Mall Intercepts

Personal interviews may be conducted at the respondents' homes or offices, or in many other places. Increasingly, personal interviews are being conducted in shopping malls. The locale for the interview generally influences the participation rate, and thus the degree to which the sample represents the general population.

Door-to-Door Interviews   The presence of an interviewer at the door generally increases the likelihood that a person will be willing to complete an interview. Because **door-to-door interviews** increase the participation rate, they provide a more representative sample of the population than mail questionnaires do. People who do not have telephones, who have unlisted telephone numbers, or who are otherwise difficult to contact may be reached using door-to-door interviews. Such interviews can help solve the nonresponse problem; however, they may underrepresent some groups and overrepresent others.

Door-to-door interviews may exclude individuals who live in multiple-dwelling units with security systems, such as high-rise apartment dwellers, or executives who are too busy to grant personal interviews during business hours. Telephoning an individual in one of these subgroups to make an appointment may make the total sample more representative; however, obtaining a representative sample of this security-conscious subgroup based on a listing in the telephone directory may be difficult.

People who are at home and willing to participate, especially if interviewing is conducted in the daytime, are somewhat more likely to be over 65 years of age and to be homemakers or retired people. These and other variables related to respondents' tendencies to stay at home may affect participation.

Callbacks   When a person selected to be in the sample cannot be contacted on the first visit, a systematic procedure is normally initiated to call back at another time. **Callbacks,** or attempts to recontact individuals selected for the sample, are the major means of reducing nonresponse error. Calling back a sampling unit is more expensive than interviewing the person the first time around, because subjects who initially were not at home generally are more widely dis-

door-to-door interview
A personal interview conducted at the respondent's home or place of business.

callback
An attempt to recontact an individual selected for a sample who was not available initially.

persed geographically than the original sample units. Callbacks in door-to-door interviews are important because not-at-home individuals (e.g., working parents) may systematically vary from those who are at home (nonworking parents, retired people, and the like).

Mall Intercept Interviews

Personal interviews conducted in shopping malls are referred to as **mall intercept interviews,** or *shopping center sampling.* Interviewers typically intercept shoppers at a central point within the mall or at an entrance and then ask respondents to come to a permanent research facility to taste new food items or view advertisements. The main reason for conducting mall intercept interviews is their lower cost. No travel is required to the respondent's home; instead, the respondents come to the interviewer, and many interviews thus can be conducted quickly.

The mall intercept interview allows the researcher to show large, heavy, or immobile visual materials, such as a television commercial, or give an individual a product to take home and use after she or he agrees to be recontacted later by telephone. Mall intercept interviews are also valuable when the cooking and tasting of food must be closely coordinated and timed to follow each other. They may also be appropriate when a consumer durable product must be demonstrated.

A major problem with mall intercept interviews is that individuals usually are in a hurry to shop, so the incidence of refusal is high—an average of 54 to 56 percent.[8] Nevertheless, the commercial marketing research industry conducts more personal interviews in shopping malls than it conducts door to door.

In a mall interview, the researcher must recognize that she or he should not be looking for a representative sample of the total population. Each mall will have its own target market's characteristics, and there is likely to be a larger bias than with careful household probability sampling. However, personal interviews in shopping malls are appropriate when the target group is similar to shoppers at the malls where the interviews take place.

Global Considerations

Willingness to participate in a personal interview varies dramatically around the world. For example, in many Middle Eastern countries, women would never consent to be interviewed by a man. Also in many countries, the idea of discussing grooming behavior and personal care products with a stranger would be highly offensive. Few people would consent to be interviewed on such topics.

The norms for appropriate business conduct also influence business people's willingness to provide information to interviewers. For example, conducting business-to-business interviews in Japan during business hours is difficult because managers, who are deeply loyal to their firm, believe they have an absolute responsibility to oversee their employees while on the job. In some cultures, when a business person is reluctant to be interviewed, it may be possible to get a reputable third party to intervene so that an interview may take place.

TELEPHONE INTERVIEWS

Telephone interviews have several distinctive characteristics that set them apart from other survey techniques. First, we will consider the advantages and disadvantages of these characteristics.

AMERITECH'S PRIVACY MANAGER

Ameritech's new phone service called Privacy Manager is intended to screen annoying sales calls from telemarketers.[9] However, it is also sure to have an impact on researchers using telephone surveys.

Ameritech's chief executive says that in product usage tests with 200 customers, reaction to Privacy Manager was off the charts. "We have never had a product test this good," says the CEO, including voice mail and caller ID. "It satisfied a need that consumers have just been pleading to have resolved."

Here's how it works: A customer needs to have a caller ID display box first, and the Privacy Manager service costs $3.95 a month. Calls normally shown on the ID screen with a name and number go right through. But any calls made from phone numbers classified as "private," "blocked," "out of area," "unavailable," or "unknown" are intercepted. A recording comes on and asks outside callers to reveal their identity by speaking their name.

Anyone who doesn't leave a name is automatically disconnected. If a caller leaves a name, the person they attempted to call hears the phone ring, and a recorded message says: "This is Privacy Manager. You have a call from . . ." and then the name of the caller. The customer is given three choices: accept the call, reject it, or play a message that says: "We don't accept telemarketing calls. Please add me to your do-not-call list."

Characteristics of Telephone Interviews

Speed   One advantage of telephone interviewing is the speed of data collection. Rather than taking several weeks for data collection (as with mail or personal interviews), hundreds of telephone interviews can be conducted literally overnight. When the interviewer enters the respondents' answers directly into a computerized system, the data processing speeds up even more.

Cost   As the cost of personal interviews continues to increase, telephone interviews are becoming relatively inexpensive. It is estimated that the cost of telephone interviews is less than 25 percent of the cost of door-to-door personal interviews. Travel time and costs are eliminated. However, the typical Internet survey is less expensive than a telephone survey.

Absence of Face-to-Face Contact   Telephone interviews are more impersonal than face-to-face interviews. Respondents may answer embarrassing or confidential questions more willingly in a telephone interview than in a personal interview. However, mail and Internet surveys, although not perfect, are better media for gathering extremely sensitive information because they can be completely anonymous. There is some evidence that people provide information on income and other financial matters only reluctantly, even in telephone interviews. Such questions may be personally threatening for a variety of reasons, and high refusal rates for this type of question occur with each form of survey research.

Although telephone calls may be less threatening because the interviewer is not physically present, the absence of face-to-face contact can also be a liability.

The respondent cannot see that the interviewer is still writing down the previous comment and may continue to elaborate on an answer. If the respondent pauses to think about an answer, the interviewer may not realize this and may go on to the next question. Hence, there is a greater tendency for interviewers to record no answers and incomplete answers in telephone interviews than in personal interviews.

Cooperation   In some neighborhoods, people are reluctant to allow a stranger to come inside the house or even stop on the doorstep. The same people, however, may be perfectly willing to cooperate with a telephone survey request. Likewise, interviewers may be somewhat reluctant to conduct face-to-face interviews in certain neighborhoods, especially during the evening hours. Telephone interviewing avoids these problems. However, some individuals refuse to participate in telephone interviews, and the researcher should be aware of potential nonresponse bias. Finally, there is some evidence that the likelihood that a call will go unanswered because a respondent is not at home varies by the time of day, the day of the week, and the month.

One trend is very clear. In the last decade, telephone response rates have dropped from 40 percent to around 15 percent.[10] Willingness to cooperate with telephone interviewing has declined over the years. In addition, it is increasingly difficult to establish contact with potential respondents, for three major reasons: (1) the proliferation of telephone numbers dedicated exclusively to fax machines and/or computers, (2) the widespread use of a non-dedicated phone line to access the Internet, and (3) the use of call-screening devices to avoid unwanted calls.[11]

Many people who own telephone answering machines will not return a call to help someone conduct a survey. Some researchers argue that leaving the proper message on an answering machine will produce return calls. The message left on the machine should explicitly state that the purpose of the call is not sales related.[12] Others believe no message should be left because researchers will reach respondents when they call back. The logic is based on the fact that answering machines are usually not turned on 100 percent of the time. Thus, if enough callbacks are made at different times and on different days, most respondents will be reached.[13] Caller ID services can have the same effect as answering machines if respondents do not pick up the phone when the display reads "out of area" or when an unfamiliar survey organization's name and number appear on the display.

Refusal to cooperate with interviews is directly related to interview length. A major study of survey research found that interviews of 5 minutes or less had a refusal rate of 21 percent; interviews of between 6 and 12 minutes had 41 percent refusal rates; and interviews of 13 minutes or more had 47 percent rates. In unusual cases a few highly interested respondents will put up with longer interviews. A good rule of thumb is to keep telephone interviews approximately 10 to 15 minutes long. In general, 30 minutes is the maximum amount of time most respondents will spend unless they are highly interested in the survey subject.

Representative Samples   Practical difficulties complicate obtaining representative samples based on listings in the telephone book. Slightly more than 96 percent of households in the United States have telephones. People without phones are more likely to be poor, aged, rural, or living in the South. Unlisted phone numbers and numbers too new to be printed in the directory are a greater problem. People have unlisted phone numbers for two reasons: because of mobility and by choice. Individuals whose phone numbers are unlisted because of a recent move differ slightly from those with published numbers. The unlisted group tends to be younger, more urban, and less likely to own a single-family dwelling. Households that maintain unlisted phone numbers by choice tend to have higher incomes. And, as previously mentioned, a number of low-income households are unlisted by circumstance. Researchers conducting surveys in areas where the proportion of unlisted phone numbers is high, such as in California (Sacramento, 71.6 percent; Oakland, 71.4 percent; Los Angeles/Long Beach, 69.8 percent), should be aware of this situation.[14] In other markets, such as Knoxville, Tennessee, where less than 16 percent of phone numbers are unlisted, this may not be a major problem. Nationally, slightly less than 30 percent of phone numbers are unlisted.

random digit dialing
Use of telephone exchanges and a table of random numbers to contact respondents with unlisted phone numbers.

The problem of unlisted phone numbers can be partially resolved through the use of random digit dialing. **Random digit dialing** eliminates the counting of names in a list (for example, calling every fiftieth name in a column) and subjectively determining whether a directory listing is a business, institution, or legitimate household. In the simplest form of random digit dialing, telephone exchanges (prefixes) for the geographic areas in the sample are obtained. Using a table of random numbers, the last four digits of the telephone number are selected. Telephone directories can be ignored entirely or used in combination with the assignment of one or several random digits. Random digit dialing also helps overcome problems due to new listings and recent changes in numbers. Unfortunately, the refusal rate in commercial random digit dialing studies (approximately 40 percent) is higher than the 25 percent refusal rate for telephone surveys that use only listed telephone numbers.

Callbacks   An unanswered call, a busy signal, or a respondent who is not at home requires a callback. Telephone callbacks are much easier to make than callbacks in personal interviews. However, as mentioned, the ownership of telephone answering machines is growing, and their effects on callbacks need to be studied.

Limited Duration   Respondents who run out of patience with the interview can merely hang up. To encourage participation, interviews should be relatively short. The length of the telephone interview is definitely limited.

Lack of Visual Medium   Because visual aids cannot be used in telephone interviews, packaging research, copy testing of television and print advertising, and concept tests that require visual materials cannot be conducted by phone. Certain attitude scales and measuring instruments, such as the semantic differential (see Chapter 10), cannot be used easily because they require the respondent to see a graphic scale.

Central Location Interviewing

Research agencies or interviewing services typically conduct all telephone interviews from a central location. They contract for WATS (Wide-Area Telecommunications Service) lines from long-distance telephone services at fixed rates, which allow them to make unlimited telephone calls throughout the entire country or within specific geographic areas. Such **central location interviewing** allows firms to hire a staff of professional interviewers and to supervise and control the quality of interviewing more effectively. When telephone interviews are centralized and computerized, an agency or business can benefit from additional cost economies.

central location interviewing
Telephone interviews conducted from a central location using WATS lines at fixed charges.

Computer-Assisted Telephone Interviewing

computer-assisted telephone interview (CATI)
A telephone interview in which answers to questions are entered directly into a computer for processing.

Advances in computer technology allow responses to telephone interviews to be entered directly into the computer in a process known as **computer-assisted telephone interviewing (CATI).** Telephone interviewers are seated at computer terminals. Monitors display the questionnaires, one question at a time, along with precoded possible responses to each question. The interviewer reads each question as it appears on the screen. When the respondent answers, the interviewer enters the response directly into the computer, and it is automatically stored in the computer's memory. The computer then displays the next question on the screen. Computer-assisted telephone interviewing requires that answers to the questionnaire be highly structured. If a respondent gives an unacceptable answer (that is, one not precoded and programmed), the computer will reject it.

Computer-assisted telephone interviewing systems include telephone management systems that select phone numbers, dial the numbers automatically, and perform other labor-saving functions. These systems can automatically control sample selection by randomly generating names or fulfilling a sample quota. A computer can generate an automatic callback schedule. A typical call management system might schedule recontact attempts to recall no answers after 2 hours and busy numbers after 10 minutes and allow the interviewer to enter a more favorable time slot (day and hour) when a respondent indicates that he or she is too busy to be interviewed. Software systems also allow researchers to request daily status reports on the number of completed interviews relative to quotas.

Computerized Voice-Activated Telephone Interviews

Technological advances have combined computerized telephone dialing and voice-activated computer messages to allow researchers to conduct telephone interviews without human interviewers. However, researchers have found that computerized voice-activated telephone interviewing works best with very short, simple questionnaires. One system includes a voice-synthesized module controlled by a microprocessor. With it the sponsor is able to register a caller's single response such as "true/false," "yes/no," "like/dislike," or "for/against." This type of system has been used by television and radio stations to register callers' responses to certain issues. One system begins with an announcement that the respondent is listening to a recorded message. Many people are intrigued with the idea of talking to a robot or a computer, so they stay on the line. The computer then asks questions, leaving blank tape in between to record the answers. If respondents do not answer the first two questions, the computer disconnects and goes to the next call.

Global Considerations

Different cultures often have different norms about proper telephone behavior. For example, business-to-business researchers have learned that Latin American business people will not open up to strangers on the telephone. Hence, researchers in Latin America usually find personal interviews more suitable than telephone surveys. In Japan, respondents consider it ill-mannered if telephone interviews last more than 20 minutes.

SELF-ADMINISTERED QUESTIONNAIRES

Many surveys do not require an interviewer's presence. Marketing researchers distribute questionnaires to consumers through the mail and in many other ways (see Exhibit 7.2). They insert questionnaires in packages and magazines. They

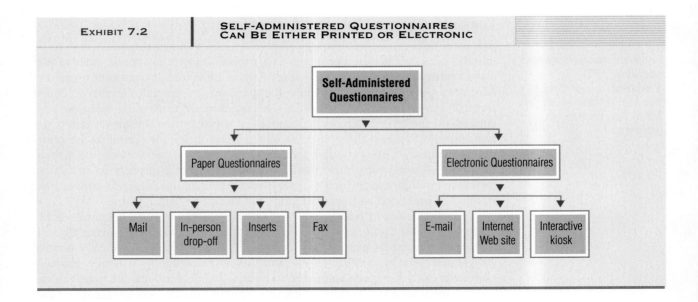

may place questionnaires at points of purchase or in high-traffic locations in stores or malls. They may even fax questionnaires to individuals. Questionnaires are usually printed on paper, but they may be posted on the Internet or sent via e-mail. No matter how the **self-administered questionnaires** are distributed, they are different from interviews because the respondent takes responsibility for reading and answering the questions.

Self-administered questionnaires present a challenge to the marketing researcher because they rely on the clarity of the written word rather than on the skills of the interviewer. The nature of self-administered questionnaires is best illustrated by explaining mail questionnaires.

self-administered questionnaire
Survey in which the respondent takes the responsibility for reading and answering the questions.

Mail Questionnaires

A **mail survey** is a self-administered questionnaire sent to respondents through the mail. This paper-and-pencil method has several advantages and disadvantages.

mail survey
A self-administered questionnaire sent to respondents through the mail.

Geographic Flexibility   Mail questionnaires can reach a geographically dispersed sample simultaneously because interviewers are not required. Respondents (such as farmers) who are located in isolated areas or those (such as executives) who are otherwise difficult to reach can easily be contacted by mail. For example, a pharmaceutical firm may find that doctors are not available for personal or telephone interviews. However, a mail survey can reach both rural and urban doctors who practice in widely dispersed geographic areas.

Cost   Mail questionnaires are relatively inexpensive compared to personal interviews and telephone surveys, though they are not cheap. Most include follow-up mailings, which require additional postage and printing costs. And it usually isn't cost-effective to try to cut costs on printing—questionnaires photocopied on poor-grade paper have a greater likelihood of being thrown in the wastebasket than those prepared with more expensive, high-quality printing.

Respondent Convenience

Mail surveys and other self-administered questionnaires can be filled out when the respondents have time; thus, there is a better chance that respondents will take time to think about their replies. Many hard-to-reach respondents place a high value on convenience and thus are best contacted by mail. In some situations, particularly in business-to-business marketing research, mail questionnaires allow respondents to collect facts, such as sales statistics, that they may not be able to recall without checking. Being able to check information by verifying records or, in household surveys, by consulting with other family members should provide more valid, factual information than either personal or telephone interviews would allow. A catalog retailer may use mail surveys to estimate sales volume for catalog items by sending a mock catalog as part of the questionnaire. Respondents would be asked to indicate how likely they would be to order selected items. Using the mail allows respondents to consult other family members and to make their decisions within a reasonable time span.

Anonymity of Respondent

In the cover letter that accompanies a mail or self-administered questionnaire, marketing researchers almost always state that the respondents' answers will be confidential. Respondents are more likely to provide sensitive or embarrassing information when they can remain anonymous.

For example, personal interviews and a mail survey conducted simultaneously asked the question "Have you borrowed money at a regular bank?" Researchers noted a 17 percent response rate for the personal interviews and a 42 percent response rate for the mail survey. Although random sampling error may have accounted for part of this difference, the results suggest that for research on personal and sensitive financial issues, mail surveys are more confidential than personal interviews.

Anonymity can also reduce social desirability bias. People are more likely to agree with controversial issues, such as extreme political candidates, when completing self-administered questionnaires than when speaking to interviewers on the phone or at their doorsteps.

Absence of Interviewer

Although the absence of an interviewer can induce respondents to reveal sensitive or socially undesirable information, it can also be a disadvantage. Once the respondent receives the questionnaire, the questioning process is beyond the researcher's control. Although the printed stimulus is the same, each respondent will attach a different personal meaning to each question. Selective perception operates in research as well as in advertising. The respondent does not have the opportunity to question the interviewer. Problems that might be clarified in a personal or telephone interview can remain misunderstandings in a mail survey. There is no interviewer to probe for additional information or clarification of an answer, and the recorded answers must be assumed to be complete.

Respondents have the opportunity to read the entire questionnaire before they answer individual questions. Often the text of a later question will provide information that affects responses to earlier questions.

Standardized Questions Mail questionnaires typically are highly standardized, and the questions are quite structured. Questions and instructions must be clear-cut and straightforward; if they are difficult to comprehend, respondents will make their own interpretations, which may be wrong. Interviewing allows for feedback from the interviewer regarding the respondent's comprehension of the questionnaire. An interviewer who notices that the first 50 respondents are having some difficulty understanding a question can report this to the research analyst so that revisions can be made. With a mail survey, however, once the questionnaires are mailed, it is difficult to change the format or the questions.

Time Is Money If time is a factor in mangement's interest in the research results, or if attitudes are rapidly changing (for example, toward a political event), mail surveys may not be the best communication medium. A minimum of 2 or 3 weeks is necessary to receive the majority of the responses. Follow-up mailings, which usually are sent when the returns begin to trickle in, require an additional 2 or 3 weeks. The time between the first mailing and the cutoff date (when questionnaires will no longer be accepted) normally is 6 to 8 weeks. In a regional or local study, personal interviews can be conducted more quickly. However, conducting a national study by mail may be substantially faster than conducting personal interviews across the nation.

Length Mail questionnaires vary considerably in length, ranging from extremely short, postcard questionnaires to lengthy, multipage booklets that require respondents to fill in thousands of answers. A general rule of thumb is that a mail questionnaire should not exceed 6 pages in length. When a questionnaire requires a respondent to expend a great deal of effort, an incentive is generally required to induce the respondent to return the questionnaire. The following sections discuss several ways to obtain high response rates even when questionnaires are longer than average.

Response Rates

Questionnaires that are boring, unclear, or too complex get thrown in the wastebasket. A poorly designed mail questionnaire may be returned by only 15 percent of those sampled; thus, it will have a 15 percent **response rate.** The basic calculation for obtaining a response rate is to count the number of questionnaires returned or completed, then divide the total by the number of eligible people who were contacted or asked to participate in the survey. Typically, the number in the denominator is adjusted for faulty addresses and similar problems that reduce the number of eligible participants.[15]

The major limitations of mail questionnaires relate to response problems. Respondents who complete the questionnaire may not be typical of all people in the sample. Individuals with a special interest in the topic are more likely to respond to a mail survey than those who are indifferent.

A researcher has no assurance that the intended subject will be the person who fills out the questionnaire. The wrong person answering the questions may be a problem when surveying corporate executives, physicians, and other professionals, who may pass questionnaires on to subordinates to complete.

Mail survey respondents tend to be better educated than nonrespondents. If they return the questionnaire at all, poorly educated respondents who cannot read and write well may skip open-ended questions (to which they are required to write out their answers). Rarely will a mail survey have an 80 to 90 percent response rate, as can be achieved with personal interviews. However, the use of

response rate
The number of questionnaires returned or completed divided by the total number of eligible people who were contacted or asked to participate in the survey.

follow-up mailings and other techniques may increase the response rate to an acceptable percentage.

Increasing Response Rates for Mail Surveys

Nonresponse error is always a potential problem with mail surveys. Individuals who are interested in the general subject of the survey are more likely to respond than those with less interest or little experience. Thus, people who hold extreme positions on an issue are more likely to respond than individuals who are largely indifferent to the topic. To minimize this bias, researchers have developed a number of techniques to increase the response rate to mail surveys. For example, almost all surveys include postage-paid return envelopes. Forcing respondents to pay their own postage can substantially reduce the response rate. Using a stamped envelope instead of a bulk rate business reply envelope increases response rates even more.[16] Designing and formatting attractive questionnaires and wording questions so that they are easy to understand also help ensure a good response rate. However, special efforts may be required even with a sound questionnaire. Several of these are discussed in the following subsections.

cover letter
Letter that accompanies a questionnaire to induce the reader to complete and return the questionnaire.

Cover Letter The **cover letter** that accompanies a questionnaire or is printed on the first page of the questionnaire booklet is an important means of inducing a reader to complete and return the questionnaire. Exhibit 7.3 illustrates a cover letter and some of the points considered by a marketing research professional to be important in gaining respondents' attention and cooperation. The first paragraph of the letter explains why the study is important. The basic appeal alludes to the social usefulness of responding. Two other frequently used appeals are asking for help ("Will you do us a favor?") and the egotistical appeal ("Your opinions are important!"). Most cover letters ensure confidentiality, invite the recipient to use an enclosed postage-paid reply envelope, describe any incentive or reward for participation, explain that answering the questionnaire will not be difficult and will take only a short time, and describe how the person was scientifically selected for participation.

A personalized letter addressed to a specific individual shows the respondent that he or she is important. Including an individually typed cover letter on letterhead rather than a printed form is an important element in increasing the response rate in mail surveys.[17]

Money Helps The respondent's motivation for returning a questionnaire may be increased by offering monetary incentives or premiums. Although pens, lottery tickets, and a variety of premiums have been used, monetary incentives appear to be the most effective and least biasing incentive. Although money may be useful to all respondents, its primary advantage may be that it attracts attention and creates a sense of obligation. It is perhaps for this reason that monetary incentives work for all income categories. Often, cover letters try to boost response rates with messages such as "We know that the attached dollar [or coin] cannot compensate you for your time. It is just a token of our appreciation." Response rates increase dramatically when the monetary incentive is to be sent to a charity of the respondent's choice rather than directly to the respondent.

Interesting Questions The topic of the research and thus the point of the questions cannot be manipulated without changing the definition of the marketing problem. However, certain interesting questions can be added to the questionnaire, perhaps at the beginning, to stimulate respondents' interest and to induce cooperation. Questions that are of little concern to the researchers, but which the

EXHIBIT 7.3 | EXAMPLE OF COVER LETTER FOR HOUSEHOLD SURVEY[18]

Official letterhead	WASHINGTON STATE UNIVERSITY PULLMAN, WASHINGTON 99968 DEPARTMENT OF RURAL SOCIOLOGY ROOM 23, Wilman Hall
Date mailed	April 19, 20XX
Inside address in matching type	Oliver Jones 2190 Fontane Road Spokane, Washington 99467
What study is about; its social usefulness	Bills have been introduced in Congress and our State Legislature to encourage the growth of rural and small town areas and slow down that of large cities. These bills could greatly affect the quality of life provided in both rural and urban places. However, no one really knows in what kinds of communities people like you want to live or what is thought about these proposed programs.
Why recipient is important (and, if needed, who should complete the questionnaire)	Your household is one of a small number in which people are being asked to give their opinion on these matters. It was drawn in a random sample of the entire state. In order that the results will truly represent the thinking of the people of Washington, it is important that each questionnaire be completed and returned. It is also important that we have about the same number of men and women participating in this study. Thus, we would like the questionnaire for your household to be completed by an adult female. If none is present, then it should be completed by an adult male.
Promise of confidentiality; explanation of identification number	You may be assured of complete confidentiality. The questionnaire has an identification number for mailing purposes only. This is so that we may check your name off of the mailing list when your questionnaire is returned. Your name will never be placed on the questionnaire.
Usefulness of study	The results of this research will be made available to officials and representatives in our state's government, members of Congress, and all interested citizens. You may receive a summary of results by writing "copy of results requested" on the back of the return envelope, and printing your name and address below it. Please do not put this information on your questionnaire itself.
Token reward for participation	
What to do if questions arise	I would be most happy to answer any questions you might have. Please write or call. The telephone number is (509) 335-8623.
Appreciation	Thank you for your assistance.
	Sincerely,
Pressed blue ballpoint signature	
Title	Don A. Dillman Project Director

respondents want to answer, may provide respondents who are indifferent to the major portion of the questionnaire with a reason for responding.[19]

Follow-Ups   The response rates for most mail surveys start off relatively high for the first two weeks after questionnaires begin to be returned, then gradually taper off. After responses from the first wave of mailings begin to trickle in, most studies use **follow-ups**—letter or postcard reminders. The follow-up letter generally asks respondents to return the questionnaire because a 100 percent response rate is important for the survey's purposes. A follow-up may include a second questionnaire or may merely be a reminder to respondents to fill out the questionnaire that was initially mailed.

follow-up
A letter or postcard reminding a respondent to return a questionnaire.

Advance Notification   Advance notification, by either letter or telephone, that a questionnaire will be arriving has been successful in increasing response rates in some situations. Advance notices that go out closer to the questionnaire mailing time produce better results than those sent too far in advance. The optimal lead time for advance notification is approximately 3 days before the mail survey is to arrive.[20]

Survey Sponsorship   Auspices bias may result from the sponsorship of a survey. One industrial marketer wished to conduct a survey of its wholesalers to learn their stocking policies and attitudes concerning competing manufacturers. A mail questionnaire sent on the corporate letterhead very likely would have received a much lower response rate than the questionnaire actually sent, which used the letterhead of a commercial marketing research firm. Sponsorship by well-known and prestigious organizations such as universities or government agencies may also significantly influence response rates.

Keying Mail Questionnaires with Codes   A marketing researcher planning a follow-up letter or postcard should not disturb respondents who already have returned the questionnaires. The expense of mailing questionnaires to those who already have responded is usually avoidable. One device for eliminating those who have already responded from the follow-up mailing list is to mark the questionnaires so that they may be keyed to identify members of the sample as respondents or nonrespondents by using code numbers. Blind keying of questionnaires on a return envelope (systematically varying the job number or room number of the marketing research department, for example) or visible code numbers on the questionnaire have been used for this purpose. Visible keying is indicated with statements such as "The sole purpose of the number on the last page is to avoid sending a second questionnaire to people who complete and return the first one." Ethical researchers key questionnaires only to increase response rates, thereby preserving respondents' anonymity.

Global Considerations

Researchers conducting surveys in more than one country must recognize that postal services and cultural circumstances differ around the world. For example, Backer Spielvogel & Bates Worldwide advertising agency conducts its Global Scan survey in 18 countries. In the United States, the questionnaire is mailed to individuals selected for the sample, but mail is not used in several other countries. In certain countries, the questionnaire may be personally delivered to respondents because of fear of letter bombs, unreliable delivery service, or low literacy rates.[21]

SELF-ADMINISTERED QUESTIONNAIRES THAT USE OTHER FORMS OF DISTRIBUTION

Many forms of self-administered, printed questionnaires are very similar to mail questionnaires. Airlines frequently pass out questionnaires to passengers during flights. Restaurants, hotels, and other service establishments print short questionnaires on cards so that customers can evaluate the service. *Tennis Magazine, Advertising Age, Wired,* and many other publications have used inserted questionnaires to survey current readers inexpensively, and often the results provide material for a magazine article.

Many manufacturers use their warranty or owner registration cards to collect demographic information and data about where and why products were purchased. Using owner registration cards is an extremely economical technique for tracing trends in consumer habits. Again, problems may arise because people who fill out these self-administered questionnaires differ from those who do not.

Greenfield Online (http://www.greenfieldonline.com) is a marketing company that conducts surveys exclusively online. This advertisement shows that the company offers a variety of services such as concept testing.

Extremely long questionnaires may be dropped off by an interviewer and then picked up later. The **drop-off method** sacrifices some cost savings because it requires traveling to each respondent's location.

Fax Surveys

With fax surveys, potential survey respondents receive and/or return questionnaires via fax machines.[22] A questionnaire inserted in a magazine may instruct the respondent to clip out the questionnaire and fax it to a certain phone number. In a mail survey, a postage-paid envelope places little burden on the respondent. But faxing a questionnaire to a long-distance number requires that the respondent pay for the transmission of the fax. Thus, a disadvantage of **fax surveys** is that only respondents with fax machines who are willing to exert the extra effort will return questionnaires. Again, people with extreme opinions will be more likely to respond.

Questionnaires can also be distributed via fax machine. These fax surveys reduce the sender's printing and postage costs and can be delivered and returned faster than traditional mail surveys. Questionnaires distributed via fax can deal with timely issues. Although most households do not have fax machines, when the sample consists of organizations that are likely to have fax machines, the sample coverage may be adequate.

E-Mail Surveys

Questionnaires can be distributed via e-mail. E-mail is a relatively new method of communication, and many individuals cannot be reached this way. However, certain projects lend themselves to **e-mail surveys,** such as internal surveys of

drop-off method
A survey method that requires the interviewer to travel to the respondent's location to drop off a questionnaire that will be picked up later.

fax survey
A survey that uses fax machines as a way for respondents to receive and return questionnaires.

e-mail survey
Surveys distributed through electronic mail.

employees or satisfaction surveys of retail buyers who regularly deal with an organization via e-mail. The benefits of incorporating a questionnaire in an e-mail include the speed of distribution, lower distribution and processing costs, faster turnaround time, more flexibility, and less handling of paper questionnaires. The speed of e-mail distribution and the quick response time can be major advantages for surveys dealing with time-sensitive issues.

Not much academic research on e-mail surveys has been conducted. Nevertheless, it has been argued that many respondents feel they can be more candid in e-mail than in person or on the telephone, for the same reasons they are candid on other self-administered questionnaires. Nevertheless, in many organizations employees know that their e-mails are not secure and "eavesdropping" by a supervisor could possibly occur. Further, maintaining respondents' anonymity is difficult, because a reply to an e-mail message typically includes the sender's address. Researchers designing e-mail surveys should assure respondents that their answers will be confidential.

Not all e-mail systems have the same capacity: Some handle color and graphics well; others are limited to text. The extensive differences in the capabilities of respondents' computers and e-mail software limit the types of questions and the layout of the e-mail questionnaire. For example, the display settings for computer screens vary widely, and wrap-around of lines may put the questions and the answer choices into strange and difficult-to-read patterns.[23] Many novice e-mail users find it difficult to mark answers in brackets on an e-mail questionnaire and/or to send a completed questionnaire using the e-mail Reply function. For this reason, some researchers give respondents the option to print out the questionnaire, complete it in writing, and return it via regular mail. Unless the

Technological innovation can change more than the way business is done in an industry—it can change entire cultures. The mechanical clock made regular working hours possible. The invention of railroads and the mass production of automobiles changed the way people thought about distance. Television changed the way we think about news and entertainment. And, because the Internet is the most important communication medium since the introduction of television, it is having a profound impact on marketing research. Self-administered polls will increasingly become electronic transactions between people and machines.[24]

research is an internal organizational survey, this, of course, requires the respondent to pay postage.

In general, the guidelines for printed mail surveys apply to e-mail surveys. However, there are some differences, because the cover letter and the questionnaire appear in a single e-mail message. A potential respondent who is not immediately motivated to respond, especially one who considers an unsolicited e-mail survey to be "spam," can quickly hit the Delete button to remove the e-mail. This suggests that e-mail cover letters should be brief and the questionnaires relatively short. The cover letter should explain how the company got the recipient's name. It should include a valid return e-mail address in the "FROM" box and reveal who is conducting the survey. Also, if the e-mail lists more than one address in the "TO" or "CC" field, all recipients will see the entire list of names. This has the potential to cause response bias and nonresponse error. When possible, the e-mail should be addressed to a single person. (The blind carbon copy, or BCC, field can be used if the same message must be sent to an entire sample.)[25]

E-mail has another important role in survey research. E-mail letters can be used as cover letters asking respondents to participate in an Internet survey. Such e-mails typically provide a password and a link to a unique Web site location that requires a password for access.

Internet Surveys

Internet survey
A self-administered questionnaire posted on a Web site.

An **Internet survey** is a self-administered questionnaire posted on a Web site. Respondents provide answers to questions displayed onscreen by highlighting a phrase, clicking an icon, or keying in an answer. Many in the survey research community believe Internet surveys are the wave of the future. Like every other type of survey, Internet surveys have both advantages and disadvantages.

This page from the SurveySite Web site (http://www.surveysite.com) shows part of an Internet survey to assess consumers' attitudes toward banner advertising. The Internet is an excellent medium for survey research on visual materials containing animation. Go to this site to take a demonstration Internet survey.

Speed and Cost-Effectiveness

Internet surveys allow marketers to reach a large audience (possibly a global one), to personalize individual messages, and to secure confidential answers quickly and cost-effectively. These computer-to-computer self-administered questionnaires eliminate the costs of paper, postage, and data entry, as well as other administrative costs. Once an Internet questionnaire has been developed, the incremental cost of reaching additional respondents is marginal. Hence, samples can be larger than with interviews or other types of self-administered questionnaires. Even with larger samples, surveys that used to take many weeks can be conducted in a week or less.

Visual Appeal and Interactivity

Surveys conducted on the Internet can be interactive. The researcher can use more sophisticated lines of questioning based on the respondents' prior answers. Many of these interactive surveys utilize color, sound, and animation, which may help to increase respondents' cooperation and willingness to spend time answering the questionnaires. The Internet is an excellent medium for the presentation of visual materials, such as photographs or drawings of product prototypes, advertisements, and movie trailers. Innovative measuring instruments that take advantage of the ability to adjust backgrounds, fonts, color, and other features have been designed and applied with considerable success.

Digital Marketing Services' Video E-Val is a proprietary technique combining a CD-ROM that is mailed to potential respondents and Internet software that controls the playing of high-quality video clips from the disk.[26] This technique allows researchers to evaluate television commercials, television programs, and other large video files without being restricted by the small percentage of potentially qualified respondents who have access to broadband communications.

Respondent Participation and Cooperation

Participation in some Internet surveys occurs because computer users intentionally navigate to a particular Web site where questions are displayed. For example, a survey of over 10,000 visitors to the Ticketmaster Web site helped Ticketmaster better understand its customer purchase patterns and evaluate visitor satisfaction with the site. In some cases individuals expect to encounter a survey at a Web site; in other cases it is totally unexpected. In some instances the visitor cannot venture beyond the survey page without providing information for the organization's "registration" questionnaire. When the computer user does not expect a survey on a Web site and participation is voluntary, response rates are low. And, as with other questionnaires that rely on voluntary self-selection, participants tend to be more interested in or involved with the subject of the research than the average person.

For many other Internet surveys, respondents are initially contacted via e-mail. Often they are members of consumer panels who have previously indicated their willingness to cooperate. When individuals receive an e-mail invitation to participate, they are given a password or a PIN number. The e-mail invitation also provides a link to a URL or instructs a user to visit a certain Web site that contains a welcome screen. Like a cover letter in a mail survey, the **welcome screen** on an Internet survey serves as a means to gain respondents' cooperation and provides brief instructions. Experienced researchers require a respondent to provide a password or PIN to move from the welcome page to the first question. This prevents access by individuals who are not part of the scientifically selected sample. Assigning a unique password code also allows the researchers to track the responses of each respondent, thereby identifying any respondent who makes an effort to answer the questionnaire more than once.

welcome screen
The first Web page in an Internet survey, which introduces the survey and requests that the respondent enter a password or PIN.

Ideally, the welcome screen contains the name of the research company and information about how to contact the organization if the respondent has a problem or concern. A typical statement might be "If you have any concerns or questions about this survey or if you experience any technical difficulties, please contact [name of research organization]."

Representative Samples   The population to be studied, the purpose of the research, and the sampling methods determine the quality of Internet samples, which varies substantially. If the sample consists merely of those who visit a Web page and voluntarily fill out a questionnaire, it is not likely to be representative of the entire U.S. population, because of self-selection error. However, if the purpose of the research is to evaluate how visitors feel about a Web site, randomly selecting every 100th visitor may accomplish the study's purpose. Scientifically drawn samples from a consumer panel or samples randomly generated in other ways can also be representative.[27]

Of course, a major disadvantage of Internet surveys is that many individuals in the general population cannot access the Internet. And, all people with Internet access do not have the same level of technology. Many people with low-speed Internet connections (low bandwidth) cannot quickly download high-resolution graphic files. Many lack sufficiently powerful computers or software that is compatible with advanced features programmed into many Internet questionnaires. Some individuals have minimal computer skills. They may not know how to navigate through and provide answers to an Internet questionnaire. For example, the advanced audio and video streaming technology of RealOne Player or Windows Media Player software can be used to incorporate a television commercial and questions about its effectiveness into an Internet survey. However, some respondents might find downloading the file too slow or even impossible; others might not have the RealOne Player or Windows Media Player software; and still others might not know how to use the streaming media software to view the commercial.

It appears that for the foreseeable future, Internet surveys sampling the general public should be designed with the recognition that problems may arise for the reasons just described. Thus, photographs, animation, or other cutting-edge technological features created on the researcher's/Web designer's powerful computer may have to be simplified or eliminated so that all respondents can interact at the same level of technological sophistication.

Because Internet surveys can be accessed anytime (24/7) from anywhere, they can reach certain hard-to-reach respondents, such as doctors. Chapter 12 discusses sampling techniques for Internet surveys.

Accurate Real-Time Data Capture   The computer-to-computer nature of Internet surveys means that each respondent's answers are entered directly into the researcher's computer as soon as the questionnaire is submitted. In addition, the questionnaire software may be programmed to reject improper data entry. For example, on a paper questionnaire a respondent might incorrectly check two responses even though the instructions call for a single answer. In an Internet survey, this mistake can be corrected interactively as the survey is taking place. Thus, the data capture is more accurate than when humans are involved.

Real-time data capture allows for real-time data analysis. A researcher can review up-to-the-minute sample size counts and tabulation data from an Internet survey in real time.

Callbacks   When the sample for an Internet survey is drawn from a consumer panel, it is easy to recontact those who have not completed the survey questionnaire. It is often a simple matter of having computer software automatically send e-mail reminders to panel members who did not visit the welcome page. Computer software can also identify the passwords of respondents who completed only a portion of the questionnaire and send those people customized messages. Sometimes such e-mails offer additional incentives to those individuals who terminated the questionnaire with only a few additional questions to answer, so that they are motivated to comply with the request to finish the questionnaire.

Personalized and Flexible Questioning   Computer-interactive Internet surveys are programmed in much the same way as computer-assisted telephone interviews. That is, the software that is used allows questioning to branch off into two or more different lines depending on a respondent's answer to a filtered question. The difference is that there is no interviewer. The respondent interacts directly with software on a Web site. In other words, the computer program asks questions in a sequence determined by the respondent's previous answers. The questions appear on the computer screen, and answers are recorded by simply pressing a key or clicking an icon, thus immediately entering the data into the computer's memory. Of course, these methods avoid labor costs associated with data collection and processing of paper-and-pencil questionnaires.

This ability to sequence questions based on previous responses is a major advantage of computer-assisted surveys. The computer can be programmed to skip from question 6 to question 9 if the answer to question 6 is no. Furthermore, responses to previous questions can lead to questions that can be personalized for individual respondents. (For example, "When you cannot buy your favorite brand, Revlon, what brand of lipstick do you prefer?") Often the respondent's name appears in questions to personalize the questionnaire. Fewer and more relevant questions speed up the response process and increase the respondent's involvement with the survey.

Use of a variety of **dialog boxes** (windows that prompt the respondent to enter information) allows designers of Internet questionnaires to be creative and flexible in the presentation of questions. Chapter 11 discusses software issues, the design of questions, and questionnaire layouts for Internet surveys.

dialog box
A window that opens on a computer screen to prompt the user to enter information.

Respondent Anonymity   Respondents are more likely to provide sensitive or embarrassing information when they can remain anonymous. The anonymity of the Internet encourages respondents to provide honest answers to sensitive questions.

Response Rates   As mentioned earlier, with a password system, people who have not participated in a survey in a pre-determined period of time can be sent a friendly e-mail reminder asking them to participate before the study ends. This kind of follow-up, along with preliminary notification, interesting early questions, and variations of most other techniques for increasing response rates to mail questionnaires, is recommended for Internet surveys.

Unlike mail surveys, Internet surveys do not offer the opportunity to send a physical incentive, such as a dollar bill, to the respondent. Incentives to respond to a survey must be in the form of a promise of a future reward—for example, "As a token of appreciation for completing this survey, the sponsor of the survey will make a sizable contribution to a national charity. You can vote for your preferred charity at the end of the survey." While some researchers have had success with promising incentives, academic research about Internet surveys is sparse, and currently there are few definitive answers about the most effective ways to increase response rates.

Security Concerns   Many organizations worry that hackers or competitors may access Web sites in order to discover new product concepts, new advertising campaigns, and other top-secret ideas. Respondents may worry whether personal information will remain private. No system can be 100 percent secure. However, many research service suppliers specializing in Internet surveying have developed password-protected systems that are very secure. One important feature of these systems restricts access and prevents individuals from filling out a questionnaire over and over again.

Kiosk Interactive Surveys

A computer with a touch screen may be installed in a kiosk at a trade show, at a professional conference, in an airport, or in any other high-traffic location to administer an interactive survey. Because the respondent chooses to interact with an on-site computer, self-selection often is a problem with this type of survey. Computer-literate individuals are most likely to complete these interactive questionnaires. At temporary locations such as conventions, these surveys often require a fieldworker to be at the location to explain how to use the computer system. This is an obvious disadvantage.

Survey Research That Mixes Modes

mixed-mode survey
Study that employs any combination of survey methods.

For many surveys, research objectives dictate the use of some combination of telephone, mail, e-mail, Internet, and personal interview. For example, the researcher may conduct a short telephone screening interview to determine whether respondents are eligible for recontact in a more extensive personal interview. Such a **mixed-mode survey** combines the advantages of the telephone survey (such as fast screening) and those of the personal interview. A mixed-mode survey can employ any combination of two or more survey methods. Conducting a research study in two or more waves, however, creates the possibility that some respondents will no longer cooperate or will be unavailable in the second wave of the survey.

Several variations of survey research use cable television channels. For example, a telephone interviewer calls a cable subscriber and asks him or her to tune in to a particular channel at a certain time. An appointment is made to interview the respondent shortly after the program or visual material is displayed. NBC uses this type of mixed-mode survey to test the concepts for many proposed new programs.

SELECTING THE APPROPRIATE SURVEY RESEARCH DESIGN

Earlier discussions of research design and problem definition emphasized that many research tasks may lead to similar decision-making information. There is no best form of survey; each has advantages and disadvantages. A researcher who must ask highly confidential questions may use a mail survey, thus sacrificing speed of data collection to avoid interviewer bias. If a researcher must have con-

Some companies establish online panels for specific audiences, including internal audiences such as their own sales reps.[28] Avon, for example, launched its AvonOpinion (http://www.avonopinion.com) program for its sales reps nearly three years ago. All Avon reps with online access are invited to join the panel, and tens of thousands of them have elected to do so—more are joining every day. Avon sends e-mail messages a minimum of every 2 weeks to randomly selected agents and encourages them to visit the specially encrypted pages on the site and complete the surveys. Certificates for Avon merchandise are given as incentives.

"The goal is to test as many items as we can before we make critical buys," says Beth Landa, product research manager. In any given month Avon speaks to at least a few hundred of its reps. Participants can view pictures—sometimes in the form of slide shows—of the products along with descriptions, and give opinions about how they think the products will sell for them.

Often Avon finds that it can get results immediately with what it dubs its "Quick Clicks." For exam-

ple, they were able to design a study, post it, invite participation, and tabulate results for a survey all in under 1 week. This online research tool replaces older research tactics where Avon commissioned research with reps in 17 malls. By moving the research online, Avon is able to poll a larger cross-section of its representatives nationwide. Quick Clicks is quicker and more convenient for reps to give feedback. Avon also sets up monthly surveys on the AvonOpinion home page so that participating panelists who haven't been queried recently don't feel as though they are being overlooked. Here visitors are polled regarding relevant and timely issues. The desired type of information comes from various sources in the company, including the marketing department. For example, a recent survey polled visitors about the company's newspaper, *Representative Times*—about content, clarity, and other issues. Other surveys have been designed to gauge convention feedback.

siderable control over question phrasing, central location telephone interviewing may be appropriate.

To determine the appropriate technique, the researcher must ask several questions: Is the assistance of an interviewer necessary? Are respondents interested in the issues being investigated? Will cooperation be easily attained? How quickly is the information needed? Will the study require a long and complex questionnaire? How large is the budget? The criteria—cost, speed, anonymity, and so forth—may differ for each project.

Exhibit 7.4 summarizes the major advantages and disadvantages of typical door-to-door, mall intercept, telephone, mail, and Internet surveys. It emphasizes the typical types of surveys. For example, a creative researcher might be able to design highly versatile and flexible mail questionnaires, but most researchers use standardized questions. An elaborate mail survey may be far more expensive than a short personal interview, but generally this is not the case.

PRETESTING

A researcher who is surveying 3,000 consumers does not want to find out after the questionnaires have been completed or returned that most respondents misunderstood a particular question, skipped a series of questions, or misinterpreted

EXHIBIT 7.4

ADVANTAGES AND DISADVANTAGES OF TYPICAL SURVEY METHODS

	Door-to-Door Personal Interview	Mall Intercept Personal Interview	Telephone Interview	Mail Survey	Internet Survey
Speed of data collection	Moderate to fast	Fast	Very fast	Slow; researcher has no control over return of questionnaire	Instantaneous; 24/7
Geographic flexibility	Limited to moderate	Confined, possible urban bias	High	High	High (worldwide)
Respondent cooperation	Excellent	Moderate to low	Good	Moderate; poorly designed questionnaire will have low response rate	Varies depending on Web site; high from consumer panels
Versatility of questioning	Quite versatile	Extremely versatile	Moderate	Not versatile; requires highly standardized format	Extremely versatile
Questionnaire length	Long	Moderate to long	Moderate	Varies depending on incentive	Moderate; length customized based on answers
Item non-response rate	Low	Medium	Medium	High	Software can assure none
Possibility for respondent misunderstanding	Low	Low	Average	High; no interviewer present for clarification	High
Degree of interviewer influence on answers	High	High	Moderate	None; interviewer absent	None
Supervision of interviewers	Moderate	Moderate to high	High, especially with central-location WATS interviewing	Not applicable	Not applicable
Anonymity of respondent	Low	Low	Moderate	High	Respondent can be either anonymous or known
Ease of callback or follow-up	Difficult	Difficult	Easy	Easy, but takes time	Difficult, unless e-mail address is known
Cost	Highest	Moderate to high	Low to moderate	Lowest	Low
Special features	Visual materials may be shown or demonstrated; extended probing possible	Taste tests, viewing of TV commercials possible	Fieldwork and supervision of data collection are simplified; quite adaptable to computer technology	Respondent may answer questions at own convenience; has time to reflect on answers	Streaming media software allows use of graphics and animation

Note: The emphasis is on *typical* surveys. For example, an elaborate mail survey may be far more expensive than a short personal interview, but this generally is not the case.

pretesting
Screening procedure that involves a
trial run with a group of respondents
to iron out fundamental problems in
the survey design.

the instructions for filling out the questionnaire. To avoid problems such as these, screening procedures, or *pretests,* are often used. **Pretesting** involves a trial run with a group of respondents to iron out fundamental problems in the instructions or design of a questionnaire. The researcher looks for such things as the point at which respondent fatigue sets in and whether there are any particular places in the questionnaire where respondents tend to terminate. Unfortunately, this stage of research may be eliminated because of costs or time pressures.

Broadly speaking, there are three basic ways to pretest. The first two involve screening the questionnaire with other research professionals; and the third—the one most often called pretesting—is a trial run with a group of respondents. When screening the questionnaire with other research professionals, the investigator asks them to look for such things as difficulties with question wording, problems with leading questions, and bias due to question order. An alternative type of screening might involve a client or the research manager who ordered the research. Often managers ask researchers to collect information, but when they see the questionnaire, they find that it does not really meet their needs. Only by checking with the individual who has requested the questionnaire does the researcher know for sure that the questionnaire will elicit the information needed. Once the researcher has decided on the final questionnaire, data should be collected with a small number of respondents (perhaps 100) to determine whether the questionnaire needs refinement.

TO THE POINT

Practice is the best of all instructors
PUBLILIUS SYRUS,
circa 42 BC

ETHICAL ISSUES IN SURVEY RESEARCH

Chapter 4 discussed marketing researchers' codes of ethics, which express researchers' obligation to protect the public from misrepresentation and exploitation under the guise of marketing research. Many ethical issues apply to survey research, such as respondents' right to privacy, the use of deception, respondents' right to be informed about the purpose of the research, the need for confidentiality, the need for honesty in collecting data, and the need for objectivity in reporting data. You may wish to reexamine Chapter 4's coverage of these issues now that various survey research techniques have been discussed.[29]

SUMMARY

The survey is a common tool for asking respondents questions. Surveys can provide quick, inexpensive, and accurate information about awareness, product knowledge, brand usage behavior, opinions, and so on.

Two major forms of error are common in survey research. The first, random sampling error, is caused by chance variation and results in a sample that is not absolutely representative of the target population. The second, systematic error, falls into two general categories. Nonresponse error, the first category, results from subjects' failing to respond to the survey. Response bias occurs when a response to a questionnaire is deliberately falsified or inadvertently misrepresented. Five specific categories of response bias exist: acquiescence bias, extremity bias, interviewer bias, auspices bias, and social desirability bias. The second category of systematic error includes administrative problems such as inconsistencies in interviewers' abilities, cheating, data-processing mistakes, and so forth.

Surveys may be classified according to method of communication. Interviews and self-administered questionnaires are used to collect survey data. Interviews may be conducted door to door, in shopping malls, or on the telephone.

Traditionally, interviews have been recorded manually, but survey researchers are increasingly using computers for this purpose.

Personal interviews are a flexible method that offer both advantages and shortcomings. Door-to-door personal interviews get high response rates, but they are also more costly to administer than other types of surveys. The presence of an interviewer may also influence subjects' responses. When a sample need not represent the national population, mall intercept interviews may reduce costs.

Telephone interviewing has the advantage of providing data fast and at a lower cost per interview. However, not all households have telephones, and not all telephone numbers are listed in directories. This causes problems in obtaining a representative sample. Absence of face-to-face contact and inability to use visual materials also limit telephone interviewing. Computer-assisted telephone interviewing from central locations can improve the efficiency of certain kinds of telephone surveys.

Traditionally, self-administered questionnaires have been distributed by mail. Today, however, self-administered questionnaires may be dropped off to individual respondents, distributed from central locations, or administered via computer. Mail questionnaires generally are less expensive than telephone or personal interviews, but they also introduce a much larger chance of nonresponse error. Several methods can be used to encourage higher response rates. Mail questionnaires must be more structured than other types of surveys and cannot be changed if problems are discovered in the course of data collection.

The Internet and other interactive media provide convenient ways for organizations to conduct surveys. Internet surveys are quick and cost-effective, but not everyone has Internet access. Because the surveys are computerized and interactive, questionnaires can be personalized and data can be captured in real time. There are some privacy and security concerns, but the future of Internet surveys looks promising.

Pretesting a questionnaire on a small sample of respondents is a useful way to discover problems while they can still be corrected.

Key Terms and Concepts

respondent
survey
random sampling error
systematic error
sample bias
respondent error
nonresponse error
nonrespondent
no contact
refusal
self-selection bias
response bias
acquiescence bias
extremity bias
interviewer bias
auspices bias

social desirability bias
administrative error
data-processing error
sample selection error
interviewer error
interviewer cheating
personal interview
probing
item nonresponse
door-to-door interview
callback
mall intercept interview
telephone interview
random digit dialing
central location interviewing

computer-assisted telephone interview (CATI)
self-administered questionnaire
mail survey
response rate
cover letter
follow-up
drop-off method
fax survey
e-mail survey
Internet survey
welcome screen
dialog box
mixed-mode survey
pretesting

Questions for Review and Critical Thinking

1. Give an example of each type of survey error listed in Exhibit 7.1.
2. A survey indicated that chief executive officers (CEOs) would prefer to relocate their businesses in Atlanta (first choice), San Diego, Tampa, Los Angeles, or Boston. The CEOs who said they were going to build the required office space in the following year were asked where they were going to build. They indicated they were going to build in New York, Los Angeles, San Francisco, or Chicago. Explain this discrepancy.
3. What potential sources of error might be associated with the following situations?
   a. In a survey of frequent flyers age 50 and older, researchers concluded that price does not play a significant role in airline travel, because only 25 percent of the respondents checked off price as the most important determinant of where and how they traveled, while 35 percent rated price as unimportant.
   b. A survey of voters finds that most respondents do not like negative political ads—that is, advertising by one political candidate that criticizes or exposes secrets about the opponent's "dirty laundry."
   c. Researchers who must conduct a 45-minute personal interview decide to offer $10 to each respondent because they believe people who will sell their opinions are more typical than people who will talk to a stranger for 45 minutes.
   d. A company's sales representatives are asked what percentage of time they spend making presentations to prospects, traveling, talking on the telephone, participating in meetings, working on the computer, and engaging in other on-the-job activities. What potential sources of error might such a question generate?
4. What aspects of consumer behavior might be too sensitive to directly question respondents about?
5. A survey conducted by the National Endowment for the Arts asked, "Have you read a book within the last year?" What response bias might be possible with this question?
6. What type of communication medium would you use to conduct the following surveys? Why?
   a. Survey of the buying motives of industrial engineers
   b. Survey of the satisfaction levels of rental-car users
   c. Survey of viewers' awareness of television commercial advertising
   d. Survey of top corporate executives
7. Evaluate the following survey designs:
   a. A researcher suggests mailing a small safe (a metal file box with a built-in lock) to respondents without the lock combination, with a note explaining that respondents will be called in a few days for a telephone interview. During the telephone interview, the respondent is given the combination and the safe may be opened.
   b. A shopping mall that wishes to evaluate its image places packets including a questionnaire, cover letter, and stamped return envelope in the mall where customers can pick them up if they wish.
   c. A floppy disk containing a questionnaire is mailed to individuals who own computers. Respondents stick the disk into their computers, answer the questions, and mail the disk back to the research company in a special mailer. Each respondent is guaranteed a monetary incentive but may increase the incentive by playing a slot machine–type game that is also mounted on the floppy disk.
   d. A mall intercept interviewing service is located in a regional shopping center. The facility contains a small room for television and movie presentations. Shoppers are used as sampling units. However, mall intercept interviewers recruit additional subjects for television commercial experiments by offering them several complimentary tickets for special sneak previews. Individuals contacted at the mall are allowed to bring up to five guests. In some cases, the complimentary tickets are offered through ads in a local newspaper.
   e. *Time* magazine opts to conduct a mail survey rather than a telephone survey for a study to determine the demographic characteristics and purchasing behavior of its subscribers.
8. What types of research studies lend themselves to the use of e-mail for survey research? What are the advantages and disadvantages of survey communication using e-mail?
9. Suppose you are the marketing research director for your state's tourism bureau. Assess the state's information needs, and identify the information you will collect in a survey of tourists who visit your state.

Exploring the Internet

1. Go to the Pew Internet and American Life page at http://www.pewinternet.org/. Several reports based on survey research will be listed. Select one of the reports. What were the research objectives? What were the first three questions on the survey?
2. Go to the Walker Information Web site (http://www.walkerinfo.com), click on Demo Center, and take one of the three surveys. Write a short report about your experience taking an Internet survey.
3. Go to the NPD Group Web site (http://www.npd.com) and click on NPD Store. What types of custom and syndicated survey research services does the company offer?
4. Go to the CASRO (Council of American Survey Research Organizations) home page

(http://www.casro.org). Select About CASRO. What are the key aspects of this research organization's mission?
5. Use a search engine such as Yahoo, Excite, or Infoseek to see what you find if you enter "telephone survey" as key words.
6. SurveyOnline is located at http://www.surveyonline.com. What unique service does this company offer?
7. To learn more about customer satisfaction surveys, go to http://www.customersat.com.
8. For links to several Web sites demonstrating online surveys, go to http://zikmund.swcollege.com.

WebSurveyor

Basic Instructions

WebSurveyor (http://www.websurveyor.com) can be used to post Internet surveys online without any hassles. There is no programming required, no need to have a Web site, and no expensive software to buy.

WebSurveyor has two components.

- The *WebSurveyor Desktop* contains software programs that allow you to design, distribute, and analyze Internet surveys.
- *WebSurveyor Server* is a hosting service that allows you to collect data via the Internet.

The WebSurveyor Desktop software is available to students who purchase new textbooks containing a WebSurveyor postcard with a serial number. Students with serial numbers should go to http://zikmund.swcollege.com, click on the textbook, click the WebSurveyor button, and follow the steps for registering. Students who need to purchase a serial number should go to http://zikmund.swcollege.com, click on the textbook, click the WebSurveyor button, and follow the steps for purchasing access to the software.

WebSurveyor gives you all the tools you need to assemble, conduct, and analyze Internet surveys.[30] The software focuses on features that make developing Internet surveys easy, but it also includes many tools that will meet the demands of advanced users. Its Survey Wizard walks you through developing each

aspect of an online survey. WebSurveyor provides free question libraries, response libraries, and sample questionnaires, all of which make assembling your unique questionnaire easy and fast.

WebSurveyor writes the questionnaire in HTML automatically and enables anyone who has a WebSurveyor account to post the questionnaire to a unique Web address at WebSurveyor.net.

After the data have been collected, WebSurveyor software analyzes the data and provides tools that automatically graph question responses.

Getting Started

An instructive tutorial explaining how to use WebSurveyor appears at http://zikmund.swcollege.com. Here we offer a brief review of the WebSurveyor process.

Getting started using WebSurveyor Desktop is quick and easy. The primary steps to getting started are

- Creating your survey
- Publishing your survey
- Analyzing your results

Creating Your Survey The quickest way to get your survey started is to use the Survey Builder Wizard. The Wizard will walk you very quickly through the steps in creating a survey using predefined templates. If you want to create your own questionnaire from scratch, you can cancel the Wizard (and even turn that option off if you like) and enter the questions manually. You can add questions to your survey by clicking on the Add button in the Question List. You can also quickly create questions using WebSurveyor's Questions Library feature.

After entering your questions you will want to confirm that your survey Detail information is correct. With those fields properly filled out you can preview your survey and change the Presentation options to enhance or change the look and feel of the questionnaire.

Once you are satisfied with the look of your survey, you can save it to a WS3 file. A WS3 file is what WebSurveyor uses to hold the definition of your survey. This is a critical file, and you should regularly back up the directory you save this file to.

Publishing Your Survey With the survey saved locally to a WS3 file, you can begin the publishing process. This takes only a matter of minutes.

Analyzing Your Results Once your survey has been published and people have begun to take it, you can begin to pull down the results for analysis. This process is covered in detail in the Analysis section of the Web site's help system.

WebSurveyor Activities
Run the WebSurveyor Desktop software, and click Example Internet Usage Survey under the heading "Open a sample survey with real data" from the Getting Started Wizard. (If the Getting Started Wizard does not appear, click Tools and then Options from the main menu, make sure "Display the Getting Started Wizard for new surveys" is checked, and then click OK. Next click File and then New from the main menu, and then click Example Internet Usage Survey under the heading "Open a sample survey with real data.")

The software will open the sample survey and prompt you to download the responses. Click the "yes" button. The desktop software will contact the WebSurveyor server and transfer the survey results to your computer. When the transfer is complete, a window will appear with information about the transfer. Click OK, and the results for the first question will automatically appear as a pie chart.

Click Preview under "Survey Editing" to get a look at the questionnaire as it appeared to the survey's respondents. After you have reviewed the questionnaire, click Analysis under Survey Results to see the actual results. You can review the results for each question in turn by using the drop-down list or arrow buttons at the top of the graphic display area.

Burke Inc. provides a number of management consulting services to clients around the world. Burke has four business units: Burke Marketing Research, Burke Customer Satisfaction Associates, Burke Strategic Consulting Group, and the Training and Development Center.

Burke Marketing Research provides full-service custom marketing research, analysis, and consulting for consumer and business-to-business product and service companies to help them understand marketplace dynamics worldwide. Services include product testing, brand equity research, pricing research, market segmentation, image and positioning studies, and a wide range of other marketing research services. Burke has been providing marketing research services to Blue Chip

companies since 1931. Burke has tremendous depth of experience in all forms of research designs, including telephone, Internet, mail, and mall intercept.

Burke Marketing Research procedures are typical of those of suppliers of custom research studies. A client may come to Burke indicating it has a marketing "problem." Burke will spend some time investigating the problem and then submit a research proposal to the client. If the client approves the proposal, Burke conducts the fieldwork and prepares a research report.

Questions

1. Outline the steps in the survey research process.
2. How might a company like Burke help a client in each step of the survey research process?

Royal Barton started thinking about an electric fishing reel when his father had a stroke and lost the use of an arm.[31] To see that happen to his dad, who had taught him the joys of fishing and hunting, made Barton realize what a chunk a physical handicap could take out of a sports enthusiast's life. Being able to cast and retrieve a lure or experience the thrill of a big bass trying to take your rig away from you were among the joys of life that would be denied Barton's father forever.

Barton was determined to do something about it—if not for his father, then at least for others who had suffered a similar fate. So, after tremendous personal expense and years of research and development, Barton perfected what is sure to be the standard bearer for all future freshwater electric reels. Forget those saltwater jobs, which Barton refers to as "winches." He has developed something that is small, compact, and has incredible applications.

He calls it the Royal Bee. The first word, obviously, is his first name. The second word refers to the low buzzing sound the reel makes when in use.

The Royal Bee system looks simple enough and probably is if you understand the mechanical workings of a reel. A system of gears ties into the gears of the spool, and a motor in the back drives the gears attached to the triggering system.

All gearing of the electrical system can be disengaged so that you can cast normally. But pushing the button for "retrieve" engages two gears. After the gears are engaged, the trigger travels far enough to touch the switch that tightens the drive belt, and there is no slip-

ping. You cannot hit the switch until the gears are properly engaged. This means you cast manually, just as you would normally fish, then you reengage the reel for the levelwind to work. And you can do all that with one hand!

The system works on a 6-volt battery that you can attach to your belt or hang around your neck if you are wading. If you have a boat with a 6-volt battery system, the reel can actually work off of the battery. There is a small connector that plugs into the reel, so you could easily use more than one of the reels with the battery. For instance, if you have two or three outfits equipped with different lures, you just switch the connector from reel to reel as you use it. A reel with the Royal Bee system can be used in a conventional manner. You do not have to use it as an electric reel unless you choose to do so.

Barton believes the Royal Bee may not be just for handicapped fishermen. Ken Cook, one of the leading professional anglers in the country, is sold on the Royal Bee. After he suffered a broken arm, he had to withdraw from some tournaments because fishing with one hand was difficult. By the time his arm healed, he was hooked on the Royal Bee because it increased bassing efficiency. As Cook explains, "The electric reel has increased my efficiency in two ways. One is for flipping, where I use it all the time. The other is for fishing topwater when I have to make a long cast. When I'm flipping, the electric reel gives me instant control over slack line. I can keep both hands on the rod. I never have to remove them to take up slack. I flip, engage the reel, and then all I have to do is push the lever with my thumb to take up slack instantly."

Cook's reel (a Ryobi 4000) is one of several that can be converted to the electric retrieve. For flipping, Cook loads his reel with 20-pound test line. He uses a similar reel with lighter line when fishing a surface lure. "What you can do with the electric reel is eliminate unproductive reeling time," Cook says.

A few extra seconds may not mean much if you are out on a neighborhood pond just fishing on the week-end. But it can mean a lot if you are in tournament competition, where one extra cast might make the difference in going home with $50,000 tucked in your pocket. "Look at it this way," Cook explains. "Let's suppose we're in clear water and it's necessary to make a long cast to the cover we want to fish with a topwater lure. There's a whole lot of unproductive water between us and the cover. With the electric reel, I make my long cast and fish the cover. Then, when I'm ready to reel in, I just press the retrieve lever so the battery engages the necessary gears, and I've got my lure back ready to make another cast while you're still cranking."

When Royal Barton retired from his veterinary supply business, he began enjoying his favorite pastimes: hunting, fishing, and developing the Royal Bee system. He realized he needed help in marketing his product, so he sought professional assistance to learn how to reach the broadest possible market for the Royal Bee system.

Questions

1. What marketing problem does Royal Barton face? What are his information needs? Outline some survey research objectives for a research project on the Royal Bee system.
2. What type of survey—personal interview, telephone interview, or mail survey—should Barton select?
3. What sources of survey error are most likely to occur in a study of this type?
4. What means should be used to obtain a high response rate?

8

OBSERVATION

What you will learn in this chapter

- To distinguish between scientific observation and casual observation.
- To discuss what can and cannot be observed.
- To understand when an observation study is the appropriate research design.
- To discuss the characteristics of observation research.
- To give examples of nonverbal behavior that can be observed.
- To discuss the various situations in which direct observation studies may take place.
- To define *response latency.*
- To discuss scientifically contrived observation.
- To discuss some ethical issues in observation studies.
- To define *physical-trace evidence.*
- To define *content analysis* and explain its purposes.
- To describe the various types of mechanical observation and methods for measuring physiological reactions.
- To discuss the UPC system and the place of scanner data in observation research.

One day, Sherlock Holmes asked Dr. Watson how many steps led up to the Baker Street apartment. Watson responded that he did not know. Holmes replied, "Ah, Watson, you see but you do not *observe.*"

Although we constantly look around us in our daily lives, like Dr. Watson, we often do not observe in a scientific sense. Holmes, however, trained himself to systematically observe the environment in order to see what others overlooked. This chapter discusses the observation method of data gathering in marketing research. ■

WHEN IS OBSERVATION SCIENTIFIC?

observation
The systematic process of recording the behavioral patterns of people, objects, and occurrences as they are witnessed.

Observation becomes a tool for scientific inquiry when it is systematically planned to achieve a formulated research purpose. Scientific observation systematically records data and relates them to well-formulated hypotheses rather than simply reflecting a set of interesting curiosities.[1]

In marketing research, **observation** is the systematic process of recording the behavioral patterns of people, objects, and occurrences as they are witnessed. No questioning or communicating with people occurs. The researcher who uses the observation method of data collection witnesses and records information as events occur or compiles evidence from records of past events.

WHAT CAN BE OBSERVED?

One can observe a wide variety of information about the behavior of people and objects. There are seven kinds of observable phenomena: physical actions, such as shopping patterns or television viewing; verbal behavior, such as sales conversations; expressive behavior, such as tone of voice or facial expressions; spatial relations and locations, such as traffic patterns; temporal patterns, such as amount of time spent shopping or driving; physical objects, such as the amount of newspapers recycled; and verbal and pictorial records, such as the content of advertisements.

The observation method may be used to describe a wide variety of behavior, but cognitive phenomena such as attitudes, motivations, and preferences cannot be observed. Thus, observation research cannot provide an explanation of why a behavior occurred or what actions were intended. Another limitation is that the observation period generally is of short duration. Behavior patterns that occur over a period of several days or weeks generally are either too costly or impossible to observe.

Domain Stores, a chain of 23 furniture stores headquartered in Norwood, Massachusetts, hired Grid II, a market research firm, to videotape consumers in one of the furniture stores. Analysis of the videotapes revealed that people shop for furniture in twos. Of the 1,034 customers who entered the store, 954 came in pairs. In addition, facial expressions and other nonverbal behavior indicated that many male customers were visibly ill at ease amid fluffed pillows and floral duvets. "The typical customer needs to be in the store at least 9 minutes to feel comfortable enough to buy," says the company's CEO. "But if the spouse or boyfriend pulls her away too soon, we lose out on the sale." As a result of the observation research, the company remodeled its 23 stores with entertainment centers where sports fans can watch live events via cable.[2]

THE NATURE OF OBSERVATION STUDIES

Marketing researchers can observe people, objects, events, or other phenomena using either human observers or machines designed for specific observation tasks. Human observation is best for a situation or behavior that is not easily predictable in advance of the research. Mechanical observation, as performed by supermarket scanners or traffic counters, can very accurately record situations or types of behavior that are routine, repetitive, or programmatic.

Human or mechanical observation may be unobtrusive; that is, it may not require communication with a respondent.[3] For example, rather than asking customers how much time they spend shopping in the store, a supermarket manager might observe and record the intervals between when shoppers enter and leave the store. The unobtrusive or nonreactive nature of the observation method often generates data without a subject's knowledge. A situation in which an observer's presence is known to the subject involves **visible observation;** a situation in which a subject is unaware that observation is taking place is **hidden observation.** Hidden, unobtrusive observation minimizes respondent error. Asking subjects to participate in the research is not required when they are unaware that they are being observed.

The major advantage of observation studies over surveys, which obtain self-reported data from respondents, is that the data do not have distortions, inaccuracies, or other response biases due to memory error, social desirability bias, and so on. The data are recorded when the actual behavior takes place.

visible observation
Observation in which the observer's presence is known to the subject.

hidden observation
Observation in which the subject is unaware that observation is taking place.

OBSERVATION OF HUMAN BEHAVIOR

Surveys emphasize verbal responses, while observation studies emphasize and allow for the systematic recording of nonverbal behavior. Toy manufacturers such as Fisher Price use the observation technique because children often cannot express their reactions to products. By observing children at play with a proposed toy, doll, or game, marketing researchers may be able to identify the elements of a potentially successful product. Toy marketing researchers might observe play to answer the following questions: How long does the child's attention stay with the product? Does the child put the toy down after 2 minutes or 20 minutes? Are the child's peers equally interested in the toy?

Behavioral scientists have recognized that nonverbal behavior can be a communication process by which meanings are exchanged among individuals. Head nods, smiles, raised eyebrows, and other facial expressions or body movements have been recognized as communication symbols. Observation of nonverbal communication may hold considerable promise for the marketing researcher. For example, with regard to customer–salesperson interactions, it has been hypothesized that in low-importance transactions, where potential customers are plentiful and easily replaced (for example, a shoe store), the salesperson may show definite nonverbal signs of higher status than the customer. When customers are scarce, as in big-ticket purchase situations (for example, real estate sales), the opposite should hold: The salesperson may show many nonverbal indicators of deference. An observation study using the nonverbal communication measures shown in Exhibit 8.1 could test this hypothesis.

EXHIBIT 8.1 | NONVERBAL COMMUNICATION: STATUS AND POWER GESTURES[4]

Behavior	BETWEEN PEOPLE OF EQUAL STATUS		BETWEEN PEOPLE OF UNEQUAL STATUS		BETWEEN MEN AND WOMEN	
	Intimate	Nonintimate	Used by Superior	Used by Subordinate	Used by Men	Used by Women
Posture	Relaxed	Tense (less relaxed)	Relaxed	Tense	Relaxed	Tense
Personal space	Closeness	Distance	Closeness (optional)	Distance	Closeness	Distance
Touching	Touch	Don't touch	Touch (optional)	Don't touch	Touch	Don't touch
Eye gaze	Establish	Avoid	Stare, ignore	Avert eyes, watch	Stare, ignore	Avert eyes
Demeanor	Informal	Circumspect	Informal	Circumspect	Informal	Circumspect
Emotional expression	Show	Hide	Hide	Show	Hide	Show
Facial expression	Smile	Don't smile	Don't smile	Smile	Don't smile	Smile

Complementary Evidence

The results of observation studies may amplify the results of other forms of research by providing complementary evidence concerning individuals' "true" feelings. Focus group interviews often are conducted behind one-way mirrors from which marketing executives observe as well as listen to what is occurring. This allows for interpretation of nonverbal behavior, such as facial expressions or head nods, to supplement information from interviews.

For example, in one focus group session concerning hand lotion, researchers observed that all the women's hands were above the table while they were casually waiting for the session to begin. Seconds after the women were told the topic was to be hand lotion, "all hands had been placed under the table or out of sight and the women's faces became tense."[5] This observation, along with the group discussion, revealed the women's anger, guilt, and shame about the condition of their hands. Although they felt they were expected to have soft, pretty hands, their housework obligations required them to wash dishes, clean floors, and do other chores that were hard on their hands.

When focus group behavior is videotaped, observation of the nonverbal communication symbols can add even more to marketers' knowledge of the situation.

Focus groups observed behind one-way mirrors are often videotaped. The ability to replay video records allows researchers to perform detailed analysis of physical actions.

DIRECT OBSERVATION

direct observation
A straightforward attempt to observe and record what naturally occurs; the investigator does not create an artificial situation.

Direct observation can produce a detailed record of events that occur or what people actually do. The observer plays a passive role. That is, there is no attempt to control or manipulate a situation—the observer merely records what occurs. Many types of data can be obtained more accurately through direct observation than by questioning. For example, recording traffic counts and/or observing the direction of traffic flows within a supermarket can help managers design store layouts that maximize the exposure of departments that sell impulse goods. A manufacturer can determine the number of facings, shelf locations, display maintenance, and other characteristics that make for better store conditions. If directly questioned in a survey, most shoppers would be unable to accurately portray the time they spend in each department. The observation method, however, could determine this without difficulty.

With the direct observation method, the data consist of records of events made as they occur. An observation form often helps keep the observations consistent and ensures that all relevant information is recorded. A respondent is not required to recall—perhaps inaccurately—an event after it has occurred; instead, the observation is instantaneous.

In many cases, direct observation is the most straightforward form of data collection (or the only form possible). The produce manager at a Jewel grocery store may periodically gather competitive price information at the Safeway and IGA stores in the neighborhood. In other situations, observation is the most economical technique. In a common type of observation study, a shopping center manager may observe the license plate (tag) numbers on cars in the parking lot. These data, along with automobile registration information, provide an inexpensive means of determining where customers live.

Certain data may be obtained more quickly or easily using direct observation than by other methods. Sex, race, and other respondent characteristics can simply be observed. Researchers investigating a diet product may use observation when selecting respondents in a shopping mall. Overweight people may be pre-screened by observing pedestrians, thus eliminating a number of screening interviews.

Recording the decision time necessary to make a choice between two alternatives is a relatively simple, unobtrusive task that can be done through direct observation. **Response latency** refers to the choice time recorded as a measure of the strength of the preference between alternatives.[6] It is hypothesized that the longer a decision maker takes to choose between two alternatives, the closer the two alternatives are in terms of preference. However, a quick decision is assumed to indicate that the psychological distance between alternatives is considerable. The response latency measure is gaining popularity now that computer-assisted data collection methods are becoming more common, because the computer can record decision times.

Errors Associated with Direct Observation

Although no interaction with the subject occurs in direct observation, the method is not error-free; the observer may record events subjectively. The same visual cues that influence the interplay between interviewer and respondent (e.g., the respondent's age or sex) may come into play in some types of direct observation settings. For example, the observer may subjectively attribute a particular economic status or educational background to the subject. A distortion of measurement resulting from the cognitive behavior or actions of the witnessing observer is called **observer bias.** For example, in a research project using observers to evaluate whether sales clerks are rude or courteous, fieldworkers may be required to rely on their own interpretations of people or situations during the observation process.

If the observer does not record every detail that describes the persons, objects, and events in a given situation, accuracy may suffer. As a general guideline, the observer should record as much detail as possible. However, the pace of events, the observer's memory, the observer's writing speed, and other factors will limit the amount of detail that can be recorded.

Interpretation of observation data is another major source of potential error. Facial expressions and other nonverbal communication may have several meanings. Does a smile always mean happiness? Does a person who is seated next to the company president necessarily enjoy high status?

Scientifically Contrived Observation

Most observation takes place in a natural setting. Observation in which an investigator intervenes to create an artificial environment in order to test a hypothesis is called **contrived observation.** Contrived observation can increase the frequency of occurrence of certain behavior patterns. For example, an airline passenger complaining about a meal or service from the flight attendant may actually be a researcher recording that person's reactions. If situations were not contrived, the research time spent waiting and observing situations would expand considerably. A number of retailers use observers called *mystery shoppers* to come into a store and pretend to be interested in a particular product or service; after leaving the store, the "shopper" evaluates the salesperson's performance.

Paco Underhill runs Envirosell, a New York consumer research company that conducts observation research. He became interested in using cameras to analyze the flow of human traffic through public places after hearing a lecture by urban geographer William Whyte. Envirosell's clients now include companies like Quaker Foods, Revlon, Hallmark Cards, and Bloomingdale's. The following is one reporter's account of what he learned about the value of observation research.

Underhill's research in retail settings led him to develop a body of observations he calls *aisle theory*.[7] Among his seminal findings is something we'll call the derriere-brush factor, although he calls it by another name. At his offices in New York, he showed me a film clip shot with a time-lapse camera aimed at a tie display in a narrow, heavily traveled aisle of the Bloomingdale's department store in Manhattan. Such aisles, meant to carry shoppers from store entrances onward into the store, are known in the retail industry as "driveways" or "power aisles."

Shoppers entered and dispersed; most zipped right by a tie display. Underhill stopped the projector. "Stand up," he commanded.

I stood.

"OK, you are standing at a counter. You are looking at ties. One of the most sensitive parts of your anatomy is your tail."

He began brushing my tail with his hand. Derriere-brush factor, he told me, "is simply the idea that the more likely you are to be brushed from the rear while you shop, the less likely you'll be converted from browser to buyer." In retail-speak the "conversion ratio" of that display or counter will be low.

Underhill's stop-action film showed how few people stopped to examine the ties in the rack. Traffic swept past the few browsers in disconcerting volume.

When Bloomingdale's chairman saw the video, he called the clerk in charge of that department and had him move the tie rack out of the driveway. Later, a Bloomingdale's vice president called Underhill and told him the chairman had personally had the sales tracked from that lone tie rack and discovered that within 6 weeks the increase had paid for Underhill's services. "That told me two things," Underhill said. "One, I wasn't charging enough, and two, the markup on ties was even more obscene than I thought."

ETHICAL ISSUES IN THE OBSERVATION OF HUMANS

Observation methods introduce a number of ethical issues. Hidden observation raises the issue of the respondent's right to privacy. For example, a firm interested in acquiring information about how women put on their bras might persuade some retailers to place one-way mirrors in dressing rooms so that this behavior may be observed unobtrusively. Obviously, such a situation raises an ethical question. Other observation methods, especially contrived observation, raise the possibility of deception of subjects.

Some people may see contrived observation as entrapment. To *entrap* means to deceive or trick into difficulty, which clearly is abusive. The difficulty is one of balancing values. If the researcher obtains permission to observe someone, the subject may not act in a typical manner. Thus, the researcher must determine his or her own view of the ethics involved and decide whether the usefulness of the information is worth telling a "white lie."

"He picks up commonsense things," said Judith Owens, vice president, marketing, of the National Retail Federation in New York, who periodically invites Underhill to show his stop-action films to the federation's many members. She watched one film of an audio store that drew mostly teenage clientele, yet placed its racks of CDs so high the kids couldn't reach them. "You watch that happen, then you hear Paco say if you drop your display by 18 inches you'll increase your productivity. Everybody says, my God, I never thought of that."

He showed AT&T that almost 20 percent of the people who came into its Phone Center stores were under 10 years old, and how salespeople spent a lot of their time simply protecting expensive phone systems displayed too close to the ground. His films showed how most people who entered a Revco drugstore failed to pick up a shopping basket and thus were automatically limited to buying only what they could carry.

Early in 1991 the Woolworth Corporation asked Underhill to study several of its Champs Sports stores to help figure out which layouts and designs worked best. Woolworth was planning a huge national expansion of the chain. It knew that sales from the rear section of each store—the hard goods section displaying such items as weights and basketballs—lagged far behind sales from other sections, but it didn't know why.

John Shanley, director of research for Woolworth, remembers how Underhill's stop-action film instantly solved the mystery. During peak sales periods a line of customers would form from the cash register to the opposite wall of the store. "It literally prevented people from going from the front to the back," Shanley recalls. "They walked up to this line, turned and walked away." As a result, all of Champs' 500 stores now feature a checkout area (known in the industry as the "cash-wrap") designed so that lines form along an axis from front to back. "All of a sudden the sales in the back of the store picked up," Shanley recalled.

But, I asked, shouldn't that barrier effect have been obvious without Underhill's help? "The obvious," Shanley answered, "isn't always that apparent."

OBSERVATION OF PHYSICAL OBJECTS

physical-trace evidence
A visible mark of some past occurrence.

Physical phenomena may be the subject of an observation study. **Physical-trace evidence** is a visible mark of some past occurrence. For example, the wear on a library book indirectly indicates which books are actually read (handled most) when checked out. A classic example of physical-trace evidence in a nonprofit setting was erosion traces:

> The floor tiles around the hatching-chick exhibit at Chicago's Museum of Science and Industry must be replaced every six weeks. Tiles in other parts of the museum need not be replaced for years. The selective erosion of tiles, indexed by the replacement rate, is a measure of the relative popularity of exhibits.[8]

Clearly, a creative marketing researcher has many options available for determining the solution to a problem.

Physical-trace evidence is the focus of a scientific project at the University of Arizona in which aspiring archaeologists sift through modern garbage: They

Direct observation of consumers of juices and juice beverages revealed that many of them poured their beverages from large bottles they had purchased into smaller empty water bottles, the kind with a push-up top. This led to the conclusion that juices packaged in smaller, convenient-to-transport bottles would find a market.[9]

examine soggy cigarette butts, empty milk cartons, and half-eaten Big Macs. Investigation of Arizona household garbage has revealed many interesting findings. For example, in Hispanic households the most popular baby food is squash.[10] It accounts for 38 percent of the strained vegetables Hispanic babies consume. In contrast, in Anglo households, peas account for 29 percent of all baby vegetables; squash ranks only above spinach, which is last. (Squash has been a dietary staple in Mexico and Central America for more than 9,000 years.) Sorting through fast-food restaurants' garbage reveals that wasted food from chicken restaurants (not counting bones) accounts for 35 percent of all food bought. This is substantially greater than the 7 percent of wasted food at fast-food hamburger restaurants.

What is most interesting about the garbage project is the comparison between the results of surveys about food consumption and the contents of respondents' garbage; garbage does not lie.[11] The University of Arizona project indicates that people consistently underreport the quantity of junk food they eat and overreport the amount of fruit and diet soda they consume. Most dramatically, however, studies show that 40 to 60 percent underreport alcohol consumption.

Counting and recording physical inventories by means of retail or wholesale audits allows researchers to investigate brand sales on regional and national levels, market shares, seasonal purchasing patterns, and so on. Marketing research suppliers offer audit data at both the retail and the wholesale levels.

An observer can record physical-trace data to discover things a respondent could not recall accurately. For example, actually measuring the number of ounces of a liquid bleach used during a test provides precise physical-trace evidence without relying on the respondent's memory. The accuracy of respondents' memories is not a problem for the firm that conducts a pantry audit. The pantry audit requires an inventory of the brands, quantities, and package sizes in a consumer's home rather than responses from individuals. The problem of untruthfulness or some other form of response bias is avoided. For example, the pantry audit prevents the possible problem of respondents erroneously claiming to have purchased prestige brands. However, gaining permission to physically check consumers' pantries is not easy, and the fieldwork is expensive. Further, the brand in the pantry may not reflect the brand purchased most often if it was substituted because of a cents-off coupon, because the subject's normal brand was out-of-stock, or for another reason.

CONTENT ANALYSIS

content analysis
The systematic observation and quantitative description of the manifest content of communication.

Content analysis obtains data by observing and analyzing the contents or messages of advertisements, newspaper articles, television programs, Web sites, and the like. It involves systematic analysis as well as observation to identify the specific information content and other characteristics of the messages. Content analysis studies the message itself; it involves the design of a systematic observation and recording procedure for quantitative description of the manifest content of communication. This technique measures the extent of emphasis on or omission of a given analytical category. For example, the content of advertisements might be investigated to evaluate their use of words, themes, characters, or space and time relationships. The frequency of appearance of women, African Americans, or other minorities in mass media has been a topic of content analysis.

Content analysis may be used to investigate questions such as whether some advertisers use certain types of themes, appeals, claims, or deceptive practices more than others or whether recent consumer-oriented actions by the Federal Trade Commission have influenced the content of advertising. A cable television programmer might do a content analysis of network programming to evaluate its competition. For example, every year researchers analyze the Super Bowl to see how much of the visual material is live-action play and how much is replay or how many shots focus on the cheerleaders and how many on spectators. The information content of television commercials directed at children can be investigated, as can company images portrayed in advertising and numerous other aspects of advertising.[13]

Study of the content of communications is more sophisticated than simply counting the items; it requires a system of analysis to secure relevant data.

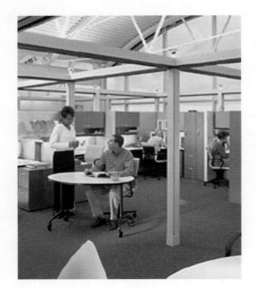

When Steelcase, an office furniture manufacturer, decided there was an opportunity for a new product specifically designed for work teams, researchers believed that observation was the best research method. Steelcase placed video cameras at various companies so its staff could observe firsthand how teams operate. After the recording period ended, the researchers exhaustively analyzed the tapes, looking for the patterns of behavior and motion that workers don't even notice themselves. The main observation was that people in teams function best if they can do some work collaboratively and some privately. These findings were utilized to design the Personal Harbor brand of modular office units. The units are similar in shape and size to a phone booth and can be arranged around a common space where a team works, fostering synergy but also allowing a person to work alone when necessary.[14]

MECHANICAL OBSERVATION

In many situations, the primary—and sometimes the only—means of observation is mechanical rather than human. Video cameras, traffic counters, and other machines help observe and record behavior. Some unusual observation studies have used motion picture cameras and time-lapse photography. An early application of this observation technique photographed train passengers and determined their levels of comfort by observing how they sat and moved in their seats. Another time-lapse study filmed traffic flows in an urban square and resulted in a redesign of the streets. Similar techniques may help managers design store layouts and resolve problems in moving people or objects through spaces over time.

Television Monitoring

television monitoring
Computerized mechanical observation used to obtain television ratings.

Perhaps the best-known marketing research project involving mechanical observation and computerized data collection is A. C. Nielsen's **television monitoring** system for estimating national television audiences. Nielsen uses a consumer panel and a sophisticated monitoring device called a PeopleMeter to obtain ratings for television programs in 18 countries.[15] Electronic boxes are hooked up to television sets to capture important information on program choices, the length of viewing time, and the identity of the viewer.

Knowing who in the family is watching allows executives to match television programs with demographic profiles. When the panel household's television set is turned on, a question mark appears on the screen to remind viewers to indicate who is watching. The viewer then uses a handheld electronic device that resembles a television remote control to record who is watching. A device attached to the television automatically sends the observed data—the viewer's age and sex and what programs are being watched—over telephone lines to Nielsen's computers.

More than 5,000 households, scientifically selected to be representative of the U.S. population, have agreed to become members of the panel and have meters placed in their homes.

Critics of the PeopleMeter argue that subjects in Nielsen's panel grow bored over time and do not always record when they begin or stop watching television. Nielsen Media Research is now working on a unique technology that will allow its PeopleMeters to scan the room, recognize each family member by his or her facial characteristics, and record when the person enters or leaves the room.

Further into the future, as digital television evolves, the current PeopleMeter measurement technologies will become obsolete. For example, Nielsen is working on more sophisticated digital cable technology that uses a set-top box decoding system. The system will "ask" what the set-top box is doing and identify the channel or display on screen. The data, invisible and inaudible to viewers, will be sent to a central processing site during normal data transmission.[16] The TiVo digital television recorder, already on the market but used by only a small percentage of the population, uses similar technology. TiVo records viewing data, such as what commercials people skip by using fast-forward, that is quite valuable to marketers.

Monitoring Web Site Traffic

Most organizations record how many people visit their Web sites. A *hit* occurs when a user clicks on a single page of a Web site. If the visitor clicks on many places to access graphics or the like, that page receives multiple hits.[17] Organizations with Web sites consisting of multiple pages find it useful to track *page views,* or single, discrete clicks on individual pages. Page views more conservatively indicate how many users visit each individual page on the Web site and may also be used to track the path or sequence of pages that each visitor follows. A variety of information technologies are used to measure Web traffic and to maintain access logs.

Jupiter Media Metrix and Nielsen//NetRatings are marketing research companies that specialize in monitoring Internet activity. The typical Internet monitoring company installs a special tracking program on the personal computers of a sample of Internet users who agree to participate in the research effort. Nielsen//NetRatings has its software installed in 225,000 computers in homes and workplaces in 26 countries. Internet monitoring enables these companies to identify the popularity of Web sites (AOL.com and Yahoo.com are among the most popular), measure the effectiveness of advertising banners, and provide other audience information. For example, a Jupiter Media Metrix study indicated that 63 percent of online shoppers stop short of completing their purchases after shipping charges are computed at the last step, known as the Checkout Line.

Scanner-Based Research

Lasers performing optical character recognition and bar code technology such as the Universal Product Code (UPC) have accelerated the use of mechanical observation in marketing research. Several syndicated services offer secondary data about product category movement generated from retail stores using scanner technology.

This technology now allows researchers to investigate more demographically or promotionally specific questions. For example, scanner research has investigated the different ways consumers respond to price promotions and how those differences affect a promotion's profitability. One primary means of implementing this type of research is through the establishment of a **scanner-based consumer panel** to replace consumer purchase diaries.

scanner-based consumer panel
A type of consumer panel in which participants' purchasing habits are recorded with a laser scanner rather than in a purchase diary.

In a typical scanner panel, each household is assigned a bar-coded card that members present to the clerk at the register. The household's code number is coupled with the purchase information recorded by the scanner. Further, as with other consumer panels, background information about the household obtained through answers to a battery of demographic and psychographic survey questions also can be coupled with the household code number.

Aggregate data, such as actual store sales as measured by scanners, are also available. These data parallel the data obtained with a standard mail diary panel, with some important improvements:

1. The data measure observed (actual) purchase behavior versus reported behavior (recorded later in a diary).
2. Substituting mechanical for human recordkeeping improves accuracy.
3. Measures are unobtrusive, eliminating interviewing and the possibility of social desirability or other bias on the part of respondents.
4. More extensive purchase data can be collected, because all UPC categories are measured. In a mail diary, respondents could not reliably record all items purchased. Because all UPC-coded items are measured in the panel, users can investigate many product categories to determine loyalty, switching rates, and so on for their own brands as well as for other companies' products and locate product categories for possible market entry.
5. The data collected from computerized checkout scanners can be combined with data about advertising, price changes, and sales promotions. Researchers can scrutinize them with powerful analytical software available from the scanner data providers.

Scanner data can show a marketer week by week how a product is doing, even in a single store, and track sales in response to local ads or promotions. Further, several organizations, such as Information Resources Inc.'s Behavior Scan System, have developed scanner panels and expanded them into electronic test market systems. These are discussed in greater detail in Chapter 9.

Advances in bar code technology have led to **at-home scanning systems** that use hand-held wands to read UPC symbols. Consumer panelists perform their own scanning after they have taken home the products. This advance makes it possible to investigate purchases made at stores that do not have in-store scanning equipment.

Measuring Physiological Reactions

Marketing researchers have used a number of other mechanical devices to evaluate consumers' physical and physiological reactions to advertising copy, packaging, and other stimuli. Researchers use such means when they believe that consumers are unaware of their own reactions to stimuli such as advertising or that consumers will not provide honest responses. Four major categories of mechanical devices are used to measure physiological reactions: (1) eye-tracking monitors, (2) pupillometers, (3) psychogalvanometers, and (4) voice pitch analyzers.

A magazine or newspaper advertiser may wish to grab readers' attention with a visual scene and then direct it to a package or coupon. Or a television advertiser may wish to identify selling points to emphasize. Eye-tracking equipment records how the subject reads a print ad or views a TV commercial and how much time is spent looking at various parts of the stimulus. In physiological terms, the gaze movements of a viewer's eye are measured with an **eye-tracking monitor,** which measures unconscious eye movements. Originally developed to

at-home scanning system
A system that allows consumer panelists to perform their own scanning after taking home products using hand-held wands that read UPC symbols.

eye-tracking monitor
A mechanical device used to observe eye movements. Some eye monitors use infrared light beams to measure unconscious eye movements.

How This Advertisement Was Read

% Noting
Each Element

★ Most Common
Starting Point

⬇ Most Common
Viewing Pattern

95%

85%

24%

63%

It's gotta be the Puppy Chow.

Purina has reformulated Puppy Chow puppy food and there's no better way to get your puppy off to ... art. It's highly digestible, so your puppy's system takes in mo ... eeds to build strong bones and muscles—and help support a heal ... mune system. New Purina Puppy Chow. The nutrition he needs now for a long, strong and exceptional life.

INCREDIBLE PUPPY FOOD.
INCREDIBLE PUPPIES.

Measurements with an eye-tracking monitor of subjects' responses to this ad for Purina Puppy Chow showed that only 24 percent of consumer viewing time was given to the body copy message and that 95 percent of the viewers started looking at the boy at the top of the ad. The red arrows show the most common viewing pattern.

measure astronauts' eye fatigue, modern eye-tracking systems need not keep a viewer's head in a stationary position. This device tracks eye movements through invisible infrared light beams that lock onto the subject's eyes. The light reflects off the eye, and eye movement data are recorded while another tiny video camera monitors which magazine page is being perused. The data are analyzed by computer to determine which components in an ad (or other stimuli) were seen and which were overlooked.

The other physiological observation techniques are based on a common principle:

> Physiological research depends on the fact that adrenalin is produced when the body is aroused. When adrenalin goes to work, the heart beats faster and more strongly, and even enlarges. Blood flows to the extremities and increases capillary dilation at the fingertips and earlobes. Skin temperature increases, hair follicles stand up, skin pores emit perspiration, and the electrical conductivity of skin surfaces is affected. Eye pupils dilate, electrical waves in the brain increase in frequency, breathing is faster and deeper, and the chemical composition of expired air is altered. This process offers a choice of about 50 different measures—the question of which measure to use is to some extent irrelevant since they are all measuring arousal.[18]

pupillometer
A mechanical device used to observe and record changes in the diameter of a subject's pupils.

A **pupillometer** observes and records changes in the diameter of a subject's pupils. A subject is instructed to look at a screen on which an advertisement or other stimulus is projected. When the brightness and distance of the stimulus from the subject's eyes are held constant, changes in pupil size may be interpreted as changes in cognitive activity that result from the stimulus (rather than from light intensity, distance from the object, or other physiological reactions to the conditions of observation). This method of research is based on the assumption that increased pupil size reflects a strong attitude toward the product or interest in the advertisement.

psychogalvanometer
A device that measures galvanic skin response, a measure of involuntary changes in the electrical resistance of the skin.

A **psychogalvanometer** measures galvanic skin response (GSR), a measure of involuntary changes in the electrical resistance of the skin. This device is based on the assumption that physiological changes, such as increased perspiration, accompany emotional reactions to advertisements, packages, and slogans. Excitement increases the body's perspiration rate, which increases the electrical resistance of the skin. The test is an indicator of emotional arousal or tension.

voice pitch analysis
A physiological measurement technique that records abnormal frequencies in the voice that supposedly reflect emotional reactions to various stimuli.

Voice pitch analysis is a physiological measurement technique that measures emotional reactions as reflected in physiological changes in a person's voice. Abnormal frequencies in the voice, caused by changes in the autonomic nervous system, are measured with sophisticated, computerized audio equipment. Computer analysis compares the respondent's voice pitch during warm-up conversations (normal range) with verbal response to questions about his or her evaluative reaction to television commercials or other stimuli. This technique, unlike other physiological devices, does not require the researcher to surround subjects with mazes of wires or equipment.

All of these devices assume physiological reactions are associated with persuasiveness or predict some cognitive response. This has not yet been clearly demonstrated, however. No strong theoretical evidence supports the argument that a physiological change is a valid measure of future sales, attitude change, or emotional response. Another major problem with physiological research involves the *calibration,* or sensitivity, of measuring devices. Identifying arousal is one thing, but precisely measuring *levels* of arousal is another. In addition, most of these devices are expensive. However, as a prominent researcher points out, physiological measurement is coincidental: "Physiological measurement isn't an exit interview. It's not dependent on what was remembered later on. It's a live blood, sweat, and tears, moment-by-moment response, synchronous with the stimulus."[19]

Each of these mechanical devices has another limitation in that the subjects are usually placed in artificial settings (watching television in a laboratory rather than at home) and know they are being observed.[20]

SUMMARY

Observation is a powerful tool for the marketing researcher. Scientific observation is the systematic process of recording the behavioral patterns of people, objects, and occurrences as they are witnessed. Questioning or otherwise communicating with them does not occur. A wide variety of information about the behavior of people and objects can be gained through observation. Seven kinds of content are observable: physical actions, verbal behavior, expressive behavior, spatial relations and locations, temporal patterns, physical objects, and verbal and pictorial records. Thus, both verbal and nonverbal behavior may be observed.

A major disadvantage of the observation technique is that cognitive phenomena such as attitudes, motivations, expectations, intentions, and preferences are not observable. Further, only overt behavior of short duration can be observed. Nevertheless, many types of data can be obtained more accurately through direct observation than by questioning respondents. Observation is often the most direct, and sometimes the only, method for collecting certain data.

Marketing researchers employ both human observers and machines designed for specific observation tasks. Human observation is commonly used when the situation or behavior to be recorded is not easily predictable in advance of the research. Mechanical observation can be used when the situation or behavior to be recorded is routine, repetitive, or programmatic. Human or mechanical observation may be unobtrusive. Human observation carries the possibility of observer bias, even though the observer does not interact with the subject.

Observation sometimes can be contrived by creating the situations to be observed. This can reduce the time and expense of obtaining reactions to certain circumstances. Contrived observation, hidden observation, and other observation research designs that might use deception often raise ethical concerns about subjects' right to privacy and right to be informed.

Physical-trace evidence serves as a visible record of past events. Content analysis obtains data by observing and analyzing the contents of messages in written and/or spoken communications. Mechanical observation uses a variety of devices to record behavior directly. Mechanical observation takes many forms. National television audience ratings are based on mechanical observation and computerized data collection. Scanner-based research is growing in popularity because of increased use of laser scanners in retail stores. Many syndicated services offer secondary data collected through scanner systems. Physiological reactions, such as arousal or eye movement patterns, may be observed using a number of mechanical devices.

Key Terms and Concepts

observation
visible observation
hidden observation
direct observation
response latency
observer bias

contrived observation
physical-trace evidence
content analysis
television monitoring
scanner-based consumer panel
at-home scanning system

eye-tracking monitor
pupillometer
psychogalvanometer
voice pitch analysis

Questions for Review and Critical Thinking

1. Yogi Berra, former New York Yankee catcher, said, "You can observe a lot just by watching." How does this statement fit in with the definition of scientific observation?
2. What are the advantages and disadvantages of observation studies compared to surveys?
3. Under what conditions are observation studies most appropriate?
4. Suggest some new uses for observation studies. Be creative!
5. A multinational fast-food corporation plans to locate a restaurant in La Paz, Bolivia. Secondary data

for this city are outdated. How might you determine the location using observation?
6. Discuss how an observation study might be combined with a personal interview.
7. The lost-letter technique has been used to predict voting behavior. Letters addressed to various political groups are spread throughout a city. The "respondent" finds an envelope, reads the address of a group supporting (or opposing) a candidate, and mails back (or throws away) the envelope. It is assumed that the respondent's action indicates a favorable (or unfavorable) attitude toward the

organization. Would this technique be appropriate in marketing research?

8. Outline a research design using observation for each of the following situations:
   a. A bank wishes to collect data on the number of customer services and the frequency of customer use of these services.
   b. A state government wishes to determine the driving public's use of seat belts.
   c. A researcher wishes to know how many women have been featured on *Time* covers over the years.
   d. A fast-food franchise wishes to determine how long a customer entering a store has to wait for his or her order.
   e. A magazine publisher wishes to determine exactly what people see and what they pass over while reading one of its magazines.
   f. A food manufacturer wishes to determine how people use snack foods in their homes.
   g. An overnight package delivery service wishes to observe delivery workers beginning at the moment when they stop the truck, continuing through delivery of the package, and ending when they return to the truck.

9. Watch the nightly news on a major network for one week. Observe how much time reporters spend on national news, commercials, and other activity. (Hint: Think carefully about how you will record the contents of the programs.)

10. Comment on the ethics of the following situations:
    a. During the course of telephone calls to investors, a stockbroker records their voices when they are answering sensitive investment questions and then conducts a voice pitch analysis. The respondents do not know that their voices are being recorded.
    b. A researcher plans to invite consumers to be test users in a simulated kitchen located in a shopping mall and to then videotape their reactions to a new microwave dinner from behind a one-way mirror.
    c. A marketing researcher arranges to purchase trash from the headquarters of a major competitor. The purpose is to sift through discarded documents to determine the company's strategic plans.

Exploring the Internet

1. The University of Arizona Department of Anthropology houses the Bureau of Applied Research in Anthropology (BARA). The garbage project described in this chapter is one of the bureau's research activities. Go to the University of Arizona's home page at http://www.arizona.edu and then go to the anthropology department in the College of Social and Behavioral Sciences. Then navigate to the BARA's garbage project. What information is available?

2. If you are interested in content analysis, go to the UCLA Television Violence Monitoring Project at http://www.media-awareness.ca/eng/med/home/ resource/ucla.htm or to the National Clearinghouse for Alcohol and Drug Information's project on Substance Use in Popular Prime-Time Television at http://www.health.org/govstudy/tvmediastudy/ index.htm.

Basically it looks like a desk lamp with a chunky smoked-glass body.[21] In fact, it is Lee Weinblatt's People Reader, a device designed to surreptitiously monitor the way people react to magazine advertising. Behind the smoked glass are two tiny, remote-controlled video cameras, one that tracks eye movements and another that monitors which page is being perused. In a nearby office, technicians measure each dismissive glance and longing gaze.

Will a high school senior unconsciously dwell on an Air Force recruitment ad featuring computer screens that look like video games? Will a middle-aged man linger over an automobile ad featuring leggy female models? The People Reader was intended to answer questions like these for companies that spend millions of dollars on advertising and, in the past, have had to depend on the accuracy of a test subject's memory.

Mr. Weinblatt is founder of the Pretesting Company in Englewood, New Jersey, which has become the leader in sleight-of-hand advertising research. He has developed an extensive bag of tricks, some of them incorporating technology originally developed for espionage. The People Reader is one; another is a mock car radio that plays prerecorded material and measures the speed with which a driver silences a commercial. There is also a television system that measures the tendency of viewers armed with remote-control devices to "zap" a particular commercial, and a computer-simulated supermarket to measure the allure of a new package. Mr. Weinblatt has hidden video cameras in a fake bar of Ivory soap, a box of cereal ("old hat now," he says), and in a ceiling sprinkler.

The unifying theme of Mr. Weinblatt's technology is eliciting responses consumers may not be aware of. Typically, people being tested are given only a limited idea—and often the wrong one—about what is actually being measured.

Since starting his company in 1985, Mr. Weinblatt has acquired an impressive list of clients, including Ralston Purina, RJR Nabisco's Planter's peanuts, S. C. Johnson's Raid insecticide, *Sports Illustrated,* and *The New Yorker.* Although Pretesting remains small, with revenues of $5.5 million, clients say Mr. Weinblatt offers them insights unlike those generated by any other advertising researchers. "I've recommended his tests many times," said Sue Le Barron, a project manager for pet food marketing research at Ralston Purina.

Traditionally, advertising research has been based on fairly overt approaches. To test a proposed television ad, for example, companies arrange to transmit the commercials to television sets of test subjects during normal programming and then interview them the next day on their ability to remember the ad and on their reactions.

Similarly, the traditional method of pretesting a new package or design is to expose it to a "focus group" of consumers who examine and react to it. Mr. Weinblatt argues that such techniques provide at best a murky picture, often failing to measure the impact of subliminal messages or, in the case of focus groups, prompting judgments in situations that don't mirror real life.

"Diagnostic research can be very useful for understanding what the problem is with a product, but it can never tell you what people are going to do in the real world," said Mr. Weinblatt. "Do people read *Newsweek* from the front or the back? How do you time the sequence of television ads? How does print stack up against TV? The questions have been piling up."

Mr. Weinblatt has been tinkering with attention-measuring devices since 1971. Armed with a master's degree in industrial psychology (and, later, in photography), he started out with the research subsidiary of the Interpublic Group of Companies Inc., which owns several major advertising agencies.

At the time, many advertising researchers were experimenting with "pupilmetrics," the measurement of pupil dilation, by filming people who were strapped into chairs and whose heads were anchored into wax molds. Mr. Weinblatt designed equipment that was less intrusive. His first assignment came from Philip Morris, which he said wanted to find the least noticeable place to mount warning labels required by the Surgeon General on a pack of cigarettes. "We found that it didn't make any difference," said Mr. Weinblatt. "Smokers don't want to see."

In 1976, Mr. Weinblatt started Telcom Research, a manufacturer of portable eye movement recorders, which he sold in 1982, just before it was about to go bankrupt. But he continued inventing increasingly unobtrusive measurement devices, and founded the Pretesting Company in 1985. Today he holds 28 patents.

To measure the chances that consumers will be attracted to a new package on crowded supermarket shelves, Mr. Weinblatt developed a computer-simulated shopping spree. Researchers evaluating a new line of dog food, for example, begin by recreating a supermarket rack in the dog food section that contains the new package. They then photograph the shelf as a whole and take close-ups of each quadrant of the shelf. This material is mixed in with similar sequences depicting the store entrance and several other supermarket sections.

People being tested are then told to "walk" through the store by reviewing slides of these images on a screen. Pressing buttons on a controller, they can move forward or backward between shelves and move in for closeups. At each section they are asked to pick out what, if anything, they would like to buy. Their answers, however, constitute only a small part of the test. The key measurements, according to Mr. Weinblatt, are based on the way they move through the slides. Unknown to the customers, a computer linked to the controller logs the amount of time spent at each picture and provides an instant tabulation of how long a person lingered at the dog food rack and at a particular part of it containing the new product. That data, in turn, can be compared with data for the rest of the supermarket and for competing products.

Mr. Weinblatt concedes there have been instances in which he incorrectly predicted that a commercial would fail. Nevertheless, he argues, his measurements offer cru-

cial information in a world of cluttered store shelves, where nine out of ten new products fail. "The typical person spends 22 minutes shopping in a supermarket that contains 18,000 products," said Mr. Weinblatt. "What we're saying is, before you bet all that money on a new product, let's do the ideal and see if people are even going to notice it."

Question
Evaluate each observation technique used by the Pretesting Company. What possible applications might each technique have?

EXPERIMENTAL RESEARCH

What you will learn in this chapter

- To define *experimentation* and discuss the requirements for making a true experiment.
- To discuss the factors that influence the choice and manipulation of the independent variables.
- To evaluate the factors that influence the selection and measurement of the dependent variables.
- To understand how to select and assign test units.
- To compare and contrast the two basic types of experimental error.
- To give examples of demand characteristics.
- To discuss how to control extraneous variables in experimental situations.
- To discuss some ethical issues in experimentation.
- To compare and contrast field and laboratory experiments.
- To distinguish between internal and external validity.
- To list the six major factors that threaten internal validity and provide examples of each.
- To outline the various quasi-experimental designs and alternative, better experimental designs.
- To understand that test marketing provides an opportunity to experiment with new marketing strategies under realistic market conditions.

Does the size of a package influence a person to increase or decrease consumption? A series of tightly controlled laboratory experiments found evidence that larger packages encourage consumers to increase the amount of the product they use. The hypothesis for one experiment was that the larger a package's size, the more a person will use on a given occasion.[1] The experiment required altering package size while holding the total supply of the product constant.

The procedure was as follows. The researchers recruited 98 adult women through local Parent-Teacher Associations (PTAs) and donated $6 to the respective organization for each participant. Two different products—Crisco oil and Creamette spaghetti—in two different sizes were selected for the study. In both cases, the larger package held twice as much of the product as the smaller package. The supply of each brand was held constant by leaving the smaller package full and using only half of the larger package. The volume of each product was determined by the package size in which it was sold.

Each subject was randomly assigned to use either a relatively small or a relatively large package, each holding identical volumes of the product. Two products were used for generalizability, and the pattern of results was expected to be similar for both products.

In individual meetings, each subject was told that researchers were collecting some basic "home economics–related" information about two different types of products. The subject was then led to one of four isolated cubicles containing either a large or a small package of one of the two products. The research assistant assigned to each cubicle did not know the purpose of the study. When the subject arrived, the research assistant read a scenario involving the use of the product: for Crisco oil, "You are frying a chicken dinner for yourself and another adult," and for Creamette spaghetti, "You are making spaghetti for yourself and another adult." The subject was asked to show how much of the product she would use in this situation and then asked how much money that use of the product would entail. After the subject left the cubicle, a researcher measured the volume of the product the subject intended to use. The procedure was repeated for all subjects.

The dependent measure was the volume of the product each subject indicated she would use. Subjects indicated their use of oil by pouring it into a frying pan; they indicated their use of spaghetti by placing it in a large (dry) pot. The volume of oil they used was measured by pouring the liquid into a narrow beaker. The volume of spaghetti was measured by holding the strands together and measuring the circumference with a finely graduated tape measure; this was later translated to an approximation of an individual count.

As was hypothesized, manipulating the package size while holding the supply of each product constant indicated that increases in a package's size were associated with increases in product usage.

Related experiments show that consumers will use more from a full container than from a half-empty one. Even when a package recommends an amount to use, as household cleaners do, research shows consumers ignore such instructions 70 percent of the time.[2]

This chapter explores the use of experimentation in marketing. ▪

THE NATURE OF EXPERIMENTS

Most students are familiar with the concept of experimentation in the physical sciences. The term *experiment* typically brings to mind an image of a chemist surrounded by bubbling test tubes and Bunsen burners. Behavioral and physical scientists have been far ahead of marketing researchers in the use of experimentation. Nevertheless, the purpose of experimental research is the same.

Experimental research allows the investigator to control the research situation so that causal relationships among variables may be evaluated. The standard marketing experimenter manipulates a single variable in an investigation and holds constant all other relevant, extraneous variables. Events may be controlled in an experiment to a degree not possible in a survey.

The researcher's goal in conducting an experiment is to determine whether the experimental treatment is the cause of the effect being measured. If a new marketing strategy (for example, new advertising) is used in a test market and sales subsequently increase in that market but not in markets where the new strategy is not employed, the experimenter can feel confident that the new strategy caused the increase in sales.

Experiments differ from other research methods in the degree of control over the research situation. In an **experiment**, one variable (the *independent variable*) is manipulated and its effect on another variable (the *dependent variable*) is measured while all other variables that may confound the relationship are eliminated or controlled. The experimenter either creates an artificial situation or deliberately manipulates a real-life situation.

One famous marketing experiment investigated the influence of brand name identification on consumers' taste perceptions. The experimenter manipulated whether consumers tasted beer in labeled or unlabeled bottles. One week respondents were given a six-pack containing bottles labeled only with letters.

experiment
A research method in which conditions are controlled so that one or more independent variables can be manipulated to test a hypothesis about a dependent variable. Experimentation allows evaluation of causal relationships among variables while all other variables are eliminated or controlled.

The following week, respondents received another six-pack with brand labels. Thus, respondents never made an actual purchase from a store but drank the beer at home at their leisure. The experimenter measured reactions to the beers after each tasting. The beer itself was the same in each case, so differences in taste perception were attributed to label (brand) influence. This example illustrates that once an experimenter manipulates the independent variable, he or she measures changes in the dependent variable. The essence of an experiment is to do something to an individual and observe the reaction under conditions that allow the reaction to be measured against a known baseline.

BASIC ISSUES IN EXPERIMENTAL DESIGN

Decisions must be made about several basic elements of an experiment. These issues are (1) manipulation of the independent variable, (2) selection and measurement of the dependent variable, (3) selection and assignment of test units, and (4) control over extraneous variables.[3]

Manipulation of the Independent Variable

independent variable
In an experimental design, the variable that can be manipulated, or altered, independently of any other variable.

The experimenter has some degree of control over the **independent variable.** The variable is independent because the experimenter can manipulate, or alter, its value to whatever he or she wishes it to be independently of any other variable. The independent variable is hypothesized to be the causal influence.

experimental treatments
Alternative manipulations of the independent variable being investigated.

Experimental treatments are the alternative manipulations of the independent variable being investigated. For example, prices of $1.29, $1.69, and $1.99 might be the treatments in a pricing experiment. Price changes, advertising strategy changes, taste formulation, and so on are typical treatments.

In marketing research, the independent variable often is a *categorical* or *classificatory variable* that represents some classifiable or qualitative aspect of marketing strategy. To determine the effects of point-of-purchase displays, for example, the experimental treatments that represent the independent variable are the different displays. Alternative advertising copy is another example of a categorical or classificatory variable. In other situations, the independent variable may be a *continuous variable*. The researcher must select the appropriate levels of that variable as experimental treatments. For example, the number of dollars that can be spent on advertising may be any number of different values.

experimental group
The group of subjects exposed to the experimental treatment.

control group
The group of subjects exposed to the control condition, that is, not exposed to the experimental treatment.

Experimental and Control Groups   In the simplest type of experiment, only two values of the independent variable are manipulated. Consider an experiment measuring the influence of advertising on sales. In the experimental condition (treatment administered to the **experimental group**), the advertising budget may be at $200,000. In the control condition (treatment administered to the **control group**), advertising may remain at zero or without change. By holding conditions constant in the control group, the researcher controls for potential sources of error in the experiment. Sales (the dependent variable) in the two treatment groups are compared at the end of the experiment to determine whether the level of advertising (the independent variable) had any effect.

Several Experimental Treatment Levels   An advertising/sales experiment using one experimental and one control group may not tell the advertiser everything he or she wishes to know about the advertising-sales relationship. If the advertiser wished to understand the functional nature of the relationship between sales and advertising at several treatment levels, additional experimental groups with advertising expenditures of $200,000, $500,000, and $1 million might be studied. This type of design would allow the experimenter to get a better idea of an optimal advertising budget.

More Than One Independent Variable   It is possible to assess the effects of more than one independent variable. In basic experimental designs, a single independent variable is manipulated to observe its effect on another single dependent variable. However, complex marketing-dependent variables such as sales, product usage, and brand preference are influenced by several factors. The simultaneous changes in independent variables such as price and advertising may have a greater influence on sales than a change in either variable alone. *Factorial experimental designs* are more sophisticated than basic experimental designs; they allow for an investigation of the interaction of two or more independent variables. Whether the experiment is basic or factorial, the purpose of marketing research experimentation is to measure and compare the effects of experimental treatments on the dependent variable.

Selection and Measurement of the Dependent Variable

dependent variable
The criterion by which the results of an experiment are judged; a variable expected to be dependent on the experimenter's manipulation of the independent variable.

The **dependent variable** is so named because its value is expected to be dependent on the experimenter's manipulation of the independent variable; it is the criterion or standard by which the results are judged. Changes in the dependent variable are presumed to be a consequence of changes in the independent variable.

Selection of the dependent variable is a crucial decision in the design of an experiment. If researchers introduce a new pink grapefruit tea mix in a test market experiment, sales volume is most likely to be the dependent variable. However, if researchers are experimenting with different forms of advertising copy appeals, defining the dependent variable may be more difficult. For example, measures of advertising awareness, recall, changes in brand preference, or sales might be used as the dependent variable, depending on the purposes of the ads. In the package size experiment dealing with Crisco oil, the dependent variable was the volume of oil that would be used. However, the dependent variable might have been the consumer's estimate of the total cost of the meal or attitude toward using a given amount of oil (a cognitive variable).

Often the dependent-variable selection process, like the problem definition process, is considered less carefully than it should be. The experimenter's choice of a dependent variable determines what type of answer is given to the research question.

In a test market, the amount of time needed for the effects to become evident should be considered in choosing the dependent variable. Sales may be measured several months after the experiment to determine if any carryover effects occurred. Changes that are relatively permanent or longer lasting than changes generated only during the period of the experiment should be considered; repeat purchase behavior may be important. Consumers may try a "loser" once, but they may not rebuy. The introduction of the original Crystal Pepsi illustrates the need to think beyond consumers' initial reactions. When Crystal Pepsi was introduced, the clear cola received high initial trial rates, but only a small percentage of customers made repeat purchases. The brand never achieved high repeat sales within a sufficiently large market segment. Brand awareness, trial purchase, and repeat purchase are all possible dependent variables in an experiment. The dependent variable therefore should be considered carefully. Thorough problem definition will help the researcher select the most important dependent variable(s).

Selection and Assignment of Test Units

Test units are the subjects, or entities, whose responses to the experimental treatment are measured or observed. Individuals, organizational units, sales territories, or other entities may be the test units. People are the most common test units in most marketing and consumer behavior experiments.

Sample Selection and Random Sampling Errors

As in other forms of marketing research, random sampling errors and sample selection errors may occur in experimentation. For example, experiments sometimes go awry even when a geographic area is specially chosen for a particular investigation. A case in point was the experimental testing of a new lubricant for outboard motors by Dow Chemical Company. The lubricant was tested in Florida and Michigan. Florida was chosen because researchers thought a warm-weather state, in which the product would have to stand up under continuous use, would prove the most demanding test. In Florida, the lubricant was a success. In Michigan, however, the story was quite different. Although the lubricant sold well and worked well during the summer, the following spring Dow discovered that in the colder northern climate the lubricant had congealed, allowing the outboard motors, idle all winter, to rust. The rusting problem never came to light in Florida, where the motors were in year-round use. Thus, some sample selection error may result from the procedure used to assign subjects or test units to either the experimental or the control group.

Random sampling error may occur if repetitions of the basic experiment sometimes favor one experimental condition and sometimes the other on a chance basis. An experiment dealing with charcoal briquets may require that the people in both the experimental and the control groups be identical with regard to level of product usage and barbecuing habits. However, if subjects are randomly assigned to conditions without knowledge of their product usage, errors resulting from differences in that usage will be random sampling errors.

Suppose a potato chip manufacturer wishes to experiment with new advertising appeals and wants the groups to be identical with respect to advertising awareness, media exposure, and so on. The experimenter must decide how to place subjects in each treatment group and which group should receive treatment. Researchers generally agree that the random assignment of participants to groups and experimental treatments to groups is the best procedure.

Randomization

Randomization, the random assignment of subjects and treatments to groups, is one device for equally distributing or scattering the effects of extraneous variables to all conditions. Thus, the chance of unknown nuisance effects piling up in particular experimental groups can be identified. The effects of the nuisance variables will not be eliminated, but they will be controlled. Randomization assures the researcher that overall repetitions of the experiment under the same conditions will show the true effects, if those effects exist. Random assignment of conditions provides "control by chance."[4] Random assignment of subjects allows the researcher to assume the groups are identical with respect to all variables except the experimental treatment.

Matching   Random assignment of subjects to the various experimental groups is the most common technique used to prevent test units from differing from each other on key variables. However, if the experimenter believes certain extraneous variables may affect the dependent variable, he or she can make sure the subjects in each group are matched on these characteristics. **Matching** the respondents on the basis of pertinent background information is another technique for controlling assignment errors. For example, in a taste test experiment for a dog food, it might be important to match the dogs into various experimental groups on the basis of age or breed. Similarly, if age is expected to influence savings behavior, a savings and loan conducting an experiment may have greater assurance that there are no differences among subjects if subjects in all experimental conditions are matched according to age.

Although matching assures the researcher that the subjects in each group are similar on the matched characteristics, the researcher cannot be certain that subjects have been matched on all characteristics potentially important to the experiment.

Repeated Measures   Experiments in which the same subjects are exposed to all experimental treatments are said to have **repeated measures.** This technique eliminates any problems due to subject differences, but it causes some other problems that we will discuss later.

Control over Extraneous Variables

The fourth decision about the basic elements of an experiment concerns control over extraneous variables. To understand this issue, it is important to understand the various types of experimental error.

In Chapter 7, we classified total survey error into two basic categories: random sampling error and systematic error. The same dichotomy applies to all research designs, but the terms *random (sampling) error* and *constant (systematic) error* are more frequently used when discussing experiments.

Constant Experimental Error from Extraneous Variables   We have already discussed random error in the context of experimental selection and assignment of test units. **Constant error** (bias) occurs when the extraneous variables or the conditions of administering the experiment are allowed to influence the dependent variables every time the experiment is repeated. When this occurs, the results will be confounded because the extraneous variables have not been controlled or eliminated.

For example, if subjects in an experimental group are always administered the treatment in the morning and subjects in the control group always receive it in the afternoon, a constant, systematic error will occur. In such a situation, the time of day—an uncontrolled extraneous variable—is a cause of constant error. In a training experiment, the sources of constant error might be the persons who do the training (operations personnel or external specialists) or whether the training is conducted on the employees' own time or on company time. These and other characteristics of the training may have an impact on the dependent variable and will have to be taken into account.

A number of extraneous variables may affect the dependent variable, thereby distorting the experiment. An example shows how extraneous variables may affect results.[5] Suppose a television commercial for brand Z gasoline shows two automobiles on a highway. The announcer states that one car has used brand Z

matching
A procedure for the assignment of subjects to groups that ensures that each group of respondents is matched on the basis of pertinent characteristics.

repeated measures
Experimental technique in which the same subjects are exposed to all experimental treatments to eliminate any problems due to subject differences.

constant error
An error that occurs in the same experimental condition every time the basic experiment is repeated; a systematic bias.

without the special additive and the other has used brand Z with the additive. The car without the special additive comes to a stop first, and the car with it comes to a stop 10 to 15 yards farther down the road. (We will assume both cars used the same quantity of gasoline.) The implication of this commercial is that the special additive (the independent variable) results in extra mileage (the dependent variable). As experimenters who are concerned with extraneous variables that could affect the result, we can raise the following questions:

1. Were the engines of the same size and type? Were the conditions of the engines the same (tuning, etc.)?
2. Were the cars of the same condition (gear ratios, fuel injector settings, weight, wear and tear, etc.)?
3. Were the drivers different? Were there differences in acceleration? Were there differences in the drivers' weights?

Because an experimenter does not want extraneous variables to affect the results, she or he must control or eliminate such variables.

demand characteristics
Experimental design procedures or situational aspects of an experiment that provide unintentional hints to subjects about the experimenter's hypothesis.

Demand Characteristics
Demand characteristics refer to experimental design procedures that unintentionally provide hints to subjects about the experimenter's hypothesis. Demand characteristics are situational aspects of the experiment that demand that participants respond in a particular way; hence, they are a source of constant error. If participants recognize the experimenter's expectation or demand, they are likely to act in a manner consistent with the experimental treatment; even slight nonverbal cues, such as a smile, may influence their reactions.

In most experiments, the most prominent demand characteristic is the person who actually administers the experimental procedures. If an experimenter's presence, actions, or comments influence subjects' behavior or sway subjects to slant their answers to cooperate with the experimenter, the experiment has **experimenter bias**. When subjects slant their answers to cooperate with the experimenter, they in effect are acting as guinea pigs and tend to exhibit behaviors that might not represent their behavior in the marketplace. For example, if subjects in an advertising experiment understand that the experimenter is interested in whether they changed their attitudes in accord with a given advertisement, they may answer in the desired direction to please him or her. This attitude change reflects a **guinea pig effect** rather than a true experimental treatment effect.

To reduce demand characteristics, the researcher typically takes steps to make it difficult for subjects to know what he or she is trying to find out. **Blinding** is used to control subjects' knowledge of whether they have been given a particular experimental treatment. In a cola taste test, one group of subjects might be exposed to the new formulation and the other exposed to the regular cola. If the subjects were blinded, all may have been told they had not been given the new formulation (or all may have been told they had received the new formulation). This technique frequently is used in medical research when subjects are given chemically inert pills (*placebos*) rather than medication.

experimenter bias
An effect on the subjects' behavior caused by an experimenter's presence, actions, or comments.

guinea pig effect
An effect on the results of an experiment caused by subjects changing their normal behavior or attitudes to cooperate with an experimenter.

blinding
A technique used to control subjects' knowledge of whether or not they have been given a particular experimental treatment.

Establishing Control of Extraneous Variables
The major difference between experimental research and other research is an experimenter's ability to hold conditions constant and manipulate the treatment. To conclude that A causes B, a brewery experimenting with a new, dark lager beer's influence on beer drinkers' taste perceptions must determine the possible extraneous variables other than the treatment that may affect the results and attempt to eliminate or

control those variables. Marketers know that brand image and packaging are important factors in beer drinkers' reactions, so the experimenter may wish to eliminate the effects associated with them. He or she may eliminate these two extraneous variables by packaging the test beers in plain packages without brand identification.

When extraneous variables cannot be eliminated, experimenters may strive for **constancy of conditions;** that is, they make efforts to expose all subjects in each experimental group to situations that are exactly alike except for the differing conditions of the independent variable. For example, experiments to measure consumers' evaluations of tissue paper softness have indicated that variation in humidity influences reactions. In this situation, holding extraneous variables constant might require that all experimental sessions be conducted in the same room at the same time of day.

If the experimental method requires that the same subjects be exposed to two or more experimental treatments, an error may occur due to the *order of presentation*. If a soft-drink company plans to test consumers' comparison of a high-caffeine, extra-sugar version of its cola versus its regular cola, one of the drinks must be tasted before the other. Consumers may tend to prefer the first drink they taste if they cannot tell any difference between the drinks. Another example is a video game manufacturer that has subjects perform two experimental tasks requiring some skill (that is, playing a game). Subjects may perform better on the second task simply because they have had some experience with the first task. **Counterbalancing** attempts to eliminate the confounding effects of order of presentation by requiring that half the subjects be exposed to treatment A first and then to treatment B while the other half receive treatment B first and then treatment A.

The random assignment of subjects and experimental treatments to groups is an attempt to control extraneous variations that result from chance. If certain

constancy of conditions
A situation in which subjects in experimental groups and control groups are exposed to situations identical except for differing conditions of the independent variable.

counterbalancing
A technique requiring that half the subjects be exposed to treatment A first and then to treatment B while the other half receive treatment B and then treatment A. This is an attempt to eliminate the confounding effects of order of presentation.

Sports Illustrated *conducts experiments to test its creative strategies and renewal materials to reveal the promotions that generate the highest response rates. For each renewal cycle,* Sports Illustrated *researchers include several control variables—source, price, amount paid, etc.—that are used to test the efficacy of renewal methods. (For example, the payment methods offered—bill me later, credit card, installment, etc.—will each elicit different responses.)*

extraneous variations cannot be controlled, the researcher must assume the confounding effects will be present in all experimental conditions with approximately the same influence. (This assumption may not hold true if the assignments were not random.) In many experiments, especially laboratory experiments, interpersonal contact between members of the various experimental groups and/or the control group must be eliminated or minimized. After the subjects have been assigned to groups, the various individuals should be kept separated so that discussion about what occurs in a given treatment situation will not become an extraneous variable that contaminates the experiment.

ETHICAL ISSUES IN EXPERIMENTATION

Experimental researchers address issues of privacy, confidentiality, deception, accuracy of reporting, and other ethical issues common to other research methods. The question of subjects' right to be informed, however, tends to be very prominent in experimentation. Research codes of conduct often suggest that the experimental subjects should be fully informed and receive accurate information. Yet experimental researchers who know that demand characteristics can invalidate an experiment may not give subjects complete information about the nature and purpose of a study. Simply put, experimenters often intentionally hide the true purposes of their experiments from subjects, perhaps by remaining silent. They then frequently debrief the subjects after the experiment. **Debriefing** is the process of providing subjects with all the pertinent facts about the nature and purpose of an experiment after the experiment has been completed.

debriefing
The process of providing subjects with all pertinent facts about the nature and purpose of an experiment after its completion.

Debriefing experimental subjects by communicating the purpose of the experiment and the researcher's hypotheses about the nature of consumer behavior is expected to counteract negative effects of deception, relieve stress, and provide an educational experience for the subject.

> Proper debriefing allows the subject to save face by uncovering the truth for himself. The experimenter should begin by asking the subject if he has any questions or if he found any part of the experiment odd, confusing, or disturbing. This question provides a check on the subject's suspiciousness and effectiveness of manipulations. The experimenter continues to provide the subject cues to the deception until the subject states that he believes there was more to the experiment than met the eye. At this time the purpose and procedure of the experiment [are] revealed.[6]

Researchers debrief subjects when there has been clear-cut deception or when they fear subjects may have suffered psychological harm from participating in an experiment (a rarity in marketing research). However, if the researcher does not foresee potentially harmful consequences in participation, she or he may omit debriefing because of time and cost considerations.[7]

laboratory experiment
An experiment conducted in a laboratory or other artificial setting to obtain almost complete control over the research setting.

Another issue that may—but typically does not—arise in marketing experiments is the subject's right to safety from physical and mental harm. Most researchers believe that if the subject's experience may be stressful or cause physical harm, the subject should receive adequate information about this aspect of the experiment *before* agreeing to participate.

FIELD AND LABORATORY EXPERIMENTS

A marketing experiment can be conducted in a natural setting (a field experiment) or in an artificial setting—one contrived for a specific purpose (a laboratory experiment). In a **laboratory experiment**, the researcher has almost complete control over the research setting. For example, subjects are recruited and brought to an advertising agency's office, a research agency's office, or perhaps a mobile unit designed for research purposes. They are exposed to a television commercial within the context of a program that includes competitors' ads, and they are not interrupted as they view the commercials. They are then allowed to purchase either the advertised product or one of several competing products in a simulated store environment. Trial purchase measures are thus obtained. A few weeks later, subjects are contacted again to measure their satisfaction and determine repeat purchasing intention. This typical laboratory experiment simulates the shopping experience and gives the consumer an opportunity to "buy" and "invest." Within a short time span, the marketer is able to collect information on decision making.

Another variation of a simulated shopping experiment involves using a representative panel of homemakers who receive a weekly visit at home from a salesperson in a mobile shopping van. This approach allows the researcher to measure trial, repeat purchase, and buying rates. Prior to the salesperson's visit the subjects are mailed a sales catalog and an order form that features the products being tested along with all the leading brands and any promotional support that is either current or being tested.

Other laboratory experiments may be more controlled or artificial. For example, a **tachistoscope** allows a researcher to experiment with the visual impact of advertising, packaging, and so on by controlling the amount of time a subject is exposed to a visual image. Each stimulus (for example, package design) is projected from a slide to the tachistoscope at varying exposure lengths ($\frac{1}{10}$ of a second, $\frac{3}{10}$, and so on). The tachistoscope simulates the split-second duration of a customer's attention in the same way a package might in a mass display.

In a **field experiment,** the researcher manipulates some variables but cannot control all the extraneous ones in the marketplace. Field experiments generally are used to fine-tune marketing strategies and to determine sales volume. For example, Betty Crocker's Squeezit (a 10 percent fruit juice drink in a squeeze bottle) could not keep up with demand in test marketing. The research showed the product's national introduction needed to be postponed until production capacity could be increased.

McDonald's conducted a field experiment to test market Triple Ripple, a three-flavor ice cream product. The product was dropped because the experiment revealed distribution problems reduced product quality and limited customer acceptance. In the distribution system the product would freeze, defrost, and refreeze. Solving the problem would have required each McDonald's city to have a local ice cream plant with special equipment to roll the three flavors into one. A naturalistic setting for the experiment helped McDonald's executives realize the product was impractical.

These examples illustrate that experiments vary in their degree of artificiality. Exhibit 9.1 shows that as experiments increase in naturalism, they begin to approach the pure field experiment, and as they become more artificial, they approach the laboratory type. The *degree of artificiality* in experiments refers to the amount of manipulation and control of the situation the experimenter uses to ensure that subjects will be exposed to the exact conditions desired.

tachistoscope
A device that controls the amount of time a subject is exposed to a visual image.

field experiment
An experiment conducted in a natural setting, where complete control of extraneous variables is not possible.

ISSUES OF EXPERIMENTAL VALIDITY

Experiments are judged by two measures. The first, internal validity, indicates whether the independent variable was the sole cause of the change in the dependent variable. The other, external validity, indicates the extent to which the results of the experiment are applicable to the real world.[8]

EXHIBIT 9.1 | THE ARTIFICIALITY OF LABORATORY VERSUS FIELD EXPERIMENTS

Internal Validity

When choosing or evaluating experimental research designs, researchers must determine whether they have internal validity and external validity. The first has to do with the interpretation of the cause-and-effect relationship in the experiment. **Internal validity** refers to the question of whether an experimental treatment was the sole cause of observed changes in the dependent variable. If the observed results were influenced or confounded by extraneous factors, the researcher will have problems making valid conclusions about the relationship between the experimental treatment and the dependent variable. If the observed results can be unhesitatingly attributed to the experimental treatment, the experiment is internally valid.

It is helpful to classify several types of extraneous variables that may jeopardize internal validity. The six major ones are history, maturation, testing, instrumentation, selection, and mortality.

History Suppose a before-and-after experiment is being conducted to test a new packaging strategy for an imported Chinese toy. If the Chinese engage in an anti-American political action that gets considerable media coverage, this action may jeopardize the validity of the experiment, because many Americans may boycott this brand of toy. This is an example of a **history effect**, which refers to specific events in the external environment between the first and second measurements that are beyond the experimenter's control. A common history effect occurs when competitors change their marketing strategies during a test marketing experiment.

A special case of the history effect is the **cohort effect,** which refers to a change in the dependent variable that occurs because members of one experimental group experienced different historical situations than members of other experimental groups. For example, two groups of managers used as subjects may be in different cohorts because one group experienced the turmoil of a corporate takeover while the other, hired after the takeover, experienced a different history and therefore may behave differently in a workplace experiment.

Maturation People change over time; that is, they undergo a process of maturation. During the course of an experiment, subjects may mature or change in some way that affects the results. **Maturation effects** are effects on the results of an experiment caused by changes in experimental subjects over time. They are a function of time rather than of a specific event. For example, during a daylong experiment, subjects may grow hungry, tired, or bored. In an experiment over a

internal validity
Validity determined by whether an experimental treatment was the sole cause of changes in a dependent variable or whether the experimental manipulation did what it was supposed to do.

history effect
The loss of internal validity caused by specific events in the external environment, occurring between the first and second measurements, that are beyond the experimenter's control.

cohort effect
A change in the dependent variable that occurs because members of one experimental group experienced different historical situations than members of other experimental groups.

maturation effect
An effect on the results of an experiment caused by experimental subjects maturing or changing over time.

THE MONKEY EVADES THE ELEPHANT

The strategy used by the makers of Formula 409 liquid cleaner to interrupt Procter & Gamble's test market and subsequent national introduction of Cinch is rather unique.[9] Although the campaign occurred several years ago, it dramatically illustrates how a small company can influence the actions of a giant one by manipulating a test market. Formula 409 was a family effort and the company's only product. When the company's president learned that Procter & Gamble would be test marketing Cinch in Denver, he did not increase advertising or lower prices for Formula 409. Indeed, he did just the opposite: He unobtrusively withdrew distribution in the Denver area. Salespeople were discouraged from restocking shelves. Thus, Procter & Gamble's test market success was overwhelming.

But wait: The marketers of Formula 409 had decided on a strategy that would discourage Procter & Gamble and other marketers in the long run. As Cinch was rolling out regionally, Formula 409's president decided to load up spray cleaner users with about a six-month supply of the product; a giant-size bottle was attached to the regular-size one at a reduced price. Since most 409 users were thus stocked up when Cinch was introduced, they did not need to buy the new product. Hence, initial sales for the giant packaged-goods marketer were disastrous. Thinking that the volume of Formula 409 was extremely small and that Denver test market results were abnormal, Procter & Gamble pulled out of the market. The president of Formula 409 had bet that Procter & Gamble was too big to notice the subtle moves of small Formula 409. It was an elephant grown so large that the monkey (Formula 409) had heard it coming and darted out of the way.

longer time span, maturation may influence internal validity because subjects grow older or more experienced or change in other ways that may influence the results. For example, suppose an experiment was designed to test the impact of a new compensation program on sales productivity. If this program were tested over a year's time, some of the salespeople probably would mature as a result of more selling experience or perhaps increased knowledge. Their sales productivity might improve because of their knowledge and experience rather than the compensation program.

testing effect
In a before-and-after study, the effect of pretesting, which may sensitize respondents or subjects when taking a test for the second time, thus affecting internal validity.

Testing **Testing effects** are also called *pretesting effects,* because the initial measurement or test alerts respondents to the nature of the experiment and respondents may act differently than they would if no pretest measures were taken. In a before-and-after study, taking a pretest before the independent variable is manipulated may sensitize respondents when they are taking the test the second time. For example, students taking standardized achievement and intelligence tests for the second time usually do better than those taking the tests for the first time. The effect of testing may increase awareness of socially approved answers, increase attention to experimental conditions (that is, the subject may watch more closely), or make the subject more conscious than usual of the dimensions of a problem.

Instrumentation Measuring the dependent variable in an experiment requires the use of a questionnaire or other form of measuring instrument. If the identical instrument is used more than once, a testing effect may occur. To avoid the effects of testing, an alternative form of the measuring instrument (for example, a questionnaire or test) may be given as the postmeasurement. Although this may reduce the testing effect, it may result in an instrumentation effect because of a change in the measuring instrument.

A change in the wording of questions, in interviewers, or in other procedures used to measure the dependent variable may cause an **instrumentation effect,** which may jeopardize internal validity. For example, if the same interviewers are used to ask questions both before and after measurement, some problems may arise. With practice, interviewers may acquire increased skill in interviewing, or they may become bored and decide to reword the questionnaire in their own terms. To avoid this problem, new interviewers are hired, but different individuals are a source of extraneous variation due to instrumentation variation. Numerous sources of instrument decay or variation are possible.

Selection   The **selection effect** is a sample bias that results from differential selection of respondents for the comparison groups, or sample selection error, addressed earlier.

Mortality   If an experiment is conducted over a period of a few weeks or more, some sample bias may occur due to **mortality,** or **sample attrition.** Sample attrition occurs when some subjects withdraw from the experiment before it is completed. Mortality effects may occur if many subjects drop from one experimental treatment group and not from other treatment or control groups. Consider a sales training experiment investigating the effects of close supervision of salespeople (high pressure) versus low supervision (low pressure). The high-pressure condition may misleadingly appear superior if those subjects who completed the experiment did very well. If, however, the high-pressure condition caused more subjects to drop out than the other condition, this apparent superiority may be due to a self-selection bias—perhaps only very determined and/or talented salespeople made it through the end of the experiment.

External Validity

The second type of validity involves the researcher's ability to generalize the results from the experiment to the marketplace or external environment. **External validity** is the ability of an experiment to generalize beyond the experiment data to other subjects or groups in the population under study. In essence, determining external validity involves a sampling question: To what extent can the results of a simulated shopping experiment be transferred to real-world supermarket shopping? Will a test market in Fort Wayne, Indiana, be representative of a nationwide introduction of the product under study? Can one extrapolate the results from a tachistoscope to an in-store shopping situation? Problems of external validity generally are related to the threat that a specific but limited set of experimental conditions will not deal with the interactions of untested variables in the real world. In other words, the experimental situation may be artificial and fail to represent the true setting and conditions in which the investigated behavior takes place. If the study lacks external validity, the researcher will have difficulty repeating the experiment with different subjects, settings, or time intervals.

If subjects in a shopping mall view a videotape that simulates an actual television program with a test commercial inserted along with other commercials, will the subjects view the commercial just as they would if it were being shown on a regular program? Some contamination probably will occur, but the experiment

instrumentation effect
An effect on the results of an experiment caused by a change in the wording of questions, in interviewers, or in other procedures used to measure the dependent variable.

selection effect
A sampling bias that results from differential selection of respondents for the comparison groups.

mortality (sample attrition) effect
A sample bias that results from the withdrawal of some subjects from the experiment before it is completed.

external validity
The ability of an experiment to generalize beyond the experiment data to other subjects or groups in the population under study.

may still be externally valid if the researcher knows how to adjust results from an artificial setting to the marketplace. Comparative norms may be established based on similar, previous studies so that the results can be projected beyond the experiment. If an experiment lacks internal validity, projecting its results is not possible. Thus, threats to internal validity may jeopardize external validity.

Trade-Offs between Internal and External Validity

Naturalistic field experiments tend to have greater external validity than artificial laboratory experiments. One problem the marketing researcher faces is that often it is necessary to trade off internal validity for external validity, because a laboratory experiment provides more control. A researcher who wishes to test advertising effectiveness via a split-cable experiment has the assurance that the advertisement will be viewed in an externally valid situation, that is, in the respondents' homes. However, the researcher has no assurance that some interruption (for example, a telephone call) will not have some influence that will reduce the internal validity of the experiment. Laboratory experiments with many controlled factors usually are high in internal validity, while field experiments generally have less internal validity but greater external validity.

CLASSIFICATION OF EXPERIMENTAL DESIGNS

The design of an experiment may be compared to an architect's plans for a structure, whether a giant skyscraper or a modest home. The basic requirements for the structure are given to the architect by the prospective owner. It is the architect's task to fill these basic requirements; yet the architect has ample room for exercising ingenuity. Several different plans may be drawn up to meet all the basic requirements. Some may be more costly than others; of two plans with the same cost, one may offer potential advantages that the second does not.[10]

basic experimental design
An experimental design in which a single independent variable is manipulated to measure its effect on another single dependent variable.

There are various types of experimental designs. If only one variable is manipulated, the experiment is a **basic experimental design.** If the experimenter wishes to investigate several levels of the independent variables (for example, four price levels) or to investigate the interaction effects of two or more independent variables, the experiment requires a *complex,* or *statistical,* experimental design.

Symbolism for Diagramming Experimental Designs

The work of Campbell and Stanley has helped many students master the subject of basic experimental designs.[11] The following symbols will be used in describing the various experimental designs:

X = exposure of a group to an experimental treatment
O = observation or measurement of the dependent variable; if more than one observation or measurement is taken, subscripts (O_1, O_2, etc.) indicate temporal order.[12]
$\boxed{R}$ = random assignment of test units; $\boxed{R}$ symbolizes that individuals selected as subjects for the experiment are randomly assigned to the experimental groups.

The diagrams of experimental designs that follow assume a time flow from left to right. Our first example will make this clearer.

Three Examples of Quasi-Experimental Designs

quasi-experimental design
A research design that cannot be classified as a true experiment because it lacks adequate control of extraneous variables.

one-shot design
An after-only design in which a single measure is recorded after the treatment is administered.

Quasi-experimental designs do not qualify as true experimental designs because they do not adequately control for the problems associated with loss of external or internal validity.

One-Shot Design

The **one-shot design**, or *after-only design*, is diagrammed as follows:

$$X \qquad O_1$$

Suppose that during a very cold winter, an automobile dealer finds herself with a large inventory of cars. She decides to experiment with a promotional scheme: offering a free trip to New Orleans with every car sold. She experiments with the promotion (X = experimental treatment) and measures sales (O_1 = measurement of sales after the treatment is administered). The dealer is not really conducting a formal experiment; she is just "trying something out."

This one-shot design is a case study of a research project fraught with problems. Subjects or test units participate because of voluntary self-selection or arbitrary assignment, not because of random assignment. The study lacks any kind of comparison or any means of controlling extraneous influences. There should be a measure of what will happen when the test units have not been exposed to X to compare with the measures of when subjects have been exposed to X. Nevertheless, under certain circumstances, even though this design lacks internal validity, it is the only viable choice.

The nature of taste tests or product usage tests may dictate the use of this design. In a taste test experiment, consumers sampled Borden ice cream from boxes and cartons. When asked which was "creamier," they invariably chose the premium-shaped carton.

One-Group Pretest–Posttest Design

one-group pretest–posttest design
A quasi-experimental design in which the subjects in the experimental group are measured before and after the treatment is administered, but there is no control group.

Suppose a real estate franchisor wishes to provide a training program for franchisees. If it measures subjects' knowledge of real estate selling before (O_1) they are exposed to the experimental treatment (X) and then measures real estate selling knowledge after (O_2) they are exposed to the treatment, the design will be as follows:

$$O_1 \qquad X \qquad O_2$$

In this example, the trainer is likely to conclude that the difference between O_2 and O_1 ($O_2 - O_1$) is the measure of the influence of the experimental treatment. This **one-group pretest–posttest design** offers a comparison of the same individuals before and after training. Although this is an improvement over the one-shot design, this experiment still has several weaknesses that may jeopardize internal validity. For example, if the time lapse between O_1 and O_2 was a period of several months, the trainees may have matured as a result of experience on the job (maturation effect). History effects also may influence this design. Perhaps some subjects dropped out of the training program (mortality effect). The effect of testing also may have confounded the experiment. For example, taking a test on real estate selling may have made subjects more aware of their lack of specific knowledge; either during the training sessions or on their own, they may have sought to brush up on material about which they realized they were ignorant.

If the second observation or measure (O_2) of salespersons' knowledge was not an identical test, the research may suffer from the instrumentation effect. If the researcher gave an identical test but had different graders for the before and after measurements, the data may not be directly comparable.

Although this design has a number of weaknesses, it is used frequently in marketing research. Remember, the cost of the research is a consideration in most business situations. Even if there will be some problems of internal validity, the researcher must always take into account questions of time and cost.

static group design
An after-only design in which subjects in the experimental group are measured after being exposed to the experimental treatment and the control group is measured without having been exposed to the experimental treatment; no premeasure is taken.

Static Group Design   In the **static group design,** each subject is identified as a member of either an experimental group or a control group (for example, exposed or not exposed to a commercial). The experimental group is measured after being exposed to the experimental treatment, and the control group is measured without having been exposed to the experimental treatment:

$$\text{Experimental group: } X \qquad O_1$$

$$\text{Control group:} \qquad\qquad O_2$$

The results of the static group design are computed by subtracting the observed results in the control group from those in the experimental group ($O_1 - O_2$).

A major weakness of this design is its lack of assurance that the groups were equal on variables of interest before the experimental group received the treatment. If the groups were selected arbitrarily by the investigator, or if entry into either group was voluntary, systematic differences between the groups could invalidate the conclusions about the effect of the treatment. For example, suppose a company that manufactures trash compactors wishes to compare the attitudes of subjects who have used a trash compactor for the first time with those who have not. If entry into the groups is voluntary, we might find that the group that receives the use of a trash compactor might have had some reason for choosing that option (for example, atypical amounts of garbage or poor garbage-collection service). Sample attrition of experimental group members who do not like trash compactors might also be a source of error.

Random assignment of subjects may minimize problems with group differences. If groups can be established by the experimenter rather than existing as a function of some other causation, the static group design is referred to as an *after-only design with control group.*

On many occasions, an after-only design is the only possible option. This is particularly true when conducting use tests for new products or brands. Cautious interpretation and recognition of the design's shortcomings may make this necessary evil quite valuable. For example, researchers conducted in-use tests of Carpet Fresh, a rug cleaner and room deodorizer. Experiments with Carpet Fresh, which originally was conceived as a granular product to be sprinkled on the floor before vacuuming, indicated that people were afraid the granules would lodge under furniture. This research led to changing the texture of the product to a powdery form.

Three Better Experimental Designs

In a formal, scientific sense, the three designs just discussed are not true experimental designs. Subjects for the experiments were not selected from a common pool of subjects and randomly assigned to one or another group. In the following discussion of three basic experimental designs, the symbol $\boxed{R}$ to the left of the diagram indicates that the first step in a true experimental design is the randomization of subject assignment.

pretest–posttest control group design

A true experimental design in which the experimental group is tested before and after exposure to the treatment and the control group is tested at the same two times without being exposed to the experimental treatment.

Pretest–Posttest Control Group Design (Before–After with Control)

The **pretest–posttest control group design,** or *before–after with control group design,* is the classic experimental design:

Experimental group: $\boxed{R}$ O_1 $\qquad X \qquad$ O_2

Control group: $\qquad$ $\boxed{R}$ O_3 $\qquad\qquad$ O_4

As the diagram indicates, subjects in the experimental group are tested before and after being exposed to the treatment. The control group is tested at the same two times as the experimental group, but subjects are not exposed to the experimental treatment. This design has the advantages of the before–after design with the additional advantages gained by its having a control group. The effect of the experimental treatment equals

$$(O_2 - O_1) - (O_4 - O_3)$$

If there is brand awareness among 20 percent of the subjects ($O_1 = 20$ percent, $O_3 = 20$ percent) before an advertising treatment and then 35 percent awareness in the experimental group ($O_2 = 35$ percent) and 22 percent awareness in the control group ($O_4 = 22$ percent) after exposure to the treatment, the treatment effect equals 13 percent:

$$(0.35 - 0.20) - (0.22 - 0.20) = (0.15) - (0.02)$$
$$= 0.13 \text{ or } 13\%$$

The effect of all extraneous variables is assumed to be the same on both the experimental and the control groups. For instance, since both groups receive the pretest, no difference between them is expected for the pretest effect. This assumption is also made for effects of other events between the before and after measurement (history), changes within the subjects that occur with the passage of time (maturation), testing effects, and instrument decay. In reality there will be some differences in the sources of extraneous variation. Nevertheless, in most cases, assuming that the effect is approximately equal for both groups is reasonable.

However, a testing effect is possible when subjects are sensitized to the subject of the research. This is analogous to what occurs when people learn a new vocabulary word. Soon they discover that they notice it much more frequently in their reading. In an experiment, the combination of being interviewed on a subject and receiving the experimental treatment might be a potential source of error. For example, a subject exposed to a certain advertising message in a split-cable experiment might say, "Ah, there is an ad for the product I was interviewed about yesterday!" The subject may pay more attention than usual to the advertisement and be more prone to change his or her attitude than in a situation with no testing effects. This weakness in the before–after with control group design can be corrected (see the next two designs).

Testing the effectiveness of television commercials in movie theaters provides an example of the before–after with control group design. Subjects are selected for the experiments by being told they are going to preview several new television shows. When they enter the theater, they learn that a drawing for several types of products will be held, and they are asked to complete a product preference questionnaire (see Exhibit 9.2). Then a first drawing is held. Next, the television pilots and commercials are shown. Then the emcee announces additional prizes and a second drawing. Finally, subjects fill out the same questionnaire about prizes. The information from the first questionnaire is the before

EXHIBIT 9.2 | PRODUCT PREFERENCE MEASURE IN AN EXPERIMENT

We are going to give away a series of prizes. If you are selected as one of the winners, which brand from each of the groups listed below would you truly want to win?

Special arrangements will be made for any product for which bulk, or one-time, delivery is not appropriate.

Indicate your answers by filling in the box like this: ■

Do not "X," check, or circle the boxes please.

Cookies		Allergy Relief Products	
(A 3-month supply, pick ONE.)		(A year's supply, pick ONE.)	
NABISCO OREO	☐ (1)	ALLEREST	☐ (1)
NABISCO OREO DOUBLE STUFF	☐ (2)	BENADRYL	☐ (2)
NABISCO NUTTER BUTTER	☐ (3)	CONTAC	☐ (3)
NABISCO VANILLA CREMES	☐ (4)	TAVIST–D	☐ (4)
HYDROX CHOCOLATE	☐ (5)	DRISTAN	☐ (5)
HYDROX DOUBLES	☐ (6)	SUDAFED	☐ (6)
NABISCO COOKIE BREAK	☐ (7)	CHLOR–TRIMETON	☐ (7)
NABISCO CHIPS AHOY	☐ (8)		
KEEBLER E.L. FUDGE	☐ (9)		
KEEBLER FUDGE CREMES	☐ (10)		
KEEBLER FRENCH VANILLA CREMES	☐ (11)		

measurement, and that from the second questionnaire is the after measurement. The control group receives similar treatment except that on the day they view the pilot television shows, different (or no) television commercials are substituted for the experimental commercials.

Posttest-Only Control Group Design (After-Only with Control)

In some situations pretest measurements are impossible. In other situations selection error is not anticipated to be a problem because the groups are known to be equal. The **posttest-only control group design**, or *after-only with control group design*, is diagrammed as follows:

Experimental group: $\boxed{R}$ X O_1

Control group: $\boxed{R}$ O_2

The effect of the experimental treatment is equal to $O_2 - O_1$.

Suppose the manufacture of an athlete's foot remedy wishes to demonstrate by experimentation that its product is better than a competing brand. No pretest measure about the effectiveness of the remedy is possible. The design is to randomly select subjects, perhaps students, who have contracted athlete's foot and randomly assign them to either the experimental or the control group. With only the posttest measurement, the effects of testing and instrument variation are eliminated. Further, researchers make the same assumptions about extraneous variables described above—that is, that they operate equally on both groups, as in the before–after with control group design.

posttest-only control group design
An after-only design in which the experimental group is tested after exposure to the treatment and the control group is tested at the same time without having been exposed to the treatment; no premeasure is taken. Random assignment of subjects and treatment occurs.

Solomon Four-Group Design By combining the pretest–posttest (before–after) with control group and the posttest-only (after-only) with control group designs, the **Solomon four-group design** provides a means for controlling the testing effect as well as other sources of extraneous variation. In the following diagram, the two Xs symbolize the same experimental treatment given to each experimental group:

$$\text{Experimental group 1:} \quad \boxed{R} \quad O_1 \quad X \quad O_2$$
$$\text{Control group 1:} \quad \boxed{R} \quad O_3 \quad \quad O_4$$
$$\text{Experimental group 2:} \quad \boxed{R} \quad \quad X \quad O_5$$
$$\text{Control group 2:} \quad \boxed{R} \quad \quad \quad O_6$$

Although we will not go through the calculations, it is possible to isolate the effects of the experimental treatment and testing in this design. Although this design allows for the isolation of the various effects, it is rarely used in marketing research because of the effort, time, and cost of implementing it. However, it points out that there are ways to isolate or control most sources of variation.

TEST MARKETING

Test marketing is an experimental procedure that provides an opportunity to test a new product or new marketing plan under realistic market conditions in order to measure sales or profit potential. Cities such as Eau Claire, Wisconsin or other small marketing areas are typical settings where a new product is distributed and marketed.

The major advantage of test marketing is that no other form of research can beat the real world when it comes to testing actual purchasing behavior and consumer acceptance of a product. For example, Benefit, an innovative cereal that General Mills claimed would reduce cholesterol, was a health-oriented product that stirred up controversy and angered some consumer activists when it was test marketed. Although Benefit contained psyllium, a soluble fiber scientifically shown to reduce cholesterol, Procter & Gamble asked the Food and Drug Administration to prevent General Mills from making health claims for Benefit and to rule that psyllium was a drug and not a food. In addition, General Mills learned that Benefit, which didn't taste all that good, appealed to a much narrower market segment than marketing strategists had envisioned.

Functions of Test Marketing

Test marketing provides two useful functions for management. First, it offers the opportunity to estimate the outcomes of alternative courses of action. Estimates can be made about optimal advertising expenditures, the need for product sampling, or how advertising and product sampling will interact. Researchers may be able to predict the sales effects of specific marketing variables, such as package design, price, or couponing, and select the best alternative action. Test marketing permits evaluation of the proposed national marketing mix.

A marketing manager for Life-Savers candies vividly portrays this function of experimentation in the marketplace:

> A market test may be likened to an orchestra rehearsal. The violinists have adjusted their strings, the trumpeters have tested their keys, the drummer has tightened his drums. Everything is ready to go. But all these instruments have not

worked in unison. So a test market is like an orchestra rehearsal where you can practice with everything together before the big public performance.[13]

A researcher may not only evaluate the outcome by investigating the product's sales volume; he or she can also investigate the new product's impact on other items within the firm's product line. Test marketing allows a firm to determine whether a new product will cannibalize sales from already profitable company lines. For example, Nabisco's cracker business is mature. The company has many brands, and it may use test marketing to make sure it is hitting the right consumer segment. A new cracker positioned at Saltine users may be a tremendous sales success, but a test market may show that the people who are actually buying it are snack cracker users and the new brand may take sales away from existing brands. In a similar situation, H. J. Heinz Company was concerned that the introduction of Heinz Salsa ketchup would take sales away from Heinz regular ketchup. Test marketing provided the necessary information, and Heinz no longer markets salsa ketchup in the United States. Test marketing is the best way to establish these market share relationships and to understand the problem of cannibalization.

The second useful function of test market experimentation is that it allows management to identify and correct any weaknesses in either the product or its marketing plan before making the commitment to a national sales launch—by which time it normally will be too late to incorporate product modifications and improvements. Thus, if test market results fall short of management's expectations, advertising weights, package sizes, and so on may be adjusted.

For example, McDonald's test marketed pizza for years. It learned competitors' reactions and the problems associated with small, individual-portion pizzas in its first test market experiment. The product strategy was repositioned, and the product testing shifted to marketing a 14-inch pizza that was not available until late afternoon. The research then focused on how consumers reacted to these pizzas sold in experimental restaurants remodeled to include "Pizza Shoppes," in which employees assembled ingredients on ready-made dough. Ultimately, McDonald's decided pizza should not be on its adult menu.

Factors to Consider in Test Market Selection

Obtaining a representative test market requires considering many factors that may not be obvious to the inexperienced researcher. Consider this observation by a vice president of a packaged-goods company:

> When I started in the business, I thought people picked cities like Columbus, Ohio, because their populations were typical. But I found the main reasons were that they were isolated media markets and the distribution patterns were such that they didn't have to worry about the chain warehouse shipping outside of Columbus. It's difficult to translate information from a city which represents 0.1 percent of the United States and multiply that to get 99.9 percent. I think it is much more important to get control of the distribution and the advertising message.[14]

As with all decisions, the objectives of the decision makers will influence the choice of alternative.

The following factors should be considered in the selection of a test market.

Population Size   The population should be large enough to provide reliable, projectable results, yet small enough to ensure that costs will not be prohibitive. New York City is not a popular test market; its size makes it unacceptable.

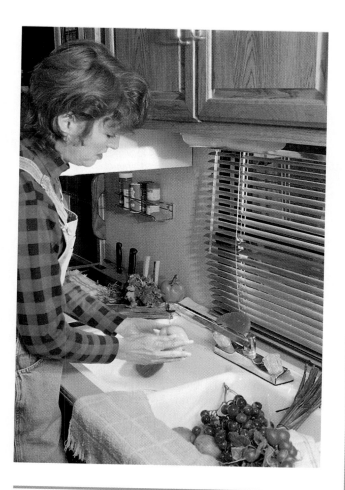

Fit is a rinse for produce from Procter & Gamble. It was in a Denver test market for more than 4 years. An initial hurdle for the new product was overcoming resistance from produce marketers and grocery retailers, who worried that Fit's advertising would arouse consumers' fears about produce safety. Another reason for the long test market was that the research showed that consumers required ample time to learn about the benefits of this unique product. Pringles, another P&G product, spent 7 years in test market.

Demographic Composition and Lifestyle Considerations

Ethnic backgrounds, incomes, age distributions, lifestyles, and other characteristics of the market should be representative of the nation or other target market. For example, test marketing on the West Coast may not be representative because people there tend to be quick to accept innovations that might not be adopted elsewhere.

Competitive Situation

Competitive market shares, competitive advertising, and distribution patterns should be typical so that test markets will represent other geographic regions. If these aspects of a test market are not representative, projectability will be difficult.

Consider the firm that test markets in one of its strongest markets. Its sales force has an easy time getting trade acceptance but may have difficulty in a market in which the firm is weak. That will influence the acceptance level, the cost of the *sell-in* (obtaining initial distribution), and the ultimate results of the test market. Hence, projecting the results of the test market into weaker markets becomes difficult.

Selecting an area with an unrepresentative market potential may cause innumerable problems. Firms probably should not test orange juice products in Florida, dairy products in Wisconsin, or antihistamines in Arizona.

Some companies test market outside the United States. Carewell Industries of Fairfield, New Jersey tested its Dentax toothbrush in Singapore. While Singapore may not have the same demographic profile as the United States, it offers extreme secrecy. It also offers a low-cost environment for launching a new product.

Media Coverage and Efficiency   Local media (television spots, newspapers) will never exactly replicate national media. However, duplicating the national media plan or one similar to it is important. Advertising in newspapers' Sunday supplements rather than in magazines does not duplicate the national plan, but such ads may provide a rough estimate of the plan's impact. Ideally, a market should be represented by the major television networks, typical cable television programming, and newspaper coverage. Some magazines have regional editions or advertising inserts.

Media Isolation   Advertising from outside communities may contaminate the test market. Further, advertising money is wasted when it reaches consumers who cannot buy the advertised product because they live outside the test area. Markets such as Tulsa, Oklahoma and Green Bay, Wisconsin are highly desirable because advertising does not spill over into other areas.

Self-Contained Trading Area   Distributors should sell primarily or exclusively in the test market area. *Spill-outs,* or shipments out of markets from chain warehouses, yield confusing shipping figures. Similarly, spill-ins (sales to shoppers from outside the territory) can confuse test market data.

Overused Test Markets   If consumers or retailers become aware of the tests, they will react differently than they normally would. Thus, one great test market should not be established. Tucson is one area now used less frequently than in the past because consumers there have displayed atypical reactions to new-product introductions. There always seemed to be a new display in the stores, and the public's reaction ceased to be average.

Loss of Secrecy   If a firm delays national introduction by test marketing, a competitor may find out about the experiment and "read" the results of the test market. The firm therefore runs the risk of exposing a new product or its plans to competitors. If the competitor finds the product easy to imitate, it may beat the originating company to the national marketplace. While Clorox Super Detergent with Bleach remained in the test market stage, Procter & Gamble (P&G) introduced Tide with Bleach nationally. Fab 1 Shot, a pouch laundry from Colgate-Palmolive, preempted Cheer Power Pouches by Procter & Gamble, but P&G wasn't sorry: Fab 1 Shot failed to be a commercial success. Although customers tried the new product, they stayed with the more traditional means of doing laundry over the long run.

Marketing research companies often select test market locations because the experiment will have a low chance of being detected by the competition. The control method of test marketing uses a "minimarket test" in a small city, using control store distribution, or forced distribution. A marketing research company that specializes in test marketing performs the entire test marketing task, including the initial sale to retailers (referred to as sell-in), warehousing, distribution, and shelving of the test product. The research company pays retailers for shelf space and therefore can guarantee distribution to stores that represent a predetermined percentage of the market's all-commodity volume (the total dollar sales for that product in a defined market). Thus, the firm is guaranteed distribution in stores that represent a predetermined percentage of the market. The control method increases the chances that the test market will be undetected.

SUMMARY

Experimental research allows the investigator to control the research situation to evaluate causal relationships among variables. In a basic experiment, one variable (the independent variable) is manipulated to determine its effect on another (the dependent variable). The alternative manipulations of the independent variable are referred to as experimental treatments.

The choice of dependent variable is crucial because this determines the kind of answer given to the research problem. In some situations, deciding on an appropriate operational measure of the dependent variable is difficult.

For experiments, random sampling error is especially associated with selection of subjects and their assignment to the treatments. The best way to overcome this problem is by random assignment of subjects to groups and of groups to treatments.

Other errors may arise from using nonrepresentative populations (for example, college students) as sources of samples or from sample mortality, or attrition, in which subjects withdraw from the experiment before it is completed. In addition, marketing experiments often involve extraneous variables that may affect dependent variables and obscure the effects of independent variables. Experiments also may be affected by demand characteristics when experimenters inadvertently give cues to the desired responses. Also, the guinea pig effect occurs when subjects modify their behavior because they wish to cooperate with an experiment.

Extraneous variables can be controlled by eliminating them or by holding them constant for all treatments. Some extraneous error may arise from the order of presentation; this can be controlled by counterbalancing the order. Random assignment is an attempt to control extraneous variables by chance.

Two main types of marketing experiments are field experiments (such as test markets) conducted in natural environments and laboratory experiments conducted in artificial settings contrived for specific purposes.

Experiments are judged by two measures of validity. One is internal validity, the question of whether the independent variable was the sole cause of the change in the dependent variable. Six types of extraneous variables may jeopardize internal validity: history, maturation, testing, instrumentation, selection, and mortality. The second measure of validity is external validity, the extent to which the results can be generalized to the real world. Field experiments are lower than laboratory experiments on internal validity but higher on external validity.

There are many different types of experimental designs. Among the better experimental designs are pretest–posttest control group design, pretest-only control group design, and the Solomon four-group design.

Test marketing is an experimental procedure that provides an opportunity to test a new product or marketing plan under realistic conditions to obtain a measure of sales or profit potential. Its major advantage as a research tool is that it closely approximates reality. Test marketing provides the opportunity to estimate the outcomes of alternative courses of action.

Key Terms and Concepts

experiment
independent variable
experimental treatments
experimental group
control group
dependent variable
test unit
random sampling error
randomization
matching
repeated measures
constant error
demand characteristics
experimenter bias
guinea pig effect

blinding
constancy of conditions
counterbalancing
debriefing
laboratory experiment
tachistoscope
field experiment
internal validity
history effect
cohort effect
maturation effect
testing effect
instrumentation effect
selection effect
mortality (sample attrition) effect

external validity
basic experimental design
quasi-experimental design
one-shot design
one-group pretest–posttest design
static group design
pretest–posttest control group
    design
posttest-only control group design
Solomon four-group design
test marketing
control method of test marketing

Questions for Review and Critical Thinking

1. Name some independent and dependent variables frequently studied in marketing.
2. A tissue manufacturer that has the fourth-largest market share plans to experiment with a 50-cents-off coupon during November. It plans to measure sales volume for November using store scanners to determine the effectiveness of the coupon. What is the independent variable? The dependent variable? Do you see any problems with the dependent variable?
3. What purpose does the random assignment of subjects serve?
4. In a test of a new coffee, three styrofoam cups labeled A, B, and C are placed before subjects. The

subjects are instructed to taste the coffee from each cup. What problems might arise in this situation?
5. What are demand characteristics? Give some examples.
6. Do you think the guinea pig effect is a common occurrence in experiments? Why or why not?
7. How may an experimenter control for extraneous variation?
8. Name the type of experiment described in the following situations, and evaluate the strengths and weaknesses of each design.
   a. A major petroleum corporation is considering phasing out its premium unleaded gasoline. It

selects Nashville, Tennessee as an experimental market in which the product might be eliminated and decides to watch product line sales results.

b. A soft-drink manufacturer puts the same brand of orange drink into two different containers with different designs. Two groups are given a package and asked to rate the drink's taste. A third group is given the orange drink in an unlabeled package and asked the same question.

c. An advertising agency pretested a television commercial with a portable television set, simulating an actual television program with the test commercial inserted along with other commercials. This program was shown to a focus group, and group discussion followed.

d. A manufacturer of a new brand of cat food tested product sampling with a trial-size package versus no sampling and three price levels simultaneously to determine the best market penetration strategy.

9. Provide an example for each of the six major factors that influence internal validity.

10. Consider a research project conducted by a company to investigate a self-contained heating and lighting source designed to be used during power failures. The product was given to the experimental subjects, who were asked to wait until dark, then turn off their heat and lights and test the product. A few days later, they were telephoned and interviewed about their opinions of the product. Discuss the external and internal validity of this experiment.

11. Evaluate the ethical and research design implications of the following study:

Sixty-six willing Australian drinkers helped a Federal Court judge decide that Tooheys didn't engage in misleading or deceptive advertising for its 2.2 beer. The beer contains 2.2 percent alcohol, compared with 6 percent for other beers.

The volunteers were invited to a marathon drinking session after the Aboriginal Legal Service claimed Tooheys advertising implied beer drinkers could imbibe as much 2.2 as desired without becoming legally intoxicated. Drunken driving laws prohibit anyone with a blood-alcohol level above 0.05 from getting behind the wheel.

But the task wasn't easy; nor was it all fun. Some couldn't manage to drink in 1 hour the required ten "middies," an Aussie term for a beer glass of 10 fluid ounces.

Thirty-six participants could manage only nine glasses. Four threw up and were excluded; another two couldn't manage the "minimum" nine glasses and had to be replaced.

Justice J. Beaumont observed that consuming enough 2.2 in an hour to reach the 0.05 level was "uncomfortable and therefore an unlikely process." Because none of the ads mentioned such extreme quantities, he ruled they couldn't be found misleading or deceptive.[15]

12. A nighttime cough relief formula contains alcohol. An alternative formulation contains no alcohol. During an experiment, subjects are asked to try the product in their homes. Alternative formulations are randomly assigned to subjects. No mention of alcohol is given in the instructions to subjects. Is this ethical?

13. What are the benefits of test marketing? When is test marketing likely? When is it unlikely?

Exploring the Internet

1. Go to http://www.apa.org/releases/tvviolence.html to find a press release about television violence and memory of advertisements.

2. Learn more about quasi-experimental designs at http://trochim.omni.cornell.edu/kb/quasiexp.htm.

At a family gathering, Dan Kessler, the manager of an I.G.A. grocery store, got into a conversation with his brother-in-law, who supervised a large number of data-entry workers at a public utility company. Kessler's brother-in-law mentioned that his company recently had begun programming background music into the data-entry room. As a result, productivity had increased, and the number of errors had decreased.

Kessler thought that playing music in a grocery store might have an impact on customers. Specifically, he thought customers might stay in the store longer if slow, easy-to-listen-to music were played. After some serious thought, he decided he should hire a marketing researcher to design an experiment to test the influence of music tempo on shopper behavior.

Questions

1. Operationalize the independent variable (that is, specify some way of measuring it).
2. What dependent variables do you think might be important in this study?
3. Develop a hypothesis for each of your dependent variables.

Dentists recommend twice-yearly checkups. Although the benefits of preventive health care have been promoted for several decades, some people visit a dentist only when they are in pain.

One dentist, Sandra Brown, had read that sending out a recall card might increase participation in the 6-month dental checkup. She thought that having patients address a standard reminder card (see Case Exhibit 9.2-1) in their own handwriting would be more effective than simply printing out a standard reminder card. She also thought a promotional message appealing to an individual's aesthetic concerns might be more appropriate than a basic reminder message.

She designed the following experiment for her dental clinic, located on the fringe of the downtown area. The clinic patients were primarily African Americans and Mexican Americans, and most were from blue-collar households. All patients were considered subjects for the experiment.

There were four experimental groups: (1) Patients who visited the dentist in May were given the standard recall card (reminding them to return in October) and asked to fill it out in their own handwriting. (2) Patients who visited the dentist in June were given a promotional recall card (to return in November) and asked to fill it out in their own hand-writing. (3) Patients who visited the dentist in July received the standard recall card (to return in December) with a typed address. (4) Patients who visited the dentist in August received the promotional recall card (to return in January) with a typed address.

Questions

1. Evaluate this experimental design.
2. What type of experimental design is this?
3. What improvements would you suggest for the experiment?

CASE EXHIBIT 9.2-1	STANDARD RECALL CARD AND THE EXPERIMENTAL PROMOTIONAL CARD

Dear Patient,
    This is to remind you that it is time for a preventive dental examination.
    Please call so that we may arrange a time that is convenient for you.

                Sandra Brown, D.D.S.

Dear Patient,
    Preventive dental examinations keep you looking your best. Your teeth are part of your good looks.
    Please call so that we may arrange a time that is convenient for you.
    Let's keep your smile looking its best.

                Sandra Brown, D.D.S.

MEASUREMENT AND ATTITUDE SCALING

BBDO, an advertising agency, has developed a measuring system to evaluate consumers' emotional responses to advertising.[1] Its Emotional Measurement System is a proprietary technique that uses photographs of actors' faces to help consumers choose their reactions to commercials. Researchers at BBDO believe that the process virtually eliminates the inherent bias in traditional copy testing. With the conventional system, consumers often underestimate their emotional responses because they feel silly putting them into words, and words are subject to varying interpretations. Thus, traditional copy tests have tended to measure thoughts rather than feelings and therefore have failed to adequately measure emotional responses.

Rather than ask consumers to choose from a simple list or write in their own words, the agency has devised a deck of 53 photos—narrowed down from 1,800—representing what BBDO calls the "universe of emotions." Each features one of six actors with different expressions ranging from happy/playful to disgusted/revolted. The deck covers a total of 26 categories of emotions.

Here's how the system works. As with most copy testing, participants are shown a single commercial or group of spots and then are given a questionnaire to test whether they remembered brand names and copy points. At any point during this process, the researchers hand out the photos. Each person is asked not to write or speak about the spot but to quickly sort through the photos, setting aside any or all that reflect how he or she feels after viewing the commercial.

Innovative techniques such as the Emotional Measurement System have improved the measurement of marketing phenomena. This chapter discusses the basic measurement issues in marketing research and attitude measurement. ∎

What you will learn in this chapter

- To explain how a researcher might answer the question "What is to be measured?"
- To define *operational definition*.
- To distinguish among nominal, ordinal, interval, and ratio scales.
- To understand the need for index or composite measures.
- To define the three criteria for good measurement.
- To understand that an attitude is a hypothetical construct.
- To explain the attitude-measuring process.
- To discuss the differences among ranking, rating, sorting, and making choices to measure attitudes and preferences.
- To explain Likert scales, semantic differentials, and many other types of attitude scales.
- To understand how to measure behavioral intentions.

An object, such as the edge of your textbook, can be measured with either side of a ruler (see Exhibit 10.1). Note that one side has inches and the other has centimeters. Thus, the scale of measurement varies depending on whether the metric side or the standard side is used. Many measurement problems in marketing research are similar to this ruler with its alternative scales of measurement. Unfortunately, unlike the two edges of the ruler, many measurement scales used in marketing research are not directly comparable.

The first question the researcher must answer is "What is to be measured?" This question is not as simple as it sounds. The definition of the problem, based on exploratory research or managerial judgment, indicates the concept to be investigated (for example, sales performance). However, a precise definition of the concept may require a description of how it will be measured, and frequently there is more than one way to measure a particular concept. For example, if researchers are conducting research to determine which factors influence a sales representative's performance, they might use a number of measures to indicate a salesperson's success, such as dollar or unit sales volume or share of accounts lost. Further, true measurement of concepts requires a process of precisely assigning scores or numbers to the attributes of people or objects.[2] The purpose of assigning numbers is to convey information about the variable being measured. Hence, the key question becomes "On what basis will numbers or scores be assigned to the concept?"

Suppose the task is to measure the height of a boy named Michael. There are a number of ways to do this:

1. We can create five categories:
   (1) Quite tall for his age
   (2) Moderately tall for his age
   (3) About average for his age
   (4) Moderately short for his age
   (5) Quite short for his age

   Then we can measure Michael by saying that because he is moderately tall for his age, his height measurement is 2.
2. We can compare Michael to ten other neighborhood children. We give the tallest child the rank of 1 and the shortest the rank of 11; Michael's height

EXHIBIT 10.1 | A TWO-SIDED RULER THAT OFFERS ALTERNATIVE SCALES OF MEASUREMENT

measurement using this procedure is 4 if he is fourth tallest among the 11 neighborhood children.

3. We can use some conventional measuring unit such as centimeters and, measuring to the nearest centimeter, designate Michael's height as 137.

4. We can define two categories of height:
   (1) A nice height
   (2) A not-so-nice height
   By our personal standard, Michael's height is a nice height, so his height measurement is 1.[3]

In each measuring situation, we have assigned a score for Michael's height: 2, 4, 137, and 1. In scientific marketing, however, research precision is the goal. These various scores differ in their precision. The researcher must determine the best way to measure what is to be investigated.

On college campuses, girl or boy watching constitutes a measurement activity: What might be a 7 to one person may be a 9 to another. Precise measurement in marketing research requires a careful conceptual definition, an operational definition, and a system of consistent rules for assigning numbers or scores.

Concepts

concept
A generalized idea about a class of objects, attributes, occurrences, or processes.

Before beginning the measurement process, a marketing researcher must identify the concepts relevant to the problem. A **concept** (or *construct*) is a generalized idea about a class of objects, attributes, occurrences, or processes. Concepts such as age, gender, and number of children are relatively concrete properties, and they present few problems in definition or measurement. Other characteristics of individuals or properties of objects may be more abstract. Concepts such as brand loyalty, personality, channel power, and so on are more difficult to define and measure. For example, brand loyalty has been measured using the percentage of a person's purchases going to one brand in a given period of time, sequences of brand purchases, number of different brands purchased, amount of brand deliberation, and various cognitive measures, such as attitude toward a brand.

Operational Definitions

operational definition
An explanation that gives meaning to a concept by specifying the activities or operations necessary to measure it.

To be measurable, concepts must be made operational. An **operational definition** gives meaning to a concept by specifying the activities or operations necessary to measure it.[4] For example, the concept of nutrition consciousness might be reflected when a shopper reads the nutritional information on a cereal package. Inspecting a nutritional label is not the same as being nutrition conscious, but it is a clue that a person *may* be nutrition conscious.

The operational definition specifies what the researcher must do to measure the concept under investigation. If we wish to measure consumer interest in a specific advertisement, we may operationally define *interest* as a degree of increase in pupil dilation. Another operational definition of interest might rely on direct responses: what people say they are interested in. Each operational definition has advantages and disadvantages.

An operational definition is like a manual of instructions or a recipe: Even the truth of a statement such as "Gaston Gourmet likes key lime pie" depends on the recipe. Different instructions lead to different results.[5]

conceptual definition
A verbal explanation of the meaning of a concept; defines what the concept is and what it is not.

An operational definition tells the investigator, "Do such-and-such in so-and-so manner."[6] Exhibit 10.2 presents a **conceptual definition** and an operational definition from a study on media skepticism.

EXHIBIT 10.2 | MEDIA SKEPTICISM:
AN OPERATIONAL DEFINITION[7]

Concept	Conceptual Definition	Operational Definition
Media skepticism	Media skepticism is the degree to which individuals are skeptical of the reality presented in the mass media. Media skepticism varies across individuals, from those who are mildly skeptical and accept most of what they see and hear in the media to those who completely discount and disbelieve the facts, values, and portrayal of reality in the media.	Please tell me how true each statement is about the media. Is it very true, not very true, or not at all true? 1. The program was not very accurate in its portrayal of the problem. 2. Most of the story was staged for entertainment purposes. 3. The presentation was slanted and unfair. 4. I think the story was fair and unbiased. 5. I think important facts were purposely left out of the story. Individual items were scored on a 4-point scale with values from 1 to 4; higher scores represented greater skepticism. Media skepticism is defined as the sum of these five scores.

RULES OF MEASUREMENT

rule
A guide that tells someone what to do.

A **rule** is a guide that tells someone what to do.[8] An example of a measurement rule might be "Assign the numerals 1 through 7 to individuals according to how brand loyal they are. If the individual is extremely brand loyal, assign a 7. If the individual is a total brand switcher with no brand loyalty, assign a 1."

Operational definitions help a researcher specify the rules for assigning numbers. If the purpose of an advertising experiment is to increase the amount of time shoppers spend in a department store, for example, *shopping time* must be operationally defined. Once shopping time is defined as the interval between entering the door and receiving the receipt from the clerk, it is relatively easy to assign numbers using a stopwatch. If a study on gasohol, a blend of ethyl alcohol and gasoline, is not concerned with a person's depth of experience but defines people as users or nonusers, it could assign a 1 for experience with gasohol and a 0 for no experience with gasohol.

The values assigned in the measuring process can be manipulated according to certain mathematical rules. The properties of the scale of numbers may allow the researcher to add, subtract, or multiply answers. In some cases, there may be problems with the simple addition of the numbers, or other mathematical manipulations may not be permissible.

TYPES OF SCALES

A **scale** is a quantifying measure, a combination of items that is progressively arranged according to value or magnitude. In other words, a scale is a continuous spectrum or series of categories. The purpose of scaling is to represent, usually quantitatively, an item's, person's, or event's place in the spectrum.

scale
A quantifying measure in the form of a combination of items that is arranged progressively according to value or magnitude.

Marketing researchers use many scales or number systems. It is traditional to classify scales of measurement on the basis of the mathematical comparisons they allow. The four types of scale are the nominal, ordinal, interval, and ratio scales.

Nominal Scale

nominal scale
A scale in which the numbers or letters assigned to objects serve as labels for identification or classification.

Number 31 on the New York Mets is Mike Piazza. Sammy Sosa is number 21 on the Chicago Cubs. These numbers nominally identify these superstars. A **nominal scale** is the simplest type of scale. The numbers or letters assigned to objects serve as labels for identification or classification. These are scales in name only. Tulsa's census tract 25 and census tract 87 are merely labels. The number 87 does not imply that this area has more people or higher incomes than number 25. An example of a typical nominal scale in marketing research would be the coding of males as 1 and females as 2. As another example, the first drawing in Exhibit 10.3 depicts the number 7 on a horse's colors. This is merely a label to allow bettors and racing enthusiasts to identify that horse.

Ordinal Scale

ordinal scale
A scale that arranges objects or alternatives according to their magnitude in an ordered relationship.

If you've been to the racetrack, you know that when your horse finishes in the "show" position, it has come in third behind the win and the place horses (see the second drawing in Exhibit 10.3). An **ordinal scale** arranges objects or alternatives

| EXHIBIT 10.3 | NOMINAL, ORDINAL, INTERVAL, AND RATIO SCALES PROVIDE DIFFERENT INFORMATION |

Nominal

Ordinal — Show, Place, Win

Interval — 1 Length, 2 Lengths, Win

Ratio — Win, 40 to 1 long shot pays $80, $2

according to their magnitude in an ordered relationship. When respondents are asked to *rank order* their shopping center preferences, they assign ordinal values to them. In our racehorse example, if we assign 1 to the win position, 2 to the place position, and 3 to the show position, we can say that 1 was before 2 and 2 was before 3. However, we cannot say anything about the degree of distance or the interval between the win and show horses or the show and place horses.

A typical ordinal scale in marketing asks respondents to rate brands, companies, or the like as excellent, good, fair, or poor. Researchers know excellent is higher than good, but they do not know by how much.

Interval Scale

The third drawing in Exhibit 10.3 depicts a horse race in which the win horse is two lengths ahead of the place horse, which is one length ahead of the show horse. Not only is the order of finish known, but the distance between the horses is known. (This example assumes a standard measure for the term *length*.) **Interval scales** not only indicate order, but they also measure order (or distance) in units of equal intervals.

The location of the zero point is arbitrary. In the Consumer Price Index, if the base year is 1993, the price level during 1993 will be set at 100. Although this is an equal-interval measurement scale, the zero point is arbitrary. The classic example of an interval scale is the Fahrenheit temperature scale. If the temperature is 80°, it cannot be said that it is twice as hot as 40°, because 80° represents not a lack of temperature but a relative point on the Fahrenheit scale. Due to the lack of an absolute zero point, an interval scale does not allow the conclusion that the number 36 is three times as great as the number 12; it allows us to conclude only that the distance from 0 to 36 is three times as great. Likewise, when an interval scale is used to measure psychological attributes, the researcher can comment about the magnitude of differences or compare the average differences on the attributes that were measured, but cannot determine the actual strength of the attitude toward an object. However, changes in concepts can be compared over time if the researcher continues to use the same scale in longitudinal research.

Ratio Scale

To be able to say that winning tickets pay 40 to 1 or that racehorse number 7 is twice as heavy as racehorse number 5, we need a ratio scale (see the fourth drawing in Exhibit 10.3). **Ratio scales** have absolute rather than relative quantities. For example, both money and weight are measured with ratio scales that possess absolute zeros and interval properties. The absolute zero represents a point on the scale where a given attribute is absent. If we hear that a person has zero ounces of gold, we understand the natural zero value for weight. In the measurement of temperature, the Kelvin scale (a ratio scale) begins at absolute zero, a point that corresponds to −273.16° on the Celsius scale (an interval scale). In distribution or logistical research, it may be appropriate to think of physical attributes such as weight or distance as ratio scales in which the ratio of scale values is meaningful. For most behavioral marketing research, however, interval scales typically are the appropriate measurements.

Mathematical and Statistical Analysis of Scales

The type of scale used in marketing research will determine the form of the statistical analysis. For example, certain operations, such as calculation of a mean (mathematical average), can be conducted only if the scale is of an interval or a ratio nature; they are not permissible with nominal or ordinal scales. Chapter 14, Basic Data Analysis, further explores how the type of scale influences the choice of the appropriate statistical technique.

INDEX MEASURES

attribute
A single characteristic or fundamental feature of an object, a person, a situation, or an issue.

index (composite) measure
A multi-item instrument that uses several variables to measure a single concept.

So far we have focused on measuring a concept with a single question or observation. Measuring brand awareness, for example, might involve one question, such as "Are you aware of _____?" However, measuring more complex concepts may require more than one question because the concept has several attributes. An **attribute** is a single characteristic or fundamental feature of an object, a person, a situation, or an issue.

Multi-item instruments for measuring a single concept with several attributes are called **index measures,** or **composite measures.** For example, one index of social class is based on three weighted variables: residence, occupation, and education. Measures of cognitive phenomena often are composite indexes of sets of variables or scales. Items are combined into composite measures. For example, a salesperson's morale may be measured by combining questions such as "How satisfied are you with your job? How satisfied are you with your territory? How satisfied are you in your personal life?" Measuring the same underlying concept using a variety of techniques is one method for increasing accuracy. Asking different questions to measure the same concept provides a more accurate cumulative measure than does a single-item estimate.

THREE CRITERIA FOR GOOD MEASUREMENT

The three major criteria for evaluating measurements are reliability, validity, and sensitivity.

Reliability

reliability
The degree to which a measure is free from random error and therefore yields consistent results.

A tailor measuring fabric with a tape measure obtains a "true" value of the fabric's length. If the tailor repeatedly measures the fabric and each time come up with the same length, it is assumed the tape measure is reliable. When the outcome of the measuring process is reproducible—that is, when similar results are obtained over time and across situations—the measuring instrument is reliable. Broadly defined, **reliability** is the degree to which a measure is free of random error and therefore yields consistent results. For example, ordinal measures are reliable if they consistently rank order items in the same manner; reliable interval measures consistently rank order and maintain the same distance between items. Imperfections in the measuring process that affect the assignment of scores or numbers in different ways each time a measure is taken, such as when a respondent misunderstands a question, cause low reliability. The actual choice among plausible responses may be governed by such transitory factors as mood, whim, or the context set by surrounding questions; measures are not always error-free and stable over time.

Validity

The purpose of measurement is to measure what we intend to measure. Achieving this obvious goal is not, however, as simple as it sounds. Consider the student who takes a test (measurement) in a statistics class and receives a poor grade. The student may say, "I really understood that material because I studied

Airline travelers put "space," especially the distance between seat backs and leg room, high on their list of preferences. Space becomes extremely important if a flight is several hours long. Plog Travel Research found that when TWA gave people more leg room, they rated the meals more favorably—even though the meals did not change. In fact, a halo effect influenced the ratings of most other characteristics, not just the food.[9] Were the measures of food quality and airline characteristics other than leg room valid?

hard. The test measured my ability to do arithmetic and to memorize formulas rather than measuring my understanding of statistics." The student's complaint is that the test did not measure *understanding* of statistics, which was what the professor had intended to measure; it measured something else.

One technique for measuring the intention to buy is the *gift method*. Respondents are told a drawing will be held at some future period for a year's supply of a certain product. Respondents report which of several brands they would prefer to receive if they won. Do the respondents' reports of the brands they would prefer to win necessarily constitute a valid measure of the brands they will actually purchase in the marketplace if they do not win the contest? Could there be a systematic bias to identify brands they wish they could afford rather than the brands they would usually purchase? This is a question of **validity**, the ability of an instrument (for example, an attitude measure in marketing) to measure what it is intended to measure. If it does not, problems will result.

Students should be able to empathize with the following validity problem. Consider the controversy about highway patrol officers using radar guns to clock speeders. A driver is clocked at 75 mph in a 55 mph zone, but the same radar gun aimed at a house registers 28 mph. The error occurs because the radar gun is picking up impulses from the electrical system of the squad car's idling engine. The house isn't speeding—and the test is not valid.

Reliability versus Validity

Let's compare the concepts of reliability and validity. A tailor using a ruler may obtain a reliable measurement of length over time with a bent ruler. A bent ruler cannot provide perfect accuracy, however, and measurements obtained with one are not valid. Thus, reliability, although necessary for validity, is not sufficient by itself. In marketing, a measure of a subject's physiological reaction to a package (for example, pupil dilation) may be highly reliable, but it will not necessarily constitute a valid measure of purchase intention.

The differences between reliability and validity can be illustrated by the rifle targets in Exhibit 10.4. An expert sharpshooter fires an equal number of rounds with a century-old rifle and a modern rifle.[10] The shots from the older gun are considerably scattered, but those from the new gun are closely clustered. The variability of the old rifle compared with that of the new one indicates that it is

validity
The ability of an instrument to measure what it is intended to measure.

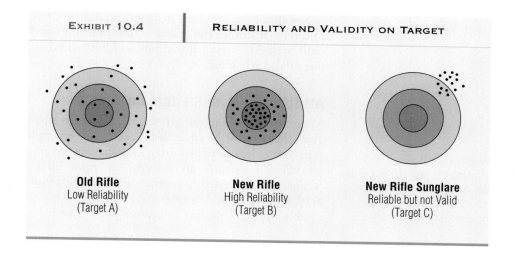

EXHIBIT 10.4 | RELIABILITY AND VALIDITY ON TARGET

Old Rifle
Low Reliability
(Target A)

New Rifle
High Reliability
(Target B)

New Rifle Sunglare
Reliable but not Valid
(Target C)

less reliable. The target on the right illustrates the concept of a systematic bias influencing validity. The new rifle is reliable (because it has little variance), but the sharpshooter's vision is hampered by glare from the sun; although consistent, the sharpshooter is unable to hit the bull's-eye.

Sensitivity

sensitivity
An instrument's ability to accurately measure variability in stimuli or responses.

The sensitivity of a scale is an important measurement concept, particularly when changes in attitudes or other hypothetical constructs are under investigation. **Sensitivity** refers to an instrument's ability to accurately measure variability in stimuli or responses. A dichotomous response category, such as "agree or disagree," does not allow the recording of subtle attitude changes. A more sensitive measure with numerous categories on the scale may be needed. For example, adding "strongly agree," "mildly agree," "neither agree nor disagree," "mildly disagree," and "strongly disagree" will increase the scale's sensitivity.

The sensitivity of a scale based on a single question or item also can be increased by adding questions or items. In other words, because index measures allow for a greater range of possible scores, they are more sensitive than single-item scales.

ATTITUDES: DEFINITION AND COMPONENTS

attitude
An enduring disposition to consistently respond in a given manner to various aspects of the world; composed of affective, cognitive, and behavioral components.

There are many definitions of *attitude*. **Attitude** usually is viewed as an enduring disposition to consistently respond in a given manner to various aspects of the world, including people, events, and objects. One conception of attitude is reflected in this brief statement: "Sally loves shopping at Sam's. She believes it's clean, conveniently located, and has the lowest prices. She intends to shop there every Thursday." This short description has identified three components of attitudes: affective, cognitive, and behavioral.

The *affective* component reflects an individual's general feelings or emotions toward an object. Statements such as "I love my Chevrolet Corvette," "I liked that book *A Corporate Bestiary*," and "I hate cranberry juice" reflect the emotional character of attitudes. The way one feels about a product, an advertisement, or an object is usually tied to one's beliefs or cognitions. The *cognitive* component represents one's awareness of and knowledge about an object. One person might feel happy about the purchase of an automobile because she believes it "gets great gas mileage" or knows the dealer is "the best in New Jersey." The *behavioral* component includes buying intentions and behavioral expectations and reflects a predisposition to action.

Attitudes as Hypothetical Constructs

hypothetical construct
A variable that is not directly observable but is measurable through indirect indicators, such as verbal expression or overt behavior.

Many variables marketing researchers wish to investigate are psychological variables that cannot be observed directly. For example, someone may have an attitude toward a particular brand of shaving cream, but we cannot observe this attitude. To measure an attitude, we must infer from the way an individual responds (by a verbal expression or overt behavior) to some stimulus. The term **hypothetical construct** describes a variable that is not directly observable but is measurable through indirect indicators such as verbal expression or overt behavior.

THE ATTITUDE-MEASURING PROCESS

ranking
A measurement task that requires respondents to rank order a small number of stores, brands, or objects on the basis of overall preference or some characteristic of the stimulus.

rating
A measurement task that requires respondents to estimate the magnitude of a characteristic or quality that a brand, store, or object possesses.

sorting
A measurement task that presents respondents with several objects or product concepts and requires them to arrange the objects into piles or otherwise classify the product concepts.

choice
A measurement task that identifies preferences by requiring respondents to choose between two or more alternatives.

A remarkable variety of techniques have been devised to measure attitudes. This variety stems in part from a lack of consensus about the exact definition of the concept. Further, the affective, cognitive, and behavioral components of an attitude may be measured by different means. For example, sympathetic nervous system responses may be recorded using physiological measures to quantify affect, but they are not good measures of behavioral intentions. Direct verbal statements concerning affect, belief, or behavior are used to measure behavioral intent. However, attitudes also may be measured indirectly using the qualitative exploratory techniques discussed in Chapter 5. Obtaining verbal statements from respondents generally requires that the respondents perform a task such as ranking, rating, sorting, or making choices.

A **ranking** task requires the respondent to rank order a small number of stores, brands, or objects on the basis of overall preference or some characteristic of the stimulus. A **rating** task asks the respondent to estimate the magnitude of a characteristic or quality that an object possesses. A quantitative score, which lies along a continuum that has been supplied to the respondent, is used to estimate the strength of the person's attitude or belief; in other words, the respondent indicates the position on one or more scales at which he or she would rate the object. A **sorting** task might present the respondent with several product concepts printed on cards and require the respondent to arrange the cards into a number of piles or otherwise classify the product concepts. Providing a **choice** between two or more alternatives is another type of attitude measurement. If a respondent chooses one object over another, the researcher can assume the respondent prefers the chosen object over the other. The following sections describe the most popular techniques for measuring attitudes.

PHYSIOLOGICAL MEASURES OF ATTITUDES

Measures of galvanic skin response, blood pressure, and pupil dilation and other physiological measures may be used to assess the affective components of attitudes. These measures provide a means of assessing attitudes without verbally questioning the respondent. In general, they can provide a gross measure of likes or dislikes, but they are not extremely sensitive measures to the different gradients of an attitude. Each of these measures is discussed elsewhere in the text.

Using rating scales to measure attitudes is perhaps the most common practice in marketing research. This section discusses many rating scales designed to enable respondents to report the intensity of their attitudes.

Simple Attitude Scales

In its most basic form, attitude scaling requires that an individual agree or disagree with a statement or respond to a single question. For example, respondents in a political poll may be asked whether they agree or disagree with the statement "The president should run for reelection." Or, an individual may indicate whether he or she likes or dislikes jalapeño bean dip. This type of self-rating scale merely classifies respondents into one of two categories; thus, it has only the properties of a nominal scale, and the types of mathematical analysis that may be used with this basic scale are limited.

Despite its disadvantages, simple attitude scaling may be used when questionnaires are extremely long, when respondents have little education, or for other specific reasons. A number of simplified scales are merely checklists: A respondent indicates past experience, preference, and the like merely by checking an item. In many cases, the items are adjectives that describe a particular object.

Most attitude theorists believe attitudes vary along a continuum. Early attitude researchers pioneered the view that the task of attitude scaling is to measure the distance between "good" and "bad," "low" and "high," "like" and "dislike," and so on. Thus, the purpose of an attitude scale is to find an individual's position on the continuum. Simple scales do not allow for fine distinctions among attitudes. Several other scales have been developed to make more precise measurements.

Category Scales

The examples just discussed are rating scales that contain only two response categories: agree/disagree. Expanding the response categories gives the respondent more flexibility in the rating task. Even more information is provided if the categories are ordered according to a particular descriptive or evaluative dimension. Consider the following question:

How often do you disagree with your spouse about how much to spend on various things?

☐ **Never**   ☐ **Rarely**   ☐ **Sometimes**   ☐ **Often**   ☐ **Very often**

category scale
A rating scale that consists of several response categories, often providing respondents with alternatives to indicate positions on a continuum.

This **category scale** is a more sensitive measure than a scale that has only two response categories; it provides more information.

Question wording is an extremely important factor in the usefulness of these scales. Exhibit 10.5 shows some common wording used in category scales. Question wording is discussed in Chapter 11.

Method of Summated Ratings: The Likert Scale

Likert scale
A measure of attitudes in which respondents rate how strongly they agree or disagree with carefully constructed statements; several scale items expressing attitudes toward an object ranging from very positive to very negative may be used to form a summated index.

Marketing researchers' adaptation of the method of summated ratings, developed by Likert, is an extremely popular means for measuring attitudes because it is simple to administer. With the **Likert scale**, respondents indicate their attitudes by checking how strongly they agree or disagree with carefully constructed statements expressing attitudes toward some object ranging from very positive to very

EXHIBIT 10.5 | SELECTED CATEGORY SCALES

Quality

Excellent	Good	Fair	Poor	
Very good	Fairly good	Neither good nor bad	Not very good	Not good at all
Well above average	Above average	Average	Below average	Well below average

Importance

Very important	Fairly important	Neutral	Not so important	Not at all important

Interest

Very interested		Somewhat interested		Not very interested

Satisfaction

Completely satisfied	Somewhat satisfied	Neither satisfied nor dissatisfied	Somewhat dissatisfied	Completely dissatisfied
Very satisfied	Quite satisfied	Somewhat satisfied	Not at all satisfied	

Frequency

All of the time	Very often	Often	Sometimes	Hardly ever
Very often	Often	Sometimes	Rarely	Never
All of the time	Most of the time	Some of the time	Just now and then	

Truth

Very true	Somewhat true	Not very true	Not at all true	
Definitely yes	Probably yes	Probably no	Definitely no	

Uniqueness

Very different	Somewhat different	Slightly different	Not at all different	
Extremely unique	Very unique	Somewhat unique	Slightly unique	Not at all unique

negative. Individuals generally choose from approximately five response alternatives—*strongly agree, agree, uncertain, disagree,* and *strongly disagree*—although the number of alternatives typically ranges from three to nine.

Consider the following example from a study of food shopping behavior:

In buying food for my family, price is no object.

Strongly disagree	**Disagree**	**Uncertain**	**Agree**	**Strongly agree**
(1)	(2)	(3)	(4)	(5)

EXHIBIT 10.6

LIKERT SCALE ITEMS FOR MEASURING ATTITUDES TOWARD PATIENTS' INTERACTION WITH A PHYSICIAN'S SERVICE STAFF [11]

1. My doctor's office staff takes a warm and personal interest in me.
2. My doctor's office staff is friendly and courteous.
3. My doctor's office staff is more interested in serving the doctor's needs than in serving my needs.
4. My doctor's office staff always acts in a professional manner.

To measure the attitude, researchers assign scores or weights to the alternative responses. In this example, weights of 5, 4, 3, 2, and 1 are assigned. (The weights, shown in parentheses, would not be printed on the questionnaire.) Strong agreement indicates the most favorable attitude on the statement, and a weight of 5 is assigned to this response. The statement given in this example is positive toward the attitude. If a negative statement toward the object (such as "I carefully budget my food expenditures") were given, the weights would be reversed, and "strongly disagree" would be assigned a weight of 5. A single scale item on a summated scale is an ordinal scale.

A Likert scale may include several scale items to form an index. Each statement is assumed to represent an aspect of a common attitudinal domain. For example, Exhibit 10.6 shows the items in a Likert scale for measuring attitudes toward patients' interaction with a physician's service staff. The total score is the summation of the weights assigned to an individual's responses. Here the maximum possible score for the index would be 20 if a 5 were assigned to "strongly agree" responses for each of the positively worded statements and a 5 to "strongly disagree" responses for the negative statement. (Item 3 is negatively worded and therefore is reverse coded.)

In Likert's original procedure, a large number of statements are generated and an item analysis is performed. The item analysis ensures that final items evoke a wide response and discriminate among those with positive and negative attitudes. Items that are poor because they lack clarity or elicit mixed response patterns are eliminated from the final statement list. However, many marketing researchers do not follow the exact procedure Likert prescribed. Hence, a disadvantage of the Likert-type summated rating method is that it is difficult to know what a single summated score means. Many patterns of response to the various statements can produce the same total score. Thus, identical total scores may reflect different attitudes because respondents endorsed different combinations of statements.

Semantic Differential

semantic differential
A measure of attitudes that consists of a series of 7-point rating scales that use bipolar adjectives to anchor the beginning and end of each scale.

The **semantic differential** is actually a series of attitude scales. This popular attitude measurement technique involves presenting a product, brand, store, or other concept followed by a series of 7-point bipolar rating scales. Bipolar adjectives, such as *good* and *bad, modern* and *old-fashioned,* and *clean* and *dirty,* anchor the beginning and the end (or poles) of the scale. The subject makes repeated judgments about the concept under investigation on each scale. Exhibit 10.7 shows a series of scales to measure attitudes toward jazz saxophone recordings.

The scoring of the semantic differential can be illustrated using the scale bounded by the anchors "modern" and "old-fashioned." Respondents are instructed to check the place that indicates the nearest appropriate adjective.

Fast—:—:—:—:—:—:—Slow

Intellectual—:—:—:—:—:—:—Emotional

Contemporary—:—:—:—:—:—:—Traditional

Composed—:—:—:—:—:—:—Improvised

Flat—:—:—:—:—:—:—Sharp

Busy—:—:—:—:—:—:—Lazy

New—:—:—:—:—:—:—Old

Progressive—:—:—:—:—:—:—Regressive

From left to right, the scale intervals are interpreted as "extremely modern," "very modern," "slightly modern," "both modern and old-fashioned," "slightly old-fashioned," and "extremely old-fashioned":

Modern—:—:—:—:—:—:—Old-fashioned

The semantic differential technique originally was developed as a method for measuring the meanings of objects or the "semantic space" of interpersonal experience. Marketing researchers have found the semantic differential versatile and have modified it for business applications. Replacing the bipolar adjectives with descriptive phrases is a frequent adaptation in product image studies. For example, the phrases "aged a long time," "not aged a long time," "not watery looking," and "watery looking" were used in a beer brand image study. A savings and loan might use the phrases "low interest on savings" and "favorable interest on savings." These phrases are not polar opposites. Consumer researchers have found that respondents often are unwilling to use the extreme negative side of a scale. Research with industrial salespeople, for example, found that in rating their own performances, salespeople would not use the negative side of the scale. Hence it was eliminated, and the anchor opposite the positive anchor showed "satisfactory" rather than "extremely poor" performance.

For scoring purposes, weight is assigned to each position on the rating scale. Traditionally scores are 7, 6, 5, 4, 3, 2, 1, or $+3, +2, +1, 0, -1, -2, -3$. Many marketing researchers find it desirable to assume the semantic differential provides interval data. This assumption, although widely accepted, has its critics, who argue that the data have only ordinal properties because the weights are arbitrary.

Exhibit 10.8 illustrates a typical **image profile** based on semantic differential data. Depending on whether the data are assumed to be interval or ordinal, the arithmetic mean or the median is used to compare the profile of one product, brand, or store with that of a competing product, brand, or store.

Numerical Scales

Numerical scales have numbers rather than semantic space or verbal descriptions as response options to identify categories (response positions). For example, if the scale items have five response positions, the scale is called a *5-point numerical scale;* a scale with seven response positions is called a *7-point numerical scale;* and so on.

image profile
A graphic representation of semantic differential data for competing brands, products, or stores, used to highlight comparisons.

numerical scale
An attitude rating scale that is similar to a semantic differential except that it uses numbers instead of verbal descriptions as response options to identify response positions.

EXHIBIT 10.8 | IMAGE PROFILE OF COMMUTER AIRLINES VERSUS MAJOR AIRLINES [13]

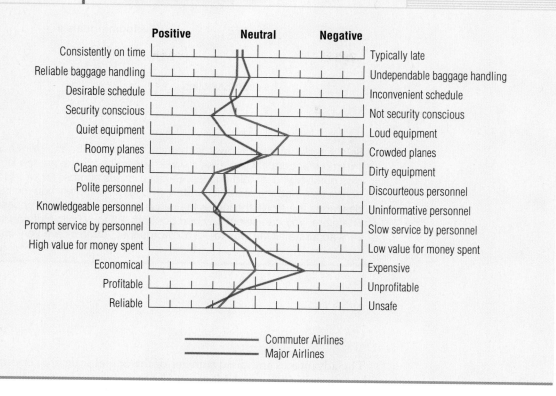

Consider the following numerical scale:

Now that you've had your automobile for about 1 year, please tell us how satisfied you are with your Ford Taurus.

Extremely satisfied 7 6 5 4 3 2 1 Extremely dissatisfied

This numerical scale uses bipolar adjectives in the same manner as the semantic differential. In practice, researchers have found that for educated populations, a scale with numerical labels for intermediate points on the scale is as effective a measure as the true semantic differential.

Stapel Scale

Stapel scale
A measure of attitudes that consists of a single adjective in the center of an even number of numerical values.

The **Stapel scale** originally was developed in the 1950s to measure the direction and intensity of an attitude simultaneously. Modern versions of the scale, with a single adjective, are used as a substitute for the semantic differential when it is difficult to create pairs of bipolar adjectives. The modified Stapel scale places a single adjective in the center of an even number of numerical values (ranging, perhaps, from +3 to −3).[14] It measures how close to or distant from the adjective a given stimulus is perceived to be. Exhibit 10.9 illustrates a Stapel scale item used in the measurement of a retailer's store image.

EXHIBIT 10.9 | A STAPEL SCALE FOR MEASURING A STORE'S IMAGE[15]

Bloomingdale's

+3
+2
+1

Wide Selection

−1
−2
−3

Select a *plus* number for words that you think describe the store accurately. The more accurately you think the word describes the store, the larger the plus number you should choose. Select a *minus* number for words you think do not describe the store accurately. The less accurately you think the word describes the store, the larger the minus number you should choose. Therefore, you can select any number from +3 for words that you think are very accurate all the way to −3 for words that you think are very inaccurate.

The advantages and disadvantages of the Stapel scale are very similar to those of the semantic differential. However, the Stapel scale is easier to administer, especially over the telephone.[16] Because the Stapel scale does not require bipolar adjectives, it is easier to construct than the semantic differential. Research comparing the semantic differential with the Stapel scale indicates that results from the two techniques are largely the same.[17]

Constant-Sum Scale

Suppose United Parcel Service (UPS) wishes to determine the importance of the attributes of accurate invoicing, delivery as promised, and price to organizations that use its service in business-to-business marketing. Respondents might be asked to divide a constant sum to indicate the relative importance of the attributes. For example:

> **Divide 100 points among the following characteristics of a delivery service according to how important each characteristic is to you when selecting a delivery company:**
>
> **Accurate invoicing** _____
>
> **Delivery as promised** _____
>
> **Lower price** _____

constant-sum scale
A measure of attitudes in which respondents are asked to divide a constant sum to indicate the relative importance of attributes.

This **constant-sum scale** works best with respondents who have high educational levels. If respondents follow the instructions correctly, the results will approximate interval measures. As the number of stimuli increases, this technique becomes increasingly complex.

Brand preference may be measured using this technique (which is similar to the paired-comparison method, discussed later), as follows:

EXHIBIT 10.10 | GRAPHIC RATING SCALE

Please evaluate each attribute in terms of how important it is to you by placing an X at the position on the horizontal line that most reflects your feelings.

Seating comfort	Not important _____	Very important
In-flight meals	Not important _____	Very important
Airfare	Not important _____	Very important

Divide 100 points among the following brands according to your preference for each brand:

Brand A _____

Brand B _____

Brand C _____

In this case, the constant–sum scale is a rating technique. However, with minor modifications it can be classified as a sorting technique.

Graphic Rating Scales

graphic rating scale
A measure of attitude that allows respondents to rate an object by choosing any point along a graphic continuum.

A **graphic rating scale** presents respondents with a graphic continuum. The respondents are allowed to choose any point on the continuum to indicate their attitude. Exhibit 10.10 shows a traditional graphic scale ranging from one extreme position to the opposite position. Typically a respondent's score is determined by measuring the length (in millimeters) from one end of the graphic continuum to the point marked by the respondent. Many researchers believe that scoring in this manner strengthens the assumption that graphic rating scales of this type are interval scales. Alternatively, the researcher may divide the line into predetermined scoring categories (lengths) and record respondents' marks accordingly. In other words, the graphic rating scale has the advantage of allowing the researcher to choose any interval desired for scoring purposes. The disadvantage of the graphic rating scale is that it provides no standard answers.

The pictorial scale is a special form of the graphic rating scale. It utilizes picture response options or other type of visual communication to portray a graphic continuum (see Exhibit 10.11). Its purpose is to enhance communication with respondents who are not highly literate, such as children.

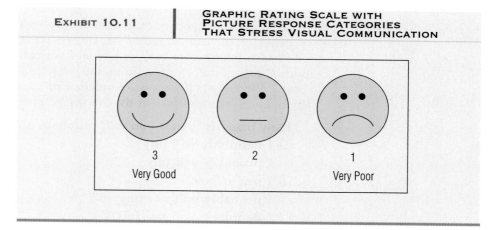

EXHIBIT 10.11 | GRAPHIC RATING SCALE WITH PICTURE RESPONSE CATEGORIES THAT STRESS VISUAL COMMUNICATION

3 — Very Good   2   1 — Very Poor

EXHIBIT 10.12

**SUMMARY OF ADVANTAGES AND
DISADVANTAGES OF RATING SCALES**

Rating Measure	Subject Must	Advantages	Disadvantages
Category scale	Indicate a response category	Flexible, easy to respond to	Items may be ambiguous; with few categories, only gross distinctions can be made
Likert scale	Evaluate statements on a scale	Easiest scale to construct	Hard to judge what a single score means
Semantic differential and numerical scales	Choose points between bipolar adjectives on relevant dimensions	Easy to construct; norms exist for comparison, such as profile analysis	Bipolar adjectives must be found; data may be ordinal, not interval
Stapel scale	Choose points on a scale with a single adjective in the center	Easier to construct than semantic differential, easy to administer	Endpoints are numerical, not verbal, labels
Constant-sum scale	Divide a constant sum among response alternatives	Approximates an interval measure	Difficult for respondents with low education levels
Graphic scale	Choose a point on a continuum	Visual impact, unlimited scale points	No standard answers
Graphic scale with picture response categories	Choose a visual picture	Visual impact, easy for poor readers	Hard to attach a verbal explanation to a response

Exhibit 10.12 summarizes the attitude–rating techniques discussed in this section.

MEASURING BEHAVIORAL INTENTION

The behavioral component of an attitude involves the behavioral expectations of an individual toward an attitudinal object. Typically this represents a buying intention, a tendency to seek additional information, or plans to visit a show-room. Category scales for measuring the behavioral component of an attitude ask about a respondent's likelihood of purchase or intention to perform some future action, using questions such as the following:

How likely is it that you will purchase a MP3 player?
☐ **I definitely will buy**
☐ **I probably will buy**
☐ **I might buy**
☐ **I probably will not buy**
☐ **I definitely will not buy**

I would write a letter to my representative in Congress or other government official in support of this company if it were in a dispute with government.

☐ **Extremely likely**
☐ **Very likely**
☐ **Somewhat likely**
☐ **Likely, about a 50–50 chance**
☐ **Somewhat unlikely**
☐ **Very unlikely**
☐ **Extremely unlikely**

The wording of statements used in these scales often includes phrases such as "I would recommend," "I would write," or "I would buy" to indicate action tendencies.

A scale of subjective probabilities, ranging from 100 for "absolutely certain" to 0 for "absolutely no chance," may be used to measure expectations. Researchers have used the following subjective probability scale to estimate the chance that a job candidate will accept a sales position:

_____	100%	**(Absolutely certain) I will accept**
_____	90%	**(Almost sure) I will accept**
_____	80%	**(Very big chance) I will accept**
_____	70%	**(Big chance) I will accept**
_____	60%	**(Not so big a chance) I will accept**
_____	50%	**(About even) I will accept**
_____	40%	**(Smaller chance) I will accept**
_____	30%	**(Small chance) I will accept**
_____	20%	**(Very small chance) I will accept**
_____	10%	**(Almost certainly not) I will accept**
_____	0	**(Certainly not) I will accept**

Behavioral Differential

behavioral differential
A rating scale instrument, similar to a semantic differential, developed to measure the behavioral intentions of subjects toward future actions.

A general instrument, the **behavioral differential,** has been developed to measure the behavioral intentions of subjects toward an object or category of objects. As in the semantic differential, a description of the object to be judged is followed by a series of scales on which subjects indicate their behavioral intentions toward this object. For example, one item might be

A 25-year-old female sales representative

Would—:—:—:—Would not

Ask this person for advice.

RANKING

Consumers often _rank order_ their preferences. An ordinal scale may be developed by asking respondents to rank order (from most preferred to least preferred) a set of objects or attributes. Respondents easily understand the task of rank ordering the importance of product attributes or arranging a set of brand names according to preference.

Paired Comparisons

paired comparison
A measurement technique that involves presenting respondents with two objects and asking them to pick the preferred object. More than two objects may be presented, but comparisons are made in pairs.

Some time ago, a chain saw manufacturer learned that a major competitor had introduced a new, lightweight (6½-pound) chain saw. The manufacturer's lightest chain saw weighed 9½ pounds. Executives wondered if they needed to introduce a 6-pound chain saw into the product line. The research design chosen was a **paired comparison**. A 6-pound chain saw was designed and a prototype built. To control for color preferences, the competitor's chain saw was painted the same color as the 9½- and 6-pound models. Respondents were presented with two chain saws at a time, then asked to pick the one they preferred. Three pairs of comparisons were required to determine the most preferred chain saw.

The following question illustrates the typical format for asking about paired comparisons:[18]

> **I would like to know your overall opinion of two brands of adhesive bandages. They are Curad and Band-Aid. Overall, which of these two brands—Curad or Band-Aid—do you think is the better one? Or are both the same?**
>
> **Curad is better** _____
> **Band-Aid is better** _____
> **They are the same** _____

If researchers wish to compare four brands of pens on the basis of attractiveness or writing quality, six comparisons $[(n)(n - 1)/2]$ will be necessary.

Ranking objects with respect to one attribute is not difficult if only a few items, such as products or advertisements, are compared. As the number of items increases, the number of comparisons increases geometrically. If the number of comparisons is too large, respondents may become fatigued and no longer carefully discriminate among them.

SORTING

Sorting tasks require that respondents indicate their attitudes or beliefs by arranging items on the basis of perceived similarity or some other attribute. Researchers at the BBDO advertising agency have consumers sort photographs of people to measure their perceptions of a brand's typical user. R. H. Bruskin Associates has used a sorting technique called AIM (Association-Identification-Measurement), which consists of arranging cards from a deck of 52. Each card reflects an element from advertising for the brand name being studied. This omnibus service measures how closely customers associate and identify these elements with a particular product, company, or advertising campaign.[19] The following condensed interviewer instructions illustrate how sorting is used in the AIM survey:

> **Thoroughly shuffle deck.**
> **Hand respondent deck.**
> **Ask respondent to sort cards into two piles:**
> > *Definitely Not Seen or Heard.*
> > *Definitely or Possibly Seen or Heard.*
> **Set aside *Definitely Not Seen or Heard* pile.**
> **Hand respondent the *Definitely or Possibly Seen or Heard* pile.**

> **Have respondent identify the item on each card in *Definitely or Possibly Seen or Heard* pile.**
>
> **Record on questionnaire.**

A variant of the constant-sum technique uses physical counters (for example, poker chips or coins) to be divided among the items being tested. In an airline study of customer preferences, the following sorting technique could be used:

> **Here is a sheet that lists several airlines. Next to the name of each airline is a pocket. Here are 10 cards. I would like you to put these cards in the pockets next to the airlines you would prefer to fly on your next trip. Assume that all of the airlines fly to wherever you would choose to travel. You can put as many cards as you want next to an airline, or you can put no cards next to an airline.**

	Cards
American Airlines	_____
Delta Airlines	_____
United Airlines	_____
Southwest Airlines	_____
Northwest Airlines	_____

SUMMARY

Marketing research problems often require the choice of an appropriate measuring system. The concept to be measured must be given an operational definition that specifies how it will be measured. There are four types of measuring scales. Nominal scales assign numbers or letters to objects only for identification or classification. Ordinal scales arrange objects or alternatives according to their magnitudes in an ordered relationship. Interval scales measure order (or distance) in units of equal intervals. Ratio scales are absolute scales, starting with absolute zeros, at which the attribute is totally absent. The type of scale determines the form of statistical analysis to use.

Index (composite) measures often are used to measure complex concepts with several attributes. Asking several questions may yield a more accurate measure than basing measurement on a single question.

Measuring instruments are evaluated based on reliability, validity, and sensitivity. Reliability is the measuring instrument's ability to provide consistent results in repeated uses. Validity is the degree to which the instrument measures the concept the researcher wants to measure. Sensitivity is the instrument's ability to accurately measure variability in stimuli or responses.

Attitude measurement is particularly important in marketing research. Attitudes are enduring dispositions to consistently respond in a given manner to various aspects of the world, including persons, events, and objects. Attitudes consist of three components: the affective, or the emotions or feelings involved; the cognitive, or awareness or knowledge; and the behavioral, or the predisposition to action. Attitudes are hypothetical constructs; that is, they are variables that are not directly observable but must be measured indirectly. Many methods for measuring attitudes have been developed, such as ranking, rating, sorting, and choice techniques.

One class of rating scales, category scales, provides several response categories to allow respondents to indicate the intensity of their attitudes. The simplest attitude scale calls for a "yes/no" or "agree/disagree" response to a single question. The Likert scale uses a series of statements with which subjects indicate agreement or disagreement. The responses are assigned weights that are summed to indicate the respondents' attitudes.

The semantic differential uses a series of attitude scales anchored by bipolar adjectives. The respondent indicates where his or her attitude falls between the polar attitudes. Variations on this method, such as numerical scales and the Stapel scale, are also used. The Stapel scale puts a single adjective in the center of a range of numerical values from +3 to −3.

Constant-sum scales require the respondent to divide a constant sum into parts, indicating the weights to be given to various attributes of the item being studied. Graphic rating scales use a continuum on which respondents indicate their attitudes.

Several scales, such as the behavioral differential, have been developed to measure the behavioral component of attitude.

People often rank order their preferences. Thus, ordinal scales that ask respondents to rank order a set of objects or attributes may be developed. In the paired-comparison technique, two alternatives are paired and respondents are asked to pick the preferred one. Sorting requires respondents to indicate their attitudes by arranging items into piles or categories.

Key Terms and Concepts

concept	index (composite) measure	category scale
operational definition	reliability	Likert scale
conceptual definition	validity	semantic differential
rule	sensitivity	image profile
scale	attitude	numerical scale
nominal scale	hypothetical construct	Stapel scale
ordinal scale	ranking	constant-sum scale
interval scale	rating	graphic rating scale
ratio scale	sorting	behavioral differential
attribute	choice	paired comparison

Questions for Review and Critical Thinking

1. What is the difference between a conceptual definition and an operational definition?
2. What descriptive statistics are allowable with nominal, ordinal, and interval scales?
3. Discuss the differences between validity and reliability.
4. Why might a researcher wish to use more than one question to measure satisfaction with a particular aspect of retail shopping?
5. Comment on the validity and reliability of the following:

   a. A respondent's report of an intention to subscribe to *Consumer Reports* is highly reliable. A researcher believes this constitutes a valid measurement of dissatisfaction with the economic system and alienation from big business.

   b. A general-interest magazine claimed that it was a better advertising medium than television programs with similar content. Research had indicated that for a soft drink and other test products, recall scores were higher for the magazine ads than for 30-second commercials.

c. A respondent's report of frequency of magazine reading consistently indicates that she regularly reads *Good Housekeeping* and *Gourmet* and never reads *Cosmopolitan*.

6. Indicate whether the following measures use a nominal, ordinal, interval, or ratio scale:
   a. Prices on the stock market
   b. Marital status, classified as "married" or "never married"
   c. Whether a respondent has ever been unemployed
   d. Professorial rank: assistant professor, associate professor, or professor
   e. Grades: A, B, C, D, or F

7. Go to the library and find out how *Sales and Marketing Management* magazine constructs its buying-power index.

8. Define the following concepts, then operationally define each one:
   a. A good bowler
   b. A television audience for *The Tonight Show*
   c. Purchasing intention for a new stereo
   d. Consumer involvement with cars
   e. A workaholic
   f. A fast-food restaurant
   g. The American Dream

9. What is an attitude? Is there a consensus concerning its definition?

10. Distinguish between rating and ranking. Which is a better attitude measurement technique? Why?

11. What advantages do numerical scales have over semantic differential scales?

12. Name some situations in which a semantic differential might be useful.

13. Should a Likert scale ever be treated as though it had ordinal properties?

14. For each of the following situations, identify the type of scale and evaluate its use:
   a. A U.S. representative's questionnaire to constituents:

   Do you favor or oppose a constitutional amendment to balance the budget?
   ☐ **Favor**   ☐ **Oppose**   ☐ **Don't know**

   b. An academic study on consumer behavior:
   Most people who are important to me think I

−3	+3
Definitely should not buy	**Definitely should buy**

   [test brand] sometime during the next week.

   c. For a psychographic statement:
   I shop a lot for specials.

Strongly agree	Moderately agree	Neutral	Moderately disagree	Strongly disagree
5	4	3	2	1

15. If a Likert summated scale has ten scale items, do all ten items have to be phrased as either positive or negative statements, or can the scale contain a mix of positive and negative statements?

16. If a semantic differential has ten scale items, should all the positive adjectives be on the right and all the negative adjectives be on the left?

17. A researcher wishes to compare two hotels on the following attributes: (1) convenience of location, (2) friendly personnel, and (3) value for money.
   a. Design a Likert scale to accomplish this task.
   b. Design a semantic differential scale to accomplish this task.
   c. Design a graphic rating scale to accomplish this task.

18. Education often is used as an indicator of a person's socioeconomic status. Historically, the number of years of schooling completed has been recorded in the *Census of Population* as a measure of education. Critics say this measure is no longer accurate as a measure of education. Comment.

 19. A researcher thinks many respondents will answer "don't know" or "can't say" if these options are printed on an attitude scale along with categories indicating agreement. The researcher omits both options on the questionnaire because the resulting data will be less complicated to analyze and report. Is this proper?

Exploring the Internet

1. SRI International investigates American consumers by asking questions about their attitudes and values. It has a Web site at which people can VALS-type themselves. To find out your VALS-type, go to http://future.sri.com.

2. The Office of Scale Research (OSR) is part of the Department of Marketing at Southern Illinois University at Carbondale. The OSR Web site provides a number of technical reports that deal with a wide variety of scaling issues. Go to http://www.siu.edu/departments/coba/mktg/osr/ and select an article from the reading list. What types of scales are listed?

3. A measure of procrastination can be found at http://www.queendom.com/tests/career/procrastination-1.html. Take this "test." Do you think this is a reliable and valid measure?

Raymond RedCorn is an Osage Indian.[20] The Ha-Pah-Shu-Tse (Osage for "red corn") restaurant in Pawhuska, Oklahoma is the only authentic Native American restaurant in the state and one of the few in the country.

The Ha-Pah-Shu-Tse restaurant opened in 1972 with a seating capacity of 8; today, after expansion, crowds of up to 90 keep RedCorn and his wife busy. They are currently marketing an Indian fry bread mix, and they are planning on increased sales for their only packaged good. Indian fry bread mix has long been a staple of the Native American diet. The bread is sweet and contains basic ingredients such as flour, shortening, and sugar.

The Restaurant

Waltena RedCorn married into the Osage tribe 47 years ago and learned how to cook from two women named Grandma Baconrind and Grandma Lookout. They must have taught her well, because customers of the Ha-Pah-Shu-Tse are not content just to eat there—they often have the RedCorns mail them fry bread mix. Raymond RedCorn finds that people who eat the unusual native dish usually request the recipe. He says, "I have not found anyone who does not like the bread." Customers aren't limited to local fans of Indian food. Because the fry bread is sold or served in restaurants and stores in Oklahoma as well as at a museum, people from as far away as Europe have tried it.

According to RedCorn, "About once a week, someone from England comes in." He serves these British customers fry bread or the restaurant's "best sellers," Indian Meat Pie or Navaho Taco, and tells them the story of fry bread and how it got him an invitation to Buckingham Palace. When he was 18 years old, he was in London for a Boy Scout Jamboree. One evening he was frying the Indian bread when the British Boy Scout organizer approached with two young men. It was only after everyone had tasted RedCorn's culinary effort that the Prince of Wales was introduced. "The Indian delegation from Oklahoma was invited to set up

their tents on the grounds at the palace and spend the weekend being entertained by the young royalty," RedCorn says.

The Product

The product as it is today took several years to perfect. The RedCorns wanted a mix that would need only the addition of water. Each batch was sent to relatives and friends for judgment on the taste until everyone was convinced it was the best it could be.

The mix, consisting of Indian flour, is already distributed in Tulsa, Bartlesville, and surrounding towns under the Ha-Pah-Shu-Tse brand name. It is packaged in 2- and 5-pound silver bags with Raymond RedCorn in Osage tribal costume pictured on the front. Directions for making the fry bread are listed on the back of the package.

The Research Problem

When planning the marketing for the Indian fry bread mix, student consultants working with the Small Business Administration suggested some attitude research. They felt that successfully marketing the Ha-Pah-Shu-Tse product depended on knowing what consumer reactions to Indian foods would be. They believed that if the image of Indian foods and consumers' awareness of them were measured, RedCorn would have a better chance of marketing his product. In addition, the student consultants felt that the name Ha-Pah-Shu-Tse violated many of the requirements for a good brand name—it was not short, simple, or easy to recall and was difficult to pronounce and spell.

Questions

1. What marketing questions must be answered as Ha-Pah-Shu-Tse plans for expansion? How can marketing research help answer those questions?
2. What type of attitude scale would you recommend? How would you generate a set of items (attributes) to be measured?
3. Does an image profile seem appropriate in this case?

An early Gallup Poll illustrates that the answer to a question frequently is a function of the question's wording.[1] "People were asked if they owned any stock. A surprisingly high degree of stock ownership turned up in interviews in the Southwest where respondents were naturally thinking of livestock. The question had to be reworded to make reference to 'securities listed on any stock exchange.'"

Many experts in survey research believe that improving the wording of questions can contribute far more to accuracy than can improvements in sampling. Experiments have shown that the range of error due to vague questions or use of ambiguous words may be as high as 20 or 30 percentage points. Consider the following illustration of the critical importance of selecting the word with the right meaning. The questions differ only in the use of the words *should, could,* and *might:*

Do you think anything *should* be done to make it easier for people to pay doctor or hospital bills?

Do you think anything *could* be done to make it easier for people to pay doctor or hospital bills?

Do you think anything *might* be done to make it easier for people to pay doctor or hospital bills?[2]

The results from the matched samples: 82 percent replied that something *should* be done, 77 percent that something *could* be done, and 63 percent that something *might* be done. A 19-percentage-point difference separated the two extremes *should* and *might*. Ironically, this is the same percentage point error as that in the *Literary Digest* poll, a frequently cited example of error associated with sampling.

This chapter outlines a procedure for questionnaire design and illustrates that a little bit of research knowledge can be a dangerous thing. ■

What you will learn in this chapter

■ To recognize that questionnaire design is not a simple task and that proper wording of relevant questions can immensely improve the accuracy of a survey.

■ To understand that the type of information needed to answer a manager's questions will substantially influence the structure and content of a questionnaire.

■ To recognize that decisions about data collection methods will influence question format and questionnaire layout.

■ To describe the difference between open-ended response questions and fixed-alternative questions.

■ To understand the guidelines that help prevent the most common mistakes in questionnaire design.

■ To discuss how the proper sequence of questions may improve a questionnaire.

■ To understand how to plan and design a questionnaire layout.

■ To recognize the importance of pretesting and revising a questionnaire.

A SURVEY IS ONLY AS GOOD AS THE QUESTIONS IT ASKS

Each stage in the interdependent marketing research process is important. However, a marketing research survey is only as good as the questions it asks. The importance of question wording is easily overlooked, but questionnaire design is one of the most critical stages in the survey research process.

"A good questionnaire appears as easy to compose as a good poem does. The end product should look as if effortlessly written by an inspired child—but it is usually the result of long, painstaking work."[3] Businesspeople who are inexperienced in marketing research frequently believe that constructing a questionnaire is a simple task. Amateur researchers find it quite easy to write short questionnaires in a matter of hours. Unfortunately, newcomers who naively believe common sense and good grammar are all one needs to construct a questionnaire generally learn that their hasty efforts were inadequate.

While common sense and good grammar are important in question writing, the art of questionnaire design requires far more. To assume people will understand the questions is a common error. Respondents simply may not know what is being asked. They may be unaware of the product or topic of interest. They may confuse the subject with something else. The question may not mean the same thing to everyone interviewed. Finally, respondents may refuse to answer personal questions. Most of these problems can be minimized, however, if a skilled researcher composes the questionnaire.

QUESTIONNAIRE DESIGN: AN OVERVIEW OF THE MAJOR DECISIONS

Relevance and *accuracy* are the two basic criteria a questionnaire must meet if it is to fulfill a researcher's purposes.[4] To achieve these ends, a researcher who is systematically planning to design a questionnaire will be required to make several decisions—typically, but not necessarily, in the following order:

1. What should be asked?
2. How should questions be phrased?
3. In what sequence should the questions be arranged?
4. What questionnaire layout will best serve the research objectives?
5. How should the questionnaire be pretested? Does the questionnaire need to be revised?

WHAT SHOULD BE ASKED?

Certain decisions made during the early stages of the research process will influence the questionnaire design. The preceding chapters stressed the need to have a good problem definition and clear objectives for the study. The problem definition will indicate the type of information that must be collected to answer the manager's questions; different types of questions may obtain certain types of information more successfully than others. Further, the communication medium used for data collection—telephone interview, personal interview, or self-administered questionnaire—will have been determined. This decision is another forward linkage that influences the structure and content of the questionnaire. The specific questions to be asked will be a function of the previous decisions.

The latter stages of the research process will have an important impact on questionnaire wording. The questions to be asked will, of course, take the form of data analysis into account. When designing a questionnaire, the researcher should consider the types of statistical analysis that will be conducted.

HOW SHOULD QUESTIONS BE PHRASED?

There are many ways to phrase questions, and many standard question formats have been developed in previous research studies. This section presents a classification of question types and provides some helpful guidelines for writing questions.

Open-Ended Response versus Fixed-Alternative Questions

Two basic types of questions can be identified based on the amount of freedom respondents have in answering.

open-ended response question
A question that poses some problem and asks the respondent to answer in his or her own words.

Open-ended response questions pose some problem or topic and ask respondents to answer in their own words. If the question is asked in a personal interview, the interviewer may probe for more information. For example:

What names of local banks can you think of offhand?

What comes to mind when you look at this advertisement?

In what way, if any, could this product be changed or improved? I'd like you to tell me anything you can think of, no matter how minor it seems.

What things do you like most about Federal Express's service?

Why do you buy more of your clothing in Nordstrom than in other stores?

How can our stores better serve your needs?

Please tell me anything at all that you remember about the BMW commercial you saw last night.

fixed-alternative question
A question in which the respondent is given specific, limited-alternative responses and asked to choose the one closest to his or her viewpoint.

Open-ended response questions are free-answer questions. They may be contrasted with **fixed-alternative questions**—sometimes called *closed questions*—which give respondents specific limited alternative responses and ask them to choose the one closest to their own viewpoints. For example:

Did you use any commercial feed or supplement for livestock or poultry in 2001?
☐ **Yes**
☐ **No**
As compared with 10 years ago, would you say that the quality of most products made in Japan is higher, about the same, or not as good?
☐ **Higher**
☐ **About the same**
☐ **Not as good**
Do you think the new homeland security restrictions have affected your business?
☐ **Yes, for the better**
☐ **Yes, for the worse**
☐ **Not especially**

WHAT A DIFFERENCE WORDS MAKE

Does advertising lower or raise prices?[5] The wording of the question influences the answer.

Consumer Attitude toward Distribution
The consumer must pay more for goods because of advertising.

No	33
Yes	39
Doubtful	17
No answer	11

Consumer Attitude toward Distribution
Advertising may cause the consumer to pay less for a product than if it were not advertised because it increases sales and makes it possible to cut the cost of production and marketing.

Yes	52
No	18
Doubtful	20
No answer	10

In which type of bookstore is it easier for you to shop—a regular bookstore or a bookstore on the Internet?

☐ **Regular bookstore**

☐ **Internet bookstore**

How much of your shopping for clothes and household items do you do in wholesale club stores?

☐ **All of it**

☐ **Most of it**

☐ **About one-half of it**

☐ **About one-quarter of it**

☐ **Less than one-quarter of it**

Open-ended response questions are most beneficial when the researcher is conducting exploratory research, especially when the range of responses is not known. Such questions can be used to learn which words and phrases people spontaneously give to the free-response question. Respondents are free to answer with whatever is uppermost in their minds. By obtaining free and uninhibited responses, the researcher may find some unanticipated reaction toward the product. Such responses will reflect the flavor of the language that people use in talking about products or services and thus may provide a source of new ideas for advertising copywriting. Also, open-ended response questions are valuable at the beginning of an interview because they allow respondents to warm up to the questioning process.

The cost of administering open-ended response questions is substantially higher than that for fixed-alternative questions because the job of editing, coding, and analyzing the data is quite extensive. As each respondent's answer is somewhat unique, categorizing and summarizing the answers is difficult. The process requires that an editor go over a sample of questions to classify the responses into some sort of scheme; then all the answers must be reviewed and coded according to the classification scheme.

Another potential disadvantage of the open-ended response question is the possibility that interviewer bias will influence the answer. While most interviewer instructions state that answers are to be recorded verbatim, rarely does even the best interviewer get every word spoken by the respondent. Thus, an interviewer tends to take shortcuts in recording the answers. But changing even a few of the respondent's words may substantially influence the results; the final answer may represent the respondent's and interviewer's combined ideas rather than the respondent's ideas alone. Also, with open-ended response questions, articulate individuals tend to give longer answers. Such respondents often are better educated and from higher income groups and therefore may not be representative of the entire population, and yet they may give a large share of the responses.

In contrast, fixed-alternative questions require less interviewer skill, take less time, and are easier for the respondent to answer. This is because answers to closed questions are classified into standardized groupings prior to data collection. Standardizing alternative responses to a question provides comparability of answers, which facilitates coding, tabulating, and ultimately interpreting the data.

Types of Fixed-Alternative Questions

Earlier in the chapter a variety of fixed-alternative questions were presented. We will now identify and categorize the various types.

The **simple-dichotomy**, or **dichotomous-alternative**, **question** requires the respondent to choose one of two alternatives. The answer can be a simple "yes" or "no" or a choice between "this" and "that." For example:

Did you make any long-distance calls last week?
☐ **Yes**   ☐ **No**

Several types of questions provide the respondent with *multiple-choice alternatives*. The **determinant-choice question** requires the respondent to choose one, and only one, response from among several possible alternatives. For example:

Please give us some information about your flight. In which section of the aircraft did you sit?
☐ **First class**
☐ **Business class**
☐ **Coach class**

The **frequency-determination question** is a determinant-choice question that asks about the general frequency of occurrence. For example:

How frequently do you watch the MTV channel?
☐ **Every day**
☐ **5–6 times a week**
☐ **2–4 times a week**
☐ **Once a week**
☐ **Less than once a week**
☐ **Never**

Attitude rating scales, such as the Likert scale, semantic differential, Staple scale, and so on, are also fixed-alternative questions. These were discussed in Chapter 10.

The **checklist question** allows the respondent to provide multiple answers to a single question. The respondent indicates past experience, preference, and the like

---

simple-dichotomy (dichotomous-alternative) question
A fixed-alternative question that requires the respondent to choose one of two alternatives.

determinant-choice question
A fixed-alternative question that requires a respondent to choose one response from among multiple alternatives.

frequency-determination question
A fixed-alternative question about general frequency of occurrence.

checklist question
A fixed-alternative question that allows the respondent to provide multiple answers to a single question by checking off items.

merely by checking off items. In many cases, the choices are adjectives that describe a particular object. Following is a typical checklist question:

Please check which of the following sources of information about investments you regularly use, if any.

☐ **Personal advice of your broker(s)**

☐ **Brokerage newsletters**

☐ **Brokerage research reports**

☐ **Investment advisory service(s)**

☐ **Conversations with other investors**

☐ **Web page(s)**

☐ **None of these**

☐ **Other (please specify)** ⎯⎯⎯⎯⎯⎯⎯⎯

A major problem in developing dichotomous or multiple-choice alternatives is the framing of the response alternatives. There should be no overlap among categories. Alternatives should be *mutually exclusive*; that is, only one dimension of an issue should be related to each alternative. The following listing of income groups illustrates a common error:

☐ **Under $15,000**

☐ **$15,000–30,000**

☐ **$30,000–55,000**

☐ **$55,000–70,000**

☐ **Over $70,000**

How many people with incomes of $30,000 will be in the second group, and how many will be in the third group? There is no way to determine the answer. Grouping alternatives without forethought or analysis is likely to diminish accuracy.

Few people relish being in the lowest category. Including a category lower than the lowest expected answers often helps to negate the potential bias caused by respondents' tendency to avoid an extreme category.

When a researcher is unaware of the potential responses to a question, fixed-alternative questions obviously cannot be used. If the researcher assumes what the responses will be but is in fact wrong, he or she will have no way of knowing the extent to which the assumption was incorrect.

Unanticipated alternatives emerge when respondents feel that closed answers do not adequately reflect their feelings. They may make comments to the interviewer or write additional answers on the printed questionnaire indicating that the exploratory research did not yield a complete array of responses. After the fact, little can be done to correct a closed question that does not provide enough alternatives; therefore, before writing a descriptive questionnaire, a researcher may find it valuable to spend time conducting exploratory research with open-ended response questions to identify the most likely alternatives. The researcher should strive to ensure sufficient response choices to include almost all possible answers.

Respondents may check off obvious alternatives, such as price or durability, if they do not see the choice they would prefer. Also, a fixed-alternative question may tempt respondents to check an answer that is more prestigious or socially acceptable than the true answer. Rather than stating that they do not know why they chose a given product, they may select an alternative among those presented, or, as a matter of convenience, they may select a given alternative rather than think of the most correct response.

Most questionnaires mix open-ended and closed questions. As we have discussed, each form has unique benefits. In addition, a change of pace can eliminate respondent boredom and fatigue.

Phrasing Questions for Self-Administered, Telephone, and Personal Interview Surveys

The means of data collection (telephone, personal interview, self-administered questionnaire) will influence the question format and question phrasing. In general, questions for mail and telephone surveys must be less complex than those used in personal interviews. Questionnaires for telephone and personal interviews should be written in a conversational style. Exhibit 11.1 illustrates how a question may be revised for a different medium.

Consider the following question from a personal interview:

Recently there has been a lot of discussion about the potential health risks to nonsmokers from tobacco smoke in public buildings, restaurants, and business offices. How serious a health threat to you personally is the inhaling of this second-hand smoke, often called *passive smoking*: Is it a very serious health threat, somewhat serious, not too serious, or not serious at all?

1. Very serious
2. Somewhat serious
3. Not too serious
4. Not serious at all
5. (Don't know)

You probably noticed that the last portion of the question is a listing of the four alternatives that serve as answers. This listing at the end is often used in interviews to remind the respondent of the alternatives, since they are not presented visually. The fifth alternative, "Don't know," is in parentheses because, although the interviewer knows it is an acceptable answer, it is not read; the researcher would prefer to "force" the respondent to choose from among the four listed alternatives.

The data collection technique also influences the layout of the questionnaire. Layout will be discussed later in the chapter.

THE ART OF ASKING QUESTIONS

No hard-and-fast rules determine how to develop a questionnaire. Fortunately, research experience has yielded some guidelines that help prevent the most common mistakes.

Avoid Complexity: Use Simple, Conversational Language

Words used in questionnaires should be readily understandable by all respondents. The researcher usually has the difficult task of adopting the conversational language of people from lower educational levels without talking down to better-educated respondents. Remember, not all people have the vocabulary of a college student; a substantial number of Americans have never gone beyond high school.

EXHIBIT 11.1 | REDUCING QUESTION COMPLEXITY BY PROVIDING FEWER RESPONSES[6]

Mail Form:

How satisfied are you with your community?

1 Very satisfied
2 Quite satisfied
3 Somewhat satisfied
4 Slightly satisfied
5 Neither satisfied nor dissatisfied
6 Slightly dissatisfied
7 Somewhat dissatisfied
8 Quite dissatisfied
9 Very dissatisfied

Revised for Telephone:

How satisfied are you with your community? Would you say you are very satisfied, somewhat satisfied, neither satisfied nor dissatisfied, somewhat dissatisfied, or very dissatisfied?

Very satisfied	1
Somewhat satisfied	2
Neither satisfied nor dissatisfied	3
Somewhat dissatisfied	4
Very dissatisfied	5

Respondents can probably tell an interviewer whether they are married, single, divorced, separated, or widowed, but providing their *marital status* may present a problem. The technical jargon of top corporate executives should be avoided when surveying retailers or industrial users. "Brand image," "positioning," "marginal analysis," and other corporate language may not have the same meaning for or even be understood by a store owner–operator in a retail survey. The vocabulary used in the following question from an attitude survey on social problems probably would confuse many respondents:

> **When effluents from a paper mill can be drunk and exhaust from factory smokestacks can be breathed, then mankind will have done a good job in saving the environment. . . . Don't you agree that what we want is zero toxicity: no effluents?**

Besides being too long and confusing, this question is leading.

Avoid Leading and Loaded Questions

Leading and loaded questions are a major source of bias in question wording. **Leading questions** suggest or imply certain answers. A study of the dry cleaning industry asked this question:

> **Many people are using dry cleaning less because of improved wash-and-wear clothes. How do you feel wash-and-wear clothes**

leading question
A question that suggests or implies certain answers.

TOO GOOD A NAME!

The Arm & Hammer brand name has been used for a number of product line extensions—for example, heavy-duty laundry detergent, oven cleaner, and liquid detergent.[7] Unfortunately, however, when the makers of Arm & Hammer baking soda launched Arm & Hammer spray deodorant and Arm & Hammer spray disinfectant, the products did not fare well, even though marketing research studies indicated that consumers had expressed positive feelings about both products. What went wrong?

Researchers who investigated the product's failures found that the Arm & Hammer name had such a strong consumer franchise that whenever it was associated with a new product or concept, consumer acceptance and buying intentions were always artificially high. When question wording included the socially desirable Arm & Hammer name, consumers were reluctant to reject it. The company had failed to realize how much response bias its name caused.

have affected your use of dry cleaning facilities in the past 4 years?

☐ **Use less**

☐ **No change**

☐ **Use more**

The potential "bandwagon effect" implied in this question threatens the study's validity. *Partial mention of alternatives* is a variation of this phenomenon:

Do small imported cars, such as Volkswagens, get better gas mileage than small U.S. cars? How do you generally spend your free time, watching television or what?

Merely mentioning an alternative may have a dramatic effect. The following question was asked in a research study for a court case (*Universal City v. Nintendo*, 1984).[8]

To the best of your knowledge, was "Donkey Kong" made with the approval or under the authority of the people who produced the *King Kong* movies?

Eighteen percent of the respondents answered "yes." In contrast, 0 percent correctly answered the question **"As far as you know, who makes 'Donkey Kong'?"**

loaded question
A question that suggests a socially desirable answer or that is emotionally charged.

Loaded questions suggest a socially desirable answer or are emotionally charged. Consider the following:

In light of today's savings–and–loan crisis, it would be in the public's best interest to offer interest-free loans to farmers.

☐ **Strongly agree**   ☐ **Agree**   ☐ **Disagree**   ☐ **Strongly disagree**

Respondents might give different answers if the loaded portion of the statement, "savings-and-loan crisis," were worded to suggest a problem of less magnitude than a crisis.

A television station produced the following 10-second spot asking for viewer feedback:

We are happy when you like programs on Channel 7. We are sad when you dislike programs on Channel 7. Write us and let us know what you think of our programming.

Few people wish to make others sad. This question is likely to elicit only positive comments.

Certain answers to questions are more socially desirable than others. For example, a truthful answer to the following classification question might be painful:

Where did you rank academically in your high school graduating class?

☐ **Top quarter**
☐ **2nd quarter**
☐ **3rd quarter**
☐ **4th quarter**

When taking personality or pyschographic tests, respondents frequently can interpret which answers are most socially acceptable even if those answers do not portray the respondents' true feelings. For example, which are the socially desirable answers to the following questions on a self-confidence scale?

I feel capable of handling myself in most social situations.

☐ **Agree**   ☐ **Disagree**

I seldom fear my actions will cause others to have low opinions of me.

☐ **Agree**   ☐ **Disagree**

Invoking the status quo is a form of loading that results in bias because most people tend to resist change.[9] An experiment conducted in the early days of polling illustrates the unpopularity of change.[10] Comparable samples of respondents were simultaneously asked two questions about the presidential succession. One sample was asked: **"Would you favor or oppose adding a law to the Constitution preventing a president from succeeding himself more than once?"** The other sample was asked: **"Would you favor or oppose changing the Constitution in order to prevent a president from succeeding himself more than once?"** To the first question, 50 percent of the respondents answered in the negative; to the second question, 65 percent answered in the negative. Thus, the public would rather add to than change the Constitution.

Asking respondents "how often" they use a product or visit a store leads them to generalize about their habits, because their behavior usually exhibits some variance. In generalizing, one is likely to portray one's *ideal* behavior rather than one's *average* behavior. For instance, brushing one's teeth after each meal may be ideal, but busy people may skip a brushing or two. An introductory **counterbiasing statement** or preamble to a question that reassures respondents that their "embarrassing" behavior is not abnormal may yield truthful responses:

Some people have the time to brush three times daily; others do not. How often did you brush your teeth yesterday?

counterbiasing statement
An introductory statement or preamble to a potentially embarrassing question that reduces a respondent's reluctance to answer by suggesting that certain behavior is not unusual.

If a question embarrasses the respondent, it may elicit no answer or a biased response. This is particularly true with regard to personal or classification data such as income or education. The problem may be mitigated by introducing the section of the questionnaire with a statement such as

To help classify your answers, we'd like to ask you a few questions. Again, your answers will be kept in strict confidence.

A question statement may be leading because it is phrased to reflect either the negative or the positive aspects of an issue. To control for this bias, the wording of attitudinal questions may be reversed for 50 percent of the sample. This **split-ballot technique** is used with the expectation that two alternative phrasings of the same question will yield a more accurate total response than will a single phrasing. For example, in a study on small-car buying behavior, one-half of a sample of imported-car purchasers received a questionnaire in which they were asked to agree or disagree with the statement **"Small U.S. cars are cheaper to maintain than small imported cars."** The other half of the import-car owners received a questionnaire in which the statement read **"Small imported cars are cheaper to maintain than small U.S. cars."**

split-ballot technique
The use of two alternative phrasings of the same question for respective halves of a sample to elicit a more accurate total response than a single phrasing would.

Avoid Ambiguity: Be as Specific as Possible

Items on questionnaires often are ambiguous because they are too general. Consider such indefinite words as *often, occasionally, regularly, frequently, many, good, fair,* and *poor.* Each of these words has many different meanings. For one person *frequent* reading of *Fortune* magazine may be reading six or seven issues a year; for another it may be two issues a year. The word *fair* has a great variety of meanings; the same is true for many other indefinite words.

Questions such as the following one, used in a study to measure the reactions of consumers to a television boycott, should be interpreted with care:

Please indicate the statement that best describes your family's television viewing during the boycott of Channel 7.
☐ We did *not* watch any television programs on Channel 7.
☐ We watched *hardly any* television programs on Channel 7.
☐ We *occasionally* watched television programs on Channel 7.
☐ We *frequently* watched television programs on Channel 7.

Some marketing scholars have suggested that the rate of diffusion of an innovation is related to the perception of product attributes such as *divisibility*, which refers to the extent to which an innovation may be tried or tested on a limited scale.[11] An empirical attempt to test this theory using semantic differentials was a disaster. Pretesting found that the bipolar adjectives *divisible–not divisible* were impossible for consumers to understand because they did not have the theory in mind as a frame of reference. A revision of the scale used these bipolar adjectives:

Testable — : — : — : — : — : — : — **Not testable**
(sample use **(sample use**
possible) **not possible)**

However, the question remained ambiguous because the meaning was still unclear.

A brewing industry study on point-of-purchase advertising (store displays) asked:

What degree of durability do you prefer in your point-of-purchase advertising?

☐ **Permanent (lasting more than 6 months)**

☐ **Semipermanent (lasting from 1 to 6 months)**

☐ **Temporary (lasting less than 1 month)**

Here the researchers clarified the terms *permanent, semipermanent,* and *temporary* by defining them for the respondent. However, the question remained somewhat ambiguous. Beer marketers often use a variety of point-of-purchase devices to serve different purposes—in this case, what is the purpose? Further, analysis was difficult because respondents were merely asked to indicate a preference rather than a *degree* of preference. Thus, the meaning of a question may not be clear because the frame of reference is inadequate for interpreting the context of the question.

A student research group asked this question:

What media do you rely on most?

☐ **Television**   ☐ **Internet**   ☐ **Radio**   ☐ **Newspapers**

This question is ambiguous because it does not ask about the content of the media. "Rely on most" for what—news, sports, entertainment?

Avoid Double-Barreled Items

double-barreled question
A question that may induce bias because it covers two issues at once.

A question covering several issues at once is referred to as a **double-barreled question** and should always be avoided. Making the mistake of asking two questions rather than one is easy—for example, **"Please indicate your degree of agreement with the following statement: 'Wholesalers and retailers are responsible for the high cost of meat.'"** Which intermediaries are responsible, the wholesalers or the retailers? When multiple questions are asked in one question, the results may be exceedingly difficult to interpret. For example, consider the following question from a survey entitled "How Do You Feel about Being a Woman?"

Between you and your husband, who does the housework (cleaning, cooking, dishwashing, laundry) over and above that done by any hired help?

☐ **I do all of it.**

☐ **I do almost all of it.**

☐ **I do over half of it.**

☐ **We split the work fifty-fifty.**

☐ **My husband does over half of it.**

The answers to this question do not tell us if the wife cooks and the husband washes the dishes.

A survey by a consumer-oriented library asked:

Are you satisfied with the present system of handling "closed-reserve" and "open-reserve" readings? (Are enough copies available? Are the required materials ordered promptly? Are the borrowing regulations adequate for students' use of materials?)

☐ **Yes**   ☐ **No**

A respondent may feel torn between a "yes" to one part of the question and a "no" to another part. The answer to this question does not tell the researcher which problem or combination of problems concerns the library user.

Consider this comment about double-barreled questions:

> Generally speaking, it is hard enough to get answers to one idea at a time without complicating the problem by asking what amounts to two questions at once. If two ideas are to be explored, they deserve at least two questions. Since question marks are not rationed, there is little excuse for the needless confusion that results [from] the double-barreled question.[12]

Avoid Making Assumptions

Consider the following question:

Should Macy's continue its excellent gift-wrapping program?
☐ **Yes**   ☐ **No**

This question has a built-in assumption: that people believe the gift-wrapping program is excellent. By answering "yes," the respondent implies that the program is, in fact, excellent and that things are fine just as they are: by answering "no," he or she implies that the store should discontinue the gift wrapping. The researchers should not place the respondent in that sort of bind by including an implicit assumption in the question.

Another frequent mistake is assuming that a respondent had previously thought about an issue. For example, the following question appeared in a survey concerning Jack-in-the-Box: **"Do you think Jack-in-the-Box restaurants should consider changing their name?"** It is very unlikely that respondents had thought about this question before being asked it. Most respondents answered the question even though they had no prior opinion concerning the name change. Research that induces people to express attitudes on subjects they do not ordinarily think about is meaningless.

Avoid Burdensome Questions That May Tax the Respondent's Memory

A simple fact of human life is that people forget. Researchers writing questions about past behavior or events should recognize that certain questions may make serious demands on the respondent's memory. Writing questions about prior events requires a conscientious attempt to minimize the problems of forgetting.

In many situations, respondents cannot recall the answer to a question. For example, a telephone survey conducted during the 24-hour period following the airing of the Super Bowl might establish whether the respondent watched the Super Bowl and then ask: **"Do you recall any commercials on that program?"** If the answer is positive, the interviewer might ask: **"What brands were advertised?"** These two questions measure *unaided recall*, because they give the respondent no clue as to the brand of interest.

If the researcher suspects the respondent may have forgotten the answer to a question, he or she may rewrite the question in an *aided-recall* format—that is, in a format that provides a clue to help jog the respondent's memory. For instance, the question about an advertised beer in an aided-recall format might be, **"Do you recall whether there was a brand of beer advertised on that program?"** or **"I am going to read you a list of beer names. Can you pick out the name of beer that was advertised on the program?"** While aided recall is not as strong a test of attention or memory as unaided recall, it is less taxing to the respondent's memory.

WHAT IS THE BEST QUESTION SEQUENCE?

The order of questions, or the question sequence, may serve several functions for the researcher. If the opening questions are interesting, simple to comprehend, and easy to answer, respondents' cooperation and involvement can be maintained throughout the questionnaire. Asking easy-to-answer questions teaches respondents their role and builds their confidence; they know this is a professional researcher and not another salesperson posing as one. If respondents' curiosity is not aroused at the outset, they can become disinterested and terminate the interview.

A mail survey among department store buyers drew an extremely poor return rate.[13] A substantial improvement in response rate occurred, however, when researchers added some introductory questions seeking opinions on pending legislation of great importance to these buyers. Respondents completed all the questions, not only those in the opening section.

In their attempt to "warm up" respondents toward the questionnaire, student researchers frequently ask demographic or classificatory questions at the beginning. This generally is not advisable, because questions that ask for personal information such as income level or education may be embarrassing or threatening to respondents. It usually is better to ask potentially embarrassing questions in the middle or at the end of the questionnaire, after a rapport has been established between respondent and interviewer.

Order Bias

Order bias can result from a particular answer's position in a set of answers or from the sequencing of questions. In political elections in which candidates lack high visibility, such as elections for county commissioners and judges, the first name listed on the ballot often receives the highest percentage of votes. For this reason, many election boards print several ballots so that each candidate's name appears in every possible position on the ballot.

Order bias can also distort survey results. For example, a questionnaire's purpose is to measure level of awareness of several charitable organizations. If Big Brothers and Big Sisters is always mentioned first, Red Cross second, and the American Cancer Association third, Big Brothers and Big Sisters may receive an artificially high awareness rating because respondents are prone to yea-saying (by indicating awareness of the first item in the list).

Asking specific questions before asking about broader issues is a common cause of order bias. For example, bias may arise if questions about a specific clothing store are asked prior to those concerning the criteria for selecting a clothing store. Suppose a respondent indicates in the first portion of a questionnaire that she shops at a store where parking needs to be improved. Later in the questionnaire, to avoid appearing inconsistent, she may state that parking is less important than she really believes it is. Specific questions may thus influence the more general ones. Therefore, it is advisable to ask general questions before specific questions to obtain the freest of open-ended responses. This procedure, known as the **funnel technique,** allows the researcher to understand the respondent's frame of reference before asking more specific questions about the level of the respondent's information and the intensity of his or her opinions.

Consider how later answers might be biased by previous questions in this questionnaire on environmental pollution:

Circle the number on the following table that best expresses your feelings about the severity of each environmental problem:

Problem	Not a Problem				Very Severe Problem
Air pollution from automobile exhausts	1	2	3	4	5
Air pollution from open burning	1	2	3	4	5
Air pollution from industrial smoke	1	2	3	4	5
Air pollution from foul odors	1	2	3	4	5
Noise pollution from airplanes	1	2	3	4	5
Noise pollution from cars, trucks, motorcycles	1	2	3	4	5
Noise pollution from industry	1	2	3	4	5

Not surprisingly, researchers found that the responses to the air pollution questions were highly correlated—in fact, almost identical.

With attitude scales, an *anchoring effect* also may occur. The first concept measured tends to become a comparison point from which subsequent evaluations are made. Randomization of items on a questionnaire susceptible to the anchoring effect helps minimize order bias.

A related problem is bias caused by the order of alternatives on closed questions. To avoid this problem, the order of these choices should be rotated if producing alternative forms of the questionnaire is possible. However, marketing researchers rarely print alternative questionnaires to eliminate problems resulting from order bias. A more common practice is to pencil in Xs or check marks on printed questionnaires to indicate where the interviewer should start a series of repetitive questions. For example, the capitalized phrases in the following question provide instructions to the interviewer to "rotate" brands, starting with the one checked:

I would like to determine how likely you would be to buy certain brands of candy in the future. Let's start with (X'ED BRAND). (RECORD BELOW UNDER APPROPRIATE BRAND. REPEAT QUESTIONS FOR ALL REMAINING BRANDS.)

Start Here:	( ) Mounds	(X) Almond Joy	( ) Snickers
Definitely would buy	−1	−1	−1
Probably would buy	−2	−2	−2
Might or might not buy	−3	−3	−3
Probably would not buy	−4	−4	−4
Definitely would not buy	−5	−5	−5

One advantage of Internet surveys is the ability to reduce order bias by having the computer randomly order questions and/or response alternatives. With complete randomization, question order is random and respondents see response alternatives in different random positions.

Asking a question that does not apply to the respondent or that the respondent is not qualified to answer may be irritating or cause a biased response because the respondent wishes to please the interviewer or avoid embarrassment. Including a **filter question** minimizes the chance of asking questions that may be inapplicable. Asking **"Where do you generally have check-cashing problems in Springfield?"** may elicit a response even though the respondent has

filter question
A question that screens out respondents who are not qualified to answer a second question.

had no check-cashing problems; he or she may wish to please the interviewer with an answer. A filter question such as **"Do you ever have a problem cashing a check in Springfield? ____ Yes ____ No"** would screen out the people who are not qualified to answer.

Another form of filter question, the **pivot question**, is used to obtain income information and other data respondents may be reluctant to provide. For example:

> **"Is your total family income over or under $50,000?" (IF UNDER, ASK) "Is it over or under $25,000?" (IF OVER, ASK) "Is it over or under $75,000?"**
>
> ☐ **Under $25,000**   ☐ **$50,001–$75,000**
> ☐ **$25,001–$50,000**   ☐ **Over $75,000**

Exhibit 11.2 gives an example of a flowchart plan for a questionnaire. Structuring the order of the questions so that they are logical will help to ensure the respondent's cooperation and eliminate confusion or indecision. The researcher maintains legitimacy by making sure that the respondent can comprehend the relationship between a given question (or section of the questionnaire) and the overall purpose of the study. Further, a logical order may aid the individual's memory. Transitional comments explaining the logic of the questionnaire may ensure that the respondent continues. Here are two examples:

> **We have been talking so far about general shopping habits in this city. Now I'd like you to compare two types of grocery stores—regular supermarkets and grocery departments in wholesale club stores.**

> **So that I can combine your answers with those of other farmers who are similar to you, I need some personal information about you. Your answers to these questions—as to all of the others you've answered—are confidential, and you will never be identified to anyone without your permission. Thanks for your help so far. If you'll answer the remaining questions, it will help me analyze all your answers.**

WHAT IS THE BEST LAYOUT?

Good layout and physical attractiveness are crucial in mail, Internet, and other self-administered questionnaires. For different reasons it is also important to have a good layout in questionnaires designed for personal and telephone interviews.

Traditional Questionnaires

Exhibit 11.3 on page 266 shows a page from a telephone questionnaire. The layout is neat and attractive, and the instructions for the interviewer (all boldface capital letters) are easy to follow. The responses "It depends," "Refused," and "Don't know" are enclosed in a box to indicate that these answers are acceptable but responses from the 5-point scale are preferred. (To see the entire questionnaire, go to the Web site of the Council of American Survey Research Organizations at http://ww.casro.org/ and check out their poll about polls).

EXHIBIT 11.2

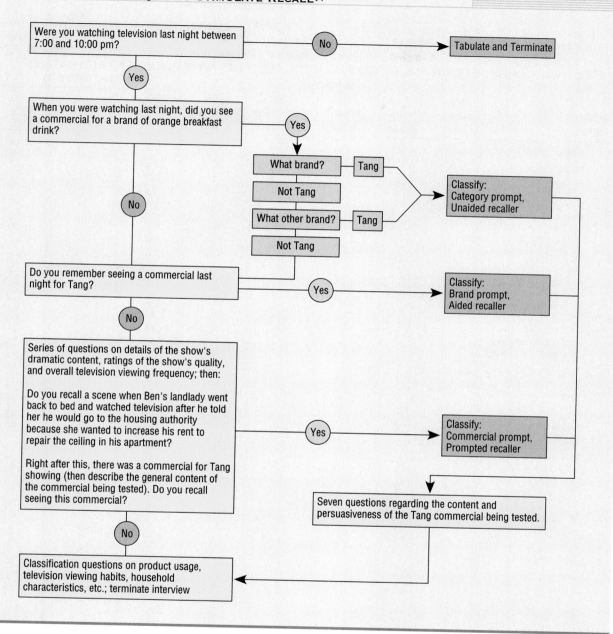

EXHIBIT 11.3 | LAYOUT OF A PAGE FROM A TELEPHONE QUESTIONNAIRE

5. Now I'm going to read you some types of professions. For each one, please tell me whether you think the work that profession does, on balance, has a very positive impact on society, a somewhat positive impact, a somewhat negative impact, a very negative impact, or not much impact either way on society. First . . . **(START AT X'D ITEM. CONTINUE DOWN AND UP THE LIST UNTIL ALL ITEMS HAVE BEEN READ AND RATED.)**

(DO NOT READ)

START HERE:	Very Positive Impact	Some-what Positive Impact	Some-what Negative Impact	Very Negative Impact	Not Much Impact	It Depends	Refused	Don't Know
[ ] Members of Congress	1	2	3	4	5	0	X	Y (24)
[ ] Business executives	1	2	3	4	5	0	X	Y (25)
[ ] Physicians	1	2	3	4	5	0	X	Y (26)
[ ] Political pollsters—that is, people who conduct surveys for public officials or political political candidates	1	2	3	4	5	0	X	Y (27)
[ ] Researchers in the media—that is, people in media such as television, newspapers, magazines and radio, who conduct surveys about issues later reported in the media	1	2	3	4	5	0	X	Y (28)
[ ] Telemarketers—that is, people who sell products or services over the phone	1	2	3	4	5	0	X	Y (29)
[ ] Used car salesmen	1	2	3	4	5	0	X	Y (30)
[ ] Market researchers—that is, people who work for commercial research firms who conduct surveys to see what the public thinks about certain kinds of consumer products or services	1	2	3	4	5	0	X	Y (31)
[ ] Biomedical researchers	1	2	3	4	5	0	X	Y (32)
[ ] Public-opinion researchers—that is, people who work for commercial research firms who conduct surveys to see what the public thinks about important social issues	1	2	3	4	5	0	X	Y (33)
[ ] College and university professors	1	2	3	4	5	0	X	Y (34)
[ ] Attorneys	1	2	3	4	5	0	X	Y (35)
[ ] Members of the clergy	1	2	3	4	5	0	X	Y (36)
[ ] Journalists	1	2	3	4	5	0	X	Y (37)

Often the rate of return can be increased by using the money that might have been spent on an incentive to improve the attractiveness and quality of the questionnaire. One expert in mail surveys suggests that questionnaires should never be overcrowded. Margins should be of decent size, white space should be used to separate blocks of print, and the unavoidable columns of multiple boxes should be kept to a minimum.[15]

Questionnaires should be designed to appear as short as possible. Sometimes it is advisable to use a booklet form of questionnaire rather than stapling a large number of pages together. In situations where it is necessary to conserve space on the questionnaire or to facilitate data entry or tabulation of the data, a multiple-grid layout may be used. The **multiple-grid question** presents several similar questions and corresponding response alternatives arranged in a grid format. For example:

multiple-grid question
Several similar questions arranged in a grid format.

Airlines often offer special fare promotions. On a vacation trip would you take a connecting flight instead of a nonstop flight if the connecting flight were longer?

	Yes	No	Not sure
One hour longer?	☐	☐	☐
Two hours longer?	☐	☐	☐
Three hours longer?	☐	☐	☐

Experienced researchers have found that it pays to phrase the title of the questionnaire carefully. In mail and other self-administered questionnaires, a carefully constructed title may capture the respondent's interest, underline the importance of the research ("Nationwide Study of Blood Donors"), emphasize the interesting nature of the study ("Study of Internet Usage"), appeal to the respondent's ego ("Survey among Top Executives"), or emphasize the confidential nature of the study ("A Confidential Survey among . . ."). The researcher should take steps to ensure that the wording of the title will not bias the respondent in the same way a leading question might.

By using several forms, special instructions, and other tricks of the trade, the researcher can design the questionnaire to facilitate the interviewer's job of following interconnected questions. Exhibits 11.4 and 11.5 illustrate portions of telephone and personal interview questionnaires. Note how the layout and easy-to-follow instructions for interviewers in questions 1, 2, and 3 of Exhibit 11.4 help the interviewer follow the question sequence. Note that questions 3 and 6 in Exhibit 11.5 instruct the interviewer to hand the respondent a card bearing a list of alternatives. Cards may help respondents grasp the intended meaning of the question and remember all the brand names or other items they are being asked about. Also, questions 2, 3, and 6 in Exhibit 11.5 instruct the interviewer that rating of the banks will start with the bank that has been checked in red pencil on the printed questionnaire. The name of the red-checked bank is not the same on every questionnaire. By rotating the order of the check marks, the researchers attempted to reduce order bias caused by respondents' tendency to react more favorably to the first set of questions. To facilitate coding, question responses should be precoded when possible, as in Exhibit 11.4.

Layout is extremely important when questionnaires are long or require the respondent to fill in a large amount of information. In many circumstances, using headings or subtitles to indicate groups of questions will help the respondent grasp the scope or nature of the questions to be asked. Thus, at a glance, the respondent can follow the logic of the questionnaire.

EXHIBIT 11.4 | **TELEPHONE QUESTIONNAIRE WITH SKIP QUESTIONS**

1. Did you take the car you had checked to the Standard Auto Repair Center for repairs?

   _1 Yes **(SKIP TO Q. 3)**   _2 No

2. **(IF NO, ASK:)** Did you have the repair work done?

   _1 Yes   _2 No

   ↓   ↓

   1. Where was the repair work done? _____   1. Why didn't you have the car repaired?
                                                       _____

   2. Why didn't you have the repair work done   _____
      at the Standard Auto Repair Center? _____   _____
      _____
      _____
      _____

3. **(IF YES TO Q. 1, ASK:)** How satisfied were you with the repair work? Were you . . .

   _1 Very satisfied

   _2 Somewhat satisfied

   _3 Somewhat dissatisfied

   _4 Very dissatisfied

   (IF SOMEWHAT OR VERY DISSATISFIED:) In what way were you dissatisfied?

   _____
   _____
   _____

4. **(ASK EVERYONE:)** Do you ever buy gas at the 95th Street Standard Center?

   _1 Yes   _2 No   **(SKIP TO Q. 6)**

5. **(IF YES, ASK:)** How often do you buy gas there?

   _1 Always

   _2 Almost always

   _3 Most of the time

   _4 Part of the time

   _5 Hardly ever

6. Have you ever had your car washed there?

   _1 Yes _2 No

7. Have you ever had an oil change or lubrication done there?

   _1 Yes _2 No

EXHIBIT 11.5 | PERSONAL INTERVIEW QUESTIONNAIRE

"Hello, my name is _____. I'm a Public Opinion Interviewer with Research Services, Inc. We're making an opinion survey about banks and banking, and I'd like to ask you . . ."

1. What are the names of local banks you can think of offhand? (INTERVIEWER: List names in order mentioned.)
   a. _____
   b. _____
   c. _____
   d. _____
   e. _____
   f. _____
   g. _____

2. Thinking now about the experiences you have had with the different banks here in Boulder, have you ever talked to or done business with . . . (INTERVIEWER: Insert name of bank checked in red below.)
   a. Are you personally acquainted with any of the employees or officers at _____?
   b. (If YES) Who is that? _____
   c. How long has it been since you have been inside _____?
      (INTERVIEWER: Now go back and repeat 2a–2c for all other banks listed.)

	(2) Talked		(2a and 2b) Know Employee Or Officer		(2c) Been in Bank in:				
	Yes	No	No	Name	Last Year	1–5	5-Plus	No	DK
Arapahoe National Bank	1	2	1	_____	1	2	3	4	5
First National Bank	1	2	1	_____	1	2	3	4	5
Boulder National Bank	1	2	1	_____	1	2	3	4	5
Security Bank	1	2	1	_____	1	2	3	4	5
United Bank of Boulder	1	2	1	_____	1	2	3	4	5
National State Bank	1	2	1	_____	1	2	3	4	5

3. (HAND BANK RATING CARD) On this card there are a number of contrasting phrases or statements— for example, "Large" and "Small." We'd like to know how you rate (NAME OF BANK CHECKED IN RED BELOW) in terms of these statements or phrases. Just for example, let's use the terms "fast service" and "slow service." If you were to rate a bank #1 on this scale, it would mean you find their service "very fast." On the other hand, a 7 rating would indicate you feel their service is "very slow," whereas a 4 rating means you don't think of them as being either "very fast" or "very slow." Are you ready to go ahead? Good! Tell me then how you would rate (NAME OF BANK CHECKED IN RED) in terms of each of the phrases or statements on that card. How about (READ NEXT BANK NAME)? . . . (INTERVIEWER: Continue on until respondent has evaluated all six banks.)

	Arapahoe National	First National	Boulder National	Security Bank	United Bank	National State
a. Service	_____	_____	_____	_____	_____	_____
b. Size	_____	_____	_____	_____	_____	_____
c. Business vs. Family	_____	_____	_____	_____	_____	_____
d. Friendliness	_____	_____	_____	_____	_____	_____
e. Big/Small Business	_____	_____	_____	_____	_____	_____
f. Rate of Growth	_____	_____	_____	_____	_____	_____
g. Modernness	_____	_____	_____	_____	_____	_____
h. Leadership	_____	_____	_____	_____	_____	_____
i. Loan Ease	_____	_____	_____	_____	_____	_____
j. Location	_____	_____	_____	_____	_____	_____

(continued)

EXHIBIT 11.5

	Arapahoe National	First National	Boulder National	Security Bank	United Bank	National State
k. Hours	____	____	____	____	____	____
l. Ownership	____	____	____	____	____	____
m. Community Involvement	____	____	____	____	____	____

4. Suppose a friend of yours who has just moved to Boulder asked you to recommend a bank. Which local bank would you recommend? Why would you recommend that particular bank?

Arapahoe National   1
First National   2
Boulder National   3
Security Bank   4
United Bank of Boulder   5
National State Bank   6
Other (Specify) _____
DK/Wouldn't   9

5. Which of the local banks do you think of as: (INTERVIEWER: Read red-checked item first, then read each of the other five.)

the newcomer's bank? _____
the student's bank? _____
the Personal Banker bank? _____
the bank where most C.U. faculty and staff bank? _____
the bank most interested in this community? _____
the most progressive bank? _____

6. Which of these financial institutions, if any, (HAND CARD 2) are you or any member of your immediate family who lives here in this home doing business with now?

Bank   1
Credit Union   2
Finance Company   3
Savings and Loan   4
Industrial Bank   5
None of these   6
DK/Not sure   7

(IF NONE, Skip to 19.)

7. If a friend asked you to recommend a place where he or she could get a loan with which to buy a home, which financial institution would you probably recommend? (INTERVIEWER: Probe for specific name.) Why would you recommend (INSTITUTION NAMED)?

Would Recommend: _____

Wouldn't   0
DK/Not Sure   9

Internet Questionnaires

Layout is also an important issue for questionnaires appearing on the Internet. A questionnaire on a Web site should be easy to use, flow logically, and have a graphic look and overall feel that motivate the respondent to cooperate from start to finish. Many of the guidelines for layout of paper questionnaires apply to Internet questionnaires. There are, however, some important differences.

With *graphical user interface (GUI) software*, the researcher can exercise control over the background, colors, fonts, and other visual features displayed on the computer screen so as to create an attractive and easy-to-use interface between the computer user and the Internet survey. GUI software allows the researcher to design questionnaires in which respondents click on the appropriate answer rather than having to type answers or codes.

Researchers often use Web publishing software, such as FrontPage, Netscape Composer, or WebSurveyor, to format a questionnaire so that they will know how it should appear online. However, several features of a respondent's computer may influence the appearance of an Internet questionnaire. For example, discrepancies between the designer's and the respondent's computer settings for screen configuration (e.g., 640 × 480 pixels versus 800 × 600 pixels) may result in questions not being fully visible on the respondent's screen, misaligned text, or other visual problems.[16] The possibility that the questionnaire the researcher/designer constructs on his or her computer may look different from the questionnaire that appears on the respondent's computer should always be considered when designing Internet surveys. One sophisticated remedy is to use the first few questions on an Internet survey to ask about operating system, browser software, and other computer configuration issues so that the questionnaire that is delivered is as compatible as possible with the respondent's computer. A simpler solution is to limit the horizontal width of the questions to 70 characters or less, to decrease the likelihood of wrap-around text.

Layout Issues   Even if the questionnaire designer's computer and the respondents' computers are compatible, there are several layout issues a Web questionnaire designer should consider. The first decision is whether the questionnaire will appear page by page, with individual questions on separate screens (Web pages), or on a scrolling basis, with the entire questionnaire appearing on a single Web page that the respondent scrolls from top to bottom. The *paging layout* (going from screen to screen) greatly facilitates skip patterns. Based on a respondent's answers to filter questions, the computer can automatically insert relevant questions on subsequent pages. If the entire questionnaire appears on one page (the *scrolling layout*), the display should advance smoothly, as if it were a piece of paper being moved up or down. The scrolling layout gives the respondent the ability to read any portion of the questionnaire at any time, but the absence of page boundaries can cause problems. For example, suppose a Likert scale consists of 15 statements in a grid-format layout, with the response categories **Strongly Agree, Agree, Disagree**, and **Strongly Disagree** at the beginning of the questionnaire. Once the respondent has scrolled down beyond the first few statements, he or she may not be able to see both the statements at the end of the list and the response categories at the top of the grid simultaneously. Thus, avoiding the problems associated with splitting questions and response categories may be difficult.

When a scrolling questionnaire is long, category or section headings are helpful to respondents. It is also a good idea to provide links to the top and bottom parts of each section, so that users can navigate through the questionnaire without having to scroll through the entire document.[17]

Whether a Web survey is in page-by-page or scrolling format, **push buttons** with labels should clearly describe the actions to be taken. For example, if the respondent is to go to the next page, a large arrow labeled "NEXT" might appear in color at the bottom of the screen.

Decisions must be made about the use of color, graphics, animation, sound, and other special features that the Internet makes possible. One thing to remember is that, although sophisticated graphics are not a problem for people with very powerful computers, many respondents' computers are not powerful enough to deliver complex graphics at a satisfactory speed, if at all. A textured background, colored headings, and small graphics can make a questionnaire more interesting and appealing, but they may present problems for respondents with older computers and/or low-bandwidth Internet connections.

With a paper questionnaire, the respondent knows how many questions he or she must answer. Because many Internet surveys offer no visual clues about the number of questions to be asked, it is important to provide a **status bar** or some other visual indicator of questionnaire length. For example, including a partially filled rectangular box as a visual symbol and a statement such as "The status bar at top right indicates approximately what portion of the survey you have completed" increases the likelihood that the respondent will finish the entire sequence of questions.

An Internet questionnaire uses windows known as dialog boxes to display questions and record answers. Exhibit 11.6 portrays four common ways of displaying questions on a computer screen. Many Internet questionnaires require the respondent to activate his or her answer by clicking on a **radio button** for a response. Radio buttons work like push buttons on automobile radios: Clicking on an alternative response deactivates the first choice and replaces it with the new response. A **drop-down box**, such as the one shown in Exhibit 11.6, is a space-saving device that allows the researcher to provide a list of responses that are hidden from view until they are needed. A general statement, such as "Please select" or "Click here," is shown initially. Clicking on the downward-facing arrow makes the full range of choices appear. If the first choice in a list, such as "Strongly Agree," is shown while the other responses are kept hidden, the chance that response bias will occur is increased. Drop-down boxes may present a problem for individuals with minimal computer skills, as they may not know how to reveal hidden responses behind a drop-down menu or how to move from one option to another in a moving-bar menu.

Checklist questions may be followed by **check boxes**, several, none, or all of which may be checked by the respondent. **Open-ended boxes** are boxes in which respondents type their answers to open-ended questions. Open-ended boxes may be designed as *one-line text boxes* or *scrolling text boxes*, depending on the breadth of the expected answer. Of course, open-ended questions require that respondents have both the skill and the willingness to keyboard lengthy answers on the computer. As in the example on page 274, some open-ended boxes are designed so that respondents can enter numbers for frequency response, ranking, or rating questions.

push button
In a dialog box on an Internet questionnaire, a small outlined area, such as a rectangle or an arrow, that the respondent clicks on to select an option or perform a function, such as Submit.

status bar
In an Internet questionnaire, a visual indicator that tells the respondent what portion of the survey he or she has completed.

radio button
In an Internet questionnaire, a circular icon, resembling a button, that activates one response choice and deactivates others when a respondent clicks on it.

drop-down box
In an Internet questionnaire, a space-saving device that reveals responses when they are needed but otherwise hides them from view.

check box
In an Internet questionnaire, a small graphic box, next to an answer, that a respondent clicks on to choose that answer; typically, a check mark or an X appears in the box when the respondent clicks on it.

open-ended box
In an Internet questionnaire, a box where respondents can type in their own answers to open-ended questions.

EXHIBIT 11.6 | ALTERNATIVE WAYS OF
DISPLAYING INTERNET QUESTIONS

Radio button

Last month, did you purchase products or services over the Internet?

○ Yes

○ No

How familiar are you with Microsoft's X-box video game player?

Know Extremely Well	Know Fairly Well	Know a Little	Know Just Name	Never Heard of
○	○	○	○	○

Drop-down box, closed position

In which country or region do you currently reside?

| Click Here | ▼ |

Drop-down box, open position

In which country or region do you currently reside?

| Click Here | ▼ |

Click Here
United States
Asia/Pacific (excluding Hawaii)
Africa
Australia or New Zealand
Canada
Europe
Latin America, South America, or Mexico
Middle East
Other

Check box

From which location(s) do you access the Internet? Select all that apply.

☐ Home
☐ Work
☐ Other Location

Please indicate which of the following Web sites you have ever visited or used. (CHOOSE ALL THAT APPLY.)

☐ E*Trade's Web site
☐ Waterhouse's Web site
☐ Merrill Lynch's Web site
☐ Fidelity's Web site
☐ Schwab's Web site
☐ Powerstreet
☐ Yahoo! Finance
☐ Quicken.com
☐ Lycos Investing
☐ AOL's Personal Finance
☐ None of the above

Open-ended, one-line box

What company do you think is the most visible sponsor of sports?

Open-ended, scrolling text box

What can we do to improve our textbook?

Below you will see a series of statements that might or might not describe how you feel about your career. Please rate each statement using a scale from 1 to 4, where 4 means "Totally Agree," 3 means "Somewhat Agree," 2 means "Somewhat Disagree," and 1 means "Totally Disagree."

Please enter your numeric answer in the box provided next to each statement. Would you say that . . . ?

A lack of business knowledge relevant to my field/career could hurt my career advancement.

My career life is an important part of how I define myself.

Pop-up boxes are message boxes that can be used to highlight important information. For example, pop-up boxes may be use to provide a privacy statement, such as the following:

IBM would like your help in making our Web site easier to use and more effective. Choose to complete the survey now or not at all.

| Complete | | No Thank You | | Privacy Statement |

Clicking on Privacy Statement opens the following pop-up box:

Survey Privacy Statement

This overall Privacy Statement verifies that IBM is a member of the TRUSTe program and is in compliance with TRUSTe principles. This survey is strictly for market research purposes. The information you provide will be used only to improve the overall content, navigation, and usability of ibm.com.

In some cases, respondents can learn more about how to use a particular scale or get a definition of a term by clicking on a link, which generates a pop-up box. One of the most common reasons for using pop-up boxes is *error trapping*, a topic discussed in the next section.

Chapter 10 described graphic rating scales, which present respondents with a graphic continuum. On the Internet, researchers can take advantage of scroll bars or other GUI software features to make these scales easy to use. For example, the graphic continuum may be drawn as a measuring rod with a plus sign on one end and a minus sign on the other. The respondent then moves a small rectangle back and forth between the two ends of the scale to scroll to any point on the continuum. Scoring, as discussed in Chapter 10, is in terms of some measure of the length (millimeters) from one end of the graphic continuum to the point marked by the respondent.

Finally, it is a good idea to include a customized thank-you page at the end of an Internet questionnaire, so that a brief thank-you note pops onto their screens when respondents click on the Submit push button.[18]

Software That Makes Questionnaires Interactive Computer code can be written to make Internet questionnaires interactive and less subject to errors. The writing of software programs is beyond the scope of this discussion. However, several of the interactive functions that software makes possible should be mentioned here.

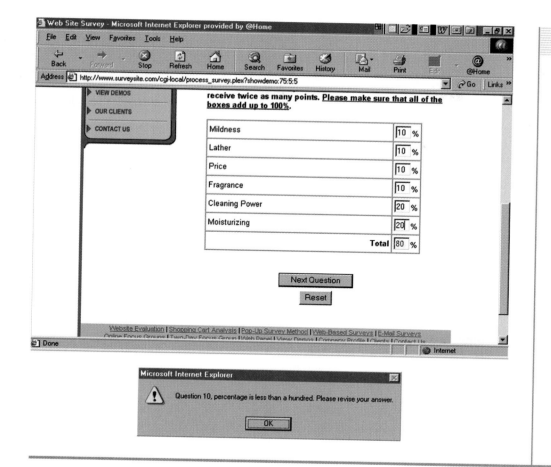

The respondent's answers to this constant-sum scale incorrectly total 80 percent—not the required 100 percent. When mistakes occur, error trapping software may cause a pop-up box to appear, with a message instructing the respondent to adjust his or her answer. With forced answering, respondents cannot skip over questions as they do in mail surveys.

As discussed in Chapter 7, Internet software allows the branching off of questioning into two or more different lines, depending on a particular respondent's answer, and the skipping or filtering of questions. Questionnaire-writing software with Boolean skip and branching logic is readily available. Most of these programs have *hidden skip logic* so that respondents never see any evidence of skips. It is best if the questions the respondent sees flow in numerical sequence.[19] However, some programs number all potential questions in numerical order, and the respondent sees only the numbers on the questions he or she answers. Thus, a respondent may answer questions 1 through 11 and then next see a question numbered 15 because of the skip logic.

Software can systematically or randomly manipulate the questions a respondent sees. **Variable piping software** allows variables, such as answers from previous questions, to be inserted into unfolding questions. Other software can randomly rotate the order of questions, blocks of questions, and response alternatives from respondent to respondent.

Researchers can use software to control the flow of a questionnaire. Respondents can be blocked from backing up, or they can be allowed to stop in mid-questionnaire and come back later to finish. A questionnaire can be designed so that if the respondent fails to answer a question or answers it with an incorrect type of response, an error message immediately appears. This is

variable piping software
Software that allows variables to be inserted into an Internet questionnaire as a respondent is completing it.

error trapping
Using software to control the flow of an Internet questionnaire—for example, to prevent respondents from backing up or failing to answer a question.

forced answering software
Software that prevents respondents from continuing with an Internet questionnaire if they fail to answer a question.

interactive help desk
In an Internet questionnaire, a live, real-time support feature that solves problems or answers questions respondents may encounter in completing the questionnaire.

called **error trapping**. With **forced answering software**, respondents cannot skip over questions as they do in mail surveys. The program will not let them continue if they fail to answer a question.[20] The software may insert a boldfaced error message on the question screen or insert a pop-up box instructing the respondent how to continue. For example, if a respondent does not answer a question and tries to proceed to another screen, a pop-up box might present the following message:

> **You cannot leave a question blank. On questions without a "Not sure" or "Decline to answer" option, please choose the response that best represents your opinions or experiences.**

The respondent must close the pop-up box and answer the question in order to proceed to the next screen.

Some designers include **interactive help desks** in their Web questionnaires, so that respondents can solve problems they encounter in completing a questionnaire. A respondent might e-mail questions to the survey help desk or get live, interactive, real-time support via an online help desk.

Some respondents will leave the questionnaire Web site, prematurely terminating the survey. In many cases sending an e-mail message to these respondents at a later date, encouraging them to revisit the Web site, will persuade them to complete the questionnaire. Through the use of software and cookies, researchers can make sure that the respondent who revisits the Web site will be able to pick up at the point where he or she left off.

Once an Internet questionnaire has been designed, it is important to pretest it to ensure that it works with Internet Explorer, Netscape, AOL, WebTV, and other browsers. Some general-purpose programming languages, such as Java, do not always work with all browsers. Because different browsers have different peculiarities, a survey that works perfectly well with one may not function at all with another.[21]

HOW MUCH PRETESTING AND REVISING ARE NECESSARY?

pretesting
Administering a questionnaire to a small group of respondents to detect ambiguity or bias in the questions or to iron out fundamental problems in the instructions or administrative procedures.

An investigator who is surveying 3,000 consumers does not want to find out after the questionnaires have been completed and returned that most respondents misunderstood a particular question, skipped a series of questions, or misinterpreted the instructions for filling out the questionnaire. To avoid problems such as these, screening procedures, or *pretests*, are often used. **Pretesting** involves a trial run in which a questionnaire is administered to a group of respondents in the target population to iron out fundamental problems in the questionnaire survey design. Here the researcher looks for such things as the point at which respondent fatigue sets in, whether there are any particular places in the questionnaire where respondents tend to terminate, and other considerations. Unfortunately, this stage of research may be eliminated because of costs or time pressures.

Broadly speaking, there are three basic ways to pretest. The first two involve screening the questionnaire with other research professionals, and the third—the one most often called *pretesting*—is a trial run with a group of respondents. When screening the questionnaire with other research professionals, the investigator asks them to look for such things as difficulties with question wording, problems with leading questions, and bias due to question order. An alternative screening process might involve a client or the manager who ordered the research. Often managers ask for information but, when they see the questionnaire, find it does not really meet their needs. Only by checking with the individual who has

BURGER FAVORITES:
A FAILURE TO COMMUNICATE

Sometimes it is just a matter of how you ask the question.[22] When Burger King sent a survey company into the field to query fast-food fanciers on whether they preferred flame-broiled or fried hamburgers, they found a three-to-one preference for the open flame, or flame-broiled method—Burger King's own. The company and its agency immediately incorporated that finding into a comparative advertising campaign.

But when Leo Shapiro, president of a marketing research company, conducted his own survey, he rephrased the question and came up with distinctly different answers. "If you have two methods of cooking and it's a verbal survey, the choice of words could influence the outcome," Shapiro said in explaining why he decided to conduct his own survey of 308 fast-food customers. An interviewer asked: "Do you prefer a hamburger that is grilled on a hot stainless-steel grill or cooked by passing the raw meat through an open gas flame?" Shapiro's researchers found that 53 percent preferred their burgers from a stainless-steel grill. This means they opted for McDonald's fried over Burger King's open flame. The interviewer then added another dimension: "The chain that grills on a hot stainless-steel griddle serves its cooked hamburg-

ers at the proper temperature without having to use a microwave oven. The chain that uses the flame puts the hamburgers into a microwave oven after they are cooked and before serving them. Just knowing this, from which of these two chains would you prefer to buy a hamburger?"

McDonald's hot stainless-steel griddles and microwaveless restaurants won again. This time they pulled in a 5½-to-1 margin over Burger King. The Burger King hamburgers do come off one at a time, so in rush periods the microwave is used to preserve the serving temperature and to melt the cheese. Burger King refuses to provide details on its survey beyond saying it was national, done by a nationally known public opinion company, that the question asked was "Do you prefer your hamburgers flame-broiled or fried?" and that they are completely satisfied with the survey.

"We found the word 'fried' was unappetizing," Shapiro said. "You don't eat fried foods. The word 'cooked' is neutral, and 'open-gas' is more precise but less appetizing [than Burger King's 'flame-broiled' description]." Shapiro stated that the most significant finding of this survey is how important the methods of cooking and serving were to the hamburger consumer.

requested the questionnaire does the researcher know for sure that the information needed will be provided.

Once the researcher has decided on the final questionnaire, data should be collected with a small number of respondents (say, 100) to determine whether the questionnaire needs further refinement. Usually the questionnaire is tried out on a group that is selected on a convenience basis and is similar in makeup to the one that ultimately will be sampled. Pretesting does not require a statistical sample; however, the researcher should not select a group too divergent from the target market (for example, selecting business students as surrogates for businesspeople). The pretesting process allows the researcher to determine whether respondents have any difficulty understanding the questionnaire and whether there are any ambiguous or biased questions. This process is exceedingly beneficial. Making a mistake with 25 or 50 subjects can avoid the potential disaster of administering an invalid questionnaire to several hundred individuals.

Counting the number of responses to each question and other means of tabulating the results of a pretest help determine whether the questionnaire will meet the objectives of the research. A **preliminary tabulation** often illustrates that although respondents can easily comprehend and answer a given question, it is inappropriate because it does not provide relevant information to help solve the marketing problem.

Many novelists write, rewrite, revise, and rewrite again certain chapters, paragraphs, or even sentences. The researcher works similarly. Rarely does he or she write only a first draft of a questionnaire. The exact number of revisions depends on the researcher's and client's judgment. The revision process usually ends when both agree that the desired information is being collected in an unbiased manner.

DESIGNING QUESTIONNAIRES FOR GLOBAL MARKETS

Now that marketing research is being conducted around the globe, researchers must take cultural factors into account when designing questionnaires. The most common problem involves translating a questionnaire into other languages. A questionnaire developed in one country may be difficult to translate because equivalent language concepts do not exist or because of differences in idiom and vernacular. For example, the concepts of uncles and aunts are not the same in the United States as in India. In India the words for *uncle* and *aunt* are different for the maternal and paternal sides of the family.[23] Although Spanish is spoken in both Mexico and Venezuela, one researcher found the Spanish translation of the English term *retail outlet* works in Mexico but not in Venezuela. Venezuelans interpreted the translation to refer to an electrical outlet, an outlet of a river into an ocean, or the passageway into a patio.

International marketing researchers often have questionnaires back translated. **Back translation** is the process of having a questionnaire that has previously been translated from one language to another translated back into the original language by a second, independent translator. The back translator is often a person whose native tongue is the language that will be used for the questionnaire. This process can reveal inconsistencies between the English version and the translation. For example, when a soft-drink company translated its slogan "Baby, it's cold inside" into Cantonese for research in Hong Kong, the result read "Small Mosquito, on the inside, it is very cold." In Hong Kong *small mosquito* is a colloquial expression for a small child. Obviously the intended meaning of the advertising message had been lost in the translated questionnaire.[24] In another international marketing research project, "out of sight, out of mind" was back translated as "invisible things are insane."[25]

As indicated in Chapter 7, literacy influences the designs of self-administered questionnaires and interviews. Knowledge of the literacy rates in foreign countries, especially those that are just developing modern economies, is vital.

SUMMARY

Good questionnaire design is a key to obtaining accurate survey results. The specific questions to be asked will be a function of the type of information needed to answer the manager's questions and the communication medium of data collection. Relevance and accuracy are the basic criteria for judging questionnaire results. A questionnaire is *relevant* if no unnecessary information is collected and the information needed to solve the marketing problem is obtained. Accurate information is reliable and valid.

Knowing how each question should be phrased requires some knowledge of the different types of questions possible. Open-ended response questions pose some question or problem and ask the respondent to answer in his or her own words. Fixed-alternative questions require less interviewer skill, take less time, and are easier to answer. In fixed-alternative questions, the respondent is given specific limited alternative responses and asked to choose the one closest to his or her own viewpoint. Standardized responses are easier to code, tabulate, and interpret. Care must be taken to formulate the responses so that they do not overlap. Respondents whose answers do not fit any of the fixed alternatives may be forced to select alternatives that do not communicate what they really mean.

Open-ended response questions are especially useful in exploratory research or at the beginning of a questionnaire. They make a questionnaire more expensive to analyze because of the uniqueness of the answers. Also, interviewer bias can influence the responses to such questions.

Some guidelines for questionnaire construction have emerged from research experience. The language should be simple to allow for variations in educational level. Researchers should avoid leading or loaded questions, which suggest answers to the respondents, as well as questions that induce them to give socially desirable answers. Respondents have a bias against questions that suggest changes in the status quo. Their reluctance to answer personal questions can be reduced by explaining the need for the questions and by assuring respondents of the confidentiality of their replies. The researcher should carefully avoid ambiguity in questions. Another common problem is the double-barreled question, which asks two questions at once.

Question sequence can be very important to the success of a survey. The opening questions should be designed to capture respondents' interest and keep them involved. Personal questions should be postponed to the middle or end of the questionnaire. General questions should precede specific ones. In a series of attitude scales, the first response may be used as an anchor for comparison with the other responses. The order of alternatives on closed questions can affect the results. Filter questions are useful for avoiding unnecessary questions that do not apply to a particular respondent. Such questions may be put into a flowchart for personal or telephone interviewing.

The layout of a mail or self-administered questionnaire can affect its response rate. An attractive questionnaire encourages a response, as does a carefully phrased title. Internet questionnaires present unique design issues. Decisions must be made about the use of color, graphics, animation, sound, and other special effects that the Internet makes possible. Finally, pretesting helps reveal errors while they can still be corrected easily.

International marketing researchers must take cultural factors into account when designing questionnaires. The most widespread problem involves translation into another language. International questionnaires are often back translated.

Key Terms and Concepts

open-ended response question
fixed-alternative question
simple-dichotomy (dichotomous-alternative) question
determinant-choice question
frequency-determination question

checklist question
leading question
loaded question
counterbiasing statement
split-ballot technique
double-barreled question

order bias
funnel technique
filter question
pivot question
multiple-grid question
push button

status bar
radio button
drop-down box
check box
open-ended box

pop-up boxes
variable piping software
error trapping
forced answering software
interactive help desk

pretesting
preliminary tabulation
back translation

Questions for Review and Critical Thinking

1. Evaluate and comment on the following questions taken from several questionnaires:

    a. A university computer center survey on SPSS usage:

    How often do you use SPSS statistical software? Please check one.

    _____**Infrequently (once a semester)**

    _____**Occasionally (once a month)**

    _____**Frequently (once a week)**

    _____**All the time (daily)**

    b. A survey of advertising agencies:

    Do you understand and like the Federal Trade Commission's new corrective advertising policy?

    _____**Yes** _____**No**

    c. A survey on a new, small electric car:

    Assuming 90 percent of your driving is in town, would you buy this type of car?

    _____**Yes** _____**No**

    If this type of _electric_ car had the same initial cost as a current "Big 3" full-size, fully equipped car, but operated at one-half the cost over a 5-year period, would you buy one?

    _____**Yes** _____**No**

    d. A student survey:

    Since the beginning of this semester, approximately what percentage of the time do you get to campus using each of the forms of transportation available to you per week?

    Walk _____
    Bicycle _____
    Public transportation _____
    Motor vehicle _____

    e. A survey of motorcycle dealers:

    Should the company continue its generous cooperative advertising program?

    f. A survey of media use by farmers:

    Thinking about _yesterday_, put an X in the box below for _each_ quarter-hour time period during which, so far as you can recall, you _personally_ listened to _radio_. Do the same for _television_.

6:00 to 10:00 A.M. by quarter-hours	6:00–6:15	6:15–6:30	6:30–6:45	6:45–7:00	7:00–7:15	7:15–7:30	7:30–7:45	7:45–8:00
Radio →								
TV →								

	8:00–8:15	8:15–8:30	8:30–8:45	8:45–9:00	9:00–9:15	9:15–9:30	9:30–9:45	9:45–10:00
Radio →								
TV →								

    If you did not watch TV any time yesterday, place an X here ☐

    If you did not listen to radio any time yesterday, place an X here ☐

    g. A government survey of gasoline retailers:

    Suppose the full-service pump selling price for regular gasoline is 132.8 cents per gallon on the first day of the month. Suppose on the 10th of the month the price is raised to 134.9 cents per gallon, and on the 25th of the month it is reduced to 130.9 cents per gallon. In order to provide the required data you should list the accumulator reading on the full-service regular gasoline pump when the station opens on the 1st day, the 10th day, and the 25th day of the month and when the station closes on the last day of the month.

h. An anti–gun control group's survey:

Do you believe that private citizens have the right to own firearms to defend themselves, their families, and their property from violent criminal attack?

____Yes   ____No

i. A survey of the general public:

In the next year, after accounting for inflation, do you think your real personal income will go up or down?

1. Up

2. (Stay the same)

3. Down

4. (Don't know)

j. A survey of the general public:

Some people say that companies should be required by law to label all chemicals and substances that the government states are potentially harmful. The label would tell what the chemical or substance is, what dangers it might pose, and what safety procedures should be used in handling the substance. Other people say that such laws would be too strict. They say the law should require labels on only those chemicals and substances that the companies themselves decide are potentially harmful. Such a law, they say, would be less costly for the companies and would permit them to exclude those chemicals and substances they consider to be trade secrets. Which of these views is closest to your own?

1. Require labels on all chemicals and substances that the government states are potentially harmful.

2. (Don't know)

3. Require labels on only those chemicals and substances that companies decide are potentially harmful.

k. A survey of voters:

Since agriculture is vital to our state's economy, how do you feel about the administration's farm policies?

Strongly favor

Somewhat favor

Somewhat oppose

Strongly oppose

Unsure

2. The following question was asked in a survey of a sample of television viewers:

We are going to ask you to classify the type of fan you consider yourself to be for different sports and sports programs.

Diehard Fan: Watch games, follow up on scores and sports news multiple times a day

Avid Fan: Watch games, follow up on scores and sports news once a day

Casual Fan: Watch games, follow up on scores and sports news occasionally

Championship Fan: Watch games, follow up on scores and sports news only during championships or playoffs

Non-Fan: Never watch games or follow up on scores

Anti-Fan: Dislike, oppose, or object to a certain sport

Does this question do a good job of avoiding ambiguity?

3. How might the wording of a question about income influence respondents' answers?

4. What is the difference between a leading question and a loaded question?

5. Design one or more open-ended response question(s) to measure reactions to a magazine ad for a Xerox photocopier.

6. Design one or more question(s) to measure how a person who has just been shown a television commercial might describe the commercial.

7. It has been said that surveys show that consumers hate advertising but like specific ads. Comment.

8. Design a complete questionnaire to evaluate a new fast-food fried chicken restaurant.

9. Design a short but complete questionnaire to measure consumer satisfaction with an airline.

10. Develop a checklist of things to consider in questionnaire construction.

11. Design a complete personal interview questionnaire for a zoo that wishes to determine who visits the zoo and how they evaluate it.

12. Design a complete self-administered questionnaire for a bank to give to customers immediately after they open new accounts.

13. Design a questionnaire for your local Big Brothers and Big Sisters organization to investigate awareness of and willingness to volunteer time to this organization.

14. Design a questionnaire for a bank located in a college town to investigate the potential for attracting college students as checking account customers.

15. The Apple Assistance Center is a hotline to solve problems for users of Macintosh computers and

other Apple products. Design a short (postcard-size) consumer satisfaction/service quality questionnaire for the Apple Assistance Center.

16. A client tells a researcher that she wants a questionnaire that evaluates the importance of 30 product characteristics and rates her brand and 10 competing brands on these characteristics. The researcher believes this questionnaire will induce respondent fatigue because it will be far too long. Should the researcher do exactly what the client says or risk losing the business by suggesting a different approach?

17. A lobbying organization designs a short questionnaire about its political position. It also includes a membership solicitation with the questionnaire. Is this approach ethical?

18. A public figure who supports cost cutting in government asks the following question in a survey: **"Do you support a presidential line item veto to eliminate waste in government?"** Is this question ethical?

Exploring the Internet

1. Visit Mister Poll at http://www.misterpoll.com, where you will find thousands of user-contributed polls on every imaginable topic from the controversial to the downright zany. What you find will depend on when you visit the site. However, you might find something such as a movie poll, where you pick your favorite film of the season. Evaluate the questions in the poll.

2. Visit Google at http://www.google.com and conduct a search using the key phrase "Questionnaire Design." How many Web sites contain this phrase? Find an interesting Web site and report on your findings.

3. A language translator (English to Spanish, French to English, etc.) can be found at http://babelfish.altavista.com/translate.dyn.

WebSurveyor Activities

Video Games
Run the WebSurveyor Desktop software, and click "From a template" under the heading "Create a new survey" from the Getting Started Wizard. (If the Getting Started Wizard does not appear, click Tools and then Options from the main menu, make sure "Display the Getting Started Wizard for New Surveys" is checked, and then click OK. Next click File and then New from the main menu, and then click "From a template" under the heading "Create a new survey.") Use the Survey Builder Wizard and click on the "Marketing Competitive Intelligence" category. Then select the Product Recall Survey template. Identify a product category that interests you (perhaps video games) and identify three or four brands in the product category (perhaps Nintendo Gamecube, Sony PlayStation, and Microsoft Xbox). Create a questionnaire using the standard template. What questions need to be added or deleted to make this questionnaire fit your research objectives?

Starry Nights
The Starry Nights questionnaire was developed using WebSurveyor's Survey Builder Wizard. The category "Marketing Customer Needs" was chosen and then "Customer Satisfaction—Consumer Service." Some

questions were modified. Using the WebSurveyor Desktop software, select File and then Open from the main menu, and then select the file named "Starry Nights.ws3." The Question List will appear. Click on "Preview" under Survey Editing to view the questionnaire as a Web page. Do other changes need to be made?

Human Resource Questionnaire
A manager used WebSurveyor's question library to create a questionnaire with 20 attitude scales. Using the WebSurveyor Desktop software, open the survey named "Human Resources.ws3." The Question List will appear. Click on "Preview" under Survey Editing to view the quesitonnaire as a Web page. Evaluate the questionnaire and, if necessary, create a revised questionnaire.

Designing Your Own Questionnaire
- Using the WebSurveyor Desktop software, design a short but complete questionnaire to measure consumer satisfaction with an airline.
- Using the WebSurveyor Desktop software, design a questionnaire for your local Big Brothers and Big Sisters organization to investigate awareness of and willingness to volunteer time to this organization.

CASE 11.1   CANTERBURY TRAVELS

Hometown, located in the north–central United States, had a population of about 50,000. There were two travel agencies in Hometown before Canterbury Travels opened its doors.

Canterbury Travels was in its second month of operations. Owner Roxanne Freeman had expected to have more business than she actually had. She decided that she needed to conduct a survey to determine how much business Hometown offered. She also wanted to learn whether people were aware of Canterbury Travels.

She thought this survey would determine the effectiveness of her advertising.

The questionnaire Roxanne Freeman designed is shown in Case Exhibit 11.1-1.

Questions
1. Critically evaluate the questionnaire.
2. Will Canterbury Travels gain the information it needs from this survey?

CASE EXHIBIT 11.1-1	TRAVEL QUESTIONNAIRE

The following questionnaire pertains to a project being conducted by a local travel agency. The intent of the study is to better understand the needs and attitudes of Hometown residents toward travel agencies. The questionnaire will take only 10 to 15 minutes to fill out at your convenience. Your name will in no way be connected with the questionnaire.

1. Have you traveled out of state?   _____Yes _____No
2. If yes, do you travel for:
      Business   Pleasure   Both
3. How often do you travel for the above?
0–1 times per month	0–1 times per year
2–3 times per month	2–3 times per year
4–5 times per month	4–5 times per year
6 or more times per month	6 or more times per year
4. How do you make your travel arrangements?
      Airline   Travel agency   Other (please specify) _____
5. Did you know that travel agencies do not charge the customer for their services?
      _____Yes _____No
6. Please rate the following qualities that would be most important to you in the selection of a travel agency:

Good   **Bad**

Free services
   (reservations, advice, and delivery of tickets
   and literature)
Convenient location
Knowledgeable personnel
Friendly personnel
Casual atmosphere
Revolving charge account
Reputation
Personal sales calls

7. Are you satisfied with your present travel agency?

Very satisfied   **Very dissatisfied**

Holiday Travel
Leisure Tours
Canterbury Travels
Other _____

(continued)

8. If not, what are you dissatisfied with about your travel agency?

Good   **Bad**

Free services
  (reservations, advice, and delivery of tickets
  and literature)
Convenient location   _____ _____ _____ _____ _____
Knowledgeable personnel   _____ _____ _____ _____ _____
Friendly personnel   _____ _____ _____ _____ _____
Casual atmosphere   _____ _____ _____ _____ _____
Revolving charge account   _____ _____ _____ _____ _____
Reputation   _____ _____ _____ _____ _____
Personal sales calls   _____ _____ _____ _____ _____

9. Did you know that there is a new travel agency in Hometown?
   _____Yes   _____No

10. Can you list the travel agencies in Hometown and their locations?
_____
_____
_____

11. Do you use the same travel agency repeatedly?

	0–1 times per month	2–3 times per month	4–5 times per month	6 or more times per month	0–1 times per year	2–3 times per year	4–5 times per year	6 or more times per year
Holiday Travel								
Leisure Tours								
Canterbury Travels								
Other (please specify)								

12. Have you visited the new travel agency in Hometown?
    _____Yes   _____No

13. If yes, what is its name? _____

14. How do you pay for your travel expenses?
    Cash   Company charge
    Check   Personal charge
    Credit card   Other _____

15. Which of these have you seen advertising for?
    Holiday Travel
    Canterbury Travels
    Other _____

16. If yes, where have you seen or heard this advertisement?

17. Would you consider changing travel agencies?
    _____Yes   _____No

The following are some personal questions about you that will be used for statistical purposes only. Your answers will be held in the strictest confidence.

18. What is your age?
    19–25   46–55
    26–35   56–65
    36–45   Over 65

(continued)

19. What is your sex?
    Male   Female
20. What is your marital status?
    Single   Divorced
    Married   Widowed
21. How long have you lived in Hometown?
    0–6 months   5–10 years
    7–12 months   11–15 years
    1–4 years   Over 15 years
22. What is your present occupation?
    Business and professional   Laborer
    Salaried and semiprofessional   Student
    Skilled worker
23. What is the highest level of education you have completed?
    Elementary school   1–2 years of college
    Junior high school   3–4 years of college
    Senior high school   More than 4 years of college
    Trade or vocational school
24. What is your yearly household income?
    $0–$5,000 $25,001–$40,000
    $5,001–$10,000 $40,001–$60,000
    $10,001–$15,000 $60,000 and above
    $15,001–$25,000

CASE 11.2   GTE AIRFONE

The questionnaire in Case Exhibit 11.2-1 was sent to a sample of frequent airline fliers.[26]

Question
Evaluate the questionnaire.

If you have used the Airfone service, please indicate your level of satisfaction with the Airfone service by circling the appropriate number below.

	Excellent 5	Good 4	Average 3	Fair 2	Poor 1
GTE Airfone service					
A1 Considering your Airfone usage, how would you rate your overall experience?	5	4	3	2	1
A2 Availability of Airfone on flights on which you've traveled	5	4	3	2	1
A3 Availability of operating instructions	5	4	3	2	1
A4 Understandability of operating instructions	5	4	3	2	1
A5 Length of time to obtain dial tone	5	4	3	2	1
A6 Ability to complete a call on the first attempt	5	4	3	2	1
A7 Transmission quality (static)	5	4	3	2	1
A8 Level of telephone background noise	5	4	3	2	1

(continued)

	Excellent 5	Good 4	Average 3	Fair 2	Poor 1
GTE Airfone service					
A9 Calls fading	5	4	3	2	1
A10 Hearing the called party clearly	5	4	3	2	1
A11 Called party hearing you clearly	5	4	3	2	1
A12 Frequency of calls disconnected	5	4	3	2	1
A13 Convenience of computer voice messages	5	4	3	2	1
A14 Current price structure	5	4	3	2	1
A15 Flight attendant helpfulness, assistance, and knowledge of the Airfone service	5	4	3	2	1
Billing					
B1 Accuracy of monthly charges	5	4	3	2	1
B2 Ease of understanding charges	5	4	3	2	1

The following questions concern your Airfone usage, airline travel, preferred charge method, and a comparison of the Airfone to cellular phones. Please answer as completely as possible.

1. In the past *year,* how often have you used the Airfone service? _____
   (Enter # Times)

2. Have you used our Seatfone product? Yes   1
   (Circle one answer)   No   2

3. Did you use the Airfone service to make urgent business calls, nonurgent business calls, or personal calls? *(Circle all that apply)*
   Urgent business calls   1
   Nonurgent business calls   2
   Personal calls   3

4. Approximately how many airline round trips do you make annually? _____
   (Enter # Times)

5. Which airline do you most frequently travel on? _____
   (Enter Name of Airline)

6. Has the Airfone service made your travel time productive and more beneficial to your completing business while in flight?
   Yes   1
   No   2
   (Circle one answer)
   If yes, please explain how _____
   _____
   _____

7. Considering the value of the Airfone service, do you feel the cost of a call is comparable to the quality of service you've experienced?
   Yes   1
   No   2
   (Circle one answer)
   If no, please explain why _____
   _____
   _____

8. Given a choice of flights with the same schedule, destination, and cost, one with the Airfone service, the other without, which flight would you choose to travel on? *(Circle one answer)*
   With Airfone   1
   Without Airfone   2

(continued)

9. Which credit cards do you own? *(Circle all that apply)*

1. American Express	4. Discover	7. UATP
2. Carte Blanche	5. Enroute	8. Visa
3. Diners Club	6. MasterCard	9. AT&T

10. Which credit card have you used in the past to pay for the Airfone service? *(Circle all that apply)*

1. American Express	4. Discover	7. UATP
2. Carte Blanche	5. Enroute	8. Visa
3. Diners Club	6. MasterCard	9. AT&T

11. Have you experienced problems activating the Airfone Service with your card(s)?
    (Circle one answer)

    Yes   1
    No   2

12. Which card would you prefer to use to pay for the Airfone service?
    (Circle all that apply)

1. American Express	4. Discover	7. UATP
2. Carte Blanche	5. Enroute	8. Visa
3. Diners Club	6. MasterCard	9. AT&T

13. Do you own a cellular phone or use a company-paid cellular phone?
    (Circle one answer)

    Yes   1
    No   2

    If yes, how does the quality of the GTE Airfone compare to that of the cellular phone? *(Circle one answer)*

    Airfone is much higher quality than cellular   1
    Airfone is somewhat higher quality than cellular   2
    Airfone is about the same quality as cellular   3
    Airfone is somewhat lower quality than cellular   4
    Airfone is much lower quality than cellular   5

14. Have you ever seen any advertising for GTE Airfone?
    If yes, what did the advertising tell you about GTE Airfone?

    Yes   1
    No   2

    _____

    _____

    If yes, where have you seen GTE Airfone advertising? *(Circle all that apply)*

    In-flight airline magazines   1
    Posters or billboards   2
    TV at airport   3
    Newspapers   4
    Business publications   5
    Card located in the seatback pocket 6
    Other   7

15. Are you aware of our Service Guarantee that provides credit when you are not satisfied with the quality of an Airfone call?
    If yes, how did you first become aware of it? *(Circle one only)*

    Yes   1
    No   2

    In-flight airline magazines   1
    Posters or billboards   2
    TV at airport   3
    Newspapers   4
    Business publications   5
    Card located in the seatback pocket 6
    Flight attendant   7
    Other   8

(continued)

These next few questions are for classification purposes only.

16. What is your job classification? *(Circle one answer)*

Professional	1
Executive	2
Managerial	3
Administrative	4
Technical	5
Other	6

17. What is your age? *(Circle one answer)*

18–24	1
25–34	2
35–44	3
45–54	4
55–64	5
65 or over	6

18. What is your sex? *(Circle one answer)*

Male	1
Female	2

19. What is your annual individual income? *(Circle one answer)*

Under $20,000	1
$20,000–$39,999	2
$40,000–$59,999	3
$60,000–$79,999	4
$80,000–$99,999	5
$100,000–$149,999	6
$150,000+	7

20. What is your level of education? *(Circle one answer)*

Attended high school	1
High school graduate	2
Some college	3
College graduate	4
Postgraduate degree	5

21. Finally, what changes/improvements would you like to see in our service?

_____

_____

Thanks again for your assistance! Please return this completed survey in the enclosed preaddressed, postage-paid envelope.

CASE 11.3 McDONALD'S SPANISH-LANGUAGE QUESTIONNAIRE

The following questions about a visit to McDonald's, originally appeared in Spanish and were translated into English.

AQUI ➔ **SE EMPIEZA**

1. **En general, ¿qué tan satisfecho/a quedó con su visita a este McDonald's hoy?** .... 😕 NADA SATISFECHO/A ① ② ③ ④ MUY SATISFECHO/A 😊 ⑤

2. **Su visita fue.......** Adentro (**A**) o en el Drive-thru (**DT**)   Ⓐ Adentro   ⒹⓉ Drive-thru
3. **Su visita fue.......** Durante el Desayuno (**D**), Almuerzo (**A**), Cena (**C**)   Ⓓ Desayuno   Ⓐ Almuerzo   Ⓐ Cena
4. **Su visita fue.......** Entre semana (**E**) o Fin de semana (**F**)   Ⓔ Entre semana   Ⓕ Fin de semana

COMIDA

5. ¿Quedó satisfecho/a con la comida que recibio hoy?   Ⓢ Si   Ⓝ No
Si NO, ¿cuál fue el problema?   Sandwich / platillo frío ◁
Favor de rellenar el(los) círculo(s) apropiado(s).
Apariencia desagradable
Mal sabor de la comida
Pocas papas en la bolsa / caja
Papas / tortitas de papa frías
Papas no bien saladas
Bebida aguada / de mal sabor

Questions

1. What is the typical process for developing questionnaires for markets in which consumers speak a different language?

2. Find someone who speaks Spanish and have him or her back translate the questions that appear above. Are these Spanish-language questions adequate?

What you will learn in this chapter

- To define *sample, population, population element,* and *census.*

- To explain why a sample rather than a complete census may be taken.

- To discuss the issues concerning the identification of the target population and the selection of a sampling frame.

- To describe common forms of sampling frames and sampling frame error.

- To distinguish between random sampling and systematic (nonsampling) errors.

- To explain the various types of systematic (nonsampling) errors that result from sample selection.

- To discuss the advantages and disadvantages of the various types of probability and nonprobability samples.

- To understand how to choose an appropriate sample design.

We all know that making a good first impression is important, because after a sample exposure people make judgments about what type of people we are. Even a member of the Polar Bear swimming club tests the early March waters of Lake Michigan with a toe before diving in. Stand in a bookstore and observe the process of sampling. A customer generally picks up a book, looks at the cover, and then samples a few pages to get a feeling for the writing style and the content before deciding whether to buy. The high school student who visits a college classroom to listen to a professor's lecture is employing a sampling technique. Selecting a university on the basis of one classroom visit may not be scientific sampling, but in a personal situation it may be a practical sampling experience. These examples illustrate the intuitive nature of sampling in everyday uses when it is impossible, inconvenient, or too expensive to measure every item in a population.

Although sampling is commonplace in daily activities, most of these familiar samples are not scientific. The concept of sampling may seem simple and intuitive, but the actual process of sampling can be quite complex. Sampling is a central aspect of marketing research, and it requires in-depth examination.

This chapter explains the nature of sampling and how to determine the appropriate sample design. ∎

SAMPLING TERMINOLOGY

sample
A subset, or some part, of a larger population.

population (universe)
Any complete group of entities that share some common set of characteristics.

The process of sampling involves using a small number of items or parts of a population to make conclusions about the whole population. A **sample** is a subset, or some part, of a larger population. The purpose of sampling is to enable one to estimate some unknown characteristic of the population.

We have defined sampling in terms of the population to be studied. A **population,** or **universe,** is any complete group—for example, of people, sales territories, stores, or college students—that shares some common set of characteristics. **Population element** refers to an individual member of a population. A **census** is an investigation of all the individual elements that make up a population—that is, a total enumeration rather than a sample.

WHY SAMPLE?

population element
An individual member of a population.

census
An investigation of all the individual elements that make up a population.

At a wine-tasting party, all guests recognize the impossibility of doing anything but sampling. However, in a scientific study whose objective is to estimate an unknown population value, why should a sample rather than a complete census be taken?

A researcher who wants to investigate a population with an extremely small number of population elements may elect to conduct a census rather than a sample because the cost, labor, and time involved would be relatively insignificant. Thus, a company that wants to assess salespeople's satisfaction with its salesforce automation system may have no pragmatic reason not to circulate a questionnaire to all 25 of its employees. In most situations, however, there are many practical reasons to sample. Sampling cuts costs, reduces labor requirements, and gathers vital information quickly.[1]

Another major reason to sample is that most properly selected samples give sufficiently accurate results. If the elements of a population are quite similar, only a small sample is necessary to accurately portray the characteristic of interest. Most of us have had blood samples taken from the finger, the arm, or another part of the body. The assumption is that the blood is sufficiently similar throughout the body that its characteristics can be determined on the basis of a sample. When the population elements are largely homogeneous, samples are highly representative of the population. Under these circumstances, almost any sample is as good as another. Even when populations have considerable heterogeneity, large samples provide sufficiently precise data to make most decisions. Of course, samples are accurate only when researchers have taken care to draw representative samples properly. We will say more about this later in the chapter.

PRACTICAL SAMPLING CONCEPTS

Researchers must make several decisions before taking a sample. Exhibit 12.1 presents these decisions as a series of sequential stages, even though the order of the decisions does not always follow this sequence. These decisions are highly interrelated.

Defining the Target Population

Once a decision has been made to sample, the first question concerns identifying the target population. What is the relevant population? In many cases, this is not a difficult question. Registered voters may be clearly identifiable. Likewise, if

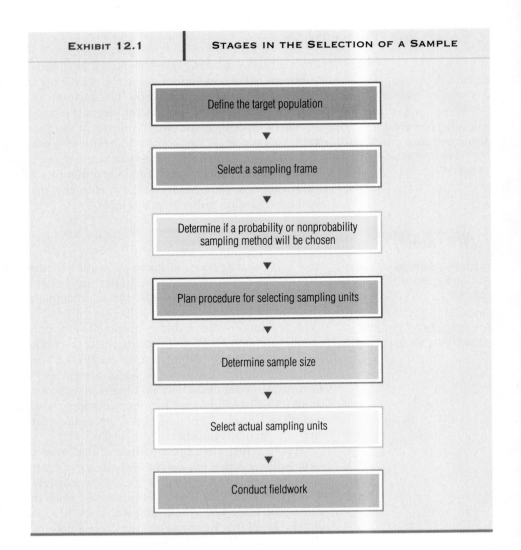

EXHIBIT 12.1 | STAGES IN THE SELECTION OF A SAMPLE

Define the target population

Select a sampling frame

Determine if a probability or nonprobability sampling method will be chosen

Plan procedure for selecting sampling units

Determine sample size

Select actual sampling units

Conduct fieldwork

a company's 106-person sales force is the population of concern, there are few definitional problems. In other cases, the decision may be difficult. One survey concerning organizational buyer behavior incorrectly defined the population as purchasing agents whom sales representatives regularly contacted. After the survey, investigators discovered that industrial engineers within the customer companies had substantially affected buying decisions, but they rarely talked with the salespeople. Frequently the appropriate population element is the household rather than an individual member of the household. This presents some problems if household lists are not available.

At the outset of the sampling process, it is vital to carefully define the target population in order to be able to identify the proper sources from which the data are to be collected. Answering questions about the crucial characteristics of the population is the usual technique for defining the target population. Does the term *comic book reader* include children under 6 years of age who do not actually read the words? Does *all persons west of the Mississippi* include people in east bank towns that border the river, such as East St. Louis, Illinois? Researchers must

HOW PRIVATE ARE MAILING LISTS?

The direct marketing and survey research industries require mailing lists to reach carefully targeted market segments.[2] Survey research companies generally purchase mailing lists that they can use for sampling purposes, or they hire a mailing list company to stuff envelopes and post surveys. Direct marketers may use credit reports, driver's license information, and voter registration records as well as other databases to compile these lists. For example, TRW Target Marketing Services, a company that originated as a service to approve individuals as creditworthy, sells mailing lists based on an individual's available credit or ownership of bank credit cards with nonzero balances.

Most credit agreements indicate that the consumer's name may be used for other purposes, and it has long been accepted practice to use credit information for purposes beyond establishing an individual's creditworthiness.

The Direct Marketing Association's Mail Preference Service allows consumers to write to have their names taken off mailing lists. However, many consumers are unaware of this service. This raises the ethical question of how to balance the right of privacy against marketing researchers' need to know.

answer the question "Whom do we want to talk to?" It may be users, nonusers, recent adopters, or brand switchers. To implement the sample in the field, tangible characteristics should be used to define the population. A baby food manufacturer might define the population of baby food purchasers as all women still capable of bearing children. However, a more specific *operational definition* would be women between ages 12 and 50. While this definition by age may exclude a few women who are capable of childbearing and include some who are not, it is still more explicit and provides a manageable basis for the sample design.

The Sampling Frame

sampling frame
A list of elements from which a sample may be drawn; also called *working population.*

In practice, a sample is drawn from a list of population elements that often differs somewhat from the defined target population. A **sampling frame** is a list of elements from which the sample may be drawn. A simple example of a sampling frame would be a list of all members of the American Medical Association. Generally it is not feasible to compile a list that does not exclude some members of the population. For example, if the student telephone directory is assumed to be a sampling frame of your university's student population, the sampling frame may exclude those students who registered late, those without phones, or those who have their telephones listed only under their roommates' or pets' names. The sampling frame is also called the *working population* because it provides the list for operational work. If a complete list of population elements is not available, materials such as maps or aerial photographs may be used as the sampling frame. The discrepancy between the definition of the population and the sampling frame is the first potential source of error associated with sample selection. We will discuss such errors later in the chapter.

Some firms, called *sampling services* or *list brokers,* specialize in providing lists or databases that include the names, addresses, phone numbers, and e-mail addresses of specific populations. Exhibit 12.2 shows a page from a mailing list company's offerings. Lists offered by companies such as this one are compiled from subscriptions to professional journals, credit card applications, warranty card registrations, and a variety of other sources. One sampling service obtained its listing of households with children from an ice cream retailer who gave away free ice cream cones on children's birthdays. (The children filled out cards with their names, addresses, and birthdays, which the retailer then sold to the mailing list company.)

A **sampling frame error** occurs when certain sample elements are excluded or when the entire population is not accurately represented in the sampling frame. One city's manager for community development, in preparation for an upcoming vote on a bond issue, used randomly generated telephone numbers as the basis for a sample survey to gauge attitudes toward capital improvements. When the bond issue failed, consultants pointed out that the appropriate sampling

sampling frame error
An error that occurs when certain sample elements are excluded from or overrepresented in a sampling frame.

EXHIBIT 12.2 | **MAILING LIST DIRECTORY PAGE**

Lists Available - *Alphabetical*

S.I.C. Code	List Title	United States Total Count	United States State Count Page	Canadian Count
	A			
5122-02	Abdominal Supports	201	‡	28
8399-03	Abortion Alternatives Organizations`	946	‡	•
8093-04	Abortion Information & Services	551	‡	•
5085-23	Abrasives	1811	‡	277
5169-04	Absorbents	145	‡	•
6541-03	Abstracters	4057	58	•
6411-06	Accident & Health Insurance	2113	‡	9
8748-52	Accident Reconstruction Service	125	‡	•
8721-01	Accountants	127392	64	6933
8721-02	Accounting & Bookkeeping General Svc	27996	64	2072
5044-08	Accounting & Bookkeeping Machines/Supls	889	‡	50
5044-01	Accounting & Bookkeeping Systems	624	‡	1230
8711-02	Acoustical Consultants	381	‡	91
1742-02	Acoustical Contractors	3063	47	433
1742-01	Acoustical Materials	878	‡	210
8999-10	Actuaries	1185	‡	•
8049-13	Acupuncture (Acupuncturists)	2921	62	493
5044-02	Adding & Calculating Machines/Supplies	5524	49	648
5044-09	Addressing Machines & Supplies	345	‡	29
5169-12	Adhesives & Glues	1187	‡	4
3579-02	Adhesives & Gluing Equipment	170	‡	204
6411-02	Adjusters	6164	57	8357
6411-01	Adjusters-Public	161	‡	•
8322-07	Adoption Agencies	1621	‡	32
8059-03	Adult Care Facilities	596	‡	•
8361-08	Adult Congregate Living Facilities	170	‡	•
7319-03	Advertising-Aerial	337	‡	26
7311-01	Advertising-Agencies & Counselors	27753	59	2552
7336-05	Advertising-Art Layout & Production Svc	457	‡	101
7331-05	Advertising-Direct Mail	6347	59	540
7311-03	Advertising-Directory & Guide	2465	‡	124
7319-01	Advertising-Displays	3441	59	571
7319-11	Advertising-Indoor	209	‡	63
7311-05	Advertising-Motion Picture	143	‡	11
7311-06	Advertising-Newspaper	4274	59	404
7312-01	Advertising-Outdoor	3052	59	297
7311-08	Advertising-Periodical	817	‡	78

S.I.C. Code	List Title	United States Total Count	United States State Count Page	Canadian Count
7313-03	Advertising-Radio	2866	59	247
7311-07	Advertising-Shoppers' Guides	392	‡	4
5199-17	Advertising-Specialties	12827	52	1648
7389-12	Advertising-Telephone	120	‡	•
7313-05	Advertising-Television	1746	‡	102
7319-02	Advertising-Transit & Transportation	179	‡	38
0721-03	Aerial Applicators (Service)	1479	‡	61
3999-01	Aerosols	158	‡	•
3812-01	Aerospace Industries	426	‡	•
	Affluent Americans		73	
5191-04	Agricultural Chemicals	549	‡	210
8748-20	Agricultural Consultants	1047	‡	474
9999-32	Air Balancing	353	‡	•
5084-64	Air Brushes	219	‡	•
4512-02	Air Cargo Service	6005	48	•
5075-01	Air Cleaning & Purifying Equipment	2055	‡	342
5084-02	Air Compressors	4358	50	717
	(See Compressors Air & Gas)			
1711-17	Air Conditioning Contractors & Systems	50951	47	2667
	Available By Brands Sold			
	Airtemp (A)	187		
	Amana (B)	1450		
	Arco Aire (2)	673		
	Armstrong/Magic Chef (C)	395		
	Arvin (4)	106		
	Bryant (D)	2223		
	Carrier (E)	5927		
	Coleman (5)	1176		
	Comfortmaker/Singer (O)	989		
	Day & Night (Z)	749		
	Fedders (H)	318		
	Heli/Quaker (3)	1977		
	Janitrol (7)	587		
	Kero-Sun (W)	2		
	Lennox (K)	4390		
	Luxaire (L)	510		
	Payne (M)	553		

In countries with less well-developed economies, such as Sri Lanka, fewer than 5 percent of households may have telephones. Telephone directories cannot serve as sampling frames in such countries.

frame would have been a list of registered voters, not adults with phones (since many might not have voted in this type of election). By including respondents who should not have been listed as members of the population, the city manager committed a sampling frame error.

Sampling Frames for International Marketing Research

The availability of sampling frames around the globe varies dramatically. Not every country's government conducts a census of population, and in some countries telephone directories are incomplete, no voter registration lists exist, and accurate maps of urban areas are unobtainable.[3] However, in Taiwan, Japan, and other Asian countries, a researcher can build a sampling frame relatively easily because those governments release some census information about individuals. If a family changes households, updated census information must be reported to a centralized government agency before communal services (water, gas, electricity, education, etc.) are made available.[4] This information is then easily accessible in the local *Inhabitants' Register*.

Sampling Units

During the actual sampling process, the elements of the population must be selected according to a certain procedure. The **sampling unit** is a single element or group of elements selected for a sample. For example, if an airline wishes to sample passengers, it may take every 25th name on a complete list of passengers. In this case, the sampling unit would be the same as the population element. Alternatively, the airline could first select certain flights as the sampling unit, then select certain passengers on each flight. In this instance, the sampling unit would contain many elements.

If the target population has first been divided into units, such as airline flights, additional terminology must be used. The term **primary sampling unit (PSU)** designates a unit selected in the first stage of sampling. Units selected in successive stages of sampling (if necessary) are called **secondary sampling units, tertiary sampling units,** and so on. When there is no list of population elements, the sampling unit

sampling unit
A single element or group of elements selected for a sample.

primary sampling unit (PSU)
A unit selected in the first stage of sampling.

secondary sampling unit
A unit selected in the second stage of sampling.

tertiary sampling unit
A unit selected in the third stage of sampling.

generally is something other than the population element. In a random digit dialing study, for example, the sampling unit will be telephone numbers.

RANDOM SAMPLING ERROR AND NONSAMPLING ERROR

random sampling error
The difference between the sample result and the result of a census conducted using identical procedures; a statistical fluctuation due to chance variations in the elements selected for a sample.

An estimation from a sample may not be exactly the same as a census count because of random sampling errors or systematic (nonsampling) errors. **Random sampling error** is the difference between the sample result and the result of a census conducted using identical procedures. Of course, the result of a census is unknown unless one is taken, which is rarely done. Random sampling error results from chance variation in the scientific selection of sampling units. The sampling units, even if properly selected according to sampling theory, may not perfectly represent the population, but generally they are reliable estimates. Our discussion of the process of randomization (a procedure designed to give everyone in the population an equal chance of being selected as a sample member) will show that because random sampling errors follow chance variations, they tend to cancel one another out when averaged. This means that properly selected samples generally are good approximations of the population. There is almost always a slight difference between the true population value and the sample value—hence, a small random sampling error. Every once in a while an unusual sample is selected because too many atypical people were included in the sample and a large random sampling error occurred. The theories behind the concept of sample reliability and other basic statistical concepts are reviewed in detail in Chapter 13. At this point, simply recognize that *random sampling error* is a technical term that refers only to statistical fluctuations due to chance variations in the elements selected for the sample.

Random sampling error is a function of sample size. As sample size increases, random sampling error decreases. Of course, the resources available will influence how large a sample may be taken. It is possible to estimate the random sampling error that may be expected with various sample sizes. Suppose a survey of approximately 1,000 people has been taken in Portland to determine the feasibility of a new soccer franchise. Assume 30 percent of the respondents favor the idea of a new professional sport in town. The researcher will know, based on the laws of probability, that 95 percent of the time a survey of slightly fewer than 900 people will produce results with an error of approximately plus or minus 3 percent. If the survey were conducted with only 325 people, the margin of error would increase to approximately plus or minus 5 percentage points. This example illustrates random sampling errors.

systematic (nonsampling) error
Error resulting from factors not due to chance fluctuations, such as the nature of a study's design and imperfections in execution.

Systematic (nonsampling) errors that lead to unrepresentative samples result primarily from the nature of a study's design and imperfections in execution. Such errors are *not* due to chance fluctuations. For example, highly educated respondents are more likely to cooperate with mail surveys than poorly educated ones, for whom filling out forms is a more difficult and intimidating task.[5] Systematic errors or biases such as these account for a large portion of errors in marketing research.

Less Than Perfectly Representative Samples

Random sampling errors and systematic errors associated with the sampling process may combine to yield a sample that is less than perfectly representative of the population. Exhibit 12.3 illustrates two nonsampling errors (sampling frame error and nonresponse error) related to sample design. The total population is represented by the area of the largest rectangle. Sampling frame errors

EXHIBIT 12.3 | ERRORS ASSOCIATED WITH SAMPLING[6]

nonresponse error
The statistical differences between a survey that includes only those who responded and a perfect survey that would also include those who failed to respond.

eliminate some potential respondents. Random sampling error (due exclusively to random, chance fluctuation) may cause an imbalance in the representativeness of the group. Additional errors will occur if individuals refuse to be interviewed or cannot be contacted. Such **nonresponse error** also may cause the sample to be less than perfectly representative. Thus, the actual sample is drawn from a population different from (or smaller than) the ideal.

PROBABILITY VERSUS NONPROBABILITY SAMPLING

There are several ways to take a sample. The main alternative sampling plans may be grouped into two categories: probability techniques and nonprobability techniques.

probability sampling
A sampling technique in which every member of the population has a known, nonzero probability of selection.

In **probability sampling**, every element in the population has a *known, nonzero probability* of selection. The simple random sample, in which each member of the population has an equal probability of being selected, is the best-known probability sample.

nonprobability sampling
A sampling technique in which units of the sample are selected on the basis of personal judgment or convenience; the probability of any particular member of the population being chosen is unknown.

In **nonprobability sampling**, the probability of any particular member of the population being chosen is unknown. The selection of sampling units in nonprobability sampling is quite arbitrary, as researchers rely heavily on personal judgment. *There are no appropriate statistical techniques for measuring random sampling error from a nonprobability sample. Thus, projecting the data beyond the sample is statistically inappropriate.* Nevertheless, on certain occasions, nonprobability samples are best suited for the researcher's purpose.

We will now explore the various types of nonprobability and probability sampling. Although probability sampling is preferred, we will discuss nonprobability sampling first to illustrate some potential sources of error and other weaknesses in sampling.

Every basketball player and fan knows that players have hot and cold streaks.[7] Players who have hot hands can't seem to miss, while those who have cold ones can't find the center of the hoop. When psychologists interviewed team members of the Philadelphia 76ers, the players estimated they were about 25 percent more likely to make a shot after they had just made one than after a miss. Nine in ten basketball fans surveyed concurred that a player "has a better chance of making a shot after having just made his last two or three shots than he does after having just missed his last two or three shots." Believing in shooting streaks, players will feed a teammate who has just made two or three shots in a row, and many coaches will bench the player who misses three in a row. When you're hot you're hot.

The only trouble is, it isn't true. When the psychologists studied detailed individual shooting records, they found that the 76ers—and the Boston Celtics, the New Jersey Nets, the New York Knicks, and Cornell University's men's and women's basketball players—were equally likely to score after a miss as after a basket. Fifty percent shooters average 50 percent after just missing three shots, and 50 percent after just making three shots.

Why, then, do players and fans alike believe that players are more likely to score after scoring and to miss after missing? In any series of 20 shots by a 50 percent shooter (or 20 flips of a coin), there is a 50-50 chance of four baskets (or heads) in a row, and it is quite possible that one person out of five will have a streak of five or six. Players and fans notice these random streaks and so form the myth that when you're hot you're hot.

The same type of thing happens with investors who believe that a fund is more likely to perform well after a string of good years than after a string of bad years. Past performances of mutual funds do not predict their future performances. When funds have streaks of several good or bad years, we may nevertheless be fooled into thinking that past success predicts future success.

The moral: Whether watching basketball, choosing stocks, flipping coins, or drawing a sample, remember the statistical principle that random sequences often don't look random. Even when the next outcome cannot be predicted from the preceding ones, streaks are to be expected.

NONPROBABILITY SAMPLING

Convenience Sampling

convenience sampling
The sampling procedure of obtaining those people or units that are most conveniently available.

Convenience sampling (also called *haphazard* or *accidental sampling*) refers to sampling by obtaining the people or units that are most conveniently available. It may be convenient and economical to set up an interviewing booth from which to intercept consumers at a shopping center. Just before elections, television stations often present person-on-the-street interviews that are presumed to reflect public opinion. (Of course, the television station generally warns that the survey was "unscientific and random" [*sic*].) The college professor who uses his or her students has a captive sample—convenient, but perhaps unwilling and unrepresentative.

Researchers generally use convenience samples to obtain a large number of completed questionnaires quickly and economically. For example, many Internet

TO THE POINT

A straw vote only shows which way the hot air blows.

O. HENRY

surveys are conducted with volunteer respondents who, either intentionally or by happenstance, visit an organization's Web site. Although a large number of responses can be obtained quickly at a low cost, selecting all visitors to a Web site is clearly convenience sampling. Respondents may not be representative because of the haphazard manner by which many of them arrived at the Web site or because of self-selection bias. The user of research based on a convenience sample should remember that projecting the results beyond the specific sample is inappropriate. Convenience samples are best used for exploratory research when additional research will subsequently be conducted with a probability sample.

Judgment Sampling

judgment (purposive) sampling A nonprobability sampling technique in which an experienced researcher selects a sample based on personal judgment about some appropriate characteristic of the sample members.

Judgment, or **purposive, sampling** is a nonprobability sampling technique in which an experienced individual selects the sample based on his or her judgment about some appropriate characteristics required of the sample member. Researchers select samples that satisfy their specific purposes, even if they are not fully representative. The consumer price index (CPI) is based on a judgment sample of market basket items, housing costs, and other selected goods and services that are expected to reflect a representative sample of items consumed by most Americans. Test market cities often are selected because they are viewed as typical cities whose demographic profiles closely match the national profile. A fashion manufacturer regularly selects a sample of key accounts that it believes are capable of providing the information needed to predict what will sell in the fall; the judgment sample is selected to achieve a specific objective.

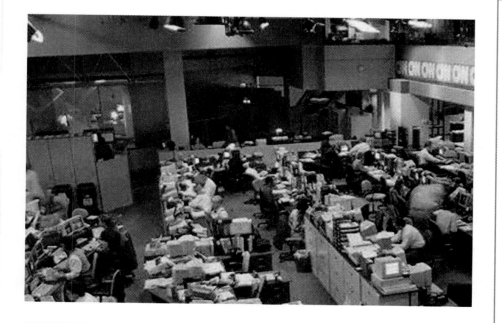

Judgment sampling often is used in attempts to forecast election results. People frequently wonder how a television network can predict the results of an election with only 2 percent of the votes reported. Political and sampling experts judge which small voting districts approximate overall state returns from previous election years; then these bellwether precincts are selected as the sampling units. Of course, the assumption is that the past voting records of these districts are still representative of the state's political behavior.

Quota Sampling

Suppose a firm wishes to investigate consumers who currently own digital versatile disk (DVD) players. The researchers may wish to ensure that each brand of DVD player/recorder is included proportionately in the sample. Strict probability sampling procedures would likely underrepresent certain brands and overrepresent others. If the selection process were left strictly to chance, some variation would be expected. The purpose of **quota sampling** is to ensure that the various subgroups in a population are represented on pertinent sample characteristics to the exact extent the investigators desire. Stratified sampling, a probability sampling procedure, also has this objective, but it should not be confused with quota sampling. In quota sampling, the interviewer has a quota to achieve. For example, an interviewer in a particular city may be assigned 100 interviews, 35 with owners of Sony DVD players, 30 with owners of Panasonic DVD players, 18 with owners of Toshiba DVD players, and the rest with owners of other brands. The interviewer is responsible for finding enough people to meet the quota. Aggregating the various interview quotas yields a sample that represents the desired proportion of each subgroup.

quota sampling
A nonprobability sampling procedure that ensures that various subgroups of a population will be represented on pertinent characteristics to the exact extent the investigator desires.

Possible Sources of Bias The logic of classifying the population by pertinent subgroups is essentially sound. However, because respondents are selected according to a convenience sampling procedure rather than on a probability basis, as in stratified sampling, the haphazard selection of subjects may introduce bias. For example, a college professor hired some of his students to conduct a quota sample based on age. When analyzing the data, the professor discovered that almost all the people in the "under 25 years" category were college educated. Interviewers, being human, tend to prefer to interview people who are similar to themselves. Quota samples tend to include people who are easily found, willing to be interviewed, and middle class. Fieldworkers are given considerable leeway to exercise their judgment concerning selection of actual respondents. Interviewers often concentrate their interviewing in areas with heavy pedestrian traffic such as downtowns, shopping malls, and college campuses. Those who interview door-to-door learn quickly that quota requirements are difficult to meet by interviewing whoever happens to appear at the door; this approach tends to overrepresent less active people who are likely to stay at home. One interviewer related a story about working in an upper-middle-class neighborhood. After a few blocks, it changed into a neighborhood of mansions. Believing that most of the potential respondents were "above his station," the interviewer skipped those houses because he felt uncomfortable knocking on doors that would be answered by servants.

Advantages of Quota Sampling Speed of data collection, lower costs, and convenience are the major advantages of quota sampling over probability sampling. Although quota sampling has many problems, carefully supervised data collection may provide a representative sample of the various subgroups within a population. Quota sampling may be appropriate when the researcher knows a certain demographic group is more likely to refuse to cooperate with a survey. For instance, if older men are more likely to refuse, a higher quota can be set for this group so that the proportion of each demographic category will be similar to the proportions in the population. A number of laboratory experiments also rely on quota sampling because it is difficult to find a sample of the general population willing to visit a laboratory to participate in an experiment.

Snowball Sampling

Snowball sampling refers to a variety of procedures in which initial respondents are selected by probability methods and additional respondents are obtained from information provided by the initial respondents.[8] This technique is used to locate members of rare populations by referrals. Suppose a manufacturer of sports equipment is considering marketing a mahogany croquet set for serious adult players. This market is certainly small. An extremely large sample would be necessary to find 100 serious adult croquet players. It would be much more economical to survey, say, 300 people, find 15 croquet players, and ask them for the names of other players. Reduced sample sizes and costs are clearcut advantages of snowball sampling. However, bias is likely to enter into the study because a person suggested by another member of the sample has a higher probability of being similar to the first person. If there are major differences between those who are widely known by others and those who are not, this technique may present some serious problems. However, snowball sampling may be used to locate and recruit heavy users, such as consumers who buy more than 50 compact disks per year, for focus groups. Since the focus group is not expected to be a generalizable sample, snowball sampling may be very appropriate.

PROBABILITY SAMPLING

All probability sampling techniques are based on chance selection procedures. Because the probability sampling process is random, the bias inherent in nonprobability sampling procedures is eliminated. Note that *random* refers to the procedure for selecting the sample; it does not describe the data in the sample. *Randomness* characterizes a procedure whose outcome cannot be predicted because it depends on chance. Randomness should not be thought of as unplanned or unscientific; it is the basis of all probability sampling techniques. In this section, we examine the various probability sampling methods.

Simple Random Sampling

Simple random sampling ensures that each element in a population will have an equal chance of being included in a sample. Drawing names from a hat and selecting the winning raffle ticket from a large drum are typical examples of simple random sampling. If the names or raffle tickets are thoroughly stirred, each name or ticket should have an equal chance of being selected. In contrast to other, more complex types of probability sampling, this process is simple because it requires only one stage of sample selection.

Although drawing names or numbers out of a fishbowl, using a spinner, rolling dice, or turning a roulette wheel may be an appropriate way to draw a sample from a small population, when populations consist of large numbers of elements, tables of random numbers (see Table A.1 in the Appendix) or computer-generated random numbers are used for sample selection.

Selecting a Simple Random Sample Suppose a researcher is interested in selecting a simple random sample of all the Honda dealers in California, New Mexico, Arizona, and Nevada. Each dealer's name is assigned a number from 1 to 105; then each number is written on a separate piece of paper, and all the slips are placed in a large drum. After the slips of paper have been thoroughly mixed, one is selected for each sampling unit. Thus, if the sample size is 35, the selection procedure must be repeated 34 times after the first slip has been selected. Mixing the slips after each selection will ensure that those at the bottom of the drum will continue to have an equal chance of being selected in the sample.

To use a table of random numbers, a serial number is first assigned to each element of the population. Assuming the population is 99,999 or less, five-digit numbers may be selected from the table of random numbers merely by reading the numbers in any column or row, moving up, down, left, or right. A random starting point should be selected at the outset. For convenience, we will assume we have randomly selected the first five digits in columns 1 through 5, row 1, of Table A.1 in the Appendix as our starting point. The first number in our sample would be 37751; moving down, the next numbers would be 50915, 99142, and so on.

The random digit dialing technique of sample selection requires that the researcher identify the exchange or exchanges of interest (the first three numbers) and then use a table of numbers to select the next four numbers.

Systematic Sampling

Suppose a researcher wants to take a sample of 1,000 from a list of 200,000 names. With **systematic sampling**, every 200th name from the list would be drawn.

The procedure is extremely simple. A starting point is selected by a random process; then every nth number on the list is selected. To take a sample of consumers from a rural telephone directory that does not separate business from residential listings, every 23rd name might be selected as the sampling interval. In the process, it is possible that Mike's Restaurant would be selected. This unit is inappropriate because it is a business listing rather than a consumer listing, so the next eligible name would be selected as the sampling unit and the systematic process would continue.

While systematic sampling is not actually a random selection procedure, it does yield random results if the arrangement of the items in the list is random in character. The problem of **periodicity** occurs if a list has a systematic pattern—that is, if it is not random in character. Collecting retail sales information every seventh day would result in a distorted sample because there would be a systematic pattern of selecting sampling units—sales for only one day of the week (perhaps Monday) would be sampled. If the first 50 names on a list of contributors to a charity were extremely large donors, periodicity might occur in sampling every 200th name. Periodicity is rarely a problem for most sampling in marketing research, but researchers should be aware of the possibility.

Stratified Sampling

The usefulness of dividing the population into subgroups, or strata, whose members are more or less equal with respect to some characteristic was illustrated in our discussion of quota sampling. The first step is the same for both stratified and quota sampling: choosing strata on the basis of existing information—for example, classifying retail outlets based on annual sales volume. However, the process of selecting sampling units within the strata differs substantially. In **stratified sampling** a subsample is drawn using simple random sampling within each stratum. This is not true of quota sampling.

The reason for taking a stratified sample is to obtain a more efficient sample than would be possible with simple random sampling. Suppose, for example, that urban and rural groups have widely different attitudes toward energy conservation, but members within each group hold very similar attitudes. Random sam-

systematic sampling
A sampling procedure in which a starting point is selected by a random process and then every nth item on a list is selected.

periodicity
A problem that occurs in systematic sampling when the original list has a systematic pattern.

stratified sampling
A probability sampling procedure in which simple random subsamples that are more or less equal on some characteristic are drawn from within each stratum of the population.

pling error will be reduced with the use of stratified sampling, because each group is internally homogeneous but there are comparative differences between groups. More technically, a smaller standard error may result from this stratified sampling because the groups will be adequately represented when strata are combined.

Another reason for selecting a stratified sample is to ensure that the sample will accurately reflect the population on the basis of the criterion or criteria used for stratification. This is a concern because occasionally simple random sampling yields a disproportionate number of one group or another and the sample ends up being less representative than it could be.

A researcher can select a stratified sample as follows. First, a variable (sometimes several variables) is identified as an efficient basis for stratification. A stratification variable must be a characteristic of the population elements known to be related to the dependent variable or other variables of interest. The variable chosen should increase homogeneity within each stratum and increase heterogeneity between strata. The stratification variable usually is a categorical variable or one easily converted into categories (that is, subgroups). For example, a pharmaceutical company interested in measuring how often physicians prescribe a certain drug might choose physicians' training as a basis for stratification. In this example the mutually exclusive strata are M.D.s (medical doctors) and O.D.s (osteopathic doctors).

Next, for each separate subgroup or stratum, a list of population elements must be obtained. (If such lists are not available, they can be costly to prepare, and if a complete listing is not available, a true stratified probability sample cannot be selected.) Using a table of random numbers or some other device, a *separate* simple random sample is then taken within each stratum. Of course, the researcher must determine how large a sample to draw for each stratum.

Cluster Sampling

cluster sampling
An economically efficient sampling technique in which the primary sampling unit is not the individual element in the population but a large cluster of elements; clusters are selected randomly.

The purpose of **cluster sampling** is to sample economically while retaining the characteristics of a probability sample. Consider the researcher who must conduct 500 interviews with consumers scattered throughout the United States. Travel costs are likely to be enormous because the amount of time spent traveling will be substantially greater than the time spent in the interviewing process. If an aspirin marketer can assume the product will work as well in Phoenix as it does in Baltimore or if a frozen pizza manufacturer assumes its product will taste the same in Texas as it does in Oregon, cluster sampling may be used.

In a cluster sample, the primary sampling unit is no longer the individual element in the population (for example, grocery stores) but a larger cluster of elements located in proximity to one another (for example, cities). The *area sample* is the most popular type of cluster sample. A grocery store researcher, for example, may randomly choose several geographic areas as primary sampling units and then interview all or a sample of grocery stores within the geographic clusters. Interviews are confined to these clusters only. No interviews occur in other clusters. Cluster sampling is classified as a probability sampling technique because of either the random selection of clusters or the random selection of elements within each cluster.

Cluster samples frequently are used when lists of the sample population are not available. For example, when researchers investigating employees and self-employed workers for a downtown revitalization project found that a comprehensive list of these people was not available, they decided to take a cluster sample, selecting organizations (business and government) as the clusters. A sample of firms within

EXHIBIT 12.4 | EXAMPLES OF CLUSTERS

Population Element	Possible Clusters in the United States
U.S. adult population	States
	Counties
	Metropolitan Statistical Areas
	Census Tracts
	Blocks
	Households
College seniors	Colleges
Manufacturing firms	Counties
	Metropolitan Statistical Areas
	Localities
	Plants
Airline travelers	Airports
	Planes
Sports fans	Football Stadiums
	Basketball Arenas
	Baseball Parks

the central business district was developed, using stratified probability sampling to identify clusters. Next, individual workers within the firms (clusters) were randomly selected and interviewed concerning the central business district. Some examples of clusters appear in Exhibit 12.4.

Ideally a cluster should be as heterogeneous as the population itself—a mirror image of the population. A problem may arise with cluster sampling if the characteristics and attitudes of the elements within the cluster are too similar. For example, geographic neighborhoods tend to have residents of the same socioeconomic status. Students at a university tend to share similar beliefs. This problem may be mitigated by constructing clusters composed of diverse elements and by selecting a large number of sampled clusters.

Multistage Area Sampling

multistage area sampling
Sampling that involves using a combination of two or more probability sampling techniques.

So far we have described two-stage cluster sampling. **Multistage area sampling** involves two or more steps that combine some of the probability techniques already described. Typically geographic areas are randomly selected in progressively smaller (lower-population) units. For example, a political pollster investigating an election in Arizona might first choose counties within the state to ensure that the different areas are represented in the sample. In the second step, precincts within the selected counties may be chosen. As a final step, the pollster may select blocks (or households) within the precincts, then interview all the blocks (or households) within the geographic area. Researchers may take as many steps as necessary to achieve a representative sample. Exhibit 12.5 graphically portrays a multistage area sampling process frequently used by a major academic

EXHIBIT 12.5 | AN ILLUSTRATION OF MULTISTAGE AREA SAMPLING[9]

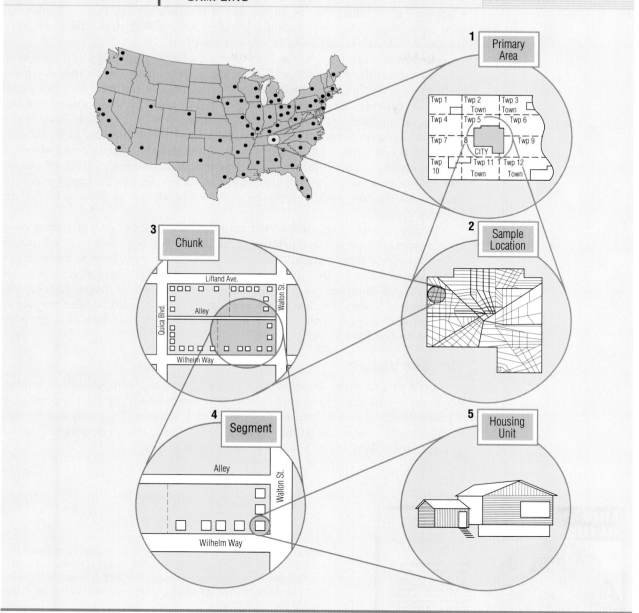

research center. Progressively smaller geographic areas are chosen until a single housing unit is selected for interviewing.

The Bureau of the Census provides maps, population information, demographic characteristics for population statistics, and so on, by several small geographical areas; these may be useful in sampling. Census classifications of small geographic areas vary, depending on the extent of urbanization within Metropolitan Statistical Areas (MSAs) or counties.

Chapter 7 mentioned the rise in the use of Internet surveys that seek information from respondents interacting with software on Web sites. There are some unique problems associated with Internet sampling.

Internet surveys allow researchers to reach a large sample rapidly. This is both an advantage and a disadvantage. Sample size requirements can be met overnight or in some cases almost instantaneously. It is possible, for instance, for a researcher to release a survey during the morning in the Eastern Standard Time zone and have all sample size requirements met before anyone on the West Coast wakes up. If rapid response rates are expected, the sample for an Internet survey should be metered out across all time zones. In addition, people in some populations are more likely to go online during the weekend than on a weekday. If the researcher can anticipate a day-of-the-week effect, the survey should be kept open long enough so that all sample units have the opportunity to participate in the research project.

A major disadvantage of Internet surveys is the lack of computer ownership and Internet access among certain segments of the population. A sample of Internet users is representative only of Internet users, who tend to be younger, better educated, and more affluent than the general U.S. population. This is not to say that all Internet samples are unrepresentative of all target populations. Nevertheless, when using Internet surveys, researchers should be keenly aware of potential sampling problems that can arise because some members of target populations do not have Internet access.

Web Site Visitors

As noted earlier, many Internet surveys are conducted with volunteer respondents who visit an organization's Web site intentionally or by happenstance. These *unrestricted samples* are clearly convenience samples. They may not be representative because of the haphazard manner by which many respondents arrived at a particular Web site or because of self-selection bias.

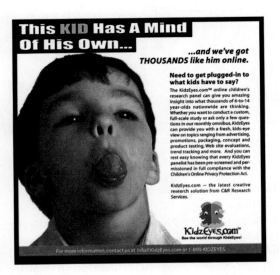

KidzEyes panelists have been prescreened and have given their permission to be surveyed online, in full compliance with the Children's Online Privacy Protection Act. It is very important that members of Internet samples opt in to receive e-mail about survey participation.

A better technique for sampling Web site visitors is to randomly select sampling units. SurveySite, a company that specializes in conducting Internet surveys, collects data by using its "pop-up survey" software. The software selects Web visitors at random and "pops up" a small Javascript window asking the person if he or she wants to participate in an evaluation survey. If the person clicks "Yes," a new window containing the online survey opens up. The person can then browse the site at his or her own pace and switch to the survey at any time to express an opinion.[10]

Randomly selecting Web site visitors can cause a problem. It is possible to overrepresent frequent visitors to a site and thus represent site visits rather than visitors. There are several programming techniques and technologies (using cookies, registration data, or prescreening) that can help accomplish more representative sampling based on site traffic.[11] Details of these techniques are beyond the scope of this discussion.

This type of random sampling is most valuable if the target population is defined as visitors to a particular Web site. Evaluation and analysis of visitors' perceptions and experiences of the Web site would be a typical survey objective with this type of sample. Researchers who have broader interests may obtain Internet samples in a variety of other ways.

Panel Samples

Drawing a probability sample from an established consumer panel or other pre-recruited membership panel is a popular, scientific, and effective method for creating a sample of Internet users. Typically, sampling from a panel yields a high response rate because panel members have already agreed to cooperate with the research organization's e-mail or Internet surveys. Often panel members are compensated for their time with a sweepstake, a small cash incentive, or redeemable points. Further, because the panel has already supplied demographic characteristics and other information from previous questionnaires, researchers are able to select panelists based on product ownership, lifestyle, or other characteristics. A variety of sampling methods and data transformation techniques can be applied to assure that sample results are representative of the general public or a targeted population.

Consider Harris Interactive Inc. The company is an Internet survey research organization that maintains a panel of more than 6.5 million individuals in the United States. In the early 21st century, Harris plans to expand this panel to between 10 million and 15 million and to include an additional 10 million people internationally.[12] A database this large allows the company to draw simple random samples, stratified samples, and quota samples from its panel members.

Harris Interactive finds that two demographic groups are not fully accessible via Internet sampling: people age 65 and older (a group that is rapidly growing) and those with annual incomes of less than $15,000. In contrast, 18- to 25-year-olds—a group that historically has been very hard to reach by traditional research methods—are now extremely easy to reach over the Internet.[13]

To ensure that survey results are representative, Harris Interactive uses a *propensity-weighting* scheme. The research company does parallel studies—by phone as well as over the Internet—to test the accuracy of its Internet data-gathering capabilities. Researchers look at the results of the telephone surveys and match those against the Internet-only survey results. Next, they use propensity weighting to adjust the results, taking into account the motivational and behavioral differences between the online and offline populations. (How propensity

Knowledge Networks (http://www.knowledgenetworks. com) was founded in 1998 by two Stanford University political science professors trying to find a way to conduct Internet surveys with samples that mirrored the U.S. population.[14] They knew the problem was that many households did not own computers or have Internet access. So they decided that the only way to get true representative samples for Internet surveys and political polls was to equip people with interactive TV devices and Internet service. In the summer of 1999, they sent out 40,000 letters, most of them containing $10 bills. The money was the teaser for the big offer: spend 10 minutes each week answering questions over the Internet, and Knowledge Networks would give the household a free Web TV, free Internet access,

and a raft of prizes doled out in various contests and raffles. If individuals were uneasy with new technology, the researchers promised not only to give them the TV and the Internet access but also to send an engineer to install the appliances. An astonishing 56 percent of the people they contacted took the offer.

Today, Knowledge Networks is the only Internet survey research company that can reach people whether or not they own computers or have ever used the Internet. By providing a consistent and convenient environment, Knowledge Networks gets consumers to share their opinions in regular multimedia surveys and provide information about the media and their own purchasing behavior.

weighting adjusts for the difference between the Internet population and the general population is beyond the scope of this discussion.)

Recruited Ad Hoc Samples

Another means of obtaining an Internet sample is to obtain or create a sampling frame of e-mail addresses on an *ad hoc* basis. Researchers may create the sampling frame offline or online. Databases containing e-mail addresses can be compiled from many sources, including customer/client lists, advertising banners on pop-up windows that recruit survey participants, online sweepstakes, and registration forms that must be filled out in order to gain access to a particular Web site. Researchers may contact respondents by "snail mail" or by telephone to ask for their e-mail addresses and obtain permission for an Internet survey. Using offline techniques, such as random digit dialing and short telephone screening interviews, to recruit respondents can be a very practical way to get a representative sample for an Internet survey. For companies anticipating future Internet research, including e-mail addresses in their customer relationship databases (by inviting customers to provide that information on product registration cards, in telephone interactions, through on-site registration, etc.) can provide a valuable database for sample recruitment.[15]

Opt-in Lists

Survey Sampling Incorporated is a company that specializes in providing sampling frames and scientifically drawn samples. The company offers more than 3,500 lists of high-quality, targeted e-mail addresses of individuals who have

opt in
To give permission to receive selected e-mail, such as questionnaires, from a company with an Internet presence.

given permission to receive e-mail messages related to a particular topic of interest. Survey Sampling Incorporated's database contains over 7 million names of Internet users who have **opted in** for limited participation. An important feature of Survey Sampling Incorporated's database is that the company has each individual confirm and reconfirm interest in communicating about a topic before the person's e-mail address is added to the company's database.[16]

By whatever technique the sampling frame is compiled, it is important not to send unauthorized e-mail to respondents. If individuals do not opt in to receive e-mail from a particular organization, they may consider unsolicited survey requests to be spam. A researcher cannot expect high response rates from individuals who have not agreed to be surveyed. Spamming is not tolerated by experienced Internet users, and it can easily backfire, creating a host of problems—the most extreme being complaints to the Internet service provider (ISP), which may shut down the survey site.

WHAT IS THE APPROPRIATE SAMPLE DESIGN?

Degree of Accuracy

Selecting a representative sample is important to all researchers. However, the degree of accuracy required or the researcher's tolerance for sampling and nonsampling error may vary from project to project, especially when cost savings or another benefit may be a trade-off for a reduction in accuracy.

For example, when the sample is being selected for an exploratory research project, a high priority may not be placed on accuracy because a highly representative sample may not be necessary. For other, more conclusive projects, the sample result must precisely represent a population's characteristics, and the researcher must be willing to spend the time and money needed to achieve accuracy.

Resources

The cost associated with the different sampling techniques varies tremendously. If the researcher's financial and human resources are restricted, certain options will have to be eliminated. For a graduate student working on a master's thesis, conducting a national survey is almost always out of the question because of limited resources. Managers concerned with the cost of the research versus the value of the information often will opt to save money by using a nonprobability sampling design rather than make the decision to conduct no research at all.

Time

A researcher who needs to meet a deadline or complete a project quickly will be more likely to select a simple, less time-consuming sample design. A telephone survey that uses a sample based on random digit dialing takes considerably less time than a survey that uses an elaborate disproportional stratified sample.

Advance Knowledge of the Population

Advance knowledge of population characteristics, such as the availability of lists of population members, is an important criterion. In many cases, however, no list of population elements will be available to the researcher. This is especially true when the population element is defined by ownership of a particular product or brand, by experience in performing a specific job task, or on a qualitative dimension. A lack of adequate lists may automatically rule out systematic sampling, stratified sampling, or other sampling designs, or it may dictate that a preliminary study, such as a short telephone survey using random digit dialing, be conducted to generate information to build a sampling frame for the primary study. In many developing countries and in smaller U.S. towns, reverse directories are the exception rather than the rule; thus, researchers planning sample designs will have to work around this limitation.

National versus Local Project

Geographic proximity of population elements will influence sample design. When population elements are unequally distributed geographically, a cluster sample may become much more attractive.

Need for Statistical Analysis

The need for statistical projections based on the sample often is a criterion. Nonprobability sampling techniques do not allow researchers to use statistical analysis to project data beyond their samples.

SUMMARY

Sampling is a procedure that uses a small number of units of a given population as a basis for drawing conclusions about the whole population. Sampling often is necessary because it would be practically impossible to conduct a census to measure characteristics of all units of a population.

The first problem in sampling is to define the target population. Incorrect or vague definition of this population is likely to produce misleading results. A sampling frame is a list of elements, or individual members, of the overall population from which the sample is drawn. A sampling unit is a single element or group of elements subject to selection in the sample.

There are two sources of discrepancy between the sample results and the population parameters. One, random sampling error, arises from chance variations of the sample from the population. Random sampling error is a function of sample size and may be estimated using the central-limit theorem, discussed in Chapter 13. Systematic, or nonsampling, error comes from sources such as sampling frame error, mistakes in recording responses, or nonresponses from persons who are not contacted or who refuse to participate.

The two major classes of sampling methods are probability and nonprobability techniques. Nonprobability techniques include convenience sampling, judgment sampling, quota sampling, and snowball sampling. They are convenient to use, but there are no statistical techniques with which to measure their random sampling error. Probability samples are based on chance selection procedures. These include simple random sampling, systematic sampling, stratified sampling, and cluster sampling. With these techniques, random sampling error can be accurately predicted.

A researcher who must determine the most appropriate sampling design for a specific project will identify a number of sampling criteria and evaluate the relative importance of each criterion before selecting a design. The most common criteria concern accuracy requirements, available resources, time constraints, knowledge availability, and analytical requirements.

Internet sampling presents some unique issues. Researchers must be aware that samples may be unrepresentative because not everyone has a computer or access to the Internet. Convenience samples drawn from Web site visitors can create problems. Drawing a probability sample from an established consumer panel or an ad hoc sampling frame whose members opt in can be effective.

Key Terms and Concepts

sample
population (universe)
population element
census
sampling frame
sampling frame error
sampling unit
primary sampling unit (PSU)
secondary sampling unit

tertiary sampling unit
random sampling error
systematic (nonsampling) error
nonresponse error
probability sampling
nonprobability sampling
convenience sampling
judgment (purposive) sampling
quota sampling

snowball sampling
simple random sampling
systematic sampling
periodicity
stratified sampling
cluster sampling
multistage area sampling
opt in

Questions for Review and Critical Thinking

1. If you decide whether you want to see a new movie or television program on the basis of the "coming attractions" or television commercial previews, are you using a sampling technique? A scientific sampling technique?
2. Name some possible sampling frames for the following:
   a. Electrical contractors
   b. Tennis players
   c. Dog owners
   d. Foreign-car owners
   e. Wig and hair goods retailers
   f. Minority-owned businesses
   g. Men over 6 feet tall
3. Describe the difference between a probability sample and a nonprobability sample.
4. In what types of situations is conducting a census more appropriate than sampling? When is sampling more appropriate than taking a census?
5. Comment on the following sampling designs:
   a. A citizen's group interested in generating public and financial support for a new university basketball arena prints a questionnaire in area newspapers. Readers return the questionnaires by mail.
   b. A department store that wishes to examine whether it is losing or gaining customers draws a sample from its list of credit card holders by selecting every 10th name.
   c. A motorcycle manufacturer decides to research consumer characteristics by sending 100 questionnaires to each of its dealers. The dealers will then use their sales records to track down buyers of this brand of motorcycle and distribute the questionnaires.
   d. An advertising executive suggests that advertising effectiveness be tested in the real world. A one-page ad is placed in a magazine. One-half of the space is used for the ad itself. On the

other half, a short questionnaire requests that readers comment on the ad. An incentive will be given for the first 1,000 responses.
   e. A research company obtains a sample for a focus group through organizations such as church groups, clubs, and schools. The organizations are paid for securing respondents; no individual is directly compensated.
   f. A researcher suggests replacing a consumer diary panel with a sample of customers who regularly shop at a supermarket that uses optical scanning equipment. The burden of recording purchases by humans will be replaced by computerized longitudinal data.
   g. A banner ad on a business-oriented Web site reads, "Are you a large company Sr. Executive? Qualified execs receive $50 for under 10 minutes of time. Take the survey now!" Is this an appropriate way to select a sample of business executives?
6. When would a researcher use a judgment, or purposive, sample?
7. A telephone interviewer asks, "I would like to ask you about race. Are you Native American, Hispanic, African American, Asian, or white?" After the respondent replies, the interviewer says, "We have conducted a large number of surveys with people of your background, and we do not need to question you further. Thank you for your cooperation." What type of sampling was used?
8. If researchers know that consumers in various geographic regions respond quite differently to a product category, such as tomato sauce, is area sampling appropriate? Why or why not?
9. What are the benefits of stratified sampling?
10. What geographic units within a metropolitan area are useful for sampling?
11. Marketers often are particularly interested in the subset of a market that contributes most to sales (for

example, heavy beer drinkers or large-volume retailers). What type of sampling might be best to use with such a subset? Why?

12. Outline the step-by-step procedure you would use to select the following:
   a. A simple random sample of 150 students at your university
   b. A quota sample of 50 light users and 50 heavy users of beer in a shopping mall intercept study
   c. A stratified sample of 50 mechanical engineers, 40 electrical engineers, and 40 civil engineers from the subscriber list of an engineering journal

13. Selection for jury duty is supposed to be a totally random process. Comment on the following computer selection procedures, and determine if they are indeed random:

   a. A program instructs the computer to scan the list of names and pick names that were next to those from the last scan.
   b. Three-digit numbers are randomly generated to select jurors from a list of licensed drivers. If the weight information listed on the license matches the random number, the person is selected.
   c. The juror source list is obtained by merging a list of registered voters with a list of licensed drivers.

 14. To ensure a good session, a company selects focus group members from a list of articulate participants instead of conducting random sampling. The client did not inquire about sample selection when it accepted the proposal. Is this ethical?

Exploring the Internet

1. Visit http://www.prb.org/ to find a Glossary of Population Terms compiled by the Population Reference Bureau.

2. Go to http://www.reversephonedirectory.com and put in your phone number. How accurate is this database?

3. Go to the U.S. Census Bureau's home page at http://www.census.gov, click on M in Subjects A to Z, and then click on Metropolitan Areas. This will take you to http://www.census.gov/population/www/estimates/metroarea.html, where you can learn about metropolitan statistical areas (MSAs) and view a complete list of MSAs.

4. Use Google to search for ski resorts. At what URL can you find a sampling frame of U.S. ski resorts?

5. Go to http://www.dartmouth.edu/~chance/ to visit the Chance course. The Chance course is an innovative program to creatively teach introductory materials about probability and statistics. The Chance course is designed to enhance quantitative literacy. Numerous videos can be played online. "Statistical Issues in Census 2000," "To Sample or Not to Sample? Why Is That the Question for Census 2000?" and "Polls" are among numerous lectures that you should find interesting.

CASE 12.1 ACTION FEDERAL SAVINGS AND LOAN CORPORATION

Steve Miles made a big move 6 months ago. He quit his job as director of retail marketing at the largest bank in the state to become marketing manager for Action Federal Savings and Loan. It had been only $3\frac{1}{2}$ years since he received his bachelor's degree in marketing at the largest university in the state, but he was bright, personable, and ambitious. Now, after several months of orientation at Action Federal (Steve called it "Mickey Mouse"), he was beginning his own marketing operations, hiring Roberta Nimoy from City University as his marketing research assistant.

Steve wanted to do an image study of each of the 13 branches of Action Federal located throughout the state. The main branch and three others were located in tall office buildings in the capital city and nearby suburbs. The other branches were located in rural areas, and their architecture was designed to fit into the surroundings. One was located in a restored colonial home.

Another, the Old Mill branch, located next to a park with a historic windmill, was designed to be compatible with the nearby river and mill.

Steve asked Roberta to develop the sampling plan for the study. After some investigation, she learned that all the accounts were listed alphabetically in the main branch's computer. She thought that a list of names and addresses could be generated by taking a sample of 1,300. The computer would be programmed to randomly select every nth name. Since the savings and loan had approximately 112,000 customers, every 86th name would be selected.

Questions
1. Evaluate Action Federal's sampling plan.
2. What alternative sampling plans might be used?

CASE 12.2 THE INTERNAL REVENUE SERVICE

The Internal Revenue Service wishes to conduct a survey on income tax cheating. The survey has several objectives:

1. To identify the extent to which taxpayers cheat on their returns, their reasons for doing so, and approaches the IRS can take to deter this kind of behavior
2. To determine taxpayers' experience of and satisfaction with various IRS services
3. To determine what services taxpayers need
4. To develop an accurate profile of taxpayers' behavior as they prepare their income tax returns
5. To assess taxpayers' knowledge and opinions about various tax laws and procedures

The federal government always wishes to be extremely accurate in its survey research. A survey of approximately 5,000 individuals located throughout the country will provide the database for this study. The sample will be selected on a probability basis from all households in the continental United States.

Eligible respondents will be adults over age 18. Within each household, an effort will be made to interview the individual who is most familiar with completing federal tax forms. When there is more than one taxpayer in the household, a random process will be used to select the member to be interviewed.

Question
Suppose you are a consultant hired to design the sample for a personal, in-home interview. Design a sample for the Internal Revenue Service survey.

DETERMINATION OF SAMPLE SIZE:
A Review of Statistical Theory

What you will learn in this chapter

- To explain the difference between descriptive and inferential statistics.

- To discuss the purpose of inferential statistics by explaining the difference between population parameters and sample statistics.

- To make data usable by organizing and summarizing them into frequency distributions, proportions, and measurements of central tendency.

- To identify and calculate the various measures of dispersion.

- To explain why the standard deviation is an important measure of dispersion.

- To identify the characteristics of the normal distribution and the standardized normal curve.

- To compute the standardized value, Z.

- To distinguish among population, sample, and sampling distributions and to identify the mean and standard deviation of each distribution.

- To explain the central-limit theorem.

- To compute confidence interval estimates.

- To understand the three factors required for specifying sample size.

- To estimate the sample size for a simple random sample when the characteristic of interest is a mean and when it is a proportion.

- To understand which nonstatistical considerations influence the determination of sample size.

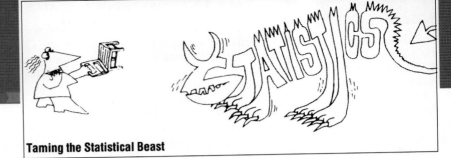

Taming the Statistical Beast

The determination of the appropriate sample size is a crucial element of marketing research. To formally identify the proper sample size, statistical theory is necessary. Unfortunately, statistics has a bad image among students.

The fear of statistics is one of college students' most universal phobias. "Stat is too difficult—I'll never pass" is a lament often heard on campus. Students postpone their statistics classes until their last semester. Statistics students are frequently subject to mental blocks; they feel like Saint George trying to tame the raging statistical dragon, as the cartoon here illustrates. There is no need, however, for students to have this dread. Statistics can be easily mastered if one learns the tricks of the trade.

Why are there so many myths about statistics? Statisticians, much like lawyers, medical doctors, and computer scientists, have developed their own jargon. Laypeople do not understand professionals' technical terms. Cynics suspect this terminology is a ploy to impress others and, possibly, to justify charging higher fees. How many fishermen have you heard say, "Hand me the reticulated lattice joined at the interstices," when they simply want a *net?*[1] Then again, when compared with professionals who use complex terminology, fishermen do not make much money.

The point is simple: If you do not understand the basics of the language, you will have problems in conversation. Statistics is the language of the marketing researcher. If administrators and marketing researchers do not speak the same language, communication will fail.

This chapter explains how to determine sample size and reviews some of the basic terminology of statistical analysis. ■

The first six sections of this chapter summarize key statistical concepts necessary for understanding the theory that underlies the derivation of sample size. These sections are intended for students who need to review the basic aspects of statistics theory. Even those students who received good grades in their elementary statistics classes probably will benefit from a quick review of the basic statistical concepts. Some students will prefer to just skim this material and proceed to page 335, where the discussion of the actual determination of sample size begins. Others need to study these sections carefully to acquire an understanding of statistics.

Descriptive and Inferential Statistics

The *Statistical Abstract of the United States* presents table after table of figures associated with numbers of births, number of employees in each county of the United States, and other data that the average person calls "statistics." These are *descriptive statistics.* Another type of statistics, *inferential statistics,* is used to make inferences about a whole population from a sample. For example, when a firm test markets a new product in Sacramento and Birmingham, it wishes to make an inference from these sample markets to predict what will happen throughout the United States. Thus, there are two applications of statistics: (1) to describe characteristics of the population or sample and (2) to generalize from the sample to the population.

Sample Statistics and Population Parameters

sample statistics
Variables in a sample or measures computed from sample data.

population parameters
Variables in a population or measured characteristics of the population.

The primary purpose of inferential statistics is to make a judgment about the population, or the collection of all elements about which one seeks information. The sample is a subset or relatively small fraction of the total number of elements in the population. It is useful to distinguish between the data computed in the sample and the data or variables in the population. The term **sample statistics** designates variables in the sample or measures computed from the sample data. The term **population parameters** designates variables or measured characteristics of the population. Sample statistics are used to make inferences about population parameters.[2] In our notation we will generally use Greek lowercase letters—for example, μ or σ—to denote population parameters and English letters, such as $\overline{X}$ or S, to denote sample statistics.

Frequency Distributions

frequency distribution
A set of data organized by summarizing the number of times a particular value of a variable occurs.

percentage distribution
A frequency distribution organized into a table (or graph) that summarizes percentage values associated with particular values of a variable.

Suppose a telephone survey has been conducted for a savings and loan association. The data have been recorded on a large number of questionnaires. To make the data usable, this information must be organized and summarized. Constructing a *frequency table,* or **frequency distribution,** is one of the most common means of summarizing a set of data. The process begins with recording the number of times a particular value of a variable occurs. This is the frequency of that value. In our survey example Table 13.1 represents a frequency distribution of respondents' answers to a question that asked how much customers had deposited in the savings and loan.

Constructing a distribution of relative frequency, or a **percentage distribution,** is also quite simple. In Table 13.2 the frequency of each value in Table 13.1 has

TABLE 13.1	FREQUENCY DISTRIBUTION OF DEPOSITS

Amount	Frequency (Number of People Who Hold Deposits in Each Range)
Under $3,000	499
$3,000–$4,999	530
$5,000–$9,999	562
$10,000–$14,999	718
$15,000 or more	811
	3,120

TABLE 13.2	PERCENTAGE DISTRIBUTION OF DEPOSITS

Amount	Percent (Percentage of People Who Hold Deposits in Each Range)
Under $3,000	16
$3,000–$4,999	17
$5,000–$9,999	18
$10,000–$14,999	23
$15,000 or more	26
	100

been divided by the total number of observations and the result multiplied by 100, to give a frequency distribution of percentages.

Probability is the long-run relative frequency with which an event will occur. Inferential statistics uses the concept of a probability distribution, which is conceptually the same as a percentage distribution except that the data are converted into probabilities (see Table 13.3).

probability
The long-run relative frequency with which an event will occur.

TABLE 13.3	PROBABILITY DISTRIBUTION OF DEPOSITS

Amount	Probability
Under $3,000	.16
$3,000–$4,999	.17
$5,000–$9,999	.18
$10,000–$14,999	.23
$15,000 or more	.26
	1.00

Proportions

proportion
The percentage of elements that meet some criterion.

When a frequency distribution portrays only a single characteristic in terms of a percentage of the total, it defines the **proportion** of occurrence. A proportion, such as the proportion of tenured professors at a university, indicates the percentage of population elements that successfully meet some standard concerning the particular characteristic. A proportion may be expressed as a percentage, a fraction, or a decimal value.

Measures of Central Tendency

On a typical day, a sales manager counts the number of sales calls each sales representative makes. He or she wishes to inspect the data to find the center, or middle area, of the frequency distribution. Central tendency can be measured in three ways—the mean, median, or mode—each of which has a different meaning.

mean
A measure of central tendency; the arithmetic average.

The Mean   We all have been exposed to the average known as the **mean**. The mean is simply the arithmetic average, and it is a common measure of central tendency.

At this point it is appropriate to introduce the summation symbol, the capital Greek letter *sigma* (Σ). A typical use might look like this:

$$\sum_{i=1}^{n} X_i$$

which is a shorthand way to write the sum

$$X_1 + X_2 + X_3 + X_4 + X_5 + \cdots + X_n$$

Below the Σ is the initial value of an index, usually i, j, or k, and above it is the final value, in this case n, the number of observations. The shorthand expression says to replace i in the formula with the values from 1 to 8 and total the observations obtained. Without changing the basic formula, the initial and final index values may be replaced by other values to indicate different starting and stopping points.

Suppose a sales manager supervises the eight salespeople listed in Table 13.4. To express the sum of the salespeople's calls in Σ notation, we just number the salespeople (this number becomes the index number) and associate subscripted variables with their numbers of calls.

TABLE 13.4	NUMBER OF SALES CALLS PER DAY BY SALESPEOPLE

Salesperson	Number of Sales Calls
Mike	4
Patty	3
Billie	2
Bob	5
John	3
Frank	3
Chuck	1
Samantha	5
Total	26

Index		Salesperson	Variable		Number of Calls
1	=	Mike	X_1	=	4
2	=	Patty	X_2	=	3
3	=	Billie	X_3	=	2
4	=	Bob	X_4	=	5
5	=	John	X_5	=	3
6	=	Frank	X_6	=	3
7	=	Chuck	X_7	=	1
8	=	Samantha	X_8	=	5

We then write an appropriate Σ formula and evaluate it:

$$\sum_{i=1}^{8} X_i = X_1 + X_2 + X_3 + X_4 + X_5 + X_6 + X_7 + X_8$$
$$= 4 + 3 + 2 + 5 + 3 + 3 + 1 + 5$$
$$= 26$$

The formula for the arithmetic mean is

$$\text{Mean} = \frac{\sum_{i=1}^{n} X}{n} = \frac{26}{8} = 3.25$$

The sum $\sum_{i=1}^{n} X$ tells us to add all the Xs whose subscripts are between 1 and n inclusive, where n equals the number of observations. The formula shows that the mean number of sales calls in this example is 3.25.

Researchers generally wish to know the population mean, μ (lowercase Greek letter *mu*), which is calculated as follows:

$$\mu = \frac{\sum_{i=1}^{n} X}{N}$$

where

N = number of all observations in the population

Often we will not have enough data to calculate the population mean, μ, so we will calculate a sample mean, $\overline{X}$ (read "X bar"), with the following formula:

$$\overline{X} = \frac{\sum_{i=1}^{n} X}{n}$$

where

n = number of observations made in the sample

More likely than not, you already know how to calculate a mean. However, knowing how to distinguish among the symbols Σ, μ, and $\overline{X}$ is necessary to understand statistics.

In this introductory discussion of the summation sign (Σ), we have used very detailed notation that included the subscript for the initial index value (i) and the final index value (n). However, from this point on, references to Σ will not include the subscript for the initial index value (i) and the final index value (n) unless there is a unique reason to highlight these index values.

median
A measure of central tendency that is the midpoint; the value below which half the values in a distribution fall.

The Median The next measure of central tendency, the **median,** is the midpoint of the distribution, or the 50th percentile. In other words, the median is the value below which half the values in the sample fall. In the sales manager example, 3 is the median because half the observations are greater than 3 and half are less than 3.

mode
A measure of central tendency; the value that occurs most often.

The Mode In apparel *mode* refers to the most popular fashion. In statistics the **mode** is the measure of central tendency that identifies the value that occurs most often. In our example Patty, John, and Frank each made three sales calls. The value 3 occurs most often, and thus 3 is the mode. The mode is determined by listing each possible value and noting the number of times each value occurs.

Measures of Dispersion

The mean, median, and mode summarize the central tendency of frequency distributions. Knowing the tendency of observations to depart from the central tendency is also important. Calculating the dispersion of the data, or how the observations vary from the mean, is another way to summarize the data. Consider, for instance, the 12-month sales patterns of the two products shown in Table 13.5. Both have a mean monthly sales volume of 200 units, but the dispersion of observations for product B is much greater than that for product A. There are several measures of dispersion.

The Range The range is the simplest measure of dispersion. It is the distance between the smallest and the largest values of a frequency distribution. Thus, for product A the range is between 196 units and 202 units (6 units), whereas for product B the range is between 150 units and 261 units (111 units).

TABLE 13.5	SALES LEVELS FOR PRODUCTS A AND B (BOTH AVERAGE 200 UNITS)	
	Units Product A	Units Product B
January	196	150
February	198	160
March	199	176
April	200	181
May	200	192
June	200	200
July	200	201
August	201	202
September	201	213
October	201	224
November	202	240
December	202	261

THE WELL-CHOSEN AVERAGE

When you read an announcement by a corporation executive or a business proprietor that the average pay of the people who work in his or her establishment is so much, the figure may mean something and it may not.[3] If the average is a median, you can learn something significant from it: Half the employees make more than that; half make less. But if it is a mean (and believe me, it may be that if its nature is unspecified), you may be getting nothing more revealing than the average of one $450,000 income—the proprietor's—and the salaries of a crew of underpaid workers. "Average annual pay of $57,000" may conceal both the $20,000 salaries

and the owner's profits taken in the form of a whopping salary.

Let's take a longer look at that one. This table shows how many people get how much. The boss might like to express the situation as "average wage $57,000," using that deceptive mean. The mode, however, is more revealing: The most common rate of pay in this business is $20,000 a year. As usual, the median tells more about the situation than any other single figure does; half the people get more than $30,000 and half get less.

Number of People	Title	Salary
1	Proprietor	$450,000
1	President	150,000
2	Vice presidents	100,000
1	Controller	57,000 ← Mean (arithmetic average)
3	Directors	50,000
4	Managers	37,000
1	Supervisor	30,000 ← Median (the one in the middle; 12 above, 12 below)
12	Workers	20,000 ← Mode (occurs most frequently)

The range does not take into account all the observations; it merely tells us about the extreme values of the distribution.

Just as people may be fat or skinny, distributions may be fat or skinny. For example, for product A the observations are close together and reasonably close to the mean. While we do not expect all observations to be exactly like the mean, in a skinny distribution they will lie a short distance from the mean, while in a fat distribution they will be spread out. Exhibit 13.1 illustrates this concept graphically with two frequency distributions that have identical modes, medians, and means but different degrees of dispersion.

The interquartile range is the range that encompasses the middle 50 percent of the observations—in other words, the range between the bottom quartile (lowest 25 percent) and the top quartile (highest 25 percent).

Deviation Scores   A method of calculating how far any observation is from the mean is to calculate individual deviation scores. To calculate a deviation from the mean, use the following formula:

$$d_i = X_i - \bar{X}$$

EXHIBIT 13.1 | LOW DISPERSION VERSUS HIGH DISPERSION

For the value of 150 units for product B for the month of January, the deviation score is -50; that is, $150 - 200 = -50$. If the deviation scores are large, we will have a fat distribution because the distribution exhibits a broad spread.

Why Use the Standard Deviation?

Statisticians have derived several quantitative indexes to reflect a distribution's spread, or variability. The *standard deviation* is perhaps the most valuable index of spread, or dispersion. Students often have difficulty understanding it. Learning about the standard deviation will be easier if we first look at several other measures of dispersion that may be used. Each of these has certain limitations that the standard deviation does not.

First is the average deviation. We compute the average deviation by calculating the deviation score of each observation value (that is, its difference from the mean), summing these scores, and then dividing by the sample size (n):

$$\text{Average deviation} = \frac{\Sigma(X_i - \bar{X})}{n}$$

While this measure of spread seems interesting, it is never used. The positive deviation scores are always canceled out by the negative scores, leaving an average deviation value of zero. Hence, the average deviation is useless as a measure of spread.

One might correct for the disadvantage of the average deviation by computing the absolute values of the deviations. In other words, we ignore all the positive and negative signs and use only the absolute value of each deviation. The formula for the mean absolute deviation is

$$\text{Mean absolute deviation} = \frac{\Sigma|X_i - \bar{X}|}{n}$$

While this procedure eliminates the problem of always having a zero score for the deviation measure, there are some technical mathematical problems that make it less valuable than some other measures; it is mathematically intractable.

Variance Another means of eliminating the sign problem caused by the negative deviations canceling out the positive deviations is to square the deviation scores. The following formula gives the mean squared deviation:

$$\text{Mean squared deviation} = \frac{\Sigma(X_i - \bar{X})^2}{n}$$

This measure is useful for describing the sample variability. However, we typically wish to make an inference about a population from a sample, and so the divisor $n - 1$ is used rather than n in most pragmatic marketing research problems.[4] This new measure of spread, called the **variance,** has the formula

variance
A measure of variability or dispersion. Its square root is the standard deviation.

$$\text{Variance, } S^2 = \frac{\Sigma(X_i - \bar{X})^2}{n - 1}$$

The variance is a very good index of the degree of dispersion. The variance, S^2, will equal zero if and only if each and every observation in the distribution is the same as the mean. The variance will grow larger as the observations tend to differ increasingly from one another and from the mean.

Standard Deviation   While the variance is frequently used in statistics, it has one major drawback. The variance reflects a unit of measurement that has been squared. For instance, if measures of sales in a territory are made in dollars, the mean number will be reflected in dollars, but the variance will be in squared dollars. Because of this, statisticians often take the square root of the variance. Using the square root of the variance for a distribution, called the **standard deviation,** eliminates the drawback of having the measure of dispersion in squared units rather than in the original measurement units. The formula for the standard deviation is[5]

standard deviation
A quantitative index of a distribution's spread, or variability; the square root of the variance for a distribution.

$$S = \sqrt{S^2} = \sqrt{\frac{\Sigma(X_i - \bar{X})^2}{n - 1}}$$

Table 13.6 illustrates that the calculation of a standard deviation requires the researcher to first calculate the sample mean. In the example with eight salespeople's sales calls (Table 13.4), we calculated the sample mean as 3.25. Table 13.6 illustrates how to calculate the standard deviation for these data.

At this point we can return to thinking about the original purpose for measures of dispersion. We want to summarize the data from survey research and other forms of marketing research. Indexes of central tendency, such as the mean, help us interpret the data. In addition we wish to calculate a measure of variability that will give us a quantitative index of the dispersion of the distribution. We have looked at several measures of dispersion to arrive at two very adequate means of measuring dispersion: the variance and the standard deviation. The formula given is for the sample standard deviation, S.

The formula for the population standard deviation, σ, which is conceptually very similar, has not been given. Nevertheless, you should understand that σ measures the dispersion in the population and S measures the dispersion in the sample. These concepts are crucial to understanding statistics. Remember, the student must learn the language of statistics to use it in a research project. If you do not understand the language at this point, review this material now.

normal distribution
A symmetrical, bell-shaped distribution that describes the expected probability distribution of many chance occurrences.

THE NORMAL DISTRIBUTION

One of the most useful probability distributions in statistics is the **normal distribution,** also called the *normal curve.* This mathematical and theoretical distribution describes the expected distribution of sample means and many other chance

TABLE 13.6		**CALCULATING A STANDARD DEVIATION:** **NUMBER OF SALES CALLS PER DAY BY** **SALESPERSONS**	

X	$(X - \bar{X})$	$(X - \bar{X})^2$
4	$(4 - 3.25) = \quad .75$	.5625
3	$(3 - 3.25) = \quad -.25$	.0625
2	$(2 - 3.25) = -1.25$	1.5625
5	$(5 - 3.25) = \quad 1.75$	3.0625
3	$(3 - 3.25) = \quad -.25$	.0625
3	$(3 - 3.25) = \quad -.25$	.0625
1	$(1 - 3.25) = -2.25$	5.0625
5	$(5 - 3.25) = \quad 1.75$	3.0625
Σ^a	a	13.5000

$$n = 8 \qquad \bar{X} = 3.25$$

$$S = \sqrt{\frac{\Sigma(X - \bar{X})^2}{n - 1}} = \sqrt{\frac{13.5}{8 - 1}} = \sqrt{\frac{13.5}{7}} = \sqrt{1.9286} = 1.3887$$

[a]The summation of this column is not used in the calculation of the standard deviation.

occurrences. The normal curve is bell shaped, and almost all (99 percent) of its values are within ± 3 standard deviations from its mean. An example of a normal curve, the distribution of IQ scores, appears in Exhibit 13.2. In this example, 1 standard deviation for IQ equals 15. We can identify the proportion of the curve by measuring a score's distance (in this case, standard deviation) from the mean (100).

standardized normal distribution
A purely theoretical probability distribution that reflects a specific normal curve for the standardized value, Z.

The **standardized normal distribution** is a specific normal curve that has several characteristics: (1) It is symmetrical about its mean; (2) the mean identifies the normal curve's highest point (the mode) and the vertical line about which this normal curve is symmetrical; (3) the normal curve has an infinite number of

EXHIBIT 13.2		**THE NORMAL DISTRIBUTION:** **AN EXAMPLE OF THE DISTRIBUTION OF** **INTELLIGENCE QUOTIENT (IQ) SCORES**

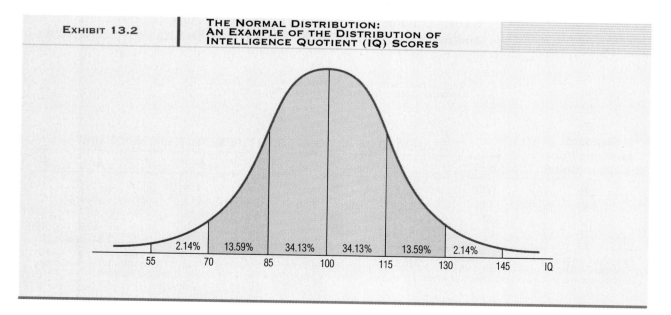

EXHIBIT 13.3 | THE STANDARDIZED NORMAL DISTRIBUTION

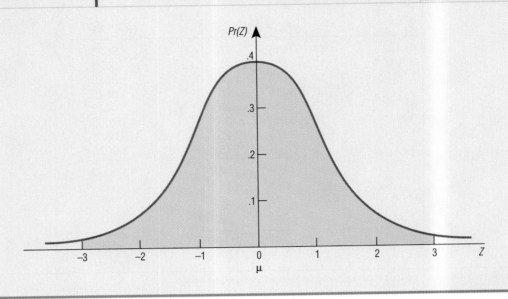

cases (it is a continuous distribution), and the area under the curve has a probability density equal to 1.0; (4) the standardized normal distribution has a mean of 0 and a standard deviation of 1. Exhibit 13.3 illustrates these properties. Table 13.7 is a summary version of the typical standardized normal table found at the end of most statistics textbooks. A more complex table of areas under the standardized normal distribution appears in Table 2 in the Appendix.

The standardized normal distribution is a purely theoretical probability distribution, but it is the most useful distribution in inferential statistics. Statisticians have spent a great deal of time and effort making it convenient for researchers to find the probability of any portion of the area under the standardized normal distribution. All we have to do is transform, or convert, the data from other observed normal distributions to the standardized normal curve. In other words, the standardized normal distribution is extremely valuable because we can translate, or

| TABLE 13.7 | THE STANDARDIZED NORMAL TABLE: AREA UNDER ONE-HALF OF THE NORMAL CURVE[a] |

Z Standard Deviations from the Mean (Units)	Z STANDARD DEVIATIONS FROM THE MEAN (TENTHS OF UNITS)									
	.0	.1	.2	.3	.4	.5	.6	.7	.8	.9
0.0	.000	.040	.080	.118	.155	.192	.226	.258	.288	.315
1.0	.341	.364	.385	.403	.419	.433	.445	.455	.464	.471
2.0	.477	.482	.486	.489	.492	.494	.495	.496	.497	.498
3.0	.499	.499	.499	.499	.499	.499	.499	.499	.499	.499

[a] Area under the segment of the normal curve extending (in one direction) from the mean to the point indicated by each row-column combination. For example, the table shows that about 68 percent of normally distributed events can be expected to fall within 1.0 standard deviation on either side of the mean (.341 times 2). An interval of almost 2.0 standard deviations around the mean will include 95 percent of all cases.

EXHIBIT 13.4

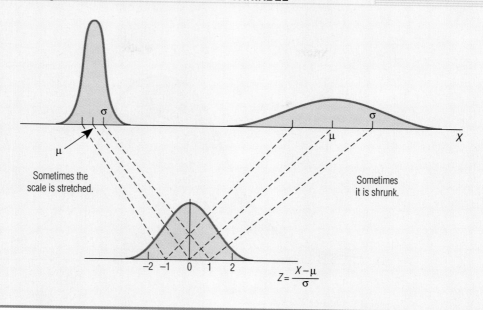

Sometimes the scale is stretched.

Sometimes it is shrunk.

$$Z = \frac{X - \mu}{\sigma}$$

transform, any normal variable, X, into the standardized value, Z. Exhibit 13.4 illustrates how to convert either a skinny distribution or a fat distribution into the standardized normal distribution. This ability to transform normal variables has many pragmatic implications for the marketing researcher. The standardized normal table in the back of most statistics and marketing research books allows us to evaluate the probability of the occurrence of many events without any difficulty.

Computing the standardized value, Z, of any measurement expressed in original units is simple: Subtract the mean from the value to be transformed and divide by the standard deviation (all expressed in original units). The formula for this procedure and its verbal statement follow. In the formula note that σ, the population standard deviation, is used for calculation.[7]

$$\text{Standardized value} = \frac{\text{Value to be transformed} - \text{Mean}}{\text{Standard deviation}}$$

$$Z = \frac{X - \mu}{\sigma}$$

where

μ = hypothesized or expected value of the mean

Suppose that in the past a toy manufacturer has experienced mean sales, μ, of 9,000 units and a standard deviation, σ, of 500 units during September. The production manager wishes to know whether wholesalers will demand between 7,500 and 9,625 units during September of the upcoming year. Because no tables in the back of the textbook show the distribution for a mean of 9,000 and a standard deviation of 500, we must transform our distribution of toy sales, X, into the standardized form using our simple formula. The following computation shows that the probability (Pr) of obtaining sales in this range is equal to .893:

EXHIBIT 13.5 | STANDARDIZED DISTRIBUTION CURVE

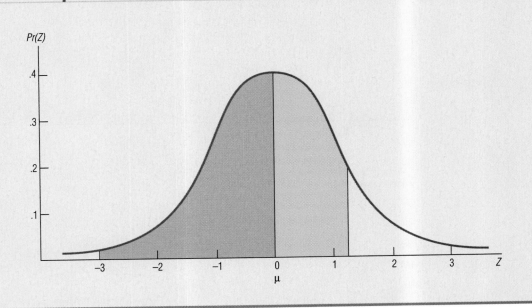

$$Z = \frac{X - \mu}{\sigma} = \frac{7,500 - 9,000}{500} = -3.00$$

$$Z = \frac{X - \mu}{\sigma} = \frac{9,625 - 9,000}{500} = 1.25$$

Using Table 13.7 (or Table 2 in the Appendix), we find that

When $Z = -3.00$, the area under the curve (probability) equals .499.

When $Z = 1.25$, the area under the curve (probability) equals .394.

Thus, the total area under the curve is .499 + .394 = .893. (The area under the curve corresponding to this computation is the shaded area in Exhibit 13.5.) The sales manager, therefore, knows there is a .893 probability that sales will be between 7,500 and 9,625.

At this point, it is appropriate to repeat that to understand statistics one must understand the language that statisticians use. Each concept discussed thus far is relatively simple, but a clear-cut command of this terminology is essential for understanding what we will discuss later on.

Now that we have covered certain basic terminology, we will outline the technique of statistical inference. However, before we do so, three additional types of distributions must be defined: population distribution, sample distribution, and sampling distribution.

POPULATION DISTRIBUTION, SAMPLE DISTRIBUTION, AND SAMPLING DISTRIBUTION

When conducting a research project or survey, the researcher's purpose is not to describe the sample of respondents, but to make an inference about the population. As defined previously, a population, or universe, is the total set, or collection, of potential units for observation. The sample is a smaller subset of this population.

A frequency distribution of the population elements is called a **population distribution**. The mean and standard deviation of the population distribution are represented by the Greek letters μ and σ. A frequency distribution of a sample is called a **sample distribution**. The sample mean is designated $\overline{X}$, and the sample standard deviation is designated S.

The concepts of population distribution and sample distribution are relatively simple. However, we must now introduce another distribution: the *sampling distribution of the sample mean*.

Understanding the sampling distribution is the crux of understanding statistics. The sampling distribution is a theoretical probability distribution that in actual practice would never be calculated. Hence, practical, business–oriented students have difficulty understanding why the notion of the sampling distribution is important. Statisticians, with their mathematical curiosity, have asked themselves, "What would happen if we were to draw a large number of samples (say, 50,000), each having n elements, from a specified population?" Assuming that the samples were randomly selected, the sample means, $\overline{X}$s, could be arranged in a frequency distribution. Because different people or sample units would be selected in the different samples, the sample means would not be exactly equal. The shape of the sampling distribution is of considerable importance to statisticians. If the sample size is sufficiently large and if the samples are randomly drawn, we know from the central–limit theorem that the sampling distribution of the mean will be approximately normally distributed.

A formal definition of the sampling distribution is as follows:

> A **sampling distribution** is a theoretical probability distribution that shows the functional relation between the possible values of some summary characteristic of n cases drawn at random and the probability (density) associated with each value over all possible samples of size n from a particular population.[8]

The sampling distribution's mean is called the *expected value* of the statistic. The expected value of the mean of the sampling distribution is equal to μ. The standard deviation of the sampling distribution of $\overline{X}$ is called the **standard error of the mean** $(S_{\overline{X}})$ and is approximately equal to

$$S_{\overline{X}} = \frac{\sigma}{\sqrt{n}}$$

To review, there are three important distributions that we must know about to make an inference about a population from a sample: the population distribution, the sample distribution, and the sampling distribution. They have the following characteristics:

	Mean	Standard Deviation
Population Distribution	μ	σ
Sample Distribution	$\overline{X}$	S
Sampling Distribution	$\mu_{\overline{X}} = \mu$	$S_{\overline{X}}$

We now have much of the information we need to understand the concept of statistical inference. To clarify why the sampling distribution has the characteristic just described, we will elaborate on two concepts: the standard error of

population distribution
A frequency distribution of the elements of a population.

sample distribution
A frequency distribution of a sample.

sampling distribution
A theoretical probability distribution of sample means for all possible samples of a certain size drawn from a particular population.

standard error of the mean
The standard deviation of the sampling distribution.

the mean and the central-limit theorem. You may be wondering why the standard error of the mean, $S_{\bar{X}}$, is defined as $S_{\bar{X}} = \sigma/\sqrt{n}$. The reason is based on the notion that the variance or dispersion within the sampling distribution of the mean will be less if we have a larger sample size for independent samples. We can see intuitively that a larger sample size allows the researcher to be more confident that the sample mean is closer to the population mean. In actual practice the standard error of the mean is estimated using the sample's standard deviation. Thus, $S_{\bar{X}}$ is estimated using $S/\sqrt{n}$.

Exhibit 13.6 shows the relationship among a population distribution, the sample distribution, and three sampling distributions for varying sample sizes. In part (a) the population distribution is not a normal distribution. In part (b) the sample distribution resembles the distribution of the population; however, there may be some differences. In part (c) each sampling distribution is normally distributed and has the same mean. Note that as sample size increases, the spread of the sample means around μ decreases. Thus, with a larger sample size we will have a skinnier sampling distribution.

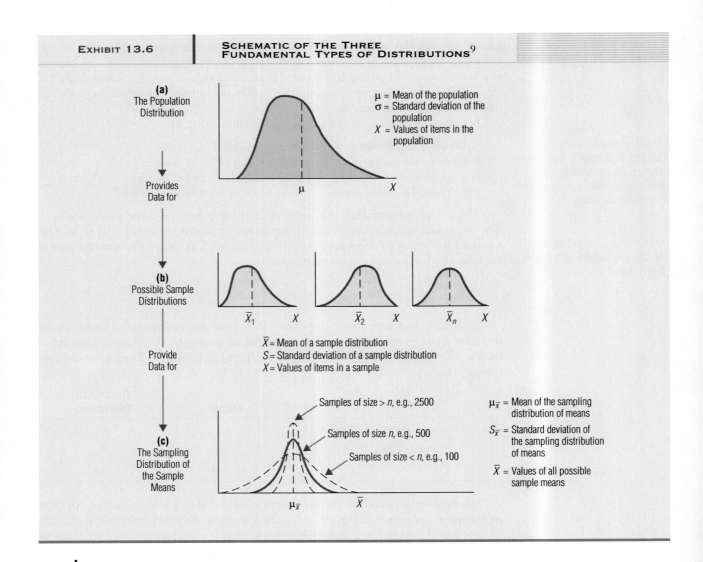

EXHIBIT 13.6

SCHEMATIC OF THE THREE FUNDAMENTAL TYPES OF DISTRIBUTIONS[9]

(a)
The Population Distribution

Provides Data for

μ = Mean of the population
σ = Standard deviation of the population
X = Values of items in the population

(b)
Possible Sample Distributions

Provide Data for

$\bar{X}$ = Mean of a sample distribution
S = Standard deviation of a sample distribution
X = Values of items in a sample

(c)
The Sampling Distribution of the Sample Means

Samples of size > n, e.g., 2500
Samples of size n, e.g., 500
Samples of size < n, e.g., 100

$\mu_{\bar{X}}$ = Mean of the sampling distribution of means
$S_{\bar{X}}$ = Standard deviation of the sampling distribution of means
$\bar{X}$ = Values of all possible sample means

CENTRAL-LIMIT THEOREM

central-limit theorem
The theory that, as sample size increases, the distribution of sample means of size *n,* randomly selected, approaches a normal distribution.

Finding that the means of random samples of a sufficiently large size will be approximately normal in form and that the mean of the sampling distribution will approach the population mean is very useful. Mathematically, this is the assertion of the **central-limit theorem,** which states: As the sample size, *n,* increases, the distribution of the mean, $\bar{X}$, of a random sample taken from practically any population approaches a normal distribution (with a mean, μ, and a standard deviation, $\sigma/\sqrt{n}$).[10] The central–limit theorem works regardless of the shape of the original population distribution (see Exhibit 13.7).

EXHIBIT 13.7

DISTRIBUTION OF SAMPLE MEANS FOR SAMPLES OF VARIOUS SIZES AND POPULATION DISTRIBUTIONS[11]

TABLE 13.8	HYPOTHETICAL POPULATION DISTRIBUTION OF TOY EXPENDITURES

Child	Toy Expenditures
Alice	$1.00
Becky	2.00
Noah	3.00
Tobin	4.00
George	5.00
Freddy	6.00

A simple example will demonstrate the central-limit theorem. Assume that a consumer researcher is interested in the number of dollars children spend on toys each month. Assume further that the population the consumer researcher is investigating consists of 8-year-old children in a certain school. In this example the population consists of only six individuals. (This is a simple and perhaps somewhat unrealistic example; nevertheless, assume that the population size is only six elements.) Table 13.8 shows the population distribution of toy expenditures. Alice, a relatively deprived child, has only $1 per month, whereas fat Freddy, the rich kid, has $6 to spend. The average expenditure on toys each month is $3.50, so the population mean, μ, equals 3.5 (see Table 13.9).

Now assume that we do not know everything about the population, and we wish to take a sample size of two, to be drawn randomly from the population of the six individuals. How many possible samples are there? The answer is 15, as follows:

$$
\begin{array}{llll}
1, 2 & & & \\
1, 3 & 2, 3 & & \\
1, 4 & 2, 4 & 3, 4 & \\
1, 5 & 2, 5 & 3, 5 & 4, 5 \\
1, 6 & 2, 6 & 3, 6 & 4, 6 \quad 5, 6
\end{array}
$$

Table 13.10 lists the sample mean for each of the possible 15 samples and the frequency distribution of these sample means with their appropriate probabili-

TABLE 13.9	CALCULATION OF POPULATION MEAN

X
$1.00
2.00
3.00
4.00
5.00
6.00
Σ $21.00

Calculations: $\mu = \dfrac{\Sigma X}{n} = \dfrac{21}{6} = 3.5 = \mu_{\bar{X}}$

| TABLE 13.10 | ARITHMETIC MEANS OF SAMPLES AND FREQUENCY DISTRIBUTION OF SAMPLE MEANS | | |

SAMPLE MEANS

Sample	ΣX	$\bar{X}$	Probability
$1, $2	$3.00	$1.50	1/15
1, 3	4.00	2.00	1/15
1, 4	5.00	2.50	1/15
1, 5	6.00	3.00	1/15
1, 6	7.00	3.50	1/15
2, 3	5.00	2.50	1/15
2, 4	6.00	3.00	1/15
2, 5	7.00	3.50	1/15
2, 6	8.00	4.00	1/15
3, 4	7.00	3.50	1/15
3, 5	8.00	4.00	1/15
3, 6	9.00	4.50	1/15
4, 5	9.00	4.50	1/15
4, 6	10.00	5.00	1/15
5, 6	11.00	5.50	1/15

FREQUENCY DISTRIBUTION

Sample Mean	Frequency	Probability
$1.50	1	1/15
2.00	1	1/15
2.50	2	2/15
3.00	2	2/15
3.50	3	3/15
4.00	2	2/15
4.50	2	2/15
5.00	1	1/15
5.50	1	1/15

ties. These sample means comprise a sampling distribution of the mean, and the distribution is *approximately* normal. If we increased the sample size to three, four, or more, the distribution of sample means would more closely approximate a normal distribution. While this simple example is not a proof of the central–limit theorem, it should give you a better understanding of the nature of the sampling distribution of the mean.

This theoretical knowledge about distributions can be used to solve two practical marketing research problems: estimating parameters and determining sample size.

ESTIMATION OF PARAMETERS

A catalog retailer, such as Horchow, may rely on sampling and statistical estimation to prepare for Christmas orders. The company can expect that 28 days after mailing a catalog, it will have received X percent of the orders it will get. With this information, it can tell within 5 percent how many ties it will sell by

Christmas. Making a proper inference about population parameters is highly practical for a marketer that must have the inventory appropriate for a short selling season.

Suppose you are a product manager for Beatrice Foods and you recently conducted a taste test to measure intention to buy a reformulated Swiss Miss Lite Cocoa Mix. The results of the research indicate that when the product was placed in 800 homes and a callback was made two weeks later, 80 percent of the respondents said they would buy it: 76 percent of those who had not previously used low-calorie cocoa and 84 percent of those who had. How can you be sure there were no statistical errors in this estimate? How confident can you be of these figures?

Students often wonder whether statistics are really used in the business world. The two situations just described provide contemporary examples of the need for statistical estimation of parameters and the value of statistical techniques as managerial tools.

Point Estimates

Our goal in using statistics is to make an estimate about population parameters. The population mean, μ, and standard deviation, σ, are constants, but in most instances of marketing research they are unknown. To estimate population values, we are required to sample. As we have discussed, $\bar{X}$ and S are random variables that will vary from sample to sample with a certain probability (sampling) distribution.

Our previous example of statistical inference was somewhat unrealistic because the population had only six individuals. Consider the more realistic example of a prospective racquetball entrepreneur who wishes to estimate the average number of days players participate in this sport each week. When statistical inference is needed, the population mean, μ, is a constant but unknown parameter. To estimate the average number of playing days, we could take a sample of 300 racquetball players throughout the area where our entrepreneur is thinking of building club facilities. If the sample mean, $\bar{X}$, equals 2.6 days per week, we might use this figure as a **point estimate**. This single value, 2.6, would be the best estimate of the population mean. However, we would be extremely lucky if the sample estimate were exactly the same as the population value. A less risky alternative would be to calculate a confidence interval.

point estimate
An estimate of the population mean in the form of a single value, usually the sample mean.

Confidence Intervals

If we specify a range of numbers, or interval, within which the population mean should lie, we can be more confident that our inference is correct. A **confidence interval estimate** is based on the knowledge that $\mu = \bar{X} \pm$ a small sampling error. After calculating an interval estimate, we can determine how probable it is that the population mean will fall within this range of statistical values. In the racquetball project the researcher, after setting up a confidence interval, would be able to make a statement such as "With 95 percent confidence, I think that the average number of days played per week is between 2.3 and 2.9." This information can be used to estimate market demand because the researcher has a certain confidence that the interval contains the value of the true population mean.

The crux of the problem for the researcher is to determine how much random sampling error to tolerate. In other words, what should the confidence interval be? How much of a gamble should be taken that μ will be included in the

confidence interval estimate
A specified range of numbers within which a population mean is expected to lie; an estimate of the population mean based on the knowledge that it will be equal to the sample mean plus or minus a small sampling error.

confidence level
A percentage or decimal value that tells how confident a researcher can be about being correct. It states the long-run percentage of confidence intervals that will include the true population mean.

range? Do we need to be 80 percent, 90 percent, or 99 percent sure? The **confidence level** is a percentage or decimal that indicates the long-run probability that the results will be correct. Traditionally, researchers have used the 95 percent confidence level. While there is nothing magical about the 95 percent confidence level, it is useful to select this confidence level in our examples.

As mentioned, the point estimate gives no information about the possible magnitude of random sampling error. The confidence interval gives the estimated value of the population parameter, plus or minus an estimate of the error. We can express the idea of the confidence interval as follows:

$$\mu = \bar{X} \pm \text{a small sampling error}$$

More formally, assuming that the researchers select a large sample (more than 30 observations), the small sampling error is given by

$$\text{Small sampling error} = Z_{c.l.} S_{\bar{X}}$$

where

TO THE POINT

A little inaccuracy sometimes saves a ton of explanation.

H. H. MUNRO (SAKI)

$$Z_{c.l.} = \text{value of } Z, \text{ or standardized normal variable, at a specified confidence level } (c.l.)$$

$$S_{\bar{X}} = \text{standard error of the mean}$$

The precision of our estimate is indicated by the value of $Z_{c.l.} S_{\bar{X}}$. It is useful to define the range of possible error, E, as follows:

$$E = Z_{c.l.} S_{\bar{X}}$$

Thus,

$$\mu = \bar{X} \pm E$$

where

$$\bar{X} = \text{sample mean}$$

$$E = \text{range of sampling error}$$

or

$$\mu = \bar{X} \pm Z_{c.l.} S_{\bar{X}}$$

The confidence interval $\pm E$ is always stated as one-half of the total confidence interval.

The following step-by-step procedure can be used to calculate confidence intervals:

1. Calculate $\bar{X}$ from the sample.
2. Assuming σ is unknown, estimate the population standard deviation by finding S, the sample standard deviation.
3. Estimate the standard error of the mean, using the formula

$$S_{\bar{X}} = \frac{S}{\sqrt{n}}$$

4. Determine the Z-value associated with the desired confidence level. The confidence level should be divided by 2 to determine what percentage of the area under the curve to include on each side of the mean.
5. Calculate the confidence interval.

The following example shows how calculation of a confidence interval can be used in preparing a demographic profile, a useful tool for market segmentation.

Suppose you plan to open a sporting goods store to cater to working women who golf. In a survey of your market area you find that the mean age ($\bar{X}$) of 100 women is 37.5 years, with a standard deviation (S) of 12.0 years. Knowing that it would be extremely coincidental if the point estimate from the sample were exactly the same as the population mean age (μ), you decide to construct a confidence interval around the sample mean using the steps just given:

1. $\bar{X} = 37.5$ years
2. $S = 12.0$ years
3. $S_{\bar{X}} = \dfrac{12}{\sqrt{100}} = 1.2$
4. Suppose you wish to be 95 percent confident—that is, assured that 95 times out of 100, the estimates from your sample will include the population parameter. Including 95 percent of the area requires that 47.5 percent (one-half of 95 percent) of the distribution on each side be included. From the Z-table (Table 2 in the Appendix), you find that .475 corresponds to the Z-value 1.96.
5. Substituting the values for $Z_{c.l.}$ and $S_{\bar{X}}$ into the confidence interval formula gives

$$\mu = 37.5 \pm (1.96)(1.2)$$
$$= 37.5 \pm 2.352$$

You can thus expect that μ is contained in the range from 35.148 to 39.852 years. Intervals constructed in this manner will contain the true value of μ 95 percent of the time.

Step 3 can be eliminated by entering S and n directly in the confidence interval formula:

$$\mu = \bar{X} \pm Z_{c.l.} \frac{S}{\sqrt{n}}$$

Remember that $S/\sqrt{n}$ represents the standard error of the mean, $S_{\bar{X}}$. Its use is based on the central-limit theorem.

If you wanted to increase the probability that the population mean will lie within the confidence interval, you could use the 99 percent confidence level, with a Z-value of 2.57. You may want to calculate the 99 percent confidence interval for the above example; you can expect that μ will be in the range between 34.416 and 40.584 years.

We have now examined the basic concepts of inferential statistics. You should understand that sample statistics such as the sample means, $\bar{X}$s, can provide good estimates of population parameters such as μ. You should also realize that there is a certain probability of being in error when you estimate a population parameter from sample statistics. In other words, there will be a random sampling error, which is the difference between the survey results and the results of surveying the entire population. If you have a firm understanding of these basic terms and ideas, which are the essence of statistics, the remaining statistics concepts will be relatively simple for you. Several ramifications of the simple ideas presented so far will permit you to make better decisions about populations based on surveys or experiments.

Random Error and Sample Size

When asked to evaluate a marketing research project, most people, even those with little marketing research training, begin by asking, "How big was the sample?" Intuitively we know that the larger the sample, the more accurate the research. This is in fact a statistical truth; random sampling error varies with samples of different sizes. In statistical terms, increasing the sample size decreases the width of the confidence interval at a given confidence level. When the standard deviation of the population is unknown, a confidence interval is calculated using the following formula:

$$\text{Confidence interval} = \bar{X} \pm Z\frac{S}{\sqrt{n}}$$

Observe that the equation for the plus or minus error factor in the confidence interval includes n, the sample size:

$$E = Z\frac{S}{\sqrt{n}}$$

If n increases, E is reduced. Exhibit 13.8 illustrates that the confidence interval (or magnitude of error) decreases as the sample size, n, increases.

We already noted that it is not necessary to take a census of all elements of the population to conduct an accurate study. The laws of probability give investigators sufficient confidence regarding the accuracy of data collected from a sample. Knowledge of the characteristics of the sampling distribution helps researchers make reasonably precise estimates.

Students familiar with the law of diminishing returns in economics will easily grasp the concept that increases in sample size reduce sampling error at a

EXHIBIT 13.8 | RELATIONSHIP BETWEEN SAMPLE SIZE AND ERROR[12]

decreasing rate. For example, doubling a sample of 1,000 will reduce random sampling error by 1 percentage point, but doubling the sample from 2,000 to 4,000 will reduce random sampling error by only another 1/2 percentage point. More technically, random sampling error is inversely proportional to the square root of *n*. (Exhibit 13.8 gives an approximation of the relationship between sample size and error.) Thus, the main issue becomes one of determining the optimal sample size.

Factors in Determining Sample Size for Questions Involving Means

Three factors are required to specify sample size: (1) the variance, or heterogeneity, of the population; (2) the magnitude of acceptable error; and (3) the confidence level. Suppose a researcher wishes to find out whether 9-year-old boys are taller than 4-year-old boys. Intuitively we know that even with a very small sample size, the correct information probably will be obtained. This is based on the fact that the determination of sample size depends on the research question and the variability within the sample.

The *variance,* or *heterogeneity*, of the population is the first necessary bit of information. In statistical terms, this refers to the *standard deviation* of the population. Only a small sample is required if the population is homogeneous. For example, predicting the average age of college students requires a smaller sample than predicting the average age of people who visit the zoo on a given Sunday afternoon. As *heterogeneity* increases, so must sample size. Thus, to test the effectiveness of an acne medicine, the sample must be large enough to cover the range of skin types.

The *magnitude of error,* or the confidence interval, is the second necessary bit of information. Defined in statistical terms as *E,* the magnitude of error indicates how precise the estimate must be. It indicates a certain precision level. From a managerial perspective, the importance of the decision in terms of profitability will influence the researcher's specifications of the range of error. If, for example, favorable results from a test market sample will result in the construction of a new plant and unfavorable results will dictate not marketing the product, the acceptable range of error probably will be small; the cost of an error would be too great to allow much room for random sampling errors. In other cases the estimate need not be extremely precise. Allowing an error of $\pm\$1,000$ in total family income instead of $E = \pm \$50$ may be acceptable in most market segmentation studies.

The third factor of concern is the *confidence level.* In our examples we will typically use the 95 percent confidence level. This, however, is an arbitrary decision based on convention; there is nothing sacred about the .05 chance level (that is, the probability of .05 of the true population parameter being incorrectly estimated). Exhibit 13.9 summarizes the information required to determine sample size.

Exhibit 13.9	STATISTICAL INFORMATION NEEDED TO DETERMINE SAMPLE SIZE FOR QUESTIONS THAT INVOLVE MEANS	
Variable	**Symbol**	**Typical Source of Information**
Standard deviation	S	Pilot study or rule of thumb
Magnitude of error	E	Managerial judgment or calculation ($ZS_{\bar{X}}$)
Confidence level	$Z_{c.l.}$	Managerial judgment

Estimating Sample Size for Questions Involving Means

Once the preceding concepts are understood, determining the actual size for a simple random sample is quite easy. The researcher

1. Estimates the standard deviation of the population
2. Makes a judgment about the allowable magnitude of error
3. Determines a confidence level

The only problem is estimating the standard deviation of the population. Ideally, similar studies conducted in the past will give a basis for judging the standard deviation. In practice, researchers who lack prior information conduct a pilot study to estimate the population parameters so that another, larger sample, of the appropriate sample size, may be drawn. This procedure is called *sequential sampling* because researchers take an initial look at the pilot study results before deciding on a larger sample to provide more precise information.

A rule of thumb for estimating the value of the standard deviation is to expect it to be one-sixth of the range. If researchers conducting a study on television purchases expected the price paid to range from $100 to $700, a rule-of-thumb estimate for the standard deviation would be $100.

For the moment, assume that the standard deviation has been estimated in some preliminary work. If our concern is to estimate the mean of a particular population, the formula for sample size is

$$n = \left(\frac{ZS}{E}\right)^2$$

where

Z = standardized value that corresponds to the confidence level
S = sample standard deviation or estimate of the population standard deviation
E = acceptable magnitude of error, plus or minus error factor (range is one-half of the total confidence interval)[13]

Suppose a survey researcher studying annual expenditures on lipstick wishes to have a 95 percent confidence level ($Z = 1.96$) and a range of error (E) of less than $2. If the estimate of the standard deviation is $29, the sample size can be calculated as follows:

$$n = \left(\frac{ZS}{E}\right)^2 = \left(\frac{(1.96)(29)}{2}\right)^2 = \left(\frac{56.84}{2}\right)^2 = 28.42^2 = 808$$

If a range of error (E) of $4 is acceptable, sample size can be reduced:

$$n = \left(\frac{ZS}{E}\right)^2 = \left(\frac{(1.96)(29)}{4}\right)^2 = \left(\frac{56.84}{4}\right)^2 = 14.21^2 = 202$$

Thus, doubling the range of acceptable error reduces sample size to approximately one-quarter of its original size. Stated conversely in a general sense, doubling sample size will reduce error by only approximately one-quarter.

Factors in Determining Sample Size for Proportions

Researchers frequently are concerned with determining sample size for problems that involve estimating population proportions or percentages. When the question involves the estimation of a proportion, the researcher requires some knowledge of the logic for determining a confidence interval around a sample proportion estimation (p) of the population proportion (π). For a confidence interval to be constructed around the sample proportion (p), an estimate of the standard error of the proportion (S_p) must be calculated and a confidence level specified.

The precision of the estimate is indicated by the value $Z_{c.l.}S_p$. Thus, the plus or minus estimate of the population proportion is

$$\text{Confidence interval} = p \pm Z_{c.l.}S_p$$

If the researcher selects a 95 percent probability for the confidence interval, $Z_{c.l.}$ will equal 1.96 (see Table 2 in the Appendix).

The formula for S_p is

$$S_p = \sqrt{\frac{pq}{n}} \qquad \text{or} \qquad S_p = \sqrt{\frac{p(1-p)}{n}}$$

where

S_p = estimate of the standard error of the proportion
p = proportion of successes
q = $1 - p$, or proportion of failures

Suppose that 20 percent of a sample of 1,200 television viewers recall seeing an advertisement. The proportion of successes (p) equals .2, and the proportion of failures (q) equals .8. To estimate the 95 percent confidence interval, we calculate

$$
\begin{aligned}
\text{Confidence interval} &= p \pm Z_{c.l.}S_p \\
&= .2 \pm 1.96 S_p \\
&= .2 \pm 1.96 \sqrt{\frac{p(1-p)}{n}} \\
&= .2 \pm 1.96 \sqrt{\frac{(.2)(.8)}{1,200}} \\
&= .2 \pm 1.96(.0115) \\
&= .2 \pm .022
\end{aligned}
$$

Thus, the population proportion (people who recall an advertisement) is estimated to be included in the interval between .178 and .222, or roughly between 18 and 22 percent, with a 95 percent confidence coefficient.

To determine *sample size* for a proportion, the researcher must make a judgment about confidence level and the maximum allowance for random sampling error. Furthermore, the size of the proportion influences random sampling error; thus, an estimate of the expected proportion of successes must be made, based on intuition or prior information. The formula is

$$n = \frac{Z_{c.l.}^2 pq}{E^2}$$

where

n = number of items in sample
$Z_{c.l.}^2$ = square of the confidence level in standard error units
p = estimated proportion of successes
q = $1 - p$, or estimated proportion of failures
E^2 = square of the maximum allowance for error between the true proportion and the sample proportion, or $Z_{c.l.}S_p$ squared

Suppose a researcher believes that a simple random sample will show that 60 percent of the population (p) recognizes the name of an automobile dealership. The researcher wishes to estimate with 95 percent confidence ($Z_{c.l.} = 1.96$) that the allowance for sampling error is not greater than 3.5 percentage points (E). Substituting these values into the formula gives

$$n = \frac{(1.96)^2(.6)(.4)}{.035^2}$$

$$= \frac{(3.8416)(.24)}{.001225}$$

$$= \frac{.922}{.001225}$$

$$= 753$$

Calculating Sample Size for Sample Proportions

In practice, a number of tables have been constructed for determining sample size. Table 13.11 illustrates a sample size table for problems that involve sample proportions (p).

The theoretical principles underlying calculation of sample sizes of proportions are similar to the concepts discussed in this chapter. Suppose we wish to take samples in two large cities, New Orleans and Miami. We wish no more than 2 percentage points of error, and we will be satisfied with a 95 percent confidence level (see Table 13.11). If we assume all other things are equal, then in the New Orleans market, where 15 percent of the consumers favor our product and 85 percent prefer competitors' brands, we need a sample of 1,222 to get results with only 2 percentage points of error. In the Miami market, however, where 30 percent of the consumers favor our brand and 70 percent prefer other brands (a less heterogeneous market), we need a sample size of 2,009 to get the same sample reliability.

Table 13.12 shows a sampling error table typical of those that accompany research proposals or reports. Most studies will estimate more than one parameter. Thus, in a survey of 100 people in which 50 percent agree with one statement and 10 percent with another, the sampling error is expected to be 10 and 6 percentage points of error, respectively.

Determining Sample Size on the Basis of Judgment

Just as sample units may be selected to suit the convenience or judgment of the researcher, sample size may also be determined on the basis of managerial judgments. Using a sample size similar to those used in previous studies provides the inexperienced researcher with a comparison with other researchers' judgments.

Another judgmental factor that affects the determination of sample size is the selection of the appropriate item, question, or characteristic to be used for the sample size calculations. Several different characteristics affect most studies, and the desired degree of precision may vary for these items. The researcher must exercise some judgment to determine which item will be used. Often the item that will produce the largest sample size will be used to determine the ultimate sample size. However, the cost of data collection becomes a major consideration, and judgment must be exercised regarding the importance of such information.

Another consideration stems from most researchers' need to analyze various subgroups within the sample. For example, suppose an analyst wishes to look at

TABLE 13.11 — SELECTED TABLES FOR DETERMINING SAMPLE SIZE WHEN THE CHARACTERISTIC OF INTEREST IS A PROPORTION[14]

SAMPLE SIZE FOR A 95 PERCENT CONFIDENCE LEVEL WHEN PARAMETER IN POPULATION IS ASSUMED TO BE OVER 70 PERCENT OR UNDER 30 PERCENT

Size of Population	Reliability			
	±1% Point	±2% Points	±3% Points	±5% Points
1,000	a	a	473	244
2,000	a	a	619	278
3,000	a	1,206	690	291
4,000	a	1,341	732	299
5,000	a	1,437	760	303
10,000	4,465	1,678	823	313
20,000	5,749	1,832	858	318
50,000	6,946	1,939	881	321
100,000	7,465	1,977	888	321
500,000 to ∞	7,939	2,009	895	322

SAMPLE SIZE FOR A 95 PERCENT CONFIDENCE LEVEL WHEN PARAMETER IN POPULATION IS ASSUMED TO BE OVER 85 PERCENT OR UNDER 15 PERCENT

Size of Population	Reliability			
	±1% Point	±2% Points	±3% Points	±5% Points
1,000	a	a	353	235
2,000	a	760	428	266
3,000	a	890	461	278
4,000	a	938	479	284
5,000	a	984	491	289
10,000	3,288	1,091	516	297
20,000	3,935	1,154	530	302
50,000	4,461	1,195	538	304
100,000	4,669	1,210	541	305
500,000 to ∞	4,850	1,222	544	306

a In these cases, more than 50 percent of the population is required in the sample. Since the normal approximation of the hypergeometric distribution is a poor approximation in such instances, no sample value is given.

TABLE 13.12 — ALLOWANCE FOR RANDOM SAMPLING ERROR (PLUS AND MINUS PERCENTAGE POINTS) AT 95 PERCENT CONFIDENCE LEVEL[15]

Response	SAMPLE SIZE						
	2,500	1,500	1,000	500	250	100	50
10 (90)	1.2	1.5	2.0	3.0	4.0	6.0	8.0
20 (80)	1.6	2.0	2.5	4.0	5.0	8.0	11.0
30 (70)	1.8	2.5	3.0	4.0	6.0	9.0	13.0
40 (60)	2.0	2.5	3.0	4.0	6.0	10.0	14.0
50 (50)	2.0	2.5	3.0	4.0	6.0	10.0	14.0

differences in retailers' attitudes by geographic region. The analyst will want to make sure to sample an adequate number of retailers in the New England, Mid-Atlantic, and South Atlantic regions to ensure that subgroup comparisons are reliable. There is a judgmental rule of thumb for selecting minimum subgroup sample size: Each subgroup to be separately analyzed should have a minimum of 100 units in each category of the major breakdowns. With this procedure, the total sample size is computed by totaling the sample sizes necessary for these subgroups.

Determining Sample Size for Stratified and Other Probability Samples

Stratified sampling involves drawing separate probability samples within the subgroups to make the sample more efficient. With a stratified sample the sample variances are expected to differ by strata. This makes the determination of sample size more complex. Increased complexity may also characterize the determination of sample size for cluster sampling and other probability sampling methods. The formulas are beyond the scope of this book. Students interested in these advanced sampling techniques should investigate advanced sampling textbooks.

A REMINDER ABOUT STATISTICS

Learning the terms and symbols defined in this chapter will provide you with the basics of the language of statisticians and researchers. As you learn more about the pragmatic use of statistics in marketing research, do not forget these concepts. The speller who forgets that *i* comes before *e* except after *c* will have trouble every time he or she must tackle the spelling of a word with the *ie* or *ei* combination. The same is true for the student who forgets the basics of the "foreign language" of statistics.

SUMMARY

Determination of sample size requires a knowledge of statistics. Statistics is the language of the researcher, and this chapter introduced its vocabulary. Descriptive statistics describe characteristics of a population or sample. Inferential statistics investigate samples to draw conclusions about entire populations.

A frequency distribution summarizes data by showing how frequently each response or classification occurs. A proportion indicates the percentage of group members that have a particular characteristic.

Three measures of central tendency are commonly used: the mean, or arithmetic average; the median, or halfway value; and the mode, or most frequently observed value. These three values may differ, and care must be taken to understand distortions that may arise from using the wrong measure of central tendency.

Measures of dispersion along with measures of central tendency can describe a distribution. The range is the difference between the largest and smallest values observed. The variance and standard deviation are the most useful measures of dispersion.

The normal distribution fits many observed distributions. It is symmetrical about its mean, with equal mean, median, and mode. Almost the entire area of the normal distribution lies within ± 3 standard deviations of the mean. Any normal distribution can easily be compared with the standardized normal, or

Z-distribution, whose mean is 0 and standard deviation is 1. This allows easy evaluation of the probabilities of many occurrences.

The techniques of statistical inference are based on the relationship among the population distribution, the sample distribution, and the sampling distribution. This relationship is expressed in the central-limit theorem.

Estimating a population mean with a single value gives a point estimate. A range of numbers within which the researcher is confident that the population mean will lie is a confidence interval estimate. The confidence level is a percentage that indicates the long-run probability that the confidence interval estimate will be correct.

The statistical determination of sample size requires knowledge of (1) the variance of the population, (2) the magnitude of acceptable error, and (3) the confidence level. Several computational formulas are available for determining sample size. Furthermore, a number of easy-to-use tables have been compiled to help researchers calculate sample size. The main reason a large sample size is desirable is that sample size is related to random sampling error. A smaller sample makes a larger error in estimates more likely.

Many research problems involve the estimation of proportions. Statistical techniques may be used to determine a confidence interval around a sample proportion. Calculation of sample size for a sample proportion is not difficult. However, most researchers use tables that indicate predetermined sample sizes.

Key Terms and Concepts

sample statistics
population parameters
frequency distribution
percentage distribution
probability
proportion
mean

median
mode
variance
standard deviation
normal distribution
standardized normal distribution
population distribution

sample distribution
sampling distribution
standard error of the mean
central-limit theorem
point estimate
confidence interval estimate
confidence level

Questions for Review and Critical Thinking

1. What is the difference between descriptive and inferential statistics?
2. The speed limits in 13 countries are as follows:

Country	Highway Miles per Hour
Italy	87
France	81
Hungary	75
Belgium	75
Portugal	75
Britain	70
Spain	62
Denmark	62
Netherlands	62
Greece	62
Japan	62
Norway	56
Turkey	56

Calculate the mean, median, and mode for these data.

3. Prepare a frequency distribution for the data in question 2.
4. Why is the standard deviation rather than the average deviation typically used?
5. Calculate the standard deviation for the data in question 2.
6. Draw three distributions that have the same mean value but different standard deviation values. Draw three distributions that have the same standard deviation value but different mean values.
7. A manufacturer of MP3 players surveyed 100 retail stores in each of the firm's sales regions. An analyst noticed that in the South Atlantic region the average retail price was $165 (mean) and the standard deviation was $30. However, in the Mid–Atlantic region the mean price was $170, with a standard deviation of $15. What do these statistics tell us about these two sales regions?

8. What is the sampling distribution? How does it differ from the sample distribution?
9. What would happen to the sampling distribution of the mean if we increased sample size from 5 to 25?
10. Suppose a fast-food restaurant wishes to estimate average sales volume for a new menu item. The restaurant has analyzed the sales of the item at a similar outlet and observed the following results:

$$\bar{X} = 500 \text{ (mean daily sales)}$$
$$S = 100 \text{ (standard deviation of sample)}$$
$$n = 25 \text{ (sample size)}$$

The restaurant manager wants to know into what range the mean daily sales should fall 95 percent of the time. Perform this calculation.
11. In the example on page 337 of research on lipstick, where $E = \$2$ and $S = \$29$, what sample size would we require if we desired a 99 percent confidence level?
12. Suppose you are planning to sample cat owners to determine the average number of cans of cat food they purchase monthly. The following standards have been set: a confidence level of 99 percent and an error of less than 5 units. Past research has indicated that the standard deviation should be 6 units. What is the required sample size?
13. In a survey of 500 people, 60 percent responded positively to an attitude question. Calculate a confidence interval at 95 percent to get an interval estimate for a proportion.
14. In a nationwide survey, a researcher expects that 30 percent of the population will agree with an attitude statement. She wishes to have less than 2 percentage points of error and to be 95 percent confident. What sample size does she need?
15. To understand how sample size is conceptually related to random sampling error, costs, and non-sampling errors, graph these relationships.
16. Suppose you are a political analyst and wish to be extremely confident that you predict the outcome of an extremely close primary election. What should the sample size be for your poll? Are there any problems involved in determining the sample size for this election?
17. A researcher expects the population proportion of Cubs fans in Chicago to be 80 percent. The researcher wishes to have an error of less than 5 percent and to be 95 percent confident of an estimate to be made from a mail survey. What sample size is required?
18. An automobile dealership plans to conduct a survey to determine what proportion of new-car buyers continue to have their cars serviced at the dealership after the warranty period ends. It estimates that 30 percent of customers do so. It wants the results of its survey to be accurate within 5 percent, and it wants to be 95 percent confident of the results. What sample size is necessary?
19. City Opera, a local opera company, wishes to take a sample of its subscribers to learn the average number of years people have been subscribing. The researcher expects the average number of years to be 12 and believes the standard deviation will be about 2 years (approximately one-sixth of the range). He wishes to be 95 percent confident of his estimate. What is the appropriate sample size?
20. Using the formula in this chapter, a researcher determines that at the 95 percent confidence level, a sample of 2,500 is required to satisfy a client's requirements. The researcher actually uses a sample of 1,200, however, because the client has specified a budget cap for the survey. What are the ethical considerations in this situation?

Exploring the Internet

1. Go to http://www.dartmouth.edu/~chance/ to visit the Chance course. The Chance course is an innovative program to creatively teach introductory materials about probability and statistics. The Chance course is designed to enhance quantitative literacy. Numerous videos can be played online.
2. Go to Lycos at http://www.lycos.com. Enter "population sampling" into the search box and then click on the Go icon. How extensive is the list of sources?
3. A random number generator and other statistical information can be found at The World Wide Web Virtual Library: Random Numbers and Monte Carlo Methods, located at http://random.mat.sbg.ac.at/links.
4. The Platonic Realms Interactive Mathematics Encyclopedia is located at http://www.mathacademy.com. It provides many definitions of statistical and mathematical terms.
5. Sample Size Calculators can be found at http://www.surveysystem.com/sscalc.htm and at http://www.svys.com/.
6. Martindale's Calculators On-Line Center site at http://www-sci.lib.uci.edu/HSG/RefCalculators.html and the Part IIA: Statistics site at http://www-sci.lib.uci.edu/HSG/RefCalculators2A.html are extremely valuable for researchers interested in statistical methods. Visit the sites and report what you find.

Coastal Star Sales Corporation is a West Coast wholesaler that markets leisure products from several manufacturers. Coastal Star has an 80-person sales force that sells to wholesalers in a six-state area, which is divided into two sales regions. Case Exhibit 13.1-1 shows the names of a sample of 11 salespeople, some descriptive information about each person, and sales performance for each of the last two years.

Questions

1. Calculate a mean and a standard deviation for each variable.
2. Set a 95 percent confidence interval around the mean for each variable.
3. Calculate the median, mode, and range for each variable.
4. Organize the data for current sales into a frequency distribution with three classes: (a) under $500,000, (b) $500,001 to $999,999, and (c) $1,000,000 and over.
5. Organize the data for years of selling experience into a frequency distribution with two classes: (a) less than five years and (b) five or more years.
6. Convert the frequency distributions from question 5 to percentage distributions.

CASE EXHIBIT 13.1-1	COASTAL STAR SALES CORPORATION: SALESPERSON DATA				

| | | | | SALES | |
| | | | | Previous | Current |
Region	Salesperson	Age	Years of Experience	Year	Year
Northern	Jackson	40	7	$ 412,744	$ 411,007
Northern	Gentry	60	12	1,491,024	1,726,630
Northern	La Forge	26	2	301,421	700,112
Northern	Miller	39	1	401,241	471,001
Northern	Mowen	64	5	448,160	449,261
Southern	Young	51	2	518,897	519,412
Southern	Fisk	34	1	846,222	713,333
Southern	Kincaid	62	10	1,527,124	2,009,041
Southern	Krieger	42	3	921,174	1,030,000
Southern	Manzer	64	5	463,399	422,798
Southern	Weiner	27	2	548,011	422,001

For the *New York Times*/CBS News Poll of American business executives, telephone interviews were conducted with 499 senior executives at companies throughout the United States.[16] The survey asked questions about their attitudes toward the political environment and its impact on business.

The sample of companies and executives was provided by Dun and Bradstreet Information Services and was randomly drawn from those listed in its nationwide database of private and publicly owned companies.

Companies with $5 million or more in annual revenues were eligible for the survey. Within each company one senior executive was interviewed. Titles eligible for the poll included owner, partner, chief executive, chairman, president, executive vice president, and senior vice president, with the first opportunity for an interview given to the most senior official.

The completed sample included 245 interviews in companies with $5 million to $99 million in annual revenue, 120 interviews in companies with $100 million to $499 million, and 134 interviews in companies with $500 million or more. The completed sample was then weighted by revenue size to reflect the actual distribution of all listed companies in the country because small companies predominate.

In theory, in 19 cases out of 20 results based on such samples will differ by no more than 6 percentage points in either direction from what would have been obtained by seeking out senior executives at all listed companies in the country with annual revenues of $5 million or more.

The potential sampling error for smaller subgroups is larger. For example, for the biggest companies, those with $500 million or more in annual revenue, it is plus or minus 9 percentage points.

Questions

1. What type of sampling method was utilized? What are the strengths and weaknesses of this procedure?
2. What confidence level was used to determine sample size?
3. Explain how to evaluate the random sampling error in the study.

BASIC DATA ANALYSIS

What you will learn in this chapter

- To understand that analysis consists of summarizing, rearranging, ordering, or manipulating data.
- To compute and explain the purposes of simple tabulations and cross-tabulations.
- To discuss how percentages help the researcher understand the natures of relationships.
- To discuss the relationship between two variables with cross-tabulation procedures.
- To explain how to elaborate and refine basic cross-tabulations.
- To discuss the nature of data transformations.
- To explain how to summarize rank-order data.
- To describe some computer software designed for descriptive analysis.
- To define *hypothesis, null hypothesis, alternative hypothesis,* and *significance level.*
- To discuss the steps in the hypothesis-testing procedure.
- To describe the factors that influence the choice of statistical method to use for analysis.

The Yankelovich Monitor conducts longitudinal surveys to track social trends.[1] According to a recent study by Yankelovich, 92 percent of kids fix their own meals sometimes. While snacks and breakfast were prepared by children most frequently, 31 percent said they even fix their own dinners. Echoing the too-busy-to-cook trend that has led to grab-and-go dinners, the child chef phenomenon has grown over the past four years. While 48 percent said they make meals for themselves most of the time (vs. 40 percent in 1995), the percentage preparing meals for the entire family has increased even higher: More than one-quarter (26 percent) do so today, compared with 15 percent in 1995.

Furthermore, it doesn't seem as if most children consider cooking a grueling chore; 92 percent of those surveyed said they like or don't mind preparing meals. Reasons cited for enjoying this task included:

Can choose the food you like	67 percent
It's fun to cook	61 percent
Can eat what you want	57 percent
Can eat as little or as much as you want	51 percent
Can invent new/different food combos	47 percent

These interesting findings illustrate the results of a typical descriptive analysis. This chapter explains how to perform descriptive analysis. ■

THE NATURE OF DESCRIPTIVE ANALYSIS

In the context of marketing research, the term *analysis* is difficult to define because it refers to a variety of activities and processes. One form of analysis consists of summarizing large quantities of raw data so that the results can be interpreted. Categorizing, or separating out the components or relevant parts of the whole data set, is also a form of analysis for comprehending patterns in the data. Rearranging, ordering, or manipulating data may provide descriptive information that will answer questions posed in the problem definition. All forms of analysis attempt to portray data so that the results may be studied and interpreted in concise and meaningful ways.

descriptive analysis
The transformation of raw data into a form that will make them easy to understand and interpret; rearranging, ordering, and manipulating data to generate descriptive information.

Descriptive analysis refers to the transformation of raw data into a form that will make them easy to understand and interpret. Describing responses or observations typically is the first stage of analysis. Averages, frequency distributions, and percentage distributions are the most common ways to summarize data.

As the analysis progresses beyond the descriptive stage, researchers generally apply the tools of inferential statistics. Univariate analysis allows researchers to assess the statistical significance of various hypotheses about a single variable.

TABULATION

Tabulation refers to the orderly arrangement of data in a table or other summary format. Counting the numbers of different responses to a question and arranging them in a frequency distribution is a simple tabulation, or *marginal tabulation*. Simple tabulation of the responses or observations on a question-by-question or item-by-item basis provides the most basic—and in many cases the most useful—form of information for the researcher. It tells the researcher how frequently each response occurs. This starting point for analysis requires the researcher to count responses or observations for each category or code assigned to a variable. Table 14.1 illustrates a **frequency table.** When this tabulation process is done by hand, it is called *tallying.* Large sample sizes generally require computer tabulation of the data.

frequency table
The arrangement of statistical data in a row-and-column format that exhibits the count of responses or observations for each category assigned to a variable.

Percentages

Whether data are tabulated by computer or by hand, percentages, cumulative percentages, and frequency distributions are useful. For example, consider Table 14.2. Most people find part B easier to interpret than part A because the percentages in part B are useful for comparing data for various time periods.

TABLE 14.1	A FREQUENCY TABLE FOR A SIMPLE TABULATION

Do you shop at IGA?

Response	Frequency
Yes	330
No	120
Total	450

TABLE 14.2

AN ILLUSTRATION OF HOW PERCENTAGES AID IN THE INTERPRETATION OF FREQUENCY DISTRIBUTIONS AND CROSS-TABULATIONS[2]

A: United States Racial and Ethnic Composition (in Thousands)

	2000	2010*	Change
Non-Hispanic White	197,061	202,390	5,329
Non-Hispanic Black	33,568	37,466	3,898
Non-Hispanic Asian/Pacific Islander	10,584	14,402	3,818
Non-Hispanic Other	2,054	2,320	266
Hispanic	31,366	41,139	9,773

B: United States Racial and Ethnic Composition (in Thousands)

	2000	Percent of Population	2010*	Percent of Population	Change	Percent Change
Non-Hispanic White	197,061	71.8	202,390	68.0	5,329	+2.7
Non-Hispanic Black	33,568	12.2	37,466	12.6	3,898	+11.6
Non-Hispanic Asian/Pacific Islander	10,584	3.9	14,402	4.8	3,818	+36.1
Non-Hispanic Other	2,054	.7	2,320	.8	266	+13.0
Hispanic	31,366	11.4	41,139	13.8	9,773	+31.2

*Projected

When a frequency distribution portrays only a single characteristic as a percentage of the total, the proportion of occurrence is defined. It may be expressed as a percentage, a fraction, or a decimal value.

When discussing percentages, researchers must be precise in their language. For example, the difference between 40 percent and 60 percent is not 20 percent, but 20 *percentage points,* or an increase of 50 percent.

Measures of Central Tendency

According to *Bride* magazine, $18,874 is the average amount brides plan to spend on their weddings.[3] This is a measure of central tendency. Describing central tendencies of the distribution with the mean, median, or mode is another basic form of descriptive analysis. These measures are most useful when the purpose is to identify typical values of a variable or the most common characteristic of a group. If knowing the average or typical performance will satisfy the information need, the mean, median, or mode should be considered.

CROSS-TABULATION

Mere tabulation of data may answer many research questions; in fact, many studies do not go beyond examining simple tabulations of question-by-question responses to a survey. Although frequency counts, percentage distributions, and averages summarize considerable information, simple tabulation may not yield the full value of the research. Most data can be further organized in a variety of ways. For example, data from a survey that samples both men and women commonly are separated into groups or categories based on sex. Analyzing results by

TABLE 14.3 | CROSS-TABULATION TABLES FROM A SURVEY ON ETHICS IN AMERICA[4]

(A) Reported Behavior (Percentage of General Public Who Have Ever Done Each Activity)

Activity	AGE		GENDER		EDUCATION	
	Under 50 Years Old	Over 50 Years Old	Men	Women	College Graduate	High School Graduate
Taken home work supplies	50	26	47	33	58	21
Called in sick to work when not ill	40	18	Not reported		36	21

(B) Reported Behavior (Percentage Who Have Ever Done Each Activity)

Activity	Business Executives	General Public
Taken home work supplies	74	40
Called in sick to work when not ill	14	31
Used company telephone for personal long-distance calls	78	15
Overstated deductions somewhat on tax forms	35	13
Driven while drunk	80	33
Saw a fellow employee steal something at work and did not report it	7	26

cross-tabulation
Organizing data by groups, categories, or classes to facilitate comparisons; a joint frequency distribution of observations on two or more sets of variables.

groups, categories, or classes is the technique of **cross-tabulation.** The purpose of categorization and cross-tabulation is to allow the inspection and comparison of differences among groups. This form of analysis also helps determine the type of relationship among variables. Since market segmentation is a major component of marketing strategy for many organizations, cross-tabulating the results of marketing research helps clarify the research findings as they pertain to market segments.

Table 14.3 summarizes several cross-tabulations from American citizens' responses to a questionnaire on ethical behavior in the United States. A researcher interested in the relative ethical perspectives of business executives and the general public can inspect this table and easily compare the two groups. The percentage table illustrates the added value of calculating percentages.

Contingency Tables

contingency table
The results of a cross-tabulation of two variables, such as answers to two survey questions.

Part A of Table 14.4 shows how the cross-tabulation of answers to two survey questions (or two variables) results in a **contingency table,** or data matrix. The frequency counts for the question "Do you shop at IGA?" are presented as column totals. The total numbers of men and women in the sample are presented as row totals. These row and column totals often are called *marginals* because they appear in the table's margins. Each of the four cells within part A represents a specific combination of the two variables. The cell that represents women who said they do not shop at IGA has a frequency count of 45.

The contingency table in part A is referred to as a 2 × 2 *table* because it has two rows and two columns. Any cross-tabulation table may be classified according

TABLE 14.4	POSSIBLE CROSS-TABULATIONS OF ONE QUESTION

(A) Cross-Tabulation of Question "Do you shop at IGA?" by Sex of Respondent

	Yes	No	Total
Men	150	75	225
Women	180	45	225
Total	330	120	450

(B) Percentage Cross-Tabulation of Question "Do you shop at IGA?" by Sex of Respondent, Row Percentage

	Yes	No	Total (Base)
Men	66.7%	33.3%	100% (225)
Women	80.0%	20.0%	100% (225)

(C) Percentage Cross-Tabulation of Question "Do you shop at IGA?" by Sex of Respondent, Column Percentage

	Yes	No
Men	45.5%	62.5%
Women	54.5%	37.5%
Total	100%	100%
(Base)	(330)	(120)

to the number of rows by the number of columns (R by C). Thus, a 3×4 table has three rows and four columns.

Percentage Cross-Tabulations

When data from a survey are cross-tabulated, percentages help the researcher understand the nature of the relationship by allowing relative comparisons. The total number of respondents or observations may be used as a **base** for computing the percentage in each cell. When the objective of the research is to identify a relationship between answers to two questions (or two variables), one of the questions is commonly chosen to be the source of the base for determining percentages. For example, look at the data in parts A, B, and C of Table 14.4. Compare part B with part C. Selecting either the row percentages or the column percentages will emphasize a particular comparison or distribution. The nature of the problem the researcher wishes to answer will determine which marginal total will serve as a base for computing percentages.

Fortunately, a conventional rule determines the direction of percentages if the researcher has identified which variable is the independent variable and

base
The number of respondents or observations (in a row or column) used as a basis for computing percentages.

which is the dependent variable: The percentages should be computed *in the direction of the independent variable*. That is, the marginal total of the independent variable should be used as the base for computing the percentages. Although survey research does not identify cause-and-effect relationships, one might argue that it would be logical to assume that a variable such as gender might predict shopping behavior, in which case independent and dependent variables may be established so as to present the most useful information.

Elaboration and Refinement

The *Oxford Universal Dictionary* defines *analysis* as "the resolution of anything complex into its simplest elements." This suggests that once the researcher has examined the basic relationship between two variables, he or she may wish to investigate this relationship under a variety of different conditions. Typically a third variable is introduced into the analysis to elaborate and refine the researcher's understanding by specifying the conditions under which the relationship between the first two variables is strongest and weakest. In other words, a more elaborate analysis asks: "Will interpretation of the relationship be modified if other variables are simultaneously considered?"

Performing the basic cross-tabulation within various subgroups of the sample is a common form of **elaboration analysis.** The researcher breaks down the analysis for each level of another variable. For example, if the researcher has cross-tabulated shopping behavior by sex (see Table 14.4) and wishes to investigate another variable (say, marital status) that may modify the original relationship, a more elaborate analysis may be conducted. Table 14.5 breaks down the responses to the question "Do you shop at IGA?" by sex and marital status. The data show that marital status does not change the original cross-tabulation relationship among women, but it does change that relationship among men. The analysis suggests that the original conclusion about the relationship between sex and shopping behavior for women be retained; the data confirm the original interpretation. However, the refinements in analysis have pointed out a relationship among men that was not immediately discernible in the two-variable case: A higher percentage of single men than married men shop at IGA. The researcher can then conclude that marital status modifies the original relationship among men—that is, that there is an interaction effect.

In this situation marital status is a moderator variable. A **moderator variable** is a third variable that, when introduced into the analysis, alters or has a contingent effect on the relationship between an independent variable and a dependent variable.

In other situations the addition of a third variable to the analysis may lead us to reject the original conclusion about the relationship. When this occurs, the

elaboration analysis
An analysis of the basic cross-tabulation for each level of a variable not previously considered, such as subgroups of the sample.

moderator variable
A third variable that, when introduced into an analysis, alters or has a contingent effect on the relationship between an independent variable and a dependent variable.

TABLE 14.5	CROSS-TABULATION OF MARITAL STATUS, SEX, AND RESPONSES TO THE QUESTION "DO YOU SHOP AT IGA?"			
	MARRIED		**SINGLE**	
	Men	**Women**	**Men**	**Women**
"Do you shop at IGA?"				
Yes	55%	80%	86%	80%
No	45%	20%	14%	20%

elaboration analysis will have indicated a **spurious relationship**—an apparent relationship between the original two variables that is not authentic. Our earlier example about high ice cream cone sales and drownings at the beach (Chapter 3) illustrated a spurious relationship.

How Many Cross-Tabulations?

Surveys may ask dozens of questions. Computer-assisted marketing researchers often indulge in "fishing expeditions," cross-tabulating every question on a survey with every other question. Thus, every possible response becomes a possible explanatory variable. All too often this activity provides reams of extra computer output, but no additional insight to management. The number of cross-tabulations should be determined early, when research objectives are stated.

DATA TRANSFORMATION

Data transformation (also called **data conversion**) is the process of changing the data from their original form to a format suitable for performing a data analysis that will achieve research objectives. Researchers often modify the values of scalar data or create new variables. For example, many researchers believe that less response bias will result if interviewers ask respondents for their year of birth rather than their age, even though the objective of the data analysis is to investigate respondents' ages in years. This presents no problem for the research analyst, because a simple data transformation is possible. The raw data coded as birth year can easily be transformed to age by subtracting the birth year from the current year.

Collapsing or combining adjacent categories of a variable is a common form of data transformation used to reduce the number of categories. For example, Likert summated scales reflect combinations of scores (raw data) from the various attitude statements. The summative score for an attitude scale with three statements is calculated as follows:

$$\text{Summative score} = \text{Variable 1} + \text{Variable 2} + \text{Variable 3}$$

This calculation can be accomplished by simple arithmetic or by programming a computer with a data transformation equation that creates a new variable for the summative score.

CALCULATING RANK ORDER

Respondents often rank order brand preferences or other variables of interest to researchers. To summarize these data for all respondents, the analyst performs a data transformation by multiplying the frequency by the rank (score) to develop a new scale that represents the summarized rank orders.

For example, suppose a manager of a frequent-flier program had ten executives rank their preferences for "dream destinations" that would be prizes in a sales promotion contest. Table 14.6 shows how the executives ranked each of four locations: Hawaii, Paris, Greece, and Hong Kong. Table 14.7 tabulates the frequencies of these rankings. To calculate a summary rank ordering, the destination with the first (highest) preference was given the lowest number (1) and the least preferred destination was assigned the highest number (4). The summarized rank orderings were obtained with the following calculations:

TABLE 14.6	INDIVIDUAL RANKINGS OF DREAM DESTINATIONS			
Executive	**Hawaii**	**Paris**	**Greece**	**Hong Kong**
1	1	2	4	3
2	1	3	4	2
3	2	1	3	4
4	2	4	3	1
5	2	1	3	4
6	3	4	1	2
7	2	3	1	4
8	1	4	2	3
9	4	3	2	1
10	2	1	3	4

TABLE 14.7	FREQUENCY TABLE OF DREAM DESTINATION RANKINGS			
	PREFERENCE RANKINGS			
Destination	**1st**	**2nd**	**3rd**	**4th**
Hawaii	3	5	1	1
Paris	3	1	3	3
Greece	2	2	4	2
Hong Kong	2	2	2	4

$$\text{Hawaii: } (3 \times 1) + (5 \times 2) + (1 \times 3) + (1 \times 4) = 20$$

$$\text{Paris: } (3 \times 1) + (1 \times 2) + (3 \times 3) + (3 \times 4) = 26$$

$$\text{Greece:} (2 \times 1) + (2 \times 2) + (4 \times 3) + (2 \times 4) = 26$$

$$\text{Hong Kong: } (2 \times 1) + (2 \times 2) + (2 \times 3) + (4 \times 4) = 28$$

The lowest total score indicates the first (highest) preference ranking. The results show the following rank ordering: (1) Hawaii, (2) Paris, (3) Greece, and (4) Hong Kong.

TABULAR AND GRAPHIC METHODS OF DISPLAYING DATA

The person who first said, "A picture is worth a thousand words" probably had graphic aids in mind. Used properly, graphic aids can clarify complex points or emphasize a message. Used improperly or sloppily, however, they can distract or even mislead. The key to effective use of graphic aids is to make them an integral part of the text. The graphics should always be interpreted in the text. This does not mean the writer should exhaustively explain an obvious chart or table, but it does mean that the text should point out the key elements of any graphic aid and relate them to the discussion in progress.

Tabular and graphic representations of the data may take a number of forms, ranging from a computer printout to an elaborate pictograph.

Tables

Tables are most useful for presenting numerical information, especially when several pieces of information have been gathered about each item discussed. The purpose of each table, however, is to facilitate the summarization and communication of the data's meaning. For example, Table 14.8 illustrates the relationships among education, income, and regional airline usage expenditures for vacation/pleasure trips. The shaded area emphasizes a key conclusion about market share. (To summarize the information in the shaded box: 32 percent of the population makes 78 percent of the expenditures.) This form of presentation simplifies interpretation.

Suppose an airline asks a question about customers' satisfaction with its baggage-handling service. In addition to showing the simple frequency for each category, most research analysts would cross-tabulate answers to the baggage-handling questions with several demographic variables such as gender, income, education, and age. Presenting multiple cross-tabulations individually in a separate table requires considerable space. Thus, many research reports use a space-saving format with either *stubheads* for rows or *bannerheads* for columns, to allow the reader to view several cross-tabulations at the same time. Table 14.9 presents several cross-tabulations in a single table with stubheads.

TABLE 14.8	REGIONAL AIRLINE USAGE FOR VACATION/ PLEASURE BY INCOME AND EDUCATION CLASS				
	Total	**Under $20,000**	**$20,000– $39,000**	**$40,000– $59,000**	**$60,000 and Over**
All consumers					
Expenditures (%)	100	10	7	16	67
Consumer units (%)	100	42	19	16	23
Index	100	26	36	100	291
Non–high school graduate					
Expenditures (%)	8	1	2	1	4
Consumer units (%)	35	21	6	4	4
Index	21	5	33	25	100
High school graduate					
Expenditures (%)	29	4	2	8	15
Consumer units (%)	30	11	6	6	7
Index	96	36	33	133	214
Attended/graduated college					
Expenditures (%)	63	5	3	7	48
Consumer units (%)	35	10	6	6	13
Index	180	50	50	116	369
				Percentage population = 32	Percentage expenditures = 78

TABLE 14.9

A STUBHEAD FORMAT ALLOWING SEVERAL CROSS-TABULATIONS TO BE INCLUDED IN A SINGLE TABLE[5]

Confidence in Church/Organized Religion

Question: I am going to read you a list of institutions in American society. Would you tell me how much confidence you, yourself, have in each one—a great deal, quite a lot, some, or very little?

The Church or Organized Religion

	Great Deal	Quite a Lot	Some	Very Little	None	No Opinion	Number of Interviews
National	42%	24%	21%	11%	1%	1%	1,528
Sex							
Men	36	27	22	13	1	1	755
Women	48	21	20	9	1	1	773
Age							
Total under 30	39	26	24	10	1	*	320
18–24 years	38	28	24	9	1	*	138
25–29 years	40	23	23	13	1	*	182
30–49 years	38	25	23	12	1	1	593
Total 50 & older	50	21	18	10	*	1	608
50–64 years	48	23	18	10	*	1	302
65 and older	52	18	18	10	1	1	306
Region							
East	33	24	28	13	1	1	388
Midwest	44	26	20	9	*	1	398
South	51	24	14	9	1	1	444
West	39	20	25	15	1	*	298
Race							
Whites	42	23	22	11	1	1	1,334
Nonwhites	45	27	18	8	1	1	184
Blacks	47	26	18	7	*	2	151
Hispanics	42	25	21	10	1	1	104

*Less than 1 percent.

Charts and Graphs

Charts translate numerical information into visual form so that relationships may be easily grasped. Although a number of standardized forms exist for presenting data in charts or graphs, the researcher may use his or her creativity to increase the effectiveness of a particular presentation. Bar charts, pie charts, line charts, and other graphic forms of presentation create strong visual impressions. Exhibit 14.1 shows simple versions of a pie chart, horizontal bar graph, vertical bar graph, and line graph.

Pie Charts   One of the most useful kinds of charts is the *pie chart,* which shows the composition of some total quantity at a particular time. Each angle, or "slice," is proportional to its percentage of the whole and should be labeled with its description and percentage. The writer should not try to include too many small slices; about six slices is a typical maximum. Companies commonly use pie charts to show how revenues were used or the composition of their sales.

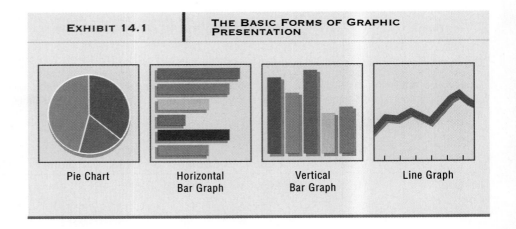

EXHIBIT 14.1 | **THE BASIC FORMS OF GRAPHIC PRESENTATION**

Pie Chart | Horizontal Bar Graph | Vertical Bar Graph | Line Graph

Line Graphs *Line graphs* are useful for showing the relationship of one variable to another. The dependent variable generally is shown on the vertical axis and the independent variable on the horizontal axis. The most common independent variable for such charts is time, but it is by no means the only one. Exhibit 14.2 depicts a multiple line graph. It shows how line graphs can display comparisons among groups over time. The line for each dependent variable

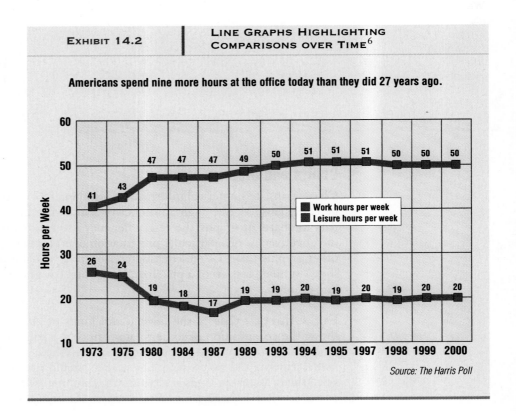

EXHIBIT 14.2 | **LINE GRAPHS HIGHLIGHTING COMPARISONS OVER TIME[6]**

Americans spend nine more hours at the office today than they did 27 years ago.

Source: The Harris Poll

WHAT WENT RIGHT?

FLORENCE NIGHTINGALE: INVENTOR OF THE PIE CHART

Florence Nightingale is remembered as a pioneering nurse and hospital reformer.[7] Less well known is her equally pioneering use of statistics to persuade people. In advocating medical reform Nightingale also promoted statistical description; she developed a uniform procedure for hospitals to report statistical information. She invented the pie chart, in which proportions are represented as wedges of a circular diagram, and she struggled to get the study of statistics introduced into higher education.

One of Nightingale's analyses compared the peacetime death rates of British soldiers and civilians. She discovered and showed that the soldiers, who lived in barracks under unhealthy conditions, were twice as likely to die as civilians of the same age and sex. She then used the soldiers' 2 percent death rate to persuade the queen and the prime minister to establish a Royal Commission on the Health of the Army. It is just as criminal, she wrote, for the army to have a mortality of 20 per 1,000 "as it would be to take 1,100 men per annum out upon Salisbury Plain and shoot them."

should be in a different color or pattern and should be clearly labeled. The researcher should not try to squeeze in too many variables; this can quickly lead to confusion rather than clarification.

Bar Charts   Bar charts show changes in the value of a dependent variable (plotted on the vertical axis) at discrete intervals of the independent variable (on the horizontal axis). A simple bar chart often presents the frequency of response to various questions. A multiple bar chart shows how multiple variables are related to the primary variable. In each case, each bar needs to be clearly identified with a different color or pattern. The researcher should not use too many divisions or dependent variables. Too much detail obscures the essential advantage of charts, which is to make relationships easy to grasp.

COMPUTER PROGRAMS FOR ANALYSIS

The proliferation of computer technology within businesses and universities has greatly facilitated tabulation and statistical analysis. Commercial statistical packages eliminate the need to write a new program every time you want to tabulate and analyze data with a computer. SAS, Statistical Package for the Social Sciences (SPSS), SYSTAT, and MINITAB are commonly used statistical packages. These user-friendly packages emphasize statistical calculations and hypothesis testing for varied types of data. They also provide programs for entering and editing data. Most of these packages contain sizable arrays of programs for descriptive analysis and univariate, bivariate, and multivariate statistical analysis. Several examples will be given in this section to illustrate how easy it is to use these statistical packages.

Microsoft Excel, Lotus 1-2-3, and Quatro Pro are spreadsheet packages that emphasize database management and allow a user to enter and edit data with minimal effort. They also incorporate some programs for descriptive analysis, graphic analysis, and limited statistical analysis. In Excel, statistical calculations can be performed using the Data Analysis and Paste Function menus shown in Exhibit 14.3. (Note: Depending on the version of Excel you have, you may have

EXHIBIT 14.3	EXCEL'S DATA ANALYSIS AND PASTE FUNCTION MENUS FOR STATISTICAL ANALYSIS

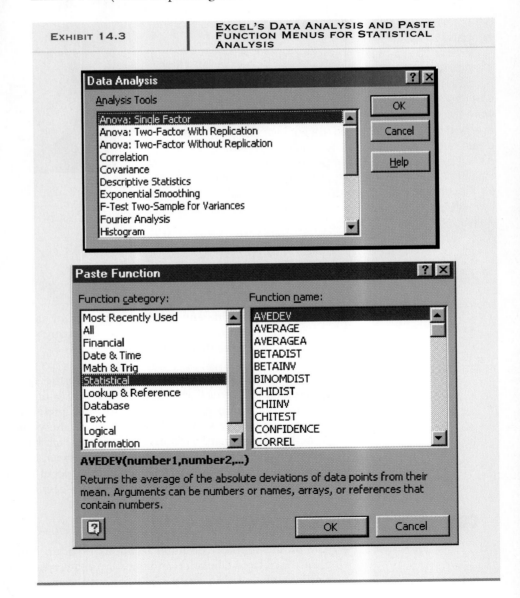

Exhibit 14.4 — SAS Computer Output of Descriptive Statistics

State = NY

Variable	N	Mean	Standard Deviation	Minimum Value	Maximum Value	Std Error of Mean	Sum	Variance	C.V.
EMP	10	142.930	232.665	12.800	788.800	73.575	1429.300	54133.0	162.782
SALES	10	5807.800	11905.127	307.000	39401.000	3764.732	58078.000	141732049.1	204.985

Key: EMP = number of employees (000)   SALES = Sales (000)

to "Add in" the statistical software applications. You will then find the enhanced functions by clicking on the Tools menu and then Data Analysis.)

Exhibit 14.4 shows an SAS computer printout of descriptive statistics for two variables: EMP (number of employees working in an MSA, or Metropolitan Statistical Area) and SALES (sales volume in dollars in an MSA) for ten MSAs. The number of data elements (N), mean, standard deviation, and other descriptive statistics are displayed.

The frequency table in Exhibit 14.5 is output from the SPSS package showing the results of a question on a survey about a commercial respondents just saw. This SPSS output gives the absolute frequency of observations, the relative frequency as a percentage of all observations, and the adjusted frequency as a percentage of the number of respondents who provided a recorded answer rather than answering "don't know" or leaving the question blank.

A histogram is similar to a bar chart. Exhibit 14.6 shows an SPSS histogram plot of purchase price data from a survey. Each bar indicates the number of purchases.

Exhibit 14.7 shows an SPSS cross-tabulation of two variables, education (EDLEVEL) and Car Country of Origin, with the row total used as a basis for percentages. (Note: The program identifies the number of respondents for whom data were not provided for both variables as missing observations.)

As you can see, statistical software programs are quite versatile, and they are extensively used in marketing research.

Exhibit 14.5 — SPSS Output Showing Frequencies[8]

Affect   Feelings about commercial you just saw

Value Label	Value	Frequency	Percent	Valid Percent	Cum Percent
liked it very much	1.00	36	6.7	6.7	6.7
liked it	2.00	169	31.3	31.6	38.3
neither liked/disliked	3.00	191	35.4	35.7	74.0
disliked it	4.00	90	16.7	16.8	90.8
disliked it very much	5.00	49	9.1	9.2	100.0
		5	.9	Missing	
	Total	540	100.0	100.0	

Valid cases   535   Missing cases   5

EXHIBIT 14.6

SPSS HISTOGRAM OUTPUT[9]

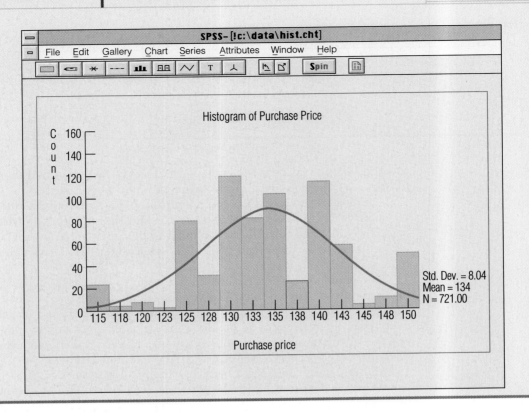

EXHIBIT 14.7

SPSS CROSS-TABULATION OUTPUT[10]

Car Country of Origin * EDUC Crosstabulation

			\multicolumn{5}{c}{EDUC}		Total
			1.00	2.00	3.00	4.00	5.00	Total
Car Country of Origin	American	Count	2	5	17	18	12	54
		% within Car Country of Origin	3.7%	9.3%	31.5%	33.3%	22.2%	100.0%
	European	Count		2	5	21	7	35
		% within Car Country of Origin		5.7%	14.3%	60.0%	20.0%	100.0%
	Japanese	Count		6	12	23	14	55
		% within Car Country of Origin		10.9%	21.8%	41.8%	25.5%	100.0%
Total		Count	2	13	34	62	33	144
		% within Car Country of Origin	1.4%	9.0%	23.6%	43.1%	22.9%	100.0%

What Is a Hypothesis?

hypothesis
An unproven proposition or supposition that tentatively explains certain facts or phenomena; a proposition that is empirically testable.

In marketing theory a **hypothesis** is an unproven proposition or supposition that tentatively explains certain facts or phenomena; it is a statement of assumption about the nature of the world. In its simplest form a hypothesis is a guess. A sales manager may hypothesize that the salespeople who are highest in product knowledge will be the most productive. An advertising manager may hypothesize that if consumers' attitudes toward a product change in a positive direction, there will be an increase in consumption of the product. Statistical techniques allow us to decide whether or not our theoretical hypothesis is confirmed by the empirical evidence.

Null and Alternative Hypotheses

null hypothesis
A statement about a status quo asserting that any change from what has been thought to be true will be due entirely to random sampling error.

alternative hypothesis
A statement indicating the opposite of the null hypothesis.

Because scientists should be bold in conjecturing but extremely cautious in testing, statistical hypotheses generally are stated in a null form. A **null hypothesis** is a statement about a status quo. It is a conservative statement that communicates the notion that any change from what has been thought to be true or observed in the past will be due entirely to random error. In fact, the true purpose of setting up the null hypothesis is to provide an opportunity for nullifying it. For example, suppose academic researchers expect that highly dogmatic (that is, closed-minded) consumers will be less likely to try a new product than will less dogmatic consumers. The researchers would generally formulate a conservative null hypothesis. The null hypothesis in this case would be that there is *no difference* between high dogmatics and low dogmatics in their willingness to try an innovation. The **alternative hypothesis** would be that there *is* a difference between high dogmatics and low dogmatics. It states the opposite of the null hypothesis.

Generally we assign the symbol H_0 to the null hypothesis and the symbol H_1 to the alternative hypothesis. The purpose of hypothesis testing is to determine which of the two hypotheses is correct. The process of hypothesis testing is slightly more complicated than that of estimating parameters because the decision maker must choose between the two hypotheses. However, the student need not worry because the mathematical calculations are no more difficult than those we have already made.

The Hypothesis-Testing Procedure

The process of hypothesis testing goes as follows. First, we determine a statistical hypothesis. We then imagine what the sampling distribution of the mean would be if this hypothesis were a true statement of the nature of the population. Next, we take an actual sample and calculate the sample mean (or appropriate statistic, if we are not concerned about the mean). We know from our previous discussions of the sampling distribution of the mean that obtaining a sample value that is exactly the same as the population parameter is highly unlikely; we expect some small difference (although it may be large) between the sample mean and the population mean. We then must determine if the deviation between the obtained value of the sample mean and its expected value (based on the statistical hypothesis) would have occurred by chance alone—say, 5 times out of 100— if in fact the statistical hypothesis had been true. In other words, we ask this question: "Has the sample mean deviated substantially from the mean of the hypothesized sampling distribution by a value large enough for us to conclude that this large a deviation would be somewhat rare if the statistical hypothesis were true?" Suppose we observe that the sample value differs from the expected value. Before we can conclude that these results are improbable (or even probable), we must have some standard, or decision rule, for determining if in fact we should reject the null hypothesis and accept the alternative hypothesis. Statisticians define this decision criterion as the *significance level*.

significance level
The critical probability in choosing between the null and alternative hypotheses; the probability level that is too low to warrant support of the null hypothesis.

The **significance level** is the critical probability in choosing between the null hypothesis and the alternative hypothesis. The level of significance determines the probability level—say, .05 or .01—that is to be considered too low to warrant support of the null hypothesis. Assuming the null hypothesis being tested is true, if the probability of occurrence of the observed data is smaller than the significance level, then the data suggest that the null hypothesis should be rejected. In other words, there has been evidence to support contradiction of the null hypothesis, which is equivalent to supporting the alternative hypothesis.

In discussing confidence intervals (the set of acceptable hypotheses), statisticians use the term *confidence level,* or *confidence coefficient,* to refer to the level of probability associated with an interval estimate. However, when discussing hypothesis testing, statisticians change their terminology and call this the *significance level,* α (the Greek letter *alpha*).

An Example of Hypothesis Testing

An example should help to clarify the nature of hypothesis testing. Suppose the Red Lion restaurant is concerned about its store image, one aspect of which is the friendliness of the service. In a personal interview customers are asked to indicate their perceptions of service on a 5-point scale, where 1 indicates "very unfriendly" service and 5 indicates "very friendly" service. The scale is assumed to be an interval scale, and experience has shown that the previous distribution of this attitudinal measurement assessing the service dimension was approximately normal.

Now, suppose the researcher entertains the hypothesis that customers feel the restaurant has neither friendly nor unfriendly service. The researcher formulates the null hypothesis that the mean is equal to 3.0:

$$H_0: \mu = 3.0$$

The alternative hypothesis is that the mean does not equal 3.0:

$$H_1: \mu \neq 3.0$$

Next, the researcher must decide on a region of rejection. Exhibit 14.8 shows a sampling distribution of the mean assuming the null hypothesis (that is, assuming $\mu = 3.0$). The darkly shaded area shows the region of rejection when $\alpha = .025$ in each tail of the curve. In other words, the *region of rejection* shows those values that are very unlikely to occur if the null hypothesis is true, but relatively probable if the alternative hypothesis is true. The values within the lighter area are called *acceptable at the 95 percent confidence level* (or 5 percent significance level, or .05 alpha level), and if we find that our sample mean lies within this region of acceptance, we conclude that the null hypothesis is true. More precisely, we fail to reject the null hypothesis. In other words, the range of acceptance (1) identifies those acceptable values that reflect a difference from the hypothesized mean in the null hypothesis and (2) shows the range within which any difference is so minuscule that we would conclude that this difference was due to random sampling error rather than to a false null hypothesis.

EXHIBIT 14.8

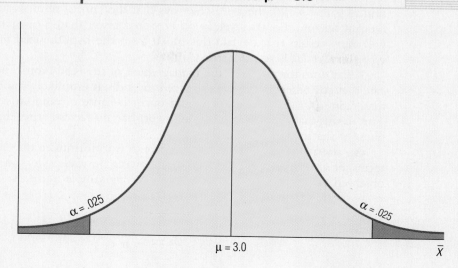

A SAMPLING DISTRIBUTION OF THE MEAN ASSUMING μ = 3.0

$\alpha = .025$ $\alpha = .025$

$\mu = 3.0$ $\bar{X}$

In our example, the Red Lion restaurant hired research consultants who collected a sample of 225 interviews. The mean score on the 5-point scale equaled 3.78. (If σ is known, it is used in the analysis; however, this is rarely true and was not true in this case.[11]) The sample standard deviation was $S = 1.5$. Now we have enough information to test the hypothesis.

The researcher has decided that the decision rule will be to set the significance level at the .05 level. This means that in the long run the probability of making an erroneous decision when H_0 is true will be fewer than 5 times in 100 (.05). From the table of the standardized normal distribution, the researcher finds that the Z score of 1.96 represents a probability of .025 that a sample mean will lie above 1.96 standard errors from μ. Likewise, the table shows that about .025 of all sample means will fall below −1.96 standard errors from μ.

The values that lie exactly on the boundary of the region of rejection are called the **critical values** of μ. Theoretically, the critical values are $Z = -1.96$ and $+1.96$. Now we must transform these critical Z-values to the sampling distribution of the mean for this image study. The critical values are

critical values
The values that lie exactly on the boundary of the region of rejection.

$$\text{Critical value—lower limit} = \mu - ZS_{\bar{X}} \text{ or } \mu - Z\frac{S}{\sqrt{n}}$$

$$= 3.0 - 1.96\left(\frac{1.5}{\sqrt{225}}\right)$$

$$= 3.0 - 1.96(.1)$$

$$= 3.0 - .196$$

$$= 2.804$$

$$\text{Critical value—upper limit} = \mu + ZS_{\bar{X}} \text{ or } \mu + Z\frac{S}{\sqrt{n}}$$

$$= 3.0 + 1.96\left(\frac{1.5}{\sqrt{225}}\right)$$

$$= 3.0 + 1.96(.1)$$

$$= 3.0 + .196$$

$$= 3.196$$

Based on the survey, $\bar{X} = 3.78$. In this case, the sample mean is contained in the region of rejection (see Exhibit 14.9). Since the sample mean is greater than the critical value, 3.196, the researcher says that the sample result is statistically significant beyond the .05 level. In other words, fewer than 5 of each 100 samples will show results that deviate this much from the hypothesized null hypothesis when in fact H_0 is actually true.

What does this mean to the management of the Red Lion? The results indicate that customers believe the service is friendly. It is unlikely (probability of less than 5 in 100) that this result would occur because of random sampling error. This means that the restaurant should worry about factors other than the friendliness of the service personnel.

An alternative way to test the hypothesis is to formulate the decision rule in terms of the Z-statistic. Using the following formula, we can calculate the observed value of the Z-statistic given a certain sample mean, $\bar{X}$:

$$Z_{obs} = \frac{\bar{X} - \mu}{S_{\bar{X}}}$$

$$= \frac{3.78 - \mu}{S_{\bar{X}}}$$

$$= \frac{3.78 - 3.0}{.1}$$

$$= \frac{.78}{.1}$$

$$= 7.8$$

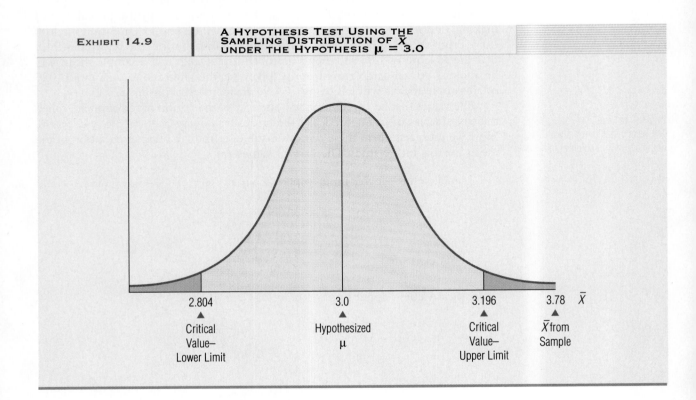

EXHIBIT 14.9

A HYPOTHESIS TEST USING THE SAMPLING DISTRIBUTION OF $\bar{X}$ UNDER THE HYPOTHESIS $\mu = 3.0$

| 2.804 | 3.0 | 3.196 | 3.78 $\bar{X}$ |
| Critical Value– Lower Limit | Hypothesized μ | Critical Value– Upper Limit | $\bar{X}$ from Sample |

In this case, the Z-value is 7.8 and we find that we have met the criterion of statistical significance at the .05 level. This result is statistically significant at the .000001 level.

THE CHI-SQUARE TEST FOR GOODNESS OF FIT

chi-square (χ^2) test
A hypothesis test that allows for investigation of statistical significance in the analysis of a frequency distribution.

Table 14.10 shows the responses to a survey to investigate awareness of a particular brand of automobile tire. This frequency distribution, or one-dimensional table from a sample of 100, suggests that the majority of the population (60 percent) is aware of the brand.

The **chi-square (χ^2)** test allows us to test for significance in the analysis of frequency distributions. Thus, categorical data on variables such as sex, education, or dichotomous answers may be statistically analyzed. Suppose, for example, that we wish to test the null hypothesis that the number of consumers aware of a certain tire brand equals the number unaware of the brand. The logic inherent in the χ^2 test allows us to compare the observed frequencies (O_i) with the expected frequencies (E_i) based on our theoretical ideas about the population distribution or our presupposed proportions. In other words, the technique tests whether the data come from a certain probability distribution. It tests the "goodness of fit" of the observed distribution with the expected distribution.

Calculation of the chi-square statistic allows us to determine whether the difference between the observed frequency distribution and the expected frequency distribution can be attributed to sampling variation. The steps in this process are as follows:

1. Formulate the null hypothesis and determine the expected frequency of each answer.
2. Determine the appropriate significance level.
3. Calculate the χ^2 value, using the observed frequencies from the sample and the expected frequencies.
4. Make the statistical decision by comparing the calculated χ^2 value with the critical χ^2 value.

To analyze the brand awareness data in Table 14.10, start with a null hypothesis that suggests that the number of respondents aware of the brand will equal the number of respondents unaware of it. Thus, the expected probability of each answer (aware or unaware) is .5. In a sample of 100, 50 people would be expected to respond yes, or aware, and 50 would be expected to respond no, or unaware. After the researcher has determined that the chi-square test is appropriate at the .05 level of significance (or some other probability level), the chi-square statistic may be calculated.

TABLE 14.10	ONE-WAY FREQUENCY TABLE FOR BRAND AWARENESS

Awareness of Tire Manufacturer's Brand	Frequency
Aware	60
Unaware	40
	100

To calculate the chi-square statistic, use the following formula:

$$\chi^2 = \sum \frac{(O_i - E_i)^2}{E_i}$$

where

χ^2 = chi-square statistic
O_i = observed frequency in the ith cell
E_i = expected frequency in the ith cell

Sum the squared differences:

$$\chi^2 = \frac{(O_1 - E_1)^2}{E_1} + \frac{(O_2 - E_2)^2}{E_2}$$

Thus, we determine that the chi-square value equals 4:

$$\chi^2 = \frac{(60 - 50)^2}{50} + \frac{(40 - 50)^2}{50}$$
$$= 4$$

Table 14.11 shows the detailed calculation for this problem.

TABLE 14.11	CALCULATING THE CHI-SQUARE STATISTIC				
Brand Awareness	Observed Frequency (O_i)	Expected Probability	Expected Frequency (E_i)	($O_i - E_i$)	$\frac{(O_i - E_i)^2}{E_i}$
Aware	60	.5	50	10	$\frac{100}{50} = 2.0$
Unaware	40	.5	50	−10	$\frac{100}{50} = 2.0$
Total	100	1.0	100	0	$\chi^2 = 4.0$

Like many other probability distributions, the χ^2 distribution is not a single probability curve, but a family of curves. These curves, although similar, vary according to the number of degrees of freedom ($k - 1$). Thus, we must calculate the number of degrees of freedom. (*Degrees of freedom* refers to the number of observations that can be varied without changing the constraints or assumptions associated with a numerical system.) We do this as follows:

$$d.f. = k - 1$$

where

k = number of cells associated with column or row data[12]

In the brand awareness problem there are only two categorical responses. Thus, the degrees of freedom equal 1 ($d.f. = 2 - 1 = 1$).

Now the computed chi-square value needs to be compared with the critical chi-square values associated with the .05 probability level with 1 degree of freedom. In Table 4 of the Appendix the critical chi-square value is 3.84. Since the calculated chi-square is larger than the tabular chi-square, the null hypothesis—that the observed values are comparable to the expected values—is rejected.[13]

CHOOSING THE APPROPRIATE TECHNIQUE

Now that we have looked at two statistical techniques for hypothesis testing, note that a number of descriptive and statistical techniques are available to assist the researcher in interpreting data. The choice of the method of analysis depends on (1) the number of variables, (2) the scale of measurement, and (3) the type of question to be answered.

Number of Variables

The number of variables to be simultaneously investigated is a primary consideration in the choice of statistical technique. A researcher who is interested only in the average number of times a prospective home buyer visits financial institutions to shop for interest rates concentrates on investigating only one variable at a time. The researcher conducts *univariate statistical analysis* when attempting to generalize from a sample about one variable at a time. Statistically describing the relationship between two variables at one time, such as the relationship between advertising expenditures and sales volume, requires *bivariate statistical analysis*. Tests of group differences and measuring the relationship (association) among variables are the subjects of Chapter 15.

Scale of Measurement

The scale of measurement on which the data are based or the type of measurement reflected in the data determines the permissible statistical techniques and appropriate empirical operations to perform. As we discussed earlier, testing a hypothesis about a mean requires interval-scaled or ratio-scaled data. We have also seen that the chi-square test can be used when the researcher employs a nominal scale to measure consumer awareness versus unawareness.

Exhibit 14.10 shows the appropriate descriptive statistics for each type of scale. It is important to remember that all statistics appropriate for lower-order scales (nominal is the lowest) are suitable for higher-order scales (ratio is the highest).

The most sophisticated form of statistical analysis for nominal-scale data is counting. Because numbers are merely labels for classification purposes, they have no quantitative meaning. The researcher tallies the frequency in each category and identifies which category contains the highest number of observations (individuals, objects, etc.). An ordinal scale provides data that may be rank ordered from lowest to highest. For example, the ranking of brand preferences generally employs an ordinal scale. Observations may be associated with percentile ranks. With ordinal data, the median may be used as the average. Because all statistical analyses appropriate for lower-order scales are suitable for higher-order scales, an interval scale may be used as a nominal scale to uniquely classify or as an ordinal scale to preserve order. In addition, an interval scale's property of equal intervals allows researchers to compare differences among scale values and to perform arithmetic operations such as addition and subtraction. Numbers may be changed, but the numerical operations must preserve order and relative magnitudes of differences. The mean and standard deviation may be calculated from true interval-scale data. A ratio scale has all the properties of nominal, ordinal, and interval scales. In addition, it allows researchers to compare absolute magnitudes,

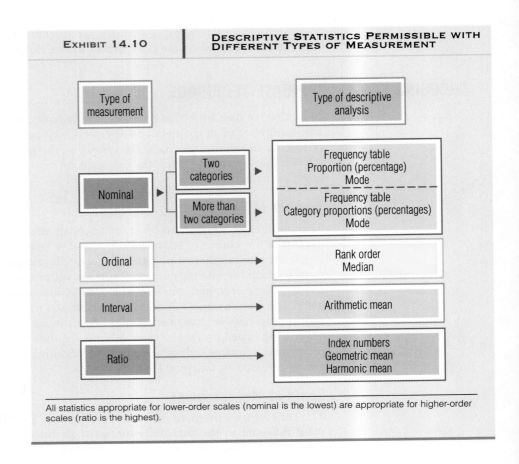

All statistics appropriate for lower-order scales (nominal is the lowest) are appropriate for higher-order scales (ratio is the highest).

because the scale has an absolute zero point. Using the actual quantities for arithmetic operations is permissible. Thus, the ratios of scale values are meaningful.

Type of Question to Be Answered

The type of question the researcher is attempting to answer is a consideration in the choice of statistical technique. For example, we already illustrated a hypothesis test for a researcher who wants to determine whether the calculated mean value of a variable differs from the expected value. Marketing researchers frequently question whether a mean, a proportion, or a distribution differs from what was expected.

Two other frequently asked questions are (1) Are there differences between two (or more) groups and (2) is there a relationship between two or more variables? These topics are discussed in the following chapter.

Exhibit 14.11 provides guidelines for selecting the appropriate statistical method. Although you may be unfamiliar with most of them, the exhibit illustrates that a variety of statistical techniques exist and the proper one may be selected based on the research situation. A complete discussion of all the relevant techniques is beyond the scope of our discussion thus far. The important point is that the researcher should anticipate the method of statistical analysis before selecting the research design and before determining the type of data to collect. Once the data are collected, the research design will reflect the initial approach to analysis of the problem.

Sample Marketing Problem	Statistical Question to Be Asked	Possible Test of Statistical Significance
Interval or Ratio Scales		
Compare actual vs. hypothetical values of average salary	Is the sample mean significantly different from the hypothesized population mean?	Z-test (if sample is large) t-test (if sample is small)
Ordinal Scales		
Compare actual evaluations and expected evaluations	Does the distribution of scores on a scale with the categories excellent, good, fair, and poor differ from the expected distribution?	chi-square test
Determine ordered preferences for all brands in a product class	Does a set of rank orderings in a sample differ from an expected or hypothetical rank ordering?	Kolmogorov-Smirnov test
Nominal Scales		
Identify sex of key executives	Is the number of female executives equal to the number of male executives?	chi-square test
Indicate percentage of key executives who are male	Is the proportion of male executives the same as the hypothesized proportion?	t-test of a proportion

SUMMARY

Descriptive analysis refers to the transformation of raw data into an understandable form. Descriptive information is obtained by summarizing, categorizing, rearranging, and other forms of analysis. *Tabulation* refers to the orderly arrangement of data in a table or other summary format. Percentages, cumulative percentages, and frequency distributions are useful. The data may be described by measures of central tendency, such as the mean, median, or mode. Cross-tabulation shows how one variable relates to another to reveal differences between groups. Such cross-tabulations should be limited to categories related to the research problem and purpose. Putting the results into percentage form facilitates intergroup comparisons.

Performing the basic cross-tabulation within various subgroups of the sample is a common form of elaboration analysis. Elaboration analysis often identifies moderator variables or spurious relationships. A moderator variable is a third variable that, when introduced into the analysis, alters or has a contingent effect on the relationship between an independent variable and a dependent variable. A spurious relationship exists when adding a third variable to the analysis indicates that the relationship between the original two variables was not authentic.

Data transformation is the process of changing data from their original form to a format that is more suitable for performing a data analysis. A data transformation is performed in order to summarize rank-order data. Rank scores are multiplied by their frequency of occurrence to develop a new scale that represents summarized rank orderings.

Tables and graphs help to simplify and clarify research data. Computer software greatly facilitates descriptive analysis. Many programs that enhance the construction of graphs and charts are available.

A hypothesis is a statement of assumption about the nature of the world. A null hypothesis is a statement about the status quo. An alternative hypothesis is a statement that indicates the opposite of the null hypothesis.

In hypothesis testing, a researcher states a null hypothesis about a population mean and then attempts to disprove it. The Z-test defines a region of rejection based on a significance level of the standardized normal distribution beyond which it is unlikely that the null hypothesis is true. If a sample mean is contained in the region of rejection, the null hypothesis is rejected.

The chi-square test allows testing of statistical significance in the analysis of frequency distributions: An observed distribution of categorical data from a sample may be compared with an expected distribution for goodness of fit.

A number of appropriate statistical techniques are available to assist the researcher in interpreting data. The choice of statistical analysis method depends on (1) the number of variables, (2) the scale of measurement, and (3) the type of question to be answered.

Key Terms and Concepts

descriptive analysis
frequency table
cross–tabulation
contingency table
base
elaboration analysis

moderator variable
spurious relationship
data transformation (data
  conversion)
hypothesis
null hypothesis

alternative hypothesis
significance level
critical values
chi-square (χ^2) test

Questions for Review and Critical Thinking

1. A survey asked respondents to respond to the statement "My work is interesting." Interpret the frequency distribution in the following SPSS output.

My work is interesting.

Category Label	Code	Abs. Freq.	Rel. Freq. (Pct.)	Adj. Freq. (Pct.)	Cum. Freq. (Pct.)
Very true	1	650	23.9	62.4	62.4
Somewhat true	2	303	11.2	29.1	91.5
Not very true	3	61	2.2	5.9	97.3
Not at all true	4	28	1.0	2.7	100.0
	•	1,673	61.6	Missing	
	Total	2,715	100.0	100.0	
Valid cases	1,042	Missing cases	1,673		

2. Use the data in the following table to (a) prepare a frequency distribution of the respondents' ages and (b) cross-tabulate the respondents' genders with cola preference.

Individual	Gender	Age	Cola Preference	Weekly Purchases
John	M	19	Coke	2
Al	M	17	Pepsi	5
Bill	M	20	Pepsi	7
Mary	F	20	Coke	2
Jim	M	18	Coke	4
Karen	F	16	Coke	4
Tom	M	17	Pepsi	8
Dawn	F	19	Pepsi	1

3. Data on the average size of a soda (in ounces) at all 30 major league baseball parks are as follows: 14, 18, 20, 16, 16, 12, 14, 16, 14, 16, 16, 16, 14, 14, 16, 20, 12, 16, 20, 12, 16, 16, 24, 16, 16, 14, 14, 12, 14, 20. The results of an Excel Descriptive Statistics analysis of these data are shown below. Interpret the output.

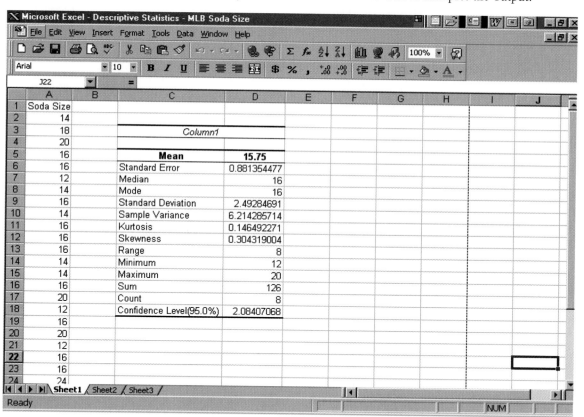

4. Interpret the following table giving the percentage of individuals on a low-fat or low-cholesterol diet by gender and age.

Age Group	Women	Men	Total
16–24	29%	13%	21%
25–34	43	25	34
35–44	46	28	37
45–54	54	32	43
55+	49	35	43

5. Visit your local computer center and see if it has SPSS, SAS, SYSTAT, or MINITAB computer packages.
6. What types of scalar data (that is, nominal, ordinal, interval, or ratio) typically are used in cross–tabulation analysis?
7. It has been argued that analysis and interpretation of data are managerial arts. Comment.
8. The data in the following tables show some of the results of an Internal Revenue Service survey of taxpayers. Analyze and interpret the data.

The last year you filed an income tax return, did you get any suggestions or information that was especially helpful to you in filing?

	Absolute Frequency	Rel. Freq. (Pct.)	Adj. Freq. (Pct.)
Yes	156	29.5	29.8
No	368	69.7	70.2
Don't know	1	.2	Missing
Not ascertained	1	.2	Missing
Blank	2	.4	Missing
	528	100.0	100.0

What kind of information was it?

	Absolute Frequency	Rel. Freq. (Pct.)	Adj. Freq. (Pct.)
Learned about energy credit	8	1.5	5.4
Learned about another deduction	46	8.7	31.3
Obtained info. about forms to use	9	1.7	6.1
Received pamphlets/forms	40	7.6	27.2
Other	44	8.3	29.9
Don't know	6	1.1	Missing
Not ascertained	2	.4	Missing
Blank	373	70.6	Missing
	528	100.0	100.0

9. What is the purpose of a statistical hypothesis?
10. What is significance level? How does a researcher choose a significance level?
11. List the steps in the hypothesis–testing procedure.
12. After a bumper crop, a mushroom grower hypothesizes that mushrooms will remain at the wholesale average price of $1 per pound. State the null hypothesis and the alternative hypothesis.
13. Assume you have the following data: H_0: $\mu = 200$, $S = 30$, $n = 64$, and $\bar{X} = 218$. Conduct a two-tailed hypothesis test at the .05 significance level.
14. Assume you have the following data: H_0: $\mu = 2,450$, $S = 400$, $n = 100$, and $\bar{X} = 2,300$. Conduct a hypothesis test at the .01 significance level.
15. The answers to a researcher's question will be nominally scaled. What statistical test is appropriate to compare the sample data with the hypothesized population data?
16. What factors determine the choice of the appropriate statistical technique?
17. A researcher plans to ask employees whether they favor, oppose, or are indifferent to a change in the company retirement program. Formulate a null hypothesis for a chi-square test, and determine the expected frequencies for each answer.

18. A data-processing analyst for a research supplier finds that preliminary computer runs of survey results show that consumers love a client's new product. The employee buys a large block of the client's stock. Is this ethical?

19. A researcher finds that in a survey of 100 people, 15 respondents answer "don't know" to a question that has "yes" and "no" as alternatives. The researcher uses 85 as a base for calculating the percentage of respondents who answer "yes" or "no." Is this the correct choice?

Exploring the Internet

1. The Megapenny Project is located at http://www. kokogiak.com/megapenny/default.asp. Visit this site to get an insight into what large numbers mean.

2. Go to http://www.spss.com and click on Industries and Market Research. What services does the company provide?

3. To see descriptive data analysis in a report on smokeless tobacco, go to the Federal Trade Commission's Bureau of Consumer Protection at http://www.ftc. gov/bcp/reports/smokeless97.htm.

4. Economagic.com's Economic Time Series Page provides links to charts and data for over 68,000 series at http://www.economagic.com.

5. The Data and Story Library is an online library of datafiles and stories that illustrate the use of basic statistics methods. The Web address is http://lib.stat. cmu.edu/ DASL/.

6. StatLib, at http://lib.stat.cmu.edu/, is a system for distributing statistical software, datasets, and information by electronic mail, FTP, and the World Wide Web.

WebSurveyor Activities

The WebSurveyor Desktop software allows you to control how results are displayed using the Chart Toolbox. Results can be displayed in the following formats: Bar, Horizontal Bar, Pie, Area, Line, Scatter, and Text.

Run the WebSurveyor Desktop software, and click Example Internet Usage Survey under the heading "Open a sample survey with real data" from the Getting Started Wizard. (If the Getting Started Wizard does not appear, click Tools and then Options from the main menu, make sure "Display the Getting Started Wizard for new surveys" is checked, and then click OK. Next click File and then New from the main menu, and then click Example Internet Usage Survey under the heading "Open a sample survey with real data.")

Using the Chart Toolbox, view the results for question 1 in each format. Which one do you prefer? Why?

Cross Tabulation Analysis

WebSurveyor's cross-tabulation feature allows you to evaluate relationships between responses to two different questions. The Cross Tabs feature of WebSurveyor Desktop is accessed through the Chart Toolbox. First click on Chart Toolbox. You can perform a Cross Tab analysis by selecting a chart type of **Text Only** on questions of the following types: Select Only One, Select All That Apply, Numeric Values, and Date Values. As soon as you change the chart type to text only, you should see a **"Cross Tab"** tab appear in the Chart Toolbox. The Example Internet Usage Survey (Sample3.ws3) was used to create the cross-tabulation shown on the next page.

Using question 1: "How long have you been using the Internet?" from the Example Internet Usage Survey opened above, perform cross-tabulation on gender, marital status, and income.

Filter

Using a filter is a great way to temporarily isolate parts of your data—for example, to view only the responses from those who answered "Male" to the question of gender and "Between 35 and 45" to the question of age.

When a filter is applied, it affects all of the analysis, reports, and data exports. You can create a filter by clicking the Set Filter . . . button in the Analysis window. Use question 6 and view only the female answers. If you understand the operation, use the filter to view the answers of divorced females.

Old School or New School

Three academic researchers investigated the idea that, in America in sports, there are two segments with opposing views on what constitutes the goal of competition (i.e., winning versus self-actualization) and the acceptable/desirable way of achieving this goal.[14] Those who believe in "winning at any cost" are proponents of sports success as a product and can be labeled "new school" (NS) individuals. The new school is founded on notions of the player before the team, loyalty to the highest bidder, and high-tech production and consumption of professional sports. On the other hand, those who value the process of sports and believe that "how you play the game matters" can be labeled "old school" (OS) individuals. The old school emerges from old-fashioned American notions of the team before the

player, sportsmanship and loyalty above all else, and competition simply for the "love of the game." The sample was drawn from attendees at a university spring season football intra-squad scrimmage.

Open the survey using the WebSurveyor Desktop software by selecting File and then Open from the main menu, select the file named "Sports.ws3," and go to Analysis. Select three questions (perhaps "most professional athletes have become too materialistic," "have no sense of loyalty to the team," and "are more interested in making money than playing the game"). Prepare a frequency distribution for each question and write a short report.

2001 Marketing Professionals Salary Survey

Open the 2001 Marketing Professionals Salary Survey using the WebSurveyor Desktop software. Click Analysis and go to the question "How did you find your last job?" What conclusions can you draw from the answers to this question?

CASE 14.1   QUALITY MOTORS

Quality Motors is an automobile dealership that regularly advertises in its local market area. It claims that a certain make and model of car averages 30 miles to a gallon of gas and mentions that this figure may vary with driving conditions. A local consumer group wishes to verify the advertising claim. To do so, it selects a sample of recent purchasers of this make and model of automobile. It asks them to drive their cars until two tanks of gasoline have been used up and to record the mileage. The group then calculates and records the miles per gallon for each car. The data in Case Exhibit 14.1-1 portray the results of the tests.

Questions

1. Formulate a statistical hypothesis appropriate for the consumer group's purpose.
2. Calculate the mean average miles per gallon. Compute the sample variance and sample standard deviation.
3. Construct the appropriate statistical test for your hypothesis, using a .05 significance level.

CASE EXHIBIT 14.1-1   MILES PER GALLON INFORMATION

Purchaser	Miles per Gallon	Purchaser	Miles per Gallon
1	30.9	14	27.0
2	24.5	15	26.7
3	31.2	16	31.0
4	28.7	17	23.5
5	35.1	18	29.4
6	29.0	19	26.3
7	28.8	20	27.5
8	23.1	21	28.2
9	31.0	22	28.4
10	30.2	23	29.1
11	28.4	24	21.9
12	29.3	25	30.9
13	24.2		

CASE 14.2   COASTAL STAR SALES CORPORATION (B)

See Coastal Star Sales Corporation (A), Case 13.1, for a description of the data.

Questions

1. Develop a hypothesis concerning the average age of the sales force at Coastal Star and test the hypothesis.
2. Calculate the mean for the previous year's sales, and use it as the basis for forming a hypothesis concerning the current year's sales. Test the hypothesis concerning the current year's sales.

The research for Downy-Q is an example of a commercial test that was conducted when an advertising campaign for an established brand had run its course.[15] The revised campaign, "Fighting the Cold," emphasized that Downy-Q was an "extra-warm quilt"; previous research had demonstrated that extra warmth was an important and deliverable product quality. The commercial test was requested to measure the campaign's ability to generate purchase interest.

The marketing department had recommended this revised advertising campaign and was now anxious to know how effectively this commercial would perform. The test concluded that "Fighting the Cold" was a persuasive commercial. It also demonstrated that the new campaign would have greater appeal to specific market segments.

Method

Brand choices for the same individuals were obtained before and after viewing the commercial. The commercial was tested in 30-second, color-moving, storyboard form in a theater test. Invited viewers were shown programming with commercial inserts. Qualified respondents were women who had bought quilts in outlets that carried Downy-Q. The results are shown in Case Exhibits 14.3-1 through 14.3-4.

Question

Interpret the data in these tables. What recommendations and conclusions would you offer to Downy-Q management?

CASE EXHIBIT 14.3-1	SHIFTS IN BRAND CHOICE BEFORE AND AFTER SHOWING OF DOWNY-Q QUILT COMMERCIAL

Question: We are going to give away a series of prizes. If you are selected as one of the winners, which of the following would you truly want to win?

Brand Choice after Commercial	BRAND CHOICE BEFORE COMMERCIAL (%)	
	Downy-Q (n = 23)	Other Brand (n = 237)
Downy-Q	78	19
Other brand	22	81

CASE EXHIBIT 14.3-2	PRE/POST INCREMENT IN CHOICE OF DOWNY-Q

Question: We are going to give away a series of prizes. If you are selected as one of the winners, which of the following would you truly want to win? (Check list.)

Demographic Group	"FIGHTING THE COLD"		NORM: ALL QUILT COMMERCIALS	
	Base	Score	Average	Range
Total audience	(260)	+15	+10	6–19
By marital status				
Married	(130)	+17		
Not married	(130)	+12		
By age				
Under 35	(130)	+14		
35 and over	(130)	+15		
By employment status				
Not employed	(90)	+13		
Employed	(170)	+18		

ADJECTIVE CHECKLIST FOR DOWNY-Q QUILT COMMERCIAL

Question: Which of these words do you feel come closest to describing the commercial you've just seen?
(Check list.)

Adjective	"Fighting the Cold" (%)	Norm: All Quilt Commercials (%)
Positive		
Appealing	18	24
Clever	11	40
Convincing	20	14
Effective	19	23
Entertaining	5	24
Fast moving	12	21
Genuine	7	4
Imaginative	7	21
Informative	24	18
Interesting	13	17
Original	7	20
Realistic	8	3
Unusual	3	8
Negative		
Amateurish	9	11
Bad Taste	4	4
Dull	33	20
Repetitious	17	16
Silly	8	19
Slow	8	7
Unbelievable	3	5
Unclear	3	2
Unimportant	14	14
Uninteresting	32	19

PRODUCT ATTRIBUTE CHECKLIST FOR DOWNY-Q

Question: Which of the following statements do you feel apply to Downy-Q?
(Mark as many or as few as you feel apply.)

Attributes	"Fighting the Cold" (%)
Extra warm	56
Lightweight	48
Pretty designs	45
Durable fabrics	28
Nice fabrics	27
Good construction	27

American Pharmaceutical Industries is a relatively well-established firm whose major source of revenue is derived from physician-prescribed drugs. Until recently most of the company's significant marketing research activities were contracted out to agencies that specialized in this type of research. However, the company has made a major decision to establish its own marketing research department under the direction of Franklin Link. Link is directly responsible to the vice president for marketing, who holds a Ph.D. in marketing. Link himself has several years of research experience with a major manufacturer of hospital and medical office supplies.

Virtually all the research American Pharmaceutical Industries has conducted in the past, and most of what it expects to conduct in the future, closely relates to very specific questions. However, at Link's suggestion, senior corporate management has approved a relatively extensive study on physician decision making with regard to the selection of drugs. Part of the data-gathering process involves personal as well as telephone interviews in which the interviewer represents himself or herself as an employee of a fictitious marketing research agency. Since some of the questions involve having physicians make evaluative statements about specific brands or drug companies, it is believed that a response bias might be introduced if American Pharmaceutical Industries were identified. Moreover, the interviewers were instructed to tell physicians that the research agency was conducting the research for its own general purposes and not for a specific client. This procedure was not discussed with George Hempel, vice president for marketing.

Physician cooperation was relatively good, and Link felt the data to be of high quality and considerable practical value. The project was completed at the end of Link's seventh month with American Pharmaceutical Industries, and he was eager to make an extensive report to senior management. Link felt that they would share his feeling about the merits of the study. Link asked Hempel if a meeting with senior management could be arranged. Hempel asked for a written report first and was provided with an extensive document. To the vice president's dismay, the report contained considerable information that directly and indirectly seriously challenged the wisdom of much of American Pharmaceutical Industries' marketing strategy for introducing new products while supporting the general strategy for well-established products. Hempel directed Link to write up a brief summary of the research results pertaining to well-established products and to make only passing reference to the implications of the research for new product marketing. This report was to serve as a substitute for the meeting Link had requested.

Question

What ethical questions about data collection and reporting of results does American Pharmaceutical Industries face?

DIFFERENCES BETWEEN GROUPS AND RELATIONSHIPS AMONG VARIABLES

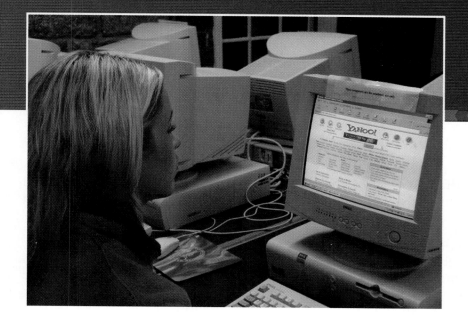

A 2001 Roper Starch Worldwide and Yahoo! Internet Life survey found that 38 percent of Internet users have a household income of more than $50,000, compared to 12 percent of those who do not go on the Internet.[1] The median age for net surfers is 38 years, versus 49 years for their so-called offline counterparts. More than one-third (37 percent) of Internet users are college graduates, compared to 11 percent of the offliners, and 26 percent hold executive or professional level jobs, compared to only 7 percent of those who don't surf the net. The majority (88 percent) own American cars and are more likely to visit travel Web sites than news, weather, or game sites. They also

- Change jobs more often than do offline consumers.
- Are more likely to run up credit card balances.
- Prefer beer and liquor to coffee.
- Appear to be more optimistic about their personal future.
- Are more likely to believe in the prospects of technological innovations, such as cars that drive themselves and portable devices that monitor health.

In the month before the survey, 74 percent of Internet consumers visited a department store, compared to 61 percent of the offline consumers. More than half (51 percent) visited a clothing store, compared to 37 percent of non–Internet users, and 40 percent made a trip to the hardware store, compared to 37 percent of the offliners. More than a third (38 percent) went to a video store, compared to 23 percent of non–Internet users, and 36 percent browsed the aisles in bookstores, compared to 16 percent of the offliners.

Making comparisons such as the preceding ones involves bivariate analysis, the topic of this chapter. The purpose of descriptive analysis is to summarize data. After summarizing the data, the

What you will learn in this chapter

- To discuss reasons to conduct test of differences.
- To understand how the type of measurement scale influences the test of difference.
- To calculate a chi-square test for a contingency table.
- To understand that analysis of variance (ANOVA) tests for differences among three or more groups.
- To give examples of marketing questions that may be answered by analyzing the associations among variables.
- To discuss the concept of the simple correlation coefficient.
- To understand that correlation does not mean causation.
- To explain the concept of bivariate linear regression.
- To discuss why multivariate regression is an important tool for analysis.

researcher may wish to measure the association between variables or test the differences between groups of objects. This chapter goes beyond univariate statistics, in which the analysis focuses on one variable at a time, and into the realm of bivariate statistics, in which the researcher is concerned with scores on two variables. The chapter also includes a brief discussion of multiple regression, a form of multivariate analysis. ■

DIFFERENCES BETWEEN GROUPS

test of differences
An investigation of a hypothesis stating that two (or more) groups differ with respect to measures on a variable.

One of the most frequently tested hypotheses states that two groups differ with respect to some behavior, characteristic, or attitude. For example, in the classical experimental design, the researcher tests differences between subjects assigned to the experimental group and subjects assigned to the control group. The survey researcher may be interested in whether male and female consumers purchase a product with equal frequency. Such tests are bivariate **tests of differences.**

Often researchers are interested in testing differences in mean scores between groups or in comparing how two groups' scores are distributed across possible response categories. We will focus our attention on these issues.

Construction of contingency tables for chi-square analysis gives a procedure for comparing the distribution of one group with that of another group. This is a good starting point from which to discuss testing of differences.

Cross-Tabulation Tables: the Chi-Square Test for Goodness of Fit

cross-tabulation (contingency table)
A joint frequency distribution of observations on two or more sets of variables.

One of the simplest techniques for describing sets of relationships is the cross-tabulation. A **cross-tabulation**, or **contingency table**, is a joint frequency distribution of observations on two or more sets of variables. This generally means that tabulation of subgroups will be conducted for purposes of comparison. The chi-square distribution provides a means for testing the statistical significance of contingency tables. It allows us to test for differences in two groups' distributions across categories.

As mentioned in Chapter 14, the chi-square test for a contingency table involves comparing the observed frequencies (O_i) with the expected frequencies (E_i). It tests the goodness of fit of the observed distribution with the expected distribution.

Table 15.1 reproduces Table 14.1. This one-dimensional table suggests that the majority of the population (60 percent) is aware of the brand. However, if we analyze the data by subgroups based on sex of respondents, as in Table 15.2, we can see the logic of cross-classification procedures. Inspection of Table 15.2 sug-

TABLE 15.1	ONE-WAY FREQUENCY TABLE FOR BRAND AWARENESS

Awareness of Tire Manufacturer's Brand	Frequency
Aware	60
Unaware	40
Total	100

TABLE 15.2	CONTINGENCY TABLE (CROSS-TABULATION) FOR BRAND AWARENESS BY SEX		
Awareness of Tire Manufacturer's Brand	**Men**	**Women**	**Total**
Aware	50	10	60
Unaware	15	25	40
Total	65	35	100

gests that most men are aware of the brand of tires, but most women are not. Thus, from our simple analysis we conclude that there is a difference in brand awareness between men and women. (It might also be stated that brand awareness may be associated with sex of respondent.)

So far we have not discussed the notion of statistical significance. Is the observed difference between men and women the result of chance variation due to random sampling? Is the discrepancy more than sampling variation? The chi-square test allows us to conduct tests for significance in the analysis of the $R \times C$ contingency table (where R = row and C = column). The formula for the chi-square statistic is the same as that for one-way frequency tables (see Chapter 14):

$$\chi^2 = \sum \frac{(O_i - E_i)^2}{E_i}$$

where

χ^2 = chi-square statistic
O_i = observed frequency in the ith cell
E_i = expected frequency in the ith cell

Again, as in the univariate chi-square test, a frequency count of data that nominally identify or categorically rank groups is acceptable for the chi-square test for a contingency table. Both variables in the contingency table will be categorical variables rather than interval- or ratio-scaled continuous variables.

We begin, as in all hypothesis-testing procedures, by formulating the null hypothesis and selecting the level of statistical significance for the particular problem. Suppose, for the preceding example, that we wish to test the null hypothesis that an equal number of men and women are aware of the brand and that the hypothesis test will be made at the .05 level of statistical significance.

In managerial terms the researchers ask whether men and women have different levels of brand awareness. Translated into a statistical question, the problem is "Is brand awareness independent of the respondent's sex?" Table 15.2 is a 2 × 2 ($R \times C$) contingency table that cross-classifies based on answers to the awareness question (rows) and the respondent's sex (columns).

To compute the chi-square value for the 2 × 2 contingency table (Table 15.2), the researcher must first identify an expected distribution for that table. Under the null hypothesis that men and women are equally aware of the tire brand, the same proportion of positive answers (60 percent) should come from both groups. In other words, the proportion of men aware of the brand would be the same as the proportion of women aware of it. Likewise, the proportion of men unaware of the brand would equal the proportion of women unaware.

There is an easy way to calculate the expected frequencies for the cells in a cross-tabulation. To compute an expected number for each cell, use the formula

$$E_{ij} = \frac{R_i C_j}{n}$$

where

R_i = total observed frequency in the ith row
C_j = total observed frequency in the jth column
n = sample size

A calculation of the expected values does not utilize the actual observed numbers of respondents in each individual cell; only the total column and total row values are used in this calculation. The expected cell frequencies are calculated as shown in Table 15.3.

To compute a chi-square statistic, use the same formula as before, but calculate degrees of freedom as the number of rows minus one $(R - 1)$ times the number of columns minus one $(C - 1)$:

$$\chi^2 = \sum \frac{(O_i - E_i)^2}{E_i}$$

with $(R - 1)(C - 1)$ degrees of freedom.

Table 15.3 shows the observed versus the expected frequencies for the brand awareness question. Using the data in Table 15.3, we calculate the chi-square statistic as follows:

$$\chi^2 = \frac{(50 - 39)^2}{39} + \frac{(10 - 21)^2}{21} + \frac{(15 - 26)^2}{26} + \frac{(25 - 14)^2}{14}$$
$$= 3.102 + 5.762 + 4.654 + 8.643$$
$$= 22.161$$

The number of degrees of freedom equals 1:

$$(R - 1)(C - 1) = (2 - 1)(2 - 1) = 1$$

From Table 4 in the Appendix, we see that the critical value at the .05 probability level with 1 $d.f.$ is 3.84. Thus, the null hypothesis is rejected. Brand awareness does not appear to be independent of the respondent's sex—in fact, the tabular value for the .001 level is 10.8, and the calculated value of 22.1 far exceeds this tabular value.

TABLE 15.3	CALCULATION OF OBSERVED VERSUS EXPECTED FREQUENCIES FOR BRAND AWARENESS PROBLEM		
Awareness of Tire Manufacturer's Brand	**Men**	**Women**	**Total**
Aware	50 (39)	10 (21)	60
Unaware	15 (26)	25 (14)	40
Total	65	35	100

Note: Expected frequencies are in parentheses. They were calculated as follows:

$$E_{11} = \frac{(60)(65)}{100} = 39 \qquad E_{12} = \frac{(60)(35)}{100} = 21 \qquad E_{21} = \frac{(40)(65)}{100} = 26 \qquad E_{22} = \frac{(40)(35)}{100} = 14$$

Proper use of the chi-square test requires that each expected cell frequency (E_{ij}) have a value of at least 5. If this sample size requirement is not met, the researcher should take a larger sample or combine (collapse) response categories.

Difference between Two Groups When Comparing Means

Researchers often wish to test a hypothesis stating that the mean scores on some interval- or ratio-scaled variable will be significantly different for two independent samples or groups. The null hypothesis about differences between groups is normally stated as follows:

$$\mu_1 = \mu_2 \quad \text{or} \quad \mu_1 - \mu_2 = 0$$

The question is whether the observed differences have occurred by chance alone. In most cases, comparisons are between two sample means $(\bar{X}_1 - \bar{X}_2)$. The formula utilized to test whether the differences are statistically significant depends on the knowledge of the value of the population standard deviation and the number of observations (sample size) in the groups. If either group is small (fewer than 30) and the population standard deviation is unknown, the researcher uses a t-test for difference of means. If the number of observations is large, the researcher uses a Z-test for difference of means to test the hypothesis.

Difference between Two Groups When Comparing Proportions

What type of statistical comparison can be made when the observed statistics are proportions? Suppose a researcher wishes to test a hypothesis that wholesalers in the northern and southern United States differ in the proportion of sales they make to discount retailers. Testing the null hypothesis that the population proportion for group 1 (π_1) equals the population proportion for group 2 (π_2) is conceptually the same as the t-test or Z-test of two means. Again, sample size is the appropriate criterion for selecting either a t-test (small sample) or a Z-test (large sample.)

The hypothesis, which is

$$H_0: \pi_1 = \pi_2$$

may be restated as

$$H_0: \pi_1 - \pi_2 = 0$$

The comparison between the observed sample proportions, p_1 and p_2, allows the researcher to ask whether the differences between two groups from random samples occurred due to chance alone.

Difference among Three or More Groups When Comparing Means

analysis of variance (ANOVA)
Analysis involving the investigation of the effects of one treatment variable on an interval-scaled dependent variable; a hypothesis-testing technique to determine whether statistically significant differences on means occur among three or more groups.

When the means of more than two groups or populations are to be compared, one-way **analysis of variance (ANOVA)** is the appropriate statistical tool. Most ANOVA problems have a nominal variable as the independent variable and an interval- or ratio-scaled variable as the dependent variable. An example of an ANOVA problem would be to compare women who work full time outside the home, those who work part time outside the home, and those who work full time inside the home on the number of hours they spend shopping in grocery stores each week. Here there is one independent variable: working status. This variable is said to have three levels: full-time employment, part-time employment, and work only within the home. Because there are three groups (levels), we cannot use a t-test or a Z-test to test for statistical significance.

If you found a variable that forecast the direction of next year's stock market with an accuracy of better than 80 percent, would you be interested in its prediction? If so, watch the Super Bowl. In 28 of the 34 years from 1967 to 2000, the stock market rose by year's end if a team from the original NFL won the championship or fell by year's end if a team from the old American Football League (now the NFL's American Football Conference) won. The value of stock market indexes appears to be associated with the football league winning the Super Bowl. Most likely this is mere coincidence, but many investors still root for teams from the original NFL.

If we have three groups or levels of the independent variable, the null hypothesis is stated as follows:

$$\mu_1 = \mu_2 = \mu_3$$

The null hypothesis is that all the means are equal. In the grocery shopping example, we are concerned with the average number of hours of three different groups of women.

As the term *analysis of variance* suggests, the problem requires comparing variances to make inferences about the means. The logic of this technique goes as follows: The variance among the means of the three groups will be large if these women differ significantly from one another in terms of number of hours spent shopping. By calculating the variance within the groups and the variance among the groups, we can determine if the means are significantly different.

RELATIONSHIPS AMONG VARIABLES

Many marketing questions deal with the association between two (or more) variables. Questions such as "Is sales productivity associated with pay incentives?", "Is socioeconomic status associated with the likelihood of purchasing a recreational vehicle?", or "Does work status relate to attitudes toward the role of women in society?" can be answered by statistically investigating the relationships between the two variables in question. In this section, we investigate how to analyze questions such as these.

In marketing, sales volume is often the dependent variable we wish to predict. The independent variables found to be associated with the dependent variable sales volume may be aspects of the marketing mix, such as price, number of salespeople, or amount of advertising, and/or uncontrollable variables, such as population or gross domestic product. For example, most managers would not be surprised to find that sales of baby strollers are associated with the number of babies born a few months prior to the sales period. In this case the dependent variable is the sales volume of baby strollers, and the independent variable is the number of babies born. The mathematical symbol X is commonly used for the independent variable, and Y typically denotes the dependent variable. It is appropriate to label dependent and independent variables only when it is assumed that the independent variable caused the dependent variable.

In many situations measures of differences, such as the chi-square test, provide information about whether two or more variables are interrelated, or associated. For example, a chi-square test between a measure of price consciousness and a measure of brand awareness provides some information about the independence or interrelationship of the two variables. Although measures such as chi-square are useful sources of information about association, statisticians have developed several other techniques with which to estimate the strength of association.

measure of association
A general term that refers to a number of bivariate statistical techniques used to measure the strength of a relationship between two variables.

The type of measure used will influence the choice of the proper statistical **measure of association.** This chapter describes simple correlation (Pearson's product-moment correlation coefficient, r) and bivariate regression. Both techniques require interval-scaled or ratio-scaled data.

Correlation Analysis

correlation coefficient
A statistical measure of the covariation, or association, between two variables.

The most popular technique for indicating the relationship of one variable to another is simple correlation analysis. The **correlation coefficient** is a statistical measure of the covariation, or association, between two variables. The correlation coefficient, r, ranges from $+1.0$ to -1.0. If the value of r equals $+1.0$, there is a perfect positive linear (straight-line) relationship. If the value of r equals -1.0, there is a perfect negative linear relationship, or a perfect inverse relationship. No correlation is indicated if r equals 0. A correlation coefficient indicates both the magnitude of the linear relationship and the direction of that relationship. For example, if we find that $r = -.92$, we know we have a relatively strong inverse relationship—that is, the greater the value measured by variable X, the lower the value measured by variable Y.

The formula for calculating the correlation coefficient for two variables X and Y is as follows:

$$r_{xy} = r_{yx} = \frac{\Sigma(X_i - \bar{X})(Y_i - \bar{Y})}{\sqrt{\Sigma(X_i - \bar{X})^2 \Sigma(Y_i - \bar{Y})^2}}$$

where the symbols $\bar{X}$ and $\bar{Y}$ represent the sample averages of X and Y, respectively.

An alternative way to express the correlation formula is

$$r_{xy} = r_{yx} = \frac{\sigma_{xy}}{\sqrt{\sigma_x^2 \sigma_y^2}}$$

where

$$\sigma_x^2 = \text{variance of } X$$
$$\sigma_y^2 = \text{variance of } Y$$
$$\sigma_{xy} = \text{covariance of } X \text{ and } Y$$

with

$$\sigma_{xy} = \frac{\Sigma(X_i - \bar{X})(Y_i - \bar{Y})}{N}$$

If associated values of X_i and Y_i differ from their means in the same direction, their covariance will be positive. If the values of X_i and Y_i tend to deviate in opposite directions, their covariance will be negative.

The simple correlation coefficient actually is a standardized measure of covariance. In the formula the numerator represents covariance and the denominator is the square root of the product of the sample variances. Researchers find the correlation coefficient useful because they can compare two correlations without regard for the amount of variance exhibited by each variable separately.

Correlation and Causation

It is important to remember that correlation does not mean causation. No matter how highly correlated the rooster's crow is to the rising of the sun, the rooster does not cause the sun to rise. A high correlation exists between teachers' salaries and the consumption of liquor over a period of years. The approximate correlation coefficient is $r = .9$. This high correlation does not indicate how much teachers drink, nor does it indicate that the sale of liquor increases teachers' salaries. It is more likely that teachers' salaries and liquor sales covary because they are both influenced by a third variable, such as long-run growth in national income and/or population.

Coefficient of Determination

If we wish to know the proportion of *variance* in Y that is explained by X (or vice versa), we can calculate the **coefficient of determination** by squaring the correlation coefficient:

$$r^2 = \frac{\text{Explained variance}}{\text{Total variance}}$$

The coefficient of determination, r^2, measures that part of the total variance of Y that is accounted for by knowing the value of X. In the example about unemployment and hours worked, $r = -.635$; therefore, $r^2 = .403$. About 40 percent of the variance in unemployment can be explained by the variance in hours worked, and vice versa.

Correlation Matrix

A **correlation matrix** is the standard form for reporting correlational results. It may be compared to a between-city mileage table, except that the research variables are substituted for cities and a coefficient of correlation is substituted for mileage. Table 15.4 shows a correlation matrix that relates some measures of sales force performance and job satisfaction to characteristics of the sales force, job attitudes from the Role Orientation Index, and territory work load.[2] You will encounter this type of matrix on many occasions. Note that the main diagonal consists of correlations of 1.00. This will always be the case when a variable is correlated with itself. The data in this example are from a survey of industrial salespeople selling steel and plastic strapping and seals used in shipping. Performance (S) was measured by identifying the salesperson's actual annual sales volume in dollars. Notice that the performance variable has a .45 correlation with the work-load variable (WL), which was measured by recording the number of accounts in the sales territory. Notice also that the salesperson's perception of job-related tension (JT) as measured on an attitude scale has a $-.48$ correlation with performance (S). Thus, when perceived job tension is high, performance is low. Of course, the correlation coefficients in these examples are moderate.

coefficient of determination (r^2)
A measure obtained by squaring the correlation coefficient; that proportion of the total variance of a variable that is accounted for by knowing the value of another variable.

correlation matrix
The standard form for reporting correlational results.

Variables	S	JS	GE	SE	OD	VI	JT	RA	TP	WL
Performance (S)	1.00									
Job satisfaction (JS)	.45[b]	1.00								
Generalized self-esteem (GE)	.31[b]	.10	1.00							
Specific self-esteem (SE)	.61[b]	.28[b]	.36[b]	1.00						
Other-directedness (OD)	.05	−.03	−.44[b]	−.24[c]	1.00					
Verbal intelligence (VI)	−.36[b]	−.13	−.14	−.11	−.18[d]	1.00				
Job-related tension (JT)	−.48[b]	−.56[b]	−.32[b]	−.34[b]	.26[b]	−.02	1.00			
Role ambiguity (RA)	−.26[c]	−.24[c]	−.32[b]	−.39[b]	.38[b]	−.05	.44[b]	1.00		
Territory potential (TP)	.49[b]	.31[b]	.04	.29[b]	.09	−.09	−.38[b]	−.26[b]	1.00	
Work load (WL)	.45[b]	.11	.29[c]	.29[c]	−.04	−.12	−.27[c]	−.22[d]	.49[b]	1.00

[a] Numbers below the diagonal are for the sample; those above the diagonal are omitted.
[b] $p < .001$.
[c] $p < .01$.
[d] $p < .05$.

Bivariate Linear Regression

bivariate linear regression
A measure of linear association that investigates a straight-line relationship of the type $Y = a + \beta X$, where X is the independent variable and a and β are two constants to be estimated.

Bivariate linear regression investigates a *straight-line relationship* of the type $Y = a + \beta X$, where Y is the dependent variable, X is the independent variable, and a and β are two constants to be estimated. The symbol a represents the Y intercept, and β is the slope coefficient. The slope β is the change in Y due to a corresponding change of one unit in X. The slope also may be thought of as *rise over run* (the rise in units on the Y-axis divided by the run in units along the X-axis).

Suppose a researcher is interested in forecasting sales for a construction distributor (wholesaler) in Florida. Further, the distributor believes a reasonable association exists between sales and building permits issued by counties. Using bivariate linear regression on the data in Table 15.5, the researcher will be able to estimate sales potential (Y) in various counties based on the number of building permits (X). To better illustrate the data in Table 15.5, we have plotted them on a scatter diagram (Exhibit 15.1). In the diagram the vertical axis indicates the value of the dependent variable, Y, and the horizontal axis indicates the value of the independent variable, X. Each single point in the diagram represents an observation of X and Y at a given point in time—that is, a paired value of X and Y. The relationship between X and Y could be "eyeballed"; that is, a straight line could be drawn through the points in the figure. However, this procedure is subject to human error: Two researchers might draw different lines to describe the same data.

The task of the researcher is to find the best means for fitting a straight line to the data. The least-squares method is a relatively simple mathematical technique for ensuring that the straight line will most closely represent the relationship between X and Y. The logic behind the least-squares technique goes as follows: No straight line can completely represent every dot in the scatter diagram; there will be a discrepancy between most of the actual scores (the dots) and the predicted score based on the regression line. Simply stated, any straight line drawn will generate errors. The least-squares method uses the criterion of

TABLE 15.5	RELATIONSHIP OF SALES POTENTIAL TO BUILDING PERMITS ISSUED	
Dealer	Y Dealer's Sales Volume (thousands)	X Building Permits
1	77	86
2	79	93
3	80	95
4	83	104
5	101	139
6	117	180
7	129	165
8	120	147
9	97	119
10	106	132
11	99	126
12	121	156
13	103	129
14	86	96
15	99	108

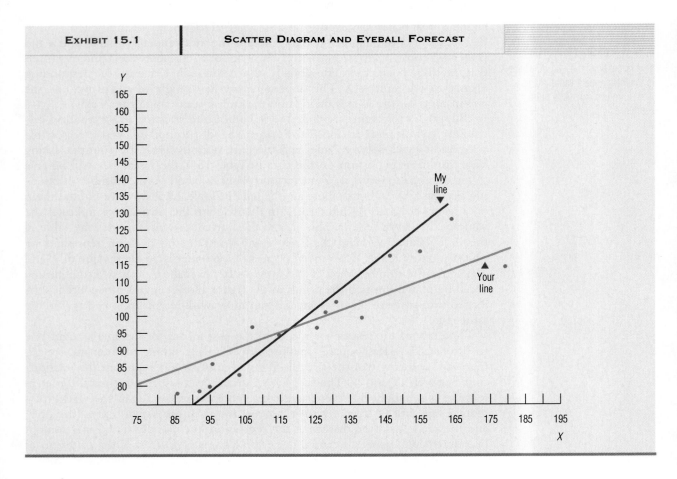

EXHIBIT 15.1 — SCATTER DIAGRAM AND EYEBALL FORECAST

attempting to make the least amount of total error in prediction of Y from X. More technically, the procedure used in the least-squares method generates a straight line that minimizes the sum of squared deviations of the actual values from this predicted regression line. With the symbol e representing the deviations of the dots from the line, the least-squares criterion is as follows:

$$\sum_{i=1}^{n} e_i^2 \text{ is minimum}$$

where

$$
\begin{aligned}
e_i &= Y_i - \hat{Y}_i \text{ (the residual)} \\
Y_i &= \text{actual value of the dependent variable} \\
\hat{Y}_i &= \text{estimated value of the dependent variable ("Y hat")} \\
n &= \text{number of observations} \\
i &= \text{number of the particular observation}
\end{aligned}
$$

The general equation for a straight line is $Y = a + \beta X$. A more appropriate estimating equation includes an allowance for error:

$$Y = \hat{a} + \hat{\beta} X + e$$

The symbols $\hat{a}$ and $\hat{\beta}$ are used when the equation is a regression estimate of the line. Thus, to compute the estimated values of α and β, we use the following formulas:

$$\hat{\beta} = \frac{n(\Sigma XY) - (\Sigma X)(\Sigma Y)}{n(\Sigma X^2) - (\Sigma X)^2}$$

and

$$\hat{a} = \bar{Y} - \hat{\beta} \bar{X}$$

where

$$
\begin{aligned}
\hat{\beta} &= \text{estimated slope of the line (the regression coefficient)} \\
\hat{a} &= \text{estimated intercept of the } Y\text{-axis} \\
Y &= \text{dependent variable} \\
\bar{Y} &= \text{mean of the dependent variable} \\
X &= \text{independent variable} \\
\bar{X} &= \text{mean of the independent variable} \\
n &= \text{number of observations}
\end{aligned}
$$

With simple arithmetic we can solve these equations for the data in Table 15.5; see Table 15.6. To estimate the relationship between the distributor's sales to a dealer and the number of building permits, we perform the following manipulations:

$$
\begin{aligned}
\hat{\beta} &= \frac{n(\Sigma XY) - (\Sigma X)(\Sigma Y)}{n(\Sigma X^2) - (\Sigma X)^2} \\[2mm]
&= \frac{15(193,345) - 2,806,875}{15(245,759) - 3,515,625} \\[2mm]
&= \frac{2,900,175 - 2,806,875}{3,686,385 - 3,515,625} \\[2mm]
&= \frac{93,300}{170,760} \\[2mm]
&= .54638
\end{aligned}
$$

TABLE 15.6 | LEAST-SQUARES COMPUTATION

	Y	Y²	X	X²	XY
1	77	5,929	86	7,396	6,622
2	79	6,241	93	8,649	7,347
3	80	6,400	95	9,025	7,600
4	83	6,889	104	10,816	8,632
5	101	10,201	139	19,321	14,039
6	117	13,689	180	32,400	21,060
7	129	16,641	165	27,225	21,285
8	120	14,400	147	21,609	17,640
9	97	9,409	119	14,161	11,543
10	106	11,236	132	17,424	13,992
11	99	9,801	126	15,876	12,474
12	121	14,641	156	24,336	18,876
13	103	10,609	129	16,641	13,287
14	86	7,396	96	9,216	8,256
15	99	9,801	108	11,664	10,692
	$\Sigma Y = 1{,}497$	$\Sigma Y^2 = 153{,}283$	$\Sigma X = 1{,}875$	$\Sigma X^2 = 245{,}759$	$\Sigma XY = 193{,}345$
	$\bar{Y} = 99.8$		$\bar{X} = 125$		

$$\begin{aligned}
\hat{a} &= \bar{Y} - \hat{\beta}\,\bar{X} \\
&= 99.8 - .54638(125) \\
&= 99.8 - 68.3 \\
&= 31.5
\end{aligned}$$

The formula $\hat{Y} = 31.5 + 0.546X$ is the regression equation used for the prediction of the dependent variable. Suppose the wholesaler is considering opening a new dealership in an area where the number of building permits equals 89. Sales in this area may be forecasted as

$$\begin{aligned}
\hat{Y} &= 31.5 + .546(X) \\
&= 31.5 + .546(89) \\
&= 31.5 + 48.6 \\
&= 80.1
\end{aligned}$$

Thus, the distributor may expect sales of 80.1 (or $80,100) in this new area.[3]

Calculation of the correlation coefficient gives an indication of how accurate the predictions are. In this example the correlation coefficient is $r = .9356$ and the coefficient of determination is $r^2 = .8754$.

Drawing a Regression Line

To draw a regression line on the scatter diagram, only two predicted values of Y need to be plotted.

Dealer 7 (actual Y value $= 129$): $\hat{Y}_7 = 31.5 + .546(165)$
$= 121.6$

Dealer 3 (actual Y value $= 80$): $\hat{Y}_3 = 31.5 + .546(95)$
$= 83.4$

EXHIBIT 15.2 | LEAST-SQUARES REGRESSION LINE

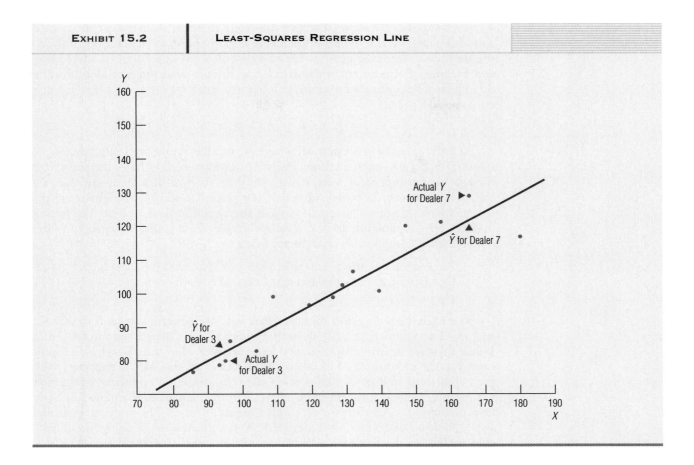

Using the data for dealer 7 and dealer 3, we can draw a straight line connecting the points 121.6 and 83.4. Exhibit 15.2 shows the regression line.

MULTIPLE REGRESSION ANALYSIS

As we have seen, the investigation of one variable at a time is referred to as *univariate analysis* and the investigation of the relationship between two variables is called *bivariate analysis*. When problems are multidimensional and involve three or more variables, we use *multivariate statistical analysis*. Multivariate statistical methods allow us to consider the effects of more than one variable at the same time. For example, suppose a forecaster wishes to estimate oil consumption for the next 5 years. While consumption might be predicted by past oil consumption records alone, adding additional variables such as average number of miles driven per year, coal production, and nuclear plants under construction may give greater insight into the determinants of oil consumption. Multivariate analysis will be illustrated in our discussion of multiple regression analysis.

Multiple regression analysis is an extension of bivariate regression analysis that allows for simultaneous investigation of the effect of two or more independent variables on a single, interval-scaled dependent variable. In the previous section, we illustrated bivariate linear regression analysis with an example concerning a construction dealer's sales volume. In that example, variations in the dependent variable were attributed to changes in a single independent variable. Reality,

multiple regression analysis
An analysis of association in which the effects of two or more independent variables on a single, interval-scaled dependent variable are investigated simultaneously.

however, suggests that several factors are likely to affect such a dependent variable. For example, sales volume might be hypothesized to depend not only on the number of building permits but also on price levels, amount of advertising, and income of consumers in the area. Thus, the problem requires identification of a linear relationship with multiple regression analysis. The multiple regression equation is

$$Y = a + \beta_1 X_1 + \beta_2 X_2 + \beta_3 X_3 + \cdots + \beta_n X_n$$

Another forecasting example is useful for illustrating multiple regression. Assume that a toy manufacturer wishes to forecast sales by sales territory. It is thought that competitors' sales, the presence or absence of a company salesperson in the territory (a binary variable), and grammar school enrollment are the independent variables that might explain the variation in sales. The data appear in Table 15.7. Following are the statistical results from multiple regression after mathematical computations have been made.

Regression equation: $Y = 102.18 + .387 X_1 + 115.2 X_2 + 6.73 X_3$
Coefficient of multiple determination (R^2): .845
F-value: 14.6

The regression equation indicates that sales are positively related to X_1, X_2, and X_3. The coefficients (βs) show the effect on the dependent variable of a 1-unit increase in any of the independent variables. The value $\beta_2 = 115.2$ indicates that an increase of \$115,200 (000 included) in toy sales is expected with each additional unit of X_2. Thus, it appears that adding a company salesperson will have a very positive effect on sales. Grammar school enrollments also may help predict sales. An increase of 1 unit of enrollment (1,000 students) indicates a sales increase of \$6,730 (000 included). A 1-unit increase in competitors' sales volume (X_1) in the territory adds little to the toy manufacturer's sales (\$387).

In multiple regression the coefficients β_1, β_2, and so on, are called *coefficients of partial regression*. Each independent variable is usually correlated with the other

TABLE 15.7		DATA FOR A MULTIPLE REGRESSION PROBLEM	
Y Sales (000)	X_1 Competitors' Sales (000)	X_2 Salesperson (1) or Agent (0)	X_3 Grammar School Enrollment (000)
222	106	0	23
304	213	0	18
218	201	0	22
501	378	1	20
542	488	0	21
790	509	1	31
523	644	0	17
667	888	1	25
700	941	1	32
869	1,066	1	36
444	307	0	30
479	312	1	22

independent variables. The correlation between Y and X_1, with the correlation that X_1 and X_2 have in common with Y held constant, is the *partial correlation.* Because the partial correlation between sales and X_1 has been adjusted for the effect produced by variation in X_2 (and other independent variables), the correlation coefficient obtained from the bivariate regression will not be the same as the partial coefficient in the multiple regression. In other words, the original value of β is the simple bivariate regression coefficient. In multiple regression, the coefficient β_1 is defined as the partial regression coefficient for which the effects of other independent variables are held constant.

As in bivariate regression, the *coefficient of multiple determination,* or multiple index of determination, indicates the percentage of variation in Y explained by the variation in the independent variables. The value of $R^2 = .845$ in our example tells us that the variation in the independent variables accounted for 84.5 percent of the variance in the dependent variable. Typically, introducing additional independent variables into the regression equation explains more of the variation in Y than it is possible to explain with fewer variables. In other words, the amount of variation explained by two independent variables in the same equation is usually greater than the variation in Y explained by either one separately.

SUMMARY

The chi-square statistic allows the researcher to test whether an observed sample distribution fits some given distribution. It can be used to analyze contingency with cross-tabulation tables. In this case, the test allows the researcher to determine whether two groups are independent. If they are not, the variables are interrelated.

Either a Z-test or a t-test for two independent samples is used to determine whether the means of two independent samples are significantly different. The t-test should be chosen over the Z-test if the population standard deviation is unknown and if the sample size is small (fewer than 30). Similarly, a t-test or Z-test for two independent samples may be used to determine whether two proportions are significantly different.

One-way analysis of variance (ANOVA) compares the means of samples from more than two populations to determine whether their differences are statistically significant.

Simple correlation is the measure of the relationship of one variable to another. The correlation coefficient (r) indicates the strength of the association of two variables and the direction of that association. Correlation does not prove causation, as variables other than those being measured may be involved. The coefficient of determination (r^2) measures the amount of the total variance in the dependent variable that is accounted for by knowing the value of the independent variable. The results of a correlation computation often are presented in a correlation matrix.

Bivariate linear regression investigates a straight-line relationship between one dependent variable and one independent variable. The regression can be done intuitively by plotting a scatter diagram of the X and Y points and drawing a line to fit the observed relationship. The least-squares method mathematically determines the best-fitting regression line for the observed data. The line determined by this method may be used to forecast values of the dependent variable given a value for the independent variable. The goodness of the line's fit may be evaluated by calculating the coefficient of determination.

Multiple regression analysis is an extension of bivariate regression analysis that allows for simultaneous investigation of the effect of two or more independent variables on a single, interval-scaled dependent variable.

Key Terms and Concepts

test of differences
cross-tabulation (contingency table)
analysis of variance (ANOVA)

measure of association
correlation coefficient
coefficient of determination (r^2)

correlation matrix
bivariate linear regression
multiple regression analysis

Questions for Review and Critical Thinking

1. What tests of difference are appropriate in the following situations?
   a. Average campaign contributions of Democrats, Republicans, and independents are to be compared.
   b. Advertising managers and brand managers have responded "yes," "no," or "not sure" to an attitude question. Their answers are to be compared.
   c. One-half of a sample received an incentive in a mail survey; the other half did not. A comparison of response rates is desired.
   d. A researcher believes that married men will push the grocery cart when grocery shopping with their wives.
2. What type of analysis should be used to analyze the following data on responses to the statement "Regulation is the best way to ensure safe products"?

	Managers	Blue-Collar Workers
Agree	58	66
Disagree	34	24
No opinion	8	10
Totals	100	100

3. A store manager's computer-generated list of all retail sales employees indicates that 70 percent are full-time employees, 20 percent are part-time employees, and 10 percent are furloughed or laid-off employees. A sample of 50 employees from the list indicates that 40 are full-time employees, 6 are part-time employees, and 4 are furloughed/laid-off employees. What statistical test should be used to determine whether the sample is representative of the population?
4. A sales force ($n = 67$) received some management-by-objectives training. The mean scores for salespeople's job performance are shown below. What type of data analysis is appropriate?

Skill	Before	After
Planning ability	4.84	5.43
Territory coverage	5.24	5.51
Activity reporting	5.37	5.42

5. The incomes of owners of trash compactors were compared with those of nonowners. The average income in a sample of 200 was as follows:

	Owners	Nonowners
$\overline{X}$	4.6	3.5

   Higher values represent higher levels of income. (Actual scaled average: less than $7,500 = 1; $7,501–$15,000 = 2; $15,001–$25,000 = 3; $25,001–$40,000 = 4; $40,001–$60,000 = 5; over $60,000 = 6.) Is a t-test appropriate?
6. An Excel Spreadsheet is reprinted on the next page. Interpret the t-test results. Are they statistically significant?

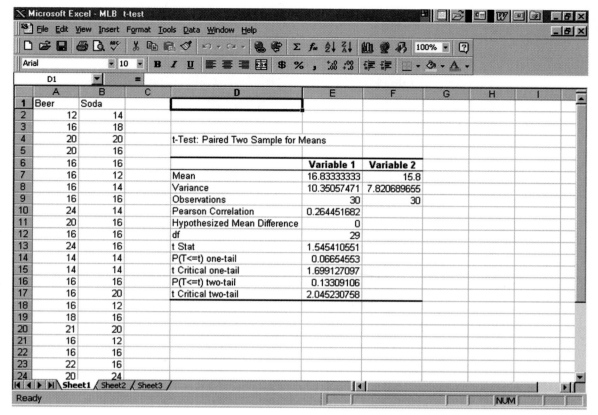

	A	B	C	D	E	F	G
1	Beer	Soda					
2	12	14					
3	16	18					
4	20	20		t-Test: Paired Two Sample for Means			
5	20	16					
6	16	16			Variable 1	Variable 2	
7	16	12		Mean	16.83333333	15.8	
8	16	14		Variance	10.35057471	7.820689655	
9	16	16		Observations	30	30	
10	24	14		Pearson Correlation	0.264451682		
11	20	16		Hypothesized Mean Difference	0		
12	16	16		df	29		
13	24	16		t Stat	1.545410551		
14	14	14		P(T<=t) one-tail	0.06654553		
15	14	14		t Critical one-tail	1.699127097		
16	16	16		P(T<=t) two-tail	0.13309106		
17	16	20		t Critical two-tail	2.045230758		
18	16	12					
19	18	16					
20	21	20					
21	16	12					
22	16	16					
23	22	16					
24	20	24					

7. The discussion in this chapter is limited to linear relationships. Try to diagram some nonlinear relationships that show *r* values of zero using the test methods shown in the text.

8. Comment on the following:
   a. Suppose Abraham Lincoln answered a survey questionnaire and indicated he had not received a grade-school diploma. The researcher found that Lincoln's educational score did not correlate highly with the expected variables. What was wrong?
   b. An international marketer has said, "When political instability increases, the price of quality increases." Is this a testable hypothesis?
   c. In 8 out of 11 years, when a racehorse won the Triple Crown (Kentucky Derby, Preakness, and Belmont Stakes), the stock market dropped.

9. A manufacturer of disposable washcloths/wipes told a retailer that sales for this product category closely correlated with sales of disposable diapers. The retailer thought he would check this out for his own sales-forecasting purposes. The researcher tells him, "Disposable washcloth/wipes sales can be predicted with knowledge of disposable diaper sales." Is this the right thing to say?

Exploring the Internet

1. Go to the Chance Web site at http://www. dartmouth.edu/~chance/ChanceLecture/ AudioVideo.html and view the very interesting streaming video "Streaks in Sports."

2. The Federal Reserve Bank of St. Louis maintains a database called FRED (Federal Reserve Economic Data). Navigate to the FRED database at http:// www.stls.frb.org/fred/index.html. Randomly select a five-year period between 1970 and 1995 and then find the correlation between average U.S. employment in retail trade and U.S. employment in wholesale trade. What statistical test is appropriate?

Springfield Electric Company is a manufacturer of electric pencil sharpeners. The company had always operated in New York and New Jersey and decided to expand beyond that region. The company president thought a new plant needed to be constructed. Seeing no need for contiguous expansion, the president favored a West Coast plant.

The marketing manager believed that sales were correlated with the number of workers employed in the geographic area; in fact, she felt that electric pencil sharpener sales were correlated with the number of white-collar workers in an area. However, all she could get were statistics for total employees. Case Exhibit 15.1-1 shows Springfield's sales of electric pencil sharp-

eners and the total number of employees in 17 Metropolitan Statistical Areas (MSAs) in New York and New Jersey. Case Exhibit 15.1-2 shows the number of employees in the MSAs in Washington, Oregon, and California. The marketing manager thought she could forecast sales for the western expansion with these data.

Questions
1. Calculate and interpret the correlation coefficient data in Case Exhibit 15.1-1.
2. Estimate the regression equation coefficient for the data (using sales as the independent variable).
3. Forecast sales in the states of California, Washington, and Oregon based on the data in Case Exhibit 15.1-2.

CASE EXHIBIT 15.1-1	DATA ON TOTAL EMPLOYEES AND SPRINGFIELD SALES IN NEW YORK AND NEW JERSEY MSAs	

Metropolitan Statistical Area	Number of Employees (thousands)	Sales
New York		
Albany–Schenectady–Troy	58.3	3,749
Binghamton	37.0	2,695
Buffalo	135.6	4,926
Elmira	12.8	2,808
Nassau–Suffolk	149.0	7,423
New York	788.8	43,401
Poughkeepsie	24.3	3,254
Rochester	139.1	8,924
Syracuse	53.6	13,119
Utica–Rome	30.8	3,151
New Jersey		
Allentown–Bethlehem–Easton	110.7	6,123
Atlantic City	8.7	2,666
Jersey City	74.2	3,210
Long Branch–Asbury Park	22.8	2,078
New Brunswick–Perth Amboy–Sayreville	78.9	2,894
Newark	252.1	14,989
Paterson–Clifton–Passaic	60.1	3,806

Metropolitan Statistical Area	Number of Employees (thousands)
Washington	
Richland–Kennewick	7.8
Seattle–Everett	123.6
Spokane	11.1
Tacoma	18.7
Yakima	8.8
Oregon	
Eugene–Springfield	18.2
Portland	90.5
Salem	12.5
California	
Anaheim–Santa Ana–Garden Grove	149.0
Bakersfield	7.1
Fresno	20.5
Los Angeles–Long Beach	750.3
Modesto	18.7
Oxnard–Simi Valley–Ventura	14.9
Riverside–San Bernardino–Ontario	51.8
Sacramento	20.5
Salinas–Seaside–Monterey	8.0
San Diego	71.4
San Francisco–Oakland	172.7
San Jose	151.1
Santa Barbara–Santa Maria–Lompoc	14.0
Santa Cruz	5.7
Santa Rosa	8.6
Stockton	20.0
Vallejo–Fairfield–Napa	7.4

CASE 15.2 CENTER FOR AMERICAN ENTERPRISE: A STUDY OF PSYCHOLOGICAL AND DEMOGRAPHIC CONTRIBUTORS TO CONSUMERISM

A few years ago the Center for American Enterprise commissioned a study to determine the causes of consumerism.[4] This was done in an effort to stem the tide of growing disenchantment with American business and its practices among a wide number of consumers.

The center, located in Dallas, Texas, was a private foundation funded by a large number of corporations to spread the ideal of the free enterprise system. It conducted a number of projects to better understand what Americans knew about business and published numerous brochures that were sent to high schools and elementary schools throughout the United States. The center believed consumerism—that is, consumer discontent—was a major problem facing business and wished to pursue it as an area of study.

Since the center did not have the expertise to properly formulate the research problem and its accompanying theory, it decided to seek outside assistance for this project. Commissioned to do the study were three professors at Southern Methodist University, Thomas, Rogers, and Michaels, who had done considerable research on the topic. The report they generated follows.

Report on Psychological and Demographic Correlates of Consumer Discontent

The study of consumerism and the allied psychological state of consumer discontent has been theoretically and empirically examined within the confines of the economic system. Although these market interfaces provide discrete areas for analyzing consumerism or consumer discontent, they may be only symptomatic of broader psychological states currently existing in society. With the exception of one study relating consumer alienation to marketing activities, little research has actively explored potential relationships between psychological states and discontent with the market system. Identification of those psychological states and demographic characteristics associated with consumer discontent would provide valuable insight into the dynamics of this phenomenon and assist in the development of constructive approaches for dealing with it from a public policy perspective.

Study Purpose

The purpose of this study is to examine the relationships among selected psychological states, demographic variables, and consumer discontent. Specific objectives of this study are threefold:

1. To determine if consumer discontent with the marketplace is rooted in more basic conceptions of an individual's life-space.
2. To determine the appropriateness of psychological constructs as potential contributors and explanatory states for investigating consumer discontent.
3. To identify demographic correlates of consumer discontent.

Method

A two-stage area sampling procedure was used to select 228 individuals from the Dallas, Texas, metropolitan area. A subsequent analysis of demographic data indicated that the sample represented a cross section of the area. Individuals were personally contacted in their homes by trained interviewers.

Respondents were given a self-administered questionnaire containing a list of 145 statements designed to measure life satisfaction, powerlessness, anomie, alienation, normlessness, social isolation, aggression, and consumer discontent. All statements were scored on a five-point Likert-type scale except for the six-point Likert-type scale of consumer discontent. Demographic data on the respondents were also collected.

Results

Results of the study are shown in Case Exhibits 15.2-1 and 15.2-2. Case Exhibit 15.2-1 presents the correlation matrix between the measures of psychological states and the consumer discontent scale. The correlations indicate that consumer discontent is indeed related to basic psychological states.

Case Exhibit 15.2-2 presents the correlation matrix between demographic variables and the consumer discontent scale. Examination of demographic variables also reveals that discontent is related to certain characteristics of the populace.

Together, the psychological and demographic correlates of consumer discontent provide a profile of the discontented consumer. Consumer discontent may be an outgrowth of more basic psychological states that reflect disassociation with society in general and specifically with the marketplace. One may speculate that dislocation in society will produce consumer discontent. Given the growing complexity of business and society, it appears that this may become an even more pervasive problem in the future and thus warrants further research at this time.

Questions

1. Interpret the results of the correlation matrix.
2. Develop a profile of the discontented consumer and the contented consumer.
3. What policy implications would you suggest based on these results?

CASE EXHIBIT 15.2-1		CORRELATION MATRIX OF SCALE RESPONSES						
(N = 228)	CD	LS	AN	AL	PO	NO	SI	AG
Consumer discontent (CD)	1.00	−.11[b]	.37[a]	.42[a]	.37[a]	.28[a]	.34[a]	.21[a]
Life satisfaction (LS)		1.00	−.44[a]	−.44[a]	−.33[a]	−.25[a]	−.44[a]	−.27[a]
Anomie (AN)			1.00	.66[a]	.56[a]	.47[a]	.54[a]	.25[a]
Alienation (AL)				1.00	.80[a]	.77[a]	.79[a]	.31[a]
Powerlessness (PO)					1.00	.46[a]	.42[a]	.15[b]
Normlessness (NO)						1.00	.42[a]	.32[a]
Social isolation (SI)							1.00	.28[a]
Aggression (AG)								1.00

[a] $p < .01$.
[b] $p < .05$; Pearson product-moment correlation coefficients.

CORRELATION OF SCALE RESPONSES WITH DEMOGRAPHIC CHARACTERISTICS

(N = 228)	CD	LS	AN	AL	PO	NO	SI	AG
Age	.13[b]	.14[b]	.10	.31[a]	.07	.29[a]	.37[a]	.13[b]
Sex[1]	−.13[b]	−.05	.02	−.15[b]	−.11	−.06	−.18[b]	.11
Race[2]	−.06	.08	.04	−.15[b]	−.13[b]	−.21[a]	−.03	−.06
Family Size	.02	−.16[a]	.21[a]	.24[a]	.11[b]	.17[b]	.27[a]	.09
Income	.31[a]	−.29[a]	.22[a]	.37[a]	.30[a]	.31[a]	.30[a]	.17[b]
Occupation[3]	−.26[a]	.08	−.20[a]	−.26[a]	−.23[a]	−.15[b]	−.23[a]	.01
Education	.15[b]	−.03	−.11	.20[a]	.27[a]	.16[b]	.06	.11

[a] $p < .01$.
[b] $p < .05$.
[1] Scored: male = 1, female = 2.
[2] Scored: Caucasian = 1, Black = 2, Mexican American = 3, other = 4.
[3] Scored: professional = 1, skilled worker = 2, unskilled worker = 3, unemployed = 4, retired = 5.

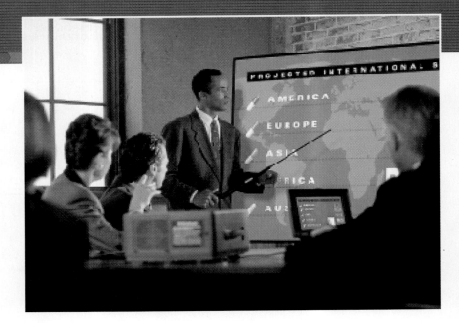

COMMUNICATING RESEARCH RESULTS:
Research Report, Oral Presentation, and Research Follow-Up

What you will learn in this chapter

- To explain how the research report is the crucial means for communicating the whole research project.
- To define the term *research report*.
- To outline the research report format and its parts.
- To explain how the oral presentation may be the most efficient means of supplementing the written report.
- To understand the importance of research follow-up.

After spending days, weeks, or even months working on a project, the researcher is likely to believe that preparation of the report is just an anticlimactic formality. After all, it seems that all the real work has been done; it just has to be put on paper. This attitude can be disastrous, however. The project may have been well designed, the data carefully collected and analyzed by sophisticated statistical methods, and important conclusions reached, but if the project is not effectively reported, all of the preceding efforts will have been wasted. Often the research report is the only part of the project that others ever see. Users of the report cannot separate the content of the project from the form in which it is presented. If people who need to use the research results have to wade through a disorganized presentation, are detoured by technical jargon they do not understand, or find sloppiness of language or thought, they probably will discount the report and make decisions without it, just as if the project had never been done. Thus, the research report is a crucial means for communicating the whole project—the medium through which the project makes its impact on decisions. This chapter explains how research reports, oral presentations, and follow-up conversations help communicate research results.[1] ■

INSIGHTS FROM THE COMMUNICATIONS MODEL

Once the data have been collected and analyzed, the researcher must become a communicator. The researcher has looked at secondary sources, gathered primary data, used statistical techniques to analyze the data, and reached conclusions. When the report on the project is written, all of these elements will affect its contents. A researcher may assume that the reader has a lot of background information on the project and produce pages and pages of unexplained tables, assuming the reader will unearth from them the same patterns the researcher observed. The report may contain technical terms such as *parameter, hypothesis test, correlation,* or *regression,* on the assumption that the reader will understand them. Or the researcher may assume that the reader lacks any background information and explain everything in sixth-grade terms, perhaps insulting the reader in the process.

When readers receive a report, they typically have not thought much about the project. They may know nothing about statistics and may have many other responsibilities. If they cannot grasp the report quickly, they may put it on the stack of "things to do someday."

Simply delivering a report to its audience is not sufficient to ensure that it gets attention. The report needs to be written so as to draw on the common experience of the researcher and the reader. Hitting that zone of common experience is the writer's responsibility, not the reader's. Unless a report is really crucial, a busy reader will not spend time and effort struggling through an inadequate or difficult-to-read document.

THE REPORT IN CONTEXT

research report
An oral presentation or written statement of research results, strategic recommendations, and/or other conclusions to a specific audience.

A **research report** is an oral presentation and/or written statement whose purpose is to communicate research results, strategic recommendations, and/or other conclusions to management and/or other specific audiences. This chapter deals primarily with the final written report that an extensive research project requires, but remember that the final report may not be the only kind prepared. A small project may require only a short oral or written report on the results. An extensive project may involve many written documents, interim reports, and a final detailed written report as well as several oral presentations.

The chapter's emphasis on the final report does not mean that other communications, such as progress reports during the course of the project, are any less important to its eventual success. And the chapter's suggestions can easily be adapted to apply to shorter, less formal reports.

REPORT FORMAT

report format
The makeup or arrangement of parts necessary to a good research report.

Although every research report is custom made for the project it represents, some conventions of **report format** are universal. They represent a consensus about the parts necessary for a good research report and how they should be ordered. This consensus is not a law, however. Every book on report writing suggests its own unique format, and every report writer has to pick and choose the parts and order that will work best for the project at hand. Many companies and universities also have in-house report formats or writing guides for writers to follow. The format presented in this chapter serves as a starting point from which a writer can shape his or her own appropriate format.

Never use a long word where a diminutive one will do.

1. Title page (sometimes preceded by a title fly page)
2. Letter of transmittal
3. Letter of authorization
4. Table of contents (and lists of figures and tables)
5. Summary
    (a)   Objectives
    (b)   Results
    (c)   Conclusions
    (d)   Recommendations
6. Body
    (a)   Introduction
          (1) Background
          (2) Objectives
    (b)   Methodology
    (c)   Results
    (d)   Limitations
    (e)   Conclusions and recommendations
7. Appendix
    (a)   Data collection forms
    (b)   Detailed calculations
    (c)   General tables
    (d)   Bibliography
    (e)   Other support material

Tailoring the Format to the Project

The format may need adjustment for two reasons: (1) to obtain the proper level of formality and (2) to decrease the complexity of the report. The format given here is for the most formal type of report, such as one for a large project done within an organization or one done by a research agency for a client company. This type of report is usually bound with a permanent cover and could be hundreds of pages long.

For less formal reports, each part is shorter and some parts are omitted. The difference may be compared to the way people's clothing varies according to the formality of the occasion. The most formal report is dressed, so to speak, in white tie and tails (or long evening gown).[2] It includes the full assortment of prefatory parts—title page, letters of transmittal, letter of authorization, and table of contents.

The next level of formality would be like an everyday business suit: parts of the prefatory material that the situation does not call for would be dropped and the complexity of the report body would be reduced. In general, as the report goes down through the sport coat, slacks, and blue jeans stages, the prefatory parts are dropped and the complexity and length of the report body are reduced.

How does the researcher decide on the appropriate level of formality? The general rule is to include all the parts needed for effective communication in the particular circumstances—and no more.[3] This factor relates to how far up in management the report is expected to go and how routine the matter is. A researcher's immediate supervisor does not need a 100-page, "full-dress" report on a routine project. However, the board of directors does not want a one-page, "blue jeans" report on a big project that backs a major expansion program. The "white-tie-and-tails" report to top management may later be stripped of some prefatory parts (and thus reduced in formality) for wider circulation within the company.

The Parts of the Report

Title Page   The *title page* should state the title of the report, for whom the report was prepared, by whom it was prepared, and the date of release or presentation.

Letter of Transmittal   The *letter of transmittal* is included in relatively formal and very formal reports. Its purpose is to release or deliver the report to the recipient. It also serves to establish some rapport between reader and writer. This is the one part of the formal report that should convey a personal or even slightly informal tone. The transmittal should not dive into the report findings except in the broadest terms. For example, it might comment generally on findings and matters of interest regarding the research. The closing section should express the writer's personal interest in the project just completed and in doing additional, related work.[4]

Letter of Authorization   The *letter of authorization* is a letter to the researcher approving the project, detailing who has responsibility for it, and describing the resources available to support it.

Table of Contents   The *table of contents* is essential to any report more than a few pages long. It should list the divisions and subdivisions of the report with page references. The table of contents is based on the final outline of the report, but it should include only the first-level subdivisions. In short reports, inclusion of only the main divisions will be sufficient. If the report contains many figures or tables, a list of these also should immediately follow the table of contents.

Summary   The *summary* briefly explains why the research project was conducted, what aspects of the problem were considered, what the outcome was, and what should be done. It is a vital part of the report. Studies indicate that nearly all managers read a report's summary, while only a minority read the rest of the report. Thus, the writer's only chance to produce an impact may be in the summary.

The summary should be written only after the rest of the report has been completed. It represents the essence of the report. It should be one page long (or, at most, two), so the writer must carefully sort out what is important enough to include. Several pages of the full report may have to be condensed into one summarizing sentence. Different parts of the report may be condensed more than others; the number of words in the summary need not be in proportion to the length of the section being discussed. The summary should be written to be self-sufficient; in fact, the summary is often detached from the report and circulated by itself.

The Body   The *body* constitutes the bulk of the report. It begins with an **introduction section** that sets out the background factors that made the project necessary as well as the objectives of the research. It continues with discussions of the methodology, results, and limitations of the study and finishes with conclusions and recommendations based on the results.

The introduction explains why the project was done and what it aimed to discover. The relevant background comes next. Enough background should be included to explain why the project was worth doing, but unessential historical factors should be omitted. The question of how much is enough should be answered by referring to the needs of the audience. A government report that will be widely circulated requires more background than a company's internal report on customer satisfaction. The last part of the introduction explains exactly what the project tried to discover. It discusses the statement of the problem and research questions as they were stated in the research proposal. Each purpose presented here should have a corresponding entry in the results section later in the report.

The second division of the body is the **research methodology section.** This section is a challenge to write because it must explain technical procedures in a manner appropriate for the audience. The material in this section may be supplemented with more detailed explanations in an appendix or a glossary of technical terms.

The **results section** should occupy the bulk of the report. This section presents those findings of the project that bear on the objectives in some logical order. The results should be organized as a continuous narrative, designed to be convincing but not to oversell the project. Summary tables and charts should be used to aid the discussion. (See Chapter 14 for a discussion of this topic.) These may serve as points of reference to the data being discussed and free the prose from excessive facts and figures. Comprehensive or detailed charts, however, should be saved for the appendix.

Because no research is perfect, its limitations should be indicated. If problems arose with nonresponse error or sampling procedures, these should be discussed. However, the discussion of limitations should avoid overemphasizing the weaknesses; its aim should be to provide a realistic basis for assessing the results.

The last division of the body is the **conclusions and recommendations section.** Conclusions are opinions based on the results, and recommendations are suggestions for action. The conclusions and recommendations should be presented in this section in more detail than in the summary, and the text should include justification as needed.

Appendix   The *appendix* presents the "too" material. Any material that is too technical or too detailed to go in the body should appear in the appendix. This includes materials of interest only to some readers or subsidiary materials not directly related to the objectives. Some examples of appendix materials are data collection forms, detailed calculations, discussions of highly technical questions, detailed or comprehensive tables of results, and a bibliography (if appropriate).

THE ORAL PRESENTATION

The conclusions and recommendations of most research reports are presented orally as well as in writing. The purpose of an **oral presentation** is to highlight the most important findings of a research project and provide clients or line managers with the opportunity to clarify any ambiguous issues by asking questions.

Introduction section
The part of the body of a report that discusses background information and the specific objectives of the research.

research methodology section
The part of the body of a report that explains the research design, sampling procedures, and other technical procedures used to collect the data.

results section
The part of the body of a report that presents the findings of the project; it includes tables, charts, and an organized narrative.

conclusions and recommendations section
The part of the body of a report that provides opinions based on the results and suggestions for action.

oral presentation
A spoken summary of the major findings, conclusions, and recommendations given to clients or line managers to provide them with the opportunity to clarify any ambiguous issues by asking questions.

During oral presentations of research reports, many presenters use transparencies that viewers in the back row cannot read.[5] In fact, some presenters use transparencies that viewers in the front row cannot read.

All viewers would be much happier if all presenters were to follow Noah's Law of Overhead Transparencies. Noah's Law says: Never, ever, under any circumstances whatsoever, put more than 40 words on a transparency. A number counts as a word. Noah's Law is called Noah's Law because when God made it rain for 40 days and 40 nights, He flooded the whole world, and no presenter should attempt that with one overhead.

Note that, in Noah's Law, 40 is the absolute upper limit. Twenty is a good average. Seven is even better. If seven words look lonely, presenters can always MAKE THE LETTERS BIGGER.

Advertising legend David Ogilvy was a devout follower of Noah's Law. He thought so highly of it that he invented and enforced Ogilvy's Corollary. Ogilvy's Corollary says: Never put anything on a transparency (or a slide or a chart) that you don't intend to read out loud to your audience word for word. He reasoned that when one message comes in on the visual channel while another comes in on the auditory channel, the audience will probably neglect one message or the other.

The oral presentation may be as simple as a short conference with a manager at the client organization's location or as formal as a report to the board of directors. The key to effective presentation in either situation is preparation.

Communication specialists often suggest that a person preparing an oral presentation should begin at the end.[6] In other words, while preparing a presentation, a researcher should think about what he or she wants the client to know when it has been completed.

The researcher should select the three or four most important findings for emphasis and rely on the written report for a full summary. The researcher needs to be ready to defend the results of the research. This is not the same as being defensive; rather, it means being prepared to deal in a confident, competent manner with the questions that arise. Remember that even the most reliable and valid research project is worthless if the managers who must act on its results are not convinced of its importance.

As with written reports, a key to effective oral presentation is adapting to the audience. Delivering an hour-long, formal speech when a 10-minute discussion is called for (or vice versa) will reflect poorly on both the presenter and the report.

Many marketing researchers view themselves as technicians who generate numbers using sophisticated research designs and statistical techniques. Unfortunately, some researchers organize their oral presentations around technical details rather than around satisfying the manager's or client's needs. In Chapter 4, we compared weather reporters and marketing researchers. The average person watching a TV weather report wants to know whether to take an umbrella to work the next day. The weather reporter provides enormous amounts of information: It's snowing in Washington, sunny in San Diego, and

Oral presentations can be enhanced with computer-generated graphics. Presentation software, such as Microsoft's PowerPoint, allows a researcher to select background design, color, bullets for highlighting, and other graphic effects that make communication of the message more effective. It is a good idea to use simple attractive graphics and to avoid overwhelming the audience with flashiness.

raining in Texas. Maps full of lines show fronts, high- and low-pressure areas, and other weather facts. This amounts to extraneous information when the viewer simply wants to avoid getting wet. Fortunately, most weather reporters eventually let us know whether rain is forecast. In a similar vein, if the client wants only an executive summary, the oral presentation should emphasize material that one would expect to find in the summary section of the written report. Managers can always ask for additional details about the methodology or clarification of the data analysis.

The principles of good speech making apply to a research presentation. Lecturing or reading to the audience is sure to impede communication at any level of formality. The presenter should refrain from reading prepared text word for word. By relying on brief notes, familiarity with the subject, and as much rehearsal as the occasion calls for, the presenter will foster better communication. She or he should avoid research jargon and use short, familiar words. The presenter should maintain eye contact with the audience and repeat the main points. Because the audience cannot go back and replay what the speaker has said, the presentation often is organized around a standard format: "Tell them what you are going to tell them, tell them, and tell them what you just told them."

Graphic and other visual aids can be as useful in an oral presentation as in a written one. Presenters can choose from a variety of media. Slides, overhead projector acetates, and on-screen computer-generated graphics are useful for larger audiences. For smaller audiences, the researcher may put the visual aids on posters or flip charts. Another possibility is to make copies of the charts for each participant, possibly as a supplement to one of the other forms of presentation.

Whatever medium is chosen, each visual aid should be designed to convey a simple, attention-getting message that supports a point on which the audience should focus its thinking. As they do in written presentations, presenters should interpret the graphics for the audience. The best slides are easy to read and interpret. Large typefaces, multiple colors, bullets that highlight, and other artistic devices can enhance the readability of charts. It is also wise for presenters to allow the audience adequate time to read and familiarize themselves with the variables presented on slides. The use of gestures during presentations can also help convey the message and make the presentation more interesting.

REPORTS ON THE INTERNET

Many clients want numerous employees to have access to research findings. One easy way to share data is to make executive summaries and reports available on a company intranet. Or, a company can use information technology on the Internet to design questionnaires, administer surveys, analyze data, and share the results in a presentation-ready format. Real-time data capture allows for beginning-to-end reporting. A number of companies offer fully Web-based research management systems—For example, zTelligence is MarketTools' online solution for capturing and reporting research findings.

THE RESEARCH FOLLOW-UP

research follow-up
Recontacting decision makers and/or clients after they have had a chance to read over a research report, in order to determine whether additional information or clarification is necessary.

Research reports and oral presentations should communicate research findings so that managers can make business decisions. In many cases, the manager who receives the research report is unable to interpret the information and draw conclusions relevant to managerial decisions. For this reason, effective researchers do not treat the report as the end of the research process. They conduct a **research follow-up**, in which they recontact decision makers and/or clients after the latter have had a chance to read over the report. The purpose is to determine whether the researchers need to provide additional information or clarify some issues that may concern management. Just as marketing research may help an organization learn about its customers' satisfaction, the research follow-up can help marketing research staffers ensure the satisfaction of their customers, marketing management.

SUMMARY

Report preparation is the final stage of the research project. It is an important stage, because the project can guide management decisions only if it is effectively communicated. The research report is the presentation of the research findings directed to a specific audience to accomplish a particular purpose.

The general format for research reports includes certain prefatory sections, the body of the report, and appended parts. The report format should be tailored to the level of formality of the particular situation.

The prefatory parts of a formal report include a title page, letters of transmittal and authorization, a table of contents, and a summary. The summary is the most often read part of a report and should include a brief statement of the objectives, results, conclusions, and recommendations. The report body includes an introduction that gives the background and objectives, a statement of methodology, and a discussion of the results, their limitations, and appropriate conclusions and recommendations. The appendix includes various material that is too specialized to appear in the body of the report.

Most research projects are reported on orally as well as in writing, so the researcher needs to prepare an oral presentation. The presentation should defend the results without being defensive. It must be tailored to the situation and the audience.

The research follow-up involves recontacting decision makers after the report has been submitted to determine whether the researchers need to provide further information or clarify any issues of concern to management.

Key Terms and Concepts

research report
report format
introduction section
research methodology section

results section
conclusions and recommendations
    section
oral presentation

research follow-up

Questions For Review and Critical Thinking

1. Why is the research report important?
2. As a manager, what degree of formality would you want from your research department?
3. Go to your library and find some research reports. How do they meet the standards set forth in this chapter?

4. How does the oral presentation of research differ from the written research report?

Exploring the Internet

1. Go to Burke Interactive's Digital Dashboard demo at http://report.burke.com/dd_demo/welcome.asp. The site contains an online customer satisfaction report for JCN Computers, a fictional personal-computer manufacturer. Evaluate the format of the online research report.
2. Go to *American Demographics* magazine's home page at http://www.marketingtools.com.

a. Browse a back issue of *American Demographics*. Find a story that appears to be a summary of research reports.
b. What research reports are available in the magazine's Marketing and Research catalog?

VALUES AND THE AUTOMOBILE MARKET

In the last decade, the luxury car segment became one of the most competitive in the automobile market. Many American consumers who purchase luxury cars prefer imports from Germany and Japan.

A marketing vice president with General Motors once commented, "Import-committed buyers have been frustrating to us." This type of thinking has led industry analysts to argue that to successfully compete in the luxury car segment, U.S. carmakers need to develop a better understanding of the consumers so that they can better segment the market and better position their products via more effective advertising. Insight into the foreign–domestic luxury car choice may result from examining owners' personal values in addition to their evaluations of car attributes, because luxury cars, like many other conspicuously consumed luxury products, may be purchased mainly for value-expressive reasons.

Industry analysts believe it would be important to assess whether personal values of consumers could be used to explain ownership of American, German, and Japanese luxury cars. Further, they believe they should also assess whether knowledge of owners' personal values provides any additional information useful in explaining ownership of American, German, and Japanese luxury cars beyond that obtained from their evaluations of the cars' attributes.

Personal values are likely to provide insights into reasons for ownership of luxury cars for at least two reasons. First, Americans have always had a very personal relationship with their cars and have used them as symbols of their self-concept. For instance, people who value a *sense of accomplishment* are quite likely to desire a luxury car that they feel is an appropriate symbol of their achievement, whereas people who value *fun, enjoyment, and excitement* are likely to desire a luxury car that they perceive as fun and exciting to drive. An advertiser trying to persuade the former segment to purchase a luxury car should position the car as a status symbol that will help its owners demonstrate their accomplishments to others. Similarly, an advertiser trying to persuade the latter segment to purchase a luxury car should position the car as a fun and exciting car to drive. In other words, effective advertising shows consumers how purchasing a given product will help them achieve their valued state, because brands tied to values will be perceived more favorably than brands that deliver more mundane benefits.

Second, when a market is overcrowded with competing brands offering very similar options—as is the case with the luxury car market—consumers are quite likely to choose between brands on the basis of value-expressive considerations.

METHOD

Data were collected via a mail survey sent to 498 consumers chosen at random from a list obtained from a syndicated research company located in an affluent county in a southern state. The list contained names of people who had purchased either a luxury American car (Cadillac or Lincoln Mercury), a luxury German car (Mercedes or BMW), or a luxury Japanese car (Infiniti or Lexus) within the last year. A cover letter explained that the survey was part of an academic research project. People were asked to return the questionnaires anonymously to a university address (a postage-paid envelope was provided with each survey). Beyond an appeal to help the researchers, respondents were not offered any other incentive to complete the surveys. Of the 498 questionnaires originally sent, 17 were returned by the post office as undeliverable. One-hundred fifty-five completed surveys were received, for a response rate of 32.2 percent.

The Survey Instrument

The survey included questions on (1) various issues that people consider when purchasing new cars, (2) importance of car attributes, (3) importance of different values, and (4) demographics (sex, age, education, and family income). Questions relating to the issues that people consider when purchasing new cars were developed through initial interviews with consumers and were measured with a 7-point Likert scale with end anchors of "strongly agree" and "strongly disagree." (See Case Exhibit 1.1.) A list of 12 car attributes was developed from the initial interviews with consumers and by consulting *Consumer Reports*. (See Case Exhibit 1.2.) The importance of each attribute was measured with a 7-point numerical scale with end points labeled "very important" and "very unimportant." The List of Values (LOV) scale in Case Exhibit 1.3 was used to measure the importance of values. Respondents were asked to rate each of the eight values (we combined fun-enjoyment and excitement into one value) on a 7-point numerical scale with end points labeled "very important" and "very unimportant."

CASE EXHIBIT 1.1	ISSUES THAT CONSUMERS CONSIDER WHEN BUYING LUXURY AUTOMOBILES

Having a luxury car is a major part of my fun and excitement.[a] (Issue 1)

Owning a luxury car is a part of "being good to myself." (Issue 2)

When I was able to buy my first luxury car, I felt a sense of accomplishment. (Issue 3)

I enjoy giving my friends advice about luxury cars. (Issue 4)

Getting a good deal when I buy a luxury car makes me feel better about myself. (Issue 5)

I seek novelty and I am willing to try new innovations in cars. (Issue 6)

I tend to buy the same brand of the car several times in a row. (Issue 7)

I tend to buy from the same dealer several times in a row. (Issue 8)

I usually use sources of information such as *Consumer Reports* in deciding on a car. (Issue 9)

I usually visit three or more dealerships before I buy a car. (Issue 10)

I would read a brochure or watch a video about defensive driving. (Issue 11)

When buying a new luxury car, my family's opinion is very important to me. (Issue 12)

My family usually accompanies me when I am shopping for a new luxury car. (Issue 13)

I usually rely upon ads and salespersons for information on cars. (Issue 14)

I usually rely upon friends and acquaintances for information on cars. (Issue 15)

When shopping for a car, it is important that the car dealer make me feel at ease. (Issue 16)

Most of my friends drive luxury import cars. (Issue 17)

Most of my friends drive luxury domestic cars. (Issue 18)

I think celebrity endorsers in ads influence people's choices of luxury cars. (Issue 19)

I would not buy a luxury car if I felt that my debt level was higher than usual. (Issue 20)

[a]Note: Subjects' responses were measured with 1 as "strongly agree" and 7 as "strongly disagree."

Attribute	Code	Attribute	Code
Comfort	Comfort	Low maintenance cost	Lomc
Safety	Safety	Reliability	Rely
Power	Power	Warranty	Warrant
Speed	Speed	Nonpolluting	Nonpol
Styling	Styling	High gas mileage	Gasmle
Durability	Durabil	Speed of repairs	Repairs

CASE EXHIBIT 1.3 | **LIST OF VALUES**

Value	Code	Value	Code
Fun-Enjoyment-Excitement	Fun	Sense of accomplishment	Accomp
Sense of belonging	Belong	Warm relationship	Warm
Being well respected	Respect	Security	Security
Self-fulfillment	Selfful	Self-respect	Selfres

The Sample

Of the 155 respondents in the sample, 58 (37.4 percent) owned an American luxury car, 38 (24.5 percent) owned a European luxury car, and 59 (38.1 percent) owned a Japanese luxury car. The majority of the sample consisted of older (85 percent were 35 years of age or above), more educated (64 percent were college graduates), and economically well-off (87.2 percent earned $65,000 or more) consumers.

THE CODE BOOK

Case Exhibit 1.4 lists the SPSS variable names and identifies codes for these variables. (Note that this data set is also available in Microsoft Excel.)

CASE EXHIBIT 1.4 | **LIST OF VARIABLES AND COMPUTER CODES**

ID—Identification number
AGE (categories are 2 = 35 years and under, 3 = 36–45 yrs, 4 = 46–55 yrs, 5 = 56–65 yrs, 6 = 65+ yrs)
SEX (1 = male, 0 = female)
EDUC—Education (1 = less than high school, 2 = high school grad, 3 = Some college, 4 = College grad, 5 = Graduate degree)
INCOME (1 = less than $35,000, 2 = $35–50,000, 3 = $50–65,000, 4 = $65,000+)
CAR—Type of luxury car (American car, European car, Japanese car)
ISSUES—The sequence of issues listed in Case Exhibit 1.1. (Strongly agree = 1; strongly disagree = 7)
ATTRIBUTES—The sequence of car attributes listed in Case Exhibit 1.2. (Very important to you = 1; very unimportant to you = 7)
VALUES—The sequence of values listed in Case Exhibit 1.3. (Very important = 1; very unimportant = 7)

ADDITIONAL INFORMATION

Several of the questions will require the use of a computerized database. Your instructor will provide information about obtaining the LUXURY data set if the material is part of the case assignment.

Questions

1. Is the sampling method adequate? Is the attitude measuring scale sound? Explain.
2. Using the computerized database with a statistical software package, calculate the means of the three automotive groups for the values variables. Do any of the values variables show significant differences between American, Japanese, and European car owners?
3. Are there any significant differences on importance of attributes?
4. Write a short statement interpreting the results of this research.

Advanced Questions

5. Are any of the value scale items highly correlated?
6. Should multivariate analysis be used to understand the data?

EMPLOYEES FEDERAL CREDIT UNION

Download the data sets for this case from http://zikmund.swcollege.com or request them from your instructor.

Employees Federal Credit Union (EFCU) is the credit union for a Fortune 500 firm. Any employee of the organization is eligible for membership in the employees' credit union.

Over the past few years, the Employees Federal Credit Union has accumulated a large amount of surplus funds, which have been invested in certificates of deposit. It has also experienced a lower loan/share ratio than other credit unions of similar size. Because of these factors, the credit union's average earnings on its investments have slowly declined and its profit margins are being squeezed. The EFCU Board of Directors decided that a research project should be conducted to determine why its members are not borrowing money from the credit union. More specifically, the research project was mandated to answer the question of why members are borrowing money from other alternative sources instead of from the credit union.

In addition to the above, the EFCU Board of Directors expressed its desire to determine what the members' attitudes were toward the overall management and operations of the credit union. It was determined that the following questions should be addressed, as well:

- How informed is the membership about the services provided by the credit union?
- Are there any differences between members who live in the area of the firm's headquarters and members who live outside of the area in opinion toward borrowing funds and the services provided by the credit union?

RESEARCH OBJECTIVES

To respond to the questions raised by the board, the following objectives were developed. The research design was formulated to address each of the objectives stated below:

- To determine the reasons why people join the credit union
- To determine the reasons why members use other financial institutions when they need to borrow funds
- To measure member attitudes and beliefs about the proficiencies of credit union employees
- To determine whether there are any perceived differences between members who live in the area of the firm's headquarters and members who live elsewhere
- To determine member awareness of the services offered by the credit union
- To measure member attitudes and beliefs about how effectively the credit union is operated

RESEARCH DESIGN AND DATA COLLECTION METHOD

The research data were collected using a mail questionnaire survey. This technique was determined to be the best method for collecting the research data for the following reasons:

- The credit union members were widely dispersed geographically.
- The board wanted to minimize the cost of conducting the research.

- Several of the questions asked in the questionnaire were of a sensitive nature.
- The board had the flexibility of being able to wait for the survey results before taking any action.

A copy of the questionnaire used to gather the research data is provided in Case Exhibit 2.1. Most of the questions were designed as structured questions because of the variation in the educational backgrounds, job functions, and interests of the members surveyed. However, the respondents were given the flexibility to answer several key questions in an unstructured format. The Likert scale was principally used where attitude measurements were requested.

CASE EXHIBIT 2.1 | **EFCU MEMBER OPINION SURVEY**

1. Are you currently a member of the Employees Federal Credit Union (EFCU)?
   Yes ( )   No ( )
   If no, please have the member of your household who is a member of the EFCU complete the questionnaire.
   If no one in your household is a member, please return the questionnaire in the enclosed prepaid envelope.
2. Why did you join the credit union? (Check as many answers as are applicable.)
   __ Convenience
   __ Higher interest rates on my savings than other financial institutions pay
   __ More personal than other facilities
   __ Wanted a readily available source for borrowing money
   __ Advertisements prompted me to join
   __ Other—please explain: _____
   _____

Statements 3 through 6 ask for your opinion of the credit union employees. Check the response that best describes your rating of the credit union employees in each category. Please check only one response for each statement.

3. The credit union employees are courteous.

Strongly disagree	Disagree	Uncertain	Agree	Strongly agree
( )	( )	( )	( )	( )

4. The credit union employees are helpful.

Strongly disagree	Disagree	Uncertain	Agree	Strongly agree
( )	( )	( )	( )	( )

5. The credit union employees are professional.

Strongly disagree	Disagree	Uncertain	Agree	Strongly agree
( )	( )	( )	( )	( )

6. The credit union employees are always available.

Strongly disagree	Disagree	Uncertain	Agree	Strongly agree
( )	( )	( )	( )	( )

7. What is your opinion about the rates the credit union is paying on its share (members/savings) accounts?
   A. Very high __   B. High __   C. Average __
   D. Low __   E. Very low __   F. No opinion __
8. What is your opinion about the rates the credit union is charging its members to borrow funds?
   A. Very high __   B. High __   C. Average __
   D. Low __   E. Very low __   F. No opinion __

---

9. How often do you receive a financial statement of your account activity?

Too often	Very often	About right	Not often enough	Never
( )	( )	( )	( )	( )

10. How would you rate the accuracy of your statements?

Excellent	Good	Fair	Poor
( )	( )	( )	( )

11. Are they easy to understand?
Yes ( )   No ( )

12. Do you feel that the credit union maintains your account information in a confidential manner?
Yes ( )   No ( )

The questions in the next set are important in determining how effective the credit union has been in communicating its different services to the members. Please answer each question honestly—remember, there are no right or wrong answers.

Circle the response that best describes your awareness of the services offered by the credit union.

Circle 1—If you were aware of the service and have used it.
Circle 2—If you were aware of the service but have not used it.
Circle 3—If you did not know this service was offered by the credit union.

	Aware and Have Used	Aware but Have Not Used	Unaware of Service
13. Regular share accounts	1	2	3
14. Special subaccounts	1	2	3
15. Christmas club accounts	1	2	3
16. Individual retirement accounts	1	2	3
17. MasterCard credit cards	1	2	3
18. Signature loans	1	2	3
19. New car loans	1	2	3
20. Late model car loans	1	2	3
21. Older model car loans	1	2	3
22. Household goods/appliance loans	1	2	3
23. Recreational loans	1	2	3
24. Share collateralized loans	1	2	3
25. IRA loans	1	2	3
26. Line of credit loans	1	2	3

27. Do you currently have a loan with the credit union?
Yes ( )   No ( )

28. During the past year, have you borrowed money from a bank or other lending source other than the credit union?
Yes ( )   No ( )
If no, go to question 30.

29. Why did you go to a source other than the credit union?
___ My loan application at the credit union was not approved.
___ The credit union did not offer this type of credit.
___ I found better loan rates elsewhere.
___ I have an established credit line elsewhere.
___ I prefer to use a local financial institution.
___ Other: _____

_____

(continued)

For statements 30 through 34, check the response that best describes your feelings about the statements. Check only one response for each statement given.

30. The credit union's loan rates are lower than those offered by other institutions.

Strongly disagree	Disagree	Uncertain	Agree	Strongly agree
( )	( )	( )	( )	( )

31. The credit union personnel will keep my personal financial information confidential.

Strongly disagree	Disagree	Uncertain	Agree	Strongly agree
( )	( )	( )	( )	( )

32. The credit union is prompt in processing loan applications.

Strongly disagree	Disagree	Uncertain	Agree	Strongly agree
( )	( )	( )	( )	( )

33. The current financial services provided by the credit union meet the needs of its members.

Strongly disagree	Disagree	Uncertain	Agree	Strongly agree
( )	( )	( )	( )	( )

34. The loan applications used by the credit union are simple and easy to complete.

Strongly disagree	Disagree	Uncertain	Agree	Strongly agree
( )	( )	( )	( )	( )

35. Which of the services provided by the credit union do you like best?

_____

36. Which of the services provided by the credit union do you like least?

_____

37. Overall, how do you feel the credit union is being managed and operated?
    A. Excellent___   B. Good___   C. Average___
    D. Poor___   E. Very poor___   F. No opinion___

38. Do you live in the headquarters area?
    Yes ( )   No ( )
    If yes, go to question 40.

39. Do you feel the credit union meets your needs as well as those of members who live in the headquarters area?
    Yes ( )   No ( )
    If no, please explain: _____
    _____

40. If you were managing the credit union, what changes would you make and what additional services, if any, would you provide? _____
    _____
    _____
    _____
    _____

We sincerely appreciate the time and effort you made in completing this questionnaire. Thank you for your help.

SAMPLING PROCEDURES

The population of the EFCU is well-defined; consequently, a simple random sample of the membership was selected. A sample size of 300 was calculated using the estimated population standard deviation based on the responses from 15 members to question 37 of the questionnaire. Question 37 was used because it capsulized the essence of the research project.

The random numbers used in making the selection of the sampling units were generated with the help of a personal computer. The sampling frame used was the January 31 trial balance listing of the EFCU membership. According to the sampling frame, EFCU had 3,531 members on that date. As a result, the 300 random numbers were generated within the range of 1 to 3,531. Each random number was matched to a corresponding number in the sampling frame, and those individuals were selected to receive copies of the survey questionnaire.

FIELDWORK

Most of the fieldwork for the research project, including all of the editing and coding of the survey data, was performed by the Supervisory Committee Chairperson. The following is a list of the (much-appreciated) assistance received during the field procedures:

- Bob Perkins obtained a copy of the most currently available listing of the membership of the EFCU.
- The payroll department prepared mailing labels for all the members in the sample who were having withholding for the credit union made out of their payroll checks.
- The credit union clerks obtained the addresses and prepared mailing labels for all the remaining individuals selected in the sample.
- Administrative assistants helped copy and collate the survey questionnaires and prepare them for mailing.
- Ron Walker mailed all of the survey questionnaires.

The survey data from the structured questions were coded based on classifications established by the researcher. The codes were input into a series of databases using an IBM personal computer and a statistical software package.

Of the 125 returned questionnaires, two were not included in the survey results. One of the questionnaires was returned without the first two pages attached, and the other questionnaire appeared to be deliberately falsified; not only were all the responses on this questionnaire at the extremes, but a number of contradictions were noted as well.

CASE EXHIBIT 2.2	CODES FOR QUESTIONNAIRE
	strongly disagree = 1, strongly agree = 5
	very high = 1, very low = 5, no opinion = 6
	too often = 1, never = 5
	excellent = 1, poor = 4
	excellent =1, very poor = 5, no answer = 6
	yes = 1, no = 2, no answer = 3
	aware and have used = 1, unaware = 3

ADDITIONAL INFORMATION

Several of the questions will require the use of a computerized database. Each variable name is represented by its question number. Q1 is the variable name for question 1, "Are you a member of the Employees Federal Credit Union?" Q2 is the variable name for question 2, etc. Case Exhibit 2.2 presents the coding. Your instructor will provide information about obtaining the EFCU data set if this material is part of the case assignment. (The data are available in SPSS or Excel format.)

Questions
1. Evaluate the research objectives.
2. Evaluate the research design in light of the stated research objectives.
3. Using the computerized database, obtain simple frequencies for the answers to each question (the answers to the open-ended questions are not included in the database).
4. Perform the appropriate cross-tabulations.
5. Perform the appropriate univariate and bivariate statistical tests after you develop hypotheses for these particular tests.

STATISTICAL TABLES

TABLE 1		RANDOM DIGITS							
37751	04998	66038	63480	98442	22245	83538	62351	74514	90497
50915	64152	82981	15796	27102	71635	34470	13608	26360	76285
99142	35021	01032	57907	80545	54112	15150	36856	03247	40392
70720	10033	25191	62358	03784	74377	88150	25567	87457	49512
18460	64947	32958	08752	96366	89092	23597	74308	00881	88976
65763	41133	60950	35372	06782	81451	78764	52645	19841	50083
83769	52570	60133	25211	87384	90182	84990	26400	39128	97043
58900	78420	98579	33665	10718	39342	46346	14401	13503	46525
54746	71115	78219	64314	11227	41702	54517	87676	14078	45317
56819	27340	07200	52663	57864	85159	15460	97564	29637	27742
34990	62122	38223	28526	37006	22774	46026	15981	87291	56946
02269	22795	87593	81830	95383	67823	20196	54850	46779	64519
43042	53600	45738	00261	31100	67239	02004	70698	53597	62617
92565	12211	06868	87786	59576	61382	33972	13161	47208	96604
67424	32620	60841	86848	85000	04835	48576	33884	10101	84129
04015	77148	09535	10743	97871	55919	45274	38304	93125	91847
85226	19763	46105	25289	26714	73253	85922	21785	42624	92741
03360	07457	75131	41209	50451	23472	07438	08375	29312	62264
72460	99682	27970	25632	34096	17656	12736	27476	21938	67305
66960	55780	71778	52629	51692	71442	36130	70425	39874	62035
14824	95631	00697	65462	24815	13930	02938	54619	28909	53950
34001	05618	41900	23303	19928	60755	61404	56947	91441	19299
77718	83830	29781	72917	10840	74182	08293	62588	99625	22088
60930	05091	35726	07414	49211	69586	20226	08274	28167	65279
94180	62151	08112	26646	07617	42954	22521	09395	43561	45692
81073	85543	47650	93830	07377	87995	35084	39386	93141	88309
18467	39689	60801	46828	38670	88243	89042	78452	08032	72566
60643	59399	79740	17295	50094	66436	92677	68345	24025	36489
73372	61697	85728	90779	13235	83114	70728	32093	74306	08325
18395	18482	83245	54942	51905	09534	70839	91073	42193	81199
07261	28720	71244	05064	84873	68020	39037	68981	00670	86291
61679	81529	83725	33269	45958	74265	87460	60525	42539	25605
11815	48679	00556	96871	39835	83055	84949	11681	51687	55896
99007	35050	86440	44280	20320	97527	28138	01088	49037	85430
06446	65608	79291	16624	06135	30622	56133	33998	32308	29434

TABLE 2

AREA UNDER THE NORMAL CURVE

z	.00	.01	.02	.03	.04	.05	.06	.07	.08	.09
0.0	.0000	.0040	.0080	.0120	.0160	.0199	.0239	.0279	.0319	.0359
0.1	.0398	.0438	.0478	.0517	.0557	.0596	.0636	.0675	.0714	.0753
0.2	.0793	.0832	.0871	.0910	.0948	.0987	.1026	.1064	.1103	.1141
0.3	.1179	.1217	.1255	.1293	.1331	.1368	.1406	.1443	.1480	.1517
0.4	.1554	.1591	.1628	.1664	.1700	.1736	.1772	.1808	.1844	.1879
0.5	.1915	.1950	.1985	.2019	.2054	.2088	.2123	.2157	.2190	.2224
0.6	.2257	.2291	.2324	.2357	.2389	.2422	.2454	.2486	.2518	.2549
0.7	.2580	.2612	.2642	.2673	.2704	.2734	.2764	.2794	.2823	.2852
0.8	.2881	.2910	.2939	.2967	.2995	.3023	.3051	.3078	.3106	.3133
0.9	.3159	.3186	.3212	.3238	.3264	.3289	.3315	.3340	.3365	.3389
1.0	.3413	.3438	.3461	.3485	.3508	.3531	.3554	.3577	.3599	.3621
1.1	.3643	.3665	.3686	.3708	.3729	.3749	.3770	.3790	.3810	.3830
1.2	.3849	.3869	.3888	.3907	.3925	.3944	.3962	.3980	.3997	.4015
1.3	.4032	.4049	.4066	.4082	.4099	.4115	.4131	.4147	.4162	.4177
1.4	.4192	.4207	.4222	.4236	.4251	.4265	.4279	.4292	.4306	.4319
1.5	.4332	.4345	.4357	.4370	.4382	.4394	.4406	.4418	.4429	.4441
1.6	.4452	.4463	.4474	.4484	.4495	.4505	.4515	.4525	.4535	.4545
1.7	.4554	.4564	.4573	.4582	.4591	.4599	.4608	.4616	.4625	.4633
1.8	.4641	.4649	.4656	.4664	.4671	.4678	.4686	.4693	.4699	.4706
1.9	.4713	.4719	.4726	.4732	.4738	.4744	.4750	.4756	.4761	.4767
2.0	.4772	.4778	.4783	.4788	.4793	.4798	.4803	.4808	.4812	.4817
2.1	.4821	.4826	.4830	.4834	.4838	.4842	.4846	.4850	.4854	.4857
2.2	.4861	.4864	.4868	.4871	.4875	.4878	.4881	.4884	.4887	.4890
2.3	.4893	.4896	.4898	.4901	.4904	.4906	.4909	.4911	.4913	.4916
2.4	.4918	.4920	.4922	.4925	.4927	.4929	.4931	.4932	.4934	.4936
2.5	.4938	.4940	.4941	.4943	.4945	.4946	.4948	.4949	.4951	.4952
2.6	.4953	.4955	.4956	.4957	.4959	.4960	.4961	.4962	.4963	.4964
2.7	.4965	.4966	.4967	.4968	.4969	.4970	.4971	.4972	.4973	.4974
2.8	.4974	.4975	.4976	.4977	.4977	.4978	.4979	.4979	.4980	.4981
2.9	.4981	.4982	.4982	.4983	.4984	.4984	.4985	.4985	.4986	.4986
3.0	.49865	.4987	.4987	.4988	.4988	.4989	.4989	.4989	.4990	.4990
4.0	.49997									

TABLE 3

DISTRIBUTION OF *t* FOR GIVEN PROBABILITY LEVELS

	LEVEL OF SIGNIFICANCE FOR ONE-TAILED TEST					
	.10	.05	.025	.01	.005	.0005
	LEVEL OF SIGNIFICANCE FOR TWO-TAILED TEST					
d.f.	.20	.10	.05	.02	.01	.001
1	3.078	6.314	12.706	31.821	63.657	636.619
2	1.886	2.920	4.303	6.965	9.925	31.598
3	1.638	2.353	3.182	4.541	5.841	12.941
4	1.533	2.132	2.776	3.747	4.604	8.610
5	1.476	2.015	2.571	3.365	4.032	6.859
6	1.440	1.943	2.447	3.143	3.707	5.959
7	1.415	1.895	2.365	2.998	3.499	5.405
8	1.397	1.860	2.306	2.896	3.355	5.041
9	1.383	1.833	2.262	2.821	3.250	4.781
10	1.372	1.812	2.228	2.764	3.169	4.587
11	1.363	1.796	2.201	2.718	3.106	4.437
12	1.356	1.782	2.179	2.681	3.055	4.318
13	1.350	1.771	2.160	2.650	3.012	4.221
14	1.345	1.761	2.145	2.624	2.977	4.140
15	1.341	1.753	2.131	2.602	2.947	4.073
16	1.337	1.746	2.120	2.583	2.921	4.015
17	1.333	1.740	2.110	2.567	2.898	3.965
18	1.330	1.734	2.101	2.552	2.878	3.922
19	1.328	1.729	2.093	2.539	2.861	3.883
20	1.325	1.725	2.086	2.528	2.845	3.850
21	1.323	1.721	2.080	2.518	2.831	3.819
22	1.321	1.717	2.074	2.508	2.819	3.792
23	1.319	1.714	2.069	2.500	2.807	3.767
24	1.318	1.711	2.064	2.492	2.797	3.745
25	1.316	1.708	2.060	2.485	2.787	3.725
26	1.315	1.706	2.056	2.479	2.779	3.707
27	1.314	1.703	2.052	2.473	2.771	3.690
28	1.313	1.701	2.048	2.467	2.763	3.674
29	1.311	1.699	2.045	2.462	2.756	3.659
30	1.310	1.697	2.042	2.457	2.750	3.646
40	1.303	1.684	2.021	2.423	2.704	3.551
60	1.296	1.671	2.000	2.390	2.660	3.460
120	1.289	1.658	1.980	2.358	2.617	3.373
∞	1.282	1.645	1.960	2.326	2.576	3.291

TABLE 4 | CHI-SQUARE DISTRIBUTION

Degrees of Freedom (d.f.)	AREA IN SHADED RIGHT TAIL (α)		
	.10	.05	.01
1	2.706	3.841	6.635
2	4.605	5.991	9.210
3	6.251	7.815	11.345
4	7.779	9.488	13.277
5	9.236	11.070	15.086
6	10.645	12.592	16.812
7	12.017	14.067	18.475
8	13.362	15.507	20.090
9	14.684	16.919	21.666
10	15.987	18.307	23.209
11	17.275	19.675	24.725
12	18.549	21.026	26.217
13	19.812	22.362	27.688
14	21.064	23.685	29.141
15	22.307	24.996	30.578
16	23.542	26.296	32.000
17	24.769	27.587	33.409
18	25.989	28.869	34.805
19	27.204	30.144	36.191
20	28.412	31.410	37.566
21	29.615	32.671	38.932
22	30.813	33.924	40.289
23	32.007	35.172	41.638
24	33.196	36.415	42.980
25	34.382	37.652	44.314
26	35.563	38.885	45.642
27	36.741	40.113	46.963
28	37.916	41.337	48.278
29	39.087	42.557	49.588
30	40.256	43.773	50.892

Example of how to use this table: In a chi-square distribution with 6 degrees of freedom (*d.f.*), the area to the right of a critical value of 12.592—i.e., the α area—is .05.

TABLE 5

CRITICAL VALUES OF $F_{v_1 v_2}$ FOR $\alpha = .05$

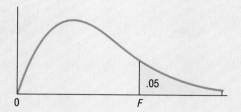

v_1 = DEGREES OF FREEDOM FOR NUMERATOR

v_2	1	2	3	4	5	6	7	8	9	10	12	15	20	24	30	40	60	120	∞
1	161	200	216	225	230	234	237	239	241	242	244	246	248	249	250	251	252	253	254
2	18.5	19.0	19.2	19.2	19.3	19.3	19.4	19.4	19.4	19.4	19.4	19.4	19.5	19.5	19.5	19.5	19.5	19.5	19.5
3	10.1	9.55	9.28	9.12	9.01	8.94	8.89	8.85	8.81	8.79	8.74	8.70	8.66	8.64	8.62	8.59	8.57	8.55	8.53
4	7.71	6.94	6.59	6.39	6.26	6.16	6.09	6.04	6.00	5.96	5.91	5.86	5.80	5.77	5.75	5.72	5.69	5.66	5.63
5	6.61	5.79	5.41	5.19	5.05	4.95	4.88	4.82	4.77	4.74	4.68	4.62	4.56	4.53	4.50	4.46	4.43	4.40	4.37
6	5.99	5.14	4.76	4.53	4.39	4.28	4.21	4.15	4.10	4.06	4.00	3.94	3.87	3.84	3.81	3.77	3.74	3.70	3.67
7	5.59	4.74	4.35	4.12	3.97	3.87	3.79	3.73	3.68	3.64	3.57	3.51	3.44	3.41	3.38	3.34	3.30	3.27	3.23
8	5.32	4.46	4.07	3.84	3.69	3.58	3.50	3.44	3.39	3.35	3.28	3.22	3.15	3.12	3.08	3.04	3.01	2.97	2.93
9	5.12	4.26	3.86	3.63	3.48	3.37	3.29	3.23	3.18	3.14	3.07	3.01	2.94	2.90	2.86	2.83	2.79	2.75	2.71
10	4.96	4.10	3.71	3.48	3.33	3.22	3.14	3.07	3.02	2.98	2.91	2.85	2.77	2.74	2.70	2.66	2.62	2.58	2.54
11	4.84	3.98	3.59	3.36	3.20	3.09	3.01	2.95	2.90	2.85	2.79	2.72	2.65	2.61	2.57	2.53	2.49	2.45	2.40
12	4.75	3.89	3.49	3.26	3.11	3.00	2.91	2.85	2.80	2.75	2.69	2.62	2.54	2.51	2.47	2.43	2.38	2.34	2.30
13	4.67	3.81	3.41	3.18	3.03	2.92	2.83	2.77	2.71	2.67	2.60	2.53	2.46	2.42	2.38	2.34	2.30	2.25	2.21
14	4.60	3.74	3.34	3.11	2.96	2.85	2.76	2.70	2.65	2.60	2.53	2.46	2.39	2.35	2.31	2.27	2.22	2.18	2.13
15	4.54	3.68	3.29	3.06	2.90	2.79	2.71	2.64	2.59	2.54	2.48	2.40	2.33	2.29	2.25	2.20	2.16	2.11	2.07
16	4.49	3.63	3.24	3.01	2.85	2.74	2.66	2.59	2.54	2.49	2.42	2.35	2.28	2.24	2.19	2.15	2.11	2.06	2.01
17	4.45	3.59	3.20	2.96	2.81	2.70	2.61	2.55	2.49	2.45	2.38	2.31	2.23	2.19	2.15	2.10	2.06	2.01	1.96
18	4.41	3.55	3.16	2.93	2.77	2.66	2.58	2.51	2.46	2.41	2.34	2.27	2.19	2.15	2.11	2.06	2.02	1.97	1.92
19	4.38	3.52	3.13	2.90	2.74	2.63	2.54	2.48	2.42	2.38	2.31	2.23	2.16	2.11	2.07	2.03	1.98	1.93	1.88
20	4.35	3.49	3.10	2.87	2.71	2.60	2.51	2.45	2.39	2.35	2.28	2.20	2.12	2.08	2.04	1.99	1.95	1.90	1.84
21	4.32	3.47	3.07	2.84	2.68	2.57	2.49	2.42	2.37	2.32	2.25	2.18	2.10	2.05	2.01	1.96	1.92	1.87	1.81
22	4.30	3.44	3.05	2.82	2.66	2.55	2.46	2.40	2.34	2.30	2.23	2.15	2.07	2.03	1.98	1.94	1.89	1.84	1.78
23	4.28	3.42	3.03	2.80	2.64	2.53	2.44	2.37	2.32	2.27	2.20	2.13	2.05	2.01	1.96	1.91	1.86	1.81	1.76
24	4.26	3.40	3.01	2.78	2.62	2.51	2.42	2.36	2.30	2.25	2.18	2.11	2.03	1.98	1.94	1.89	1.84	1.79	1.73
25	4.24	3.39	2.99	2.76	2.60	2.49	2.40	2.34	2.28	2.24	2.16	2.09	2.01	1.96	1.92	1.87	1.82	1.77	1.71
30	4.17	3.32	2.92	2.69	2.53	2.42	2.33	2.27	2.21	2.16	2.09	2.01	1.93	1.89	1.84	1.79	1.74	1.68	1.62
40	4.08	3.23	2.84	2.61	2.45	2.34	2.25	2.18	2.12	2.08	2.00	1.92	1.84	1.79	1.74	1.69	1.64	1.58	1.51
60	4.00	3.15	2.76	2.53	2.37	2.25	2.17	2.10	2.04	1.99	1.92	1.84	1.75	1.70	1.65	1.59	1.53	1.47	1.39
120	3.92	3.07	2.68	2.45	2.29	2.18	2.09	2.02	1.96	1.91	1.83	1.75	1.66	1.61	1.55	1.50	1.43	1.35	1.25
∞	3.84	3.00	2.60	2.37	2.21	2.10	2.01	1.94	1.88	1.83	1.75	1.67	1.57	1.52	1.46	1.39	1.32	1.22	1.00

v_2 = DEGREES OF FREEDOM FOR DENOMINATOR

TABLE 6

CRITICAL VALUES OF $F_{v_1 v_2}$ FOR $\alpha = .01$

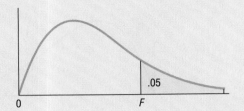

v_1 = DEGREES OF FREEDOM FOR NUMERATOR

v_2	1	2	3	4	5	6	7	8	9	10	12	15	20	24	30	40	60	120	∞
1	4,052	5,000	5,403	5,625	5,764	5,859	5,928	5,982	6,023	6,056	6,106	6,157	6,209	6,235	6,261	6,287	6,313	6,339	6,366
2	98.5	99.0	99.2	99.2	99.3	99.3	99.4	99.4	99.4	99.4	99.4	99.4	99.4	99.5	99.5	99.5	99.5	99.5	99.5
3	34.1	30.8	29.5	28.7	28.2	27.9	27.7	27.5	27.3	27.2	27.1	26.9	26.7	26.6	26.5	26.4	26.3	26.2	26.1
4	21.2	18.0	16.7	16.0	15.5	15.2	15.0	14.8	14.7	14.5	14.4	14.2	14.0	13.9	13.8	13.7	13.7	13.6	13.5
5	16.3	13.3	12.1	11.4	11.0	10.7	10.5	10.3	10.2	10.1	9.89	9.72	9.55	9.47	9.38	9.29	9.20	9.11	9.02
6	13.7	10.9	9.78	9.15	8.75	8.47	8.26	8.10	7.98	7.87	7.72	7.56	7.40	7.31	7.23	7.14	7.06	6.97	6.88
7	12.2	9.55	8.45	7.85	7.46	7.19	6.99	6.84	6.72	6.62	6.47	6.31	6.16	6.07	5.99	5.91	5.82	5.74	5.65
8	11.3	8.65	7.59	7.01	6.63	6.37	6.18	6.03	5.91	5.81	5.67	5.52	5.36	5.28	5.20	5.12	5.03	4.95	4.86
9	10.6	8.02	6.99	6.42	6.06	5.80	5.61	5.47	5.35	5.26	5.11	4.96	4.81	4.73	4.65	4.57	4.48	4.40	4.31
10	10.0	7.56	6.55	5.99	5.64	5.39	5.20	5.06	4.94	4.85	4.71	4.56	4.41	4.33	4.25	4.17	4.08	4.00	3.91
11	9.65	7.21	6.22	5.67	5.32	5.07	4.89	4.74	4.63	4.54	4.40	4.25	4.10	4.02	3.94	3.86	3.78	3.69	3.60
12	9.33	6.93	5.95	5.41	5.06	4.82	4.64	4.50	4.39	4.30	4.16	4.01	3.86	3.78	3.70	3.62	3.54	3.45	3.36
13	9.07	6.70	5.74	5.21	4.86	4.62	4.44	4.30	4.19	4.10	3.96	3.82	3.66	3.59	3.51	3.43	3.34	3.25	3.17
14	8.86	6.51	5.56	5.04	4.70	4.46	4.28	4.14	4.03	3.94	3.80	3.66	3.51	3.43	3.35	3.27	3.18	3.09	3.00
15	8.68	6.36	5.42	4.89	4.56	4.32	4.14	4.00	3.89	3.80	3.67	3.52	3.37	3.29	3.21	3.13	3.05	2.96	2.87
16	8.53	6.23	5.29	4.77	4.44	4.20	4.03	3.89	3.78	3.69	3.55	3.41	3.26	3.18	3.10	3.02	2.93	2.84	2.75
17	8.40	6.11	5.19	4.67	4.34	4.10	3.93	3.79	3.68	3.59	3.46	3.31	3.16	3.08	3.00	2.92	2.83	2.75	2.65
18	8.29	6.01	5.09	4.58	4.25	4.01	3.84	3.71	3.60	3.51	3.37	3.23	3.08	3.00	2.92	2.84	2.75	2.66	2.57
19	8.19	5.93	5.01	4.50	4.17	3.94	3.77	3.63	3.52	3.43	3.30	3.15	3.00	2.92	2.84	2.76	2.67	2.58	2.49
20	8.10	5.85	4.94	4.43	4.10	3.87	3.70	3.56	3.46	3.37	3.23	3.09	2.94	2.86	2.78	2.69	2.61	2.52	2.42
21	8.02	5.78	4.87	4.37	4.04	3.81	3.64	3.51	3.40	3.31	3.17	3.03	2.88	2.80	2.72	2.64	2.55	2.46	2.36
22	7.96	5.72	4.82	4.31	3.99	3.76	3.59	3.45	3.35	3.26	3.12	2.98	2.83	2.75	2.67	2.58	2.50	2.40	2.31
23	7.88	5.66	4.76	4.26	3.94	3.71	3.54	3.41	3.30	3.21	3.07	2.93	2.78	2.70	2.62	2.54	2.45	2.35	2.26
24	7.82	5.61	4.72	4.22	3.90	3.67	3.50	3.36	3.26	3.17	3.03	2.89	2.74	2.66	2.58	2.49	2.40	2.31	2.21
25	7.77	5.57	4.68	4.18	3.86	3.63	3.46	3.32	3.22	3.13	2.99	2.85	2.70	2.62	2.53	2.45	2.36	2.27	2.17
30	7.58	5.39	4.51	4.02	3.70	3.47	3.30	3.17	3.07	2.98	2.84	2.70	2.55	2.47	2.39	2.30	2.21	2.11	2.01
40	7.31	5.18	4.31	3.83	3.51	3.29	3.12	2.99	2.89	2.80	2.66	2.52	2.37	2.29	2.20	2.11	2.02	1.92	1.80
60	7.08	4.98	4.13	3.65	3.34	3.12	2.95	2.82	2.72	2.63	2.50	2.35	2.20	2.12	2.03	1.94	1.84	1.73	1.60
120	6.85	4.79	3.95	3.48	3.17	2.96	2.79	2.66	2.56	2.47	2.34	2.19	2.03	1.95	1.86	1.76	1.66	1.53	1.38
∞	6.63	4.61	3.78	3.32	3.02	2.80	2.64	2.51	2.41	2.32	2.18	2.04	1.88	1.79	1.70	1.59	1.47	1.32	1.00

v_2 = DEGREES OF FREEDOM FOR DENOMINATOR

TABLE 7

**CRITICAL VALUES OF THE
PEARSON CORRELATION COEFFICIENT**

	LEVEL OF SIGNIFICANCE FOR ONE-TAILED TEST			
	.05	.025	.01	.005
	LEVEL OF SIGNIFICANCE FOR TWO-TAILED TEST			
d.f.	.10	.05	.02	.01
1	.988	.997	.9995	.9999
2	.900	.950	.980	.990
3	.805	.878	.934	.959
4	.729	.811	.882	.917
5	.669	.754	.833	.874
6	.622	.707	.789	.834
7	.582	.666	.750	.798
8	.549	.632	.716	.765
9	.521	.602	.685	.735
10	.497	.576	.658	.708
11	.476	.553	.634	.684
12	.458	.532	.612	.661
13	.441	.514	.592	.641
14	.426	.497	.574	.623
15	.412	.482	.558	.606
16	.400	.468	.542	.590
17	.389	.456	.528	.575
18	.378	.444	.516	.561
19	.369	.433	.503	.549
20	.360	.423	.492	.537
21	.352	.413	.482	.526
22	.344	.404	.472	.515
23	.337	.396	.462	.505
24	.330	.388	.453	.496
25	.323	.381	.445	.487
26	.317	.374	.437	.479
27	.311	.367	.430	.471
28	.306	.361	.423	.463
29	.301	.355	.416	.456
30	.296	.349	.409	.449
35	.275	.325	.381	.418
40	.257	.304	.358	.393
45	.243	.288	.338	.372
50	.231	.273	.322	.354
60	.211	.250	.295	.325
70	.195	.232	.274	.303
80	.183	.217	.256	.283
90	.173	.205	.242	.267
100	.164	.195	.230	.254

Greek Letters

α (alpha)	level of significance or probability of a Type I error
β (beta)	probability of a Type II error or slope of the regression line
μ (mu)	population mean
ρ (rho)	population Pearson correlation coefficient
Σ (summation)	take the sum of
π (pi)	population proportion
σ (sigma)	population standard deviation
χ^2	chi–square statistic

English Letters

$d.f.$	number of degrees of freedom
F	F-statistic
n	sample size
p	sample proportion
$Pr(\ )$	probability of the outcome in the parentheses
r	sample Pearson correlation coefficient
r^2	coefficient of determination (squared correlation coefficient)
R^2	coefficient of determination (multiple regression)
S	sample standard deviation (inferential statistics)
$S_{\overline{X}}$	estimated standard error of the mean
S_p	estimated standard error of the proportion
S^2	sample variance (inferential statistics)
t	t-statistic
X	variable or any unspecified observation
$\overline{X}$	sample mean
Y	any unspecified observation on a second variable, usually the dependent variable
$\hat{Y}$	predicted score
Z	standardized score (descriptive statistics) or Z-statistic

A

acquiescence bias A category of response bias that results because some individuals tend to agree with all questions or to concur with a particular position.

administrative error An error caused by the improper administration or execution of the research task.

advocacy research Research undertaken to support a specific claim in a legal action.

alternative hypothesis A statement indicating the opposite of the null hypothesis.

analysis of variance (ANOVA) Analysis involving the investigation of the effects of one treatment variable on an interval-scaled dependent variable; a hypothesis-testing technique to determine whether statistically significant differences on means occur among three or more groups.

applied research Research undertaken to answer questions about specific problems or to make decisions about particular courses of action.

at-home scanning system A system that allows consumer panelists to perform their own scanning after taking home products using hand-held wands that read UPC symbols.

attitude An enduring disposition to consistently respond in a given manner to various aspects of the world; composed of affective, cognitive, and behavioral components.

attribute A single characteristic or fundamental feature of an object, a person, a situation, or an issue.

auspices bias Response bias that results because respondents are influenced by the organization conducting the study.

B

back translation The process of translating a questionnaire into another language and then having a second, independent translator translate it back to the original language.

backward linkage A term implying that the later stages of the research process influence the early stages.

base The number of respondents or observations (in a row or column) used as a basis for computing percentages.

basic experimental design An experimental design in which a single independent variable is manipulated to measure its effect on another single dependent variable.

basic (pure) research Research conducted to expand the boundaries of knowledge itself or to verify the acceptability of a given theory.

behavioral differential A rating scale instrument, similar to a semantic differential, developed to measure the behavioral intentions of subjects toward future actions.

bivariate linear regression A measure of linear association that investigates a straight-line relationship of the type $Y = a + \beta X$, where X is the independent variable and a and β are two constants to be estimated.

bivariate statistical analysis Data analysis and hypothesis testing involving the simultaneous investigation of two variables.

blinding A technique used to control subjects' knowledge of whether or not they have been given a particular experimental treatment.

browser A software program with a graphical user interface that enables the user to display Web pages as well as navigate the Internet.

business intelligence software Computer programs that permit managers to restructure and analyze data in extensive data warehouses to discover significant patterns and relationships.

C

callback An attempt to recontact an individual selected for a sample who was not available initially.

case study method An exploratory research technique that intensively investigates one or a few situations similar to the problem situation.

categorical (classificatory) variable A variable that has a limited number of distinct values.

category scale A rating scale that consists of several response categories, often providing respondents with alternatives to indicate positions on a continuum.

causal research Research conducted to identify cause-and-effect relationships among variables.

census An investigation of all the individual elements that make up a population.

central-limit theorem The theory that, as sample size increases, the distribution of sample means of size n, randomly selected, approaches a normal distribution.

central location interviewing Telephone interviews conducted from a central location using WATS lines at fixed charges.

check box In an Internet questionnaire, a small graphic box, next to an answer, that a respondent clicks on to choose that answer; typically, a check mark or an X appears in the box when the respondent clicks on it.

checklist question A fixed-alternative question that allows the respondent to provide multiple answers to a single question by checking off items.

chi-square (χ^2) test A hypothesis test that allows for investigation of statistical significance in the analysis of a frequency distribution.

choice A measurement task that identifies preferences by requiring respondents to choose between two or more alternatives.

client Term often used by a research department to refer to line management for whom it performs services.

cluster sampling An economically efficient sampling technique in which the primary sampling unit is not the individual element in the population but a large cluster of elements; clusters are selected randomly.

code of ethics A set of guidelines that states the standards and operating procedures for ethical practices by researchers.

coefficient of determination (r^2) A measure obtained by squaring the correlation coefficient; that proportion of the total variance of a variable that is accounted for by knowing the value of another variable.

cohort effect A change in the dependent variable that occurs because members of one experimental group experienced different historical situations than members of other experimental groups.

compromise design An approximation of an experimental design, which may fall short of the requirements of random assignment of subjects or treatments to groups.

computer-assisted telephone interview (CATI) A telephone interview in which answers to questions are entered directly into a computer for processing.

computer-interactive survey Data collection method in which the respondent completes a self-administered questionnaire displayed on the monitor of a computer. Respondents interact directly with a computer programmed to ask questions in a sequence determined by respondents' previous answers.

computer map A two- or three-dimensional map generated by a computer to portray demographic, sales, or other data.

concept A generalized idea about a class of objects, attributes, occurrences, or processes.

concept testing Any exploratory research procedure that tests some sort of stimulus as a proxy for an idea about a new, revised, or repositioned product, service, or strategy.

conceptual definition A verbal explanation of the meaning of a concept; defines what the concept is and what it is not.

conclusions and recommendations section The part of the body of a report that provides opinions based on the results and suggestions for action.

conclusions and report preparation stage The stage in which the researcher interprets information and draws conclusions to be communicated to decision makers.

concomitant variation The way in which two phenomena or events vary together.

confidence interval estimate A specified range of numbers within which a population mean is expected to lie; an estimate of the population mean based on the knowledge that it will be equal to the sample mean plus or minus a small sampling error.

confidence level A percentage or decimal value that tells how confident a researcher can be about being correct. It states the long-run percentage of confidence intervals that will include the true population mean.

constancy of conditions A situation in which subjects in experimental groups and control groups are exposed to situations identical except for differing conditions of the independent variable.

constant error An error that occurs in the same experimental condition every time the basic experiment is repeated; a systematic bias.

constant-sum scale A measure of attitudes in which respondents are asked to divide a constant sum to indicate the relative importance of attributes.

consumer panel A longitudinal survey of the same sample of individuals or households to record their attitudes, behavior, or purchasing habits over time.

content analysis The systematic observation and quantitative description of the manifest content of communication.

content provider A party that furnishes information on the World Wide Web.

contingency table The results of a cross-tabulation of two variables, such as answers to two survey questions.

continuous variable A variable that has an infinite number of possible values.

contrived observation Observation in which the investigator creates an artificial environment to test a hypothesis.

control group The group of subjects exposed to the control condition—that is, not exposed to the experimental treatment.

control method of test marketing A "minimarket test" using forced distribution in a small city. Retailers are paid for shelf space so that the test marketer can be guaranteed distribution.

controlled store test A hybrid between a laboratory experiment and a test market; test products are sold in a small number of selected stores to actual customers.

convenience sampling The sampling procedure of obtaining those people or units that are most conveniently available.

cookies Small computer files that a content provider can save onto the computer of someone who visits its Web site.

correlation coefficient A statistical measure of the covariation, or association, between two variables.

correlation matrix The standard form for reporting correlational results.

counterbalancing A technique requiring that half the subjects be exposed to treatment A first and then to treatment B while the other half receive treatment B and then treatment A. This is an attempt to eliminate the confounding effects of order of presentation.

counterbiasing statement An introductory statement or preamble to a potentially embarrassing question that reduces a respondent's reluctance to answer by suggesting that certain behavior is not unusual.

cover letter Letter that accompanies a questionnaire to induce the reader to complete and return the questionnaire.

critical values The values that lie exactly on the boundary of the region of rejection.

cross-check A comparison of data from one source with data from another source to determine the similarity of independent projects.

cross-functional teams Teams composed of individuals from various organizational departments, such as engineering, production, finance, and marketing, who share a common purpose.

cross-sectional study A study in which various segments of a population are sampled and data are collected at a single moment in time.

cross-tabulation Organizing data by groups, categories, or classes to facilitate comparisons; a joint frequency distribution of observations on two or more sets of variables.

custom research A marketing research study designed for an individual client and tailored to the client's unique needs.

customer relationship management (CRM) A decision support system that brings together numerous pieces of information about customers and their relationship with the company.

D

data Facts or recorded measures of certain phenomena.

data conversion The process of changing the original form of data to a format suitable to achieve the research objective; also called data transformation.

data-gathering stage The stage in which the researcher collects the data.

data mining The use of powerful computers to dig through volumes of data to discover patterns about an organization's customers and products. It is a broad term that applies to many different forms of analysis.

data-processing and analysis stage The stage in which the researcher performs several interrelated procedures to convert data into a format that will answer management's questions.

data-processing error A category of administrative error that occurs because of incorrect data entry, incorrect computer programming, or other procedural errors during the data-processing stage.

data transformation (data conversion) The process of changing the original form of data to a format suitable to achieve the research objective.

database A collection of raw data arranged logically and organized in a form that can be stored and processed by a computer.

database marketing The use of customer databases to promote one-to-one relationships with customers and create precisely targeted promotions.

debriefing The process of providing subjects with all pertinent facts about the nature and purpose of an experiment after its completion.

decision making The process used to resolve a problem or to choose from alternative opportunities.

decision support system A computer-based system that helps decision makers confront problems through direct interaction with databases and analytical software programs.

degrees of freedom The number of observations minus the number of constraints or assumptions needed to calculate a statistical term.

demand characteristics Experimental design procedures or situational aspects of an experiment that provide unintentional hints about the experimenter's hypothesis to subjects.

dependent variable The criterion by which the results of an experiment are judged; a variable expected to be dependent on the experimenter's manipulation of the independent variable.

depth interview A relatively unstructured, extensive interview in which the interviewer asks many questions and probes for in-depth answers.

descriptive analysis The transformation of raw data into a form that will make them easy to understand and interpret; rearranging, ordering, and manipulating data to generate descriptive information.

descriptive research Research designed to describe characteristics of a population or phenomenon.

determinant-choice question A fixed-alternative question that requires a respondent to choose one response from among multiple alternatives.

dialog box A window that opens on a computer screen to prompt the user to enter information.

direct observation A straightforward attempt to observe and record what naturally occurs; the investigator does not create an artificial situation.

director of marketing research The head of a research department, who provides leadership and integrates staff-level activities by planning, executing, and controlling the marketing research function; sometimes called director of marketing information systems.

discussion guide A document prepared by a focus group moderator that contains remarks about the nature of the group and outlines the topics or questions to be addressed.

door-to-door interview A personal interview conducted at the respondent's home or place of business.

double-barreled question A question that may induce bias because it covers two issues at once.

double-blind design A technique in which neither the subjects nor the experimenter knows which are the experimental and which the controlled conditions.

drop-down box In an Internet questionnaire, a space-saving device that reveals responses when they are needed but otherwise hides them from view.

drop-off method A survey method that requires the interviewer to travel to the respondent's location to drop off a questionnaire that will be picked up later.

E

e-mail Electronic mail used to communicate over the Internet.

e-mail survey Survey distributed through electronic mail.

elaboration analysis An analysis of the basic cross-tabulation for each level of a variable not previously considered, such as subgroups of the sample.

electronic data interchange (EDI) The linking of one company's computer system with another company's system to allow the sharing of data and software.

electronic test markets A system of test marketing that measures results based on Universal Product Code data; often scanner-based consumer panels are combined with high-technology television broadcasting systems to allow experimentation with different advertising messages via split-cable broadcasts or other technology.

environmental scanning Information gathering and fact finding designed to detect indications of environmental changes in their initial stages of development.

error trapping Using software to control the flow of an Internet questionnaire—for example, to prevent respondents from backing up or failing to answer a question.

experience survey An exploratory research technique in which individuals who are knowledgeable about a particular research problem are questioned.

experiment A research method in which conditions are controlled so that one or more independent variables can be manipulated to test a hypothesis about a dependent variable. Experimentation allows evaluation of causal relationships among variables while all other variables are eliminated or controlled.

experimental group The group of subjects exposed to the experimental treatment.

experimental treatments Alternative manipulations of the independent variable being investigated.

experimenter bias An effect on the subjects' behavior caused by an experimenter's presence, actions, or comments.

exploratory research Initial research conducted to clarify and define the nature of a problem.

expressive behavior A type of behavior that can be scientifically observed, such as tone of voice or facial expression.

external data Data created, recorded, or generated by an entity other than the researcher's organization.

external validity The ability of an experiment to generalize beyond the experiment data to other subjects or groups in the population under study.

extremity bias A category of response bias that results because some individuals tend to use extremes when responding to questions.

eye-tracking monitor A mechanical device used to observe eye movements. Some eye monitors use infrared light beams to measure unconscious eye movements.

F

fax survey A survey that uses fax machines as a way for respondents to receive and return questionnaires.

field experiment An experiment conducted in a natural setting, where complete control of extraneous variables is not possible.

filter question A question that screens out respondents who are not qualified to answer a second question.

fixed-alternative question A question in which the respondent is given specific, limited-alternative responses and asked to choose the one closest to his or her own viewpoint.

focus group interview An unstructured, free-flowing interview with a small group of people.

follow-up A letter or postcard reminding a respondent to return a questionnaire.

forced answering software Software that prevents respondents from continuing with an Internet questionnaire if they fail to answer a question.

forecast analyst The person who provides technical assistance such as computer analysis to forecast sales.

forward linkage A term implying that the early stages of the research

process influence the design of the later stages.

frequency-determination question A fixed-alternative question about general frequency of occurrence.

frequency distribution A set of data organized by summarizing the number of times a particular value of a variable occurs.

frequency table The arrangement of statistical data in a row-and-column format that exhibits the count of responses or observations for each category assigned to a variable.

ftp File Transfer Protocol; a software program that allows users to establish an interactive file transfer session with a remote host's computer system so that they can read and download full-text versions of files from the remote system.

funnel technique Asking general questions before specific questions in order to obtain unbiased responses.

G

global information system An organized collection of computer hardware, software, data, and personnel designed to capture, store, update, manipulate, analyze, and immediately display information about worldwide business activity.

graphic rating scale A measure of attitude that allows respondents to rate an object by choosing any point along a graphic continuum.

guinea pig effect An effect on the results of an experiment caused by subjects changing their normal behavior or attitudes to cooperate with an experimenter.

H

Hawthorne effect An unintended effect on the results of a research experiment caused by the subjects knowing that they are participants.

hidden observation Observation in which the subject is unaware that observation is taking place.

history effect The loss of internal validity caused by specific events in the external environment, occurring between the first and second measurements, that are beyond the experimenter's control.

home page The introductory page or opening screen of a Web site.

host Any computer that has access to other computers on the Internet. One or more people may log on to a host computer through their personal computers.

hyperlinks Connections from one Web page to other Web pages, which may be on any computer connected to the Internet.

hypothesis An unproven proposition or supposition that tentatively explains certain facts or phenomena; a probable answer to a research question.

hypothetical construct A variable that is not directly observable but is measurable through indirect indicators, such as verbal expression or overt behavior.

I

iceberg principle The principle that the dangerous part of many marketing problems is neither visible to nor understood by marketing managers.

image profile A graphic representation of semantic differential data for competing brands, products, or stores, used to highlight comparisons.

independent variable In an experimental design, the variable that can be manipulated, or altered, independently of any other variable; a variable expected to influence a dependent variable.

index (composite) measure A multi-item instrument that uses several variables to measure a single concept.

index number Score or observation recalibrated to indicate how it relates to a base number.

index of retail saturation A calculation that describes the relationship between retail demand and supply.

information Any body of facts in a format suitable for decision making or in a context that defines the relationship between two pieces of data.

instrumentation effect An effect on the results of an experiment

caused by a change in the wording of questions, in interviewers, or in other procedures used to measure the dependent variable.

interactive help desk In an Internet questionnaire, a live, real-time support feature that solves problems or answers questions respondents may encounter in completing the questionnaire.

interactive medium A medium, such as the Internet, that a person can use to communicate with and interact with other users.

internal and proprietary data Secondary data that originate inside the organization.

internal validity Validity determined by whether an experimental treatment was the sole cause of changes in a dependent variable or whether the experimental manipulation did what it was supposed to do.

Internet A worldwide network of computers that allows users access to information and documents from distant sources.

Internet survey A self-administered questionnaire posted on a Web site.

interpretation The process of making pertinent inferences and drawing conclusions concerning the meaning and implications of a research investigation.

interval scale A scale that both arranges objects according to their magnitudes and distinguishes the ordered arrangement in units of equal intervals.

interviewer bias A response bias that occurs because the presence of the interviewer influences answers.

interviewer cheating The practice by interviewers of filling in fake answers or falsifying questionnaires.

interviewer error Mistakes made by interviewers who fail to record survey responses correctly.

intranet A company's private data network that uses Internet standards and technology.

introduction section The part of the body of a report that discusses background information and the specific objectives of the research.

item nonresponse Failure by a respondent to answer a question on a questionnaire.

J

judgment (purposive) sampling A nonprobability sampling technique in which an experienced researcher selects a sample based on personal judgment about some appropriate characteristic of the sample members.

L

laboratory experiment An experiment conducted in a laboratory or other artificial setting to obtain almost complete control over the research setting.

leading question A question that suggests or implies certain answers.

Likert scale A measure of attitudes in which respondents rate how strongly they agree or disagree with carefully constructed statements; several scale items expressing attitudes toward an object ranging from very positive to very negative may be used to form a summated index.

link A connection to another screen or document.

loaded question A question that suggests a socially desirable answer or that is emotionally charged.

longitudinal study A survey of respondents conducted at different times, thus allowing analysis of changes over time.

M

mail survey A self-administered questionnaire sent to respondents through the mail.

mall intercept interview A personal interview conducted in a shopping mall or other high-traffic area.

manager of customer quality research The person who specializes in conducting surveys to measure consumers' satisfaction and perceptions of product quality.

manager of decision support systems The person who supervises the collection and analysis of sales data and other recurring data.

market tracking The observation and analysis of trends in industry volume and brand share over time.

marketing concept The marketing philosophy that stresses a consumer orientation, emphasizes long-range profitability, and suggests the integration and coordination of marketing and other organizational functions.

marketing research The systematic and objective process of generating information to aid in making marketing decisions.

matching A procedure for the assignment of subjects to groups that ensures that each group of respondents is matched on the basis of pertinent characteristics.

maturation effect An effect on the results of an experiment caused by experimental subjects maturing or changing over time.

mean A measure of central tendency; the arithmetic average.

measure of association A general term that refers to a number of bivariate statistical techniques used to measure the strength of a relationship between two variables.

median A measure of central tendency that is the midpoint; the value below which half the values in a distribution fall.

mixed-mode survey Study that employs any combination of survey methods.

mode A measure of central tendency; the value that occurs most often.

model building The use of secondary data to help specify relationships between two or more variables; it can include the development of descriptive or predictive equations.

moderator The person who leads a focus group discussion.

moderator variable A third variable that, when introduced into an analysis, alters or has a contingent effect on the relationship between an independent variable and a dependent variable.

mortality (sample attrition) effect A sample bias that results from the withdrawal of some subjects from the experiment before it is completed.

multiple-grid question Several similar questions arranged in a grid format.

multiple regression analysis An analysis of association in which the effects of two or more independent variables on a single, interval-scaled dependent variable are investigated simultaneously.

multistage area sampling Sampling that involves using a combination of two or more probability sampling techniques.

N

neural network A form of artificial intelligence in which a computer is programmed to mimic the way that human brains process information.

no contact A person who is not at home on the first or second contact, or who is otherwise inaccessible.

nominal scale A scale in which the numbers or letters assigned to objects serve as labels for identification or classification.

nonprobability sampling A sampling technique in which units of the sample are selected on the basis of personal judgment or convenience; the probability of any particular member of the population being chosen is unknown.

nonrespondent A person who is not contacted or who refuses to cooperate in the research.

nonresponse error The statistical differences between a survey that includes only those who responded and a perfect survey that would also include those who failed to respond.

normal distribution A symmetrical, bell-shaped distribution that describes the expected probability distribution of many chance occurrences.

not-at-home A person who is not at home on the first or second attempt at contact.

null hypothesis A statement about a status quo asserting that any change from what has been thought to be true will be due entirely to random sampling error.

numerical scale An attitude rating scale that is similar to a semantic differential except that it uses numbers, instead of verbal descriptions, as response options to identify response positions.

O

observation The systematic process of recording the behavioral patterns of people, objects, and occurrences as they are witnessed.

observer bias A distortion of measurement resulting from the cognitive behavior or actions of a witnessing observer.

one-group pretest–posttest design A quasi-experimental design in which the subjects in the experimental group are measured before and after the treatment is administered, but there is no control group.

one-shot design An after-only design in which a single measure is recorded after the treatment is administered.

online focus group A focus group whose members carry on their discussion through an Internet chat room.

open-ended box In an Internet questionnaire, a box where respondents can type in their own answers to open-ended questions.

open-ended response question A question that poses some problem and asks the respondent to answer in his or her own words.

operational definition An explanation that gives meaning to a concept by specifying the activities or operations necessary to measure it.

opt in To give permission to receive selected e-mail, such as questionnaires, from a company with an Internet presence.

oral presentation A spoken summary of the major findings, conclusions, and recommendations, given to clients or line managers to provide them with the opportunity to clarify any ambiguous issues by asking questions.

order bias Bias caused by the influence of earlier questions in a questionnaire or by an answer's position in a set of answers.

ordinal scale A scale that arranges objects or alternatives according to their magnitude in an ordered relationship.

P

paired comparison A measurement technique that involves presenting respondents with two objects and asking them to pick the preferred object. More than two objects may be presented, but comparisons are made in pairs.

percentage distribution A frequency distribution organized into a table (or graph) that summarizes percentage values associated with particular values of a variable.

performance-monitoring research Research that regularly, sometimes routinely, provides feedback for evaluation and control of marketing activity.

periodicity A problem that occurs in systematic sampling when the original list has a systematic pattern.

personal interview An interview that gathers information through face-to-face contact with individuals.

physical actions A type of behavior that can be scientifically observed, such as shopping patterns or television viewing.

physical-trace evidence A visible mark of some past occurrence.

picture frustration A version of the TAT that uses a cartoon drawing for which the respondent suggests a possible dialogue between the characters.

pilot study A collective term for any small-scale exploratory research technique that uses sampling but does not apply rigorous standards.

pivot question A filter question used to determine which version of a second question will be asked.

point estimate An estimate of the population mean in the form of a single value, usually the sample mean.

pop-up boxes In an Internet questionnaire, boxes that appear at selected points and contain information or instructions for respondents.

population (universe) Any complete group of entities that share some common set of characteristics.

population distribution A frequency distribution of the elements of a population.

population element An individual member of a population.

population parameters Variables in a population or measured characteristics of the population.

posttest-only control group design An after-only design in which the experimental group is tested after exposure to the treatment and the control group is tested at the same time without having been exposed to the treatment; no premeasure is taken. Random assignment of subjects and treatment occurs.

preliminary tabulation A tabulation of the results of a pretest to help determine whether a questionnaire will meet the objectives of the research.

pretest–posttest control group design A true experimental design in which the experimental group is tested before and after exposure to the treatment and the control group is tested at the same two times without being exposed to the experimental treatment.

pretesting Screening procedure that involves a trial run with a group of respondents to iron out fundamental problems in the survey design.

primary sampling unit (PSU) A unit selected in the first stage of sampling.

probability The long-run relative frequency with which an event will occur.

probability sampling A sampling technique in which every member of the population has a known, nonzero probability of selection.

probing The verbal prompts made by an interviewer when the respondent must be motivated to communicate his or her answer more fully; used to get respondents to enlarge on, clarify, or explain answers.

problem definition stage The stage in which management seeks to identify a clear-cut statement of the problem or opportunity.

program strategy The overall plan to conduct a series of marketing research projects; a planning activity that places each marketing project in the context of the company's marketing plan.

projective technique An indirect means of questioning that enables a respondent to project beliefs and feelings onto a third party or an inanimate object or into a task situation.

proportion The percentage of elements that meet some criterion.

proprietary marketing research The gathering of new data to investigate specific problems.

psychogalvanometer A device that measures galvanic skin response, a measure of involuntary changes in the electrical resistance of the skin.

pupillometer A mechanical device used to observe and record changes in the diameter of a subject's pupils.

push button In a dialog box on an Internet questionnaire, a small outlined area, such as a rectangle or an arrow, that the respondent clicks on to select an option or perform a function, such as Submit.

push technology Internet information technology that automatically delivers personalized content to the viewer's desktop, using computer software known as smart agents.

Q

quasi-experimental design A research design that cannot be classified as a true experiment because it lacks adequate control of extraneous variables.

quota sampling A nonprobability sampling procedure that ensures that various subgroups of a population will be represented on pertinent characteristics to the exact extent the investigator desires.

R

radio button In an Internet questionnaire, a circular icon, resembling a button, that activates one response choice and deactivates others when a respondent clicks on it.

random digit dialing Use of telephone exchanges and a table of random numbers to contact respondents with unlisted phone numbers.

random error An error that occurs because of chance; statistical fluctuations in which repetitions of the basic experiment sometimes favor one experimental condition and sometimes the other.

random sampling error The difference between the sample result and the result of a census conducted using identical procedures; a statistical fluctuation due to chance variations in the elements selected for a sample.

randomization A procedure in which the assignment of subjects and treatments to groups is based on chance.

ranking A measurement task that requires respondents to rank order a small number of stores, brands, or objects on the basis of overall preference or some characteristic of the stimulus.

rating A measurement task that requires respondents to estimate the magnitude of a characteristic or quality that a brand, store, or object possesses.

ratio scale A scale that has absolute rather than relative quantities and an absolute zero where a given attribute is absent.

refusal A person who is unwilling to participate in a research project.

reliability The degree to which a measure is free from random error and therefore yields consistent results.

repeated measures Experimental technique in which the same subjects are exposed to all experimental treatments to eliminate any problems due to subject differences.

report format The makeup or arrangement of parts that are necessary to a good research report.

research analyst The person responsible for client contact, project design, preparation of proposals, selection of research suppliers, and supervision of data collection, analysis, and reporting activities.

research assistant The person who provides technical assistance with questionnaire design, analysis of data, and so on.

research design A master plan that specifies the methods and procedures for collecting and analyzing needed information.

research design stage The stage in which the researcher determines a framework for the research plan of action by selecting a basic research method.

research follow-up Recontacting decision makers and/or clients after they have had a chance to read over a research report, in order to determine whether additional information or clarification is necessary.

research methodology section The part of the body of a report that explains the research design, sampling procedures, and other technical procedures used to collect the data.

research objective The researcher's version of the marketing problem; it explains the purpose of the research in measurable terms and defines standards for what the research should accomplish.

research proposal A written statement of the research design that includes a statement of the purpose of the study and a detailed, systematic outline of procedures associated with a particular research methodology.

research report An oral presentation or written statement of research results, strategic recommendations, and/or other conclusions to a specific audience.

research sophistication A stage in which managers have considerable experience in the proper use of research techniques.

research supplier A commercial marketing research service that conducts marketing research activity for clients.

respondent The person who answers an interviewer's questions or provides answers to written questions.

respondent error A category of sample bias resulting from some respondent action or inaction such as nonresponse or response bias.

response bias A bias that occurs when respondents either consciously or unconsciously tend to answer questions with a certain slant that misrepresents the truth.

response latency The amount of time it takes to make a choice between two alternatives; used as a measure of the strength of preference.

response rate The number of questionnaires returned or completed divided by the total number of eligible people who were contacted or asked to participate in the survey.

results section The part of the body of a report that presents the findings of the project; it includes tables, charts, and an organized narrative.

role-playing technique A projective technique that requires the subject to act out someone else's behavior in a particular setting.

rule A guide that tells someone what to do.

S

sample A subset or some part of a larger population.

sample bias A persistent tendency for the results of a sample to deviate in one direction from the true value of the population parameter.

sample distribution A frequency distribution of a sample.

sample selection error An administrative error caused by improper sample design or sampling procedure execution.

sample statistics Variables in a sample or measures computed from sample data.

sampling distribution A theoretical probability distribution of sample means for all possible samples of a certain size drawn from a particular population.

sampling frame A list of elements from which a sample may be drawn; also called working population.

sampling frame error An error that occurs when certain sample elements are excluded from or overrepresented in a sampling frame.

sampling stage The stage in which the researcher determines who is to be sampled, how large a sample is needed, and how sampling units will be selected.

sampling unit A single element or group of elements selected for a sample.

scale A quantifying measure in the form of a combination of items that is arranged progressively according to value or magnitude.

scanner-based consumer panel A type of consumer panel in which participants' purchasing habits are recorded with a laser scanner rather than in a purchase diary.

scientific method Systematic techniques or procedures used to analyze empirical evidence in an unbiased attempt to confirm or disprove prior conceptions.

search engine A computerized directory that allows anyone to search the World Wide Web for information in a particular way.

secondary data Data that have been previously collected for some purpose other than the one at hand.

secondary sampling unit A unit selected in the second stage of sampling.

selection effect A sampling bias that results from differential selection of respondents for the comparison groups.

self-administered questionnaire Survey in which the respondent takes the responsibility for reading and answering the questions.

self-selection bias A bias that occurs because people who feel strongly about a subject are more likely to respond than people who feel indifferent about it.

semantic differential A measure of attitudes that consists of a series of 7-point rating scales that use bipolar adjectives to anchor the beginning and end of each scale.

sensitivity An instrument's ability to accurately measure variability in stimuli or responses.

sentence completion method A projective technique in which respondents are required to complete a number of partial sentences with the first word or phrase that comes to mind.

server A computer that provides services on the Internet.

significance level The critical probability in choosing between the null and alternative hypotheses; the probability level that is too low to warrant support of the null hypothesis.

simple-dichotomy (dichotomous-alternative) question A fixed-alternative question that requires the respondent to choose one of two alternatives.

simple random sampling A sampling procedure that assures each element in the population of an equal chance of being included in the sample.

single-source data Diverse types of data offered by a single company. The data are usually integrated on the basis of a common variable such as geographic area or store.

site analysis techniques Techniques that use secondary data to select the best locations for retail or wholesale operations.

smart agent software Software capable of learning an Internet user's preferences and automatically searching out information in selected Web sites and then distributing it.

snowball sampling A sampling procedure in which initial respondents are selected by probability methods and additional respondents are obtained from information provided by the initial respondents.

social desirability bias Bias in responses caused by respondents' desire, either conscious or unconscious, to gain prestige or appear in a different social role.

societal norms Codes of behavior adopted by a group that suggest what a member of that group ought to do under given circumstances.

software Various types of programs that tell computers, printers, and other hardware what to do.

Solomon four-group design A true experimental design that combines the pretest–posttest with control group design and the posttest-only with control group design, thereby providing a means for controlling the interactive testing effect and other sources of extraneous variation.

sorting A measurement task that presents respondents with several objects or product concepts and requires them to arrange the objects into piles or otherwise classify the product concepts.

spatial relations and locations Physical distance and other physical patterns, such as traffic counts, studied in scientific observation.

split-ballot technique The use of two alternative phrasings of the same question for respective halves of a sample to elicit a more accurate total response than a single phrasing would.

spurious relationship An apparent relationship between two variables that is not authentic.

standard deviation A quantitative index of a distribution's spread, or variability; the square root of the variance for a distribution.

standard error of the mean The standard deviation of the sampling distribution.

standardized normal distribution A purely theoretical probability distribution that reflects a specific normal curve for the standardized value, Z.

standardized research service A research organization that has developed a unique methodology for investigating a specialty area, such as advertising effectiveness.

Stapel scale A measure of attitudes that consists of a single adjective in the center of an even number of numerical values.

static group design An after-only design in which subjects in the experimental group are measured after being exposed to the experimental treatment and the control group is measured without having been exposed to the experimental treatment; no premeasure is taken.

status bar In an Internet questionnaire, a visual indicator that tells the respondent what portion of the survey he or she has completed.

stratified sampling A probability sampling procedure in which simple random subsamples that are more or less equal on some characteristic are drawn from within each stratum of the population.

streaming media Multimedia content, such as audio or video, that can be accessed on the Internet without being downloaded first.

survey A method of collecting primary data in which information is gathered by communicating with a representative sample of people.

syndicated service A marketing research supplier that provides standardized information for many clients.

systematic error Error resulting from some imperfect aspect of the research design or from a mistake in the execution of the research.

systematic sampling A sampling procedure in which a starting point is selected by a random process and then every nth item on a list is selected.

T

tachistoscope A device that controls the amount of time a subject is exposed to a visual image.

telephone interview An interview that gathers information through telephone contact with respondents.

television monitoring Computerized mechanical observation used to obtain television ratings.

temporal patterns In scientific observation, the length of time required for an act or event to occur, such as the amount of time spent shopping or driving.

tertiary sampling unit A unit selected in the third stage of sampling.

test marketing An experimental procedure that provides an opportunity to measure sales or profit potential for a new product or to test a new marketing plan under realistic marketing conditions.

test of differences An investigation of a hypothesis stating that two (or more) groups differ with respect to measures on a variable.

test unit An entity whose responses to experimental treatments are being observed or measured.

testing effect In a before-and-after study, the effect of pretesting which may sensitize respondents or subjects when taking a test for the second time, thus affecting internal validity.

thematic apperception test (TAT) A projective technique that presents a series of pictures to research subjects and asks them to provide a description of or a story about the pictures.

third-person technique A projective technique in which the respondent is asked why a third person does what she or he does or what he or she thinks about a product. The respondent is expected to transfer his or her attitudes to the third person.

time series design An experimental design used when experiments are conducted over long periods of time. It allows researchers to distinguish between temporary and permanent changes in dependent variables.

total quality management A business philosophy that emphasizes market-driven quality as a top organizational priority.

tracking study A type of longitudinal study that uses successive samples to compare trends and identify changes in variables such as consumer satisfaction, brand image, or advertising awareness.

U

Uniform Resource Locator (URL) A Web site address that Web browsers recognize.

V

validity The ability of an instrument to measure what it is intended to measure.

variable Anything that may assume different numerical or categorical values.

variable piping software Software that allows variables to be inserted into an Internet questionnaire as a respondent is completing it.

variance A measure of variability or dispersion. Its square root is the standard deviation.

verbal behavior A type of behavior that can be scientifically observed, such as sales conversations.

visible observation Observation in which the observer's presence is known to the subject.

voice pitch analysis A physiological measurement technique that records abnormal frequencies in the voice that supposedly reflect emotional reactions to various stimuli.

W

Web site One or more Web pages with related information about a particular topic.

welcome screen The first Web page in an Internet survey, which introduces the survey and requests that the respondent enter a password or PIN.

word association test A projective technique in which the subject is presented with a list of words, one at a time, and asked to respond with the first word that comes to mind.

World Wide Web (WWW) A portion of the Internet that is a system of computer servers that organize information into documents called Web pages.

CHAPTER 1

1. Adapted with permission from Sara Eckel, "Cheese Whiz: A Fresh Ad Strategy Transforms Easy Mac into an Appetizing Product for Moms and Teens," *American Demographics*, March 2001, p. S14.

2. American Marketing Association, *Report of the Committee on Definitions of Marketing Research*, 1987.

3. Adapted from the definition of research in American Marketing Association, Committee on Definitions, *Marketing Definitions: A Glossary of Marketing Terms* (Chicago: American Marketing Association, 1960), p. 17; American Marketing Association, *Report of the Committee on Definitions of Marketing Research*, 1987. The official AMA definition is as follows: "Marketing research is the function which links the consumer, customer, and public to the marketer through information—information used to identify and define marketing opportunities and problems; generate, refine, and evaluate marketing actions; monitor marketing performance; and improve understanding of marketing as a process. Marketing research specifies the information required to address these issues; designs the method for collecting the information; manages and implements the data collection process; analyzes the results; and communicates the findings and their implications."

4. Sonia Reyes, "Ian Friendly: Groove Tube," *BrandWeek*, October 16, 2000, pp. M111-M116.

5. Adapted from Jon Berry, "The Art of Rubbermaid," *Adweek*, March 16, 1992, p. 24.

6. Stephanie Thompson, "EZ Being Green: Kids' Line Is Latest Heinz Innovation," *Advertising Age*, July 10, 2000, pp. 3, 5; Greg Farrell, "What's Green, Easy to Squirt? Ketchup," *USA Today*, July 10, 2000, p. 2b; and Kristen Hays, "Heinz Gooses an Old Flavor with a New Color," *Marketing News*, July 31, 2000, p. 24.

7. Courtesy of General Electric Corporation.

8. For a detailed discussion of marketing strategy and tactics, see William G. Zikmund and Michael d'Amico, *Marketing*, 7th Edition (Cincinnati: South-Western, 2001), Chapter 2.

9. Thomas C. Kinnear and Ann R. Root, eds., *1994 Survey of Marketing Research* (Chicago: American Marketing Association, 1995), p. 43.

10. Ian P. Murphy, "Aided by Research, Harley Goes Hog Wild," *Marketing News*, December 2, 1996, p. 16; and Jerry Shriver, "Richer, Older Harley Riders Like Everyone Else," *USA TODAY*, March 8-10, 2002, p. 2A.

11. N. Carroll Mohn, "Pricing Research for Decision Making," *Marketing Research*, Winter 1995, pp. 11-12.

12. David Churchill, "Cabin Pressures," *Management Today*, October 1, 1994, p. 96.

13. Adapted with permission from "Super Bowl Delivers Attentive Viewers Who Remember the Advertising," http://www.ipsos-asi.com/website/index.php?department_id=5&sub_cat=18&subsub_cat=0&pageid=108, downloaded February 14, 2002.

14. Carmen Hensch and Enrique Gil, "Authentically Mexican Las Palmas Wows Cooks," Special Advertising Section, *BrandWeek*, August 21, 2000, pp. 3-4.

15. For a more extensive discussion of this issue, see Zikmund and d'Amico, *Marketing*.

16. Jack Honomichi, "Growth Stunt," *Marketing News*, June 4, 2001, p. H4.

17. "You Say Tomato, I Say Tomahto," *Express Magazine*, Spring 1992, p. 19.

18. William G. Zikmund and Michael d'Amico, *Effective Marketing* (Cincinnati: South-Western, 2002), p. xxxii.

19. Adapted from Louis E. Boone and David L. Kurtz, *Contemporary Marketing* (Ft. Worth: Harcourt, 2001), pp. vc17-vc18.

20. Information from Ben & Jerry's Web page at http://www.benjerry.com; LearNet's Video *Ben & Jerry's*; and a press release from Ben & Jerry's, February 20, 1997.

CHAPTER 2

1. Adapted with permission from Sarah L. Roberts-Witt, "Gold Diggers," *PC Magazine,* February 20, 2001, pp. ibiz 6-7.

2. H. G. Wells, "The Brain: Organization of the Modern World," 1940.

3. Stewart Deck, "What Is CRM?" *Darwin Online,* May 16, 2001, http://www.darwinmag.com/learn/curve/column.html?ArticleID=104, downloaded June 5, 2001.

4. whatis.com, http://whatis.techtarget.com/definition/0,289893,sid9_gci213567,00.html.

5. Steven Crofts, "Business Intelligence," special advertising section, *Fortune,* October 27, 1997, p. s4.

6. The following is a more detailed explanation of data warehousing: "Bill Inmon is often quoted and referenced for his ideas on data warehouses. . . . In Inmon's eyes a warehouse has a multi-tiered structure of data/information . . . which includes examples from employee data. Snapshots of current, detailed data from operational systems are extracted, reformatted, and loaded to the warehouse tables. These detailed data form the basis, the foundation for the other layers. Then, from the detailed data can be developed one or more layers of summarized data tables (which he would call 'lightly summarized' and 'highly summarized'). Also, as detailed data are historically accrued in the warehouse, the older snapshots can be archived to a historical layer. Inmon also adds a supporting element of metadata—descriptions of the data and of the data transformation rules—to the mix. This descriptive/help information enables much greater understanding of the data by all warehouse users." Source: Michael Bosworth, "Rolling Out a Data Warehouse Quickly at Umass: A Simple Start to a Complex Task," *Cause/Effect,* Spring 1995. See also Bill Inmon, "The Structure of the Information Warehouse," *Data Management Review,* August 1993, pp. 5-8.

7. Bill Gates, *The Road Ahead* (New York: Viking Penguin, 1995).

8. For an extensive listing of databases, see the annual *Gale Directory of Databases* (Detroit: Gale Research, Inc., two volumes).

9. Nielsen//NetRatings http://www.eratings.com/news/20000907.htm, downloaded May 16, 2001.

10. Patrick A. Moore and Ronald E. Milliman, Western Kentucky University, "Application of the Internet in Marketing Education," paper presented to the Southwest Marketing Association, Houston, Texas, 1995.

11. Charles S. Parker, *Understanding Computers Today and Tomorrow* (Fort Worth, TX: Dryden Press, 1998), p. 69.

12. "Three Visions of an Electronic Future," *New York Times,* March 24, 1996, p. F-22.

13. Paul Schneider, "Behind Company Walls: It's the Intranet," *Arizona Business Gazette,* March 7, 1996.

14. Adapted with permission from Jennier deJony, "View from the Top," *Inc. Technology #1,* 1995, downloaded from the Internet July 3, 1998.

CHAPTER 3

1. Audits & Surveys, *Report to Retailers and Marketers,* 2000, www. surveys.com; and Jean Halliday, "Imports Lap Up Auto Spending," *Advertising Age,* June 11, 2001, p. S14.

2. Barry Janoff, "Brands of the Land," *BrandWeek,* April 20, 2001, p. 28.

3. Becky Ebenkamp, "For Whom the Bell Tolls," *BrandWeek,* May 7, 2001, p. 22.

4. Claire Selltiz, Lawrence S. Wrightsman, and Stuart W. Cook, *Research Methods in Social Relations* (New York: Holt, Rinehart and Winston, 1976), pp. 114–115.

5. Phillip J. Runkel and Joseph E. McGrath, *Research on Human Behavior: A Systematic Guide to Method* (New York: Holt, Rinehart and Winston, 1972), p. 2.

6. A. Einstein and L. Infeld, *The Evolution of Physics* (New York: Simon and Schuster, 1942), p. 95.

7. Robert F. Mager, *Preparing Instructional Objectives* (Belmont, CA: David S. Lake Publishers, 1984).

8. Russell L. Ackoff, *Scientific Method* (New York: John Wiley and Sons, 1962), p. 71.

9. Patrick Coyne, "ACD Conference on Interactive Media," *Communication Arts,* vol. 36, no. 8 (January/February 1995), p. 140.

10. Pretests of full-blown surveys and experiments also are considered pilot studies. These smaller versions of the formal studies generally are used to refine techniques rather than for problem definition and hypothesis clarification.

11. Carol Vogel, "Dear Museumgoer: What Do You Think?" *New York Times,* December 20, 1992, pp. H-1, H-32.

12. David Todd, "Special Report: Youth Marketing: Dentyne Ice Locks Lips with Youth Target," *Strategy: The Canadian Marketing Report,* May 8, 2000, p. B14, http://www.strategymag.com/articles/20000508/youth-dentyneice.asp, downloaded January 28, 2001.

13. Julian Simon, *Basic Research Methods in Social Science: The Art of Empirical Investigation* (New York: Random House, 1969), p. 4.

14. Based on *A General Taxpayer Opinion Survey,* Office of Planning and Research, Internal Revenue Service, March 1980.

CHAPTER 4

1. Lee Adler and Charles S. Mayer, *Managing the Marketing Research Function* (Chicago: American Marketing Association, 1977), p. 18.

2. James B. Stuart, R. J. Reynolds Tobacco Company, personal communication.

3. Eli P. Cox III, *Marketing Research: Information for Decision Making* (Englewood Cliffs, NJ: Prentice-Hall, 1979) pp. 54–55.

4. Thomas C. Kinnear and Ann Root, eds., 1994 *Survey of Marketing Research* (Chicago: American Marketing Association, 1995).

5. Kathie Julian and Sarah Coffer, "Kaleidoscope of Change," *Marketing Research,* Fall 1996, pp. 8–14.

6. Job titles vary substantially in industry. This title could also be *supervisor of research, manager of research, project director,* or *senior research analyst* in a larger firm with several levels of management.

7. Vincent P. Barabba, "Market Research Technique—What, Why, Who, Where, When, and How?" *Harvard Business Review,* June 14, 1989.

8. For alternative perspectives, see Kenneth C. Schneider's excellent article "Marketing Research Industry Isn't Moving toward Professionalism," *Marketing Educator,* Winter 1984, pp. 1, 6; Steven J. Skinner, O. C. Ferrell, and Alan J. Dubinsky, "Organizational Dimensions of Marketing-Research Ethics," *Journal of Business Research* 16 (1988), pp. 209–223; and Patrick E. Murphy and Gene R. Laczniak, "Traditional Ethical Issues Facing Marketing Researchers," *Marketing Research,* March 1992, pp. 8–21.

9. Lawrence D. Wiseman, "The Present Value of Future Studies," speech to the Advertising Research Foundation, March 1980.

10. C. Merle Crawford, "Attitudes of Marketing Executives toward Ethics in Marketing Research," *Journal of Marketing,* April 1970, pp. 46–52; Ishmael P. Akaah and Edward A. Riordan, "Judgments of Marketing Professionals about Ethical Issues in Marketing Research: A Replication and Extension," *Journal of Marketing Research,* February 1989, pp. 112–120.

11. Leo Bogart, "The Researcher's Dilemma," *Journal of Marketing,* January 1962, pp. 6–11.

12. Cynthia Crossen, *Tainted Truth* (New York: Simon & Schuster, 1994), p. 95.

13. H. Keith Hunt, "The Ethics of Research in the Consumer Interests: Panel Summary," ed. Norleen M. Ackerman, *Proceedings of the American Council of Consumer Interests Conference,* 1979, p. 152.

14. Fred W. Morgan, Jr., "Judicial Standards for Survey Research: An Update and Guidelines," *Journal of Marketing,* January 1990, pp. 59–70.

15. Robert Bezilla, Joel B. Haynes, and Clifford Elliot, "Ethics in Marketing Research," *Business Horizons,* April 1976, pp. 83–86.

16. John Harwood and Daniel Pearl, "U.S. Midterm Elections: U.S. Politicians Yell Foul Over Phone Polling Method," *Wall Street Journal Europe,* November 11, 1994.

CHAPTER 5

1. Reprinted with permission from Jeff Green, "The PT Cruiser's Storied History," *BrandWeek,* October 16, 2000, pp. M68–M70.

2. Dave Fusaro, "Food Products of the New Millennium," *Prepared Foods,* January 1, 1996.

3. David Schwartz, *Concept Testing: How to Test New Product Ideas before You Go to Market* (New York: AMACOM, 1987), p. 57.

4. Gary Hamel and C. K. Prahalad, "Corporate Imagination and Expeditionary Marketing," *Harvard Business Review,* July–August 1991, p. 85.

5. "Light Says Problem Research Will Give More Benefits Than Benefit Research," *Marketing News,* September 20, 1975, p. 7.

6. Adapted from Michael A. Hitt, R. Duane Ireland, and Robert E. Hoskisson, *Strategic Management: Competitiveness and Globalization Concepts,* 2nd ed. (Mason, OH: South-Western, 1995), p. 82.

7. Carol Vogel, "Dear Museumgoer: What Do You Think?" *New York Times,* December 20, 1992, p. H-1.

8. Belkist Padilla, "Projective Techniques: Do They Work in the Hispanic Market?" *Quirk's Marketing Research Review,* Article Number 0483, April 1999.

9. Based on the discussion in John M. Hess, "Group Interviewing," in *New Science of Planning,* R. L. King, Ed. (Chicago: American Marketing Association, 1968), p. 194.

10. Steve Rabin, "How to Sell across Cultures," *American Demographics,* March 1, 1994, p. 56.

11. Rebecca Piirto Heather, "Future Focus Groups," *American Demographics,* January 1, 1994, p. 6.

12. http://www.realnetworks.com/getstarted/index.html, downloaded June 30, 2001.

13. Nicholas Negroponte, "Being Anonymous," *Wired,* October 1998, p. 216.

14. Casey Sweet, "Anatomy of an Online Focus Group," *Quirk's Marketing Research Review,* December 1999, Article Number 0548.

15. Kate Maddox, "Virtual Panels Add Real Insights for Marketers," *Advertising Age,* June 29, 1998, p. 34.

16. Jon Rubin, "Online Marketing Research Comes of Age," *BrandWeek,* October 30, 2000, p. 28.

17. Adapted from Tibbett Speer, "Nickelodeon Puts Kids Online," *American Demographics,* January 1, 1994, p. 16.

18. Robert F. Hartley, *Marketing Mistakes* (Columbus, OH: Grid, 1976), p. 87.

19. The Iowa Poll, August 1977.

20. James McNeal, *The Kids Market: Myths and Realities* (Ithaca, NY: Paramount Market Publishers, 1999), p. 245.

21. Philip Kotler, "Behavioral Models for Analyzing Buyers," *Journal of Marketing,* October 1965, pp. 37–45.

22. Ronald Alsop, "Advertisers Put Consumers on the Couch," *Wall Street Journal,* May 13, 1988, p. 19.

23. William G. Zikmund and William J. Lundstrom, *A Collection of Outstanding Cases in Marketing Management* (St. Paul, MN: West Publishing, 1979). All rights reserved.

CHAPTER 6

1. Excerpts reprinted with permission from John Ritter, "Calif. Racial Data Shifts: Becomes the First Big State with No Ethnic Majority," *USA TODAY,* March 30, 2001, p. 1A.

2. The idea for Exhibit 6.1 came from Robert W. Joselyn, *Designing the Marketing Research Project* (New York: Petrocelli/Charter, 1977).

3. "Rising Stars in Frozen Pizza," *Milling & Baking News,* November 26, 1996, p. 30.

4. Theresa Howard, "Coca-Cola Hopes Taking New Path Leads to Success," *USA TODAY,* March 6, 2001, p. 6b.

5. Bette Harrison, "Retro Activity: As Generation Y Plumbs Parents' Culture, the Kids Claim Birdies and Bowling, with a Twist," *Atlanta Constitution,* October 27, 1998, p. F1.

6. Lee Fleming, "Digital Delivery: Pushing Content to the Desktop," Digital Information Group, January 31, 1997.

7. "How Smart Agents Will Change Selling," *Forbes ASAP,* August 28, 1995, p. 95.

8. "How Smart Agents Will Change Selling."

9. "Datawatch," *Advertising Age,* January 18, 1993, p. I-12.

10. This section is based on Michael Levy and Barton Weitz, *Retail Management* (Homewood, Il.: Richard D. Irwin, 1992), pp. 357–358.

11. Based on information from DataMind's home page at http://www.datamindcorp.com.

12. Srikumar S. Rao, "Technology: The Hot Zone," *Forbes,* November 18, 1996.

13. Excerpt reprinted with permission from Janet Novack, "The Data Miners," *Forbes,* February 12, 1996, Reprinted by permission of Forbes Magazine. © 2002 Forbes Inc.

14. John Foley, "Squeezing More Value from Data," *InformationWeek,* December 9, 1996.

15. IBM Business Intelligence Data Mining Product Discovery, http://www.ibm.com.

16. Todd Wasserman, Gerry Khermouch, and Jeff Green, "Mining Everyone's Business," *Brandweek,* February 28, 2000, p. 34; and Ira

Sager, "Big Blue Wants to Mine Your Data," *Business Week,* June 3, 1996.

17. Based on information from DataMind's home page at http://www.datamindcorp.com.

18. "Going with the Grain," *Advertising Age,* September 11, 1995, p. 3.

19. Jack Neff, "Wal-Mart Takes Stock in RetailLink System," *Advertising Age,* May 21, 2001, p. 6.

20. The description of the data bank is reprinted from information that can be accessed from the NTDB home page.

21. Reprinted from Louis E. Boone and David L. Kurtz, *Contemporary Marketing,* 10th ed. (Mason, OH: South-Western, 2001), pp. vc7–vc8.

22. This historical material and additional details may be found at http://www.census.gov/acsd/www/history.html.

CHAPTER 7

1. Adapted with permission from Sara Eckel and Alison Stein Wellner, "For Wannabe Chefs, Pictures Speak Louder than Words," *American Demographics,* March 2001, p. S15.

2. Paul B. Sheatsley, "Survey Design," in *Handbook of Marketing Research,* Robert Ferber, Ed. (New York: McGraw-Hill, 1974), p. 66.

3. From Willard I. Zangwill, "Manager's Journal: When Customer Research Is a Lousy Idea," *Wall Street Journal,* March 8, 1993, p. A12.

4. Peter Tuckel and Harry O'Neill, "The Vanishing Respondent in Telephone Surveys," a paper presented at the 56th annual conference of the American Association of Public Opinion Research (AAPOR) in Montreal, May 17–20, 2001.

5. Douglas Aircraft, *Consumer Research* (undated), p. 13.

6. Adapted with permission from Barbara Buell, "The Effect of Expecting to Evaluate on Quality and Satisfaction Evaluations," *Stanford Business,* May 2000, Volume 68, Number 3. The research was based on Chezy Ofir and Itamar Simonson, *GSB Research Paper #1608,* Stanford University, Graduate School of Business, July 1999.

7. John Frieman and Edgar Butler, "Some Sources of Interviewer Variance in Surveys," *Public Opinion Quarterly,* Spring 1976, pp. 79–81.

8. "Your Opinion Counts," *1986 Refusal Rate Study* (Indianapolis: Walker Marketing Research, 1986).

9. Adapted with permission from Sally Beattie, "Ameritech's New Phone Service Aims to Keep Telemarketers at Bay," *Wall Street Journal,* September 23, 1998, p. 10.

10. Jon Rubin, "Online Marketing Research Comes of Age," *BrandWeek,* October 30, 2000, p. 28; and Michael Lewis, "The Two-Bucks-a-Minute Democracy," *New York Times Magazine,* November 5, 2000, p. 65.

11. Peter Tuckel and Harry O'Neill, "The Vanishing Respondent in Telephone Surveys," a paper presented at the 56th annual conference of the American Association of Public Opinion Research (AAPOR) in Montreal on May 17–20, 2001.

12. Peter Tuckel and Trish Shukers, "The Answering Machine Dilemma," *Marketing Research,* Fall 1997, pp. 5–9.

13. P. S. Tuckel and B. M. Finberg, "The Answering Machine Poses Many Questions for Telephone Survey Research," *Public Opinion Quarterly,* Summer 1991.

14. "Sacramento Is Most Unlisted," *The Frame,* March 1997, a quarterly newsletter published by Survey Sampling, Inc., http://www.worldopinion.com/the_frame/index.html.

15. For various response rate calculations, see Frederick Wiseman and Maryann Billington, "Comment on a Standard Definition of Response Rates," *Journal of Marketing Research,* August 1984, pp. 336–338. Also, the researcher may wish to take into account the possibility of respondents registering opinions twice. See Thomas J. Steele, Warren L. Schwendig, and Nina M. Ray, "Do Multi-Wave Mailings Lead to Multi-Response in Mail Surveys?" *Applied Marketing Research,* Spring 1989, pp. 15–20; and Thomas J. Steele, W. Lee Schwendig, and

John A. Kilpatrick, "Duplicate Responses to Multiple Survey Mailings: A Problem," *Journal of Advertising Research,* March 1992.

16. Don A. Dillman, *Mail and Internet Surveys: The Tailored Design Method* (New York: John Wiley and Sons, 2000), p. 173.

17. David R. Schaefer and Don A. Dillman, "Development of a Standard E-Mail Methodology: Results of an Experiment," *Public Opinion Quarterly,* Vol. 62, No. 3 (Fall 1998), p. 378.

18. Don A. Dillman, *Mail and Telephone Surveys: The Total Design Method* (John Wiley and Sons, 1978), p. 209.

19. For an interesting article dealing with this issue, see Michael Geurts and David Whitlark, "A Little Inducement Goes a Long Way," *Marketing Research: A Magazine of Management and Applications,* Summer 1994, pp. 13–15.

20. For an empirical research study that deals with this issue, see Ronald D. Taylor, John Beisel, and Vicki Blakney, "The Effect of Advanced Notification by Mail of a Forthcoming Mail Survey on Response Rates, Item Omission Rates and Response to Speed," paper presented at the 1984 Convention of the Southern Marketing Association, New Orleans, LA.

21. Lewis C. Winters, "International Psychographics," *Marketing Research: A Magazine of Management and Applications,* September 1992, p. 48.

22. For a complete discussion of fax surveys, see the excellent article by John P. Dickson and Douglas L. Maclachlan, "Fax Surveys: Return Patterns and Comparison with Mail Surveys," *Journal of Marketing Research,* February 1996, pp. 108–113.

23. Dillman, *Mail and Internet Surveys,* pp. 369–372.

24. Neil Postman, *Technopoly: The Surrender of Culture to Technology* (New York: Vintage Books, 1993), pp. 6–15; and James P. Ronda, "Thomas Moran and the Eastern Railroads," *The Gilcrease Journal,* Spring/Summer 1997, p. 38.

25. http://www.websurveyor.com/learn_howto.asp, downloaded May 14, 2001.

26. http://www.dmsdallas.com/cust_research/videval.html, downloaded April 23, 2001.

27. "Recent Research Confirms Online Surveys Are a Viable Means of Reaching General Population," Digital Marketing Services, Inc., September 17, 1998, http://www.dmsdallas.com/press_room.html, downloaded April 24, 2001.

28. "Real-Time and Online Research Is Paying Off," *Direct Marketing,* Vol. 63, No. 1 (May 2000), p. 58. Copyright © 2000 Hoke Communications, Inc.

29. For an interesting empirical study, see Ishmael P. Akaah and Edward A. Riordan, "The Incidence of Unethical Practices in Marketing Research: An Empirical Investigation," *Journal of the Academy of Marketing Sciences,* Spring 1990, pp. 143–152.

30. http://www.websurveyor.com/prod_features.asp, downloaded July 26, 2001.

31. Based on material that originally appeared in C. C. Risenhoover, "A Bee and His Reel," *Bassmaster Magazine;* Bob Bledsoe, "Inventor's Latest Line Hooks Some Converts," *Tulsa Tribune,* September 20, 1984, p. 6C; and Stan Fagerstrom, "A Reel with a Motor," *Pro Bass,* April 1985, p. 61.

CHAPTER 8

1. Claire Selltiz, Lawrence S. Wrightsman, and Stuart W. Cook, *Research Methods in Social Relations* (New York: Holt, Rinehart and Winston, 1976), p. 251.

2. Joshua Macht, "The New Market Research," *Inc.,* July 1998, pp. 92–93.

3. E. J. Webb, Donald T. Campbell, Richard D. Schwartz, and Lee Sechrest, *Unobtrusive Measures: Nonreactive Research in the Social Sciences* (Chicago: Rand McNally, 1971).

4. Nancy M. Henley, *Body Politics: Power, Sex, and Nonverbal Communication* (New York: Simon & Schuster, 1977), p. 181.

5. Glen L. Urban and John R. Hauser, *Design and Marketing of New Products* (Englewood Cliffs, NJ: Prentice-Hall, 1980), p. 129.

6. Tyzoon T. Tyebjee, "Response Latency: A New Measure for Scaling Behavior and Preferences," *Journal of Marketing Research,* February 1979, pp. 96–101.

7. Erik Larson, "Attention Shoppers: Don't Look Now But You Are Being Tailed." Copyright 1993 by Erik Larson.

8. Webb et al., *Unobtrusive Measures.*

9. Bill Abrams, *The Observational Research Handbook* (Chicago: NTC Business Books, 2000), p. 14.

10. William Rathje and Cullen Murphy, "Garbage Demographics," *American Demographics,* May 1992, pp. 50–53.

11. Witold Rybczynski, "We Are What We Throw Away," *New York Times Book Review,* July 5, 1992, pp. 5–6.

12. Howard B. Waitzkin, "Information Giving and Medical Care," *Journal of Health and Social Behavior,* Vol. 26 (1985), pp. 81–101.

13. For an excellent discussion of the inherent problems of content analysis, see Camille P. Schuster, "Content Analysis, Interactive Data, and Reliability," paper presented at the American Marketing Association Conference on Research Methods and Causal Modeling, February 27–March 2, 1983.

14. Justin Martin, "Ignore Your Customer," *Fortune,* May 1, 1995, p. 126.

15. http://www.acnielsen.com, downloaded July 5, 2001.

16. Press release, "ACNielsen Unveils 'Future-Proofing' Technologies; TV Ratings System Revamped for Digital Era," March 10, 1999, http://acnielsen.com/news/asiapacific/au/1999/19990310.htm, downloaded July 5, 2001.

17. http://www.mra-net.org/docs/resources/technology/buzzwords.cfm, downloaded April 24, 2001.

18. "Live, Simultaneous Study of Stimulus, Response Is Physiological Measurement's Great Virtue," *Marketing News,* May 15, 1981, pp. 1, 20.

19. Herbert B. Krugman's statement as quoted in "Live, Simultaneous Study of Stimulus," p. 1.

20. For an expanded discussion of physiological research, see James A. Muncy, "Physiological Responses of Consumer Emotions: Theory, Methods, and Implications for Consumer Research," paper presented at the American Marketing Association Marketing Educators' Conference, 1987.

21. Edmund L. Andrews, "Delving into the Consumer Unconscious," *New York Times,* July 22, 1990, p. F-9. Copyright © 1990 by The New York Times Company.

CHAPTER 9

1. Brian Wansink, "How and Why a Package's Size Influences Usage Volume." Trace Discussion Paper TI 95-1, Timbergen Instituet, Amsterdam-Rotterdam, The Netherlands.

2. Anne G. Perkins, "Package Size: When Bigger Is Better," *Harvard Business Review,* March–April 1995, p. 14.

3. Vernon Ellingstad and Norman W. Heimstra, *Methods in the Study of Human Behavior* (Monterey, CA: Brooks/Cole, 1974), pp. 61–62.

4. Barry F. Anderson, *The Psychological Experiment: An Introduction to the Scientific Method* (Belmont, CA: Brooks/Cole, 1971), p. 28.

5. M. Venkatesan and Robert J. Holloway, *An Introduction to Marketing Experimentation: Methods, Applications and Problems* (New York: The Free Press, 1971), p. 14.

6. Alice M. Tybout and Gerald Zaltman, "Ethics in Marketing Research: Their Practical Relevance," *Journal of Marketing Research,* November 1974, pp. 357–368.

7. Daniel Toy, Jerry Olsen, and Lauren Wright, "Effects of Debriefing in Marketing Research Involving 'Mild' Deceptions," *Psychology and Marketing,* Spring 1989, pp. 65–85.

8. This section is based on Donald T. Campbell and Julian C. Stanley, *Experimental and Quasi-Experimental Designs for Research* (Chicago: Rand McNally, 1963), pp. 5–9.

9. B. J. Winer, *Statistical Principles in Experimental Design* (New York: McGraw-Hill, 1979), p. 1.

10. Campbell and Stanley, *Experimental and Quasi-Experimental Designs,* pp. 13–25.

11. The term *observation* is used in the most general sense. Although most marketing experiments use some form of measurement other than direct observation of some dependent variable, the terminology used by Campbell and Stanley is used here because of its traditional nature.

12. *Market Testing Consumer Products* (New York: National Industrial Conference Board, 1967), p. 13.

13. Sally Scanlon, "The True Test," *Sales and Marketing Management* (March 1979), p. 57.

14. Reprinted with permission from Geoffrey Lee Martin, "Drinkers Get Court Call" *Advertising Age,* May 20, 1991. Copyright © 1991 Crain Communications Inc.

CHAPTER 10

1. Gary Levin, "Emotion Guides BBDO's Ad Tests,"*Advertising Age,* January 29, 1990, p. 12.

2. Jum C. Nunnally, *Psychometric Theory* (New York: McGraw-Hill, 1967), p. 2.

3. Sarah M. Dinham, *Exploring Statistics: An Introduction for Psychology and Education* (Monterey, CA: Brooks/Cole, 1976), p. 3.

4. This definition is adapted from Fred N. Kerlinger, *Foundations of Behavioral Research* (New York: Holt, Rinehart and Winston, 1973), p. 31.

5. Barry F. Anderson, *The Psychology Experiment* (Monterey, CA: Brooks/Cole, 1971), p. 26.

6. Fred N. Kerlinger, *Behavioral Research: A Conceptual Approach* (New York: Holt, Rinehart and Winston, 1979), p. 41.

7. Adapted from Michael D. Cozzens and Noshir S. Contractor, "The Effect of Conflicting Information on Media Skepticism," *Communications Research,* August 1987, pp. 437–451.

8. Kerlinger, *Behavioral Research,* p. 428.

9. Cathy Lynn Grossman, "Passenger-Jet Designers Ponder Pie-in-the-Sky Idea," *USA TODAY,* April 18, 1995, p. 3D.

10. Keith K. Cox and Ben M. Enis, *The Marketing Research Process* (Pacific Palisades, CA: Goodyear, 1972), pp. 353–355; and Fred N. Kerlinger, *Foundations of Behavioral Research,* 3rd ed. (Fort Worth: Holt, Rinehart and Winston, 1986).

11. Stephen W. Brown and Teresa A. Swarts, "A Gap Analysis of Professional Service Quality," *Journal of Marketing,* April 1989, p. 95.

12. Joel Huber and Morris B. Holbrook, "Using Attribute Ratings for Product Positioning: Some Distinctions Among Compositional Approaches," *Journal of Marketing Research,* November 1979, p. 510.

13. J. Richard Jones and Sheila I. Cocke, "A Performance Evaluation of Commuter Airlines: The Passengers' View," *Proceedings: Transportation Research Forum,* Vol. 22 (1981), p. 524.

14. Irving Crespi, "Use of a Scaling Technique in Surveys," *Journal of Marketing,* July 1961, pp. 69–72.

15. Dennis Menezes and Norbert F. Elbert, "Alternative Semantic Scaling Formats for Measuring Store Image: An Evaluation," *Journal of Marketing Research,* February 1979, pp. 80–87; and Irving Crespi, "Use of a Scaling Technique in Surveys," *Journal of Marketing,* July 1961, pp. 69–72.

16. Del I. Hawkins, Gerald Albaum, and Roger Best, "Stapel Scale or Semantic Differential in Marketing Research?" *Journal of Marketing Research,* August 1974, pp. 318–322.

17. Menezes and Elbert, "Alternative Semantic Scaling Formats for Measuring Store Image."

18. Yoram Wind, Joseph Denny, and Arthur Cunningham, "A Comparison of Three Brand Evaluation Procedures," *Public Opinion Quarterly,* Summer 1979, p. 263.

19. R. H. Bruskin Associates, 303 George Street, New Brunswick, NJ.

20. Adapted from Kay Goggin, "Indian Family Sells Food," *Stillwater News Press,* October 17, 1979, p. 24.

CHAPTER 11

1. Charles W. Roll, Jr., and Albert H. Cantril, *Polls: Their Use and Misuse in Politics* (New York: Basic Books, 1972), p. 106.

2. Stanley L. Payne, *The Art of Asking Questions* (Princeton, NJ: Princeton University Press, 1951), pp. 8-9. The reader who wants a more detailed account of question wording is referred to this classic book on that topic.

3. Paul L. Erdos, *Professional Mail Surveys* (New York: McGraw-Hill, 1970), p. 37.

4. Donald P. Warwick and Charles A. Lininger, *The Sample Survey: Theory and Practice* (New York: McGraw-Hill, 1975), p. 127.

5. Stephen A. Greyser and Raymond A. Bauer, "What a Difference Words Make: Americans and Advertising," *Public Opinion Quarterly,* Spring 1966, pp. 69-78.

6. Don A. Dillman, *Mail and Telephone Surveys: The Total Design Method* (John Wiley and Sons, 1978), p. 209.

7. Adapted from the September 20, 1982 issue of *Advertising Age.*

8. Fred W. Morgan, "Judicial Standards for Survey Research: An Update and Guidelines," *Journal of Marketing,* January 1990, pp. 59-70.

9. Payne, *The Art of Asking Questions,* p. 185.

10. Roll and Cantril, *Polls,* pp. 106-107.

11. The other product attributes are *relative advantage, compatibility, complexity,* and *communicability.* See Thomas S. Robertson, *Innovative Behavior and Communication* (New York: Holt, Rinehart and Winston, 1971), pp. 46–47.

12. Payne, *The Art of Asking Questions,* pp. 102–103.

13. Erdos, *Professional Mail Surveys,* p. 59.

14. "General Foods Corporation: Tang Instant Breakfast Drink (B)," © 1978 F. Stewart DeBruicker and Harvey N. Singer, The Wharton School, University of Pennsylvania.

15. This section relies heavily on Erdos, *Professional Mail Surveys.*

16. Don A. Dillman, *Mail and Internet Surveys: The Tailored Design Method* (New York: John Wiley and Sons, 2000), pp. 357–361.

17. Sarah J. Young and Craig M. Ross, "Web Questionnaires: A Glimpse of Survey Research in the Future," *Parks & Recreation,* Vol. 35, No. 6 (June 2000), p. 30.

18. Young and Ross, "Web Questionnaires."

19. http://www.decisionanalyst.com/online/surtech.htm, downloaded February 6, 2001.

20. http://www.decisionanalyst.com/online/surtech.htm, downloaded February 6, 2001.

21. Matt Michel, "Controversy Redux," *CASRO Journal,* http://www.decisionanalyst.com/publ_art/contredux.htm, downloaded February 8, 2001.

22. Adapted from Christy Marshall, "Here's the Word on Surveys About Burger Favorites," *Advertising Age,* March 21, 1983.

23. Philip R. Cateora, *International Marketing* (Homewood, IL, Richard D. Irwin, 1990), pp. 387–389.

24. Cateora, *International Marketing*, pp. 387–389.

25. Subhash C. Jain, *International Marketing* (Boston: PWS Kent, 1990), p. 338.

26. GTE Airfone, authorization for limited use granted by GTE Airfone, Inc.

CHAPTER 12

1. Morris James Slonim, *Sampling in a Nutshell* (New York: Simon and Schuster, 1960), p. 3.

2. Adapted from "The Private Debate," *Advertising Age,* October 17, 1988, pp. 12–13; and Diane K. Bowers, "The Privacy Challenger," *Marketing Researcher,* September 1991, p. 61.

3. Philip R. Cateora, *International Marketing* (Homewood, IL: Irwin, 1990), pp. 384–385.

4. Sabra E. Brock, "Marketing Research in Asia: Problems, Opportunities, and Lessons," *Marketing Research,* September 1989, p. 47.

5. Seymour Sudman, *Applied Sampling* (New York: Academic Press, 1976), p. 17.

6. Adapted from Keith K. Cox and Ben M. Enis, *The Marketing Research Process* (Pacific Palisades, CA: Goodyear, 1972); and Danny N. Bellenger and Barnet A. Greenberg, *Marketing Research: A Management Information Approach* (Homewood, IL: Irwin, 1978), pp. 154–155.

7. From David G. Myers, *Exploring Psychology* (Worth, 1990), p. 471.

8. Sudman, *Applied Sampling*, pp. 210–222.

9. From *Interviewer's Manual, Revised Edition* (Ann Arbor, MI: Survey Research Center, Institute for Social Research, University of Michigan, 1976), p. 36. Reprinted by permission.

10. http://www.surveysite.com.

11. "Frequently Asked Questions about Conducting Online Research: New Methodologies for Traditional Techniques," Council of American Survey Research Organizations, http://www.casro.org/faq.cfm, February 8, 2001.

12. Gloria Mellinger, "Harris Interactive Inc.," *World Opinion Research Profiles,* July 18, 2000.

13. Mellinger, "Harris Interactive Inc."

14. Michael Lewis, "The Two-Bucks-a-Minute Democracy," *New York Times Magazine,* November 5, 2000, p. 65; and http://www.knowledgenetworks.com.

15. "Frequently Asked Questions about Conducting Online Research: New Methodologies for Traditional Techniques."

16. http://www.ssisamples.com, January 3, 2001.

CHAPTER 13

1. Morris James Slonim, *Sampling in a Nutshell* (New York: Simon & Schuster, 1960), pp. 1–2.

2. Most of the statistical material in this book assumes that the population parameters are unknown, which is the typical situation in most applied research projects.

3. Darrell Huff and Irving Geis, *How to Lie with Statistics* (New York: W. W. Norton, 1954), p. 33.

4. The reasons for this are related to the concept of degrees of freedom, which will be explained later. At this point, disregard the intuitive notion of division by *n,* because it produces a biased estimate of the population variance.

5. An alternative version of this formula is easier to use in computation:

$$S = \sqrt{\frac{\sum_{i=1}^{n} X_i^2 - \frac{\left(\sum_{i=1}^{n} X_i\right)^2}{n}}{n - 1}}$$

Rather than computing each deviation and summing, one can find the sum and sum of squares of the observations, substitute them into the formula, and evaluate. Many pocket calculators have features that make it easy to accumulate $\sum_{i=1}^{n} X_i$ and $\sum_{i=1}^{n} X_i^2$ at the same time.

6. Thomas H. Wonnacott and Ronald J. Wonnacott, *Introductory Statistics* (New York: John Wiley & Sons, 1969), p. 70. Reprinted with permission.

7. In practice, most survey researchers will not use this exact formula. A modification of the formula, $Z = (X - \mu)/S$, using the sample standard deviation in an adjusted form, is frequently used.

8. William L. Hayes, *Statistics* (New York: Holt, Rinehart and Winston, 1963), p. 193.

9. Adapted from D. H. Sanders, A. F. Murphy, and R. J. Eng, *Statistics: A Fresh Approach* (New York: McGraw-Hill, 1980), p. 123.

10. Thomas H. Wonnacott and Ronald J. Wonnacott, *Introductory Statistics,* 2nd ed. (New York: John Wiley & Sons, 1972), p. 125.

11. Ernest Kurnow, Gerald J. Glasser, and Frederick R. Ottman, *Statistics for Business Decisions* (Homewood, IL: Irwin, 1959), pp. 182–183.

12. Fred N. Kerlinger, *Foundations of Behavioral Research* (New York: Holt, Rinehart & Winston, 1986), p. 117.

13. Note that the derivation of this formula is (1) $E = ZS_{\bar{X}}$, (2) $E = ZS/\sqrt{n}$, (3) $\sqrt{n}ZS/E$, (4) $n = (ZS/E)^2$.

14. Nan Lin, *Foundations of Social Research* (New York: McGraw-Hill, 1976), p. 447. Copyright © 1976 by Nan Lin. Used with permission.

15. Lin, *Foundations of Social Research.*

16. "How the Poll Was Conducted," *The New York Times,* December 13, 1992, p. Y19. Copyright © 1992 by The New York Times Company. Reprinted by permission.

CHAPTER 14

1. Excerpt reprinted with permission from "Chef Boy-ar-dee," *BrandWeek,* May 3, 1999, p. 22. © 1998–1999 VNU Business Media Inc. Used with permission.

2. Reprinted by permission from *American Demographics,* June 2000, p. 72.

3. Becky Ebenkamp, "For Whom the Bell Tolls," *BrandWeek,* May 7, 2001, p. 22.

4. From Roger Ricklefs, "Ethics in America," *The Wall Street Journal,* October 31, 1983, pp. 33, 42; November 1, 1983, p. 33; November 2, 1983, p. 33; and November 3, 1983, pp. 33, 37.

5. From "Confidence in Church/Organized Religion," *The Gallup Report 238,* July 1985, p. 4.

6. Reprinted from "Time Off," *American Demographics,* March 2001, p. 24.

7. Adapted from David G. Meyers, *Exploring Psychology* (New York: Worth Publishers, 1990), p. 464.

8. This output is from the SPSS Student Version.

9. From *Real Stats Real Easy: SPSS for Windows.* Copyright © 1992, SPSS, Inc.

10. This output is from the SPSS Student Version.

11. Technically the *t*-distribution should be used when the population variance is unknown and the standard deviation is estimated from

sample data. However, with large samples it is convenient to use the Z-distribution, because the t-distribution approximates the Z-distribution.

12. The reader with an extensive statistics background will recognize that there are a few rare cases in which the degrees of freedom do not equal $k - 1$. However, these cases will rarely be encountered by readers of this level of book, and to present them would only confuse the discussion here.

13. An example of how to use the chi-square table is given in Table A.4 of the appendix.

14. This material was created by Ajay Sukhdial, Oklahoma State Universty; Damon Aiken, Butler University; and Lynn Kahle, University of Oregon. Additional details can be found in "Are You Old School? A Scale for Measuring Sports Fans' Old-School Orientation," *Journal of Advertising Research,* in press.

15. Adapted with permission from Melvin Prince, *Consumer Research for Management Decisions* (New York: John Wiley and Sons, 1982), pp. 163–166.

16. Randall L. Schultz, Gerald Zaltman, and Philip C. Burger, *Cases in Marketing Research* (Ft. Worth: Dryden Press, 1975), pp. 229–230.

CHAPTER 15

1. Reprinted with permission from "New Study Paints a Detailed Picture of the Online Shopper," *The Food Institute Report,* March 26, 2001, p. 3.

2. See Richard P. Bagozzi, "Salesforce Performance and Satisfaction as a Function of Individual Difference, Interpersonal and Situational Factors," *Journal of Marketing Research,* November 1978, pp. 517–531.

3. This is a point estimate. A confidence interval can be calculated for this sales estimate; however, the topic is beyond the scope of this book.

4. Copyright © 1981, Dr. William J. Lundstrom, reprinted with permission.

CHAPTER 16

1. The first draft of this chapter was written by John Bush, Oklahoma State University. It originally appeared in William G. Zikmund, *Business Research Methods* (Hinsdale, IL: Dryden Press, 1984), and is adapted with permission.

2. David M. Robinson, *Writing Reports for Management Decisions* (Columbus, OH: Merrill, 1969), p. 294.

3. Robinson, *Writing Reports,* p. 297.

4. This discussion is based on Robinson, *Writing Reports,* pp. 300, 338–339, and Jessamon Dawe and William Jackson Lord, Jr., *Functional Business Communication* (Englewood Cliffs, NJ: Prentice-Hall, 1968), p. 414.

5. Adapted with permission from William D. Wells, "Noah's Law of Overhead Transparencies," *ACR Newsletter,* June 1993, p. 10. Association for Consumer Research, College of Business Administration, Valdosta State University, Valdosta, GA.

6. "A Speech Tip," *Communication Briefings,* Vol. 14, No. 2, p. 3.